Teaching Race in the European Renaissance

A Classroom Guide

Teaching Race in the European Renaissance

A Classroom Guide

Edited by

Matthieu Chapman

Anna Wainwright

Arizona State University

Tempe, Arizona

2023

Teaching Race in the European Renaissance: A Classroom Guide was published in 2023 by ACMRS Press at Arizona State University in Tempe, Arizona.

This book is available online at https://asu.pressbooks.pub/race-in-the-european-renaissance-classroom-guide/

ISBN: 978-0-86698-835-3 (hardcover)
ISBN: 978-0-86698-836-0 (paperback)

A catalog record for this book has been created by the Library of Congress.

Hardcover and paperback editions are printed in the United States of America.

Contents

Introduction

MATTHIEU CHAPMAN AND ANNA WAINWRIGHT

> *"History is not the past. It is the present.*
> *We carry our history with us. We *are* our history.*
> *If we pretend otherwise ... we literally are criminals."*[1]
> — James Baldwin

In November 2019, three pathbreaking scholars in English early modern race studies, Kim F. Hall, Ayanna Thompson, and Kimberly Coles, co-authored a clarion call to arms for their colleagues. Published on the website of the Modern Language Association, "BlackkkShakespearean: A Call to Action for Medieval and Early Modern Studies," was a welcome jolt to the broader academic community. It reminds us that the very "assertion that studying medieval and early modern periods sheds light on the foundational texts of a so-called Western civilization has made the fields attractive to far-right extremists."[2] Turning their attention to the "crisis of the humanities," the three scholars tie recent drops in enrollments and the ever-present anxiety about the decline of the humanities directly to the lack of diversity in the fields of medieval and early modern studies. The world is not, they insist, "as it was imagined by the University of Chicago's Great Books Program of the 1940s" — nor is the contemporary American student body the same as it was once constructed by the legally enforced "separate but equal" epistemology established in *Plessy v Ferguson* (1896) and overturned in *Brown v the Board of Education of Topeka* (1954). In order for our fields to remain relevant and transformative, there is both a

1. James Baldwin, *The Cross of Redemption: Uncollected Writings* (New York: Vintages Books, 2011), 125.
2. Kimberly Anne Coles, Kim F. Hall, and Ayanna Thompson, "BlacKKKShakespearean: A Call to Action for Medieval and Early Modern Studies," last modified November 19, 2019. https://profession.mla.org/blackkkshakespearean-a-call-to-action-for-medieval-and-early-modern-studies/

"practical and ethical imperative" to expand the study of the past, the way it is taught, and who teaches it. We could not agree more.

Volume Origins

The production of this interdisciplinary collection on how to teach race in the European Renaissance was bracketed by two very American events which, nevertheless, are most relevant to the subject matter at hand.[3] The first was the Unite the Right rally in Charlottesville on August 11 and 12, 2017; the second, the attack on the Capitol Building in Washington D.C. on January 6, 2021. Both deadly events transpired in cities with a storied history. Charlottesville, founded in 1762, was home to two of America's founding fathers, Thomas Jefferson and James Monroe, who lived within its limits while serving as Governor of Virginia. Both chose to commute across the mountains to Richmond to conduct governmental business rather than leave behind their home in the lush forests of the Shenandoah Valley. Despite a population of little more than 48,000 today, the city boasts two UNESCO World Heritage Sites, Jefferson's plantation of Monticello and the prestigious university he founded after leaving presidential office, the University of Virginia. The city's deep significance to American history is perhaps why white supremacists chose Charlottesville as the location where they would "Unite the Right" in the summer of 2017 in ostensible protest over the removal of Confederate monuments.[4] With

3. A note on word choice. Throughout this volume, the editors and chapter authors use the terms "Renaissance" and "early modern" somewhat interchangeably, to denote the period between roughly 1400 and 1650 in Europe. While the volume is primarily concerned with this period, we also refer regularly to the Middle Ages and the medieval period, which we generally identify as between the fifth and fifteenth centuries. As we explore in this introduction, we are also aware of the way these modern periodizations themselves are often conflated and stereotyped in popular culture, and in political discourse. We use "American" here to mean "of the United States." We have tried to remain conscious throughout this volume of the bad habit academics in the United States, including we two, have of conflating "America" with the United States.
4. Dara Lind. "Unite the Right, the violent white supremacist rally in Charlottesville, explained," August 14, 2017. *Vox.com*. https://www.vox.com/2017/8/12/16138246/charlottesville-nazi-rally-right-uva.

polo collars popped high and tiki torches held higher, these domestic terrorists – dubbed the "alt-right" by mass media – took to the streets, spewing hate-filled rhetoric from hate-filled hearts. One young woman, Heather Heyer, was killed when James Alex Fields, Jr., drove his car intentionally into a crowd of counter-protestors; many others were beaten and injured. The spectacular violence of the march recalled the early twentieth century, when the Ku Klux Klan and other groups would march openly through American streets, nooses in hand, in search of Black and brown citizens to hang from trees as both advertisement and affirmation of their belief in the superiority of the white race. In the flash of a flame from a two-dollar party store accessory, Charlottesville was forever repositioned in the American consciousness. No longer was this the birthplace of "all men are created equal." Now the uglier side of city's history – the slavery, the lynching, the violence – came to the fore. These white supremacists sought to assert exclusive ownership of the present by appropriating the past: the American Dream, that promise of life, liberty, and the pursuit of happiness dreamed up by the country's forefathers, was theirs alone.

Charlottesville was still on the minds of many the following spring, including scholars of the early modern period. During a roundtable on teaching race at the 2018 Renaissance Society of America Annual Meeting in New Orleans, numerous audience members began their questions with "In this post-Charlottesville world ... " The roundtable participants – many of whom appear in this volume – were not as willing as the audience to view this particular white supremacist rally as a watershed moment in American history. While the events of Charlottesville were shocking to many Americans both inside and outside of the academy, met with cries of "this isn't the America I know!" for many others, the violent march in August 2017 was but the latest example in a long line of white supremacist attempts to appropriate the past as a political tool.

Our students see images from the periods we term the Middle Ages and Renaissance almost every day in popular culture; what they see, almost without exception, is a whitewashed version of a period of enormous diversity. The growing awareness in our field of how the history of racism – both American and globally – intersects with the study of the Middle Ages and Renaissance in particular, along with the conversations that occur between scholars about this violence, are too often contained to hotel conference rooms hundreds of miles from our classrooms. The whitewashing of imagery and ideas from the premodern periods both in popular culture and by open white supremacists thus goes undiscussed in classrooms, as well as unchallenged. So too does the role of nineteenth-century nationalism and the construct of "Western Civilization" in classes on ancient Greece and Rome, Renaissance Italy, and Elizabethan England, as well as the deep cultural investment many have in propagating a linear narrative that leads directly to the neoclassical monuments and statehouses across the country. And while many of us who study the past know just how fundamental racial, religious, national, and ethnic diversities were to the fabric of premodern Europe, white supremacists rewrite history, spinning a tale of Renaissance racial purity and casting it as a societal, cultural, and ethnic ideal for contemporary America. Indeed, many of them arrived in Charlottesville in full Crusader regalia, complete with chainmail, helmets, and swords. Marching with shields and banners bearing premodern symbols — the red cross on a white background of the Knights Templar, runes from the Elder Futhark — they offered a false and dangerous narrative of history to consumers of mass media, from Fox News and Breitbart to CNN and Twitter. These mostly young, mostly male, white Americans offered the public an inaccurate pre-modern European history in their all-white image, presenting themselves as the modern manifestation of "white knights" of yore. Indeed, the term "white knight" itself, while positive to many, has nefarious, racialized undertones.[5] The "whiteness" of these knights is not divine, but rather relational. And while it does signal a moral cause of medieval crusaders, that morality establishes its whiteness as an antithesis to a series of darkened, racialized Others. In both the Medieval and modern senses, these cavaliers battle for the sanctity of their imagined white homelands and the mythological purity of their white race.

Since the public outcry over Charlottesville, the longstanding historical trend of weaponizing an idealized white past to legitimize racist ideas

5. On the white knight and race in the premodern, see especially Heng 2018, 191–209.

has become more difficult for people to ignore.[6] In February of 2019, when Maryland police uncovered a white nationalist Coast Guard Lieutenant's stockpile of arms and documented plans to start a race war, they also uncovered writings that hearkened to fantastical visions of restoring a racially "pure" Viking homeland to America.[7] In the March 2019 massacre at a mosque in Christchurch, New Zealand, the mass murderer covered his gun with the scratched-in names of "inspirational" figures from Western history who crusaded against Muslims. These included not just medieval warriors but early modern figures such as the Renaissance Venetian duke Sebastiano Venier, who played a central role in the Christian victory over the Muslim Ottoman Empire at the Battle of Lepanto in 1571, and Ernst Rüdiger von Starhemberg, a leader in the Battle of Vienna against the Ottomans in 1683. And on January 6, 2021, a white supremacist mob – whipped into a frenzy over false allegations of a stolen presidential election – invaded the neoclassical Capitol building in Washington D.C. to "stop the steal." The insurrectionists included the man dubbed the "QAnon Shaman," whose costume mixed appropriated symbols from cultures indigenous to the American continent with medieval Nordic ones.[8]

From slavery and colonization to the fight for Civil Rights and the epidemic of extrajudicial police violence against Black bodies, white supremacy has always governed our nation and guided both its discourse

6. David M. Perry, "How to Fight 8Chan Medievalism – and Why We Must," last modified June 27, 2019. https://psmag.com/ideas/how-to-fight-8chan-medievalism-and-why-we-must-notre-dame-christchurch.
7. Isaac Stanley Becker, "'They Hate White Males': A Norwegian Mass Murderer Inspired the Coast Guard Officer Accused of Plotting Terror, Feds Say," last modified February 21, 2019. https://www.washingtonpost.com/nation/2019/02/21/they-hate-white-males-norwegian-mass-murderer-inspired-coast-guard-officer-plotting-terror-feds-say/.
8. We detest the media's uncritical deployment of this appropriated titled. This man is not a Shaman. He is a terrorist. And describing him as a Shaman is the type of uncritical cultural, racial, and ethnic appropriation that continues to support and perpetuate white supremacist violence through the supposedly mundane and quotidian.

and its conscience.[9] What makes the trajectory from Charlottesville to January 6th unique is that these events eschewed the veil of plausible deniability that usually conceals the racist underpinnings of American society and unabashedly embraced the myth of America as a whites-only nation. It is no coincidence that this primetime racism has come in the same years as the openly manufactured panic over the way the history of race in the United States is taught. Since August of 2020, right-wing media have led a "Crusade" against a new public enemy: critical race theory in American schools. While the sophisticated legal framework developed in the final decades of the last century by scholars including, among others, Kimberlé Crenshaw and Derrick Bell, is not actually being taught in most K-12 classrooms, that is very much beside the point. "CRT" is now used as a cudgel for any mention made of race or racism in American history by teachers, and 42 states have proposed or passed laws forbidding the mention of terms like "implicit bias," "systemic racism," etc. Members of the New Hampshire State Legislature recently proposed a bill that would update a McCarthy-era "loyalty oath" for public school teachers, by which they would have to swear not only to indoctrinate their students in Communism, but also any "theory" that suggests America was founded on racism.[10] The 1619 Project, conceived and spearheaded by the Pulitzer-prize winning journalist and Macarthur fellow Nikole Hannah-Jones, argues that 1619, the year the first enslaved Black Africans arrived

9. While the literature on the history of American racism and white supremacy is of course vast, a helpful initial reading list for both teachers and students looking to learn more about the ways in which racism, especially antiblack racism, has been legislated into American law might include Nikole Hannah-Jones' *The 1619 Project: A New American Origin Story* (WH Allen, 2021); Eric Foner, *Reconstruction: America's Unfinished Revolution, 1863–1877* (Harper Collins, 1988); Heather McGhee, *The Sum of Us: What Racism Costs Everyone and How We Can Prosper Together* (Penguin, 2021); Carol Anderson, *The Second: Race and Guns in a Fatally Unequal America* (Bloomsbury, 2021); Michelle Alexander, *The New Jim Crow: Mass Incarceration in the Age of Colorblindness* (The New Press, 2012); Isabel Wilkerson, *Caste: The Origins of Our Discontents* (Random House, 2020).
10. https://www.nhpr.org/nh-news/2021-12-03/teacher-loyalty-bill-would-restrict-how-u-s-history-especially-racism-can-be-discussed-in-school.

on North American soil, is a more accurate starting point for American history than 1776. Although the 1619 project is purely history and has no connection to Critical Race Theory, it, too, has become a flashpoint.[11]

Teaching the history of race and racism in the United States is under fierce attack. But racism and white supremacy are by no means America-only problems. Quite the contrary: racism and white supremacy pre-date the United States as a nation, regardless of whether one considers its founding to be 1776 or 1619. Education in the diverse history of premodern Europe — and its central role in the creation of the racialized modern society in which we live — is key to understanding the history of racism and shattering the mythological narratives of racial purity embraced by white supremacists. Indeed, the very historical symbols that hate groups deploy in support of their narratives are often grounded in a history that runs counter to such myths. The round, golden shield emblazoned with a black eagle that appeared in so many newspapers and media reports from the march on Charlottesville was the standard originally borne by Saint Maurice — a Black Roman general of African descent.[12] The classics scholar Sarah Bond was targeted in 2017 by white supremacists online for reminding readers of *Hyperallergic*, one of the world's most popular online magazines of contemporary art, that the seemingly pure-white statues of ancient Greece and Rome were originally painted to demonstrate the many different ethnicities of antiquity, among other meanings.[13]

In their attempts to remake the past into an idealized, racially homogeneous vision for the future, contemporary American white supremacists thus draw attention to the problematic nature of "history" itself.

11. Katie Robertson, "Nikole Hannah-Jones Denied Tenure at University of North Carolina," *New York Times*, May 19, 2021. https://www.nytimes.com/2021/05/19/business/media/nikole-hannah-jones-unc.html.
12. Becky Little, "How Hate Groups Are Hijacking Medieval Symbols While Ignoring the Facts Behind Them," last modified September 3, 2018. https://www.history.com/news/how-hate-groups-are-hijacking-medieval-symbols-while-ignoring-the-facts-behind-them.
13. Colleen Flaherty, "Threats for What She Didn't Say," last modified June 19, 2017. https://www.insidehighered.com/news/2017/06/19/classicist-finds-herself-target-online-threats-after-article-ancient-statues

While it would be simpler to dismiss the problem of contemporary white supremacy and its relationship to the European past as a handful of radical terrorist organizations and far-right extremists, the ways in which the history of the period has been recorded, written, and legitimized by academia has long played a role in these bad faith appropriations. In recent years, resistance to early modern race studies — which has been instigated and produced overwhelmingly by scholars of color — has made its way into contentious debates over inclusion in conferences, often resulting in violence for those who dare to challenge the white status quo.[14] Scholars of color who have dared to transgress the white-limed walls and ivory towers of pre-modern histories have been met with resistance ranging from passive aggressive condescension to virulent hostility to outright racism. From public accusations that they owe their jobs to their race[15] to assertions that they don't belong,[16] the evidence and argumentation of scholars of color and their attempts to de-anachronize race in pre-modern history have encountered an onslaught of emotion and white fragility.

Even with the obstacles to this work, over the past twenty-five years, scholars such as Kim F. Hall, Margo Hendricks, Ania Loomba, and Joyce Green MacDonald, and many others cited in the pages that follow, have worked diligently to problematize racially homogeneous constructions of premodern histories. These scholars have wielded evidence of racial thought with nuanced precision, uncovering the non-white presence buried within the whitewashed past. In doing so, they have challenged the white supremacist appropriation of a history that belongs to us all, and

14. Jennifer Schuessler. "Medieval Scholars Joust With White Nationalists. And One Another." *New York Times*. May 5, 2019. https://www.nytimes.com/2019/05/05/arts/the-battle-for-medieval-studies-white-supremacy.html.

15. See Dan-el Padilla Peralta, "Some thoughts on AIA-SCS 2019," last modified January 7, 2019. https://medium.com/@danelpadillaperalta/some-thoughts-on-aia-scs-2019-d6a480a1812a.

16. Nahir I. Otaño Gracia, "Lost in Our Field: Racism and the International Congress on Medieval Studies," last modified July 24, 2018. https://medievalistsofcolor.com/race-in-the-profession/lost-in-our-field-racism-and-the-international-congress-on-medieval-studies/.

opened up numerous fields of study to a more accurate, inclusive, and intellectually engaging history.[17]

The truth is that we all teach race in our classrooms, even if we do not do so consciously. We can either directly wrestle with the elephant in the room and through our struggle create something productive; or we can ignore the elephant, and in doing so, perpetuate a whitewashed history, alienating many of the students in our increasingly diverse classrooms.[18] More often than not, the elephant remains in a corner while students are taught one of the myriad versions of early modern European history in which the word "race" — and its multifaceted manifestations in multiple intersecting discourses — is absent from discussion. On occasion, the topic might sneak into the room, concealed by the handkerchief in *Othello* or the black skin of a demon in Dante's *Inferno*, but absent larger contextualization and direct engagement in the classroom, the issues of race in the texts that students read become divorced from the world around them, relegated to a past that is not a part of "history." To ignore race is to ignore the extraordinary opportunity to make the past accessible and relevant to today's students, and to lose sight of a crucial tool for providing not only a more nuanced and accurate history, but also a more compassionate, progressive, and antiracist present.

But how does one incorporate race into a class on the premodern when race is not their area of scholarly expertise? We recognize the tension and

17. While Renaissance Race Studies is a growing and exciting field, the majority of work produced comes from the Anglophone tradition, either written in or engaging with sources in the English language. Although present, Renaissance Race Studies has a much smaller foothold in other national traditions. We recognize this imbalance and the problems inherent with it and are hopeful this volume will help inspire scholars in those fields to pursue future work on race in their national traditions.
18. From 1976 to 2008, the distribution of race among college undergraduates shifted immensely. In 1976, 82% of undergraduates were white. By 2008, that number was down to 63.2%, with every other racial group seeing an increase in their proportion of students. In addition, the percentage of 18–24-year-olds in every non-white racial group continued to increase through 2018. See https://nces.ed.gov/pubs2010/2010015/tables/table_24_1.asp and https://nces.ed.gov/programs/coe/pdf/coe_cpb.pdf.

anxiety that can come with attempting to bring race into classroom discussion. Without proper training, this task can be damaging — the students' education and the teacher's status are both at stake. Discussing race openly immediately transforms the classroom into a political space; in today's political climate, we understand the discomfort and danger that accompanies discussion of differentials of power in history in the past and today, as the raft of laws that attempt to outlaw any discussion of race in the classroom attest. We believe that the consequences of erasure, however, far outweigh the comfort of depoliticization — and that the more educators who bring the topic up, the less taboo it will be for future scholars and students. Ayanna Thompson and Laura Turchi have already asked teachers of Shakespeare, "Who benefits from a race-free, gender-free, sexuality-free and ability-free approach [in the classroom]? ... Is it sufficient to espouse the value of diversity and not touch upon it in a Shakespeare unit?" Nahir I. Otaño Gracia likewise queries in an editorial on MedievalistsOfColor.com: "What has academia lost? What have we lost by allowing racism to hurt people of color? ... For one, we lose the scholarship of people who never return." We encourage all educators to brave the discomfort in an effort to embrace those voices before they are lost. It is our responsibility to show students not only why the humanities matter today, but that they belong to them.

For those intrepid adventurers who wish to journey into the perhaps uncharted waters of race in the European Renaissances, we offer this book as a guide. What follows is a collection of essays, exercises, and lesson plans designed to be a star chart to help teachers navigate through these choppy waters both safely and productively, not only in the college classroom but in the high school one as well. While the gears of the academy slowly turn and the pool of scholars specializing in race in the European Renaissances slowly expands, this book will allow those already on the seas a beacon through which to shine light on the diverse bodies that contributed to the diverse European Renaissances, in various disciplines and topics of early modern history and literature. You may find yourself serving as a life raft for your students, letting them know "I see you, I hear you" — an ally in their struggles both inside and outside of the classroom.

The breadth of topics found in this volume are designed to open doors into discussing race in your classes on Renaissance topics regardless of your specialty or focus. Whether you are teaching literature, culture, art history, or music, are exploring Britain, Italy, France, or the Iberian Peninsula, this volume offers tools for combating white supremacy and diversifying your curriculum to incorporate the diverse bodies and voices that made the Renaissances periods of immense artistic, social, cultural, and scientific growth. Some essays are positioned to speak directly to students as assigned reading, but all are aimed at teachers, and many can be used across national traditions and subject matter.

Mapping Race: Britain from Shakespeare to Aphra Behn

The vocabularies and ideas of race with which Americans are most familiar, including the ways in which race intersects with skin color, nation, religion, and gender, exist in a continuum with those found in the Early Modern British Isles. This grammar, although originating from studies of Early Modern England, resonates throughout Anglophone studies of other early modern nations and cultures. To familiarize the reader with the varying discourses on race to be discussed in the following chapters of this section, Matthieu Chapman offers a brief description of and review of literature for each to help the reader expand on and contextualize the ideas presented. Chapman breaks down early modern British racial thinking into ten distinct but often overlapping discourses: blood and genealogy, nation, religion, color, gender, transnational constructions, processes and actions, pseudo-science, materiality, and metaphysics, designed to help teachers find ways to incorporate race into discussions of any of those topics that may occur in their classrooms.

Once the reader is familiar with the discourses on race in the early modern British Isles, the section turns toward the most familiar relic of the period to appear in modern classrooms: William Shakespeare. Maya Mathur's "When Students Recognize Gender but not Race: Addressing the Othello-Caliban Conundrum" offers a lesson helping students to unpack the networks of racial and gendered violence in Shakespeare's *Othello* and *The Tempest*. Mathur's chapter guides professors and students through multiple primary sources from George Best, Richard Hakluyt, and others to help students understand how colonial and patriarchal oppression manifests across and throughout the racial and gender spectrums.

Matthieu Chapman and Joshua Kelly then deploy contemporary critical race theory and Lacanian psychoanalysis in "Sight-Reading Race in Early Modern Drama: Dog Whistles, Signifiers, and the Grammars of Blackness" to argue that the early modern English audience's familiarity with the genealogy of racial signifiers that appeared in devil characters on the stage allowed the audience to "see dog-whistles" of race where conventional blackening techniques may not have appeared. They analyze the intersection of racial, gendered, and religious discourses to unpack the semiotics of the staged witches in Shakespeare's *Macbeth* to argue that the figures contain a confluence of signs that made them read to the audience as the unrepresentable Black woman.

To limit the teaching of race in Renaissance English literature to the Bard, however, would be to do a disservice to the diversity of materials, thoughts, and scholars working on race in the time and period. The next three chapters argue for how race appears in three other literary titans of Early Modern Britain. First is Dennis Austin Britton's "Teaching Spenser's Darkness: Race, Allegory, and the Making of Meaning in *The Faerie Queene*," in which he tackles how to work through the allegory and racializations evident in a text often accompanied by interpretative anxiety. Next, in "Causing Good and Necessary Trouble with Race in Milton's Comus (Especially for BIPOC students in Early Modern English Classrooms)," Reginald A. Wilburn applies Congressman John Lewis's famous term "good trouble" to teaching Milton in the early modern English classroom, especially for BIPOC students. Jennifer Lodine-Chaffey then turns to Aphra Behn with "Teaching Aphra Behn's *Oroonoko* as Execution Narrative." Lodine-Chaffey shows educators how to use primary source documents related to slave rebellions and executions to re-read the connections between race, humanity, and violence present in Behn's novella.

Closing out the section on the British Isles are two pieces that move beyond the bounds of the literary world and examine the larger culture of Renaissance Britain. In "'The Present Terror of the World': The Ottoman Empire in the English Imaginary," Ambereen Dadabhoy tracks the ambivalent attitudes of envy and alterity present between Britain and the Middle East in the early modern world by analyzing Richard Knolles's compendium *The Generall Historie of the Turkes* and its influence on *Othello*.

Her analysis unpacks the racializing logics that undergird the ambivalence between the two kingdoms, and she argues that these same logics undergird America's current "War on Terror," bridging the gaps between the early modern and the world of today's classrooms. And lastly, Amrita Dhar's "When They Consider How Their Light Is Spent: Intersectional Race and Disability Studies in the Classroom" shows educators how to use two sonnets of the same name, "When I Consider How My Light Is Spent," written centuries apart – one by early modern poet John Milton and one by modern poet Tyehimba Jess – to create intersectional awareness between race and disability studies for modern students.

Continental Europe

While there has been significantly less work done on race in continental Europe than in England during the Renaissance, the essays in this section are a sign of the growing attention to the subject in multiple national traditions, including Italian, French, Spanish, German, and Portuguese. Anna Wainwright opens the Italian section with an overview of how race can be addressed in the Italian Renaissance classroom. Discussions might include the racialization of Ottoman Turks after the "Fall" of Constantinople in 1453; Christopher Columbus's role in the racialization of Italian Americans in the nineteenth-century United States; Italy's participation in the slave trade; the Black African presence on the peninsula; and "lyric whiteness" in Petrarch.[19] Suzanne Magnanini then offers instructors a way to explore an understudied component of Giambattista Basile's classic book of fairy tales, *Lo cunti de li cunti*, or *The Pentameron*, in "Ogres and Slaves: Giambattista Basile's Fairy Tales of Race." She centralizes the often-ignored character of Lucia, a Black enslaved girl who becomes princess through trickery and is generally read as a "negative exemplum" in contrast with the white Zoza. Magnanini guides teachers through how to use the book of fairy tales, which finds its way into many a college class-

19. On "lyric whiteness," see Kim F. Hall, "'These bastard signs of fair': Literary Whiteness in Shakespeare's Sonnets," in *Post-Colonial Shakespeares*, edited by Ania Loomba and Martin Orkin (Routledge, 2003), 64–83.

room both within and outside of Italian Studies, to address the broad questions: “How might a literary genre grounded in “long ago” and “far away” fantasies allow us to examine the complex social historical realities of race and slavery in the early modern Mediterranean? How do gender and genre shape representations of race?” In “The Black Attendant in Titian’s ‘Diana and Actaeon’ and in Modern Oblivion,” geared toward students, Patricia Simons situates the artist Titian’s famous representation of Diana and Acteon from 1559 within the broader intersecting contexts of race, gender, and trade in Venice. Simons challenges existing scholarship on the painting’s myopic focus on whiteness by analyzing the presence of a Black female servant in the context of recent art history scholarship on the popularity of the Black female attendant in Italian Renaissance painting. In doing so, Simons argues for a new, more nuanced reading of the figure that does not reduce her to the position of “aesthetic foil” to Diana’s glaring whiteness, or, alternately, to an allegorical representation without historical meaning or value. Instead, Simons focuses her attention on this Black servant, thus allowing for a consideration of her relative autonomy in the piece. In “Whitewashing the Whitewashed Renaissance: Italian Renaissance Art through a *Kapharian Lens*,” Rebecca Howard next offers teachers a way to study the “whitewashed Renaissance” through the important works of contemporary Black artist Titus Kaphar, which focus on incorporating the Black subject into canonical works of art. Used together, Simons’ and Howard’s pieces offer teachers a productive new way to approach and incorporate the study of race into Italian Renaissance art history, tying it to contemporary considerations of how European art has consistently erased or ignored non-white subjects. Shifting from visual art to music, Emily Wilbourne offers students important new work on seventeenth-century Florence with the case study of Buonaccorsi “the Moor,” an enslaved Black singer at the Medici court, in “Gio: Buonaccorsi ‘the Moor’: An Enslaved Black Singer at the Medici Court.” Wilbourne makes clear that “race and racial difference were an important part of Florentine court life,” as well as demonstrating the obvious similarities between Renaissance racist stereotypes and those today, often left unexplored in the Italian context. These six pieces together argue compellingly for the urgency of integrating and centralizing race in Italian Renaissance Studies.

Turning to France, Anna Klosowska examines the use of blackface or *barbouillage* in early modern lyric poetry, visual arts, and theater produced in Paris, and its relationship to French engagement with the slave trade. Taking as her point of entry French imitations of Giambattista Marino's poem *La bella schiava*, she offers instructors a host of primary sources that make plain the popularity and cultural impact of anti-blackness in Renaissance Paris, and also highlights new and important scholarly work in early modern critical race studies.[20] The next chapter moves from Paris to France's colonial project in the Americas. In "Learning to Listen: A New Approach to Teaching Early Modern Encounters in the Americas," Charlotte Daniels and Katherine Dauge-Roth discuss the ways in which Bowdoin's French Studies program overhauled their instruction of canonical literature in order to incorporate Indigenous responses to French colonialism and imperialism. This thoughtful and activist approach to linguistic and cultural instruction offers a powerful model for all instructors of foreign languages, whose students must constantly contend with expressing themselves on issues of import while faced with linguistic instability. Moving from French culture to German, Noam Andrews's "Racial Profiling: Delineating the Renaissance Face" draws on scientific discourses from around the world to argue that the delineations between races and ethnicities found in phrenology, physiognomy, and other pseudoscientific discourses predate the Enlightenment and originated in the early modern period through the example of Albrecht Dürer.

Global Renaissances

The Renaissance was, of course, a time of travel and movement; this was a primary factor in the way race was understood and theorized. In "Contextualizing Race in Leonard Thurneysser's Account of Portugal," Carolin Alff offers a comparative analysis of the varying cultures observed by the

20. Of particular note, she highlights Noémie Ndiaye's *Scripts of Blackness: Early Modern Performance Culture and the Making of Race* (University of Pennsylvania Press, 2022), which is required reading for any instructor who wants to talk about early modern race on the Continent with their students.

Swiss-German traveler and scholar during his time in Portugal, and the ways in which he deploys a racial discourse in both the content and structure of his manuscript to separate humans from animals. Dana Leibsohn and Barbara Mundy then take up the Transatlantic discourses of race and colonization in their essay, "Settler Colonialism, Families, and Racialized Thinking: *Casta* Painting in Latin America." Using casta paintings, which depicted the sixteen-category race-based caste system that structured society in early modern Spanish Mexico, as the objects of analysis, Leibsohn and Mundy argue that ideas of nation, race, blood, and indigeneity were varyingly fixed and fluid, destabilizing the widespread notion of the colonial "other."

Two further articles provide techniques for incorporating contemporary technologies and materials. Lisandra Estevez's "Teaching Race in the Global Renaissance Using Local Art Collections" offers a practical, adaptable case study for encouraging both teachers and students to engage with local museum resources to analyze structures of race across time and space and contextualize the local and the modern within larger, more complex, global and temporal contexts. And finally, Elizabeth Spragins's "Podcasting Las Casas and Robert E. Lee: A Case Study in Historicizing Race" guides teachers through using podcasts both as teaching aid and assignment to get students to engage with centuries-long discourses of nation, blood purity, honor, and religious orthodoxy that undergirded race from the Western Mediterranean, to colonial New Spain, to twenty-first century Charlottesville, Virginia.

Beyond the Early Modern: Global Pasts and Presents

In the last section, the volume expands the temporal frame of Renaissance Race Studies with three chapters that explore ways in which contemporary classrooms and performances engage with and echo early modern constructions of race. First, Marjorie Rubright and Amy Rodgers present "*American Moor*: *Othello*, Race, and the Conversations Here and Now," an analysis of the performance of Keith Hamilton Cobb's groundbreaking *American Moor* at UMASS Amherst. Their conversation engages with the ways in which the shifting racialization of Othello intertwines with racial politics in contemporary America, ultimately arguing that the eponymous

Moor has become Black cultural property. Next up, Roya Biggie's "Mapping Race Digitally in the Classroom" offers educators a method for helping students understand that notions of race do not develop in a vacuum by using digital mapping techniques. Closing out the volume are Ann Christensen and Laura Turchi. Their chapter, "Editing the Renaissance for an Antiracist Classroom," argues that educators must re- and un-edit classroom editions of early modern texts along with their students so that they may all engage in proactive discussions of the language that is racist and sexist. Instead of dismissing the language as a product of its time, Christensen and Turchi offer methods for working with the students to address not only the early modern contexts of this language, but also how it interacts with the world today.

COVID Classrooms and Looking Ahead

The pieces in this volume were finalized during a pandemic that has disproportionately harmed communities of color in the US: there has been much talk that the country is suffering from the "twin pandemics" of COVID-19 and racism. While some academics joked on Twitter about how much writing Shakespeare got done during his own era's plague, many scholars, some in this volume, took this time to host and present in antiracist teaching workshops that incorporated early modern work and tied today's racism and white supremacy to the longstanding racializations we have mentioned.[21] In this COVID-19 moment of social distancing and isolation, masked classrooms and the politicization of vaccine mandates at universities, early modern critical race studies is more important than ever. Pandemics, like white supremacy, are nothing new — and they are connected, in the violence perpetrated against the bodies of those oppressed and erased from history. Students looking to understand the pandemic will have to understand white supremacy, and its historical trajectory, as well.

21. Of particular note, Ambereen Dadabhoy gave numerous Zoom presentations on the importance of race in the Renaissance classroom, including "Cultivating an Anti-Racist Pedagogy" at the Folger Shakespeare Library. https://ambereendadabhoy.com/.

This project is intentionally open-access, and the current pieces of the volume are intended as a beginning, an introduction for how to teach race in the European Renaissance based on the field as it stands at the beginning of 2023. As early modern critical race studies continues to grow and a new generation of scholars pushes the field forward, it is our hope that this volume will grow as well, as will discussions of race in the Early Modern/Renaissance classroom.

Acknowledgements

MATTHIEU CHAPMAN AND ANNA WAINWRIGHT

This volume began as a roundtable, "Teaching Race in the Renaissance" at the 2018 Renaissance Society of America Annual Conference in New Orleans. We are grateful to the participants of that roundtable, Dennis Britton, Amrita Dhar, Jeanette Fregulia, Roya Biggie, Dennis Looney, and Miles Parks Grier, as well as to Alison Frazier, who helped to organize the panel. Thanks also to Ian Smith, who offered his strong support despite being prevented from chairing the panel due to inclement weather, and to Jyotsna Singh, who stepped up in his place. We are also grateful to Dennis Britton for talking through the structure of the volume at an early point, and his encouragement throughout the process.

Heartfelt thanks to Virginia Cox and Janet Smarr for reading our initial proposal for the volume, their astute comments, and their continued mentorship of our work. Matt would like to thank Julia Schleck, Miles Parks Grier, Joshua Kelly (who also contributed to this volume), and Bernadette Andrea for offering their guidance and feedback on both the ideas contained within and finding this book a home. Anna would like to thank Bernadette Andrea, Amy Boylan, Jessica Goethals, Shannon McHugh and Melissa Swain for their thoughtful suggestions for the Italian portion of this book, and Elissa Weaver, Suzanne Magnanini, and Emily Wilbourne for early conversations on early modern Italy and race.

Funding for this volume was generously provided by our universities. At the University of New Hampshire, we would like to thank the Center for the Humanities, the Italian Studies Quasi-endowment, and the College of Liberal Arts. At SUNY-New Paltz, we thank the School of Fine and Performing Arts.

We are grateful to have found a home for this volume at ACMRS Press, and we would like to thank Ayanna Thompson for including us in the Press' broader publishing initiative. Thanks also to Roy Rukkila and Geoffrey Way for their steady, expert hands.

Finally, we would like to thank our wonderful contributors for your chapters, your patience, and your perseverance. We are so lucky to have gone through this journey with you, and we thank you for remaining committed to this project throughout the difficult first years of the Covid-19 pandemic. Students and instructors alike are now fortunate to have your scholarship in their hands and their classrooms.

Mapping Race in Early Modern Europe

MATTHIEU CHAPMAN

Who owns history?

While the question may seem facetious or even non-sensical (for how can someone own a time period?), this question as well as any sums up the stakes of studying early modern Europe. With the global rise of nationalist movements and white supremacist discourse, extremist groups whose names I do not wish to publicize or legitimize by listing them here have sought to appropriate the Medieval and Renaissance periods in Europe as their white property. In doing so, they falsely mythologize these historical eras as periods of cultural superiority that are inextricably linked to a false narrative of racial purity. As such, they seek to claim this history as solely their property and use it as a guide to build what they view as a better tomorrow lacking diversity and inclusivity.

I wish this discourse was contained solely to hate groups, but unfortunately, the insidious belief of racial purity and pre-modern (and perhaps even modern) Europe as white property permeate academic settings as well. To even begin to discuss the racist roots of academic constructs such as "Western Civilization" and "Otherness" unleashes a blowback from the majority white, male fields that publicly joke about their homogeneity.[1] Renaissance Race Studies has, from nascent stages in the 1990s, been subject to claims of irrelevance and anachronism from Renaissance Studies writ-large, most specifically New Historicists, who claim that history and literature were inextricable.[2] Ian Smith takes these debates to task, how-

1. J. Clara Chan, "Medievalists, Recoiling from White Supremacy, Try to Diversify the Field," *Chronicle of Higher Education*. 16 July 2017, https://www.chronicle.com/article/Medievalists-Recoiling-From/240666.
2. For examples of how Renaissance Studies attempted to kneecap Renaissance Race Studies, see Stephen Greenblatt, "Racial Memory and Literary History," *Publications of the Modern Language Association of America* (2001): 48–63; and William C. Jordan "Why "Race"? *Journal of Medieval and Early Modern Studies* 31.1 (2001): 165–173; among others.

ever, arguing that, "Fetishizing historical accuracy is to claim the high moral ground of sound scholarship, a position from which to disguise resistance to race work, from which to promote a singular perspective and methodology as acceptable while placing firm restrictions on others."[3] In other words, the calls for "historical accuracy" are less about methodology than they are about access, ownership, and power. These calls for "historical accuracy" rarely take the time to offer caveats and critiques of the standards for "accuracy" and to identify who had the privilege of recording the evidence that positivists use to construct "history."

Yet still, the community of premodern critical race scholars persists. Even more, we flourish. Over the past decade, as more non-white scholars enter into these fields that are historically homogeneous both in terms of gender and race, major organizations in Medieval and Renaissance Studies have engaged in conflict over the field's inherent racism. While some of these conflicts have borne productive fruit, such as the Renaissance Society of America beginning to offer diversity grants for attending their annual conference and the Shakespeare Association of America giving voice to Race Studies in their 2019 plenary session, those who call out the racism often suffer greater attacks than those who perpetrate the racism.[4]

The conflict over the role of race in the study of pre-modern Europe has led scholars of Renaissance England to begin asking the very question that begins this introduction: who owns history? Margo Hendricks's 2007 article, "Race: A Renaissance Category?" avoids the deployment of color to argue for the primacy of race in Renaissance Studies and instead looks at the ways in which the category structured Renaissance identities through

3. Ian Smith, "We Are Othello: Speaking of Race in Early Modern Studies," *Shakespeare Quarterly* 67.1 (2016): 104–124.
4. See "An Open Letter in Support of a Besieged Academic," *National Association of Scholars* 16 Aug. 2018, https://www.nas.org/blogs/dicta/an_open_letter_for_a_besieged_academic; Peter Wood, "Anatomy of a Smear," *Inside Higher Ed.* 30 Sep. 2018, https://www.insidehighered.com/views/2018/09/10/slurring-medieval-scholar-attempt-silence-those-who-disagree-opinion; Dorothy Kim, "Medieval Studies Since Charlottesville." *Inside Higher Ed.* 30 Aug. 2018, https://www.insidehighered.com/views/2018/08/30/scholar-describes-being-conditionally-accepted-medieval-studies-opinion.

its interaction with lineage, inheritance, and the Renaissance theory of "generation," in which notions of illegitimacy of the father brought forth by a lack of resemblance could be explained by attributing the difference to the mother's imagination.[5] Hendricks thus challenges the notion that Renaissance England was a period of "racial purity" by establishing race as an ordering mechanism for English identity and society without collapsing into a discourse purely of color. Arthur Little, Jr., has even gone as far as to openly ask the questions, "Is Shakespeare or the Renaissance/early modern period white property?... Is there something of a *working* assumption in early modern studies that the early modern period ... is a field for the *unmarked*, that is for "white" scholars and those who can so masterfully transform themselves?"[6] With this, Little is challenging all of us to think of race not only as a deviation from an assumed white normativity, but also to think about the ways in which that assumed normativity structures our knowledge of premodern history and the present structure of the academy.

As the field of early modern studies continues to becomes more accessible to diverse ways of thinking and diverse bodies, scholars in the field that previously excluded or denigrated such perspectives have begun to create new spaces. Although times are changing and the academy is becoming more progressive in many ways, albeit with significant backlashes, the study of race in the Renaissance still faces resistance. At this point, however, the arguments against race as a valid category of analysis for early modern studies have largely been debunked; yet, the tired clichés of anachronism and the dangerous assumptions of racial purity persist. The anxiety around scholarship on race in early modern England has led to the unfortunate but understandable use of scare-quotes to surround the term, a problematic device that has been called out by scholars such

5. Margo Hendricks, "Race: A Renaissance Category?" A *Companion to English Renaissance Literature and Culture* (New York: Wiley, 2010), 535–544.
6. Arthur L. Little, Jr., "Re-Historicizing Race, White Melancholia, and the Shakespearean Property," *Shakespeare Quarterly* 67.1 (2016): 84–103; 88.

as Kim F. Hall, Margo Hendricks, Patricia Parker, Matthieu Chapman, and others.[7]

With the rise of white nationalist thought and fascist violence against racial minorities, the stakes for studies of race in pre-modern periods have never been higher. Along with these raised stakes, however, comes an increased threat of violence and anger that can destabilize and undermine any attempts at productive conversation. So how does one discuss race in a period that a majority of both the academic and broader communities consider occurred prior to race? More importantly, how do we bring the potential tinderbox of race into our classrooms in a constructive way that accounts for the knee jerk aversion to these discussions?

Renaissance Race Studies agrees with New Historicism that race in Renaissance Europe did not function the same way it does today. That said, to assume that the vast network of racialized thought that existed in Renaissance Europe exists in a temporal vacuum that has no influence or genealogy with the modes of racialized thinking that exist in today's world is the far more dangerous fallacy. The field of Renaissance Race Studies has largely come to embrace the challenges presented by claims of anachronism and, as such, has utilized varying methodologies to unpack a multifaceted network of intersecting discourses in early modern Europe that deploy racialized grammars to articulate varying identities and subjectivities. These grammars address not only the physical being, but the diverse and complex network of racial thinking that encapsulates multiple forms of difference including the physical, the genealogical, the metaphysical, and the psychic.

In the past few years, the catchphrase "Race Before Race" has become a productive framework for displacing the Enlightenment as the origin of racial thinking and working beyond the often bad-faith claims of anachronism. Prominent organizations such as the Folger Shakespeare Library,

7. See Kim F. Hall, *Things of Darkness: Economies of Race and Gender in Early Modern England* (Ithaca, NY: Cornell UP, 1995), 6–7; Margo Hendricks and Patricia Parker, eds., *Women, "Race," and Writing in the Early Modern Period* (New York: Routledge, 1994) 1–3; Matthieu Chapman, *Anti-Black Racism in Early Modern English Drama: The Other "Other"* (New York: Routledge, 2016), 7–9.

the Arizona Center for Medieval and Renaissance Studies, and Shakespeare's Globe in London have all held symposia, lectures, and other events under the banner of "Race before Race" with the purpose of expanding awareness of the discourse concerning race in the early modern era and its impact and influence on racial thinking today. This framework analyzes the vast network of inter-connected discourse, vocabularies, and practices that structured social order prior to the Enlightenment's pseudo-scientific invention of race while offering a direct challenge to the Enlightenment's long-standing (and fallacious) position as the era that birthed racial discourse.[8]

Unpacking the myriad ways in which race existed before race is perhaps best accomplished by examining and describing the individual threads of racialized discourse that Europeans deployed to construct social order. In her introduction to *Shakespeare, Race, and Colonialism*, Ania Loomba describes the "Vocabularies of Race" that articulate difference in early modern England. She identifies three primary streams of discourses that deploy a racializing vocabulary to construct difference: 1. "Skin, colour, religion, and community"; 2. "cross-cultural encounters"; and 3. "gender, class and national differences."[9] While Loomba's taxonomy provides a port from which to launch our exploration, in the almost twenty years since her review of both early modern and modern literature that deploys racializing discourse, scholars working on race in Renaissance England have not only offered new cartographies of racial vocabulary, but have also charted new waters in the exploration and unpacking of racial thinking that existed in the period. While these streams rarely appear independent from one another, I find it useful to discuss these streams as

8. The period of the Enlightenment (1650 to mid-1800s) gave birth to notions of "scientific racism," a belief that races could be separated into various species through Anthropology, Phrenology, Craniometry, and other disciplines and pseudo-sciences. Although long debunked by science, the works during this period from the likes of Henri de Boulainvilliers, Carl Linnaeus, Georges Cuviers, Arthur Schopenhauer are often fallaciously considered to be the genesis of racial thinking because they were among the first to describe, codify, and classify solid racial categories, even though these categories and the criteria used to establish them were unscientific and bigoted.
9. Ania Loomba, *Shakespeare, Race, and Colonialism* (Oxford: Oxford UP, 2002), 6.

individual categories. Going forward, I will offer a new and expanded vocabularies of race for Renaissance Europe that divides Loomba's streams into their individual tributaries and also accounts for the advancements in the field since Loomba's description.

This new vocabulary outlines ten different modes of racial thought in Early Modern Europe: *blood and genealogy, nation, religion, color, gender, transnational constructions, processes and actions, pseudo-scientific, materiality*, and *subjectivity*. With such a broad spectrum of racial thought present in Early Modern Europe, it would be impossible to include a comprehensive review of the literature. Rather, this chapter is meant to serve as an introduction to and foundation for discussing Early Modern European conceptions of race in contemporary classrooms. Although I define each of the threads individually, the network of racial thought is so interconnected that, while I categorize the works into one framework, each work mentioned includes multiple iterations of race in their analyses. Lastly, while the sources I used to decipher these modes comes primarily from the study of race in Early Modern England, these discourses appear throughout the continent, and the pieces in this collection engage with these modes regardless of geographical area of analysis.

Grammars of Racial Difference in Early Modern Europe

The earliest uses in the English language of the term race to describe human difference comes in the Earl of Surrey's 1547 translation of the ancient Roman poet Virgil's Aeneid.[10] In this context, the term race refers to the *blood and genealogy* (bloodlines and kinship) of the varying tribes of Italy: the Trojans, the Rutulians, and the Ausonians. Jean Feerick's *Strangers in Blood* argues that the emergence of skin color-based designations of race depend on "the decline of a deeply established system of difference that places a metaphysical value on bloodline independent of

10. Virgil Certain bokes of Virgiles Aeneis (transl. Earl of Surrey) 1st edition of bk. II; new edition of bk. IV, 1557 (1 vol.). [London]: Apud Ricardum Tottel. Cum priuilegio ad imprimendum solum STC 24798.

color, complexion, or culture."[11] The discourse of tribe and kinship found in the Earl of Surrey's translation of Virgil would later come to manifest through the interpretation of *nation*, particularly national difference, as racial difference. Scott Oldenburg uses this understanding of race to argue for intersection between blackness, family genealogy, and national identity in his 2001 article, "The Riddle of Blackness in England's National Family Romance."[12] Oldenburg uses numerous examples from early modern texts of Black characters representing the negation of goodness to argue that these characters represent the negative aspects of Oedipal transference, thus leaving the positive aspects, which read white, as the enabling transference that constructs a racialized English national identity.[13] Also in this stream is John Michael Archer's *Old Worlds: Egypt, Southwest Asia, India, and Russia in Early Modern English Writing.*[14] Archer analyzes English travel narratives and dramatic texts to argue that the English not only used racialized distinctions to rank within a taxonomy New World peoples and cultures, but also interpreted and constructed racialized differences between themselves and the Old World cultures and nations described in Archer's title.

In each of these works on blood and nation as racial categories, *color* is already finding its way into the discourse through the deployment of blackness. These color markers distinguishing peoples in early modern England find their way into the discourse on race primarily through *religion*, specifically religious discourses, the third stream of racial thought in the period. Manicheanism, which posited a universe constructed along a divide between light and dark, was one of the most widespread religions

11. Jean E. Feerick, *Strangers in Blood: Relocating Race in the Renaissance* (Toronto: Toronto UP, 2010) 5.
12. Scott Oldenburg, "The Riddle of Blackness in England's National Family Romance," *Journal for Early Modern Cultural Studies* 1.1 (Spring/Summer 2001): 46–62.
13. Oldenburg, "The Riddle of Blackness," 59.
14. John Michael Archer's *Old Worlds: Egypt, Southwest Asia, India, and Russia in Early Modern English Writing* (Stanford: Stanford UP, 2001).

in the world between the third and seventh centuries.[15] These ideas found their way into Christianity in the fourth century through St. Augustine's interpretations of biblical texts.[16] This division persisted for over a millennium into early modern England, where both in texts and in performance, dramatists and players represented God as light and the Devil as black. In *The Devil and the Sacred in English Drama* 1350–1642, John D. Cox argues that the "binary distinction between God and the devil became the model for a series of parallel positions that influenced thinking about science, history, religion, and politics,"[17] and of course, race. Dennis Britton's *Becoming Christian: Race, Reformation, and Early Modern English Romance* offers one of the most compelling articulations of the intersection of religion and race in England, arguing that "the Church of England's baptismal theology transformed Christians and "infidels" into distinctive races."[18] He concludes that "[l]abels like "Jew," "Turk," and "Moor" embrace both racial and religious identities" that make it difficult, if not impossible, to know if the term is meant to describe a person's ethnicity, culture, religion, or all of the above.[19] Robert Hornback's *Racism and Early Blackface Comic Performance* continues the conversation between religious and nationalist discourses on race, arguing that "Renaissance nationalism was frequently proto-racist — a kind of Christian nationalism allied, paradoxically, to racist/prejudiced constructions of pan-European whiteness aiming to colonize, subjugate, plunder, exploit, and/or expel dark-com-

15. For further discussion of the influence of Manicheanism on English religion, see Joseph R. Washington. *Anti-blackness in English Religion*, 1500–1800 (Lewiston, NY: Edwin Mellen, 1984).
16. See Matthieu Chapman, *Anti-Black Racism in Early Modern English Drama: The Other "Other"* (New York: Routledge, 2016), 36–39.
17. John Cox, *The Devil and the Sacred in English Drama* 1350–1642 (Cambridge: Cambridge UP, 2000), 6.
18. Dennis Austin Britton, *Becoming Christian: Race, Reformation, and Early Modern English Romance* (New York: Fordham UP, 2014), 4.
19. Britton, *Becoming Christian*, 6.

plexion Strangers … "[20] These works, while offering distinct viewpoints on the matter, each prioritize religion in their discussion of racialization.

The division between black and white that originated in religious texts would eventually find grounding in the physical body and manifest as skin color as a means of articulating racialized difference. Sujata Iyengar's *Shades of Difference: Mythologies of Skin Color in Early Modern England* argues that notions of race as related to embodiment and skin color can only be understood in their historical, geographical, and literary contexts.[21] For Iyengar, the literary contexts, the construction of myths and narratives of difference, played the primary role in the creation of color-based racial identities.[22] Cristina Malcolmson's *Studies of Skin Color in the Early Royal Society: Boyle, Cavendish, Swift* also takes a skin-color based approach to analyzing race; however, instead of relying on literature, Malcolmson looks at the relationships between science, government, colonialism, and the slave trade that produced ideas about race.[23] Imtiaz Habib takes an archival approach to racialized color difference in *Black Lives in the English Archives: Imprints of the Invisible.*[24] This collection of historical documents referencing dark-complexioned people in England includes an analysis of the role the archive played in the construction of racial difference in early modern England.

Recently, scholars such as Gary Taylor, Arthur Little, Jr., and David Sterling Brown have begun to re-interpret the color divide of early modern race studies to decentralize whiteness as the normative, un-racialized body. Gary Taylor's *Buying Whiteness: Race, Culture and Identity from Columbus to Hip Hop* is a survey of five centuries of literary texts, art, and popular culture that seeks to examine the formation of whiteness

20. Robert Hornback, *Racism and Early Blackface Comic Traditions: From the Old World to the New* (New York: Springer, 2018), 271.
21. Sujata Iyengar, *Shades of Difference: Mythologies of Skin Color in Early Modern England* (Philadelphia: Cambridge University Press, 2004).
22. Iyegnar, *Shades of Difference*, 1.
23. Cristina Malcolmson, *Studies of Skin Color in the Early Royal Society: Boyle, Cavendish, Swift* (Burlington, VT: Ashgate, 2013).
24. Imtiaz Habib, *Black Lives in the English Archives, 1500–1677: Imprints of the Invisible* (Burlington, VT: Ashgate, 2008).

as a racial category.[25] Arthur Little's *Re-Historicizing Race, White Melancholia, and the Shakespearean Property* argues that the English subject constructed an ideal version of whiteness that was unattainable by the subject, thus racializing the subject in relation to their own whiteness and producing an existential melancholia.[26] Patricia Akhimie's *Shakespeare and the Cultivation of Difference* analyzes racial discourse and thought in Shakespearean works that do not contain a character who is othered by their skin tone.[27]

The Manichean binaries or black and white, good and evil, God and Devil would also lead to the development of *gender* as a racialized difference in early modern English thought. Kim F. Hall's *Things of Darkness: Economies of Race and Gender in Early Modern England* is among the works that influenced not only arguments of gender as a racialized construct, but the field of Renaissance Race Studies as a whole. Hall argues that "the polarity of light and dark articulates ongoing cultural concerns over gender roles and shifting trade structures" and that "dark and light, rather than being mere indications of Elizabethan beauty standards or markers of moral categories, became in the early modern period the conduit through which the English began to formulate notions of "self" and "other.""[28] Joyce Green MacDonald's *Women and Race in Early Modern Texts* examines the racial identities of female characters, audiences, and writers in early modern England to argue that gender and racial formations inform each other.[29] Lara Bovilsky's *Barbarous Play: Race on the English Renaissance Stage* examines shifts in individual identity on the

25. Gary Taylor, *Buying Whiteness: Race, Culture and Identity from Columbus to Hip Hop* (New York: Palgrave, 2005).
26. Arthur L. Little, Jr., "Re-Historicizing Race, White Melancholia, and the Shakespearean Property." *Shakespeare Quarterly* 67.1 (2016): 84–103.
27. Patricia Akhimie. *Shakespeare and the Cultivation of Difference: Race and Conduct in the Early Modern World* (New York: Routledge, 2018).
28. Kim F. Hall, *Things of Darkness: Economies of Race and Gender in Early Modern England.* (Ithaca, NY: Cornell UP, 1995): 2.
29. Joyce Green MacDonald, *Women and Race in Early Modern Texts* (Cambridge: Cambridge UP, 2002).

Renaissance stage, arguing that these shifts reveal deep parallels between the categories of race and gender in early modern England.[30]

In the last few years, scholars have recognized that the Early Modern period does not fit so easily into the nation state analysis that academia has relied on since the 1940s and have begun to shift to an approach to the past that engages with notions of "connected histories" and other *transnational constructions*. Connected histories do not assume that nation-states existed in a vacuum that produced homogeneous and independent cultures and societies, but rather prefers to operate under the assumptive logic that the world is interconnected through travel, trade, commerce, and culture. Studies of race in early modern England have also recently begun to engage in connected histories of the topic that seek to uncover and analyze the trans-national and trans-cultural exchanges that inform ideations of race. Susan D. Amussen's *Caribbean Exchanges: Slavery and the Transformation of English Society*, 1640-1700 explores the circulation of race between England and the Caribbean, arguing that Caribbean slaveowning practices informed the construction of England's racial whiteness.[31] The collection *Early Modern Black Diaspora Studies*, edited by Cassander L. Smith, Nicholas Jones, and Miles Parks Grier, creates a bridge between Black studies and early modern studies by examining the interconnectedness of notions of blackness as they relate to culture, bodies, and history across national boundaries ranging from England to Spain to the Caribbean.[32]

In addition to the bodily conceptions of race, scholars have begun to argue that certain *processes and actions* in early modern England intersected with and produced racialized discourse. Ayanna Thompson's *Performing Race and Torture on the Early Modern Stage* analyzes scenes of torture in early modern drama to argue that the torture of racialized flesh

30. Lara Bovilsky, *Barbarous Play: Race on the English Renaissance Stage* (Minneapolis: U of Minnesota P, 2008).
31. Susan Amussen, *Caribbean Exchanges: Slavery and the Transformation of English Society*, 1640–1700 (Chapel Hill: UNC Press, 2007).
32. Cassander L. Smith, Nicholas R. Jones, and Miles P. Grier, eds., *Early Modern Black Diaspora Studies: A Critical Anthology* (New York: Springer, 2018).

reveals a paradoxical idea of race as both a construction and essential in the eyes of the early modern English subject.[33] Ian Smith's *Race and Rhetoric in the Renaissance: Barbarian Errors* argues that the early modern English subject used language as a marker of civility to separate themselves from barbarous Africans, thus making language inextricably linked with the formation of racial identities.[34] Also in this category is Elizabeth Spiller's *Reading and the History of Race in the Renaissance*. Spiller argues that the early modern English subject understood reading as something that happened both in and to the body, and thus what you read could change what you were, including altering one's racial identity.[35]

This period also had its share of *pseudo-scientific* discourses on race. English translations of classical texts reignited interest in Climate Theory, which posited that skin color was a product of geographical latitude, and Humoral Theory, which argued that color was reflective of an internal imbalance between the bodily fluids of phlegm, blood, black bile, and yellow bile. Mary Floyd-Wilson's *English Ethnicity and Race in Early Modern Drama* argues that the early modern English subject re-interpreted and re-imagined these discourses to alter their original depiction of the English as "impressible, barbaric, and inversely defined by the traits and temperament of dark peoples on the other side of the world."[36] Race was such a powerful tool for structuring society that the English subject rewrote science to affirm white superiority.

In addition to the physical body and bodily practice, scholars have also argued that *materiality* and certain materials were racialized as part of English subject formation, thus creating a discourse in which materials play a role in racial identity formation. Virginia Mason Vaughan's *Performing Blackness on English Stages, 1500–1800* argues that the ways in which

33. Ayanna Thompson, *Performing Race and Torture on the Early Modern Stage* (New York: Routledge, 2013).
34. Ian Smith, *Race and Rhetoric in the Renaissance: Barbarian Errors* (New York: Springer, 2009).
35. Elizabeth Spiller, *Reading and the History of Race in the Renaissance* (Cambridge: Cambridge UP, 2011).
36. Mary Floyd-Wilson, *English Ethnicity and Race in Early Modern Drama* (Cambridge: Cambridge UP, 2003), 5.

the stage portrayed blackness, including costumes, cosmetics, narrative tropes, character types, and physical performances all played a role in English racial formations.[37] Andrea Stevens's *Inventions of the Skin: The Painted Body in Early English Drama* 1400–1642 discusses the use of blackface cosmetics on the English stage to portray race and how it allowed the ideas of the characters' racial formation to circulate into society as a whole.[38] Ian Smith's seminal "Othello's Black Handkerchief" argues that both scholars and practitioners have appropriated the handkerchief in *Othello* to construct a formation of blackness that denies black subjectivity.[39]

On the notion of *subjectivity*, recently scholars have begun to use modern Critical Race Theory to unpack racial logics in early modern England and challenge that not only is race a category of human, but also race is used to define what it means to be human. Matthieu Chapman's *Antiblack Racism in Early Modern English Drama: The Other "Other"* uses contemporary Afro-Pessimist Theory to argue that chattel slavery in America is the product of the English constructing their humanity through antiblackness, thus rendering Black Africans as ontologically inhuman.[40]

This is by no means an exhaustive list of the scholarship that addresses race in early modern England, but rather is meant to provide a foundation for understanding the myriad conceptualizations of race in early modern England and the work currently being done on the topic. Unpacking the discursive threads deployed by these scholars provides a useful vocabulary for discussing race throughout early modern Europe. The multifaceted, intersecting network of racialized discourses in early modern England manifest throughout the scholarly spectrum, leaving no field of inquiry untouched and no body, regardless of the descriptors used, unmarked. To discuss history is to discuss humanity, and to discuss

37. Virginia Mason Vaughan, *Performing Blackness on English Stages, 1500–1800* (Cambridge: Cambridge UP, 2005).
38. Andrea Stevens, *Inventions of the Skin* (Edinburgh: Edinburgh UP, 2013).
39. Ian Smith, "Othello's Black Handkerchief." *Shakespeare Quarterly* 64.1 (2013): 1–25.
40. Matthieu Chapman. *Anti-Black Racism in Early Modern English Drama: The Other "Other"* (New York: Routledge, 2016).

humanity is to discuss race. To approach discussions of race in the Renaissance, however, requires expanding the vocabularies with which we typically approach race in the modern era. I encourage you to proceed through this volume not only questioning what it means for a body to be raced in early modern England and elsewhere, but also the different ways in which bodies, ideas, and imaginations can be raced and what it means in those cases in which race goes unremarked. As you approach the forthcoming chapters on England and texts from early modern England in your classes, think beyond race as purely a difference in skin color and keep in mind the many different ways in which race appears in early modern English society, culture, and politics as well as the texts, discourses, knowledge, and performances they produce.

Questions for Discussion

1. Think of the texts you know from early modern England that deal with race. Which of these categories appear in those texts? How do they appear?
2. How do these individual strains of racial grammar intersect and diverge in the discourse, texts, and performances of early modern England?
3. Are there other grammars of difference in early modern England that intersect with or could be better articulated through race?
4. In what ways do these grammars manifest in other regional, national, and geographical discourses? What other strains of racialized grammar do other nations deploy to construct difference?
5. While contemporary discourse often defines race purely through difference in skin color, this difference is often discussed in relation to these categories. In what ways do these early modern English categories of race continue to manifest today?

When Students Recognize Gender but Not Race: Addressing the Othello-Caliban Conundrum

MAYA MATHUR

Carol Mejia-LaPerle ended her talk at the 2019 RaceB4Race symposium, "Race and Periodization," with the following question: "As we commit to anti-racist efforts in our thinking, researching, and teaching, what materials, archives, histories and experiences can we put *beside* each other?"[1] She suggested that juxtaposing historical documents, contemporary texts, and experiential narratives might offer one avenue for exploring the continuities between past and present attitudes toward race. Katherine Gillen and Lisa Jennings make a similar claim when they call on teachers to decolonize Shakespeare by highlighting the racist contexts and colonial legacies of his plays; facilitating intersectional readings of his work; assigning responses to his plays by BIPOC artists and critics; and providing students with opportunities to engage creatively with his work.[2] The layered approach that Meija-LaPerle and Gillen and Jennings mention is vital at a time when well-funded white supremacist and anti-immigrant campaigns seek to ban discussions of race and racism in the classroom.[3] The antiracist approaches to teaching that they advocate are an important rejoinder to the attempts to silence discussions about race and racism in early modern literature.

1. Carol Mejia LaPerle, "Dark Will, Race, and Affect: Philosophical Histories of Will and Critical Race Studies," *Race and Periodization*, Washington DC, 2019.
2. Katherine Gillen and Lisa Jennings, "Decolonizing Shakespeare? Towards an Antiracist, Culturally Sustaining Praxis," *The Sundial*, 26 Nov. 2019, accessed 27 Jan. 2020, https://medium.com/the-sundial-acmrs/decolonizing-shakespeare-toward-an-antiracist-culturally-sustaining-praxis-904cb9ff8a96.
3. Recent legislation against discussions in Florida, Texas, and Oklahoma's public schools represents just one instance of a broader campaign to suppress antiracist texts and practices.

In the Predominantly White Institution (PWI) where I teach, this silence often stems from my students' lack of experience, and resultant discomfort, with conversations about race. This reluctance is evident in their responses to *Othello* (1603–1604) and *The Tempest* (1611), plays that chronicle the oppression that their non-white characters, Othello, a Moor, and Caliban, an Indigenous figure, face at the hands of white Europeans.[4] On the surface, Othello and Caliban are quite different. Othello is a respected general in Venice while Caliban is a servant to Prospero and Miranda, the banished Duke of Milan and his daughter who occupy his island. Despite the external difference in their circumstances, Othello and Caliban share one trait: their persecution is predicated on their desire for white women. Othello's position in Venice is threatened when he marries Desdemona, the daughter of Brabantio, a Venetian senator, and shattered completely after he murders her at the instigation of his ensign, Iago. On a related note, Caliban loses his freedom when he tries to rape Miranda in an attempt to wrest control of the island from Prospero.

The oppression of non-white men who display hostility towards white women represents a conundrum for many of my students: Should they sympathize with Othello and Caliban after their abuse of Desdemona and Miranda? Would they condone the violence against Desdemona and Miranda in doing so? How should the men in power, such as Brabantio, Iago, and Prospero, who enable gendered violence but do not perpetrate it, be treated? The students in my courses on Shakespeare have typically responded with sympathy to the mistreatment of Desdemona and Miranda but been more equivocal in their response to the racial hostility directed at Othello and Caliban. On the one hand, student sympathy towards Desdemona and Miranda, whose male guardians habitually silence them, is understandable. Indeed, for students coming of age in the #MeToo era, privileging Desdemona's and Miranda's plight over the hostility directed towards Othello and Caliban may appear to be the natural, even feminist, position to take when interpreting *Othello* and *The Tempest*. At the same time, their unwillingness to extend similar consideration

4. I use the term "non-white" when referring to both Othello and Caliban. I am grateful to Matthieu Chapman for his suggestions on terminology.

towards Othello and Caliban suggests a concomitant failure to recognize and acknowledge their suffering.[5]

In this essay, I explore the potential reasons for my students' silence and discuss strategies to help create greater awareness of race and racism in *Othello* and *The Tempest*. As David Sterling Brown notes, however, teachers do their students a disservice if they focus on how race affects minority characters while ignoring its impact on white characters.[6] Just as important, Kim F. Hall maintains that "concentrating only on the 'other' may not be antiracist since it does not necessarily engage in issues of power." [7] Taking these arguments as a starting point, I draw attention to the ways in which privilege informs and protects white characters even as it isolates and marginalizes non-white characters in *Othello* and *The Tempest*.

I assign these texts, and the historical materials that accompany them, with the awareness that my students' overlapping identities will generate a wide variety of responses, from experiences of white fragility — feelings of discomfort or resistance to conversations about race — to distress at the long history of racial oppression that is reflected in the plays.[8] I seek

5. David Sterling Brown identifies a similar dynamic in critical responses to *The Merchant of Venice* and *Titus Andronicus* in "The 'Sonic Color Line': Shakespeare and the Canonization of Sexual Violence against Black Men," *The Sundial*, 16 Aug. 2019, accessed 17 March 2021, https://medium.com/the-sundial-acmrs/the-sonic-color-line-shakespeare-and-the-canonization-of-sexual-violence-against-black-men-cb166dca9af8. On the lack of sympathy for Othello's epilepsy, see Justin P. Shaw, "'Rub Him About the Temples': *Othello*, Disability, and the Failures of Care," *Early Theater* 22.2 (2019): 172–173. These essays connect premodern and contemporary methods for policing Black men and can be productively assigned when teaching *Othello*.
6. David Sterling Brown, "(Early) Modern Literature: Crossing the Color-Line," *Radical Teacher* (2016): 69–77.
7. Kim F. Hall, "Teaching Race and Gender," *Shakespeare Quarterly* 47.4 (1996): 461. Eric De Barros makes a related point when he suggests that instructors should find strategies to help students confront their biases instead of seeking to reduce their discomfort with discussing issues of race, "Teacher Trouble: Performing Race in the Majority White Shakespeare Classroom," *Journal of American Studies* 54.1 (2020): 79.
8. See Robin DiAngelo, "White Fragility," *International Journal of Critical Pedagogy* 3.3 (2011): 57.

to address these responses to the play with a content note on my syllabus that I read during the first class session and reiterate whenever we read texts that involve language or imagery that students may find upsetting. The note states, "Your well-being is important to me, as is your success in the course. You should be aware that the texts we study are early representations of early modern race-thinking; that is, they traffic in religious and racial stereotypes that may be emotionally challenging to read. Some of the texts we read also contain references to sexual violence and ableist language and imagery. I will flag these texts before we read them and will be available to discuss your reactions to them." I try not to assume that white students will be unaware of the racist discourse in the plays or that non-white students will wish to discuss racist elements of the text.[9] Instead, I seek to be mindful of the multiplicity of student reactions the play might generate while facilitating a discussion about the roles that privilege and oppression play in the materials under examination.

In the balance of this essay, I outline strategies that I use to raise awareness of the intersections of race and gender in *Othello* and *The Tempest* in a course on Shakespeare and race. The questions I asked myself when designing the course were as follows: What tools could I use to create greater awareness of how racial injustice intersects with gendered violence in *Othello* and *The Tempest*? What methods could I employ to illustrate the harm that is inflicted on non-white characters in these plays and generate greater awareness of the structural oppression they face? I address these questions through a layered methodology that includes historicizing representations of race, close reading raced and gendered language in the plays, exploring visual representations of the plays, and investigating the treatment of race and gender in modern adaptations. This approach to course design has helped generate more complex discussions of the stereotypes about race and gender presented in these plays and the extent to which Othello and Caliban can resist them. While I developed these strategies for a course on Shakespeare and race, the

9. On *Othello*'s resonance for students of color, see Francesca Royster, "Rememorializing Othello: Teaching *Othello* and the Cultural Memory of Racism," *Approaches to Teaching Shakespeare's* Othello, edited by Peter Erickson (New York: MLA Press, 2005), 53–61.

units on historicizing, close reading, visualizing, and adapting the plays that I discuss below may be modified for discussions of *Othello* and *The Tempest* in high school and college classrooms.

Historicizing Race

There is a rich history of scholarship on Othello and Caliban as raced figures. While I recommend a selection of this scholarship to my students, I have found that teaching Ayanna Thompson's essay, "Did the Concept of Race Exist for Shakespeare?" in concert with Ibram X. Kendi's chapter, "Human Hierarchy," can help illustrate how ideas about race were formed and circulated in the early modern period.[10] Kendi's chapter provides the context for early modern race-making by explaining how classical theories of racial difference and early modern treatises that were used to justify the transatlantic slave trade.[11] Thompson's essay introduces readers to the concept of race-making or racecraft, the process through which racial ideologies were constructed, and examines their circulation in Shakespeare's plays. Taken together, these texts help students understand the ways in which early modern Europeans created racial categories to justify enslavement and colonization in Africa, Asia, and the Americas.[12] These essays provide the context for the historical documents that students engage with when studying *Othello* and *The Tempest* and provide them

10. Ayanna Thompson, "Did the Concept of Race Exist for Shakespeare and his Contemporaries?" *The Cambridge Companion to Shakespeare and Race* (New York: Cambridge University Press, 2021), 7–8. Ibram X. Kendi, *Stamped from the Beginning: The Definitive History of Racist Ideas in America* (New York: Penguin, 2016), 20–21.
11. In the preface to his book, Kendi classifies ideas about race into three groups, segregationist, or the belief in racial hierarchies, assimilationist, the belief that marginalized groups should adopt the cultural values of those in power, and antiracist, the belief that all races are equal (4–5). I find it useful to outline these categories and ask students where they would situate the characters in *Othello* and *The Tempest* in relation to them.
12. The inconsistencies of early modern race-making are also illustrated in Ania Loomba and Jonathan Burton's anthology, *Race in Early Modern England: A Documentary Companion* (New York: Palgrave Macmillan, 2007).

with the tools to critically analyze these artifacts. Teaching the essays at the beginning of the semester helps students recognize when characters are echoing the racial ideologies of their time and when they are challenging its tenets.

I provide students with some of the cultural contexts for *Othello* by assigning the anonymous ballad, "The Lady and the Blackamoor" (c.1569–1570) and an excerpt from George Best's *Discourse of Discovery* (1578), at the beginning of class discussion on the play.[13] The ballad features a villainous Moor who responds to being chastised by the lord he serves by kidnapping his master's wife and children and gleefully plotting their deaths. The ballad rehearses a series of stereotypes about Moors as dishonest, rapacious, and bloodthirsty that I use to frame the close-reading of the text.[14] Students reading the ballad alongside Act 1, Scene 1 of the play can point to the similarities between the disgruntled Moor and Iago, and note the contrast between him and Othello. These contrasts can be used to suggest that Shakespeare was challenging established images of Moorish violence in his initial construction of Othello.

Interestingly, *Othello* does not simply reverse the positions of ensign and lord from "The Lady and the Blackamoor."[15] The second document we study, George Best's *Discourse of Discovery*, complicates Shakespeare's portrayal of Othello and Iago in other ways. In the excerpt we read, George Best offers three reasons to account for the blackness of the people who inhabit the Torrida Zone, whom he refers to variously as either

13. All references to the play are from William Shakespeare, *Othello: Text and Contexts*, ed. Kim F. Hall (Boston: Bedford/St. Martin's, 2007). The excerpts from "The Lady and the Blackamoor" and *Discourse of Discovery* that I assign are from the chapter, "Race and Religion," in the Cultural Contexts section of the volume.
14. Hall, 197-203.
15. Patricia Fumerton offers an excellent account of the ballad's recirculation in prose accounts about the threat that enslaved people posed to slaveholders in eighteenth-century Georgia, The Moving Violation of "The Lady and the Blackamoor." *The Broadside Ballad in Early Modern England* (Philadelphia: University of Pennsylvania Press, 2020), 273–274. Excerpts from the prose account might be taught alongside the ballad to illustrate the process by which a sensational work of fiction may be repackaged as a truthful account in the service of race-making.

Black Moors or Ethiopians — the hot climate in which they live, a natural infection that they pass on to their heirs, and a consequence of sin stemming from Cham's disobedience of his father, Noah, which was punished in the black skin of his children, but ultimately settles on the curse of Cham as the most satisfactory explanation for this condition. Best writes, "And of this black and cursed Chus came all these black Moors which are in Africa, for ... Africa remained for Cham [Ham] and his black son, Chus, and was called Chamesis, after the father's name, being perhaps a cursed, dry, sandy and unfruitful ground, fit for such a generation to inhabit. Thus, you see that the cause of the Ethiopians' blackness is the curse and natural infection of blood."[16] I assign Best's *Discourse* toward the end of class discussion on *Othello* in order to ask a series of open-ended questions on the extent to which Best's theories of race, especially his notion of infection and sin, inform the play. These might include the following: Which characters infect, and which characters are infected? How does the notion of infection shift and change during the course of the play? Is the infection literal, figurative, or a combination of the two conditions? Students often focus on Othello's increasing consciousness of his blackness as well as Desdemona's growing association with her mother's Black maid, Barbary, to view the play as confirming Best's theory by locating blackness as a metaphorical infection that Othello passes on to Desdemona. Still others read against the grain of Best's treatise by describing Iago as the source of an infection that damages the characters he comes into contact with his racist and misogynist beliefs. Using these materials can sensitize students to the ways in which *Othello* might destabilize Best's race-making even as it appears to confirm his views.

I employ similar methods when teaching *The Tempest* in relation to early modern narratives about colonization. I begin by having students read excerpts from two documents, Richard Hakluyt's *Reasons for Colonization* and Michel de Montaigne's "Of the Cannibals," from the Bedford/St. Martin's edition of *The Tempest* (2000). I assign Hakluyt's treatise early in our discussion of the play since the author uses it to advocate for England's assertion of religious and military authority over the Americas. For

16. Hall, 193.

Hakluyt, this exercise of hard and soft power will supply England with a regular supply of cheap commodities and provide its manufacturers with a ready market in which to sell their goods. As he asserts when writing of Indigenous groups who may be reluctant to trade with the English, "they shall not dare to offer us any great annoy but such as we may easily revenge with sufficient chastisement to the unarmed people there."[17]

After they read Hakluyt's text, I ask students to outline his central claims regarding the land that is about to be colonized as well as its inhabitants. Then, we consider the extent to which Hakluyt's formulation is applicable to Prospero, Trinculo, and Stefano's plans for the island and its inhabitants in *The Tempest*. Students note that, unlike Hakluyt, who was invested in extracting material wealth from the Americas, the play's colonizers are more interested in exploiting the workers that the island provides. Students point to the magic that Prospero harnesses from Ariel and his fellow spirits as well as the labor he extracts from Caliban as signs of his status as a colonizer. I also ask students to list the strategies that Prospero uses to maintain his power, especially with a rebel like Caliban in his midst. Finally, students compare Prospero's successful exertion of his authority with Trinculo and Stefano's comic attempts to play the colonizer with Caliban. As they note, Trinculo's desire to profit by displaying Caliban's body in England and Stefano's desire to be king of the island are comic instantiations of Hakluyt's playbook for conquest. Reviewing a text like Hakluyt's *Reasons* generates awareness of the ease with which European characters asserted their authority over the natives they encountered and illustrates the dehumanizing nature of colonial contact. Situating Caliban within the discourse of colonization thus creates greater awareness of the cycle of labor and punishment that he endures on the island and helps frame his desire to escape it.

The relationship between Montaigne's "Of the Cannibals" and *The Tempest* is more complicated. Montaigne's essay champions what he sees as the egalitarian government of the Tupinamba people in Brazil — and by extension other Indigenous people in the Americas — whom he repre-

17. All references are from William Shakespeare, *The Tempest*, edited by Gerald Graff and James Phelan (New York: Bedford/St. Martin's, 2000), 126.

sents as free from the corrupting influence of Europe's political, legal, and economic institutions. As Montaigne notes, the inhabitants of the Americas are "a nation ... that hath no kind of traffic, no knowledge of letters, no intelligence of numbers, no name of magistrate, nor of politic superiority; no use of service, of riches, or of poverty; no contracts, no successions, no partitions, no occupation but idle."[18] Montaigne's view finds an unlikely advocate in Gonzalo, the king of Naples's counselor, whose folly in imagining a democratic kingdom in which he can anoint himself king is mocked by Antonio and Sebastian, the play's villains. Gonzalo's speech echoes Montaigne's, especially in the suggestion that the island would involve "no kind of traffic / ... no name of magistrate / Letters should not be known; riches, poverty / And use of service, none" (2.1.145–148). The affinities between Montaigne and Gonzalo's words, like the alignments between Hakluyt and Prospero, Trinculo, and Stefano, can generate important discussions about Shakespeare's engagement with discourses of colonization.

I accordingly ask students to read this exchange and consider the following questions in light of Montaigne's essay: Should we take Gonzalo's vision of a society in which all things are held in common seriously? Or, should we agree with Antonio and Sebastian that the system that Gonzalo imagines is unworkable in practice? If we agree with the play's villains, are we also complicit in their view that the only system of government possible is one that is built on conquest? Most students respond to this question by suggesting that Shakespeare sets Gonzalo up to be mocked by the readers. They are less certain of how to read Antonio and Sebastian's vision of authority, a vision that Caliban shares when he calls on Stefano to murder Prospero and seize the island from him. Caliban's thirst for violence, like his assault on Miranda, aligns him with the usurping younger brothers, Antonio and Sebastian, and against the seemingly benevolent patriarchs, Prospero and Alonso. Placing Hakluyt and Montaigne in conversation with the characters who are disempowered in *The Tempest* can provide students with insight into why they rebel and how their political

18. Graff and Phelan, 120.

beliefs have shaped their rebellion – beliefs that originate in Europe and not the island.[19]

Close Reading for Race/Gender

Historical documents help students theorize the oppressive regimes within which Othello and Caliban operate, but they do not do enough to disrupt the racial baggage – the unacknowledged or unconsidered assumptions about race – that students bring to the classroom.[20] This baggage is shaped by a media landscape in which racial, religious, and gender "outsiders" are treated with suspicion, whether this involves rhetoric that defends the police killing of unarmed Black men, upholds anti-immigrant sentiments, or supports legislation targeting transgender communities. Students raised to be uncritical recipients of social media may buy into negative stereotypes about marginalized communities just as often as they might question them.[21] The messages that students receive online might make them more susceptible to the pronouncements of characters like Prospero and Iago than those of outsiders like Othello and Caliban. Moreover, students may grow to question the oppressive ideologies of Iago and Prospero, but rarely question the moral authority of the plays' heroines, Desdemona and Miranda. Indeed, once virtue is aligned with racial and gender superiority, it becomes constitutive of a dramatic ideal that Desdemona and Miranda embody and that Othello and Caliban cannot live up to.

19. For a discussion of European beliefs about the inhabitants of the Americas and their attitude toward Indigenous property rights respectively, see essays by John Gillies and Patricia Steed in *The Tempest and Its Travels* edited by Peter Hulme and William H. Sherman (Philadelphia: University of Pennsylvania Press, 2000), 180–219.
20. I am grateful to Elisa Oh for outlining the "pre-formed and bone-deep conceptions of race" that students bring to the classroom in the RaceB4Race Symposium, "Race and Periodization," Washington DC, September 2019.
21. On the divergence of Black and white opinion on race and policing, see Ian F. Smith "We are Othello: Speaking of Race in Early Modern Studies," *Shakespeare Quarterly* (Spring 2016): 116–117.

To start, I create greater awareness of unacknowledged structures of exclusion in the plays by introducing students to the concepts of privilege and intersectionality outlined by Peggy McIntosh and Kimberlé Crenshaw in their seminal work on race and gender.[22] In her essay, "White Privilege and Male Privilege," McIntosh defines privilege as a series of unearned advantages that confers power on the dominant group. Kimberlé Crenshaw's definition of intersectionality offers a necessary complication of McIntosh's work by highlighting the overlapping axes of oppression to which non-white women are often subjected. I introduce students to the concepts developed by these authors in order to illustrate the privileges that white women and non-white men may have on account of their race and gender and to differentiate their position from those of two non-white women, Desdemona's Black nursemaid, Barbary, and Caliban's mother, Sycorax, who are marginalized because of their race and gender. I draw attention to these overlapping axes of privilege and oppression at the beginning of the semester so that students are better prepared to recognize them and chart their circulation in the characters and language of the plays.

I ask students to consider how these concepts operate in *Othello* and *The Tempest* through a series of close-reading activities that examine how white male power is upheld and whether white women like Desdemona, Emilia, and Miranda, who have race privilege but experience gender subordination, can exercise similar authority. In addition, these activities are designed to uncover how racial privilege is used to demonize Othello and Caliban. My goal for this exercise is to help students recognize the history and genealogy of racism that is situated in the language of the plays and that they may not recognize as racialized.[23] Often, these activities involve examining the racialized language that white characters use to vil-

22. Peggy McIntosh, "White Privilege and Male Privilege," *Privilege: A Reader*, ed. Michael Kimmel (New York: Routledge, 2017), 29, 36–37. Kimberlé Crenshaw, "Demarginalizing the Intersections of Race and Sex," *University of Chicago Legal Forum* 1 (1989): 143, 159.
23. For an excellent resource on the way language is used to idealize whiteness and demonize blackness, see Farah Karim-Cooper, "Anti-Racist Shakespeare," *Shakespeare's Globe*, 26 May 2020. www.shakespearesglobe.com/discover/blogs-and-features/2020/05/26/anti-racist-shakespeare. Accessed 10 Jan. 2020.

ify Othello and Caliban. For instance, I have students interrogate the axes of privilege in *Othello* through its opening sequence where Iago, Roderigo, and Brabantio use a series of racial epithets to describe the relationship between Othello and Desdemona. I ask the class to catalogue the stereotypes of race that emerge in this exchange. These epithets include Iago and Roderigo's dehumanizing references to Othello as "the thick lips," "black ram," "Barbary horse," and "devil" (1.1.67, 91, 93, 113), and Brabantio's accusation that Othello is a "foul thief," a "thing," and practitioner "of arts inhibited" who has trapped his daughter by witchcraft (1.2.62, 72, 79).[24] I use close-reading activities such as this one to draw students' attention to the stereotypes about Moors that white men circulate in the play.

I follow this close reading of the play's opening scene with an examination of Othello and Desdemona's description of their union in Act 1, Scene 3. As students note, the couple challenge Iago's portrayal of their relationship by casting Othello as the desired guest and Desdemona as the desiring subject. The contrast between Iago's representation and Othello's self-fashioning begin to blur in the play's later acts as Othello grows more susceptible to manipulation and begins to see himself through Iago's racist gaze. The change in Othello's persona makes it easier for students to focus on Othello's gullibility in the face of Iago's fabricated evidence about Desdemona and Cassio. I seek to challenge this perspective by asking students to chronicle Othello's account of the marital, professional, and psychological losses he suffers on account of Iago's resentment.[25] I do so in order to highlight Othello's humanity at a point in the play when he appears to be transforming into the violent "other" that Iago envisions for the audience. My task as an instructor is to interrupt audience complicity with characters like Iago and illustrate the methods that he uses to perpetuate racist and misogynist beliefs about Othello and Desdemona until they are echoed by other characters in the play.

24. I remind students of the content note on my syllabus before we engage in close-reading activities that involve racist language or forms of sexual violence.

25. Othello's exchange with Iago in 3.3.350–379 is instructive in this regard because Othello uses it to connect his loss of Desdemona with his loss of reputation in the Venetian army.

One final strategy I use to unpack the play's racist framework is the exchange between Othello and Emilia that follows Desdemona's murder in Act 5, Scene 2. Here, Emilia echoes Iago's language regarding Moors by tarring Othello with a list of racial slurs, including "devil," blacker devil," "gull," and "dolt," as she proclaims him a murderer (5.2.135, 137, 170). My students' concern with Othello's treatment of Desdemona means that they often end up identifying with Emilia, who becomes a proto-feminist heroine of sorts when she outlines the patriarchal double standard that allows men to mistreat their wives (4.3.85–102). This structure of sympathy means that students often end up sharing her critique of Othello as "the blacker devil" just as much as they become complicit with Iago's stereotypical image of him (5.2.135). In this context, I ask students to consider what Emilia's words reveal about the politics of race and gender in the play. I want my students to notice that while Emilia is supposed to be subordinate to the men in the play, her racial privilege also gives her greater moral authority over Othello at the play's conclusion. The final speech we look at is Lodovico's at the end of the play, which confirms Emilia's perspective by erasing Othello's legacy and transferring his wealth to Cassio. Lodovico's speech demonstrates that, despite their claims of color blindness, the Venetian authorities were always grooming potential heirs from within their ranks in order to reduce Othello's importance to the state.

Caliban experiences no such fall from grace in *The Tempest*. His place at the bottom of the social hierarchy is evident to the audience the moment he emerges from the rock where Prospero has imprisoned him. Like Othello, Caliban is described in terms that racialize him, strip him of his humanity, and render him an object of ridicule. In a series of exchanges that we examine in class, Prospero and Miranda refer to Caliban as a "whelp," "slave," "villain," "tortoise," and "savage" when they first describe him for the audience (2.1.283, 311, 316, 319, 358). Stefano and Trinculo, the drunken butler and jester who become Caliban's temporary companions on the island, likewise address him as "mooncalf," "monster," and "servant monster," terms that designate his status as an outsider even among those at the bottom of the Neapolitan social ladder (2.2.128, 140; 3.2.3).[26] The epithets used to describe Caliban carry negative associations similar to those about Othello's skin color and his status as a Moor. The most specific of these designations, surprisingly, comes from Miranda. In her only direct speech to Caliban, the compassion that Miranda shows for the victims of the tempest disappears as she blames Caliban's "vile race" for his ingratitude toward her father and herself (1.2.361).[27] Caliban seems to confirm Miranda's perspective of him as a "thing most brutish" when he gleefully admits that he tried to assault Miranda in order to wrest control of the island (1.2.360, 352–54). Miranda's chastisement of Caliban, coupled with Caliban's lack of shame about his reported assault on her, sets up a conflict as to whether he deserves to be sentenced to a lifetime of labor and imprisonment. My goal when teaching the play is to foster greater awareness of Caliban's position by highlighting the similarities between his plans to usurp power and Prospero's methods for controlling his enemies.

I also invite students to interrogate Prospero's narrative about his benevolence toward Miranda, Ariel, and Caliban in in Act 1, Scene 2. Students read or perform these scenes in small groups, making note of those moments when Prospero's performance of kindness appears insincere or unpersuasive. In studying Prospero's initial speech to Miranda, where he reveals the reasons for their exile on the island, students often comment that Prospero chides her for being inattentive or interrupting him before he puts her into a temporary sleep as he issues his instructions to Ariel (1.2.25–116). Likewise, students note that Prospero shifts from praising Ariel's skill in raising the tempest that forces his enemies onto the island to threatening Ariel when he demands his freedom (1.2.189-305). Student responses to Prospero's exchange with Caliban are more compli-

26. All quotes are taken from *The Tempest: A Case Study in Critical Controversy*, eds. Gerald Graff and James Phelan (New York: Bedford/St. Martin's, 2000).

27. On the manner in which Caliban is raced, see Matthieu Chapman, "Red, White, and Black: Shakespeare's *The Tempest* and the Structuring of Racial Antagonisms in Early Modern England and the New World," *Theatre History Studies*, vol. 39 (2020): 8, and Ania Loomba, *Shakespeare, Race, and Colonialism* (Oxford and New York: Oxford University Press, 2002), 35 and

cated; they note that Prospero reserves the harshest criticism for Caliban, whose demand for freedom he counters with a laundry list of the crimes that he has committed (1.2.324–379). I follow this exchange by introducing students to the popular psychological classification of parenting styles as authoritarian, authoritative, and permissive, and then use these categories to interrogate Prospero's claim that he is a good parent surrounded by ungrateful children (1.2.93–97).[28] Students note that Prospero shifts from the more positive category of authoritative with Miranda, where he is both responsive to questions and rule-oriented, to shades of authoritarianism with Ariel and Caliban, to whose appeals he is unresponsive and rejecting. These popular categories can illustrate the inconsistencies in Prospero's rhetoric and explain why Ariel, Caliban, and Miranda seek to challenge his authority.

Another method I use to challenge Prospero's demonizing of Caliban is to examine his relationship with the comic duo of Trinculo and Stefano, which covers Act 2, Scene 2 and Act 3, Scene 2 of the play. We explore these scenes in order to consider Caliban's political agency when he is outside Prospero's sphere of influence. In the first scene, Trinculo and Stephano both consider enriching themselves by enslaving and transporting Caliban to Europe (2.2.14-67). In the second scene, Caliban presents a formal petition to Stefano, where he asks him to kill Prospero and promises him ownership of the island and control of Miranda in return for his efforts (3.2.82–98). As we read through these scenes, I ask students to ponder the following questions: What structures of authority inform Trinculo and Stefano's relationship with Caliban? Does Caliban replace one ruler with another or does this scene reflect his growing agency? What, if anything, does Caliban achieve through his failed rebellion? I use these questions to highlight not only how white privilege empowers Stephano and Trinculo to treat Caliban as their property, but also how their author-

28. The American Psychological Association's description of these categories is available at "Parenting Styles," https://www.apa.org/act/resources/fact-sheets/parenting-styles (accessed 26 Nov. 2019). For a recent analysis of these categories, see Sofie Kuppens and Eva Ceulemans, "Parenting Styles: A Closer Look at a Well-Known Concept." *Journal of Child and Family Studies* 28 (2019): 168–181.

ity is destabilized when they forge an alliance with Caliban. Finally, we examine Caliban's ambiguous role at the end of the play. Will Caliban be taken to England and displayed as a captive? Will he finally get what he desires and become ruler of the island? In our closing discussion on the play, I have students generate an ending for Caliban. The play, especially when read through a postcolonial lens, affords readers more room to question Prospero's authority and endows Caliban with more freedom to shape his story.

Visualizing Race/Gender

Reading strategies can help complicate the familiar racial stereotypes that can influence students' reactions to non-white characters. Pairing a close investigation of the text with images that are based on it can also help reveal the manner in which generations of artists have shaped popular responses to the plays. I accordingly conclude class discussion of *Othello* with two images that are informed by its final scene, George Noble's engraving of Othello and Desdemona and the John Massey Wright/Timothy Stansfield Engleheart engraving of Othello, Desdemona, and Emilia, both of which were printed in John Boydell's *Shakespeare Gallery*, a collection of images from the plays, in 1797.[29] In the first engraving, a shamefaced Othello refuses to look at the sleeping Desdemona before he murders her. In the second, Desdemona and Emilia are situated beside one another while Othello is placed on the margins of the scene.

I display these images after we compare Othello's final speech, in which he asks the assembled Venetians to measure his service to the state against his misdeeds (5.2.347–366), with Lodovico's speech, a list of decrees punishing Iago, dividing Othello's estate, and announcing Cassio's promotion (5.2.372–382). Lodovico's primary reference to Othello and Desdemona is a demand that the "tragic loading of this bed" be hidden so that its contents will cease to disturb the viewer (5.2.374). Artistic representations of the play tend to ignore both Othello's plea and Lodovico's orders by magnifying the murderous contents of the bed and Othello's

29. These images are reprinted in Hall, 7, 17, 178.

role in producing it. I encourage students to pay close attention to the play of light and shade in these images and consider whose point of view they reproduce. Do they reflect Iago's negative portrait of the relationship between Othello and Desdemona; Othello's plea for accurate representation of their union; or Lodovico's clinical account of their deaths? Students observe that the images come closest to sharing Iago's perspective on the couple; they do so by situating Desdemona and Emilia in a pool of light while shrouding Othello in darkness as he turns his gaze away from the audience. The visual documents thus perpetuate the erasure of Othello's status as a noble general by emphasizing the threat that he poses to white femininity.[30]

I follow a similar path in discussions of Act 1, Scene 2 of *The Tempest* by using Henry Fuseli's popular depiction of Prospero, Miranda, and Caliban, from John Boydell's Shakespeare Gallery to enhance our discussion of the play.[31] The engraving features a clothed Prospero with Miranda behind him pointing toward a naked, muscular, and combative Caliban, who crouches aggressively on a rock as Ariel bathed in light looks on from above. I display this image alongside the speech between Prospero, Miranda, and Caliban, which places Prospero's rhetoric of betrayal by Caliban alongside Caliban's defense of his actions as a form of resistance to colonization (1.2.324–378). Along with discussing Prospero's rhetoric in the speech, I ask students to debate whether Prospero has the right to imprison Caliban and whether Caliban has the right to defend himself — even to attack Miranda — in defense of his freedom. Once I have listed students' responses on the board, I shift the conversation to the image

30. Francesca Royster addresses the gaps in Lodovico's final speech by asking students to create their own epitaphs for Othello, 59. On Othello's fear that he will be unable to find a sufficiently sympathetic white narrator to tell his story, see Smith, 112. For an important counter-narrative that highlights the racism directed toward Othello, see the short film, "Dear Mr. Shakespeare," directed by Shola Amoo, 2017, accessed 5 Nov. 2021, https://vimeo.com/183218909.
31. Peter Simon, "The Enchanted Island Before the Cell of Prospero – Prospero, Miranda, Caliban, and Ariel." *The American Edition of Boydell's Illustrations of the Dramatic Works of Shakespeare* (1797), The Metropolitan Museum of Art. Accessed 10 Sept. 2019 https://www.metmuseum.org/art/collection/search/365591.

and ask students to consider the following questions: Which aspects of the exchange between Prospero, Miranda, and Caliban does the artist keep, and which ones does he exclude? Why does the artist add Ariel to the scene? How does the artist use light and shadow to distinguish virtuous characters from villainous ones? As students note, the image cements conventional readings by placing Prospero, and Miranda, who are bathed in light, on one side and situating Caliban, who is cast in shadow, on the other. Like the artistic portrayals of Othello, those involving Caliban choose to contrast his interlocutors' virtue with his inhumanity. Placing images of Othello and Caliban alongside investigations of Shakespeare's text drives home the message that, far from neutral representations, visual documents can help reinforce the long history of racist representation in which these characters are embedded.

Adaptations of Race/Gender

While artists and filmmakers have often reinforced racist images of Othello and Caliban, twentieth- and twenty-first-century playwrights have a history of resisting such portrayals. In my course, Shakespeare and Race, I assign two adaptations of *Othello*, Paula Vogel's *Desdemona: The Story of a Handkerchief* (1987) and Djanet Sears' *Harlem Duet* (1997), and one of *The Tempest*, Aimé Cesaire's *Une Tempete*, or *A Tempest* (1969). These plays revise Shakespeare's texts by telling his stories from the perspective of its marginal characters, primarily white women in the case of Vogel, nonwhite women in the case of Sears, and Caliban in the case of Cesaire. While the adaptations reflect and expand on the source, they are not necessarily utopian alternatives to the race and gender problems that trouble *Othello* and *The Tempest*. Reading these texts alongside Shakespeare's thus allows for a productive conversation on the ways in which racist and sexist tropes are perpetuated and challenged by contemporary writers.

The first adaptation I assign, Paula Vogel's *Desdemona*, is a feminist text that centers on the conversations about marriage and sexuality between three female characters from *Othello*: Desdemona, Emilia, and Bianca. Unlike Shakespeare's Desdemona, who prefers Othello to her other suitors and remains faithful to him, Vogel's Desdemona confesses to having enjoyed many lovers before she met Othello and engaging with many more once she is bored with him. She gains access to these lovers through Bianca, a sex worker who helps Desdemona explore her sexual desires by giving her access to her clients.[32] Vogel's play champions Desdemona's right to explore her sexual desires but ends up reproducing the problematic racial dynamics of *Othello* by representing Othello as exotic fodder for his wife's appetite and a forbidding presence that she ultimately seeks to escape. While the play fulfills many students' desire for a less submissive heroine by creating a Desdemona who places her desires over her husband's demands, it also reinforces Shakespeare's portrait of Othello as the embodiment of Black male jealousy.[33] When I teach the text, I ask students to examine the ways in which Desdemona, Emilia, and Bianca's roles are expanded as well as the way Othello's role is limited in the play. These conversations help draw students' awareness both to Vogel's refusal to correlate femininity with virtue and her tendency to associate Black masculinity with violence. *Desdemona* thus offers an important lesson on the pitfalls that writers face when they seek to privilege *Othello*'s depiction of gender while ignoring its toxic racial politics.

Djanet Sears's *Harlem Duet* (1997), a prequel to *Othello*, provides an important corrective to the erasure of race in Vogel's text. The play, which is set in Harlem in 1861, 1928, and the 1990s, focuses on the conversations between two composite characters, a Black woman named Billie and a Black man named Othello, who leaves her for a white woman. The majority of the play focuses on the conversations between a grief-stricken Bil-

32. For an instance of Vogel's intensification of Desdemona's sexual desires, see Scene 11 where her Desdemona confesses, "I simply lie still there in the darkness taking them all into me. I close my eyes and in the dark of my mind – oh, how I travel," *Desdemona: A Play About a Handkerchief*, in *Adaptations of Shakespeare*, eds. Daniel Fischlin and Mark Fortier (New York: Routledge, 2000), 243. Keith Hamilton Cobb's play, *American Moor* (2016), offers an important counter-narrative to Vogel's reading of Othello and may be taught in conjunction with or as an alternative to Vogel's text. The play focuses on an African American actor's desire to humanize Othello for theater audiences who have been subjected to misperceptions of his character by white directors (New York: Methuen, 2020).
33. On Desdemona's treatment of Othello as an exotic "other" and her disappointment at his embracing of Venetian values, see Vogel, Scene 11, 242.

lie who is struggling to come to terms with Othello's engagement to a white woman named Mona. Billie accuses Othello of marrying Mona out of a desire to erase his racial identity and find acceptance in the white community. Othello rejects her accusation and suggests, instead, that his relationship with Mona and position as a professor at Columbia University are proof that they live in a color-blind world (Act 1, Scene 7). Othello's claims for assimilation are ironic in this context: the audience is aware that his plans to travel to Cyprus with his wife, Mona, and a colleague, Yago, will result in his death. *Harlem Duet* draws attention to the contrast between Billie's fierce attachment to the Black community and Othello's desire to erase his racial identity. I draw students' attention to these issues by asking the following questions when we discuss the play: Why does Othello choose to marry Mona when he shows evidence of his continued desire for Billie? To what extent is Othello's choice dictated by a desire to assimilate to white society? Does Sears' play share Billie's point of view that Othello's quest is futile, and that white acceptance can only be earned through the assertion of Black power? Class discussion of *Harlem Duet* opens up important conversations about the steep price that members of marginalized communities pay both for their decision to reject the culture of the majority, as Billie does, and for their desire to assimilate to it, as is the case for Othello. Vogel's *Desdemona* and Sears' *Harlem Duet* are important companion pieces to *Othello*, since they help reflect on the manner in which Shakespeare's Desdemona and Othello are trapped by the patriarchal and white supremacist societies to which they belong.[34]

34. Toni Morrison's play, *Desdemona* (2011) is an excellent adaptation to teach in conjunction with *Othello*. The play reflects on the events in *Othello* by adding a number of female characters who are mentioned but never seen in Shakespeare's play, including Barbary/Sa'ran, Desdemona's non-white maid; Soun, Othello's mother; and Madame Brabantio, Desdemona's mother (London: Oberon Books, 2018). Together, these characters draw attention to both Othello's violence against Desdemona and Desdemona's race and class privilege in relation to Barbary and Emilia.

Martinique-born writer Aime Cesaire's *Une Tempete*, or A *Tempest* (1969) performs a similarly important function as *Harlem Duet*.[35] Written during the twentieth-century movement for decolonization, Cesaire's play is told from the perspective of Caliban, who is transformed into a revolutionary with the power to raise an army of the island's flora and fauna to assist him in his battle against Prospero. The narrative also transforms Prospero into the classic colonizer, whose consciousness of the "white man's burden" compels him to remain on the island and attempt to reassert his authority in the face of Caliban's revolt. The play ends without victory on either side, with Prospero and Caliban locked in an endless struggle for supremacy. A *Tempest* is far from balanced: its focus on the battle between Prospero and Caliban, the play gives short shrift to Miranda, who is dismissed by both men.[36] The play nonetheless helps students reflect on the unjust structure of power in Shakespeare's play and on the colonial regimes that England established in the centuries after it was first performed.

I assign adaptations of *Othello* and *The Tempest* to illustrate the ways in which twentieth-and twenty-first-century writers have rewritten Shakespeare in order to address their concerns with his work. The adaptations also demonstrate that Shakespeare's plays are living artifacts that students can reshape to suit their needs.[37] I present students with the opportunity to engage creatively with the texts they have read through a final project in which they can update Shakespeare for their time. Students have responded to this prompt by rewriting specific scenes and narrative arcs; creating Spotify playlists, Instagram accounts, and TikTok videos for

35. On *Harlem Duet*'s engagement with *Othello*, see Nedda Mehdizadeh, "Othello in Harlem: Transforming Theater in Djanet Sears's *Harlem Duet*," *Journal of American Studies* 54 (2020): 14.
36. On the problems with minimizing Miranda's role in A *Tempest*, see Jyotsna Singh, "Caliban versus Miranda: Race and Gender Conflicts in Post-Colonial Writings of *The Tempest*," *Feminist Readings of Early Modern Culture: Emerging Subjects*, Eds. Valerie Traub, M.L. Kaplan, and D. Callaghan (Cambridge: Cambridge University Press, 1996), 205–206.
37. I also remind students to bring their awareness of racial stereotypes that they have studied to bear on their creative projects, especially if they choose to represent nonwhite characters in the play.

individual characters; activities that are especially useful for reframing discussions of race and gender in Shakespeare.

Discussions that address Shakespeare and race may help students engage with topics that they might otherwise shy away from, but they cannot erase the broader implications of racial bias. Studying the play's historical context, its racist language, and visual documents, however, will help students reflect more carefully on the interpretive strategies that they use to talk about race in Shakespeare. A layered approach to reading *Othello* and *The Tempest*, such as the one I share here, can help students unpack the coded language that is used to demonize its non-white characters and shift sympathy toward their white oppressors. Examining the plays in light of primary documents from the early modern period helps students understand how contemporary discussions about travel, climate, religion, and skin color informed conceptions of character. Likewise, exploring eighteenth- and nineteenth-century images of the plays demonstrates how artists dehumanized Othello and Caliban in a manner that continues to influence popular depictions of the play.[38] Finally, teachers can enhance discussions of *Othello* and *The Tempest* by examining adaptations that focus on the perspectives of their marginalized characters. While a set of reading materials may not shift the perspectives on race and gender that students bring to the classroom, they can, nonetheless, challenge conventional modes of reading. By placing historical texts, visual documents, and literary appropriations in conversation with the textual study of *Othello* and *The Tempest*, teachers can provide students with the tools to recognize the pernicious effects of racism in the literature they read in class and develop strategies to combat its influence outside the classroom.

38. On the persistence of racist tropes associated with *Othello* in the popular podcast, *Serial*, see Vanessa Corredera, "'Not a Moor Exactly:' Shakespeare, *Serial*, and Modern Constructions of Race," *Shakespeare Quarterly* (Spring 2016): 38–40.

Suggested Further Reading

Akhimie, Patricia. *Shakespeare and the Cultivation of Difference: Race and Conduct in the Early Modern World.* New York: Routledge, 2020.

Chapman, Matthieu. "Away, You Ethiop!": A *Midsummer Night's Dream* and the Denial of Black Affect — A Song to Underscore the Burning of Police Stations." In *Race and Affect in Early Modern English Literature*, edited by Carol Meija LaPerle. ACMRS Press, 2022. https://doi.org/http://doi.org/10.54027/GJYM2659

Dadabhoy, Ambereen. "The Unbereable Whiteness of Being in Shakespeare." *Postmedieval: A Journal of Medieval Cultural Studies* 11, (2020): 228–235. https://doi.org/10.1057/s41280-020-00169-6

Erickson, Peter, and Kim F. Hall. "A New Scholarly Song": Rereading Early Modern Race." *Shakespeare Quarterly* 67, no.1 (Spring 2016): 1–13.

Hendricks, Margo. "Race: A Renaissance Category?" In *A New Companion to English Renaissance Literature and Culture*, edited by Michael Hattaway, 535–44. 2 vols. New York: Wiley/Blackwell, 2010.

MacDonald, Joyce Green. "Finding *Othello*'s African Roots through Djanet Sears's *Harlem Duet*." In *Approaches to Teaching Shakespeare's* Othello, edited by Peter Erickson and Maurice Hunt, 202–20. New York: Modern Language Association, 2005.

Smith, Ian. "Othello's Black Handkerchief." *Shakespeare Quarterly* 64, no.1 (Spring 2013): 1–25.

Thompson, Ayanna. "Othello/YouTube." In *Shakespeare on Screen:* Othello, edited by Sarah Hatchuel and Nathalie Vienne Guerrin, 1–16. Cambridge: Cambridge University Press, 2015.

Figure 1. Engraving of *Othello*, 5.2, by Henry Singleton (1793).
Singleton, Henry. *Yet I'll not shed her blood* (London: C. Taylor, 1793). Used by permission of the Folger Shakespeare Library under a Creative Commons Attribution-ShareAlike 4.0 International License

Figure 2. Engraving of *Othello*, 5.2, by John Massey Wright/Timothy Stansfield Engleheart.

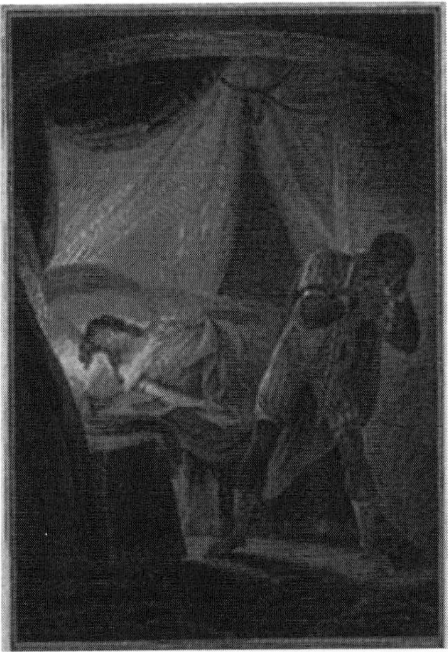

Figure 3. Engraving from *Othello*, 5.2, by George Noble. George Noble. Othello, Act V, Scene 2 (London: J.&J. Boydell, 1800). Used by permission of the Folger Shakespeare Library under a Creative Commons Attribution-ShareAlike 4.0 International License.

Figure 4. Engraving from *The Tempest*, 1.2, by Henry Fuseli.
Fuseli, Henry. *The Tempest*, act I, scene 2. Used by permission of the Folger Shakespeare Library under a Creative Commons Attribution-ShareAlike 4.0 International License.

Figure 5. Watercolor from *The Tempest*, 2.2, by Johann Heinrich Ramberg. Johann Heinrich Ramberg, *The Tempest*, act II, scene 2. Used by permission of the Folger Shakespeare Library under a Creative Commons Attribution-ShareAlike 4.0 International License.

Sight-Reading Race in Early Modern Drama: Dog Whistles, Signifiers, and the Grammars of Blackness

MATTHIEU CHAPMAN AND JOSHUA KELLY

Introduction

On Sunday, July 14, 2019, United States President Donald Trump tweeted the following:

> "So interesting to see 'Progressive' Democrat Congresswomen, who originally came from countries whose governments are a complete and total catastrophe, the worst, most corrupt and inept anywhere in the world (if they even have a functioning government at all), now loudly ... " (1/3)
>
> " ... and viciously telling the people of the United States, the greatest and most powerful Nation on earth, how our government is to be run. Why don't they go back and help fix the totally broken and crime infested places from which they came. Then come back and show us how ... " (2/3)
>
> " ... it is done. These places need your help badly, you can't leave fast enough. I'm sure that Nancy Pelosi would be very happy to quickly work out free travel arrangements!" (3/3)[1]

The progressive Democratic Congresswomen to whom he is referring are Alexandria Ocasio-Cortez (Representative from New York's 14th district), Ilhan Omar (Representative from Minnesota's 5th district), Ayanna Pressley (Representative from Massachusetts's 7th district), and Rashida Tlaib (Representative from Michigan's 13th district). These four women have

1. Trump, Donald. (@realDonaldTrump). 2019. Twitter, July 14, 2019. 7:27 a.m. https://twitter.com/realDonaldTrump/status/1150381396994723841.

many things in common. Each of them won their congressional seat in 2019. Each of them is an American citizen (all of them except for Ilhan Omar was born in the United States. Omar naturalized from Somalia in 2000 when she was seventeen years old). Most importantly, however, each of them is a woman of color.

Many news outlets including CNN, *The Boston Globe*, and *The New York Times* immediately called out the tweets for what they were: a racist attack designed to mobilize Trump's white supremacist base through "dog whistle politics."[2] In their article "Populism as Dog-Whistle Politics: Anti-Elite Discourse and Sentiments toward Minorities," Harvard professor Bart Bonikowski and University of California–Berkeley professor Yueran Zhang illustrate the concept of dog-whistles:

> "Dog-whistle politics" refers to the use of ostensibly innocuous discursive cues that prime more insidious outgroup hostilities, particularly among those who share the ideological predilections of the speaker. In practice, such coded language often evokes racially charged attitudes, but it has also been used in religious and anti-immigrant discourse. The metaphor is a reference to high-pitched dog-training whistles that use frequencies inaudible to humans.[3]

Donald Trump, while not explicitly mentioning race, deployed discursive tactics that listeners would invariably hear as a remark on race while still giving himself plausible deniability.

Although the phrase dog-whistling became popular in relation to political campaigns of the 1980s, the linguistic processes and discursive ambiguity that produce the dog-whistle effect have a history that go as far back as the Elizabethan Age. This essay uses psychoanalyst Jacques

2. Paul Krugman. "Racism Comes Out of the Closet." *The New York Times*, July 15, 2019, https://www.nytimes.com/2019/07/15/opinion/trump-twitter-racist.html.
3. Bart Bonikowski and Yueran Zhang. "Populism as Dog-Whistle Politics: Anti-Elite Discourse and Sentiments towards Minorities." *Harvard.edu/files*. https://scholar.harvard.edu/files/bonikowski/files/bonikowski_and_zhang_-_populism_as_dog-whistle_politics.pdf.

Lacan's theories of semiotics, along with other models, and contemporary critical race theory to reveal how certain signs performed on the early modern stage engaged in visual dog-whistling, which allowed early modern audiences to sight-read race; to "see" race where it may not have been explicitly performed through blackening cosmetics and materials — or by Black bodies.

Such an analysis will serve not just as a necessary inquiry for scholars of performance philosophy, theatre history, and race studies, but also as an accessible tool for teachers of Shakespeare and Renaissance theatre to better help their students understand the complex and underdiscussed performances of blackness on the early modern stage. In teaching and discussing race in Renaissance England, it is important to not only address the period in a vacuum, but to also acknowledge the continuum of racial thinking that began in the medieval period and continues to today. While simply reading today's conceptions of race onto the past would, of course, be too simplistic, ignoring the afterlives and echoes of early modern racial thinking would be far more dangerous.

We will begin with a brief explanation of visual cues and semiotics — a system of recognizable codes — to show how Trump's tweets function as dog-whistling, and then will explore how we can use textual cues from early modern historical sources to read race in bodies that may otherwise be considered to be unraced. After an overview of numerous primary documents and dramatic sources which create a genealogy of racial semiotics — textual dog-whistles — we will use an analysis of the witches in *Macbeth* as our case-study to show how those cues persevere in the Shakespearean canon. We've chosen this play because the witches of *Macbeth* exist chronologically and semiotically at the intersection of "black" and "female" in a way that reinforces racial thinking of the Black woman as foreign, dangerous, and impossible to incorporate into civil society — in other words, in a way that foreshadows the political attacks of Donald Trump. Also, because *Macbeth* is still a commonly used touchstone of the English-speaking theatrical canon and frequently required reading in undergraduate English and drama courses, it is doubly useful as a starting point for demonstrating the necessity of understanding (and teaching) racial semiotics in Shakespeare: to learn to hear dog-whistles when they are blasted in our most-used texts.

Visual Signs, Linguistics, and Semiotics in Early Modern England

The history of signs is one of endless replacement: in order to understand one series of symbols, one needs another language of interpretation. Accepting that the quest for a universally understood language is a pipe-dream, we are left with are genealogies of interpretation — crossroads of expression in signs and symbols which allow us to follow meaning as it is defined from one instance to another. This field is called semiotics.

While semiotics has developed into a discipline with its own specializations and philosophies of thought, more broadly it incorporates all forms of interpretive abstracts, from letters to sounds to metaphor. As Umberto Eco says in his pivotal *Semiotics and the Philosophy of Language* (1986):

> A specific semiotics is, or aims at being, the 'grammar' of a particular sign system, and proves to be successful insofar as it describes a given field of communicative phenomena as ruled by a system of signification. Thus there are 'grammars' of American Sign Language, of traffic signals, of a playing-card 'matrix' for different games of a particular game (for instance, poker). These systems can be studied from a syntactic, a semantic, or a pragmatic point of view.[4]

It is important to understand how a semiotic grammar is identified by its *legibility* among those who understand its signs — it is not labelled as a cogent sign system by any other body save those who can read it. If it can do this, then it can have predictive and explanatory power about (and for) those capable of that reading. Signifiers and referents (symbols that stand in representation of ideas — from words to numbers to abstract codes)

4. Umberto Eco. *Semiotics and the Philosophy of Language*. (Bloomington: Indiana University Press, 1986), 5.

exist in a relationship with one another, but they also exist within a grammar in which they are constructed in relation to one another.[5]

The most accessible form of related grammar comes, of course, from common language, and the "existence of a certain rule (or code) enabling both the sender and the addressee to understand the manifestation in the same way must, of course, be presupposed if the transmission is to be successful," that we "take as signs also words, that is the elements of verbal language."[6] In this way, semiotics both incorporates — and is separate from — linguistics, for it includes verbal language but allows for the fact that any modality of sign carries interpretive potential. So, while we interpret signs that we speak and see, we are also able to interpret the grammar through which these signs are produced. Reading these grammatical slippages between spoken/represented signs and other signs with which they discursively relate to a deleterious effect produces the dog-whistle.

Semiotics bursts into sociopolitical and psychological discourses when it is assumed that we recognize our social and political selves, as well as our psychological Selves, by legible signifiers that we share with others. It is for this reason that semiotics and Lacanian signifiers (a system of signs whose meanings are understood by specific audiences) become primary methods for performance philosophy and criticism: a practice based entirely on varying modes of symbolism and representation. It is often the case in drama that what is presented to an audience are not simply intended or unintended messages, but messages simultaneously intended for different audiences or even legible codes otherwise implanted. It is this very concept of Otherness which brings us to Lacan.

In his paper given to the Rome Congress at the Institute of Psychology, University of Rome, in 1953, psychoanalyst Jacques Lacan outlines the "temptation that presents itself to the analyst to abandon the foundation of speech, and this precisely in areas where its use, verging on the inef-

5. In structural explanations of these ideas — like that of Saussure — the sign is the sum of the signified (meaning) and the signifier (referent), which produces a message or significant for those capable of connecting the two.

6. Eco, *Semiotics*, 16.

fable, would seem to require examination more than ever."[7] Aware of the separation between real, imaginary, and symbolic conditions, Lacan underscores the necessity for the psychoanalyst of truly understanding speech. In particular, this is because speech has the potential to betray a semiotic system used by the unconscious ("The unconscious is structured like a language," in his famous formulation), which the analyst is bound to interpret:

> Even if it communicates nothing, discourse represents the existence of communication; even if it denies the obvious, it affirms that speech constitutes truth ... Thus the psychoanalyst knows better than anyone else that the point is to figure out [*entendre*] to which "part" of this discourse the significant term is relegated.[8]

For Lacan, such interpretation is an exercise in understanding the language of the Other, for which the unconscious is used as discourse.[9] In Lacan's "big Other," one finds the objective spirit of "trans-individual socio-linguistic structures configuring the fields of inter-subjective interactions," including "ideas of anonymous authoritative power and/or knowledge (whether that of God, Nature, History, Society, State, Party, Science ...)."[10] That this relationship between signifiers and signs, constituted by the signifier and the signified, is ultimately subjective is part of the complexity of human socio-psychological development: "Language brings with it the arbitrary nature of the sign and differential relations among signs ... So it is for Lacan."[11] For Lacan, indeed, language itself is the act of differentiation.

7. Jacques Lacan, *Ecrits*, translated by Bruce Fink. (New York: W.W. Norton & Company, 2006), 202.
8. Lacan, *Ecrits*, 209.
9. Lacan, *Ecrits*, 16.
10. "Jacques Lacan." *Stanford Encyclopedia of Philosophy*, last modified July 10, 2018. https://plato.stanford.edu/entries/lacan/#OthOedComSex.
11. Paul H. Fry. *Theory of Literature* (New Haven: Yale University Press, 2012), 173.

> The first network, that of the signifier, is the synchronic structure of the language material in so far as each element takes on its precise usage therein by being different from the others; this is the principle of distribution that alone regulates the function of the elements of language [*langue*] at its different levels, from the phonematic pair of oppositions to compound expressions, the task of the most modern research being to isolate the stable forms of the latter.
>
> The second network, that of the signified, is the diachronic set of the concretely pronounced discourses, which historically affects the first network, just as the structure of the first governs the pathways of the second. What dominates here is the unity of signification, which turns out never to come down to a pure indication of reality [*réel*], but always refers to another signification. In other words, signification comes about only on the basis of taking things as a whole [*d'ensemble*].[12]

The socio-linguistic structures of the Other are often documented in the artifacts which make up the study of history and literature, and careful examination can teach us the grammars involved in any given system. Conclusions by performance philosophers and theatre historians have already shown the potential of reading semiotics of blackness within these primary sources for the early modern period. In *Performing Race and Torture on the Early Modern Stage* (2008), Ayanna Thompson posits that "a racialized epistemology does not necessarily have to be based on a semiotically charged interpretation of color so much as a semiotically charged interpretation of bodiliness."[13] Building from this, Matthieu Chapman's study of the performances of blackness in the early modern period, *Anti-Black Racism in Early Modern English Drama* (2017), makes the case that subjectivity itself was racially based during this time and that recognition of one's self was dependent on fluency in this particular grammar.

12. Lacan, *Ecrits*, 345.
13. Ayanna Thompson, *Performing Race and Torture on the Early Modern Stage* (New York: Routledge, 2008), 4.

Those who lacked semiotic reciprocity were systematically inhuman, "a being that lacks the capacity for definition, a true anti-human, the antagonist against which all human identities find a stable base for identification."[14] In (literally) other words, the Other in this sense is that which is not myself. For Renaissance England, alterity is one of the dominant grammars of blackness, and vice versa.

Absence, then, forms a sign by which early modern subjects understand "blackness" to be a substituted meaning – alterity, anti-human, or even "unthought," as Saidiya Hartman writes: "that every attempt to emplot the slave in a narrative ultimately resulted in his or her obliteration."[15] Contrast this against the observation of Lynda Boose, who writes in "The Getting of a Lawful Race: Racial Discourse and the Unrepresentable Black Woman":

> The black man is representable. But within Europe's symbolic order of dominance and desire, the black woman destroys the system, essentially swallowing it up within *the signification of her body*.[16] [Italics, ours.]

Although from completely different fields and theoretical backgrounds, these two quotes intersect in their assumptive logic of blackness: that the symbolic order through which not only narratives, but also the notions of narrative itself, are constructed are incompatible with – and cannot account for – the emplotment of black flesh. Developing fluency in other signifiers of blackness within the early modern period, then, allows us to illustrate this incapability of *direct* representation for Black women. As Boose goes on to remind us about Shakespearean drama in particular:

14. Matthieu Chapman, *Anti-Black Racism in Early Modern English Drama* (New York: Routledge, 2017), 23.
15. Saidiya V. Hartman and Frank B. Wilderson III, "The Position of the Unthought," *Qui Parle*, 13, No. 2. (Spring/Summer 2003): 184.
16. Lynda E. Boose, "The Getting of a Lawful Race: Racial Discourse in Early Modern England and the Unrepresentable Black Woman," in *Women, "Race," and Writing in the Early Modern Period*, ed. Margo Hendricks and Patricia Parker (New York: Routledge, 1994), 47.

> Even on occasions where the black woman-white male yoking occurs in the main plot, the racial narrative nonetheless remains repressed, retarded from full articulation by its dissipation into figures like Shakespeare's Cleopatra or Marlowe's Dido, both of whom are only by the remotest suggestion represented as being Negro ... By contrast to the way that repeated allusions to both skin color and physiognomy foreground the racial identity of the black male figure in *The Merchant of Venice*, *Titus Andronicus*, and *Othello*, the unrepresentability of Cleopatra's racial status is what gets foregrounded by *Antony and Cleopatra*'s use of only two such allusions, both of which obfuscate rather than situate the issue.[17]

What Boose may be unintentionally framing for us is the fact that signifiers of blackness were, in the case of *Antony and Cleopatra*, no longer merely textual. It may be that in original performances of the play, grammars of blackness had developed into the Lacanian signified without the implicit use of mere language in the first network. In other words, blackness could have been signified in ways that the absence of direct text may not reveal, and in the disparity between dichotomous (or seemingly unrelated) meanings would exist a visual dog-whistle.

Our work will be to examine a different play. If we do not look at the linguistic product but rather the structures which undergird that labor — the black woman was represented through a confluence of signs — we will find that a series of dog-whistles are instantly cogent.

One such sign is the witch.

Witches in England

To understand how this grammar produces the unrepresentable Black woman in the early modern subject's imagination requires a bit of history on the status of witches and devils in the early modern English imagination and the development of representations of blackness on the stage of that time.

17. Boose, "The Getting of a Lawful Race," 47.

People living in Renaissance England were developing a remarkable semiotic awareness in terms of race and national identity, and the arbitrary interchange of those signifiers was not only wide-spread, but part-and-parcel of a strengthening need for social identity. As John Jeffries Martin maintains in *Myths of Renaissance Individualism* (2004), "Renaissance identities were almost always anxious identities, uncertain about the boundaries between … the inner and outer 'self'" and whose boundaries were in constant flux and could be interpreted as "something that linked one person, by the logic of resemblance … to family, craft, city and nation," or "a screen … behind which one should … conceal one's thoughts and beliefs," or "something remarkably permeable".[18] As we add, such a subjectivity was eager to utilize an assumed ontology of blackness deeply inseminated in English cultural history by this time.

For centuries, blackness and evil were mutual signifiers in England, appearing in the Medieval period and deriving from the Manichaean doctrine that the universe was constructed along a binary between light and dark: that light is the province of godliness and darkness with evil.[19] Augustine of Hippo echoed this distinction in his work, "offering a proto-Lacanian analysis of the symbolic order" by equating that which was of God to be good, and "if things are deprived of goodness, *they will have no being at all*."[20] In *Anti-Blackness in English Religion in* 1500–1800, Joseph Washington explains how this Manichean schism persisted in Europe and shifted the social attitude toward various forms of blackness, describing "the propensity of the English in their public and private writings to equate black people not with humans but with devils." [21] Accordingly, absence of direct representation and amalgams of black signification resulted in roughly four hundred years of "Moors, devils, witches, and the

18. John Jeffries Martin, *Myths of Renaissance Individualism*. (London: Palgrave MacMillan, 2004), 13–14.
19. Chapman, *Anti-Black Racism*, 35.
20. Chapman, *Anti-Black Racism*, 35.
21. Joseph R. Washington, *Anti-Blackness in English Religion* 1500–1800. (Lewiston: Edwin Mellon Press, 1984), 39.

black body all at one time or another occup[ying] the position of absence that defined English subjectivity."[22]

In the case of witches, "blackness" becomes the linguistic sign by which their evil is recognized. The *Etymologiae* of Isidore of Seville describes witches as "transformed from humans."[23] And, though it seems he was incorrect about this particular citation, Heinrich Kramer claimed in his 1486 *Malleus Maleficarum* that Isidore of Seville *also* said:

> Witches are so called on account of the blackness of their guilt, that is to say, their deeds are more evil than those of any other malefactors. [Isidore] continues: They stir up and confound the elements by aid of the devil, and arouse terrible hailstorms and tempests. Moreover, he says they distract the minds of men, driving them to madness, insane hatred, and inordinate lusts.[24]

While — to the best of our knowledge — Isidore said nothing of the sort, the *Malleus Maleficarum*, with its astonishing number of black referents, became "the continental treatise most influential in England."[25] King James I of England, in his 1597 witch-hunting treatise *Daemonologie* narrates a story in which "he granted that the deuill had appeared vnto him in the night before, appareled all in blacke."[26]

The discourse on witches further reveals the psychic threat that the early modern subject associated not just with the sexualized female body,

22. Washington, *Anti-Blackness in English Religion*, 39.
23. Isidore of Seville. *The Etymologies of Isidore of Seville*. Translators: Stephen A. Barney, W.J. Lewis, J.A. Beach, and Oliver Bergof (Cambridge: Cambridge University Press, 2006), 346.
24. Heinrich Kramer and James Sprenger, *The Malleus Maleficarum: Translated with an Introduction, Bibliography & Notes by the Reverend Montague Summers*, accessed November 11, 2019. http://www.malleusmaleficarum.org/downloads/MalleusAcrobat.pdf, 39.
25. John L. Teall, "Witchcraft and Calvinism in Elizabethan England: Divine Power and Human Agency," *Journal of the History of Ideas*, 23, no. 1. (March 1962): 23.
26. James I. *Daemonologie in the Forme of a Dialogie Diuided into three Bookes*. Robert Walde-graue, Printer to the Kings Majestie, 1597. Hosted by *ProjectGutenberg.org*. http://www.gutenberg.org/files/25929/25929-pdf, 78. Accessed November 11, 2019.

but specifically with the female body's potential for interbreeding with darkness. Such a fear is not purely misogynist, as Margaret Denike claims in *The Devil's Insatiable Sex: A Genealogy of Evil Incarnate* (2003) but is also anti-miscegenation. In numerous instances, confessions from witch trials describe the devil with which the woman was said to have a relationship. In the 1645–1647 case of Elizabeth Southerne, for instance, the Dunwich peddler claims to have "met the divell midsomer last like a black boy 10 years old."[27] Or, more vividly, from Marie "wife of *Henrie Smith*," who "confirmed by her owne Confession" that the Devil "appeared vnto her amiddes these discontentments, in the shape of a blacke man, and willed that she should continue her malice."[28]

On the matter of demonic miscegenation and its legacy in English consciousness and drama, Julia Garrett provides the most succinct overview:

> [W]hile trials did not generally produce evidence about the most fantastical witch practices – including orgiastic sabbaths, copulation with the devil ... such material was hardly absent from English culture altogether. Learned writers in England frequently addressed such matters in their treatises, while publishers made the major Continental tracts available in a variety of vernacular languages, occasionally offering English translations. King James I ... provides an account of ... the obscene kiss [on the arse] required of the Devil's converts.

And it was none other than

> Thomas Aquinas "who first propounded the possibility that a demon as a succubus could capture semen from a man and as an incubus subsequently use it to impregnate a woman" (18), and Stu-

27. Clive Holmes, "Women: Witnesses and Witches" in *New Perspectives on Witchcraft, Magic, and Demonology, Volume 4: Gender and Witchcraft*, ed. Brian P. Levack (New York: Routledge, 2001), 133.
28. Alexander Roberts, "A Treatise of Witchcraft ... " d. 1620, accessed November 11, 2019. Hosted by https://quod.lib.umich.edu/e/eebo/A10802.0001.001/1:4?rgn=div1;view=fulltext.

> art Clark identifies such concerns about whether "demonic sexuality [could] result in genuine miscegenation" (190)[29]

In this way, witches came to symbolize a very real threat to assumptions about subjectivity by representing the threat of miscegenation between the subject and the abject (or in inhuman non-subject) upon which that subjectivity is constructed. This challenges the boundaries of what defines the human. The early modern English subject's anxiety over the potential for miscegenation corrupting or destroying their being can be seen in the discourse of witches. Fearing the incorporation of blackness, which we have shown was already established as the binary opposition of the self and community, the early modern English subject was determined to avoid a collapse of both subjectivity and society.

This potential for incorporation, even if only available through supernatural means, was troublesome enough to constructions of humanity that it resulted in the blackening of the women, marking witches as null entities with no legal or ontological recourse because of their sexualized relationship with blackness. Evidence for the perceived blackness of witches exists in the legal process and punishment for witchcraft. When scholar Margaret Denike questions, "How is it that, despite their alleged incompetence and incapacity, which justified women's exclusion from inquisitorial and legal processes in most European countries, women could be brought before ecclesiastical and secular courts in unprecedented numbers and convicted of crimes of witchcraft that bore the harshest penalties as yet known in Western legal history?", she is referring to the fact that in most witch trials, the accused was completely at the mercy of society; men, women, and children all had equal status as witnesses against crimes of witchcraft.[30] Witchcraft was such a threat that it was labelled a *crimen exceptum* or "exceptional crime," meaning there was "no restriction on the use of torture to extort confessions and no right for

29. Julia M. Garrett, "Witchcraft and Sexual Knowledge in Early Modern England," *Journal for Early Modern Cultural Studies*, 13, no. 1 (Winter 2013): 36.
30. Margaret Denike, "The Devil's Insatiable Sex: A Genealogy of Evil Incarnate," *Hypatia*, 18, no. 1 (January 2009): 14.

suspects to appeal their convictions. Nor was there any process of appeal, and hence no scrutiny of the evidence and no procedure for recourse to a centralized higher court. There were also relaxed rules for the use of witnesses, which entailed, for example, that women and children could testify in trials for the first time."[31]

What accounts for this exception? As opposed to other crimes, the association with blackness rendered witches guilty at the word of an informant; hence, upon accusation, the witch lost the capacity for interlocution. This made witchcraft (black arts and black magic) unique in that the accused was excommunicated from civil society; the crime was considered so severe an affront to accepted and expected bounds that participation warranted the removal of the accused from society. In many cases, the end result of a witchcraft trial was death, with "casual" estimates as low as 50,000 witches being killed in Europe from 1400–1700.[32]

This separation of witches from civil society and occupation of a position that coincides with blackness made its way from society to the stage and became readable in the scenes and signifiers of early modern drama. By the time witches began appearing on stage, with drama historian Thomas Berger citing Robert Greene's 1587 play *Alphonsus of Aragon* as the earliest play with a witch character, the Black body already existed both in society and on the stage.[33] Witches, then, were no longer the corporeal manifestation of scandalized relationality, but rather became beings defined through their scandalous relations with blackness. Witches in drama, while blackened, are not Black, but rather inhabit a location outside of civil society but still within the symbolic order. Witches inhabit a space of *severed* relationality, not *a priori* absent relationality — removed from the discourse of Black semiotics but recognizable through dog-whistling Black grammar. Despite the appearance of

31. Denike, "The Devil's Insatiable Sex," 33.

32. Alan Kors and Edward Peters, *Witchcraft in Europe, 400–1700: A Documentary History* (Philadelphia: University of Pennsylvania Press, 2000), 17.

33. Thomas L. Berger, William C. Bradford, and Sidney L. Sondergard, *An Index of Characters in Early Modern English Drama: Printed Plays, 1500-1660* (Cambridge: Cambridge University Press, 1998), 112.

the Black body as the corporeal representation of blackness on the stage, the stage witch still maintained remnants of the Black ontology within its onstage presence.

The first appearance of witches on the early modern stage coincides with the appearance on stage of the black body, both occurring in 1587. As Virginia Mason Vaughan writes in *Performing Blackness on English Stages: 1500–1800*, "In the 1580s and 1590s a crucial shift took place from the simple *display* of blackened devils and Moorish kinds to the white actor's *impersonation* of black characters."[34] The fact that the dramatic practice of using blackface to directly portray the devil specifically and damnation generally was commonplace by this point can be seen in a number of production documents and playtexts themselves. Andrea Stevens records that:

> Surviving guild accounts . . . list payments for black paint used in mystery plays, indicating that face-blackening agents number among the first known uses of theatrical paint. Drapers' accounts from Coventry record payments for blacking the faces of devils and damned souls: "item payde for blacckyng of the Sowles facys 'V' Itm pd for Collering ye blacke Soils faces"; "payd for penttyng of the blake soles faces."[35]

While the dramatic representation of witches functioned differently than the representation of devils in that they are not pure abjects, we can still see remnants of grammars of blackness manifested in their staging through their physical and narrative exile from civil society. The majority of witches in early modern English drama conform to two basic conventions that derive from the public perception: they maintain an association

34. Virginia Mason Vaughan, *Performing Blackness on English Stages*, 1500–1800 (Cambridge: Cambridge University Press, 2008), 35.
35. Andrea Stevens, "Mastering Masques of Blackness: Jonson's 'Masque of Blackness,' The Windsor Text of 'The Gypsies Metamorphosed,' and Brome's 'The English Moor,'" *English Literary Renaissance*, 39, no. 2. (Spring 2009): 401.

with devils and blackness and exist separate from mainstream society.[36] It is in this connecting space between "witch" and "blackness" – a space well-traversed by this time in English subjectivity, that the dog-whistle exists. In *Macbeth* – it is of low enough pitch to be heard by human ears.

Dog-Whistles and Blackness in *Macbeth*

That *Macbeth* is an early modern English play containing witches at all would, from the argument above, require one to accept the text as part of the legacy of Black semiotic performance. However, some useful insights and supportive arguments can be found in previous scholarship on blackness in *Macbeth*, as well as through new interpretive reading. The seemingly contradictory nature of the witches' blackness has been commented on by scholars, but not thoroughly addressed. The 2010 collection *Weyward Macbeth*, edited by Scott L. Newstok and Ayanna Thompson, insightfully analyses the racial aspect of the play *Macbeth*, with the first two contributions to the book by Thompson and Celia R. Daileader addressing the blackness of the witches. Daileader's article "Weird Brothers: What

36. Garrett argues that "Renaissance dramatists such as Thomas Middleton, Thomas Heywood, Ben Jonson, Thomas Dekker, and John Marston all incorporated [witches' miscegenation] into their work" (Garrett, 36). Thomas Berger cites twenty-six plays from 1550–1660 containing characters listed in the *dramatis personae* or described in the text specifically as witches, as opposed to the terms conjuress, enchantress, and sorceress which have different connotations (Berger, 1998). Both Dietmar Tatzl and Stephen Greenblatt comment on the relationship, or lack thereof, between witches and civil society as they appear in drama. Greenblatt claims that "witchcraft functioned as an important factor in creating the average man or woman, who perceived themselves in relation to that concept but always from a dualistic distance" (Dietmar Tatzl, *"Secret, Black, and Midnight Hags:" The Conception, Presentation, and Function of Witches in Renaissance Drama* [Vienna: Wilhelm Braumuller Universitats-Verlagsbuchhandlung, 2005], 4); Tatzl argues that "the majority of witchcraft plays present witches as malevolent figures who interfere with the natural and divine order of the universe, threaten the stability of society or practice harmful sorcery" (Tatzl, 55). Both of these quotes mirror the position of witches in society at large, not only as existing in a space outside of civil society, but as entities upon which the subject and civil society can seek to establish definitions.

Thomas Middleton's *The Witch* Can Tell Us About Race, Sex, and Gender in *Macbeth*" interrogates the early modern conventions surrounding the staging of witches in a manner that signals the liminal space of witches in the semiotic system of blackness. Daileader raises the issue of the witches being referred to as Black, but not being presented as Black, stating:

> Though Macbeth calls the witches 'secret, black, and midnight hags' (4.1.64), neither they nor 'black Hecate' (3.2.42) seem to have been blacked up. On the one hand, this is not surprising given the moral blackness of the human characters ... On the other hand, the Renaissance commonplace about the Devil's blackness would seem to require it.[37]

The convention of black devils cited by Daileader is one of the factors that allow witches to exist simultaneously as structurally blackened and theatrically non-Black. The relationality between witches and conceptions of abject blackness reveals ways in which the early modern subject could conceptualize abject blackness independent of aesthetic blackness; on the stage, one does not have to be "blacked up" to be Black, but rather the social energy circulated through the stage allows witches to be perceived as abjects in spite of their aesthetics – this is the early modern version of a dog-whistle.[38]

While the individual performances of those signifiers may be difficult to track, textual and linguistic cues *do* still appear in the play itself. Serving as double entendre able to rouse collective social memory of blackness, passages adopt striking new poignance when viewed through this historical lens. These include Malcolm's description of "Devilish Macbeth," who like the Devil unto witches, "By many of these trains hath sought to win me / Into his power." At a servant who comes to bear news of

37. C.R. Daileader, "Weird Brothers: What Thomas Middleton's *The Witch* Can Tell Us about Race, Sex, and Gender in *Macbeth*," in *Weyward Macbeth. Signs of Race*, edited by A Thompson and S.L. Newstok (New York: Palgrave Macmillan, 2010), 14.
38. For a discussion of social energy in early modern English drama, see Stephen Greenblatt, *Shakespearean Negotiations: The Circulation of Social Energy in Renaissance England* (Berkeley: University of California Press, 1988), 6–7.

the approaching army, Macbeth screams: "The devil damn thee black ... " "Black spirits" accompany "black Hecate" during the witches' dance. And, of course, upon first seeing the witches, Banquo famously describes their inhumanity as they who "look not like the inhabitants o' the earth, / And yet are on't? Live you?"[39]

So strong is this recognition of Black grammar that it has even created these associations without intent. Moralizing on the separation between black magic and miracles in 1932, a scholar for *The Journal of English and Germanic Philology* writes: "The witches exude evil. Essentially they are linked with whatever forces of evil exist ... The same mysterious evil is in African wizardry today, unconnected with any of the existing religions, a malignant power that defies analysis."[40] Such connections raise questions about the ways in which many popular representations of witchcraft in commercial drama have further Otherized semiotics of blackness from general spellcraft to distinctly Black traditions of "dark magic" such as voodoo, hoodoo, and African shamanism.

Dog-whistling is ultimately the defining convention of blackness in *Macbeth* as well as a thematic device, for it is a play in which such blackness (the prophesying of the witches) creates an unchangeable plot of characters who see that which is/isn't — the spectral dagger (which he has not, yet *sees* still), the ghost of Banquo, and others. Black magic, as much as blackness itself, exists at the threshold of those versed in its manifestations, and growing awareness of this parallax is articulated by Macbeth himself when he says:

> Stars, hide your fires;
> Let not light see my black and deep desires:
> The eye wink at the hand; yet let that be,
> Which the eye fears, when it is done, to see.[41]

39. Act IV, Scene Three; Act V, Scene Three; Act IV, Scene One, and Act I, Scene Three, respectively. All quotes from MIT's Shakespeare archive, *The Tragedy of Macbeth*. http://shakespeare.mit.edu/macbeth/full.html.
40. Mildred Tonge. "Black Magic and Miracles in *Macbeth*." *The Journal of English and Germanic Philology*, 31, no. 2. (1932): 236.
41. Act I, Scene Four.

That which is evil and inspired by evil incarnate is jointly manifested in blackness, that which would be left unknown, and is counterpoised against the known, the good, and the moral — the identity of Macbeth hangs in this balance. What the eye cannot bear to look at, the hand must still do in darkness, regardless, though the eye still knows what is happening. It is in this same balance that all the semiotics we have discussed find potential for understanding.

The Subject, Semiotics, and Us

Semiotics morph over time, and the signifiers of blackness in early modern English drama are no exception. However, what has not changed is the fact that blackness and its association with evil as assumed by a measurable portion of English-speaking society is still prevalent enough to demand the use of dog-whistles in contemporary political discourse. It was Lee Atwater, campaign manager for President George H.W. Bush in 1988, who infamously revealed the G.O.P.'s coordinated use of the tactic in public spheres.

> You start out in 1954 by saying, 'Nigger, nigger, nigger.' By 1968 you can't say 'nigger' — that hurts you. Backfires. So you say stuff like forced busing, states' rights and all that stuff. You're getting so abstract now [that] you're talking about cutting taxes, and all these things you're talking about are totally economic things and a byproduct of them is [that] blacks get hurt worse than whites. And subconsciously maybe that is part of it. I'm not saying that. But I'm saying that if it is getting that abstract, and that coded, that we are doing away with the racial problem one way or the other. You follow me — because obviously sitting around saying, 'We want to cut this,' is much more abstract than even the busing thing, and a hell of a lot more abstract than 'Nigger, nigger.'[42]

42. Bob Herbert, "Impossible, Ridiculous, Repugnant." *The New York Times*. October 6, 2005, accessed February 2, 2020. https://www.nytimes.com/2005/10/06/opinion/impossible-ridiculous-repugnant.html

It is a small performative leap from the dog-whistling described by Atwater to the tweets of Donald Trump with which we opened.[43] Political conclusions aside, what the scope of this chapter demonstrates is that, in the history of Black signifiers, there exists a relationship between the obfuscation of Black humanity and this long history of dog-whistles. The early modern period of English drama is one moment in which that evolving saga of Black semiotics is documented – and *Macbeth* exists as one demonstrable artifact of that genealogy.

Our field is rife with discussion, argument, and engagement of the themes of representation, blackness, minstrelsy, and embodiment, yet in the rooms where such discourse seems most open and vibrant – our classrooms and rehearsal halls – those themes are conspicuously absent when exploring this popular text. Whether approached as a literary text or a playscript, *Macbeth* concentrates the interval of time between the early modern period and our own through its documented Black dehumanization. What's more, while the practice of dehumanizing blackness through coded semiotics is widespread in modern political discourse, as examples from Atwater to Trump reveal, we find it all the more necessary for teachers, scholars, and practitioners of drama to examine how history has deafened us to such dog-whistles and break their spells.

43. The use of dog-whistles continue to be an identity-resolving tool in British politics as well, as prime Minister Boris Johnson compared women in burqas to "letterboxes" and "bank robbers." Jessica Elgot, "Boris Johnson Accused of 'Dog-Whistle' Islamophobia Over Burqa Comments," *The Guardian*. August 6, 2018. Accessed October 20, 2021. https://www.theguardian.com/politics/2018/aug/06/boris-johnsons-burqa-remarks-fan-flames-of-islamophobia-says-mp. He is also reported to have referred to the fictional Kenyan ancestry of Barack Obama and described Black citizens as "piccaninnies" with "watermelon smiles."

Bibliography

@realDonaldTrump. "So interesting to see "Progressive" Democrat Congresswomen, who originally came from countries whose governments are a complete and total catastrophe, the worst, most corrupt and inept anywhere in the world (if they even have a functioning government at all), now loudly ... " *Twitter*, July14, 2019, 5:27 a.m., https://twitter.com/realdonaldtrump/status/1150381394234941448?lang=en

Berger, Thomas L., William C. Bradford, and Sidney L. Sondergard. *An Index of Characters in Early Modern English Drama: Printed Plays, 1500–1660*. Cambridge: Cambridge University Press, 1998.

Bonikowski, Bart, and Zhang, Yueran. "Populism as Dog-Whistle Politics: Anti-Elite Discourse and Sentiments towards Minorities." Hosted at *Harvard.edu/files*. https://scholar.harvard.edu/files/bonikowski/files/bonikowski_and_zhang_-_populism_as_dog-whistle_politics.pdf. Retrieved 3 Nov. 2019.

Boose, Lynda E. "The Getting of a Lawful Race: Racial Discourse in Early Modern England and the Unrepresentable Black Woman." In *Women, "Race," and Writing in the Early Modern Period*. edited by Margo Hendricks and Patricia Parker. New York: Routledge, 1994.

Chapman, Matthieu. *Anti-Black Racism in Early Modern English Drama*. New York: Routledge, 2017.

Eco, Umberto. *Semiotics and the Philosophy of Language*. Bloomington: Indiana University Press, 1986.

Denike, Margaret. "The Devil's Insatiable Sex: A Genealogy of Evil Incarnate." *Hypatia* 18, no. 1 (January 2009): 10–43.

Elgot, Jessica. "Boris Johnson Accused of 'Dog-whistle' Islamophobia Over Burqa Comments." *The Guardian*. August 6, 2018.

Fry, Paul H. *Theory of Literature*. New Haven: Yale University Press, 2012.

Garrett, Julia M. "Witchcraft and Sexual Knowledge in Early Modern England." *Journal for Early Modern Cultural Studies* 13, no. 1 (Winter 2013): 32–72.

Greenblatt, Stephen. *Shakespearean Negotiations: The Circulation of Social Energy in Renaissance England*. Berkeley: University of California Press, 1988.

Hartman, Saidiya V., and Frank B. Wilderson III. "The Position of the Unthought." *Qui Parle* 13, no. 2. (Spring/Summer 2003): 183–201.

Herbert, Bob. "Impossible, Ridiculous, Repugnant." *The New York Times*, October 6, 2005. https://www.nytimes.com/2005/10/06/opinion/impossible-ridiculous-repugnant.html Retrieved February 2, 2020.

Holmes, Clive. "Women: Witnesses and Witches." In *New Perspectives on Witchcraft, Magic, and Demonology, Volume 4: Gender and Witchcraft*, edited by Brian P. Levack. New York: Routledge, 2001.

Hornback, Robert. "The Folly of Racism: Enslaving Blackface and the "Natural" Fool Tradition." *Medieval & Renaissance Drama in England* 20, (2007): 46–84.

Isidore of Seville. *The Etymologies of Isidore of Seville*. Translated by Stephen A. Barney, W.J. Lewis, J.A. Beach, and Oliver Bergof. Cambridge: Cambridge University Press, 2006.

James I. *Daemonologie in the Forme of a Dialogie Diuided into three Bookes*. Robert Walde-graue, Printer to the Kings Majestie, 1597. Hosted by *ProjectGutenberg.org*. http://www.gutenberg.org/files/25929/25929-pdf.pdf. Retrieved November 1, 2019.

"Jacques Lacan." *Stanford Encyclopedia of Philosophy*. July 10, 2018, accessed November 1, 2019. https://plato.stanford.edu/entries/lacan/#OthOedComSex

Kors, Alan and Peters, Edward. *Witchcraft in Europe, 400–1700: A Documentary History*. Philadelphia: University of Pennsylvania Press, 2000.

Kramer, Heinrich, and James Sprenger. *The Malleus Maleficarum: Translated with an Introduction, Bibliography & Notes by the Reverend Montague Summers*. http://www.malleusmaleficarum.org/downloads/MalleusAcrobat.pdf. Retrieved November 11, 2019.

Krugman, Paul. "Racism Comes Out of the Closet." *The New York Times*, July 15, 2019. https://www.nytimes.com/2019/07/15/opinion/trump-twitter-racist.html

Lacan, Jacques. *Ecrits*. Translated by Bruce Fink. New York: W.W. Norton & Company, 2006.

Martin, John Jeffries. *Myths of Renaissance Individualism*. London: Palgrave MacMillan, 2004.

Poitevin, Kimberly. "Inventing Whiteness: Cosmetics, Race, and Women in Early Modern England." *Journal for Early Modern Cultural Studies* 11, no. 1. (Spring/Summer 2011): 59–89.

Stevens, Andrea. "Mastering Masques of Blackness: Jonson's 'Masque of Blackness,' The Windsor Text of 'The Gypsies Metamorphosed,' and Brome's 'The English Moor.'" *English Literary Renaissance* 39, no. 2. (Spring 2009): 396–426.

Tatzl, Dietmar. *"Secret, Black, and Midnight Hags": The Conception, Presentation, and Function of Witches in Renaissance Drama.* Vienna: Wilhelm Braumuller Universitats-Verlagsbuchhandlung, 2005.

Teall, John L. "Witchcraft and Calvinism in Elizabethan England: Divine Power and Human Agency." *Journal of the History of Ideas* 23, no. 1. (March 1962): 21–36.

Tonge, Mildred. "Black Magic and Miracles in *Macbeth*." *The Journal of English and Germanic Philology* 31, no. 2. (1932): 234–246.

Thompson, Ayanna. *Performing Race and Torture on the Early Modern Stage*. New York: Routledge Press, 2008.

Vaughan, Virginia Mason. *Performing Blackness on English Stages, 1500–1800*. Cambridge: Cambridge University Press, 2008.

Washington, Joseph R. *Anti-Blackness in English Religion 1500–1800*. Lewiston: Edwin Mellon Press, 1984.

Teaching Spenser's Darkness: Race, Allegory, and the Making of Meaning in *The Faerie Queene*

DENNIS AUSTIN BRITTON

I begin classes on Edmund Spenser's *Faerie Queene* where most teachers begin, Spenser's letter to Raleigh:

> SIR *knowing how doubtfully all* Allegories *may be construed, and this booke of mine, which I have entituled the* Faery Queene, *being a continued* Allegory, *or darke conceit, I have thought good aswell for avoyding of gealous opinions and miscostructions, as also for your better light in reading thereof, (being so by you commanded,) to discover unto you the general intention and meaning, which in the whole course thereof I have fashioned, without expressing of any particular purposes or by accidents therein occasioned.* (714)[1]

Of course, there is much to focus on in the letter to Raleigh, but first on Spenser's list of things that need to be explained is the allegorical nature of his work.[2] I draw my students' attention to allegory as "darke conceit"

1. All quotations from *The Faerie Queene* are from Edmund Spenser, *The Faerie Queene*, edited by A. C. Hamilton, second edition (New York: Routledge, 2001). Parenthetical citation will appear in the essay. Letterforms have been modernized (i/j and u/v), but original spellings have been maintained. Spelling was not fixed in the early modern period, but Spenser uses archaic spellings and words to represent his poem as an artifact from the past.
2. We also spend time discussing Spenser's claims that "*The generall end therefore of all the booke is to fashion a gentleman or noble person in vertuous and gentle discipline*" (714). As I describe in this chapter, I ask students to think about the ways in which English gentlemen are being fashioned in opposition to "dark" characters in the poem. I also discuss Spenser's sources, especially *Orlando Furioso* and *Gerusalemme liberata*, to draw attention to the ways they represent conflicts between Christians and Muslims.

that contains within it the potential for "jealous opinions" and "misconstructions." Halfway through the opening sentence of the letter, we take time to pause. On the one hand, Spenser's rendering of poetic figuration as dark is entirely conventional. In *The Defense of Poesy*, Philip Sidney writes that "there are many mysteries contained in poetry, which of purpose were written darkly, lest by profane wits it should be abused," while in *The Art of English Poesie*, George Puttenham offers that allegories produce "a duplicitie of meaning or dissimulation vnder couert and darke intendments."[3] Darkness as it relates to poetry, figures of speech, and allegory functions somewhat differently in Sidney and Puttenham. While Sidney asserts that darkness is created by poetic figures more generally to safeguard "mysteries" from "profane" wits, Puttenham suggests that "duplicitie of meaning and dissimulation" and darkness are specific to allegory — and with his language of duplicity and dissimulation, we have a useful preamble for later classroom discussions of Duessa. What is common to Sidney, Puttenham, and Spenser, nevertheless, is the link between poetic figuration and darkness, a darkness that certain classes of readers — aided by *proper* modes of reading and interpretation — can overcome.

I do not assume that my students know what allegory is, nor what it means for Spenser to call it the "darke conceit." In addition to drawing students' attention to passages from Sidney and Puttenham, I provide them M. H. Abrams's trusty definition from *A Glossary of Literary Terms*: "An allegory is a narrative in which the agents and action, and sometimes the setting as well, are contrived both to make coherent sense on the 'literal,' or primary level of signification, and also to signify a second, correlated order agents, concepts, or event."[4] Abrams's definition itself requires unpacking, but what I hope students get from Abrams is that allegories tell two stories at once and recall the duplicity described by Puttenham.

3. Philip Sidney, *The Defense of Poesy*, in *Sir Philip Sidney: Selected Prose and Poetry*, edited by Robert Kimbrough, second edition (Madison: University of Wisconsin Press, 1983), 99–158, at 157; and George Puttenham, *The Art of English Poesy: A Critical Edition*, edited by Frank Whigham and Wayne A. Rebhorn (Ithaca, NY: Cornell University Press, 2007), 238.
4. M. H. Abrams, *A Glossary of Literary Terms*, fourth edition (New York: Holt, Rinehart, and Watson, 1981), 4.

But I also use Abrams to highlight the fact that there is a story that resides on the literal level, and that that story is worth thinking about on its own terms. While there is nothing particularly radical about asking students to pay attention to the relationships between characters, places, and actions and "agents, concepts, or events," I want students to consider why a story about knights, ladies, and monsters *must* be interpreted as signifying the becoming of the White English Protestant nation, how the ideological work of the poem almost forces readers to make certain connections between characters and concepts in order to produce "correct" interpretations of the poem and reject the dark ones.[5]

Interpretation, after all, is a primary source of Spenserian anxiety. If it was obvious that the Fairy Queen should be read as "*the most excellent and glorious person of our soveraine the Queene*" (716) and that Belphoebe, too, should be read as signifying aspects of Elizabeth I, Spenser would have no need to explain it in the letter. Spenser recognizes that allegories are prone to be interpreted in a manner that departs from the author's intention. But here, interpretations that depart from those intended by the author point to a reader who is unable to master darkness. Through his letter and his narrator, Spenser seeks to guide the reader toward specific interpretations. As the literary critic Susanne Lindren Wofford puts it, "While the poem textualizes its meanings by directing attention to the openness, instability, and generativity of signs as signs, and to the tropological exchanges within and among signs, the allegory works in an opposed way, putting into action what we might call the narrator's hegemonic desire to enforce assent to dominant traditional discourses and to the political and social power they affirm."[6] If Spenser (and the narrator) were to have his way, our teaching of *The Faerie Queene* might be reduced to helping students do little more than grasp what we presumed to be

5. I deliberately capitalize "White" following the suggestion of the historian Nell Irvin Painter and others who argue that doing so draws attention to White as a racialized identity. See Painter's "Capitalize 'White', Too," *The Washington Post*, July 7, 2020, https://www.washingtonpost.com/opinions/2020/07/22/why-white-should-be-capitalized/.
6. Susanne Lindgren Wofford, *The Choice of Achilles: The Ideology of Figure in the Epic* (Stanford: Stanford University Press, 1992), 222.

the poet's intended meaning, to helping them read his allegory "correctly." To do this, however, would be grossly out of line with scholarly attention — especially after the influential poststructuralist theorist Roland Barthes killed authors — to various ways that meaning may evade intention, and the ways in which the allegorical mode is unable to maintain exact equivalency between what Renaissance scholar Harry Berger called many years ago the allegorical "Image" and "Idea."[7] But I want to suggest that resistance to what seems to be Spenser's intended meaning is all the more necessary for understanding the construction of race in his poem, especially as it emerges in connection to knowledge and interpretation. The letter links "misconstruction" of meaning to the darkness of/in/surrounding the reader. The poem wants to lead readers to the light of "correct" interpretation, which often emerges through vanquishing dark, racialized characters who hold wrong knowledge.[8]

I give my students what seems to be a simple task: trace images of lightness and darkness, whiteness/fairness and blackness, in the poem; chart who and what are associated with light and dark; and pause at moments when the poem mentions objects or activities related to reading and interpretation. This tracing, of course, is assisted by having students read portions of Kim F. Hall's *Things of Darkness: Economies of Race and*

7. Harry Berger, *The Allegorical Temper: Vision and Reality in Book 2 of Spenser's* Faerie Queene (New Haven: Yale University Press, 1957), 22. On tensions, contradictions, and polysemy within the allegory, also see, for example, James Norhnberg, *The Analogy of The Faerie Queene* (Princeton: Princeton University Press, 1977); Wofford, *The Choice of Achilles*; Gordon Teskey, *Allegory and Violence* (Ithaca, NY: Cornell University Press, 1996); and Judith H. Anderson, *Reading the Allegorical Intertext: Chaucer, Shakespeare, Spenser, and Milton* (New York: Fordham University Press, 2011). Guiding students solely toward "intended meaning" would also ignore the self-consciousness that literary critics often read as inherent to the poem.
8. Here we might think about Acrasia's Bower of Bliss, which since Stephen Greenblatt has been read as pointing toward the Americas. See Greenblatt's "To Fashion a Gentleman: Spenser and the Destruction of the Bower of Bliss" in *Renaissance Self-Fashioning* (Chicago: University of Chicago Press, 1980), 157–92; David Read, *Temperate Conquests; Spenser and the Spanish New World* (Detroit: Wayne State University Press, 2000); and Joan Pong Linton, *Romance of the New World: Gender and the Literary Formations of English Colonialism* (Cambridge: Cambridge University Press, 2006).

Gender in Early Modern England.[9] Giving students the task of tracing this imagery is especially useful for engaging Book 1 and its project to differentiate Protestant truth from Catholic falsehood. Doing so, I believe, not only provides students with a concrete activity that offers an entryway into the poem, but it also allows the class to discuss the racialization of knowledge production and interpretation.

Edmund Spenser's epic is a generator of epistemic whiteness, akin to various projects of racialization wherein, as philosopher George Yancy argues, "whiteness is deemed the transcendental norm, the good, the innocent, the pure, while blackness is the diametrical opposite. This is the twisted fate of the Black body vis-à-vis white forms of disciplinary control, processes of white racist embodied habituation, and epistemic white world-making."[10] *The Faerie Queene*, through all of the self-consciousness about its allegory, is a useful site for witnessing the process of "epistemic white world-making," and for examining how Spenser employs allegory as a form of disciplinary control in order to produce specific kinds of meanings. Analyzing the relationship between allegory and meaning, the literary critic Gordon Teskey argues, "Meaning is an instrument used to exert force on the world as we find it, imposing on the intolerable, chaotic otherness of nature a hierarchal order in which objects appear to have

9. Kim F. Hall, *Things of Darkness: Economies of Race and Gender in Early Modern England* (Ithaca, NY: Cornell University Press, 1995). I rarely teach *The Faerie Queene* outside of a sophomore-level Medieval-Renaissance survey. In that course, I might only assign a few pages from Hall's introduction. But just asking students to read, and then discussing, a few pages is enough to provide an elementary understanding of how race is constructed through images of fairness and darkness.

10. George Yancy, *Black Bodies, White Gazes: The Continuing Significance of Race in America*, second edition (Lanham, MD: Rowman & Littlefield, 2017), 3. Yancy's focus on White worldmaking is especially evocative here given critical interest in Spenser's worldmaking. See, for example, Patrick Cheney and Lauren Silberman, eds., *Worldmaking Spenser: Explorations in the Early Modern Age* (Lexington: University of Kentucky Press, 2000), especially essays by Elizabeth Jane Bellamy, David J. Baker, and Heather Dubrow in sections "Policing Self and Other: Spenser, the Colonial, and the Criminal." On worldmaking in early modern Europe in Spenser and beyond, and worldmaking as precursor to European imperialism, see Ayesha Ramachandran, *The Worldmakers: Global Imagining in Early Modern Europe* (Chicago: University of Chicago Press, 2015).

inherent 'meanings.'"[11] Following Teskey, scholars who work on Spenser are now attending to connections between the messiness of allegorization and racialization. Ross Lerner argues that Spenser's poem "reveals how the unstable project of racialization must continually fail to reduce individuals and communities to the meanings they are supposed to embody, just as readers of *The Faerie Queene* will continue to discover the gaps and unassimilable narrative materials that unsettle the poem's allegorical edifice."[12] In a similar vein, Benedict S. Robinson writes, "Perhaps the world projected by racial discourse is itself an allegorical fiction. But allegory also surely disrupts the smooth functioning of racial signifiers in the very thoroughness with which it sublimates the physicality of the body."[13] Both Ross and Robinson suggest that *The Faerie Queene* is an ideal site for unpacking the illogic of racialization precisely because Spenser's epic often questions what "seems" and what bodies signify. By examining how the poem's assignments of lightness and darkness work in the service of fashioning the White/light English Protestant gentleman, I believe students are able to see how one particular project of racial, religious, and national self-definition mandated the darkening of others. I also hope this exercise helps students examine how the poem racializes meaning making and interpretation. My primary aim in this chapter, then, is not only to provide a way to teach how race works in *The Faerie Queene*, but also to argue that we have a responsibility to provide students with the analytical tools for recognizing the ways Spenser's epic attempts to train readers how to interpret the world through an epistemology of English Protestant whiteness.

11. Gordon Teskey, 2. Teskey focuses on how this violence plays itself out in relation to gender.
12. Ross Lerner, "Allegorization and Racialization in *The Faerie Queene*," in the special issue "Spenser and Race," edited by Dennis Austin Britton and Kimberly Anne Coles, *Spenser Studies* 35 (2021): 107–32, at 124.
13. Benedict S. Robinson, "'Swarth' Phantastes: Race, Body and Soul in *The Faerie Queene*," in the special issue "Spenser and Race," edited by Dennis Austin Britton and Kimberly Anne Coles, *Spenser Studies* 35 (2021): 133–51, at 134.

Images of dark and light come up immediately in Book 1, and students may note in the epic invocation that the poet calls on the "holy virgin chief of nyne" (1.Proem.2), Cupid,

> And with them eke, O Goddesse heavenly bright,
> Mirrour of grace and Majestie divine,
> Great Ladie of the greatest Isle, whose light,
> Like *Phoebus* lampe throughout the world doth shine,
> Shed they faire beames into my feeble eyen,
> And raise my thoughtes too humble and too vile
> To thinke of that true glorious type of thine,
> The argument of mine afflicted stile:
> The which to heare, vouchsafe, O dearest dread a while.
> (1.Proem.4)

We begin with Spenser's following of epic convention. I give them invocations from Homer, Virgil, and Tasso — especially since Spenser mentions them as sources of inspiration — as points of comparison. We focus on Spenser's deification of Elizabeth and his comparison of her to Phoebus. Without Elizabeth's "faire beames," the poet claims his "thoughts" will be "too humble and too vile / To thinke of that true glorious type of thine." The poet's own mental processes are highlighted here; without the sovereign's "light," a metaphorical rendering of royal favor and approval of his artistic enterprise, the poet, his thoughts, and the poem reside in an implied darkness. It is here that the poem links light and monarchal power, and perhaps to imperial ambition — if we are to believe that Elizabeth's light, like Phoebus', shines on the whole world.

We then move on to the opening stanzas of canto 1 and analyze the description of Redcrosse Knight alongside images of St. George and the Dragon. Both because the poem does not identify Redcrosse as St. George until canto 10 and because most students are unfamiliar with the legend and its iconography, I draw attention to what the description of Redcrosse would likely have called to the minds of Spenser's first readers. We look at a variety of Medieval and Renaissance images of St. George and the

Figure 1. Master of Sir John Folstof, "Saint George and the Dragon," 1430–1440, Book of Hours, Ms. 5 (84.ML.723), fol. 33v., J. Paul Getty Museum, Los Angeles. Digital image courtesy of the Getty's Open Content Program.

Dragon, including an imaged from an illuminated manuscript by Master of Sir John Folstof (figure 1) and Raphael's painting (figure 2):[14]

14. Both images have a specific English connection. The Master of Sir John Folstof gets his name from the manuscript he illuminated belonging to Sir John Folstof. In Raphael's painting, St. George wears the blue garter of the English Order of the Garter with the

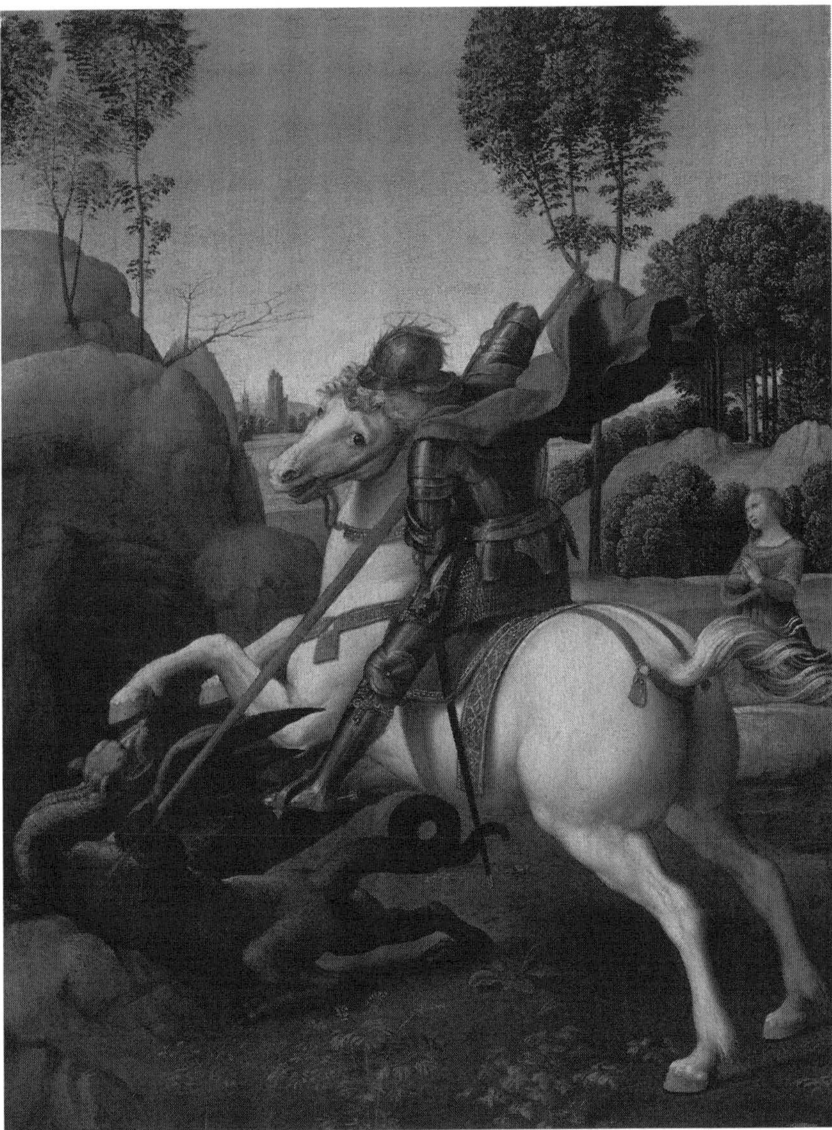

Figure 2. Raphael. *Saint George and the Dragon*, c. 1506. National Gallery of Art, Washington. Courtesy of the National Gallery of Art, Washington.

order's motto, HONI (*Honi soit qui mal y pense*, disgraced be he who thinks ill of it). The painting was made for King Henry VII's emissary, Gilbert Talbot.

Students notice similarities among representations: the light-reflecting sheen of St. George's armor, the whiteness of his horse, the whiteness of the princess, her red dress, and the darkness of the dragon. In Master of Sir John Folstof's image, students will also note similarity between St. George's breastplate and shield, the St. George's Cross (though usually identified by them as the English flag), and the description of Redcrosse:

> And on his breast a bloudie Crosse he bore,
> The deare remembrance of his dying Lord,
> For whose sweete sake the glorious badge he wore,
> And dead as living ever him ador'd:
> Upon his shield the like was also scor'd,
> For soveraine hope, which in his helpe he had:
> Right faithfull true was in deede and word,
> But of his cheere did seeme too solemne sad;
> Yet nothing did him dread, but ever was ydrad.
> (1.1.2)

It almost appears that Spenser was looking at Master of Sir John Folstof's illustration when composing Book 1, even to the description of the knight's "sad" expressions. But what I want students to take away here is a preliminary understanding of iconographic traditions, the way certain stories, characters, people, creatures, and settings are repeatedly represented. Although in many ways meaning presupposes figuration in *The Faerie Queene*, meaning making is assisted by shared expectations established through generic and iconographic traditions.

Following our analysis of Redcrosse, we discuss Una, in whom the colors black and white come into explicit contact:

> A lovely Ladie rode him faire beside,
> Upon a lowly Asse more white then snow,
> Yet she much whiter, but the same did hide
> Under a vele, that wimpled was full low,
> And over all a blacke stole shee did throw,
> As one that inly mournd: so was she sad
> And heavie sat upon her palfrey slow:

> Seemed in heart some hidden care she had,
> And by her in a line a milkewhite lambe she lad.
> (1.1.4)

Una is superlatively white. Here is a good place to ask students to think about the relationship between the literal and the figurative, between the chromatic image they are asked to imagine, and that to which it is supposed to point. Students can easily see that – in a single stanza! – images of whiteness abound, even as they note that the whiteness described is impossible to see/imagine/perceive: how can an ass be whiter than snow, and then how can a woman be whiter than a whiter-than-snow ass? Here Spenser seems obsessed with creating a figure who is whiter than white. But as the imagery asks us to visualize a whiteness that is whiter than white, the description points to something that exist beyond the level of the merely chromatic.

Given the task of charting images of lightness/whiteness and darkness/blackness, students will likely note as well that Una is covered by a "black stole." Upon this recognition, Una's special allegorical status becomes evident – not all characters in the poem exist on the same allegorical level. By way of the black stole, Spenser teaches the reader how to interpret the color of surfaces. While wearing black garments is certainly a conventional sign of mourning, the narrator makes it a point to inform us that she wears the black stole "As one that inly mournd." The narrator, as Spenser does in the letter to Raleigh, wants to make sure readers interpret correctly and isn't content to leave interpretation solely to the reader's ability to decipher color symbolism. Una becomes a figure for allegory itself; she is covered by darkness that the reader must see beyond to understand the truth she represents, even as the outer, surface layer points toward something internal.[15]

15. This reading is also supported by the editor's, A. C. Hamilton's, gloss: "by **more white then snow** with truth (in Ripa 1603:501, *Verità* is *vestita di color bianco*) and with faith cf. x 13.1); and by her **vele** with the truth that remains veiled to the fallen" (32, note to stanza 4). And yet, Spenser's figure of truth is not clothed in white, but is white herself clothed in black, a distinction that is worth asking students to consider. Nonetheless, the gloss echoes Sidney's suggestion that poetic figuration conceals the truth from

I will also ask students what it means that Una sits "faire beside" Redcrosse. Does "fair" describe Una's appearance or the manner in which she rides? Here is another good place to direct students to Hall's *Things of Darkness* and the *Oxford English Dictionary* (OED), where they will encounter a dizzying number of definitions for "fair" as an adjective, any number of which might be in play here: for example, "Beautiful to the eye; of attractive appearance; good-looking" (def. A.I.1), "Excellent, admirable; good, desirable; noble, honourable; reputable" (def. A.I.6), "Expressing or expressive of gentleness or peaceable intention; kind, mild" (def. A.II.8), "Open to view, plainly visible; clear, distinct" (def. A.II.9.b), "In accordance with propriety; appropriate, fitting; seemly, becoming" (def. A.II.13), and "Of hair or complexion: light as opposed to dark in colour. Of a person: having such colouring" (def. A.IV.17). Arguably, however, these varied meanings all bear on Una's characterization; although there are multiple ways to read "faire besides," all understandings of fair adhere to each other in Una's oneness. She is White because she is fair in her looks, character, and behaviors.

It is worth me saying quite explicitly here that the arguments and assertions above are based on a conviction that projects of racialization are variously aligned with, contained in, and transmitted through iconographic traditions, Christian typology, conventional color symbolism, and generic/poetic conventions.[16] Moreover, I assert, *The Faerie Queene* does

those for whom it is not intended. Hamilton also cites the art historian Roy Strong, who notes that black and white are traditionally the colors associated with perpetual virginity, and thus this depiction of Una also points toward Elizabeth I. On the significance of the relationship between Una's whiteness and her black stole that is complementary to my own, see Robinson, "'Swarth' Phantates," 145–46. Robinson, as I do below, also suggests that we read this in relation to a later moment in the poem when the narrator tells us "As white seemes fairer, match with blacke attone" (3.9.2).

16. Kimberly Anne Coles and I have argued, "The question is not whether whiteness or blackness is attached to actual bodies that are white or black: the question is whether this moral encoding attaches at all. And what happens when we entertain the possibility that it might?" ("Beyond the Pale," *Spenser Review* 50.1.5 [Winter 2020]. http://www.english.cam.ac.uk/spenseronline/review/item/50.1.5. Accessed February 13, 2021). In the article we posed this as a question of "possibility" because we were

not simply employ these; it produces hermeneutics, or modes of interpretation, that shape how readers read. It works to make the color "white" appear "fair" – in all senses of the word, as described above – by repeatedly darkening people, places, and concepts. For example, using a simile to apologize for telling the story of Paridell and Helenore in Book 3, the narrator notes that evil examples are useful, "As white seemes fairer, match with blacke attone" (3.9.2). We might well ask how something can appear visually fairer than white; the simile suggests that the fairness of whiteness can only be perceived through its relationship to blackness – a perception that critical race studies has variously illuminated. As such, Spenser's project needs blackness; just as whiteness cannot seem fair based solely on its chromatic quality, the fairness of English Protestants and the values they hold is only perceptible with the aid of blackness.

All of this becomes especially evident when Redcrosse and Una encounter Errour. Given the poem's very careful uses of light and dark, the sudden tempest and darkening of the sky that leads Redcrosse, Una, and the dwarf "to seeke some covert nigh at hand" in "A shadie grove" (1.1.7) signals the character's movement into a deeply allegorical space. But as they encounter Errour and the darkness surrounding her character, the reader also encounters what I suggest is the poem's first explicit racialization of knowledge. The dwarf suggests that it would be best to leave Errour alone, "Fly fly (quoth then / The fearefull Dwarfe:) this is no place for living men" (1.1.13),

> But Full of fire and greedy hardiment,
> The youthfull knight could not for ought be staide,
> But forth unto the darksom hole he went,
> And looked in: his glistering armor made
> A little glooming light, much like a shade,
> By which he saw the ugly monster plaine,
> Halfe like a serpent horribly displaide,

writing to an audience of skeptical, if not hostile, Spenserians. Nevertheless, Coles and I are certain that this moral encoding does attach to real bodies in the early modern period.

> But th'other halfe did womans shape retaine,
> Most loathsome, filthie, foule, and full of vile disdaine.
> (1.1.14)

Redcrosse's light is not as strong as it should be, and in noting that his "glooming light" is "much like a shade," the narrator may even suggest that there is a degree of darkness within him.[17] Dark as his light may be, it nevertheless allows Redcrosse to see the "ugly monster plaine." Here is another place to have students consult the OED, which will allow them to see that Spenser's use of "plaine" is anything but plain. Yet, what is perhaps the most obvious understanding of "plaine" — "Clear to the senses or the mind; evident, manifest, obvious; easily perceivable or recognizable" (*OED*, plain adj. 2. III.7) — is also the most nonsensical: how is Redcrosse able to see Errour clearly or plainly in the dark? That "plaine" should primarily be read in this way is also suggested by the usage of the word in stanza 16: "For light she hated as deadly bale, / Ay wont in desert darknes to remaine, / Where plain none might her see, nor she see any plaine" (1.1.16). Errour resides in the darkness so that she does not have to be seen or see others — she's minding her own business! Here again, students see how darkness is meant to obscure clarity: surprisingly, Errour, like Una, becomes a figure for allegory itself.

Errour as a figure for allegory, however, is more explicitly linked to issues of interpretation, especially since "plaine" can also mean "Of which the meaning is evident; simple, easily intelligible, readily understood" (*OED*, plain adj. 2. III.9.a). Considering this meaning of "plaine," perhaps Errour is a figure that is easily understood even if she is not clearly seen. For those of us interested in the workings of ideology and White supremacy, the troubling implications of this formulation are apparent: what is already understood to be true has little to do with what is really there and is placed in the shadows. There is no need for Redcrosse or the White Protestant reader to really *see* Errour because she already signifies error; all that really seems to matter is what she already means within the allegory, what is "easily intelligible, readily understood."

17. Hamilton suggests this in his gloss (34, note to stanza 14).

That Errour is a figure related to meaning making and interpretation is also emphasized in her connection to books. After Redcross "grypt her gorge,"

> Therewith she spewd out of her filthie maw
> A floud of poyson horrible and blacke,
> Full of great lumps of flesh and gobbets raw,
> Which stunck so vildly, that it forst him slacke
> His grasping hold, and from her turne him backe:
> Her vomit full of bookes and papers was,
> With loathly frogs and toades, which eyes did lacke,
> And creeping sought way in the weedy gras:
> Her filthy parbreake all the place defiled has.
> (1.1.20)

Errour's blackness is internal — a few stanzas later readers learn that she has "cole black blood" (1.1.24) that nearly overwhelms Redcrosse. We also see that this blackness is comprised of "books and papers" and blind "frogs and toades." Editor A. C. Hamilton's gloss makes it clear that here we are supposed to see Errour and the filth she spews as signifying the Roman Catholic Church and its doctrines.[18] The oddness of Errour's vomit itself signals that we should read allegorically, and there is little reason not to read Errour as figuring Roman Catholicism — the blindness of Errour's children can certainly be interpreted as pointing to what Protestants saw as the Roman Catholic refusal or inability to accept the truth. Yet, what I want students to consider here, again, are the bodies in which ideas and concepts are lodged — and the details attributed to those bodies matter. Errour is seen as dark, even if it is only because she resides in the shadows, her internal fluids are black, and a few stanzas later we learn that she has serpent children who are "Deformed monsters, fowle, and blacke as inke" (1.1.23). If Una is the whitest character in *The Faerie Queene*, Errour is the blackest.

18. Hamilton, 36 note to stanza 20.

The narrator continues to demonize Errour through an epic simile in Stanza 21:

> As when old father *Nilus* gins to swell
> With timely pride above the *Aegyptian* vale,
> His fattie waves doe fertile slime outwell,
> And overflow each plaine and lowly dale:
> But when his later spring gins to avale,
> Huge heapes of mudd he leaves, wherein there breed
> Ten thousand kindes of creatures partly male
> And partly femall of his fruitful seed;
> Such ugly monstrous shapes elswher may no man reed.
> (1.1.21)

We stop and pay attention to the first of many epic similes in the poem — indeed, one of my teachers taught me to pay special attention to the political and ideological work done through epic similes.[19] I ask, is it significant that the poem's first epic simile points toward Egypt and Africa? What connections might the poem be making between Errour/error and Africanness? And, although when it comes to metaphors and similes, we tend to read the vehicle as describing the tenor, to what extent does the tenor denigrate the vehicle — does Errour's blackness blacken an Africa that in many ways was already understood as Black?

When Spenser needs an image of black monstrous fecundity, he turns to Africa. This turning can be illuminated by Kim Hall's aforementioned discussion of "trope of blackness": the use of the trope could be "applied not only to dark-skinned Africans but to Native Americans, Indians, Spanish and even Irish and Welsh as groups that needed to be marked as

19. My classes with Susanne L. Wofford have greatly influenced how I read *The Faerie Queene*. Considering this simile, she writes, "In contrast to the allegory's tendencies as an extended metaphor to make its divergent material seem to have a deeper 'affinitie,' the similes often insinuate a suppressed interpretation that the allegory does not easily countenance" (291). Wofford sees this at work in the fact that while Redcrosse is surely meant to defeat error, Errour as breeder creator of books and paper's and strangeness makes her a figure of the poem itself.

'other.' However, ... in these instances it still draws its power from England's ongoing negotiations of African difference and from the implied color comparison therein."[20] Africa was already metonymic for various types of otherness that were rendered visibly Black. In Spenser's simile, Errour's blackness aligns with African blackness – and African blackness does not need to be mentioned outright because it is already assumed. In many ways, Errour herself seems to be African: they both are associated with liquidness, and while the Nile produces "such ugly monstrous shapes elswher may no man reed," Errour's children are described as "Deformed monsters, fowle, and blacke as inke."[21]

Errour and Africa are yoked further through the language of reading, texts, and printing: the Nile produces shapes (characters, if you will) that can only be read there, and Errour vomits books and papers and has children "blacke as inke." Literary critic Miles P. Grier's discussion of "inkface" is especially useful here. Noting that "black as ink" was a common simile in the early modern period, Grier argues, "By relating the histories of racial thought and the technologies of reading and writing, the inkface concept enables a rich account of performances of literacy as rituals of an elastic racial category of illiterate, legible blacks" and "to link a person to ink was to designate her as one who could never be an insightful reader because she was meant *to be read* by a white expert."[22] In Spenser's allegory, Errour becomes a figure of *ill*-literacy, producer of both corrupted

20. Hall, *Things of Darkness*, 7.
21. We also take time to discuss Errour's gender, dangerous fecundity, and reproductive capacity and capability. The groundbreaking work on race in early modern texts by Kim F. Hall, Ania Loomba, Margo Hendricks, Patricia Parker, Francesca Royster, Arthur Little Jr., and Joyce Green MacDonald has shown us the varied ways in which race was constructed through and alongside gender discourse.
22. Miles P. Grier, "Inkface: The Slave Stigma in England's Early Imperial Imagination," in *Scripturalizing the Human: The Written as the Political*, edited by Vincent L. Wimbush (New York: Routledge, 2015), 193–220, at 195. Playing on the relationship between character as a symbol that represents language and as distinguishing features of a person's or people's mental or moral qualities, Grier also asserts that "Inkface, the metonymic play that represents 'blackness' as marked signifiers in a European characterology, was critical to an early modern English imperial project" (196).

texts and interpretation. At the same time, the poem's allegory works hard to make Errour legible vis-à-vis Africa, virtually insisting that English readers focus on what Errour and Africa produce while making sure that they are read with disgust and as absolutely unlike the texts that they encounter "elswher." Black corporality becomes textuality, made legible through figuration; the religious allegory necessitates a particular reading, and the epic simile that finds numerous correspondences between the allegorical "Image" — to use Harry Berger's language here again — and the simile's vehicle shape how the vehicle is itself read. Within the religious allegory, Africa informs how Errour is to be read, and Errour informs how Africa is to be read. I am thus arguing that here Spenser's allegory quite deliberately invokes Africa as a cite of legible illegibility. Spenser's yoking of images of blackness with the reference to Africa itself tell us that Africa and blackness *can* be yoked together, and that in this yoking they produce an image of that which is to be understood as signifying that which is "other" to epistemologies of whiteness. And, more to the purpose of this article, this is worth exploring with our students; we can use texts like *The Faerie Queene* not only to examine constructions of racial difference in late-sixteenth-century England, but also to show students how texts attempt to train readers to read through racial epistemologies.

Of course, there are many more episodes in *The Faerie Queene* where students can see how the allegory seemingly requires the application of light/white and dark/black to characters. But this examination of Book 1, canto 1 shows that tracing this chromatic application can help students see reading and interpretation as racializing practices; via allegory, an epistemology of whiteness dictates how literary characters are read, even as the very act of reading the allegory trains readers in that epistemology. This is not to say that differences between "Image" and "Idea" do not problematize the ways the allegory produces this epistemology. The varied critical conversations about such difference in fact make *The Faerie Queene* an ideal site for witnessing the incoherence of racist epistemologies. Providing students with a deeper understanding of literary genre, mode, forms, and tropes — with which Spenserians have traditionally been obsessed — gives students tools for dissecting how racist epistemologies work, and how they produce the conditions that determine how people are colored and then read.

Discussion Questions

1. In what ways does the poem racialize men and women differently?
2. *The Faerie Queene* contains numerous non-human characters like Errour. How are racialized identities shaped through the relationships between humans and non-humans?
3. Spenser's *Faerie Queene* is an epic poem. Why might epic be an especially fitting genre to help define racial identity?

Further Reading

Britton, Dennis Austin, and Kimberly Anne Coles. "Spenser and Race: An Introduction." Special issue, "Spenser and Race," edited by Dennis Austin Britton and Kimberly Anne Coles. *Spenser Studies* 35 (2021): 1–19.

Chapman, Matthieu. "Staging Blackness: The Impossibility of Interlocution." In *Anti-Black Racism in Early Modern English Drama: The Other "Other,"* 33–66. New York: Routledge, 2017.

Hall, Kim F. "Beauty and the Beast of Whiteness: Teaching Race and Gender." *Shakespeare Quarterly* 47 (1996): 461–75.

Sanchez, Melissa E. "'To Giue Faire Colour': Sexuality, Courtesy, and Whiteness in The Faerie Queene." "Spenser and Race," edited by Dennis Austin Britton and Kimberly Anne Coles. *Spenser Studies* 35 (2021): 245–84.

Thompson, Ayanna. "Afterword: Me, The Faerie Queene, and Critical Race Theory." Special issue, "Spenser and Race," edited by Dennis Austin Britton and Kimberly Anne Coles. *Spenser Studies* 35 (2021): 285–90.

Teaching Aphra Behn's *Oroonoko* as Execution Narrative[1]

JENNIFER LODINE-CHAFFEY

Aphra Behn's 1688 novella *Oroonoko, or The Royal Slave* offers high school and post-secondary teachers a unique opportunity to explore late-seventeenth-century race relations with their students. As a semi-autobiographical piece written by an Englishwoman, *Oroonoko* draws readers in through its sympathetic treatment of the enslaved African prince and his wife, Imoinda. Recent scholarly articles have stressed the usefulness of this text for teaching about racism, seventeenth-century travel narratives, and representations of gender.[2] While these are valuable ways to engage with the text, I want to suggest a further option. By looking closely at Behn's depiction of Oroonoko's execution, we can further students' understanding of the construction of race relations through the lens of execution practices in the New World.

Written as both a romantic court intrigue narrative and an "eye-witness" account of British colonial practices in Surinam (which they occupied from 1650 to 1667), *Oroonoko* tells the story of an African prince's life, enslavement, and horrific death. Aphra Behn (1640–1689), a Restora-

1. The author would like to thank the editors of this volume, as well as Stephanie Bauman, Rob Bauer, Vanessa Cozza, Tracey Hanshew, Kirk McAuley, and Donna Potts, for their advice and comments in relation to this work.

2. For examples of teaching practices focused on racial issues see Robin R. Bates, "Using *Oroonoko* to Teach the Corrosive Effects of Racism," *English Language Overseas Perspectives and Enquiries* 3, no. 1–2 (2006): 157–68 and Derek Hughes, "*Oroonoko* and Blackness," in *Approaches to Teaching Behn's Oroonoko*, ed. Cynthia Richards and Mary Ann O'Donnell (New York: The Modern Language Association of America, 2011), 57–64. For an approach to teaching *Oroonoko* as an early travel narrative, see Margarete Rubik, "Teaching *Oroonoko* in the Travel Narrative Course," in *Approaches to Teaching Behn's Oroonoko*, 118–23. Jane Spencer provides a useful discussion of Behn's gender and her place in the canon in "Behn and the Canon," in *Approaches to Teaching Behn's Oroonoko*, 194–99.

tion-era English dramatist and poet and one of the first British women to make a living by her pen, recounts Oroonoko's tragic fall in a narrative that traces his love for and loss of the beautiful Imoinda, enslavement through trickery, sale to colonists in Surinam, rebellion against his British owners, and eventual execution. Perhaps the most striking/shocking passage of the novel is the scene of Oroonoko's death. In gruesome language, Behn relates that as the African prince tranquilly smokes a pipe, his body is progressively dismembered:

> [T]he Executioner came, and first cut off his Members [genitals], and threw them into the Fire; after that, with an ill-favoured Knife, they cut his Ears, and his Nose, and burn'd them; he still Smoak'd on, as if nothing had touch'd him; then they hack'd off one of his Arms, and still he bore up, and held his Pipe; but at the cutting off the other Arm, his Head sunk, and his pipe drop'd, and he gave up the Ghost, without a Groan, or a Reproach.[3]

What strikes the reader about this account is not just the violence enacted on the slave's body, but the curious lack of reaction to physical pain displayed by Oroonoko himself. Despite the intense physical agony he must be experiencing, the prince refuses to give voice to his torture.

Students are often shocked by Behn's description of Oroonoko's execution and the prince's stoic behavior.[4] In our contemporary society,

3. Aphra Behn, *Oroonoko, or The Royal Slave*: A *True History*, in *Oroonoko*: A *Norton Critical Edition*, ed. Joanna Lipking (New York: W. W. Norton & Company, 1997), 64. Behn's inclusion of the pipe, while perhaps unintentional, suggests parallels between the tobacco commonly grown in the New World. For more on the connections between the African prince and American tobacco, see Susan B. Iwanisziw, "Behn's Novel Investment: 'Oroonoko': Kingship, Slavery and Tobacco in English Colonialism," *South Atlantic Review* 63, no. 2 (Spring 1998): 75–98.
4. For more on this topic, see the following: Sean McEvoy, "The Ethics of Teaching Tragic Narratives," in *Teaching Narrative*, ed. Richard Jacobs (Cham, Switzerland: Palgrave Macmillan, 2018), 55–69 and Jack Halberstam, "Trigger Happy: From Content Warning to Censorship," *Signs: Journal of Women in Culture and Society* 42, no. 2 (Winter 2017): 535–42.

instructors at all levels should consider the possibility that some students may find the gruesome violence enacted upon Behn's central character not only shocking, but also viscerally disturbing. While I believe that Behn intends Oroonoko's execution to alarm and upset the reader in order to evoke sympathy for the executed prince, instructors may want to consider providing some warning about representations of violence and their potential impacts before analyzing capital punishments in the early modern period. However, providing full trigger warnings, as ethnicity and gender theorist Jack Halberstam argues, "reduces the viewer to a defenceless, passive, and inert spectator who has no barriers between herself and the flow of images that populate her world."[5] Indeed, while it is important to be sensitive to individuals in our classrooms, it is also imperative that students confront our shared historical past. The power of teaching works that represent violence like Behn's *Oroonoko*, I argue, is that it encourages reflection on human morality and mortality and it asks us to interrogate values in the past and today. Additionally, students should understand that violence against black bodies in historical sources and literary texts is related to and implicated in twenty-first-century racism.

With these provisos, I seek to move beyond the initial shock of the final scene in Behn's *Oroonoko* to analyze the importance of execution rituals and question why these practices mattered in the greater Caribbean world.[6] In my class and throughout this essay, I focus on the connections between racism and corporal punishment in order to re-examine the history and origins of antiblack oppression. In particular, Behn's novella explicitly links execution and racial formation, thereby highlighting the disproportional historical punishment of people of color, which students must grapple with not only in my class but also in our modern world.To provide students with a grasp of execution theory and practice so they

5. Halberstam, "Trigger Happy," 541.
6. Although technically part of South America, Surinam is usually designated by scholars as part of the greater Caribbean due to the area's cultural and historical similarities to the islands in the Caribbean Sea. See J. R. McNeill, *Mosquito Empires: Ecology and War in the Greater Caribbean, 1620–1914* (Cambridge: Cambridge University Press, 2010) and Patrick Taylor, ed. *Nation Dance: Religion, Identity, and Cultural Difference in the Caribbean* (Bloomington, IN: Indiana University Press, 2001).

can more readibly think through the connections between race and punishment, I assign supplementary readings that help guide our discussions of Oroonoko's death and its possible meanings. These readings include primary source documents about British executions in London during the seventeenth century, an article by noted historian Richard Price about Surinam slave punishments that contains a contemporary account of a slave execution, and a short reading from theorist Michel Foucault about executions from his influential study *Discipline and Punish*. In addition, I ask students to put these sources in conversation and individually work on theorizing Oroonoko's behavior in writing before attending a class session that breaks students into groups to jointly work on the possible meanings of Oroonoko's execution in Behn's text. Finally, students are asked to consider poet and engraver William Blake's images of slaves undergoing punishment included in John Gabriel Stedman's 1796 *Narrative, of a Five Years' Expedition, against the Revolted Negroes of Surinam*. By focusing on Oroonoko's execution and Blake's engravings, students begin to question their own ideas about slavery and race relations during the long eighteenth century.

Most twenty-first-century students initially come to *Oroonoko* with fixed ideas about slavery based on more recent American history. Often informed by master narratives about slavery and its connection to Southern cotton plantations and general assumptions that all "good" people viewed slavery as morally wrong, students tend to initially read Behn's text as containing an abolitionist message and assume that resistance to slavery is based on the belief that slavery is inherently evil. Their prolonged engagement with *Oroonoko*, however, complicates this simplistic reading. My hope is for students to gain important realizations about Behn's novella that provide them with greater understanding of historical slavery and racism, how early modern depictions of Black peoples usually reinforced ideologies of white racial dominance, the importance of the Caribbean world in the slave trade, and the racial construction of execution practice that contributed to the growth of later prejudices.

Establishing Historical Context: Assigned Readings

To obtain a broader understanding of how executions worked in seventeenth-century Great Britain, I assign the anonymous account of John Marketman's 1680 hanging. This document not only details Marketman's murder of his wife, but also describes his final actions before death. What I hope students gain from this text is that for the common British man or woman, public executions generally included a number of rituals missing from the accounts of Afro-Caribbean slave executions. For instance, the condemned in Britain received religious instruction and were expected to express sinfulness and repentance on the scaffold. Often narratives noted sympathetic reactions from the audience. In contrast to *Oroonoko*, the account of Marketman's execution focuses not on the grisly details of his death, but instead on his remorse. According to the anonymous author, in his "long speech," Marketman lamented his disobedience to his parents, his "Youthful days [spent] in Profanation of the Sabbath," his "Debaucheries beyond expression," and his failure to emulate his wife's virtuous behavior. Notably, Marketman ended his last statement by asking that "all should pray to the Eternal God for His everlasting welfare," and "[recommending] his Soul to the Almighty."[7] His scaffold speech, which humanizes Marketman by alluding to his spiritual condition and familial ties, is typical of many accounts during this time period and is readily available from the database of scanned primary sources, Early English Books Online.[8]

7. Anonymous, *The True Narrative of the Execution of John Marketman, Chrynrgian, of Westham in Essex, for Committing a Horrible & Bloody Murther Upon the Body of his Wife, That Was Big with Child When He Stabbed Her* (London: s.m., 1680), 4. For access to this source, visit the University of Michigan's Early English Books Online Text Creation Partnership, which provides scholars with editions of early modern works for research purposes (https://quod.lib.umich.edu/e/eebogroup/).
8. For other useful accounts of the execution behavior of seventeenth-century British men and women that showcase repentance, warnings to the crowd, and a final prayer, see the following: Anonymous, *News from Islington, or, The Confession and Execution of George Allin, Butcher* (London, 1674), 1–6; Anonymous, *The True Narrative of the Confession and Execution of Elizabeth Hare ...* (London, 1683) 1–4; Anonymous, *A true and per-*

To further students' understanding not only of typical British executions, but also executions in the New World, and their intersections with race and with the way the British punished Black slaves in the New World, I include an online article from the historian, Richard Price. In "Violence and Hope in a Space of Death: Paramaribo," Price explains the gruesome 1710 dismemberment and capital punishment of a runaway slave as seen through the eyes of J. D. Herlein, a Dutch traveler. Quoting Herlein, Price describes the execution of the man in vivid detail:

> He was lain on the ground, his head on a long beam. The first blow he was given, on the abdomen, burst his bladder open, yet he uttered not the least sound; the second blow with the axe he tried to deflect with his hand, but it gashed the hand and upper belly, again without his uttering a sound. The slave men and women laughed at this, saying to one another, 'This is a man!' Finally, the third blow, on the chest, killed him. His head was cut off and the body cut in four pieces and dumped in the river.[9]

fect relation of the grand traytors execution .... Together with their severall speeches and confessions (London: Printed for William Gilbertson, 1660), 1; and Anonymous, *A True Narrative of the Confession and Execution of Several Notorious Malefactors at Tyburn on Wednesday April the 16th 1684* (London, 1684), 1–4. For more information on the English ritual of execution see J. A. Sharpe, "'Last Dying Speeches': Religion, Ideology and Public Execution in Seventeenth-Century England," *Past and Present* 107 (May 1985): 144–67 and Katherine Royer, *The English Execution Narrative, 1200–1700* (London: Pickering & Chatto, 2014). For instructors without access to Early English Books Online, the following sources are open access and readily available to all scholars: English Broadside Ballad Archive (http://ebba.english.ucsb.edu/), The Proceedings of the Old Bailey, 1674–1913 (https://www.oldbaileyonline.org/), and Una McIlvenna's Execution Ballads (https://omeka.cloud.unimelb.edu.au/execution-ballads/).

9. Richard Price, "Violence and Hope in a Space of Death: Paramaribo" *Common-Place* 3, no. 4 (July 2003), n.p. http://www.common-place-archives.org/vol-03/no-04/paramaribo/. A similar description of a late-eighteenth-century execution of a Koromantyn slave is provided in Bryan Edward's history of the West Indies. See Edwards, *The History, Civil and Commercial, of the British Colonies in the West Indies*, Vol. 2, London: John Stockdale, 1793, 98.

I suggest that students connect this anonymous slave's execution behavior to Oroonoko's conduct and notice that both enslaved individuals refuse to give voice to their pain, and that neither account provides the last dying speech their contemporaries in Great Britain usually delivered. In addition, this text stresses the reactions of the crowd, who applaud the dying man's stoicism. While this detail is not present in Behn's text, the "slave men and women" watching the execution in Herlein's account attest to the bravery of the victim, suggesting that his silence is heroic and a sign of courage, and in this case, manliness.[10]

Finally, I add to this short packet a section from theorist Michel Foucault's seminal work that presents his interpretation of public execution as a "theatre of punishment" where the state inscribes its power on the body of the criminal and forces him or her to confess and repent. For Foucault, the executed body attests to the truth of the sentence and the ritual of execution belongs "to the ceremonies by which power is manifested."[11] The political display of the tortured body and death of the condemned affirmed the power of the sovereign through "a policy of terror," meant to reassert the monarch's power over the physical bodies of his subjects. For Foucault, executions publicized the ruler's authority and worked to instill the people's fear and obedience. Likewise, the last dying speeches of the condemned authenticated the sentence of the law.[12] Foucault also argues that torture needs to meet three conditions: it must produce measurable pain, it should mark the victim physically, and it needs to "form part of a ritual."[13] I encourage students to question Oroonoko's execution in light of these theories and to ask themselves two questions: does

10. While fewer accounts of the punishments of Caribbean slave women exist, John Gabriel Stedman does mention one eighteenth-century female slave at Paramaribo who was given 400 lashes and "bore them without a complaint." Thus, it is likely that female slaves exhibited similar stoic behaviors when executed. See Stedman, *Narrative of a Five Years' Expedition against the Revolted Negroes of Surinam*, vol. 2, 2nd ed. (London: J. Johnson & Thomas Payne, 1813), 198.
11. Michel Foucault, *Discipline and Punish: The Birth of the Prison*, trans. Alan Sheridan (New York: Pantheon Books, 1977), 47.
12. Foucault, *Discipline and Punish*, 66.
13. Foucault, *Discipline and Punish*, 33–34.

Oroonoko's tortured body function as a sign of the planters' authority? And does Oroonoko's refusal to acknowledge his suffering diminish the torture he and the reader experience? By asking these questions, students confront the violence enacted on Oroonoko not only as a clear racializing of Black bodies through execution practices, but also as evidence of the ways that literature and the visual arts influenced and continue to influence the dehumanization and objectication of Black individuals.

Theorizing Colonial Executions of Enslaved Individuals: Assignment and Discussion

Three class days are spent on the text of *Oroonoko*. The first day is a general introduction to Aphra Behn's writings and biography, as well as a guided discussion of the first half of the novella. This class discussion will include questions of genre, as well as an overview of themes of nobility, slavery, and the colonial project. At the end of this class, I provide the students with a collection of documents (including Marketman's execution narrative, Price's article, and a chapter from Foucault's seminal work) to consider in conjunction with Behn's novel. I ask them to carefully read these short pieces and write/craft answers to the following questions:

1. How is Oroonoko's execution different from the 1680 execution of John Marketman? How is it the same?
2. What do you notice about Herlein's description of the 1710 execution of a runaway slave in Paramaribo? How is this execution similar to or different from Oroonoko's execution?
3. What is Price's central argument about slave executions? Do you agree or disagree?
4. How does Foucault interpret execution? How might we apply these ideas to Oroonoko's actions during his public punishment and subsequent execution?
5. Why do you think Behn depicts Oroonoko as a silent sufferer? Why doesn't he cry out during his sufferings?

During the second class period, students meet in groups of three to five to compare notes and come up with possible reasons for Oroonoko's execution behavior and jointly answer the five questions I posed. I spend time visiting with each group to ascertain their involvement with the supplementary materials, Behn's text, and the questions. I ask each group to turn in their answers at the end of the class period.

During the third class period focusing on *Oroonoko*, I go through the students' answers in class and present differing views of the prince's execution behavior based on student analysis. In this way, students become active participants in the classroom, guiding the discussion and offering historically and theoretically informed interpretations of *Oroonoko* based on the assigned readings. This session thus uses a dialogic approach that takes into account both the students' response and my own approach to the text. Building on this opening exercise, I present a guided lecture with relevant artwork. I thereby provide students with further examples of both British executions and Caribbean slave executions and outline the differences in practice between the Old and the New World. With my students' assistance, I break down the different representations, noting the preparation for death and the expectation of a final speech for contemporary British men and women. I also provide an example of a depiction of the scaffold speech and execution from a contemporary British pamphlet (see figure 1). We discuss the audiences of these public spectacles and contemplate the responses to both Old and New World executions. I review Price's and Foucault's understandings of public punishments and ask students how they interpret Oroonoko's death. For instance, do they see his refusal to show pain as an act of defiance against white supremacy? Or is he adopting British martyrdom traditions? I also ask the students if the depiction of Oroonoko is biased because of Aphra Behn's race, gender, or class. Through this discussion, students question the possible meaning of Oroonoko's and other enslaved individuals's behavior under torture in light of its filtration through a European lens.

Performance and race scholar Ayanna Thompson points out that during the seventeenth century, dramatic representations of the torture of African bodies depicted "the racialized body as something accessible,

Figure 1. Anonymous, *A true and perfect relation of the grand traytors execution, as at severall times they were drawn, hang'd, and quartered at Charing-crosse, and at Tiburne. Together with their severall speeches and confessions which every one of them made at the time of their execution.* London: Printed for William Gilbertson, 1660. RB 233064, The Huntington Library, San Marino, California.

controllable, and penetrable."[14] Indeed, Thompson notes that playwright Thomas Southerne's 1695 adaptation of Behn's novella, *Oroonoko: A Tragedy*, worked as an early abolitionist piece not only because it positioned Oroonoko's torture as inhumane and cruel, but also because it "constantly [restaged] the abjection of the racialized victim."[15] This portrayal of Oroonoko as the abject victim of violence, although highlighting the prince's heroism and the injustice of his treatment, is always framed through the gaze of the white audience; thus, while Southerne's play may challenge racism, it also provides white viewers with the power to determine the nature of Oroonoko's racial makeup, be it essentialized or constructed.[16] Behn, as a white female narrator, similarly positions herself as the controlling subject, for it is through her gaze that we encounter Oroonoko and through her words that we think through his racialized position in Surinam's society.

14. Ayanna Thompson, *Performing Race and Torture on the Early Modern Stage* (New York: Routledge, 2008), 53.
15. Thompson, *Performing Race*, 65.
16. Thompson, *Performing Race*, 51–73.

I end the class with a presentatin of Blake's engravings from Stedman's 1796 *Narrative, of a Five Years' Expedition, against the Revolted Negroes of Surinam* (see figure 2 and figure 3). Blake's depictions of African bodies complement the discussion by providing visual representations of torture. Like Behn, Blake looks at the punishment of Africans through a European lens. These images can further the discussion of the racist aspects of punishment in the greater Caribbean world. I ask students to consider how the slaves are represented in Blake's artwork: Do these engravings, for instance, offer sympathetic portrayals of slaves? How are these Africans responding to torture and punishment? What is Blake's intent in creating these images?[17] By asking these questions, I want students to consider Blake's attempt to sympathize with African peoples as well as his eroticization of the black body.[18]

These two conflicting strategies used by Blake to frame the torture of black people, in a similar fashion to Behn's construction of Oroonoko, invite viewers to both identify with the suffering individual and to objectify and "other" the person experiencing torture. Based on eyewitness accounts of punishments, both images I present to students feature the brutal treatment of Black slaves in the Dutch colony of Surinam. At the center of each image is the body of a Black man or woman hanging from a tree or gallows; both appear to gaze away from the viewer as if focused on their pain and each is in a state of undress. Because he presents them as nearly naked Blake seems to accentuate their innocence by symbolically linking them to nature; additionally, the postures of the Black man and woman appear almost erotic due to the curve of their bodies and the aestheticization of their torture. While blood appears in each image, dripping from the ribs of the man and striping the body of the woman, realistic gore remains absent and bodies are not skeletal, but instead appear

17. This approach is suggested by Mary Ann O'Donnell in her guide to materials in *Approaches to Teaching Behn's Oroonoko*, 9.

18. For a more in-depth study of Blake's eroticization of the Surinam slaves, see Marcus Wood, *Slavery, Empathy, and Pornography* (Oxford: Oxford University Press, 2002).

Figure 2. Detail from William Blake's illustration John Gabriel Stedman, *Narrative, of a Five Years' Expedition, against the Revolted Negroes of Surinam*, copy 2, object 2 (Bentley 499.2) "A Negro hung alive by the Ribs to a Gallows."

strong and hardy, suggesting that the original white viewers could more easily gaze upon and romanticize the figures.[19]

19. For further discussion of Blake's use of eroticized Black bodies in his work, see Mario Klarer, "Humanitarian Pornography: John Gabriel Stedman's Narrative of a Five Years Expedition Against the Revolting Negroes of Surinam (1796)," *New Literary History* 36, no. 4 (Autumn 2005): 559–87 and Debbie Lee, *Slavery and the Romantic Imagination* (Philadelphia: University of Pennsylvania Press, 2002), 99–105. See also Anne K. Mellor's contention that rather than highlighting the tortures endured by Black Africans, Blake

Figure 3. Detail from William Blake's illustration John Gabriel Stedman, *Narrative, of a Five Years' Expedition, against the Revolted Negroes of Surinam*, copy 2, object 8 (Bentley 499.2) "Flagellation of a Female Samboe Slave."

actually "erased the violence against the black body" in his engravings for Stedman's narrative by omitting the punishing overseers, limiting the blood loss, and leaving out details from the textual account like vultures feeding on the male victim's corpse. See Mellor, "Blake, Gender and Imperial Ideology: A Response," in *Blake, Politics, and History*, ed. Jackie DiSalvo, G. A. Rosso, and Christopher Z. Hobson (New York: Garland, 1998), 351–52.

Outcomes: Confronting Racism in Behn's Text

As stated at the outset of this piece, by comparing Oroonoko's execution to Blake's engravings, I hope that students will rethink their assumptions about race relations and slavery in the transatlantic world. Although many historians have claimed that the development of classical racism, or the idea that humans could be divided into different subspecies or "races" and that some of these "races" were superior to others did not fully develop until the late eighteenth century, such arguments need reassessment. Much recent scholarship on historical understandings of race rightly points out that early modern writers privileged whiteness and deliberately constructed language and institutions in support of European dominance.[20] Literary critics such as Ian Smith, for instance, establish the earlier Elizabethan obsession with skin color as a mark of cultural difference, noting that for sixteenth- and seventeenth-century writers and performers "race signifie[d] not an abstract essence but a doing, a verbal performance ... a continuous pursuit of subjection."[21] Likewise, critical race theory expert Kim F. Hall shows that the English language helped to establish racial difference, justify the exploitation of non-white peoples, and enable white individuals — men in particular — to define and for-

20. Earlier accounts of African peoples, for instance, present a view of Black people as sexually promiscuous and animalistic. Leo Africanus' *A Geographical Historie of Africa*, written during the sixteenth century and first translated into English in 1600, offered the following description of Africans: "The Negros likewise leade a beastly kinde of life, being utterly destitute of the use of reason, of dexteritie of wit, and of all artes. Yea they so behave themselves, as if they had continually lived in a forrest among wilde beasts. They have great swarmes of harlots among them; whereupon a man may easily conjecture their manner of living." See Leo Africanus, *A Geographical Historie of Africa, Written in Arabicke and Italian by John Leo a More, borne in Granada, and brought up in Barbarie*, trans. John Pory (London: George Bishop, 1600), 42. For a wide range of early modern texts dealing with race, see *Race in Early Modern England: A Documentary Companion*, ed. Ania Loomba and Jonathan Burton (London: Palgrave Macmillan, 2007).
21. Ian Smith, "Barbarian Errors: Performing Race in Early Modern England," *Shakespeare Quarterly* 49, no. 2 (Summer 1998): 171.

mulate their identity by comparing themselves to racial "others."[22] More recently, literary scholar Miles P. Grier argues that not only language and performance, but also early modern English book printing, enabled the reading of Black bodies as less than white bodies within the developing racial hierarchy. According to Grier, "inkface," which he defines as the "shared field of blackface performance, tattooing, writing, and printing ... helped Britons struggling with memories of their own past as tattooed slaves in ancient Rome by transferring the ink mark of servility to other ethnicities as a property of their character."[23] Thus, while the connections between slavery and race remained emergent rather than fully formed during the seventeenth century, early modern Europeans used a variety of texts, symbols, performances, and actions to essentialize and denigrate Black Africans, which in turn allowed for the development of racialized slavery.[24]

While Behn expresses sympathy with her tragic prince, she never suggests that slavery is an evil institution. Instead, her focus throughout is on

22. Kim F. Hall, *Things of Darkness: Economies of Race and Gender in Early Modern England* (Ithaca: Cornell University Press, 1995).
23. Miles P. Grier, "Inkface: The Slave Stigma in England's Early Imperial Imagination," in *Scripturalizing the Human: The Written as the Political*, edited by Vincent L. Wimbush (New York: Routledge, 2015), 195.
24. Important scholarship on race in the early modern period has and continues to improve our understanding of blackness and race relations in this era. In addition to the texts mentioned above, see the following: Ania Loomba, *Gender, Race, Renaissance Drama* (Manchester: Manchester University Press, 1989); Joyce Green MacDonald, *Women and Race in Early Modern Texts* (Cambridge: Cambridge University Press, 2002); Sujata Iyengar, *Shades of Difference: Mythologies of Skin Color in Early Modern England* (Philadelphia: University of Pennsylvania Press, 2005); Jyotsna G. Singh, ed., *A Companion to the Global Renaissance: English Literature and Culture in the Era of Expansion* (Chichester: Wiley-Blackwell, 2009); Elizabeth Spiller, *Reading and the History of Race in the Renaissance* (New York: Cambridge University Press, 2011); Arthur L. Little Jr., "Re-Historicizing Race, White Melancholia, and the Shakespearean Property," *Shakespeare Quarterly* 67, no. 1 (Spring 2016): 84–103; Matthieu Chapman, *Anti-Black Racism in Early Modern English Drama: The Other "Other"* (New York: Routledge, 2017); and Cassander L. Smith, Nicholas R. Jones, and Miles P. Grier, ed. *Early Modern Black Diaspora Studies: A Critical Anthology* (Cham, Switzerland: Palgrave Macmillan, 2018).

Oroonoko's social status. His enslavement and his execution are wrong, she seems to insist, because of his position as an elite personage, not because of any fundamental immorality of slavery.[25] Indeed, Oroonoko himself, as a prince, owned slaves prior to his capture following indigenous African practices. As literary scholar Gary Gautier convincingly argues, Behn rendered slavery "as a class relation and not a race relation," even in its nascent British trans-Atalantic context.[26] Students should be aware, however, that Behn's text inhabits a liminal space in time, and that slavery in the Atlantic world increasingly became based on blackness during the eighteenth century, and that racism was operative in early modern England.[27] In short, Behn was writing about race even if she believed her work reflected class issues rather than racial differences.

Additionally, I stress that Behn's novel and its depictions of Oroonoko's punishments and execution place it firmly within the realm of Caribbean texts, as well as Caribbean methods of racial formation and terror. The colonial Caribbean world was a unique place. As historian Thomas W. Krise notes, the form of slavery practiced in the Caribbean "was radically different from the forms of slavery that existed in the rest of the world for thousands of years; it was large-scale and commercial and involved colonies in which the enslaved vastly outnumbered the free population."[28]

25. Gary Gautier, in his comparison of Behn's novella, Defoe's *Robinson Crusoe*, and Olaudah Equiano's biography, posits a similar argument, noting that "the commercial order, in assigning Oroonoko to the vertical rank of slave without regard to blood quality, fails to assign his identity in a culturally intelligible way." See Gautier, "Slavery and the Fashioning of Race in *Oroonoko*, *Robinson Crusoe*, and Equiano's *Life*," *The Eighteenth Century: Theory and Interpretation* 42, no. 2 (2001): 161–79, at 165.
26. See Gautier, "Slavery and the Fashioning of Race," 163.
27. For more on the development of Atlantic slavery and its connection to race, see Edward B. Rugemer, "The Development of Mastery and Race in the Comprehensive Slave Codes of the Greater Caribbean during the Seventeenth Century," *The William and Mary Quarterly* 70, no. 3 (July 2013): 429–58.
28. Thomas W. Krise, "Oroonoko as a Caribbean Text," in *Approaches to Teaching Behn's Oroonoko*, ed. Cynthia Richards and Mary Ann O'Donnell (New York: The Modern Language Association of America, 2011), 93. For more on seventeenth- and eighteenth-century slavery in the Caribbean, see Charles C. Mann, 1493: *Uncovering the New World Columbus Created* (New York: Vintage Books, 2012), 93–95, 99–116.

As many scholars have argued, the sugar trade that flourished in the Caribbean during the eighteenth century and owed its success to slave labor provided Great Britain with a significant economic advantage over its competitors. In addition, the sugar trade perpetuated and expanded the slave trade to continue producing sugar cane. Because the Caribbean planters were outnumbered by their slaves, fear was an instrument of control. Therefore, executions like Oroonoko's became strategic public means of "terrifying and grieving" Afro-Caribbean slaves "with frightful spectacles of a mangled king."[29] Behn's details about Oroonoko's punishment, including his stoic endurance, reflect actual historical events. In addition to the account of Herlein, numerous Caribbean texts note the superhuman fortitude displayed by tortured and executed slaves as well as the horrific tortures used to instill obedience in the enslaved population.[30]

With this history in mind, I return to the execution of Oroonoko. I ask students to consider both the way that Oroonoko is executed and the way that he responds to his public torture and death — and how both are racialized. For instance, students should notice that while most British executions in the late seventeenth century involved hanging (except for severe cases of treason), the tortures devised for African slaves were often extremely brutal, harkening back to medieval and early modern punishments no longer used in Great Britain. The account of John Marketman's execution helps students understand a typical contemporary hanging. Unlike Oroonoko, who is forcibly tied to the post where he will be executed, Marketman is led to the gallows by his weeping mother. And while

29. Behn, *Oroonoko*, 65.

30. In his 1667 study of Surinam, for example, George Warren notes that African slaves "manifest their fortitude, or rather obstinacy in suffering the most exquisite tortures [that] can be inflicted upon them, for a terror and example to others without shrinking." See George Warren, *An Impartial Description of Surinam upon the Continent of Guiana in America: With a History of Several Strange Beasts, Birds, Fishes, Serpents, Insects, and the Customs of that Colony*, etc. (London, 1667), 19. For a particularly disturbing account of slave punishments, see Trevor Burnard, *Majesty, Tyranny, and Desire: Thomas Thistlewood and His Slaves in the Anglo-Jamaican World* (Chapel Hill and London: The University of North Carolina Press, 2004).

Oroonoko is given a tobacco pipe to smoke during his demise, Marketman is met by a minister, who provides comforting words of forgiveness and hope for eternal life. As an African man (and as Behn notes, a non-Christian), Oroonoko is deemed unworthy of the comforts given Marketman and is denied an opportunity to provide a final statement.[31]

Marketman's death is presumably over relatively quickly. Oroonoko's execution, on the other hand, is cruelly prolonged rather than mercifully swift. As the passage I quoted above conveys, he is slowly killed by the removal of his body parts one after another.[32] Importantly, the first items removed are his genitals, which Leslie Richardson interprets as the white planters' attempt "to efface his manhood and his humanity" and "an early example of the ideological impulse to feminize nonwhite men in relation to European men."[33] Oroonoko's execution, therefore, is meant to function

31. For executed slaves in British colonial outposts few if any records of ritual speeches exist, leading historian Diana Paton to surmise that because the slaves were considered outside of civilized society by their European overseers and unaccustomed to accepted European execution rituals they "would have been unlikely to produce the 'appropriate' penitent speech of the condemned sinner." See Paton, "Punishment, Crime, and the Bodies of Slaves in Eighteenth-Century Jamaica," *Journal of Social History* 34, no. 4 (Summer 2001): 923–954, here 943–944. It should also be noted that Oroonoko's status as a religious other by virtue of both his ethnicity and choice means that his approach to death and the afterlife remain unarticulated perhaps because Behn lacks the language to accurately represent the prince's beliefs. Additionally, the Christianization of racial others during this time period was a matter of debate. As Lauren Shook points out, the expansion of the British Atlantic coincided with the classification of "those that looked, acted, and worshipped differently than them, couching those differences in religious rhetoric"; additionally, such rhetoric implied that African people, due to their descent from Noah's son, Ham, were incapable of true salvation. See Shook, "[L]ooking at me my body across distances': Toni Morrison's *A Mercy* and Seventeenth-Century European Religious Concepts of Race," in *Early Modern Black Diaspora Studies: A Critical Anthology*, edited by Cassander L. Smith, Nicholas R. Jones, and Miles P. Grier (Cham, Switzerland: Palgrave Macmillan, 2018), 159, 160 and David M. Whitford, *The Curse of Ham in the Early Modern Era: The Bible and the Justifications for Slavery* (Burlington: Ashgate, 2009).
32. Behn, *Oroonoko*, 64–65.
33. Leslie Richardson, "Teaching *Oroonoko* at a Historically Black University," in *Approaches to Teaching Behn's Oroonoko*, 128.

as a fearful and dehumanizing spectacle. By losing the part of himself that denotes his manhood, Oroonoko loses a part of his identity. After the removal of his genitals, Oroonoko suffers the loss of his ears and then his nose, which further serves to "other" him. Finally, the executioner cuts off his arms. All these maimings serve to disempower Oroonoko and deprive him of the body parts that relate most fully to his identity as a human, and a man. Yet, the prince's stoic behavior may discredit the white men's attempt to humiliate and subjugate him. Students should analyze their interpretations of the type of execution in terms of its effectiveness. Does Oroonoko's behavior during his execution ultimately serve the interests of the planters? Does it uphold Oroonoko's innate nobility? Or does Oroonoko's approach to his execution do something else entirely?

Despite his dignity and heroic demeanor, Oroonoko's execution conduct needs to be analyzed as a possibly racist construction, due perhaps in part to Behn's subject position as a white female author. I want students to understand that his silence is ambiguous and offers multiple meanings.[34] For instance, literary critic Roy Eriksen points out the similarities between Oroonoko and early modern Protestant and Catholic martyrs, who often met their ends with stoic silence that, while signifying resistance to the theological and political ruling party, upheld traditional Christian beliefs by mimicking Christ's behavior on the cross.[35] Additionally, numerous scholars have noted the parallels between Oroonoko and the executed English king Charles I, viewing Behn's novella "as a (straight-

34. As Cheryl Glenn argues in her study of silence, choosing not to speak is often a strategic choice that can communicate empowerment and resistance just as often as it disempowers. See Glenn, *Unspoken: The Rhetoric of Silence* (Carbondale: Southern Illinois University Press, 2004).

35. Roy Eriksen, "Between Saints' Lives and Novella: The Drama of Oroonoko, or the Royal Slave (1688)" in *Aphra Behn and Her Female Successors*, ed. by Margarete Rubik, (Münster: LIT, 2001), 123. For more on sixteenth- and seventh-century martyrdom, see Sarah Covington, *The Trail of Martyrdom: Persecution and Resistance in Sixteenth-Century England* (Notre Dame: University of Notre Dame Press, 2003); Andrea McKenzie, *Tyburn's Martyrs: Execution in England, 1675–1775* (London: Hambledon Continuum, 2007); and John R. Knott, *Discourses of Martyrdom in English Literature, 1563–1694* (Cambridge: Cambridge University Press, 1993).

forward) royalist allegory," and, seemingly, a reminder of the Stuart king's attempt to frame himself as a martyr prior to his execution.[36]

Conversely, Oroonoko's stoicism under torture can be read as an act of defiance. Oroonoko's refusal to cry out may signify his denial of white planters' power over his body and mind. As historian Thomas W. Krise explains, stories of slave stoicism "remind us that people were criticizing the imperial enterprise from the beginning and that the Africans who were forced to settle in the New World … had vibrant and ancient cultures that both resisted the spread of imperialism and contributed to the richly mixed culture that developed in the Caribbean."[37] By remaining silent during his execution, Oroonoko may subtly critique the injustice of his treatment and offer other slaves a model of passive resistance.[38]

In conclusion, by comparing Behn's depiction of Oroonoko's torture and death to contemporaneous British executions, students gain a greater understanding of seventeenth- and eighteenth-century racism within the greater Caribbean world and its relationship to metropolitan England. *Oroonoko* is not an easy read emotionally or intellectually for modern students. Instead, it is a complex text that forces students to visualize the

36. Megan Griffin, "Dismembering the Sovereign in Aphra Behn's Oroonoko," *English Literary History* 86, no. 1 (Spring 2019): 107–33, at 108.

37. Krise, "*Oroonoko* as a Caribbean Text," 96. Reports of similar execution behaviors by African slaves followed the 1675 rebellion in Barbados. Jenny Shaw relates that before his burning, the West African slave Tony persuaded his fellow victims to "not speak one word more." According to Shaw, this rhetoric of silence "became a source of strength for Tony, and for others who took heart from his show of defiance" and in the West African belief that death would return them to their homelands. See Shaw, *Everyday Life in the Early English Caribbean: Irish, Africans, and the Construction of Difference* (Athens: The University of Georgia Press, 2013), 135–37.

38. Natalie Zemon Davis points out that West African slaves in Surinam would have been familiar with ordeals meant to establish the guilt or innocence of an individual based on their physical reactions to pain. Therefore, Oroonoko's heroism may reflect his training to endure pain and his understanding of Gold Coast rituals that stressed silence and relied on the body's manifestation of signs. See Natalie Zemon Davis, "Judges, Master, Diviners: Slaves' Experience of Criminal Justice in Colonial Suriname," *Law and History Review* 29, no. 4, Law, Slavery, and Justice: A Special Issue (November 2011): 925–984, at 963–64.

horrific treatment of an enslaved man and confront the historical realities of racial slavery. By placing the moment of Oroonoko's death in conversation with contemporaneous European execution narratives, I hope to instill in students a greater understanding of how racism impacted not only the lives of Caribbean slaves, but their deaths as well.

Thinking about the brutality enacted on Black bodies in our shared and fraught past in the Anglophone world often brings up connections to the current and continued dehumanization of and violence against Black individuals. Recent events in the United States, from the murder of George Floyd by a police officer to the shooting of Ahmaud Arbery by white supremacists remind us that the perpetration of violence on Black people continues. Beyond their shock at the inhumane treatment of Oroonoko, students recognize a persistent theme throughout western history — white people have consistently othered Black people in an attempt to rationalize their colonist oppression and to justify their continued use of violence against Black people. Perhaps, though, what is most apparent to students engaging deeply with Behn's novella is the way that Oroonoko's anguish is rendered as a spectacle for consumption by the implicitly white reader, just as Blake's engravings offer viewers images of Black suffering. These imaginative spaces, while multifaceted and capable of producing sympathy, also function to induce trauma for Black people and other racialized subalterns. The display of Oroonoko's pain thereby propagates a narrative of Black illegibility that continues to silence Black voices and render the suffering individual as an unreadable other. In contrast to the relatively more "merciful" executions of white British men and women, which allowed for public repentance and familial involvement, the corporal punishment of Oroonoko is graphic and debasing. As the quote I shared at the beginning of the essay shows, the prince's execution strips him of his identity and denies him a chance at communal redemption. By reading texts like *Oroonoko*, my hope is that students will confront the history of antiblack oppression and dehumanization and identify the biases and complacency that still exist within our world.

Suggestions for Further Reading

Behn, Aphra. *Oroonoko, or The Royal Slave*. in *Oroonoko: A Norton Critical Edition*, edited by Joanna Lipking. New York: W. W. Norton & Company, 1997.

Krise, Thomas W. "*Oroonoko* as a Caribbean Text." In *Approaches to Teaching Behn's Oroonoko*, edited by Cynthia Richards and Mary Ann O'Donnell, 92–98. New York: The Modern Language Association of America, 2011.

Little, Arthur L., Jr. "Re-Historicizing Race, White Melancholia, and the Shakespearean Property." *Shakespeare Quarterly* 67, no. 1 (Spring 2016): 84–103.

McEvoy, Sean. "The Ethics of Teaching Tragic Narratives." In *Teaching Narrative*, edited by Richard Jacobs, 55–69. Cham, Switzerland: Palgrave Macmillan, 2018.

Miller, Shannon. "Executing the Body Politic: Inscribing State Violence onto Aphra Behn's *Oroonoko*." In *Violence, Politics, and Gender in Early Modern England*, edited by Joseph P. Ward, 173–206. New York: Palgrave MacMillan, 2008.

Rivero, Albert J. "Aphra Behn's 'Oroonoko' and the 'Blank Spaces' of Colonial Fictions." *Studies in English Literature, 1500–1900* 39, no. 3, Restoration and Eighteenth Century (Summer 1999): 443–62.

Causing Good and Necessary Trouble with Race in Milton's *Comus*

REGINALD A. WILBURN

The following essay aims to raise greater pedagogical awareness about the redemptive role English professors can play by "causing good and necessary trouble" with race in a seventeenth-century text like John Milton's *Comus*. *Comus* tells the story of a Lady's heroic resolve to remain virginally chaste while lost in the woods and separated from her two brothers. She remains chaste despite her encounter with the bestial demigod, Comus, a monstrous antagonist, who, according to Barbara Lewalski, "embodies ... the seductive power of false rhetoric and the threat of rape" among other things.[1] After encountering Comus and resisting his lecherous seductions, the unnamed Lady and protagonist of the masque falls prey to his supernatural spell. Sabrina, a woodland nymph, rescues the Lady from Comus at masque's end. Her intervention allows the story to end on a favorable and positive note. Lewalski, commenting on the 1645 "reformed Masque," notes this revised version of the poem particularly explores "the nature of temptation, the problem of deception and illusion in the fallen world, and the danger of taking false pleasures for true ones."[2] Milton's masque explores more than these moral vices. In addition to telling a story of women's heroic chastity, it narrates fictions that ideologically negate blackness in the seventeenth century.

Causing good and necessary trouble with race and *Comus* in our contemporary moment provides rich opportunities for continually illuminating "how Milton plays a crucial role in popular culture, and, in turn, how popular culture adapts and transforms Milton."[3] It is this "pop Milton" that Knoppers and Semenza expressly identify as having a more than rele-

1. Barbara Lewalski, *The Life of John Milton: A Critical Biography* (Blackwell, 2003), 63.
2. Lewalski, *The Life of John*, 63.
3. Laura Lunger Knoppers and Gregory Colon Semenza, "Introduction," *Milton in Popular Culture* (Palgrave, 2006), 5.

vant "place in scholarship and the classroom."[4] When English professors committed to antiracist pedagogical approaches develop close-reading strategies focused on interrogating and explicating Milton's tropological influence on antiblack rhetoric in the mid- to late-seventeenth century, they position their students and scholar-citizens to cultivate a stronger appreciation of the canonical author's enduring literary value.

Additionally, adopting this pedagogical approach contributes to maximizing the kinds of student learning outcomes that hold power for enriching the transhistorical value of one of the most preeminent of poets in English tradition. Critic Angelica Duran comments on Milton's instructional significance in this regard when she recognizes, "paradoxically, the feminism, multiculturalism, and globalism that have contributed to the growth in the canon that has squeezed out Milton from some survey courses also have increased the benefits of his inclusion."[5] Further recalling her attraction to "Milton's works as a first-generation United States citizen," Duran theorizes "a large number of college-bound high schoolers, college students, and autodidacts turn to what used to be unabashedly called great English literature to understand academic culture, learn professional discourse, and define anglophone culture against and within their heritage culture."[6] Milton, from this vantage point of cultural re-mastery, becomes known in a very special way by reading communities whose positionality often locates them as situated at the margins of academia and elsewhere in society.

Assignments and discussions that invite critical inquiry of what will later be discussed as Milton's British Africanisms, create democratic spaces for the care of marginalized students in the early modern classroom. These pedagogical practices also school and educate a broader population of students to re-evaluate the formal English they speak, read,

4. Knoppers and Semenza, "Introduction," 4.
5. Angelica Duran, "Milton and the Undergraduate British Literature Survey Course: Who, Where, When, How, and, by All Means, Why?" in *Approaches to Teaching Milton's Shorter Poetry and Prose*, Ed. Peter C. Herman, (The Modern Language Association, 2007), 48.
6. Duran, "Milton and the Undergraduate British Literature Survey Course," 48–49.

and study. Ultimately, this critical re-evaluation of language in literature empowers scholar-citizens to comprehend and apprehend a greater understanding of the ways a ruling language inflected with racist ideologies can undermine the most noble forms of patriotism and civic duty. It is in this respect that early modern English professors specializing in seventeenth-century literature hold promise for redeeming America by daring to "cause good and necessary trouble" with the word work of race in a minor yet major poem like Milton's *Comus*.

The late US Representative John Lewis (1940–2020) famously exhorted publics to acclimate themselves to causing what he repeatedly deemed "good and necessary trouble" as a most patriotic of civic duties. The iconic Civil Rights statesman was known for oratorically stirring up this civic trouble at various university commencement exercises. In a testament to his life of integrity and service, Lewis pre-arranged the issuing of his final patriotic mandate to a wide public audience. On July 30, 2020, the day he was funeralized, Lewis' Op-Ed piece for *The New York Times* commended Black Lives Matter protestors for the unrelenting social activism they displayed throughout the previous months. Their protests, in the aftermath of George Floyd, Breonna Taylor, and Ahmaud Arbery's murders, he writes, "filled [him] with hope about the next chapter of the great American story."[7] Inasmuch as Lewis' Op-Ed piece holds unique relevance for the widest of global audiences, it likewise enlarges the investigative terrain whereby early modern English professors specializing in seventeenth-century literature and committed to upholding the enduring value of the humanities in higher education can rewrite bold possibilities for the future of languages, literatures, and diverse global cultures.

Milton, as research scholars of English know, remains an icon in the literary tradition. He enjoys this stature of preeminence in no small part due to his success in dignifying the English language through his signature poem in the epic tradition, *Paradise Lost* (1667). This literary achievement crowned his native language with honor and global prestige both in and beyond his lifetime. Milton's dignifying of English culture and language

7. John Lewis, "John Lewis: Together, You Can Redeem the Soul of Our Nation," *The New York Times*, July 30, 2020.

also occurred at a time when his country's engagement in the trading of African slaves began to flourish. These dynamics of synchronic intertextuality merit scholarly examination on the basis of a poetic self-authorship that announces itself through Milton's tropological use of antiblack rhetoric. In *Comus*, this rhetoric of antiblack bias reverberates and accumulates as a result of the then-young poet's myriad British Africanisms.

Toni Morrison's *Playing in the Dark: Whiteness and the Literary Imagination* interrogates the literary phenomenon she regards as "American Africanism." This trope reflects "the ways in which a nonwhite Africanlike (or Africanist) presence or persona was constructed in the United States" to include the wide and varied "imaginative uses this fabricated presence served."[8] *Playing in the Dark* focuses exclusively on American Africanisms, highlighting the numerous ways race and antiblackness resurface throughout prized canonical texts in American literature. Even when Black characters do not physically appear or are not represented in these works, Morrison contends, Africanist presence yet exists. Africanist people, she contends, exist as (in)visible through tropological objects like rice, cotton, sugar. Because enslaved black labor was required to sow, till, and harvest these staples of US commerce and wealth, Africanist presence, as Morrison theorizes, must be acknowledged as a shaping presence of race in these literary works. *Playing in the Dark* examines these "American Africanisms" while acknowledging the existence of a European counterpart that proves equally pernicious on the literary pages of white-authored texts. Teaching students the art of close reading literary texts, race and the cultural forces of synchronic intertextuality associated with England's enslavement of Africans throughout the seventeenth century with a nuanced acknowledgement of the growing prestige of the English language make scholarly interrogations of whiteness and Milton's British Africanisms a novel experience of literary study.

Such a study likewise attests to the enduring instructional value of the humanities as a disciplinary platform of exemplary citizenship and leadership. This is because, as Morrison additionally acknowledges, "there

8. Toni Morrison, *Playing in the Dark: Whiteness and the Literary Imagination*, (Vintage Books, 1992), 6.

also exists, of course, a European Africanism with a counterpart in colonial literature."[9] These seemingly innocuous racialized snubs reverberate, demean, and denigrate blackness throughout numerous early modern texts in English. As a result, it is not difficult to imagine the myriad ways these British Africanisms are apt to trigger and offend BIPOC student-readers in early modern English classrooms when any of these canonical texts are assigned and discussed. BIPOC students need not be present in early modern English classroom for Milton's British Africanisms to work to deleterious ends. All students are educationally disenfranchised when culturally responsive teaching focused on noting the word work of race that British Africanisms reverberating throughout the texts of a canonical author like Milton is overlooked, neglected, abandoned, or forsaken.

In their noteworthy collection, *Re-Membering Milton* (1989), literary critics Mary Nyquist and Margaret W. Ferguson argued for a body of scholarship that would dignify England's premier Christian and epic poet of liberty in ways unprecedented prior to the 1990s. Specifically, they sought to "foster the conditions needed for a more engaged as well as more theoretically and historically informed, critical literature" on his expansive body of religious, political, and literary writing.[10] In their introduction, Nyquist and Ferguson consider Milton "the most impressive and notorious of self-authored authors," further asserting he participated in modes of "political and religious radicalism [that] revealed features of an emerging bourgeois class-consciousness in ways that have yet to be fully explored."[11] Carolivia Herron's landmark contribution to the collection offered the first essay of Milton criticism to survey and address "complex critical questions about cross-cultural influence" relative to the epic writer's "enabling and inhibiting" influence on African American authors.[12] Published examinations of race and Black lives in Milton Studies have

9. Morrison, *Playing in the Dark*, 38.
10. Mary Nyquist and Margaret W. Ferguson, "Preface," in *Re-Membering Milton: Essays on the Texts and Traditions*. (Methuen, 1988), xvi.
11. Mary Nyquist and Margaret W. Ferguson, "Preface," in *Re-Membering Milton*, xiii.
12. Carolivia Herron, "Milton and Afro-American Literature," in *Re-Membering Milton: Essays on the Texts and Traditions*, Eds. Mary Nyquist and Margaret W. Ferguson, (Methuen, 1988), 280.

increased to a minimal degree since Herron's article. Given the paucity of this scholarship, one has to wonder: to what extent do discussions of race and Black lives take place in early modern English classrooms? Moreover, how do professors respond when BIPOC students in early modern English courses dare to raise their hands and voice their opinions and queries about the British Africanisms they might see operating and reverberating in these canonically privileged, white-authored texts?

If discussions of race and blackness in these classes seldom happen if at all, the failure to introduce them as points of scholarly consideration and examination constitute missed pedagogical opportunities that prove most unfortunate. The missed opportunity proves especially unfortunate given the abundance of British Africanisms Milton rhetorically deploys in *Comus* and other of his works. Whenever this pedagogical oversight or neglect occurs, it disenfranchises twenty-first-century students from entrepreneurially explicating the forces of synchronic intertextuality that denigrate racial blackness in the early modern period at a time when English language, literature, and culture were being dignified by preeminent white authors of literary tradition. Of particular note, this was a period in literary history when England's participation in the transatlantic slave trade showed no signs of waning and in fact increased from the second half of the century onwards. This dynamic has theoretical implications for assessing the extent to which Milton's dignifying of the English language benefits from increased poetic negations of blackness, particularly throughout the seventeenth century. To teach these and other racially inflected dynamics of synchronic intertextuality is to "cause good and necessary trouble with race." Commensurate with John Lewis' patriotic mandate, instigating pedagogical trouble with Milton's *Comus* holds radical potential for "redeeming the soul of the nation" through a culturally responsive remastery of English and its literary traditions.

Teaching the word work of race and anti-blackness in *Comus* rather than the great epic poem, *Paradise Lost*, makes sense for a couple of reasons. First, it is a shorter work, and, arguably, more accessible to student readers. Thus, English professors have greater pedagogical luxury to mine the text for its rhetorical stock of British Africanisms without having to ensure students understand the largeness of Milton's ideas, the numerous conventions germane to epic, and the density of poetic form, philosophy, and political allegory that makes this poem so great if not foreboding to beginning scholars. Second, the concentration of British Africanisms reverberating throughout *Comus* makes the discussion of antiblackness rich with scholarly possibilities for students invested in mining the limitations of the English language that is our inheritance in global culture. Third, and of particular relevance, Milton composes and publishes *Comus* in a period where England's trading in black flesh was on the rise. If forces of synchronic intertextuality help to shape the meaning of language and culture in any material way, then the word work of race in *Comus* throughout the 1630s and 1640s provides a critical contextual lens useful for understanding the trouble with language and racializing discourse as penned by a young writer who was well on the way to becoming the literary icon long revered across the centuries of time.

Milton's British Africanisms and the literary microaggressions they may provoke, then, serve as an exclusive educational training ground for cultivating ennobled global citizenship. Early modern English professors can satisfy this high pedagogical calling by teaching forms of radical re-reading of race in white-authored literature that cross-culturally echoes the "active rewritings" of Milton modeled by various authors in African American tradition.[13] Employing these popular culture approaches to teaching *Comus* and other pieces of Milton's writings clarify the anachronistic importance of critical race pedagogy as a pedagogical method for making him matter in the aftermath of George Floyd's, Breonna Taylor's, and Ahmaud Arbery's tragic murders.

The phrase and contemporary political movement known as "Black Lives Matter" registers so palpably in contemporary consciousness as to cast new racial meaning on the rhetorical, lexical, and semantic "things of darkness" Kim Hall, a leading scholar of race in the English Renaissance, examines. Concerning the literary scripts of antiblackness in these texts, Hall's groundbreaking work argues, "the trope of blackness had a broad arsenal of effects in the early modern period."[14] However this racial trope may have been used, Hall maintains it "still draws its power from England's

13. Herron, "Milton and Afro-American Literature," 280.

14. Hall, *Things of Darkness*, 6.

ongoing negotiations of African difference and from the implied color comparison therein."[15] Her theory holds particular relevance for critical race readings of *Comus*, a 1,023-lined poem containing more than 103 unique words and figures of darkness and negated blackness. Milton frequently used words like "night," "dark," and "shade" throughout the poem for a total of nineteen, twelve, and eight times respectively. Phrases like "in thick shelter of black shades embowered," "of Stygian darkness spets her thickest gloom," "Dark-veiled Cotyotto," "sable cloud," "Dim darkness and this leavy labyrinth," and "in double night of darkness and of shades," reflect several of the multiple clusters Milton assembles to negate blackness either directly or figuratively (*Comus* 61; 129; 221; 278; 335). A range of other words like "drear," "shady," "smoke," "smoky," "nocturnal," and "tawny" contribute to negating blackness in the poem. Milton even has one of his characters castigate "all the monstrous forms / 'Twixt Africa and Ind[ia]" who are believed to accompany Comus' riotous behavior (605–606).

Composed in 1634 and performed at Ludlow Castle, Milton's experimental masque is a dramatic work that generically hearkens back to medieval times. By the early modern period, court masques were "modified" and transformed "by characteristics borrowed from civic pageants, chivalric customs, sword-dances, and the religious drama."[16] Court masques like these typically functioned at the entertainment level of elaborate spectacle. Performed at Ludlow Castle before John and Frances Egerton, the Earl and countess of Bridgewater respectively, *Comus* was written with the couple's "only unmarried daughter," the fifteen-year-old Lady Alice Egerton in mind.[17] Given these contexts, it is not likely that the average reader would expect Milton's masque to have little or anything material to do with race or themes of antiblackness.

15. Hall, *Things of Darkness*, 7.
16. William Harmon and C. Hugh Holman, A *Handbook to Literature*, 8th Edition, (Prentice Hall, 2000), 308.
17. Lynne A. Greenberg, "The 'Unowned' Lady: Teaching *Comus* and Gender," in *Approaches to Teaching Milton's Shorter Poetry and Prose*, edited by Peter C. Holman, (The Modern Language Association, 2007), 153.

Nor does *Comus* contain physiognomically black characters. However, its first 240 lines tells a kind of racial story that paves pedagogical paths for teaching blackness as a dehumanizing intertext of race throughout the remainder of this "great minor poem" from Milton's canon.[18] For instance, the opening setting introduces readers to a geographical landscape enshrouded in figures of darkness connotatively conveying racial undertones of antiblack bias. Because *Comus* has as its theme a focus on women's heroic chastity, Milton's British Africanisms reveal subtexts of race and whiteness too hyper-visible across the poem's 1,023 lines not to be interrogated or deconstructed. As a critical close reading of *Comus* will evidence, Milton's tropological engagements with the word work of race in an advancing language destined for global prestige reveals his style of playing poetically in the darkness of his whitened imagination.

Milton's British Africanisms throughout *Comus* thus prove central to the racialized workings of seventeenth-century synchronic intertextuality. Specifically, their concentrated presence throughout the work showcases the young and ambitious laureate poet's commitment to putting figures of poetic blackness into greater racial formation at a critical period of the seventeenth century. By the time Milton composed and revised *Comus*, England's ongoing and escalating participation in the trading of African slaves had been operating for nearly a century. For instance, Winthrop Jordan, the American historian, identifies the "Protestant Reformation in England" as launching a "complex development" in the sixteenth century that involved a partnership between the "taut Puritan and the bawdy Elizabethan."[19] The age, which, according to him, "we usually think of in terms of great literature – [and] Milton and Shakespeare" more specifically, was also "driven by the twin spirit of adventure and control," one where "adventurous Elizabethans embarked upon voyages of discovery overseas" and interpreted the Africans they encountered as savages, beasts, and

18. Christopher Kendrick, "Milton and Sexuality: A Symptomatic Reading of *Comus*" in *Re-Membering Milton: Essays on the Texts and Traditions*, edited by Mary Nyquist and Margaret W. Ferguson, (Methuen, 1988), 46.
19. Winthrop D. Jordan, *White Over Black: American Attitudes toward the Negro: 1550–1812*, (UNC Press, 1968), 40.

sexually lecherous.[20] Historians John Hope Franklin and Alfred A. Moss, Jr., also comment on England's growing interest in slavery. Their narrative account of African American history highlights the extent to which England, as a growing empire, enjoyed its territorial hold on the Caribbean at key moments in the seventeenth century. Franklin and Moss further explain "the English secured control of St. Christopher in 1623, Barbados in 1625, and Nevis, Antigua, and Montserrat in the 1630s" before winning "one of the great prizes" in 1655 "by driving the Spaniards out of Jamaica."[21] English language and culture advanced, prospered, and flourished amid these hegemonic encounters with blackness.

England's enslavement and trading of Africans, when coupled with the proliferation of antiblack racial signs reverberating throughout a work like *Comus*, invites transformational learning opportunities for twenty-first-century students. The dynamic specifically positions students to examine racial processes of synchronic intertextuality in mid-seventeenth-century writings and by a premier white canonical author like Milton. Cultivating these skills in language use and meaning production ultimately prepares students to approach literary works with the pedagogical goal of helping them to remaster words, phrases, and ideological ideas with the kind of linguistic excellence Milton demands of strong readers. Strong readers place a "premium on individual acts of attention and composition" in the course of balancing a "difficult mix of authority and humility" when approaching densely resistant texts in particular.[22] Early modern English professors who effectively teach students to read race closely and critically help to strengthen students' humanistic proficiencies through the exercising of right, sound, and judicious reasoning. This pedagogical approach also exhibits culturally responsive care for the educational souls of BiPOC students who may find Milton's literary microaggressions of antiblack bias throughout *Comus* triggering.

20. Jordan, *White Over Black*, 40.

21. John Hope Franklin and Alfred A. Moss Jr., *From Slavery to Freedom: A History of African Americans*, seventh edition. (McGraw Hill, 1994), 43.

22. David Bartholomae and Anthony Petrosky, "Introduction," in *Ways of Reading* (Bedford/St. Martin's Press, 2014), 7; 9.

(Literary) Microaggressions, Pedagogy, and Troubling Milton's Canonical Authority

Charles Pierce, a noted professor of education and psychiatry, coined the term "microaggressions." The concept denotatively refers to the "subtle, stunning, often automatic, and non-verbal exchanges," which, generally are considered as "put downs" by racialized individuals who bear the brunt of these social infractions.[23] Derald Wing Sue, a professor of counseling psychology, has elaborated upon the term's definition, emphasizing the phenomenon as "brief, everyday exchanges that send denigrating messages to people of color because they belong to a racial minority group."[24] Raced individuals likely experience microaggressions daily in their various social interactions with whites. The "subtle snubs or dismissive looks, gestures and tones" they are apt to experience in predominantly white settings often are "so pervasive and automatic in daily conversations and interactions" as to be dismissed by those who may feel disempowered by these (perceived) affronts to one's humanity.[25] At other times, such microaggressions may register to the recipient of these acts as being "innocent or innocuous" in intent or effect.[26] These slights may seem minimal in the moment. Yet, microaggressions often prove "detrimental to persons of color because they impair performance in a multitude of settings by sapping the psychic and spiritual energy of [addressees] and by creating inequities" in the process.[27]

Literature classrooms sometimes play geographical host to the circulation of microaggressions of antiblack bias that routinely surface in literary texts by canonical white authors in English. Literary microaggressions tend to surface in peculiar ways throughout early modern seventeenth-

23. Chester Pierce, Jean Carew, Diane Pierce-Gonzalez, and Deborah Wills, "An Experiment in Racism: TV Commercials," in *Television and Education*, edited by Chester Pierce (Sage, 1978), 66.
24. Derald Wing Sue, "Racial Microaggressions in Everyday Life: Implications for Clinical Practice" *American Psychology* 62.4, 273.
25. Sue, "Racial Microaggressions, 273.
26. Sue, "Racial Microaggressions, 273.
27. Hall, *Things of Darkness*.

century literature, where figures of darkness indicative of antiblack bias operate as "economies of race" according to Hall. As Hall explains further, such economies "set the stage for the longer process by which preexisting literary tropes of blackness" throughout the early modern period "profoundly interacted with the fast changing economic relations of White Europeans and their darker 'others.'"[28] Thus, intensive study of Milton's British Africanisms merit ongoing investigative study for millennial English majors, who, for the sake of an ennobled citizenship modeled by Representative Lewis, should never be allowed to forget the linguistic role that race plays in strengthening the forces of seventeenth-century synchronic intertextuality.

Seventeenth-century English literature highlights the increased flourishing of a language and culture that little more than a century prior was deemed globally inferior to those of ancient Greek and Latin civilizations. As mentioned above, the seventeenth century is also a period where England's growing participation in the slave trade increased and flourished. These hostile encounters, then, have dire synchronic consequences for contemporary readings of English culture, its literary productions, and the diasporic descendants of enslaved blacks who speak, read, and study a colonialist language rhetorically loaded with no short supply of poetic Africanisms constitutive of antiblack bias. Gregory Machacek is useful here in terms of exploring the benefits associated with investigating Milton's poetic language and its meaning-making properties relative to an intertextual project grounded in a study of synchronic semiotics. In *Milton and Homer: 'Written to Aftertimes,'* Machacek traces a trail of substituted allusions for the phrase "Heavenly Muse" in line 6 from Book 1 of *Paradise Lost*. The phrase resurfaces in substituted form as "the Spirit of Oreb or Sinai," and later, as "the Christian Holy Spirit."[29] This allusive trail of substituted terms within a literary work provides a template for conceptualizing a cognitive field for playing with race and blackness

28. Kim F. Hall, *Things of Darkness: Economies of Race and Gender in Early Modern England*, (Cornell University Press, 1995), 4.
29. Gregory Machacek, *Milton and Homer: "Written to Aftertimes"* (Duquesne University Press, 2011), 24.

within the realm of Milton's white imagination and audience members who, throughout time, fail to see race operating on these grounds of linguistic contention.

A similar phenomenon along interpretive axes of race and antiblackness occurs on implied and inferential levels of meaning throughout *Comus*. Instructing students in the art and science of investigating these intertextual allusions for negated blackness exposes the word work of race and antiblackness Milton operationalizes so frequently throughout the masque. Astute readers of *Comus* may see and recognize a similar operation resurfacing throughout the poem relative to a semiotics of racial Otherness. Not unlike Milton's repeated substitutions for his "Heavenly Muse" phrase, a semiotics of racial Otherness reverberates "so flagrantly" throughout *Comus* as to "call attention to" various signs of antiblackness that likewise "cast [these signifying tropes] into relief" to the point of "utterly exhausting them."[30] In our post-George Floyd moment, how might our pedagogical approaches to teaching English literature involve the word work of race that is necessary for troubling the language of its barbarous errors of black negation?

An email to me from Hamilton Griffin, a second-year West Point cadet, clarifies what is at stake should early modern English professors forsake the sacred trust of schooling today and tomorrow's scholar-citizens in race through the liberal arts, humanities, and literary studies. Cadet Griffin served as president of the Black Culture and Arts Forum at his military institution in the 2020–2021 academic year. During the fall semester, he invited me to address members of the undergraduate student organization. His communication to me noted he and his peers read my article, "'Getting Uppity with Milton; or Because My Mom Politely Asked was Milton Racist?,'" finding its arguments both provocative and timely.[31] Cadet Griffin especially noted the article "raises a host of questions dealing with how [Black-identified students] should regard not just microaggressions in literature, but the overall dehumanization of black people." His state-

30. Machacek, *Milton and Homer*, 24.

31. See Reginald A. Wilburn, "Getting 'Uppity' with Milton; or Because My Mom Politely Asked: 'Was Milton Racist?'" in *Milton Studies* 62.2 (2020): 266–279.

ment reveals the kind of psychic educational negotiations Black students, in particular, may feel compelled to deal with, navigate, and overcome when confronting any number of literary microaggressions encountered in certain English literature classrooms. When it comes to reading, studying, and openly discussing the works of some of the most revered canonmakers in English tradition, the dynamic of literary microaggressions can prove stultifying to the point of causing the "emotional devastation" that bell hooks elsewhere identifies as "soul murder."[32]

Traditions of literary history make canonical white authors like Milton nearly unavoidable in discipline-specific curricula. The "things of darkness" reverberating throughout these authors' texts may sometime go unchecked by professors or students. As a result, those bearing the brunt of these canonized literary microaggressions may simply have to "deal with" the alienating effects of an inhibiting language system "just to get by" and academically succeed for and within the educational moment. In light of these psychosomatic negotiations students like Cadet Griffin encounter, one wonders in the name of providing students a premium educational experience the extent to which white canonical authors' (in)visible intertexts of negated blackness potentially hit too close to home for BIPOC scholars and their peers' existential or ontological good? This pedagogical conundrum might empower English professors committed to antiracist pedagogies to "cause good and necessary trouble" with race in white-authored canonical texts of privileged literary periods. Milton is one seventeenth-century author whose writings may be taught through this pedagogical context. His stock of British Africanisms affords students unique opportunities to identify, explore, and explicate the numerous literary microaggressions and poetic emphases that thematically negate blackness throughout the early modern period.

New English majors may not know, understand, or respect the revered Milton who yet ranks as an icon in English tradition. For this reason, introducing him prior to assigning a work like *Comus* may be in order, especially in the post-George Floyd moment where pronouncements of "Black lives matter" may foster an even greater consciousness about the value

32. bell hooks, *We Real Cool: Black Men and Masculinity*, (Routledge, 2004), 15.

of Africanist people in society than prior to 2014. At this historical juncture of Black consciousness, do new English majors know Milton ranks alongside Geoffrey Chaucer and William Shakespeare as a member of a rather elite triumvirate in English literature? Are they cognizant of the snippets of criticism spanning the seventeenth and twentieth centuries that extols him as sublime and his epic equally so? As a case in point, critic Stephen Dobranski, writing about Milton's relevance "today" notes in his introduction to a special issue of *Milton Studies* that the seventeenth-century writer remains "without equal," further asserting a work like *Paradise Lost* survives as "the greatest single poem written in English."[33]

A second thing millennial students should know about Milton prior to studying what I call the "word work" of race in *Comus* is that his later long epic poem, *Paradise Lost*, constitutes the canonical achievement in belles-lettres that dignified English on a scale unrivaled by previous literary texts. Milton's epic globally dignified English by demonstrating the capaciousness and grandness of a language that poetically could live up to the high demands of culture and express a nation's glory in the most exalted form of poetry. Moreover, Milton achieved this heroic literary accomplishment while nearly blind. It is also worth considering that today's twenty-first-century students may not realize that English, prior to the 1600s, was deemed a paganistic and culturally inferior language. Appropriated from "classical rhetoric and grammar," notions of linguistic barbarism, according to Ian Smith, typically denoted "linguistic vices [and] errors in language that were specifically associated with foreigners or cultural outsiders."[34] The English language was coming more into vogue by the second decade of the seventeenth century. Herein lies what Smith astutely recognizes as the "'Renaissance' racial matrix: [a] dynamic circulation of a static paradigm as the articulation of English mastery" that emerges not long after the language itself was deemed inferior and barbarous in comparison to Greek and Latin.[35] Spoken primarily

33. Stephen Dobranski, "Milton Today, Part 1," in *Milton Studies* v.
34. Ian Smith, *Race and Rhetoric in the Renaissance: Barbarian Errors*, (Palgrave Macmillan, 2009), 1.
35. Smith, *Race and Rhetoric*, 3.

by so-called uneducated classes, English gained and began to enjoy high cultural status throughout the seventeenth century and beyond. One recognizes the traces of this linguistic anxiety in Milton's prefatory "Verse" to *Paradise Lost*. Of particular note, his defense for composing the epic in unrhymed blank verse leads him to justify this aesthetic choice of "neglect" as culturally synonymous with the works of Homer and Virgil. Like them, Milton eschews rhyme in his great epic poem, believing the poetic element reflects "the inventions of a barbarous age."[36]

Milton, who possessed a privileged and formidable education, would have been well acquainted with the greatest writers from antiquity down to his present age. He absorbed some of the best these precursors and near contemporaries offered. Undoubtedly, he was "used by" those who influenced him and transformed those influences "into something altogether [his] own."[37] The epic *Paradise Lost*, like other literary genres Milton explored, shows him excelling at this mastery of "literary strangeness," a "mode of originality" mastered by "only a few figures" who across the annals of history have been regarded as capable of "fight[ing] relatively free of the anxiety of influence."[38] New English majors may not know the cultural weight and significance of a work like *Paradise Lost*. Nor might they understand it is through this signature work that Milton is understood largely as dignifying the English language by heroic turns and at a time when the culture had only recently begun to come in vogue.

Inasmuch as he is worthy to be praised, Milton merits critique as well. He is worthy to be critiqued on account of his injurious British Africanisms like those reverberating throughout *Comus*. These abuses of language contribute to why select African American authors throughout literary history respond to Milton as though he were an "inhibiting" canonical influence in tradition. For instance, when Herron recognizes Milton as having an "inhibiting" influence on certain African American writers, she,

36. John Milton, "the Verse." *Paradise Lost*, Norton Critical Edition, Gordon Teskey, Ed. (Norton, 2000), 2.
37. Harold Bloom, *The Western Canon: The Books and School of the Ages* (Riverhead Books NY, 1994), 170.
38. Bloom, *The Western Canon*, 3; 9.

no doubt, refers to the intertexts and metalanguage of race contemporary students are apt to recognize when reading him.[39] Adopting and refining this pedagogical approach exposes Milton's literary microaggressions of antiblack bias for what they are: triggering mechanisms of poetic speech that survive as a reproach to the young canonical poet and the nation he so proudly dignified through words and numerous figures of negated darkness.

Teaching and Decolonizing Milton's British Africanisms in *Comus*

Forces of synchronic intertextuality make it rather difficult to imagine a moralizing work on virginal chastity like *Comus* could in any way consider Black women of the period as virtuous. Synchronic intertextuality, according to Gregory Machacek, involves textual interrelations governing "the semiotic practices in effect in a particular culture at a particular historical moment."[40] When we consider England's growing participation in the slave trade throughout the 1630s and 1640s, it becomes unpardonable to overlook the extent and degree to which discourses of race and antiblackness may have contributed to the heinous acts of Africanist subjugation that a developing English language helped to sanction as ideologically licit. One suspects the capture, enslavement, and rape of African women during this period necessarily complicated the possibility of performing favorable moralistic readings of Black female subjects in particular. As Winthrop D. Jordan explains, "the case with English confrontation with Negroes" concerns a colonialist society mired "in a state of rapid flux, undergoing important changes in religious values, and comprised of men who were energetically on the make and acutely and often uncomfortably self-conscious of being so."[41] Particularly from the time of the Eng-

39. Carolivia Herron, "Milton and Afro-American Literature" in *Re-Membering Milton: Essays on the Texts and Traditions*, edited by Mary Nyquist and Maragret W. Ferguson, (Methuen, 1988), 280.
40. Gregory Machacek, *Milton and Homer: 'Written to Aftertimes'* (Duquesne University Press, 2011), 25.
41. Jordan, *White Over Black*, 43.

lish Reformation to the Elizabethan period and beyond in the seventeenth century, English culture's confrontation with a people they considered "less technologically advanced [and] markedly different in appearance and culture" led them to conceive those they encountered and enslaved with "radically contrasting qualities of color, religion, and style of life, as well as animality and a peculiarly potent sexuality."[42] These racial formations in language and synchronic intertextuality occur within a dynamic of proliferating signs, rhetorical figures, and flawed semiotic readings of and about Africanist blackness throughout the early modern period.

Critical raced readings of darkness throughout *Comus* reveal Milton's tropological operations of marginalizing Black women and their filial issue. This marginalizing sign system marks a supernatural character like Circe as a dark child of the sun and a mother too figuratively racialized as Black to be considered chaste, virtuous, or reflecting ideal standards typically ascribed to patriarchal perceptions and conceptions of white femininity in early modern England. A signature motif in "the classic story of slavery," according to Saidiya Hartman, involves "wayward lines of descent" sired by white men in power whose sexual vices often proved "phantasmal."[43] Interestingly, "sexual connotations embodied in the terms *bestial* and *beastly* were considerably stronger in Elizabethan English than" Jordan associated with US culture at the close of the 1960s.[44] Against the cultural backdrop of these seventeenth-century racial contexts, millennial student-scholars are primed to perform critical interrogations of whiteness as distorted projections of the blackness Milton negates in *Comus* through his exhaustive supply of British Africanisms.

Before darkening Circe's maternal character, Milton first grounds his masque in a series of poetic British Africanisms. As early as the fifth line, *Comus* is bound to resonate with a racial tenor of antiblackness. An attendant spirit descends from "the starry threshold of Jove's court," lighting upon this "dim spot / Which men call earth" (1; 5). She descends from

42. Jordan, *White Over Black*, 43.

43. Saidiya Hartman, *Lose Your Mother: A Journey Along the Atlantic Slave Route*, (Farar, Straus, and Giroux 2007), 76; 77.

44. Jordan, *White Over Black*, 33.

Jove's starry celestial regions to fulfill an "errand" for which she would not otherwise "soil these pure ambrosial weeds / With the rank vapours of [earth's] sin-worn mould" (15; 16–17). Her reading of the earthly sphere grounds this descriptive setting in an atmospheric climate of antiblack bias where a developing trope of negated darkness serves as a figure of scenic debauchery. These opening lines also present earth as a dichotomous setting, one starkly contrasted from Heaven's celestially luminescent regions. Playing with figures of geographical darkness and light, Milton characterizes Earth as a moral climate mired in sin.

Guiding students in the explicating and deconstructing of these figures can lead to some rather surprising discoveries relative to Milton's style of playing in the dark with negated blackness. For example, Milton symbolically underscores the dichotomous relationship between the opening light and dark atmospheric setting by racializing England as a nationalist landscape of optic whiteness. This "representation of literary and cultural whiteness" encourages an interrogative reading of England as stereotypically pure and distinct from a so-called dark continent populated by Africans.[45] The attendant spirit makes this reading evident by referring to Neptune's "imperial rule of all the sea-girt isles" and boasting that England's national landscape exists as "the greatest and the best of all the main" that the god of the sea "quarters to his blue-haired deities" (21; 28–29). Furthermore, her boastful pride in England's "old and haughty nation" soon leads her to comment on the masque's main characters, the "fair offspring" who have been "nursed in princely lore" and are headed to "attend their father's state / And new-entrusted sceptre" (33; 34; and 35).

Fair, in this instance, highlights the characters' pale skin tones within the very passage that racializes England as metonymically white. Milton scholars such as Barbara Lewalski's comments on the masque's nationalist undertones do not specifically address race yet underscore the word workings of race in the masque by noting as significant Milton's dedicating *Comus* to Bridgewater. Dedicating *Comus* to Bridgewater contributes to constructing the masque's story "as a representative of the ancient British

45. AnaLouise Keating, "Interrogating 'Whiteness,' (De)constructing 'Race'" in *Teaching African American Literature: Theory and Practice* (Routledge, 1998), 195–96.

nation" in the process.[46] David Lowenstein concurs, arguing *Comus* reveals young Milton's literary investments in "mythopoeic representations" at a moment "in the [poet's] early career" where readers see him "rethinking in dramatic poetry, the ethics, politics, of English nationhood to a degree that has not been fully appreciated."[47] Milton's attitudes about his country would undergo several permutations in the decades beyond the 1630s, Loewenstein continues. Nevertheless, in *Comus*, contemporary audiences note a young poet of growing prominence "already devoting his imaginative energies to reconceiving the symbolism of familial and national representation."[48] These linguistic codes spur a concretizing recognition of the racializing tropological schema reverberating in subsequent lines of *Comus*. Echoing the racial signs of the times, Milton's contrasting figures of light and darkness work in tandem with idealized conceptions of white nationhood as a poetic mechanism for denigrating black geographies like the 'shady' darkness of the ominous woods where Comus dwells as a hellish outcast and exilic figure.[49]

Three lines following the passage on British nationhood, Milton's attendant spirit introduces audiences to an ominous wooded setting. The Lady and her brothers are depicted as making their way "through the perplexed paths of this drear wood" and its "nodding horror of whose shady brows / Threats the forlorn and wand'ring passenger" (37; 38–39). Descriptions like "drear," "horror," and "shady brows" intensify the atmospheric gloom of the wooded setting, infusing the scene with a sense of ominous foreboding that the narrating spirit has poetically forecasted. If anything favorable could be expected of this darkened setting, Jove would have little to no reason for dispatching the attendant spirit to aid the siblings' "defence and guard" (42). That her divine assistance is needed at all only under-

46. Keating, "Interrogating 'Whiteness,' (De)constructing 'Race,'" 77.
47. David Loewenstein, "Milton's Ludlow *Maske* and Remaking English Nationhood" in *Making Milton: Print, Authorship, and Afterlives* Eds. Emma Depledge, John S. Garrison, and Marissa Nicosia, (Oxford University Press, 2021), 78; 79.
48. Loewenstein, "Milton's Ludlow *Maske*," 79.
49. While, on the one hand, referring to the wooded area that provides the setting for *Comus*, I also use the term "shady" to denote "deceitful, underhanded, and/or evil practices" as is common in twentieth-century Black vernacular.

scores the gloom and doom signified by these darkened woods. The ensuing forty-seven lines underscore the pedagogical importance of closely reading and examining Milton's British Africanisms in *Comus* "for its hidden and overt racial meanings" of negated black difference.[50] In these lines, Milton's attendant spirit racially profiles Comus as descending from a maternal genealogical line bewitched with supernatural vice.

The attendant spirit characterizes Comus by his bad filial association with Circe. First, Milton takes poetic license and racial liberties with Greek myth by imbuing his classical source material with inflections of supernatural deviance. This poetic decision further inflects Milton's stock of British Africanisms with added resonances of black and negated difference. The spirit's limited focus and characterization of Bacchus, Comus' father, makes apparent that Circe is to be understood as largely responsible for her son's deviant nature. Bacchus, audiences learn, was the first to extract "the sweet poison of misused wine" which he took from Circe's "charmed cup" (45; 51). Like Adam in *Paradise Lost*, he succumbs to fallenness at the hands of an Eve-like temptress. Although the attendant spirit faults Bacchus for drinking Circe's sin-inducing beverage, she devotes more space to emphasizing Circe's fallen nature by darkening and maligning the maternal figure as a racially Othered care giver and nurturer.

The attendant spirit not only introduces Circe as a witch but darkens the maternal character by referring to her as a "daughter of the Sun" (51). Twinning the vice of supernatural evil with an imagistic portrayal of Circe as a child of the sun characterizes this bewitching mother figure with a physiognomic complexion distinctly darker than the phenotype ascribed to the Lady and her brothers. Moreover, if Circe is to be understood as a direct filial descendant of the sun, such characterization shades in the visual direction of a complexional blackness too darkened by the radiating light of an intensely warm sun. This designation also darkens Circe, potentially conjuring associations with the African continent and its torrid climate attributable to the central star of the solar system.

Homer's *Odyssey* geographically situates Circe on Aeaea, an island located west of Italy in the Mediterranean yet just north of continental

50. Keating, "Interrogating 'Whiteness,' (De)constructing 'Race,'" 189.

Africa. In the seventeenth century and at the time Milton writes *Comus*, Africa already functioned as a tropological sign of negated blackness. Thus, by taking allusive poetic license with Circe and associating her with a torrid geographical climate like continental Africa, Milton, in a sense, displaces the maternal witch from the Mediterranean island named in the Homeric source. This allusive mode of characterization highlights Circe's bewitching maternal nature as evil and wayward. Its poetic properties also solidify a tropological grammar of antiblack bias in *Comus* while portraying Circe as a maternal archetype tainted under a bad rhetorical sign of Africanist presence and racial otherness.

Negated as a type of supernatural seductress, Circe invites racialized readings of disfigured and maddened disability in the masque. The men she beguiles undergo bestial metamorphosis. According to the narrator, "whoever tasted" the beverage she offers "lost his upright shape, / And downward fell into a groveling swine" (lines 52–53). Already Africanized by her filial association with the sun and her supernatural vice, Circe racially sponsors the bestial disfigurement of the men she successfully seduces. This aspect of characterization further amplifies semiotic readings of a bewitching blackness that transforms the corporeal shape of her victims and drives them to maddened states of disability. Theorizing connections between blackness and madness, Theri Pickens advises readers of *Black Madness::Mad Blackness* to "learn to think madly, Blackly."[51] For Pickens, "madness and blackness have a complex constellation of relationships," one she theorizes as "constituted within the fissures, breaks, and gaps in critical and literary texts."[52] A goal of her theoretical project aims to encourage scholars to "read Blackness and madness alongside each other," particularly as conjoined properties where "race and disability [often] intersect."[53] Pickens' theory certainly applies to a close critico-race reading of Circe's effect on the men she seduces. The theory applies to the monstrous child Circe births and nurtures as well.

51. Their Alyce Pickens, *Black Madness::Mad Blackness*, (Duke University Press, 2019), xi.

52. Pickens, *Black Madness*, 3.

53. Pickens, *Black Madness*, 13; 23.

Circe seduces Bacchus, "gaze[s] upon his clust'ring locks," and eventually bears "a son / Much like his father but his mother more / Whom therefore she brought up and Comus named" (54; 56–58). This backstory surrounding Comus' birth suggests Circe, alone, bears the blame for the monstrous child's disfigured appearance and defiled or debauched nature. Similarly, she may be understood as transmitting the vice symbolically associated with her racial Otherness and moral vice to her son. This mode of negatively characterizing Comus as a result of Circe's symbolic nature anticipates the American "grammar" Hortense Spillers, in her influential article "Mama's Baby, Papa's Maybe," theorizes as the post-natal condition of Black mothers' relations to dynamics of US slavery. Spillers contends the children of Black women are "touched and handled" by their mothers. This "perceived matriarchal pattern" whereby enslaved mothers and their children often find themselves caught "in a state of social 'pathology'" useful for subsequent "pornotroping" in global culture, emerges as the consequence of paternal particularities associated with the "peculiar institution."[54] In a system where white slaveholding fathers typically withhold legal rights of heirship to the Black children they sire and Black fathers can be sold miles away, Black biological mothers or their surrogates, generally are left to raise one's filial descendants. Comus anticipates this racial grammar in a seventeenth-century canonical work written, performed, and revised in an era where England's ongoing participation in the slave trade was on the rise.

Comus grows and matures, having been schooled and well versed in his mother's supernatural arts. According to the narrator, Comus roams "the Celtic and Iberian fields" before settling within "this ominous wood" and its "thick shelter of black shades embowered" (60; 61; and 62). As with the setting at the outset of the masque, this dark and shady bower extends the negative interpretive associations with bewitched blackness that Circe transmit to her son at birth. The poem evidences the extent to which Circe's supernatural blackness touches her son when noting the

54. Hortense Spillers, "Mama's Baby, Papa's Maybe: An American Grammar Book," in *Black, White, and In Color: Essays on American Literature and Culture* (University of Chicago Press, 2003), 205; 206.

grown Comus "excels his mother at her mighty art" (63). That he practices a variation of his mother's witchcraft and within an embowered geographical setting of ominous darkness intensifies the signifying power of Milton's British Africanisms relative to Comus' character and his figuratively marginalized identity along racial lines in the masque.

Like his mother, Comus beckons "weary travellers" to ruin and destruction by tempting them with "orient liquor" (64; 65). His victims likewise undergo bestial metamorphoses as a result of consuming a poisonous beverage that transforms their "human count'nance … / Into some brutish form of wolf, or bear, / Or ounce, or tiger, hog, or bearded goat" (68; 70–71). Interestingly, they are unable to "perceive their foul disfigurement" (74). Their inability to see their bestially transformed selves as they are in reality means these bewitched victims live within perpetual states of maddened blackness. This racialized madness manifests more palpably as a result of their tendency to "boast themselves more comely than before" (75). Physically disfigured and mentally disabled from seeing themselves as and for who they really are, Comus' brutish rout evidence Milton's poetic commingling of race and disability as blended signs of blackened debauchery. They also glory homoerotically in the appreciation of their fallen metamorphosed state. Of particular note, they "roll with pleasure in a sensual sty" of debased folly (77). Within this mixed constellation of racially coded signs, Comus' rout of fallen and bestial and monstrously disfigured men magnify Milton's British Africanisms with a greater clarity of antiblack bias.

Comus and his rout pose moral threats to wayfaring travelers "favoured of high Jove" (78). Given the religious and moral threats they pose to the allegorical British citizens in the masque, Comus dispatches the attendant spirit to Earth as a type of divine protectorate. The attendant spirit dutifully fulfills these earthly errands, assisting those who "pass through" the "advent'rous glade" of Milton's ominous setting and providing them "safe convoy" through its woods lest they fall prey to Comus' evil machinations (79). Having established the onset of conflict in the masque, the attendant spirit brings the poem's introductory section to a close. Milton next turns to a poetic strategy of racializing the setting and characterization with percussive sounds of Africanist rhythm.

Just prior to Comus' entrance, the attendant spirit "hear[s] the tread / Of hateful steps" then hides to view the unfolding incidents (92). The stage directions and lines 93 through 144 reinforce codes of Africanist Otherness by characterizing Comus and his crew's riotous tread through the woods as musically reflecting syncopated sounds of blackness. The group enters the grounds "like sundry sorts of wild beasts, but otherwise like men and women." Their "riotous and unruly noise" peals the atmosphere with thunderous decibels that tropologically announce the alterity of Africanist presence. Milton inflects this antiblack reading of the wild and unruly crew by suddenly breaking from the stately meter of heroic blank verse.

Comus speaks in iambic tetrameter in stark contrast to the attendant spirit's heroic blank verse. Occasionally, Comus deviates from iambic tetrameter. When he does, his lines extend beyond the metrical feet accorded to blank verse, often containing eleven or more syllables. The sudden shift from blank verse to iambic tetrameter calls tropological attention to itself since Milton's figurative economies of racial characterization have worked successfully to frame the bestial demigod in an interpretive image of negated and deviant blackness. Editor of the *Riverside Milton* Roy Flannagan contends Comus' use of iambic tetrameter corresponds to "conventions of the Elizabethan theater for supernatural beings."[55] Another rhetorical difference Comus' deviant rhythm makes throughout this passage concerns Milton's rebellious altering of the masque's oral and aural soundscapes. These rebellious lines create linguistic choppiness and infuse the masque with truncated syncopated rhythms of barbarous dissonance. Akin to the supernatural nature of his character, his alternative rhetorical style troubles the ominous setting as demonic grounds that relay verbal echoes of what Katherine McKittrick astutely theorizes as the racialized "sayability of geography." These supernatural inflections of race and antiblackness in *Comus* cohere with racialized readings of the ominous woods and the monstrous rout simultaneously.

55. Roy Flannagan, ed., *The Riverside Milton* (Houghton Mifflin, 1998), 128.

Milton denigrates black percussive music elsewhere in his canon as well. Stanzas XXIII and XXIV in "On Christ's Nativity" and line 394 from Book 1 of *Paradise Lost* provide two examples where Milton demonizes Black music for its percussive difference. Contemporary novelist, Ishmael Reed, critiques Milton on the very basis of this manner of British Africanisms in *Mumbo Jumbo*. As I reference in "Getting Uppity with Milton," a character in Reed's novel censures Milton for the antiblack references to Africanist music appearing in lines from the poem, "On Christ's Nativity." Interpreting lines from Milton's poem as expressive of a disdain for the timbrelled, percussive, and syncopated music associated with ancient Egyptian civilization, Reed's narrator "recognizes these sonic rhythms" as repulsive to the epic writer.[56] As a result, the narrator believes English professors revere this racist Milton as an "amulet" and "talisman" who proves useful for excluding Black people from their academic departments.[57] Interpretively deeming these instances of poetic language as racist, Reed performs an interrogative clapback in literary tradition that responds to Milton's microaggressions of Africanist music and its percussive cultural stylings. BIPOC students might find and enjoy similar emancipatory joy when English professors create lesson plans that invite all of us to clap back at Milton on the literal, implied, and inferential levels of semiotic meaning throughout *Comus* and other works by the epic writer and his seventeenth-century contemporaries.

Comus further breaks from the established form of speech by resorting to rhyming couplets in this passage of deviant meter. This deviance by rhyming couplets especially differentiates him from the whiteness of Milton's racially privileged characters. As per the introduction of this passage above, Milton's apology for "The Verse" to *Paradise Lost*, breaks with poetic convention in English by dignifying his nation's language and culture through a rejection of rhyme. Milton's decision to consign Comus to speaking in rhyming couplets dehumanizes the demigod further as a barbarous racial Othered thing and maddened figure of symbolic blackness. This Africanist feature of musical blackness accords with Reed's poetic

56. Wilburn, "Getting Uppity with Milton," 272.
57. Wilburn, "Getting Uppity with Milton," 272.

hateration of Milton in *Mumbo Jumbo* while advancing Ian's cultural analyses of so-called barbarous language that synchronically impacts racial meaning in the early modern period. Milton's prefatory "Verse" further denigrates a poetics of rhyme as useful for "set[ting] off wretched matter and lame meter."[58] In other words, the epic writer associates rhyme as a figure of abject disability. According to this logic, Milton perceives rhyme and Comus' use of it as a poetic sign of physical inferiority. Comus' metrical "feet," in this instance, symbolically connote the poet's disenfranchising support of an ableist worldview that already are conjoined with signifiers of racial Otherness. Close readings of lines 93 through 144 alongside students provide pedagogical opportunities for students to read and hear these tropological resonances and echoes of antiblack bias. More specifically, Milton's acoustic Africanisms in this section of the poem racially profile his dark-child characters through musical modes of percussive and syncopated blackness.

Comus' choppy meter of blackened racial disability changes and reverts to heroic blank verse (unrhymed iambic pentameter) only upon hearing the approaching tread of what he perceives may be a lost virginal maiden. "Break off, break off, I feel the different pace / Of some chaste footing hear about this ground" he exclaims (145–146). In this moment of rhetorical artifice, that is, Comus adopts the stately rhythms of heroic blank verse. His now affected English signals a duplicitous exercise of doubled vocal consciousness. In the seminal literary work, *The Souls of Black Folk* (1903), W. E. B. Du Bois coins the concept "double consciousness" to express African Americans' "sense of always looking at one's self through the eyes of others, of measuring one's soul by the tape of a world that looks on in amused contempt and pity."[59] Du Bois, writing within US sociological contexts, explains this condition of white supremacist culture causes racially discriminated individuals to "ever feel" the twoness of "souls," "thoughts," and "warring ideals in one dark body."[60] These strivings

58. Milton, "The Verse," 2.
59. W. E. B. Du Bois, *The Souls of Black Folk*, edited by Henry Louis Gates and Terri Hume Oliver (W. W. Norton, 1999), 11.
60. Du Bois, *The Souls of Black Folk*, 11.

occur at the expense of ontologically laboring to enjoy being both Black and American.

An anachronistic pre-working of this racial dynamic occurs in Milton's masque when Comus suddenly shifts to speaking elevated poetic English. It is as if he knows far too well that the soft tread of a perceived white and virginally chaste maiden demands or deserves an affected speech pattern suitable to the racial privilege she enjoys in early modern English culture. He sustains this stately rhythm of unrhymed speech for the next twenty-five lines as a preparatory method of rhetorical trickery. He intends to figuratively enslave the Lady by cheating her "eye with blear illusion" and the relaying of "false presentments" (155; 56).

The Lady also calls attention to the racial tenor of musical difference upon her arrival on the scene. "This way the noise was, if mine ear be true," she states, adding, "Methought it was the sound / Of riot, and ill-managed merriment," (170; 171–172). Adding to her assessment of the racialized soundscape, she equates the riotous crew's musical merriment to "the jocund flute, or gamesome pipe," which, she finds, "Stirs up among the loose unlettered hinds" (173–174). Such music provides incorrigible accompaniment for the "wanton" dancing she abhors (176). Music of this sort also leaves the Lady "loath / To meet the rudeness and swilled insolence / Of such late wassailers" (177–179). These discriminating sentiments about the racially Othered music she scoffs at work in concert with and supplement her rather natural style of speaking in the exalted metrical rhythms of heroic blank verse. Devoting pedagogical time for studying these various instances of coded rhetorical speech throughout the first 229 lines of *Comus* allows for detailed interrogations and analyses of whiteness that facilitate additional opportunities for deconstructing race a la Milton's myriad British Africanisms. As literary microaggressions, these features of poetic language expose early modern English for its various rhetorical postures of pitting notions of white purity against presumptive interpretations that denigrate blackness as naturally hedonistic and immoral.

The remaining plot leaves more than enough room for English professors to cause continued trouble with Milton and race in *Comus*. Explications of the geographic setting, Circe and Comus' respective characterizations and the masque's denigrating critiques of Black musical expressivity unmasks a "hidden curriculum" of racial meaning production throughout this short canonical work. This (in)visible yet hidden tropological system of racial signs requires rigorous activities of literary deconstruction, ultimately requiring students to read race critically in literary texts as scholarly artists. Anthony Abraham Jack defines a "hidden curriculum" as an instructional set of academic survival skills "full of unwritten rules, unexplained terms, and a whole host of things that insiders take for granted."[61] This system of social negotiating principles often comes second nature to students from privileged socio-economic backgrounds. It not only tests students' "intellectual chops but their ability to navigate the social world" of institutions "where the rewards of such mastery are often larger and more durable than those that come from acing an exam."[62] Milton's British Africanisms in *Comus* reveal a hidden curriculum of myriad poeticized racial meanings. Making these signifiers of darkened meaning more visible to readers' critically astute eyes awakens Milton's text beyond some students' interpretive imaginations.

Prepping for academic discussions of this hidden curriculum in *Comus* easily lends itself to a two- or three-day teaching unit. After orienting students to Milton's canonical stature in English literature, pedagogical exercises devoted to studying and discussing the masque's first 229 lines offers fascinating opportunities for interrogating whiteness and racist projections of antiblack bias. Subsequent units might afford students opportunities for text-mining, interrogating, and deconstructing the more than 500 British Africanisms that may be (in)visibly hidden throughout the remainder of the poem. Text-mining, as Kenton Rambsy explains in his examination of select short fiction by Zora Neale Hurston and Richard Wright, aids scholars to "analyze words, clusters of words, and word densities" in texts toward illuminating how literary artists "represent language."[63] Lesson plans that introduce text-mining *Comus* for its

61. Anthony Abraham Jack, *The Privileged Poor: How Elite Colleges are Failing Disadvantaged Students*, (Harvard University Press, 2019), 190.
62. Jack, *The Privileged Poor*, 86.
63. Kenton Rambsy, "Text-Mining Short Fiction by Zora Neale Hurston and Richard Wright Using Voyant Tools." CLA*Journal*, 59(3), (2016): 251.

linguistic figures and related "things of darkness," likewise assists students to explicate Milton's masque for its technique of casting discriminatory and signifying "shade" on Black identity. Equally important, this pedagogical approach "makes ... shifting language patterns" of race hypervisibly "apparent from the beginning of [Milton's] story in relation to the end."[64] This dynamic holds especially along multiple axes of interpretation where race, gender, sexuality, and disability tend to collide throughout *Comus*.

It should be noted that the pedagogical point of interrogating and deconstructing Milton's British Africanisms in *Comus* and seventeenth-century literature should not serve the interest of banishing the canonical epic writer from the English curriculum. Rather, I see the benefit of adopting this recommended pedagogical goal as assisting transformative scholar-citizens like the students we teach to remaster the English language Milton dignified more than 350 years ago. Elsewhere I have defined this skill of remastering Milton as a sophisticated interpoetic intelligence performed by some of the most erudite authors and readers across the annals of African American literary history. My article on Josephine Brown's biography of her father, William Wells Brown, explores the meaning and value that Milton's *Comus* had for the former fugitive slave, antislavery orator, playwright, and novelist.[65] My future scholarship will add to this dearth in scholarship by examining Milton's *Comus* as intertextually valuable to Frederick Douglass, and the unsung musical virtuoso, Roland Hayes. Both appropriate snippets of *Comus*, evidencing performances of Black intertextual remastery with Milton that reinterpret him in expressive forms of revisionary cultural excellence. By including the appropriate passages from Wells Brown's Travel Narrative, Douglass's speech, "The Nation's Problem: An Address Delivered in Washington, D.C., on 16 April 1889," and Hayes' musical rendition, "Comus: Preach Me Not your Musty Rules," early modern English professors committed to antiracist pedagogy can cause a whole lot of good, necessary, and uppity trouble with Mil-

64. Rambsy, "Text-Mining Short Fiction," 255.
65. See Reginald A. Wilburn, "The Return of William Wells Brown: A Heroic Black Miltonist in Elizabeth Josephine Brown's Miltonic Biography of Her Father," in *Women (Re)Wrting Milton*, edited by Mandy Green and Sharihan Al-Akhras (Routledge, 2021), 73–90.

ton in their syllabi and classrooms. Causing trouble with Milton in these entrepreneurial ways "enable[s] readers to enter into a transhistoric conversation that extends forward and backward" in a manner that Angelica Duran recognizes as "at once global and intensely personal."[66]

Notwithstanding the triggering nature of Milton's British Africanisms throughout *Comus*, Wells Brown, Douglass, and Hayes' performances of Miltonic remastery make an added case for pedagogically causing good and necessary trouble with race in the epic writers' seventeenth-century masque. Although poets of the English word throughout the seventeenth century contributed to the developing and flourishing of a major literature while negating blackness, processes of synchronic intertextuality could not deter a "misrepresented people" from dignifying the language anew.[67] Wells Brown, Douglass, and Hayes' remastered appropriations of *Comus* can teach twenty-first-century students that a critical place and space exists for interrogating the whiteness of an English language system. Interrogating the privileged whiteness of our English language system can help all of us to re-member Milton as a pedagogical consequence of causing good and necessary trouble with the literary icon even if by anachronistic pedagogical methods. This is because Milton, "canonical writer *par excellence*, continues to thrive" in global circles of social activism.[68]

Ultimately, causing this good and uppity trouble with Milton's *Comus* affords students the twenty-first-century skills necessary for undertaking roles of transformative global citizenship in the now and hereafter. In our present age, it is not uncommon for students, parents, university administrators, and members of society at large to minimize the worth and enduring value of English literary studies as a discipline. Additionally, it is too easy for those not in the know to summarily dismiss disciplines of languages, literatures, and cultures as little more than a recreational luxury. Certainly, in this post-George Floyd, Breonna Taylor, and Ahmaud Arbery

66. Duran, "Milton and the Undergraduate," 48.
67. Stevie Wonder, *Bambooozled* Sound Recording.
68. Laura Lunger Knoppers and Gregory Colon Semenza, "Introduction," in *Milton in Popular Culture*, 5.

moment, ours is a discipline deserving not of knee-jerking defense but of unequivocal respect for what expertise in language can do for global civilization when remastered in the hearts, minds, and wills of those who dedicate themselves to its rigorous study. In a 2014 commencement address at Emory University, Representative Lewis offered a precursory gospel of revolt and civil disobedience that predated the Op-Ed piece in *The New York Times* referenced earlier in this essay. In that address, Representative Lewis instructed graduating members of his audience to

> use your education. You have wonderful teachers, wonderful professors, researchers. Use what you have. Use your learning. Use your tools to help make our country and make our world a better place, where no one will be left out or left behind.

As this snippet makes clear, Representative Lewis regarded professors as indispensable educational resources for redeeming the soul of the nation. Each semester presents new opportunities for early modern English professors committed to antiracist pedagogies to perform this salvific work of educational patriotism. When early modern English professors dare to teach students to decode race through critical close readings of a work like *Comus*, we do something far more heroic than merely dignifying Milton and the language he crowned with global prestige. Rather, through a "reconstruction of instruction" we resurrect canons of literature anew, interrogating a stockpile of British Africanisms in the service of doing justice to all humanity by and through language with high critico-creative skill.

"The Present Terror of the World": The Ottoman Empire in the English Imaginary

AMBEREEN DADABHOY

To claim that the terrorist attacks on the United States on September 11, 2001, changed the world, is far from hyperbole. Those attacks and the United States' swift military response on what it deemed its "War on Terror," inaugurated a new era in US militarism, nationalism, and patriotism, while simultaneously recuperating and refashioning centuries old tropes of cultural and religious conflict between Islam and Christianity. Five days after the attacks, during a presidential address to the country, George W. Bush, announced "We're a nation that can't be cowed by evil-doers [...] This crusade, this war on terrorism is going to take a while."[1] Bush's construction of the terrorists as "evil-doers," evacuated the possible political underpinnings of their violence, and his equation of his war with medieval European incursions into the near east, the crusades, successfully yoked religion to politics.[2] Religious difference and its attendant form of cultural and racial othering became a vital tenet of the logics animating this conflict. Moreover, Bush's words point to the protean and temporally dislocated quality of the ensuing war: "evil-doers" and terrorists being sufficiently severed from specific and particular nation-states necessitated an elastic policy toward warfare. Nonetheless, even as War on Terror logics — the needs of the security state over and above the constitutional protections of the citizenry and international human rights

1. "Remarks by the President upon Arrival," on September 16, 2001. https://georgewbush-whitehouse.archives.gov/news/releases/2001/09/20010916-2.html.
2. I do not mean to suggest that the European crusades were not performing this very same ideological feat, only that as that conflict is conjured in the popular Euro-American imaginary, the political aims of the Frankish kingdoms, to maintain outposts in that region for political power, seem to have been lost.

mandates – seemed to supersede geography; this war could be fought in any location, wherever a threat to US national security presented itself. It was, at the same time, confined to geographies with Muslim majority populations; first Afghanistan, then Iraq, and, in the hands of future presidents, the theater of war moved expansively across the "Islamic worlds" of Africa, the Middle East, and South Asia. Thus, very easily facilitating the slippage from War on Terror to War on Islam.

In this essay, I would like to turn back the clock by several centuries and deliberate on the possible premodern sources of the kind of conflict Bush's rhetoric and the War on Terror activates, that between Christendom and *Dar al-Islam*, the world of Islam, to excavate the links between the United States' ongoing War on Terror (over twenty years at the time of this writing) and the "Terrour," that the Ottoman Empire elicited in its European neighbors. Specifically, I examine Richard Knolles monumental compendium, *The Generall Historie of the Turkes, from the first beginning of that nation to the rising of the Othoman Familie: with all the notable expeditions of the Christian Princes against them. Together with* THE LIVES AND CON*quests of the Othoman Kings and Emperours Faithfullie collected out of the best Histories, both auncient and moderne, and digested into one continual Historie until this present year* 1603, which announces in its title, not only the ongoing and seemingly endless nature of Ottoman aggression, but also frames the imperial ambitions of the Ottomans in Europe as a religious conflict. Knolles's text is important to investigate because of the allusions and references that intimate it as a source text for William Shakespeare's *Othello* (1603).[3] The *Generall Historie*'s catalogue of Ottoman sultans, the social and cultural composition of the empire, and its conquests in Europe and Asia offered fertile historical context for Shakespeare's appropriation of Cinthio's *Gli Hecatommithi* into his own play about imperial conflict, exogamous marriage, and early

3. Ambereen Dadabhoy, "The Moor of America: Approaching the Crisis of Race and Religion in the Renaissance and the Twenty-First Century." *Teaching Medieval and Early Modern Cross-Cultural Encounters*. Palgrave Macmillan, New York, 2014. 123–40; and Virginia Mason Vaughan, Vaughan, "Supersubtle Venetians: Richard Knolles and the Geopolitics of Shakespeare's Othello." *Visions of Venice in Shakespeare* 1 (2011): 19.

modern racism. Knolles's ambivalent framing of the Ottoman Empire evidences Shakespeare's own approach to identity and subjectivity within the schema of imperial domination and his construction of "the Turk" as an Other menacing the culture and society of the (Christian) eastern Mediterranean. Fully cognizant of the problem of correlating the two different historical and imperial conflicts, I propose in this study to show how European incursions into and aggressions with Muslim geographies and regimes have maintained strategic discursive similarities, which facilitate European and US community and nation-building efforts and support for increased militarism. Knolles's *Generall Historie*, then, discloses the alignment between discourses of religion, culture, and race as they cohere around the figure of "the Turk," and offers an ambivalent space through which to interrogate the religio-racial logics of our own War on Terror.

Modern and Premodern Terror

At this juncture, a reader of this collection might wonder how and why the War on Terror speaks to teaching race in the early modern period. The scholarly turn toward the Near East, particularly the Ottoman Empire in the 1990s and beyond, has opened up new avenues for interpreting early modern identity in the Mediterranean, particularly identity that is racially Othered as non-white and non-European.[4] These studies have focused on

4. See, for example the work of Daniel Vitkus, "Turning Turk in Othello: The Conversion and Damnation of the Moor." *Shakespeare Quarterly* 48.2 (1997): 145–76; Emily C. Bartels, "Making More of the Moor: Aaron, Othello, and Renaissance Refashionings of Race." *Shakespeare Quarterly* 41.4 (1990): 433–54; Michael Niell, " 'Mulattos,' 'Blacks,' and 'Indian Moors': Othello and Early Modern Constructions of Human Difference." *Shakespeare Quarterly* 49.4 (1998): 361–74; Ania Loomba, *Gender, Race, Renaissance Drama.* Manchester University Press, 1989; Jonathan Burton, *Traffic and Turning: Islam and English Drama, 1579–1624.* University of Delaware Press, 2005; Matar, Nabil. *Turks, Moors, and Englishmen in the Age of Discovery.* Columbia University Press, 2000; Barbour, Richmond. *Before Orientalism: London's Theatre of the East, 1576-1626.* Vol. 45. Cambridge University Press, 2003; MacLean, Gerald. *Looking East: English Writing and*

the imprecision of racial markers and the fluidity that attends to early modern English and European taxonomies of human difference. While I agree with some of these scholars that imprecision, fluidity, and even incoherence mark the writing of race — of whiteness and non-whiteness — by European writers, travelers, and playwrights, I also claim that focusing on cultural and religious difference can work to deracinate racially Otherized bodies in the period and to defuse the material, affective, and symbolic power that race mobilizes and exerts. What I hope to offer here, then, is a way for teachers and students to investigate the intersection of race and religion, to see how certain identities get racialized, to understand how racialization is a process of making Others who can then be controlled and oppressed either ideologically or materially.

The majority of our students now have no living memory of the terrorist attacks on September 11, 2001, and perhaps the early years of the War on Terror, such as the invasion of Iraq.[5] What prior knowledge can we then assume they bring to our class discussions when we ask them to think about how these early modern conflicts are connected to our contemporary ones? A possible answer, after almost two decades of this war, relies on the cultural and religious stereotypes about Islam and Muslims that are popular in our society: that Muslims are terrorists; that Muslim women are oppressed; that Islam is religion of violence; that Muslims hate "the West"; that Muslims should not be trusted. As a Muslim woman, these stereotypes are not easy for me to rehearse here, and they are only the proverbial tip of the iceberg when we think of the damaging construction of Islam and Muslim identity in the West in the wake of the War on Terror; however, they are important to catalogue, even in brief because they give us an opportunity to understand the intellectual and emotional limits of our students' comprehension of and orientation toward the topic. The political stakes of an approach that tackles religious alterity as it operates

the Ottoman Empire before 1800. Springer, 2007; and Andrea, Bernadette. *Women and Islam in Early Modern English Literature*. Cambridge University Press, 2008.

5. I recognize that here I am speaking of a so-called traditional-aged student group between 18–22. Such age groupings might not obtain for many instructors at institutions with more age diversity in their student populations.

in the Renaissance and early modern periods are fraught and can elicit as much discomfort as conversations about racial difference. Indeed, what I am trying to suggest is that these are imbricated categories and to facilitate a discussion on one will be to do so on the other. Preparing ourselves for what our students do and do not know about identity is vital to creating a classroom environment that will be attentive to our students' needs; our pedagogical goals regarding the elastic, fluid, and somatically located construction of race in the period; and to combatting the repetition of damaging stereotypes in our discussions.

My own experience teaching race and religion in early modern English drama suggests that our students need us to offer nuance to the polemical ways in which racial and religious differences have been mobilized in the period and in the historical record to suggest a bifurcated geopolitical early modern period, where there was either the West and the rest, or the realm of Christendom and worlds of Islam.[6] To rely on such tidy and false constructions of the early modern period, particularly the early modern Mediterranean, would allow a neat mapping of our War on Terror onto that period because the United States and its western allies have reproduced such stark binaries in their justifications for this conflict.[7] The relatively uncomplicated and unnuanced presentation of the War on Terror in our public discourse suggests the kind of nationalistic ideological point of view that may inhere in our students. When we teach texts like William Shakespeare's *Othello* that seem to conjure the fault lines of the War on Terror in different geographic and temporal registers we encounter a very contemporary cultural dilemma. How do we frame and contour their

6. I teach at Harvey Mudd College, a small Liberal Arts college, which focuses on STEM education. My students are non-majors and I often teach generalist courses. For further examples of my teaching on race please see: Ambereen Dadabhoy "Skin in the Game: Teachin Race in Early Modern Literature" *Studies in Medieval and Renaissance Teaching*. Vol 27.2, 2020; Ambereen Dadabhoy "The unbearable whiteness of being (in) Shakespeare." *postmedieval* 11.2 (2020): 228–35.
7. I use "our" here to indicate my own global and political positioning as someone who resides in the United States and is a citizen of this country. While I am vehemently opposed to the war, there are many ways in which I am coerced politically into supporting it.

experience of a play that traffics in political, imperial, and military aims that mimic our own? Writing about teaching *Othello* on September 12, 2001, Michael Galchinsky chronicles the play's relevance to that moment:

> Here was this early modern play set in Venice, the "world trade center" of its time, a place where all sorts of people from all sorts of cultures come to exchange goods, money, even husbands and wives. Here was Venice under attack by the Turks, the Christian West under attack by the Islamic East. Here was a War set in Cyprus, at the precise geographic midpoint between Venice and Constantinople, between West and East. True, we saw that the war is quickly decided before it has even begun — God resolves it in favor of the West by sending a providential storm to rout the Turks. But we also saw that although God seems to cast his vote for Venice, the end of the war does not signal the end of the East/West conflict in the play. Rather the conflict is internalized as a domestic dispute within Venice itself.[8]

Galchinsky rehearses familiar scripts, deploying the play's binary oppositions to offer an historical lexicon for the national trauma. The conclusions he draws from the plot about divine favor auger the crusade rhetoric marshaled by Bush, activating the notion of a religious mandate underpinning imperial, political conflicts. As Galchinsky's students moved through the play, however, they observed both Iago's manipulation which fostered the racism and Othering that the text engages in, as well as the historical continuities about "the dehumanizing effects of class hatred and xenophobia; the suspicion of immigrants heightened by war; the difficulty of finding language that can bridge differing ideologies in a multi-ethnic and multi-religious world."[9] Such continuities were necessary in the immediate aftermath of the tragedy and remain strategically pragmatic

8. Michael Galchinsky. "On Poetry and Terror: Shakespeare on September 12." *South Atlantic Review* 66.4 (2001): 141–44, at 142. Galchinsky is a professor of literature and human rights at Georgia State University.
9. Galchinsky, 144.

as pedagogical aids to foster empathy and promote the relevance of the Shakespearean text. However, even as we demonstrate the sedimented historical trajectory of the conflicts animating Shakespeare's play, we run the risk of reifying the differences and conflicts between these cultures. We evacuate historical, cultural, and local particularity and assign meaning to a teleological vision of history and an overarching narrative of "the clash of civilizations."[10]

As pedagogical practice, then, it seems incumbent that we deliberately adopt a critical and ambivalent approach toward such seemingly conciliatory hermeneutics.

Richard Knolles's *The Generall Historie of the Turkes . . . digested into one continual Historie until this present year* 1603, I propose, offers a corrective that exposes both the particular and transcendent qualities of the conflicts motivating much of *Othello* and our own War on Terror. A cursory study of the *Generall Historie* discloses Knolles's ideological investments in representing the Ottoman Empire as a dangerous and threatening enemy. Knolles dedicates his text to King James I of England not only because James is his monarch, but also because of James's antagonistic position toward the Ottoman Empire which manifested in his poem, *Lepanto* (1591), celebrating the Holy League's defeat of Ottoman naval forces at that eastern Mediterranean location.[11] Knolles's "induction unto the Christian reader," further establishes the global threat of the Ottoman Empire, which "is from a small beginning become the greatest terror of the world, and holding in subjection many great and mightie kingdoms in Asia, Europe, and Affricke, is grown to that height of pride, as that it threateneth destruction unto the rest of the kingdoms of the earth;

10. Huntington, Samuel P. "The clash of civilizations?" *Culture and Politics*. Palgrave Macmillan, New York, 2000. 99-118.
11. James' tribute to the Holy League's victory over the Ottoman Empire was memorialized in *His Majesties Lepanto or Heroicall Song*, London: 1603. While the poem was published the same year as Knolles, *Generall Historie*, it was written while he was king of Scotland (1567–1625); Richard Knolles, *The Generall Historie of the Turkes*, London: 1603.

laboring with nothing more than the weight of itself."[12] Knolles catalogues the prodigious grasp of the Ottoman Empire,

> In greatnesse whereof is swallowed up both the name and Empire of the Sarasins [Saracens], the glorious Empire of the Greeks, the renowned kingdoms of Macedonia, Pelepneses, Epirus, Bulgaria, Servia, Bosna, Armenia, Cyprus, Syria, Aegypt, Judea, Tunes, Argiers, Media, Mesopotamia [Iraq], with a great part of Hungarie, as also of the Persian kingdome [Iran], and all those churches, places so much spoken of in holy scripture (the Romanes only excepted;) and in briefe, so much of Christendome as farre exceedeth that which is thereof at this day left.[13]

In his prefatory pages, Knolles frames the greatness and glory of the Ottoman Empire in terms of its successful conquests throughout much of the Mediterranean world, both classical and contemporary. Knolles claims an exception for the Roman Empire which ironically highlights the Ottoman Empire's capacity to fully rival and be successor to that great, classical Eurasian empire. These initial remarks expose anxiety about and fear of cultural and political domination. While James's *Lepanto* rehearsed a pan-European victory over Ottoman forces, Knolles's text, an assemblage of European material into English, conveys the continued real, material danger posed by the Ottoman Empire. Hence, hundreds of pages later we read a passage that echoes the one above, an act of repetition that affirms power of the Ottoman Empire and the anxiety it generates in those who would stand against it:

> It now so proudly trimupheth, as if it should never have end: at the beautie whereof the world woondereth, and the power thereof quaketh: within the greatness whereof are contained no small portions of Asia, Europe, and Africke, but even the most famous and fruitfull kingdoms thereof: no part of the world left untouched

12. Knolles, "To the Reader," no pagination.
13. Knolles, "To the Reader," no pagination.

> but America only; not more fortunate with her rich mines, than in that she is so farre from so great and dangerous an enemy.[14]

Returning, again and again, to what he sees as Ottoman global imperial domination, Knolles registers both fear and admiration. In pointing out the vast swathes of land and people under Ottoman power, he displays his own "imperial envy"[15] and desire, for the fledgling empire of the English can in way compare to the size and glory of the Ottoman.

Knolles's taxonomy of the Ottoman Empire and its greatness nonetheless operates through the polarities of fear, which I have charted above, and desire, to which I now turn. Even as he recounts the global scale of the Ottoman threat, he seems compelled to identify the causes, beyond militarism, that forge Ottoman superiority. That such moments follow swiftly on the heels of his descriptions of Ottoman imperial expansion signal the connection Knolles conceives between the political and military cohesion of the empire. Indeed, immediately after his initial tally of Ottoman territorial control Knolles shifts to "the causes of the Turks greatness," in and of themselves "not depending on the improvident carelessness, weaknesse, discord, or imperfections of others." This qualification is telling: it admits to the inherent of power, control, and superiority of the Ottomans. Chief among the reasons Knolles grants is

> a rare unitie and agreement amonst them, as well in the manner of their religion (if it be so called) as in matters concerning their state (especially in all their enterprises to be taken in hand for the augmenting of their Empire) as that thereof they call themselves Islami, that is to say, men of one mind, or at peace among themselves; so as it is not to be marveled, if thereby they grow strong themselves, and dreadful to others: joyne unto this their courage, conceived by the wonderfull successe of their perpetuall

14. For ease of reading, I've changed all of u/v and i/j to their modern spellings. Knolles, 132.
15. MacLean, Gerald. *Looking East: English Writing and the Ottoman Empire before 1800*. Springer, 2007. (iv).

> fortune, their notable vigilancie in taking advantage of every occasion for the enlarging of their Monarchie, their frugalitie and temperateness in their diet and other manner of living, their straight observing of their ancient militarie discipline, their cheerefull and almost incredible obedience unto their princes and Sultans; such, as in that point no nation in the world was to be worthily compared unto them: all great causes why their empire hath so mightily increased and so long continued.[16]

Ottoman unity in multiple arenas, military discipline, religious cohesion, and political harmony is everything that Europe and England are not at the beginning of the seventeenth century. From Knolles's vantage point as an Englishman, in a nation troubled by political and religious discord, not to mention a military in disarray and colonial enterprises on the brink of failure, Ottoman power and the Ottoman body politic appear remarkably sound and enviable. Rather than an excoriating portrayal of dangerous menace, Knolles's text betrays a desire for the social, cultural, and imperial stability found within the vast borders of the Ottoman Empire. Such stability is further emphasized at the end of every chapter in the *Generall Historie*, where Knolles offers a timeline juxtaposing the reign of the Ottoman sultan who is the subject of the chapter with his European counterparts. Hence, the end of his disquisition on Sultan Süleyman, Knolles lists a chronology of European rulers who were his contemporaries:

16. Knolles, "To the Reader," no pagination.

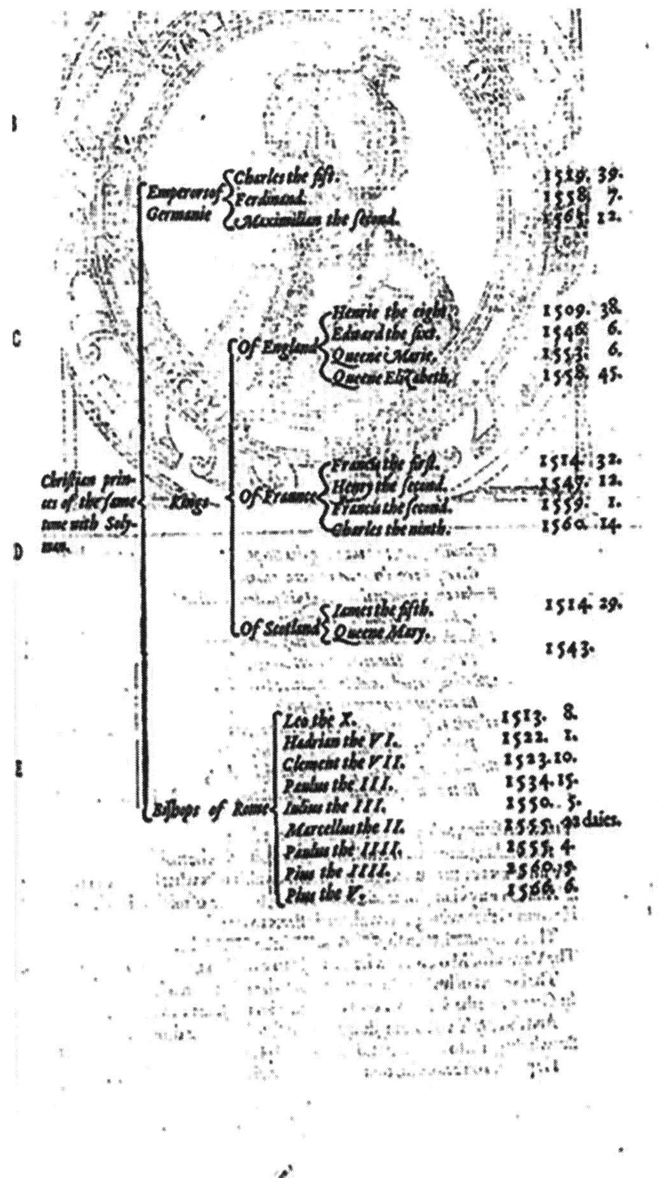

Christian princes of the same time with Solyman.

Emperors of Germanie
- Charles the fift. 1519. 39.
- Ferdinand. 1558. 7.
- Maximilian the second. 1565. 12.

Kings

Of England
- Henrie the eight. 1509. 38.
- Edward the sixt. 1546. 6.
- Queene Marie. 1553. 6.
- Queene Elizabeth. 1558. 45.

Of France
- Francis the first. 1514. 32.
- Henry the second. 1547. 12.
- Francis the second. 1559. 1.
- Charles the ninth. 1560. 14.

Of Scotland
- James the fifth. 1514. 29.
- Queene Mary. 1543.

Bishops of Rome
- Leo the X. 1513. 8.
- Hadrian the VI. 1522. 1.
- Clement the VII. 1523. 10.
- Paulus the III. 1534. 15.
- Iulius the III. 1550. 5.
- Marcellus the II. 1555. 22 daies.
- Paulus the IIII. 1555. 4.
- Pius the IIII. 1560. 5.
- Pius the V. 1566. 6.

Figure 1. Richard Knolles, *Generall Historie* (London, 1603). European rulers during the reign of Sultan Süleyman.

Emperors of Germany		Charles V	1519.	39
		Ferdinand	1558.	7
		Maximillian II	1565.	12
	Of England	Henry VIII	1509.	38
		Edward VI	1546.	6
		Mary	1553.	6
		Elizabeth	1558.	45
	Of France	Francis I	1514.	32
		Henry II	1547.	12
		Francis II	1559.	1
		Charles IX	1560.	14
	Of Scotland	James V	1514.	29
		Mary, Scots	1543.	20
Bishops of Rome		Leo X	1513.	8
		Hadrian VI	1522.	1
		Clement VII	1523.	10
		Paulus III	1534.	15
		Julius III	1550.	5
		Marcellus II	1555.	22 days
		Paulus IV	1555.	4
		Pius IV	1560.	5
		Pius V	1566.	6

Table 1. Transcription of Knolles, p. 825.

What such an accounting discloses is the stability and strength of the Ottoman Empire. Süleyman's long reign, from 1520–1566 survived a succession of European rulers, signaling once more the imperial superiority of the Ottoman Empire. Even as the ideological scaffolding of the *Generall Historie* posits a binary opposition between the realm of Christendom and the dominions of the Ottoman Empire, such moments of desire, admiration, and envy breakdown the tidy divisions Knolles seeks to concretize. Furthermore, as a text engaged with its own particular War on Terror, conceived of in terms of imperial expansion and cultural annihilation, the *Generall Historie* displays an ambivalence that seems to prohibit its recruitment into the kinds of logics that govern our own War on Terror. In other words, the tropes of cultural assimilation and destruction motivating the *Generall Historie*'s antagonistic orientation toward the Ottoman Empire, may strike us a deeply familiar and suggest a linear historical trajectory that yokes the Ottoman Empire to "radical Islamic fundamentalism," or jihadism; however, the text's own polysemy, its desire and admiration for unity, stability, and strength embodied in not only the figure of the sultan but also in its aggressive and successful militarism indicate important points of difference. While I did not advance the notion that Knolles's *Generall Historie* is a pro-Ottoman text, I do hope to complicate neat readings that allow the past to be instrumentalized in order to present the worlds of Islam as monolithic and unchanging.

Like contemporary discourses on the War on Terror, the *Generall Historie* engages in acts of racializing that depend on the barbarism of "the Turk." These moments seem to racialize via the process of estrangement, to make radically foreign in order to imbue a form of racial difference that is otherwise invisible.[17] In the Ottoman context, race becomes less about somatic difference than about ethnicity, culture, and religion. By no means should the elasticity of racial discourses signal that somatic, bodily, and/or epidermalized ideas about race were not in the process of being developed in the period. Rather, this elasticity points to the contingency and availability of race as a discourse to create Others, develop social and cultural hierarchies, and demarcate the boundaries of inclusion within the

17. Previously, I have claimed that early modern English drama often featured Muslims as Moors because that offered a clear way to racialize Islam and locate it in visible difference. See Dadabhoy, "Two Faced," 126–27.

body of the emerging European nation states. The racializing on display in Knolles's depiction of the terror of "the Turk" manifests in cultural practices that locate this subjectivity beyond the bounds of European civilization.

One Ottoman practice that routinely comes under scrutiny in European writing about the empire and is also mobilized by Knolles is that of fratricide, which was the normal mode of Ottoman succession. As Knolles presents it, this battle royale among the sons of the sultan to win the imperial seat emblematizes the cruelty of "the Turk," highlighting the inhumanity of that identity:

> As for the kind of law of nature, what can be thereunto more contrarie, than for the father most unnaturally to embrue his hands in the bloud of his owne children? And the brother to become the bloudie executioner of his owne bretheren? A common matter among the Othoman Emperours. All which most execrable and inhumane murthers they coeur with the pretended safetie of their state, as thereby freed from feare of all aspiring competitors (the greatest torment of the mighttie) and by the preservation of the inegritie of their Empire, which they thereby keepe whole and entire unto themselves, and so deliver it as it were by hand from one to another, in no part dismembered or impaired.

The Ottomans did practice fratricide among the possible heirs of the reigning sultan because they did not adhere to the precepts of primogeniture as was common in European monarchies. The royal Ottoman princes, the *shehzades*, were usually appointed governorships upon their majority, to learn how to become political and military leaders. Upon the demise of the sultan, each *shehzade* would return from his province to claim the throne, often by gaining approval of the jannisary corps and always by murdering any rival.[18] Knolles takes special care here to emphasize the brutality by focusing on the bloody tyranny of this practice: what is par-

18. Caroline Finkel, *Osman's Dream: The History of the Ottoman Empire*. Hachette UK, 2007, 196.

ticularly inhumane is that brother or father should shed the blood of one with whom he shares blood. As the text presents it: fratricide is an utter violation of nature and its command. Thus, the Ottoman imperial dynasty is outside the bounds of nature and natural law, rendered radically Other by their adherence to such lethal customs.

These moments encode the logics of Othering mobilized by Knolles to create radical difference between European norms, mores, and values, and those of the Ottomans. Indeed, Shakespeare deploys a similar strategy at the end of *Henry* IV, *Part* 2, when the newly crowned Hal, now Henry V [1413–1422], imperiously declares: "Brothers, you mix your sadness with some fear. / This is the English, not the Turkish court; / Not Amurath an Amurath succeeds, / But Harry Harry."[19] In signaling the benevolence of his rule, Henry V draws a comparison between the English and the Ottoman court, assuring his brothers of their safety. Nonetheless, in making the comparison, he also signals similitude, claiming that just as the Ottoman throne has successfully passed from father to son for centuries, so, too, have the English achieved dynastic stability. Henry's juxtaposition evokes the Ottomans as imperial models.[20] Shakespeare's ambivalence here mimics Knolles's own orientation toward the Ottoman Empire, for at the close of his lengthy chapter on Sultan Süleyman, Knolles offers a brief description of the sultan that appears ideologically neutral: "he was of stature tall, of feature slender, long necked, his color pale and wan, his nose long and hooked, of nature ambitious and bountiful, more faithful of his word and promise than were most part the Mahometan kings his progenitors; wanting nothing worthy of so great an Empire, but that wherein all happiness is contained, faith in Christ Jesus."[21] His final words about Sultan Süleyman, the Magnificent as he was called in

19. William Shakespeare, *Henry IV Part Two*. Ed. René Weis. New York: Oxford University Press, 1997 (5.2.46–49).
20. Shakespeare might be signaling the reign of Murad III [1575–1595], who was sultan during the reign of Elizabeth I; however, its just as likely that "Amurath," is being used as a generic name for an Ottoman sultan, especially since Murat III was succeeded by Mehmet III [1595–1603]. Barbour, 23; and Robinson, Benedict S. "Harry and Amurath." *Shakespeare Quarterly* 60.4 (2009): 399–424.
21. Knolles, 824.

Europe, exhibit the ambivalence characteristic of this text. His language catalogues the sultan's physical appearance in terms absent of markers of somatic, racial Othering and highlight the nobility of his character. He is admirable in all ways except for one: his religious difference. That religion, then, becomes the vehicle for locating difference. If the *Generall Historie* cannot counter the greatness of the Ottoman Empire, then its rhetorical strategy and ideological investment is in posing this Other, foreign, and alien empire as a terror incompatible with the values and culture of England and Europe, which seem to rest here on religion, on Islam.

Othello's War on Terror

As I conclude my exploration of the affinities, alignments, and ambivalences in the mobilization of War on Terror discourse in our contemporary moment and the early modern period, I would like to return to Shakespeare's *Othello* because the play seems to endorse the ideological projects and investments of both historical moments. On its surface, the play reiterates the binary oppositions that attend to the logics of the War on Terror writ large and that serve as the moral and political high ground from which Europe, Christendom, and/or the United States can launch its offensive or defensive attack on the foreign, encroaching Other. Indeed, the first act of the play with its fierce debate as to that target of Ottoman imperial aggression, whether they sail for Rhodes or Cyprus establishes the Ottoman threat as possible cultural annihilation.[22] Moreover, Othello's "theft" of Desdemona, as her father represents their elopement, is positioned as an extension of "the Turks'" potential siege of Cyprus, linking race to religion and both discourses to the Ottomans in order to establish their alterity.[23] This unnuanced and flat approach facilitates the "clash of civilizations" reading which transforms the Ottomans

22. At the time of the play's composition, both Rhodes (1522) and Cyprus (1573) had been incorporated into the Ottoman Empire.
23. See for example, Brabantio's lines, "So let the Turk of Cyprus us beguile" in response to the Duke advising him that Desdemona's illicit marriage to Othello is not that bad. William Shakespeare. Ed. Kim F. Hall *Othello*. New York: Bedford St. Martin, 2007 (1.3.213).

into outsiders and invaders rather than the dominant imperial power in the eastern Mediterranean. Simply exploring the play through its binaries also lends credence to the notion that that there were unified entities called Christendom and the Islamic world, historical fictions that elide the deep internecine schisms and wars that characterize the early modern formations of both religions. Indeed, this Christian unity rings particularly hollow in the English context, which is emerging from its own religious and political conflict. Finally, the polarities Shakespeare develops further disguise the cultural and political intimacies between Venice and the Ottoman Empire, this alliance so objectionable in European eyes, that Venice was called "the Turk's courtesan."[24] To be sure, Shakespeare's play neglects these distinctions in the only scene that ostensibly takes up the matter of the Ottoman threat.[25]

I close with *Othello*, then, because it demonstrates its own particular brand of War on Terror logics. The play offers one of the few moments in an early modern English / Shakespeare classroom — or in a course tracing the historical development of race from the premodern — where the past and the present neatly align in their political and cultural investments. It remains worth considering how performances of *Othello* that locate the play in the present day — knowingly or unknowingly — reiterate War on Terror logics in production.[26] When the senators deliberate on the target of "Turkish," military aggression, to what extent might Venice's own militarism, as exhibited through costuming and props, the fundamentals of staging, conjure the contemporary War on Terror, yoking the early modern to the modern? The play mobilizes and facilitates these problematic

24. Lucette Valensi. *The Birth of the Despot: Venice and the Sublime Porte*. Cornell University Press, 1993, 20.
25. William Shakespeare. *Othello*, edited by Michael Neill. New York: Oxford World Classics, 2006 (1.3).
26. I would argue that all contemporary productions of *Othello* access the visual semiotics of the War on Terror. See for example Iqbal Khan's *Othello* for the Royal Shakespeare Company in 2015, where the scenes of torture that precede the so-called temptation scene of 3.3 harness the brutality of the "enhanced interrogation" techniques deployed by the CIA on terrorist detainees in Guantanomo, forms of torture that included water boarding.

continuities, making it incumbent on teachers, then, to augment the play with the historical context that illuminates the complexities and contingencies underpinning the seemingly straightforward political and imperial conflict animating the play's early scenes. Using Knolles's *Generall Historie* in our classroom as a parallel text offers a possible antidote, forcing us to interrogate our own reconstructions of the past to suit our present.

Discussion Questions

1. What are the interpretive or analytical benefits of thinking through the ideas that animate our current War on Terror in an early modern context?
2. How does reading historical texts alongside imaginative ones produce knowledge about the ideas that created the forms of power and domination upon with the construction of racial, cultural, and religious differences rely?
3. How do totalizing terms like Christendom and Islamic World contribute to the ways that the premodern past is constructed along racial and religious lines that are always in conflict? Are there other ways beyond these binaries of looking at moments of encounter in the early modern past?

Suggestions for Further Reading

Andrea, Bernadette Diane. *Women and Islam in Early Modern English Literature.* Cambridge: Cambridge University Press, 2007.

Awan, Imran, and Islam Issa. "'Certainly the Muslim is the very devil incarnation': Islamophobia and The Merchant of Venice." *The Muslim World* 108, n.3 (2018): 367–86.

Bayoumi, Moustafa. *This Muslim American Life: Dispatches from the War on Terror.* New York: New York University Press, 2015.

Brummett, Palmira Johnson. *Mapping the Ottomans: Sovereignty, Territory, and Identity in the Early Modern Mediterranean.* Cambridge: Cambridge University Press, 2015.

Butler, Judith. *Frames of War When Is Life Grievable?* London: Verso, 2009.

Dadabhoy, Ambereen. "Two Faced: The Problem of Othello's Visage." *Othello: The State of Play* (2014): 121–48.

Das, Nandini, et al. "Keywords of Identity, Race, and Human Mobility in Early Modern England." (2021): 359.

Erickson, Peter, and Maurice Hunt, eds. *Approaches to Teaching Shakespeare's Othello*. New York: Modern Language Association of America, 2005.

Faroqhi, Suraiya. *Approaching Ottoman History: An Introduction to the Sources*. Cambridge: Cambridge University Press, 1999.

Goffman, Daniel. *The Ottoman Empire and Early Modern Europe*. Cambridge: Cambridge University Press, 2002.

Hall, Kim F. "Beauty and the Beast of Whiteness: Teaching Race and Gender." *Shakespeare Quarterly* 47, no.4 (1996): 461–75.

Kumar, Deepa. *Islamophobia and the Politics of Empire*. Chicago: Haymarket Books, 2012.

Pratt, Mary Louise. *Imperial Eyes: Travel Writing and Transculturation*. 2nd ed. London: Routledge, 2008.

Said, Edward W. *Covering Islam: How the Media and the Experts Determine How We See the Rest of the World*. Rev. ed., 1st Vintage books ed. New York: Vintage Books, 1997.

———. *Orientalism*. 25th anniversary edition. With a new preface by the author. New York: Vintage Books, 1994.

Schülting Sabine, et al. *Early Modern Encounters with the Islamic East: Performing Cultures*. Farnham: Ashgate Pub, 2012.

When They Consider How Their Light Is Spent: Intersectional Race and Disability Studies in the Classroom

AMRITA DHAR

Being the visibly non-white and audibly foreigner-sounding person in the room can have some peculiar advantages, such as being permitted a refusal to consider race as a sort of unspeakable in mixed settings in the US. Thus it was, that faced with the apparent difficulty of talking about race in a class of Black and white and brown young people some years ago, I decided that our collective task could be made more and not less intuitive, more and not less accessible, if we added another ostensibly difficult topic, disability, to our discussion. This is where I went – to two poems that I had recently read side-by-side and could not stop thinking about: John Milton's "When I consider how my light is spent" and Tyehimba Jess's "When I consider how my life is spent." They are sonnets, both, and although written centuries apart, they bear the same name. To study them together is to note, between poets, the workings of influence and defiance, reverence and anger, answer and question, accord and grief. As one student later told me, reading the two poems together is like "seeing the work of poetry in action" – as she explained, registering that poets read poets and write what they read, and in any case, "write life, you know?"

This essay is a reflection and an account of how the compressed power of these sonnets can be used pedagogically to interrogate ideas of physical ability, race, agency, and justice. Led by my experience in the classroom, I offer in this essay, first, that these two superlative poems, when read together, enable intersectional awareness of race and disability. As such, they promote discussion about the profound interlocking between premodern and current conceptions of bodily and intellectual integrity. The side-by-side study of these two poems allows students to link literary production across time and place in a grounded and graspable manner; they make real for students the poetic, creative, and human businesses of influence, imitation, criticism, and departure. Secondly, I make a recommendation in this essay for the study of poetry as a political, socially responsive, and urgent artform.[1] This recommendation is not so much a distinct argument here as an essay-long mood and assertion. I make this assertion as someone who grew up surrounded by poetry in multiple languages, with, first, the conviction that poetry is one of the most important forms of human resistance to oppression and, next, that educators should treat it as such in classrooms. I consider this point especially important to stress now, when undergraduate students in the US often remark on poetry as difficult to read or analyze, while the same resistance is not offered by them, for instance, to novels or short stories or even essays in theory and criticism.[2] Finally and cumulatively, I advance in this essay that a mutually informing conversation between race and disability theories opens up both areas of study in rigorously generative directions. Indeed, I argue that the study of any form of marginalization — which is not "out there" in some abstract elsewhere, but everywhere around us in our racist, sexist, ableist societies — is only enriched by deliberately making space for discussion of how a particular kind of marginalization oper-

1. See, for instance, the former Poet Laureate of the United States, Tracy K. Smith, explain why "Political Poetry Is Hot Again" — and always was, for those in need of language for political thought and action: https://www.nytimes.com/2018/12/10/books/review/political-poetry.html (*The New York Times*, December 10, 2018). See also her "Introduction: This Is Why" in Tracy K. Smith, sel., *American Journal: Fifty Poems for our Time* (Minneapolis: Graywolf Press, in association with the Library of Congress, 2018).
2. In a recent advanced undergraduate seminar that I taught on "Movements, Migrations, and Memories," the syllabus mostly contained readings in prose — including poems, novels, graphic novels, creative non-fiction essays, and critical essays — and my students, all operating at the advanced level, found the material accessible and discussable. It was the poetry that seemed to be, in the words of one student, something to "get it over with" before moving on to more interesting/accessible materials (classroom conversation, February 2020). Other classroom exchanges I have had confirm my sense that students frequently see poetry as something *not* for everyone. The usual manner of putting it, however, is in personal terms: that *they* are "not good at" poetry, or that poetry is not for *them*.

ates in conjunction with other forms of marginalization.[3] The more we as educators connect the dots between the various forms of structural marginalization in operation, the better our students are equipped as citizens of the world we inhabit together. I end the essay with specific pedagogical suggestions and questions for the classroom.

Two Sonnets

Here are the poems. I offer them along with a content warning for violence, police brutality, and grief.

"When I consider how my light is spent"
John Milton
When I consider how my light is spent,
E're half my days, in this dark world and wide
And that one Talent which is death to hide,
Lodg'd with me useless, though my Soul more bent
To serve therewith my Maker, and present
My true account, least he returning chide,
Doth God exact day labour, light deny'd
I fondly ask; but patience to prevent
That murmur, soon replies, God doth not need
Either man's work or his own gifts, who best
Bear his milde yoke, they serve him best, his State
Is Kingly. Thousands at his bidding speed
And post o'er Land and Ocean without rest:
They also serve who only stand and waite.[4]

3. This assertion is directly indebted to Kimberlé Crenshaw's teachings in intersectionality, a critical framework emerging from the theory, practice, and activism of Black feminism. For important recent conversations in this field – conversations led by Crenshaw – see the podcast on *Intersectionality Matters*: https://aapf.org/podcast.
4. Sonnet XVI [19], reproduced from John Milton, *The Complete Works*, Vol. III, *The Shorter Poems*, eds Barbara Kiefer Lewalski and Estelle Haan (Oxford: Oxford University Press, 2012; corrected impression 2014), 245.

"When I consider how my light is spent"
Tyehimba Jess

I squint through the glaucoma of my right eye
to watch the YouTube video of Frankie Taylor,
arrested on a DUI, strapped down in a restraining chair,
beaten unconscious and half blind by the police
of Eastpointe, Michigan. The officer put on his light
blue rubber glove, and in a shout that slowly shrugged
into bureaucratic chant, told Taylor to "stop resisting"
13 times — once for each blow to Frankie's left eye
until it was pummeled into bloody darkness.
We share a darkness, Frankie and I. Turns out his
blinded eye also had glaucoma, an affliction
more common for those of dark American hue —
this is my true account. But my question chides:
Who labors day and night to deny my darkness light?[5]

I presented my content warnings in class. My students stayed, listened, worked with me. We read Milton's poem first — but did not stop to unpack it. Then, we read Jess's poem, for which Milton's poem is made both reason and reason for departure. Again, we did not stop — yet. I mentioned that I wanted to do an in-class collaborative close reading of *both* poems: each poem individually, first, and then we would place them in conversation with each other. I explained that I wanted us to purposefully investigate what "happens" to each poem when we reckon with its centuries-spanning namesake, its other.

Milton scholarship is old and rich, but there is not much discussion in it of Milton's lived blind condition during the writing of some of our landmark poetry in the English language: *Paradise Lost* (1667), *Paradise Regained* (1671), and *Samson Agonistes* (1671).[6] The sonnet I have tran-

5. "When I consider how my light is spent," reproduced from the "Proceedings of the Annual Meeting of the Milton Society of America, 2017."
6. The only clear exceptions in book-length work are Eleanor Gertrude Brown's older work *Milton's Blindness* (New York: Columbia University Press, 1934), and William

scribed, also known as the sonnet "On His Blindness" (a title supplied by later editorial interjection; in Milton's lifetime, it was published as Sonnet "XVI" in his 1673 volume, *Poems*), makes a critical elision of Milton's blind condition impossible, but in a class of non-English-majors and where most if not all of the class was reading this poem for the first time, there arose the question of whether the poet was, in fact, blind. After all, the word "blind" never occurs in the poem.[7] Even if it did, my students and I knew, for we had recently discussed, the easy slippage possible between matter and metaphor when it comes to words such as "light" and "dark," "day" and "night," "seeing" and "blind." Indeed, even outside such ocularcentrism in the day-to-day English we still use, the metaphorical valences of disability — any disability — remain profuse and problematic.[8]

I told my students that the poet was, in fact, blind. I also explained some details of what we know of Milton's life and time: that Milton lived in seventeenth-century England; that he was a practicing poet and polemic; that he went blind as an adult, in his early-to-mid forties, never fully knowing the physiological reasons for his visual loss; that it took him a long time, nearly eight years, to go from initial limited-sighted-ness to total and irreversible absence of sight; that the loss itself, slow but sure, was accompanied by hope, desire, despair, and longing. What follows now is something of the exchange between my students and me. As in any classroom with active and engaged learners, my students asked questions

Poole's recent *Milton and the Making of* Paradise Lost (Cambridge, MA: Harvard University Press, 2017). I am currently writing on Milton's blindness and his poetry for my book on *Milton's Blind Language* (work in progress).

7. Neither do the words "sight" or "eye." The poem is carried by the metaphorical affordances of the juxtaposed "light" and "light deny'd."
8. Society's needs to "explain" disability — the how and the why of it — makes disability especially susceptible to metaphorical uses; however, these metaphors usually work to further remove the actual experiences of disability from discourse. See David Mitchell and Sharon Snyder's *Narrative Prosthesis: Disability and the Dependencies of Discourse* (Ann Arbor: University of Michigan Press, 2001) for pioneering work in this respect.

of me and each other, answered one another, waited for my questions, heard my questions but jumped ahead, and asked their own.[9]

"But the 'God' here is actual God, right?"

"Must be, it also says 'maker' here."

Yes, I answered.

"Is he [Milton] talking to himself about why he is blind?"

Yes, I said – that is a great way to put it.

"Is he asking why God made him blind?"

Is he? – I asked back. Let's read those lines again.

"I feel like he's asking what he's supposed to do now."

"He's blind – is he saying he's 'useless' now?"

Is he saying *he* is useless, or that something "lodg'd" with him is useless? – I interposed.

And so we went, talking through the sonnet's initial build and then the *volta*: "*but* patience / to prevent that murmur" (my emphasis). We noted that a different force, "patience" – was this patience as Patience, personified, or simply the poet's own patience? – was presented as stepping in to resolve for the poet something of his feelings of conflict.

And what does this "patience" say or "reply"? – I asked.

"It stuck out to me too that he says 'replies' – does that mean the poet asked a question? To 'patience' directly?"

"Patience is speaking on God's behalf ... ?"

"Is 'patience' God?"

"No, 'patience' can't be God, 'patience' is saying what God needs."

"Actually, doesn't need."

We thus arrived at the famous final lines of the sonnet, and its very end, with its single-syllable words, only the "only" and "also" even extending into two syllabus: "They also serve who only stand and wait." I pointed out that if we read the line without the only two disyllabic words in it, we should have on our hands an even sparser, more intense, no-arguments-brooked statement: they serve who stand and wait. As I spoke, I found myself, as often in my classroom presence, scanning/stressing as I spoke.

9. My students' comments/questions are in quote marks in the exchanges documented in this essay.

In my own pared construction of this line, the perfect iambic pentameter of the original had converted into an emphatic spondaic trimeter: **they serve/ who stand/ and wait**.

"Ooof!"

Would he like to explain that assessment? — I asked my student, although and perhaps because his reaction made me smile.

"I mean, he wants to be okay with his blindness."

Just as traditional Milton scholarship has not dealt sufficiently with disability, so too has race scholarship, whether in premodern critical race studies or current-day critical race studies, not often contended centrally and explicitly with disability.[10] Yet, disability is a strangely accessible topic — perhaps because, as disability studies scholar Tobin Siebers points out, a disability identity is the one bodily identity that any of us may at any given point, and potentially suddenly, come to inhabit:

> The presence of disability creates a different picture of identity — one less stable than identities associated with gender, race, sexuality, nation, and class — and therefore presenting the opportunity to rethink how human identity works. I know as a white man that I will not wake up in the morning as a black woman, but I could wake up as a quadriplegic, as Mark O'Brien did when he was six

10. The exceptions therefore stand out with particular brilliance. See, for instance, the work of Justin Shaw in premodern critical race studies: "'Rub Him About the Temples': *Othello*, Disability, and the Failures of Care," *Early Theatre* 22.2 (2019): 171–84. See also the volume on *Monstrosity, Disability, and the Posthuman in the Medieval and Early Modern World* edited by Richard Godden and Asa Simon Mittman (New York: Palgrave Macmillan, 2019). In scholarship concerned with more recent literature, see, for instance, Sami Schalk's *Bodyminds Reimagined: (Dis)Ability, Race, and Gender in Black Women's Speculative Fiction* (Durham: Duke University Press, 2018); Therí A Pickens's *Black Madness: Mad Blackness* (Durham: Duke University Press, 2019); C. Riley Snorton's *Black on Both Sides: A Racial History of Trans Identity* (Minneapolis: University of Minnesota Press, 2017); David L. Eng and Shinhee Han's *Racial Melancholia, Racial Dissociation: On the Social and Psychic Lives of Asian Americans* (Durham: Duke University Press, 2019); and Jason Farr's *Novel Bodies: Disability and Sexuality in Eighteenth-Century British Literature* (New Brunswick: Rutgers University Press, 2019). Book-length work at the confluence of premodern disability and race studies is still awaited.

> years old (O'Brien and Kendall 2003). Able-bodiedness is a temporary identity at best, while being human guarantees that all other identities will eventually come into contact with some form of disability identity.[11]

I had earlier brought Siebers's scholarship into this class, in the form of the Introduction to his book *Disability Theory* (2008). In this groundbreaking monograph, Siebers outlines the "ideology of ability," the almost-entirely-unexamined societal assumption that bodies *must* ideally be perfectible and perfected and perfect, present and able and presentable. As Siebers points out, "[d]isability identity stands in uneasy relationship to the ideology of ability, presenting a critical framework that disturbs and critiques it. [...] Disability creates theories of embodiment more complex than the ideology of ability allows."[12] Many days after our class session with Siebers's work, one student wrote to me that the discussion had been important for her because she did not earlier imagine that something as "expected" and "normal" as ability could be so because of an ideology: "Just knowing that ability is an idea is incredible."[13] Even later, another student walked out with me after class ended and said that understanding disability as something that can be invisible and "unavailable to me" (to the student) but nevertheless present ("there") had helped her relationship with a family member.

From Siebers and the "ideology of ability," we turned to Jess's sonnet. As we had done with Milton's poem, we re-read and read aloud this poem. It ended: "Turns out his/ blinded eye also had glaucoma, an affliction/ more common for those of dark American hue –/ this is my true account. But my question chides:/ Who labors day and night to deny my darkness light?" And without fully knowing why, but myself at the mercy of the

11. See Siebers, *Disability Theory* (Ann Arbor: University of Michigan Press, 2008): 5. See also Mark O'Brien and Gillian Kendall, *How I Became a Human Being: A Disabled Man's Quest for Independence* (Madison: University of Wisconsin Press, 2003).
12. See Siebers, *Disability Theory*, 9.
13. My student's assessment proves correct Siebers's claim that ideology doesn't allow its critiques to be registered. "Ideology does not permit the thought of contradiction necessary to question it" (*Disability Theory*, 8).

momentum of the poem, its true account, and its ask for accountability, I departed from what I had written in my lesson plan ("Work through Jess's poem line by line in a close reading") and asked the class: so, who labours day and night to deny this darkness light? Again, I caught myself stressing the words as though I was scanning the poem's last line: **who la/**bours **day/ and night/** to de/**ny this/ dark**ness/ **light**?[14]

What ensued was a discussion on racism, police brutality, and state-sanctioned violent disabling of individuals from marginalized communities. In brief, this was one of the most generative discussions of race *or* disability that I have known. Today, as I recall the swiftness with which the conversation got under way, I assert that it is precisely the fact of race and disability being on our table together that enabled the class to tackle them both, and to tackle them with political consciousness and critical capaciousness.

Scholars of disability studies on both sides of the Atlantic – the post-civil-rights US and temporally aligned UK were early leaders in this field – now concede that the interdisciplinary field of disability studies as pursued in the global North has been overwhelmingly and even dangerously white and bourgeois.[15] Thus, it was striking to me that of all the confer-

14. In another class, we had just looked at the opening of *Paradise Lost*, and debated between "**till/ one great/**er **man**" and "till/ **one great/**er **man**" (Book 1, l. 4). Of course, in Jess's poem it is "my darkness," not "this darkness" – with the "my" setting off a brilliant internal rhyme with the following "deny." But "this" served to ask my question.
15. For important checks, balances, correctives, and turns away from white-centric experience and scholarship and, sometimes, away also from the colonising global North, see the direction-setting work of, among others, Chris Bell, "Introducing White Disability Studies: A Modest Proposal," *The Disability Studies Reader*, ed. Lennard Davis, 2nd ed. (New York: Routledge, 2006): 275–82; Jasbir Puar, *The Right to Maim: Debility, Capacity, Disability* (Durham: Duke University Press, 2017); Julie Avril Minich, *Accessible Citizenships: Disability, Nation, and the Cultural Politics of Greater Mexico* (Philadelphia: Temple University Press, 2014) and "Enabling Whom?" *Lateral* 5.1 (2016), https://doi.org/10.25158/L5.1.9; Nirmala Erevelles, *Disability and Difference in Global Contexts: Enabling a Transformative Body Politic* (New York: Palgrave, 2011) and "Race," *Keywords for Disability Studies*, eds. Rachel Adams, Benjamin Reiss, and David Serlin (New York: New York University Press, 2015), https://keywords.nyupress.org/disability-studies/essay/race/; Subini Ancy Annamma, David Connor, and Beth Ferri, "Dis/ability critical

ences and seminars I had so far attended, it was in this undergraduate classroom composed mainly of individuals *not* otherwise trained in disability studies that we addressed the intersections of disability, race, systemic and targeted violence, and disablement carried out in the name of the law.

If few students in this general education class had earlier read extensively in Milton, even fewer seemed to have heard of or read Jess. Yet, Jess did not need as much of an introduction as Milton had, for the contemporaneity of his work made it easier for the students to know just where the poet was coming from. No student asked who Jess was, or where he was writing from; I later volunteered the information that Jess was a US author who in 2017 received the Pulitzer Prize for Poetry. For the duration of our discussion, Jess was simply a poet who had written for us in our time — and there he remained. It was his poem that had our attention.

Who la/bours **day/ and night/** to de/**ny this/ dark**ness/ **light**? Sometimes my students answered my questions directly, sometimes indirectly.

"This is not disability in the same way [as in the previous poem] at all."

Why not? — I asked.

"It's violent."

It was this simplicity and accuracy in my student's statement that allowed me to mention something fundamental also about race-making: that it's violent — because the point of it is to establish hierarchy. Medieval studies scholar Geraldine Heng's definition of race-making as a practice of strategic essentialism in order to create hierarchy is crucially pertinent here.[16] This commonality of *process* is where race intersects most pow-

race studies (DisCrit): theorizing at the intersections of race and dis/ability," *Race Ethnicity and Education* 16:1 (2013): 1–31, https://doi.org/10.1080/13613324.2012.730511; Karen Nakamura, *Deaf in Japan: Signing and the Politics of Identity* (Ithaca: Cornell University Press, 2006) and *A Disability of the Soul: An Ethnography of Schizophrenia and Mental Illness in Contemporary Japan* (Ithaca: Cornell University Press, 2013); and Sona Hill Kazemi, "Whose Disability (Studies)? Defetishizing Disablement of the Iranian Survivors of the Iran-Iraq War by (Re)Telling their Resilient Narratives of Survival," *Canadian Journal of Disability Studies* 8.4 (2019): 195–227.

16. See *The Invention of Race in the European Middle Ages* (Cambridge: Cambridge University Press, 2018), especially "Beginnings," 1–14, for an excellent overview of the Euro-

erfully with disability; in disability-making, too, is involved a practice of strategic essentialism, and a strategic *exclusion* on the basis of that essentialism — and the point of the exercise is to establish or reinforce hierarchy and a withholding of access.

But why was I suddenly talking not so much about race as race-*making*, and not so much about disability as disability-*making*?

Because neither race nor disability was born in the void; neither dropped from the sky. We must think about race because race-making has already happened, because race-*ism* is real; we must think about disability because disability-making has already taken place, because able-*ism* is real. Only, the processes of race-making and disability-making are very good at not *seeming* as such, very good at disappearing into mainstream history or circumstance or "norm" or "culture" or "tradition" or "just how things are." In other words, infrastructural race-making or racism is hardly ever put under scrutiny when we study history or policy or science or technology or business, or even art or fantasy or poetry. It is only the demands for inclusion and equity — when they happen, *if* they happen — that are marked. And whenever these demands for inclusion and equity are marked, they are perceived as political. When occasionally achieved, those demands for inclusion are even hailed as "milestones" — as the abolition of slavery is, or the achievement of the women's vote in the US. But the fact that the exclusion was itself political, deliberate, clear in its priorities of establishing or maintaining hierarchy, escapes notice in most teachings of history, policy, science, technology, and art. But no exclusion is ever inadvertent; an individual or a system *always* plans it. Race-making is real.

In disability studies, we have a slightly better handle on things: we know that impairment does not equal disability. It is when a social system *makes* of an impairment — such as blindness, or a missing limb, or a chronic illness — a lack and a problem and a restriction to access and participation

pean dedication to race-making and the development of a racialized view of the world. Relatedly: for a clear enumeration of the stakes of race-making in the US, see Ibram X. Kendi's phenomenal *Stamped from the Beginning: The Definitive History of Racist Ideas in America* (New York: Nation Books, 2016).

that it becomes a disability. Thus, we notice disability in the making; we register the process of disability-making. But in this field, too, the paucity of layered political dialogue, and the absence of activist and scholarly voices from non-white communities, means that we don't come anywhere near contending with the multitudinous horrifying intersections at which disability-making takes place. These are not horrors to turn away from — again, they did not materialize out of the ether; human-engineered systems of hierarchy and exclusion created these horrors. Rather, they are matters that we must pay attention to. A Dalit man who attends a wedding feast in Uttarakhand and eats in the presence of upper-caste guests is ritually humiliated and evicted, then ambushed after leaving the gathering; next morning, his mother finds him half-dead outside their house; nine days later, the man dies.[17] It is a civilising example to other Dalits to not get above their positions. A woman who has brought inadequate dowry to her newly-married-into household in Bangladesh, and whose family comes short of making the full "gift" to the in-laws after the wedding, has acid thrown on her face.[18] It is consequence for her party's failing an evolving agreement. An eighteen-month-old baby girl in Kashmir is shot at with a pellet gun and blinded in one eye by the Indian armed forces when she, in her mother's arms, tries to escape tear gas, also deployed by the army, the keepers of the peace.[19] It is retribution for the toddler's keeping the wrong religion, the wrong geography, and the wrong company. A man of dark American hue is strapped to a chair and punched in the face, an eye, repeatedly, by a keeper of the law in the US. It is reprimand, according to the keeper of the law — whose own hue is not in question because he is simply a keeper of the law who is lawfully sorting matters out after

17. See Vineet Khare, "The Indian Dalit man killed for eating in front of upper-caste men," *BBC News*, 20 May 2019, https://www.bbc.com/news/world-asia-india-48265387.
18. See Eric Nee, "Survivor of an Acid Attack," *Stanford Social Innovation Review* (Summer 2014), https://ssir.org/articles/entry/survivor_of_an_acid_attack, https://doi.org/10.48558/v0s4-ng62.
19. See Malik Sajad, "An 18-Month-Old Victim in a Very Old Fight," *The New York Times*, 19 January 19, 2019, https://www.nytimes.com/2019/01/19/opinion/sunday/kashmir-conflict.html.

the arrest of a man for Driving Under the Influence – for resisting while restrained.

It is only when we are willing and able to note these workings of multiple marginalizations, often decisively abetted by the state, that we can discuss together the parallel mechanisms of race-*making* and disability-*making*, and similarly note how one route of discrimination facilitates another.

The Work of Racism, the Work of Ableism

"'Who labors day and night to deny my darkness light?' I mean, he's right, this police officer is doing a lot to make this darkness happen!"

Yes, he is, I said. It is worth noting this. Racism is a matter of its own labour: deliberate racist labour. Jess's poem allows us to see an example of the work that a racist must put in in order to commit racist actions.[20] Racism takes work: racist work. And I want us to remember that ignorance (the "I did not know"), which is often invoked as an "unwitting" reason for racist actions, is also fostered through a particular kind of labour. That is to say: if there is a lot of evidence on a particular issue, and we still deny that evidence, or steer ourselves and our communities away from that evidence, then our ignorance is a result of careful cultivation and dedicated labour. One has to be committed to one's ignorance in order to preserve it in the face of overwhelming evidence. Therefore, the cultivation of ignorance is also racist work. It is one thing to actually not know – and this is *not* a common state for anyone paying attention – but it is another to go out of one's way to not know, or to claim that one does not know.

After a brief silence: "But what do you do if you really did not know?"

20. Looking over the sheer work that goes into racism, scholar David Sterling Brown poignantly writes: "Yet harmed, too, in the process of executing anti-Black racism is the white self, which leads me to wonder: Do white people understand how their irrational fear of and disdain for Black people actually manifests as a form of self-hate and, perhaps more damagingly, self-harm?" See his "'Don't Hurt Yourself': (Anti)Racism and White Self-Harm" in the *Los Angeles Review of Books*, 6 July 2021, https://lareviewofbooks.org/article/antiracism-in-the-contemporary-university/#_ftn2.

That is a good question. My answer is: you apologize, step back, and do your homework. As long as you are not defending or cultivating your ignorance, you're all right. Do your homework.

Some more silence.

Let me give you an example from my part of the world, I said. Where I come from, which is supposed to be postcolonial — India gained political independence from the British in 1947 — we talk often of something called decolonization. You can probably guess what it means: it is an effort to shed the vestiges of colonialism. The thing is, we talk about decolonization *knowing* that every single person has to put in the work every single day. There is no achieved state with decolonization. The work of decolonization is never "done." That's okay. We are not free of the colonial.[21] When something is part of the air for centuries, it cannot just go away one day because there has been a transfer of political power. In fact, it may never fully go away, because the roots of our state systems and our mindscape are so deeply plugged into the colonial. So, actual decolonization is a never-ending process. It is a matter of doing one's learning, or *un*-learning, every day. It is the same with antiracism.

Yet another silence, and then: "I don't want to offend anyone, you know."

That is a good thing to want to do: not offend. However, I should tell you that it is not possible to *never* give offence. Like with any other learning, one is liable to make mistakes. The point is to learn from the mistakes, and move on, and not give up on the work of learning. It is also important to know that calling people out — unless there was deliberate and

21. Those with privilege in India like to claim that we are truly in a postcolonial moment. My analogy for them is that they are like the self-professed "colour-blind" of the US who "don't see race" because they don't have to see race. Many upper-caste Indians like to claim that we are "past all that with caste" and that "caste does not matter anymore" in India. To this, I ask: In whose India? For a comparable study focused on the United States, see also Isabel Wilkerson's *Caste: The Origins of Our Discontents* (New York: Random House, 2020). Wilkerson's appropriation of the term "caste" for race relations in the most imperial current-day entity of the global North is problematic, and yet she is right to assert that the word "racism" fails to denote or account for the systematic oppression that Black people continue to face in the United States, and to therefore reach for another term, a different vocabulary.

wilfull wrongdoing, of course – is usually not personal. Calling people out in a manner of calling people in is a matter of extending the conversation and helping our collective learning.[22] If anyone calls you out on something because they have been offended, apologize, learn the lesson, and move on. They simply want you to know better.

"Did this author know of Milton's poem?"

What do you think?

"Yes."

"Yes, I mean, it's even the same title."

"And it's about blindness. He knows."

"And it's fourteen lines, like the other one."

Yes, it's a sonnet. This might sound like a digression, since we haven't spoken today about metrical units – but stay with me. Do you know what "stanza" means?

"Like in a poem?"

Yes.

"It's used in poems."

"It's a kind of verse ... ?"

Yes, a stanza is a unit of verse. And yes, the word refers to the basic metrical unit of a poem. A poem can have several stanzas in it. In a sonnet, which is fourteen lines, there's technically only one stanza. The poem is a stanza. But what does the word "stanza" literally mean?

My students waited for me to continue.

In Italian – the language from which the sonnet form entered other languages – the word *stanza* means "room." Another US poet, Phyllis Levin, has this lovely formulation about the sonnet. A sonnet, Levin says, is a room forever "haunted by the presence of its former occupants."[23] Levin

22. I am indebted to Laura Seymour for pointing out to me the similarities between a compassionate and thoughtful "calling out" and "calling in".
23. "It may help to conceptualize the sonnet as a room (or stage) that can be divided in a number of different ways to serve many functions. Since its overall dimensions and circumference do not change, whatever occurs within that space will always be determined to some degree by its size and haunted by the presence of its former occupants. Even if we rearrange, replace, or remove some of the furniture, the marks will still be there to remind us of how things were positioned in the past." See the Introduction in

is referring to the fact that the sonnet is one of the most widely known verse forms in the world, and a form which enjoys a distinction as one that writers flex poetic muscles in. It is a form that exacts poetic discipline, a form that authors have returned to over generations, either for stand-alone creations/poems or for "cycles"/groups of poems following a particular theme or story. Notable sonnet cycles in English go all the way back to early modern authors such as playwright and poet William Shakespeare, and Catholic-turned-Anglican preacher and metaphysical poet John Donne.[24] In recent times, the US writer Marilyn Hacker has used a sonnet cycle to great effect in the telling of a twentieth-century lesbian love story, and US author Terrance Hayes writing in the post-Trump-election moment has documented in seventy sonnets of the same name a resonant narrative of risk, recursive history, and Black belonging.[25] What I'm getting at is: the choice of the sonnet form is never by chance – it is a form that is difficult to pull off well, and a form that comes with a lot of baggage, because it has centuries of history. The choice of the sonnet form is by intention.

"So he [Jess] has definitely read the Milton poem!"

Yes, I said, he has. And Jess wants us to know that he has.[26] Why is this important?

"Milton is a biggie, isn't he? Like, a famous poet?"

Phyllis Levin, ed., *The Penguin Book of the Sonnet: 500 Years of a Classic Tradition in English* (London: Penguin, 2001): xxxviii.

24. Shakespeare's *Sonnets* was first printed as a sequence in 1609; Donne's series of "Holy Sonnets" was published posthumously in his 1633 *Poems*.
25. See Hacker's *Love, Death, and the Changing of the Seasons* (New York: W. W. Norton) and Hayes's *American Sonnets for My Past and Future Assassin* (New York: Penguin, 2018).
26. When next I teach these poems, I shall mention that Jess has possibly also read his Richard Wilbur, who, in turn, has read his Milton. See Wilbur's 1967 poem "A Miltonic Sonnet for Mr. Johnson on His Refusal of Peter Hurd's Official Portrait" in his *Collected Poems, 1943–2004* (Orlando: Harcourt, 2004): 221. Wilbur knows that Milton used the sonnet for public commentary. Wilbur uses it to write for the President of his country: "Wait, Sir, and see how time will render you/ Who talk of vision but are weak of sight" (ll. 11–12). It is notable that Wilbur, too, uses the words "vision" and "sight" for their metaphorical valences.

I agree. Milton's status as one of the pre-eminent poets in the English language means that Jess's ability to "do" Milton is itself a statement of Jess's poetic ambition. And Milton is already one of the most ambitious poets that ever lived. Jess's signaling that he wants to share space with Milton is a means of his laying claim to a specific poetic tradition.

What else could we say about Jess's having read his Milton?

"He's using his poem to talk to the other one."

Exactly — and what is the conversation? What similarities and differences can we mark?

"This one is not about his [the author's] blindness, he's telling us about another person, Frankie Taylor."

"And this one is not about *going* blind, and as [another student] said, this one is about a different kind of blindness. It's violent."

Yes, and yes. This is worth underlining, for one of Jess's achievements in this poem is precisely this elucidation of how disability and race intersect. For understanding this poem, and by extension, understanding the world in which the person named in this poem, Frankie Taylor, lives, we cannot consider Taylor's disability — a violently inflicted disability — and race as *unrelated* from one another. As such, this poem provides a cue for readers to think of other situations where specific marginalized identities forcefully intersect with other marginalized identities. Thus, this poem trains us to develop an intersectional awareness of marginalization — namely, that any form of marginalization can be used to *further* endanger and hurt.

I wanted to make another point about the disability-making as we see it in horrible "action" in this poem. The use of state-sanctioned — indeed, state-invented and state-finessed — violence in order to impair and disable a state's citizens is not new. Some citizens/members of any given state are always more "equal" than other citizens/members, depending on status, financial reach, politics, background, religion, ethnicity, and various realities of difference and dis/empowerment. Jess's poem's narration and witnessing of state violence, even as Jess consciously picks up a poem by Milton and talks back to that seventeenth-century sonnet, should remind us of the early modern (in the West, the fifteenth, sixteenth, and seventeenth centuries) practice of punitive disabling carried out by the state. State punishments such as blinding, and the cutting off of ears, hands, nose, or tongue, were a reality for the England that Shakespeare lived in and that Milton, in the generation following Shakespeare's, inherited. Executions were still publicly performed, capital punishment still meted out through horrific body- and mind-breaking means. The police officer abusing Frankie Taylor has history behind him. In disability studies today, we have mostly forgotten that state-imparted or state-endorsed disability, mutilation, and sometimes, breaking-until-death have been time-honoured means of keeping a population under obedience, bringing a people to heel, and generating terror and personal censorship. In the overwhelming majority of disability studies discussions of the twenty-first century, we consider congenital disabilities (the "born that way" discourse) and sudden-onset disabilities (the "this can happen to a person peacefully living their life and minding their own business" discourse) in our search for structural reform – when we search for structural reform at all. We tend to forget that just as the means of racism have changed but racism itself thrives in our unequal world, so too have many means of disabling changed but disabling policies and practices continue to determine our lives today.[27] Even when scholars such as Jasbir Puar, for example, lay clear the lines of continuity between state-sanctioned methods of disabling, maiming, and debilitating, indeed, even when she does this work with hemispherical expansiveness and rigorous precision, we still largely ignore the everyday ramifications of this violence in our individualistic, capitalist society.

But on the point of the connections between violence, the state, and what can be made to count as legal, let me bring you back to the poem, back to both poems, to think about justice and accountability. Let us also look at form. Where is the *volta*, the turn, in Jess's poem?

There was some counting, underlining, writing.

27. This is related to why countries like the US are so eager to jump into wars. Wars produce terrible bodily and cognitive disabilities, but since there is no significant and ongoing pressure to truly and fully take measure of this cost of war, wars remain easy for the US to declare and enter. Of course, wars are also made easy by the country's collective investment in them. In 2022, the US military budget is over $740 billion. See https://www.defense.gov/cj/.

"Turns out his/ blinded eye also had glaucoma ... "

It was now my turn to be silent for a moment.

Yes, that is absolutely a turn, I finally said, although I had thus far not quite noticed it as such in my own readings. That is where the poem turns from a narration of incident to a narration of background and a narration of context and a narration of lived history. Thank you. And good work with the looking, for it makes sense to search for the turn close to the point where the sonnet's octet meets the sestet. Talking about which, what happens at the precise point where the octet meets the sestet?

"A 'bloody darkness'!"

"And in the next line, it says, 'We share a darkness, Frankie and I.' He [Jess] uses the word 'darkness' to talk about the blindness but also race."

"He also brings up glaucoma again."

"He says it's more common among African-Americans."

"I did not know that."

"And this [glaucoma] is something he [Jess] has in common with Frankie Taylor."

"This [glaucoma] is *another* thing that they have in common."

Yes, and yes. And there is yet another turn. Can you find it? Jess even uses the same word to set off that turn as Milton used in his poem: "but." As in Milton's poem, there is only one "but" in Jess's poem.

"This is my true account. *But* my questions chides ... "

"Oh, Milton uses 'chide,' too! – but it's God [who chides] in that poem."

Well spotted. And look at the contradiction Jess sets up: between a "true account" and his own question, "my question," that "chides." Why should a true account be followed by a chiding?

"Because this is not a blindness to be okay with."

"Could we say that Jess is calling Milton out, in a way?"

Classrooms: The History of Ideas

My class ended, as classes sometimes do, somewhat abruptly. I barely had time to pull various threads together and say out loud my emphasis on intersectional thinking, and to thank my students. But, as often, my students left the room talking to one another about the material we had just been through. I made my own notes that evening.

I want to teach these poems again, for there are further threads to explicitly discuss, depending on the purpose of the class.

In a class on ideas, history, and ideology, we should talk about, for instance:

> What is the difference between conceptions of divine and human justice?
>
> What is a true account?
>
> Where is the line between what is legal and what is ethical?
>
> What is justice?
>
> What does it mean for a blind person to wait for justice? (And which blind person are we talking about? The moment we phrase it like that – about a blind person waiting for justice – are we implicitly defaulting to whiteness for personhood?)
>
> What does it mean for a Black person – specifically, a Black person of the twenty-first century US – to wait for justice? And how long are they supposed to wait?
>
> What does it mean for a Black person to present their true account, when their truth has been historically denied in the making of a nation?
>
> What do we understand by history? What have we been taught in our schools, and who wrote the "true" accounts we have grown up reading? Whose truth did we read? Whose truth did we unwittingly, or wittingly, turn away from, erase?

Classrooms: Theory

A class on theory is another excellent venue for discussion of these poems; it is through texts that theory comes alive. In this sort of class, I should scaffold a discussion of Milton's and Jess's poems with, or position the poetry to directly precede, readings in critical race theory and disability theory. Accessible introductions to the topics of critical race studies and disability studies have existed for two decades.[28] As I have indicated, these poems taken together facilitate not only a discussion of critical race theory and disability theory, they also encourage a propulsive intersectionality animating that critical acquaintance.

Further: bringing these two poems into a class focused on theory makes it possible for students to register what we lose – or deliberately exclude – when we generate and use theory along a single analytical lens or selected analytical lenses at the expense of others. I contend that all the four critical lenses – of gender, race, sexuality, and disability – that currently lend themselves most emphatically to activist and institutional energies in our world, do so for good reason, and that they must be supported as areas of further growth in the academy and the social sphere. Gender, race, sexuality, and disability are matters of what is profoundly owned or disowned *in the body*; they are therefore matters of what can be viscerally targeted in instances of discrimination and by oppressive structures. They underpin or exacerbate a host of other relatively more mobile but often no less crucial markers of inclusion or exclusion, such as age, social class, religious orientation, cultural background, medical history, post/partum status, financial standing, im/migration, un/documentation, and un/imprisonment record. As teachers, it is our job not only to make sure that our students develop awareness of all four key critical lenses for considering the world and its complex and interlocking texts, but also to facilitate students' recognition of how these critical lenses talk to each other and to other brackets of segregation, belonging, and omission. There is no greater collective intellectual skill that we can impart today than one which teaches our students to work together toward a just future.

28. See Richard Delgado and Jean Stefancic, eds, *Critical Race Theory: An Introduction* (New York: New York University Press), of which the first edition was published in 2001. This book is currently in its third edition, published in 2017. The first edition of the *Disability Studies Reader*, edited by Lennard Davis, (New York: Routledge) was published in 1997. This book is currently in its fifth edition, published in 2016.

The following are some questions to bring into a class on theory and criticism:

> What is race?
>
> What does it mean to think of race in terms of language?
>
> What is disability?
>
> What does it mean to think of disability in terms of language?
>
> What makes an individual "raced"?
>
> What is the opposite of "raced"?
>
> What makes an individual "disabled"?
>
> What is the opposite of "disabled"?
>
> What relationships exist between race-making and disability-making?
>
> What are the other intersections – other than disability – that we can note with race in these poems?
>
> What are the other intersections – other than race – that we can note with disability in these poems?

Classrooms: Poetry

Milton's and Jess's poems are, of course, powerfully at home in a class on poetry. Here are some questions for that class:

> How do sentences work in the poems? (Milton's sonnet only has two sentences. Jess's poem has five. How do the sentences function as units of thought?)

How does rhyme work in Milton's poem? What is the rhyme scheme? What does an examination of the prosody of the poem open up about its meaning?

How does rhyme work in Jess's poem? What does an examination of the prosody of the poem open up about its meaning? Is there a rhyme scheme? Does it make sense to think in terms of a rhyme scheme when most of the rhyme is internal to lines and run-ons? (How many internal rhymes can you find? How many assonances can you find?)

What is the architecture of the two poems? How is thought/content distributed across units such as the octet and the sestet?

How do lines end, pause, or run on in the poems? How does that set the pace of the poems?

Jess's poem is a brilliant exposition of how run-on lines can be used for doubling sense and images – one image/sense activated where the line breaks, and another activated as the sentence "resumes" in the next line. Can you find these doubled images and multiplied meanings? (For instance, where "The officer put on his light/ blue rubber glove," the word "light" works as a possible noun until the end of that first line, but the run-on converts the word into an adjective. The image changes as we read, deepening the poetic "land"-scape and the scope of the story. For the "shout that slowly shrugged/ into bureaucratic chant," how is the violent indifference of "shrugged" converted into violent action in the next line?) Is there anything comparable to this pulled-forth intensity in Milton's poem? (Note, too, that Milton is a complete master of enjambment in his defining 1667 epic poem *Paradise Lost*. Is Jess again "doing" Milton, in a way, when he uses enjambment to such powerful effect in *his* poem?)

In both Milton's and Jess's poems, the word "light" is used precisely twice. But no two uses of the word are toward exactly the same meaning. What meanings are they, and what are the material and metaphorical affordances of each "light"?

Similarly, can we analyse the word "dark"? Both poems only use that word once. (Note: Jess's poem also takes on "darkness" itself.)

How can we analyse "labour"/"labor"?

In both Milton's and Jess's poems, how do the poets deploy readerly/listenerly expectation? Are there specific ideas/words/phrases that the poem teaches us to expect? (For instance, how does Milton's assertion of being at "half my days," or half his lifespan, at the moment of writing this poem run up against the invocation to death? In Jess's poem, how does his assertion that "We share a darkness, Frankie and I" pick up and deflect readers' anticipation of mentions of race and ocular difference? Given Jess's use of his poem to talk back to Milton's poem, and in our world's context of racist police brutality and murder, could Jess's use of "darkness" allow a reader *not* to think of death?)

Literary criticism has many forms, and poetry is one of them. How does Jess's poem function as literary criticism of Milton's poem? What happens to Milton's poem, now that Jess has written a poem of the same name?

Similarly, what happens to Jess's poem when we read it with Milton's poem? In the wake of Jess's poem, how is Milton's poem reanimated for the twenty-first century? (And how would Milton's poem read if a student read it *after* reading Jess's poem? Could we chronologically foreground the "after"-poem and lead "back" to the earlier one?)

Social criticism and political protest have many forms, and poetry is one of them. Milton and Jess both know this. Milton's 1673 *Poems* contained the explicitly political Sonnets 11: "A Book was writ of late call'd Tetrachordon," 12: "I did but prompt the age to quit their cloggs," and 18, "On the Late Massacher in Piemont": "Avenge O Lord thy slaughter'd Saints." His uncollected poems include Sonnets 15: "Fairfax, whose name in armes through Europe rings" and 16: "Cromwell, our cheif of men." Jess's collections *Leadbelly* (2005) and *Olio* (2016) both contain poems exploring Black US identities at the intersections of music, orality/aurality, slavery, history, blindness, melancholy, and anger. The "Blind Boone" poems in *Olio* are particularly compelling in this respect. How can we read the two poems at hand in the context of Milton's and Jess's oeuvres of poetry as politics and protest?

What other current-day poets can we place Milton and Jess as sonneteers in conversation with? (For a recent example, there is outstanding work by Jericho Brown: "The Tradition," "The Water Lilies," and the genre-expanding "Duplex" poems in his 2019 collection, *The Tradition*. Like Jess, Brown received the Pulitzer Prize for Poetry. And there is, as I have already mentioned, the diamond-hard precision of Terrance Hayes's *American Sonnets*. Every poem in that collection has the same name: "American Sonnet for My Past and Future Assassin" – but the assassins are as wide-ranging as the history that produced them. See particularly the poems beginning "The black poet would love to say," "But there never was a black male hysteria," "Probably twilight makes blackness dangerous," and "Probably all our encounters are existential.")

What other current-day poets can we place Milton and Jess as protest poets in conversation with? (We live in a time of great poetic richness in the US. For recent examples of superb poetry of protest and witnessing, we have work by Tracy K. Smith, Ilya Kaminsky, Javier Zamora, Natalie Diaz, Joy Harjo, N. Scott Moma-

> day, Layli Long Soldier, and Danez Smith, to name only some contemporary practitioners.)[29]
>
> From Jess's example, we may understand that contemporary and Black scholars and makers of poetry read their Milton and their early modern poetry. Correspondingly, do we have examples of early modern scholars of poetry reading their Black and contemporary poets, and writing about them?[30] What examples can we name of authors and scholars of poetry examining influence and belonging across centuries — for instance, as Miller Oberman does when he translates/transcreates from Old English poetry into contemporary English?[31]

"But are students ready for these discussions?" "Will they understand?" These are not hypothetical questions; I have been asked them by white and able-bodied colleagues and administrators who themselves felt unready, uncomfortable, or both. I answer those questions in the affirmative, by example of everything I have mentioned of my classes. But in general terms, too, I say yes; our students are ready and *expect* to enter the conversation.

29. For only the most recent collections in this embarrassment of riches, see Smith's *Wade in the Water* (Minneapolis: Graywolf Press, 2018); Kaminsky's *Deaf Republic* (Minneapolis: Graywolf Press, 2019); Zamora's *Unaccompanied* (Port Townsend: Copper Canyon Press, 2017); Diaz's *Postcolonial Love Poem* (Minneapolis: Graywolf Press, 2020); Harjo's *An American Sunrise* (New York: W. W. Norton, 2019); Momaday's *The Death of Sitting Bear* (New York: HarperCollins, 2020); Long Soldier's *Whereas* (Minneapolis: Graywolf Press, 2017); and Smith's *Don't Call Us Dead* (Minneapolis: Graywolf Press, 2017).
30. I don't know that there are many. But scholars of early modern poetry *should* read their contemporary poets, and particularly their contemporary BIPOC poets, and write about them. As scholars of early modern poetry, we are scholars of poetry. This is our work.
31. See Oberman's collection *The Unstill Ones* (Princeton: Princeton University Press, 2017).

Teaching Race in Renaissance Italy

ANNA WAINWRIGHT

How do we, as students and teachers of the Italian Renaissance, talk about race? What *was* race in Renaissance Italy, and how does it relate to race in the United States today? Most students who enter the classroom on the first day of a course on the Italian Renaissance will not be anticipating any discussion of race. When I first ask students in my survey course on medieval and Renaissance Italian culture what they think when they hear the term "Renaissance," they tend to offer up answers that demonstrate just how ingrained the collective — and selective — understanding of the period is. They talk about rebirth; an opposition with the "Dark Ages"; beautiful art; the "Renaissance man." Images that students select in a first assignment to represent what they think of the era reveal a fairly uniform visual perspective of the Italian Renaissance. Two of the most frequently chosen images are Da Vinci's Vitruvian man (see figure 1) and Botticelli's *The Birth of Venus* (see figure 2). Both images, which present idealized human forms, male and female respectively, reinforce a visual vocabulary of the period that centers whiteness and the able-bodied, and suggests homogeneity as ideal. It is a visual paradigm that has been steadily bolstered in the intervening 500 years, intertwined with the myth of the Renaissance "individual" imposed on us by historian Jacob Burckhardt a century and a half ago, which persists in the popular imagination despite having been dismantled by scholars of the period in the intervening years.[1]

1. Jacob Burckhardt published what would become the ur-text of Renaissance Studies, his influential *Die Cultur der Renaissance in Italien* in 1860, translated as *The Civilization of the Renaissance in Italy* in 1878. On the evolution on Italian Renaissance historiography from Burckhardt on, see especially Virginia Cox, *A Short History of the Italian Renaissance*, (I.B. Tauris, 2015); John Jeffries Martin, "The Renaissance: Between Myth and History," in *The Renaissance: Italy and Abroad*, ed. John Jeffries Martin (Routledge, 2003), 1–24.

This is certainly how the Italian Renaissance continues to be presented in many an American college classroom. Students often come away from such with a cast of characters that is only slightly expanded from that with which they arrived — an assortment of old, dead white men (and perhaps a few women) who reinforce their notion that the past has nothing to do with them. (This is, of course, in the United States; in most Italian classrooms, the women don't generally make an appearance either.) This discrepancy has only become more pronounced as the student body in American higher education, along with the general U.S. population, has changed. As literary critics Kimberly Ann Coles, Kim F. Hall and Ayanna Thompson observe in their manifesto "BlacKKKShakespearean: A Call to Action for Medieval and Early Modern Studies," "Future students, the pool from which we must recruit our majors, look less and less like the cohort of previous generations for whom our current degrees were constructed."[2] What is more, as Coles, Hall, and Thompson make clear, it is both "practical and ethical" to make race visible in the early modern classroom, as "the occlusion of race as an object of study in our research and in our classrooms aids white nationalist narratives." This call to teachers of English literature is just as meaningful for instructors of Italian Studies, both in the United States and in Italy. Why is it important, after all, that students learn what happened in sixteenth-century Florence if it doesn't connect in some way to their own lives, their own experiences, and the world in which they live today? I say this not to dismiss learning about the past "for its own sake" out of hand but to underline the disconnect students often feel with the way history is presented to them — and to suggest that the Italian Renaissance has more to do with their present than they have been led to believe, including the way race is weaponized in Italy today, and even in the United States.

Race as a concept and part of Renaissance life, however, has not been a central conversation in scholarship on Italy. This has made it difficult

2. Coles, Kimberly Anne, Kim F. Hall and Ayanna Thompson, "BlacKKKShakespearean: A Call to Action for Medieval and Early Modern Studies," MLA Profession, Fall 2019. https://profession.mla.org/blackkkshakespearean-a-call-to-action-for-medieval-and-early-modern-studies/.

for instructors to know where to start if they *do* want to bring the subject of race to the classroom. But the primary sources are brimming with racialized references: Petrarch extolled a white beauty, Dante condemned Mohammed to Hell, and Ariosto and Tasso both marshaled crusading themes and deified the violent expeditions of Christopher Columbus in their respective epics (and Tasso borrowed from the *Aethiopica* to create his heroine Clorinda, a white woman born to Black Ethiopian royalty). Racialized narratives around non-Italians, especially Muslims, Jews, and Black Africans, as well as the violent oppression of ethnic and religious minorities throughout the city-states, influenced this cultural production, and are important parts of Italian Renaissance history. Enslaved Black Africans were being bought and sold across the peninsula by the fifteenth century. Isabella d'Este (1474–1539), the "First Lady of the Renaissance," was asking her favorite buyer to find her a young girl "as Black as possible."[3] The Venetian Ghetto was established to confine Jews in 1516, with Rome following suit in 1555.[4] By the end of the sixteenth century, the Jesuits forbade Jewish and Muslim converts (and their children) to Catholicism from entering the order.[5] As scholar Nancy Bisaha and others have shown, the concept of "Europe" itself developed from Italian humanists like Enea Silvio Piccolomini (1404–1464, the future Pope Pius II), who set Christian Europeans in opposition to the Ottoman "Turks" and other Muslims. "The Turkish race," Piccolomini wrote in his 1458 treatise *Europea*, "is Scythian and uncivilized"; Christian Europeans therefore had to be united against them. (Indeed, this call for Christian, European unity against the "Muslim menace" continued on in treatises and political ora-

3. Paul Kaplan, "Isabella d'Este and black African women," in *Black Africans in Renaissance Europe*, edited by T.F. Earle and K.J.P Lowe (Cambridge University Press, 2005), 125–154, esp. 134.
4. On the Venetian ghetto see Dana E. Katz, *The Jewish Ghetto and the Visual Imagination of Early Modern Venice*, (Cambridge University Press, 2017); on the Roman ghetto, Kenneth R. Stow, *Theater of Acculturation: The Roman Ghetto in the Sixteenth Century*, (University of Washington Press, 2015).
5. Peter A. Mazur, *Conversion to Catholicism in Early Modern Italy*, (Routledge, 2019), 19.

tions throughout the sixteenth century.)[6] This wealth of evidence, however, has not led to much scholarly discussion of a broader pattern of racial formation present in early modern Italy, nor does it tend to be what students think of when they think of "Renaissance Italy."[7]

Yet models for this kind of work exist in adjacent fields. For the last three decades, scholars in English literature have argued the case for race as a central strain of identity formation in the Renaissance.[8] Instructors and students now have a rich world of scholarly literature with which to engage critically on race with William Shakespeare, with John Milton, and with Aphra Behn, among other sixteenth- and seventeenth-century English authors, as other essays in this collection demonstrate. Indeed, it is worth noting that some of the most straightforward engagement of the presence of race in early modern Italian literature has come not from Italianists, but from scholars who have pioneered the study of race in English literature. Kim F. Hall's two groundbreaking studies of white beauty in English Petrarchism (1996 and 2003) — in which she argues that lyric poetry's codification of a particular brand of white beauty is intrinsically linked to white supremacy — remain perhaps the most useful interventions into whiteness in Petrarch's lyric itself.[9] Dennis Britton has recently observed that many of the racial anxieties and ambiguities evident in

6. Nancy Bisaha, *Europe* (c. 1400–1458) (Catholic University of America Press, 2020), 30. On the continuation of this rhetoric in the Italian context, see Wainwright, Anna Wainwright, "A Simple Virgin Speaks: Authorial Identity and Perusasion in Isabella Cervoni's Oration to Pope Clement VIII" *The Italianist*, 37, no. 1 (2017): 1–19.
7. The scholar Deborah Parker has spoken to the lack of diversity amongst scholars of Italian Studies, and the importance of change in the field. See her June 2018 article in Inside Higher Ed, https://www.insidehighered.com/views/2018/06/21/paucity-asians-and-other-minorities-teaching-and-studying-italian-and-other-foreign.
8. Cf. the editors' introduction to the volume, especially footnote ix. On the importance of early modern **critical** race studies, see especially Margo Hendricks' keynote at the Folger/Race B4 Race conference on Race and Periodization in September 2019, https://www.folger.edu/institute/scholarly-programs/race-periodization/margo-hendricks.
9. Kim F. Hall, "'These bastard signs of fair': Literary Whiteness in Shakespeare's Sonnets" in *Post-Colonial Shakespeares*, edited by Ania Loomba and Martin Orkin (Routledge, 2003), 65.

Shakespeare's *Othello* were already present in the Italian novella on which it is based, Cinthio's *Un capitano moro*. Othello, Britton argues, is one of Shakespeare's most "Italian" plays, *including* in its attention to race: "it is set in Italy, it draws from Italian sources, it employs an Italian mode of dramatic composition, and it attempts to translate to its English audience Italian notions of race."[10] That *Othello* — perhaps the Renaissance play most famous for the centrality of race to its plot — originates in an Italian novella is not much discussed in Italian Studies.[11] And yet *Un capitano moro* is not an aberration; Italian literature is filled with stories in which racial difference plays a starring role, as I discuss below.

One way to change the disconnect between the evidence and the popular perception of the Italian Renaissance is to start talking about race in the classroom, introducing students to the ways in which the period and the study of it have been complicit in how race works in our world today. The essays on Renaissance Italy in this collection offer a way into teaching race in the Italian context in art history, literature, and music. They should help instructors present the Italian Renaissance in ways that open up the past to new generations of students — not by anachronistically shoehorning in considerations of race, but by expanding and updating our syllabi to include the myriad ways in which race was present and in formation during the Italian Renaissance. As my co-editor Matthieu Chapman and I state in the introduction to this volume, we are always teaching race in the classroom, whether we do so intentionally or not. By not speaking out loud with our students about race, we are reinforcing "walls of whiteness"

10. Dennis Austin Britton, "*Contaminatio*, Race, and Pity in *Othello*" in *Rethinking Shakespeare Source Study*, edited by Dennis Austin Britton and Melissa Walter (Routledge, 2018), 46.
11. One important push in early modern critical race studies is to push beyond *Othello* as Shakespeare's "race play" *par excellence*. David Sterling Brown has recently argued for a broader consideration of race in Shakespeare, especially around whiteness, and has coin the term "The Other Race Plays." David Sterling Brown, "White Hands: Gesturing Toward Shakespeare's *Other* 'Race Plays,'" Shakespeare Association of America 2019 Plenary, "Looking Forward: New Directions in Early Modern Race Studies."

around white students, and excluding BIPOC students from a history that is theirs, too.[12]

This volume comes at a time when numerous fields are rethinking their complicity in racism and white supremacy, including Classics and Medieval Studies.[13] Scholars of the Italian Renaissance, too, must acknowledge the field's role in the history of white supremacy in the academy, as well as in American higher education. There is a through line from the Roman Empire to Mussolini's fascism, to today's white supremacy in America and Europe, and it runs right through the Italian Renaissance. We cannot uncritically present Italian humanism's belief in their rightful inheritance of the classical past, for example, without acknowledging how that belief has been weaponized; nor can we consider texts by Dante, Ariosto, and Tasso without considering their role in the long history of Orientalism.

The pieces on Italy in this volume identify ways in which instructors might use Italian Renaissance materials to talk about race in the early modern world and today, and I would suggest that many chapters outside the borders of the Italian section of this volume would also be excellent

12. Brunsma, Brown and Placier argue that "white students enter historically white colleges and universities (HWCUs) surrounded by invisible walls that protect them from attacks on white supremacy," and that these protective walls are generally reinforced through their education. David L. Brunsma, Eric S. Brown, and Peggy Placier, "Teaching Race at Historically White Colleges and Universities: Identifying and Dismantling the Walls of Whiteness," *Critical Sociology*, 39, no. 5 (2012): 717–38. These "walls of whiteness" are becoming ever more visible, however, as state legislatures across the United States pass laws banning discussions of racism and white supremacy in the classroom, as we discuss in the introduction to this volume.
13. On the debate in Classics see especially Dan-el Padilla Peralta, "Espistemide: the Roman Case," in *Classica: Revista Brasiliera de Estudos Classicos*, 33, no. 2 (2020): 151–86, and Patrice D. Rankine, "The Classics, Race, and Community-Engaged or Public Scholarship" in *American Journal of Philology*, 140, no. 2 (2019); on medievalism see the debate over the term "Anglo-Saxon" and its role in white supremacist discourse, especially Mary Rambaran-Olm, "Misnaming the Medieval: Rejecting 'Anglo-Saxon' Studies," November 4, 2019, https://www.historyworkshop.org.uk/misnaming-the-medieval-rejecting-anglo-saxon-studies/.

guides for lectures and activities in an Italian Renaissance classroom.[14] What I would like to add here are a few reasons why one might incorporate discussions of race into a standing Medieval and Renaissance syllabus – whether literature, history, or art history – and why, in many ways, this is just as important as or more so than developing a whole class on race in the Italian Renaissance. One reason is that, as many who write on teaching race in general have observed, race is a subject that almost always makes some students uncomfortable. Many American students, especially white students, have been taught that acknowledging race aloud is rude, awkward, or wrong. Moreover, white students have also been implicitly taught that race has nothing to do with them.[15] While more and more colleges and universities are instituting diversity requirements, many students will not voluntarily take a class with race in the title. In the college curriculum, race tends to be something that is only expected to be addressed in certain classes, in certain disciplines, by certain professors, for certain students. This structural inequity forces yet more labor onto scholars of color, and reinforces the notion that "race" is something only people of color have to think about, study, or teach. It is unfair to limit the heavy lifting on antiracist pedagogy to a few courses and professors, and doing so contributes to the further siloing of discussions of race. Intentionally including race in a class on the Italian Renaissance not only gives students a clearer picture of the past, but also fights against the compartmentalization of race in American higher education.

Dennis Looney, author of *Freedom Readers: The African American Reception of Dante Alighieri and the "Divine Comedy,"* observed at a panel at the Renaissance Society of America in 2018 that, in diversifying syllabi, instructors must be attentive to tokenism. It is not enough to devote one class period, or even one week, of the semester to issues of race in a class

14. I would suggest especially Ambereen Dadabhoy's piece on *Othello* and the present-day War on Terror; Roya Biggie's essay on mapmaking with students; and Amrita Dhar's discussion of the intersection of race and disability; and Anna Klosowska's chapter on French imitations of Marino's *La bella schiava*.
15. On this, see Karen Elias and Judith C. Jones, "Two Voices from the Front Lines: A Conversation about Race in the Classroom," in *Race in the College Classroom*, edited by Bonnie TuSmith and Maureen T. Reddy (Rutgers University Press, 2002), 8.

(or to gender or class, for that matter); indeed, this tends to reinforce the idea for students that race is an issue that does not have to do with other aspects of study. (On a practical note, what happens if a student just happens to miss *that* class?) Rather, race should be integrated into a syllabus so that it is always present and up for discussion — since, as critical race scholars have amply shown, it is always already present.

For instructors committed to the idea that race is evident in Italian canonical texts and can only enrich classroom discussion, the next important question, then, is how we might define race in the Italian Renaissance with our students. Fortunately, there are ample and important resources for considering race in the early modern period, and they can be applied to the Italian context with judicious attention to context. As indicated above, I take as my basis the foundational work done in early modern English critical race studies by scholars such as Britton, Chapman, Hall, and Margo Hendricks, among many others, who have shown through their incisive and insightful scholarship how race existed and developed in Renaissance England.[16] Particularly productive for considering what we mean by "race" in the early modern period is Ian Smith's grounding definition as "the product of several, often interrelated, categories of identification, a complex amalgam of codes that can be mobilized to ratify group exclusion and marginalization."[17] This "complex amalgam of codes" in the Italian context included skin color, geography, lineage (both literary and familial), and religion. It can also be productive to think critically with students about whiteness in the early modern period. One of my students recently observed that the whiteness of one's skin seems to switch from a desirable attribute only for women to one desirable for all. "Textur[ing] the flat surface of whiteness" as Sujata Iyengar describes it, also helps

16. For a comprehensive list of early modern critical race scholarship, see editors' introduction to this volume, footnote ix.

17. Ian Smith, *Race and Rhetoric in the Renaissance: Barbarian Errors* (Palgrave Macmillan, 2010), 3.

students understand why the history of race in the Italian Renaissance is essential even for a mostly (or entirely) white classroom.[18]

In addition to the essays in this collection that offer ways into thinking about race through the Italian Renaissance painter Titian, through the novellas of Giambattista Basile, the poetry of Giambattista Marino and his French imitators, and through Florentine music history, what might be some ways to integrate the discourse on race into an existing syllabus? In a module on Dante, we can talk about the violence against Mohammed and Ali in the *Inferno* through Edward W. Said's keen analysis in *Orientalism*, and also learn how Black American authors engaged with Dante through selections from Dennis Looney's *Freedom Readers*.[19] Petrarch's lyric can be read through the lens of "lyric whiteness," with help from Hall's work, as can any discussion of depictions of white women in Italian Renaissance art, from the Virgin Mary to Botticelli's Judith and her maidservant. When we teach Ariosto and Tasso, we should make the connection to Columbus and the way in which he was used to bolster an imaginary Italian imperial legitimacy in the sixteenth century and compare that to how he was used to confirm the whiteness of Italian Americans in the nineteenth and twentieth centuries.[20] Indeed, it is worth pausing here (and in the classroom) to consider Columbus, and the role his representation in early modern as well as contemporary culture might play in a class on the Renaissance. The way the Italian Renaissance has been filtered and weaponized in American history comes into particularly sharp relief when it comes to the Italian sailor, who was born in Genoa in 1451, just two years before the Fall of Constantinople to the Ottomans. While he is often taught more as an avatar for Spanish imperialism than

18. Sujata Iyengar, "Strangeness: Early Modern European Women and the Invention of Whiteness" in *Early Modern Literary Studies*, 2020, 2.
19. Said memorably points out that the Orientalizing impulse, which we think of as predominantly a phenomenon of the nineteenth and twentieth centuries, began much earlier, and points to Dante as an early perpetrator. Edward Said, *Orientalism* (Vintage, 1978), 68.
20. On Columbus in Tasso, see especially Jane Tylus, "Reasoning Away Colonialism: Tasso and the Production of the *Gerusalemme liberata*" *South Central Review* 10, no. 2 (1993): 100–114.

Italian identity in the American high school classroom, this was not the case in sixteenth- and seventeenth-century Italy, nor has it been the case for the Italian American community over the course of the last century.[21] This knowledge adds depth and context to the conversations students hear on more left-leaning campuses every October over the urgency for a shift from Columbus Day to Indigenous People's Day, and offers more information to students on campuses that celebrate the holiday unquestioningly. Columbus Day itself might be a product of nineteenth-century racialized anxieties in the US, but Columbus has long been fertile ground for aggrandizing Italy's place in imperial history, from Tasso's paean to him in Canto 16 of *Gerusalemme liberata* to lesser-known epics of the seventeenth century, in which Columbus is not only praised for his "discovery" of the New World, but was written into the story of the 1492 Fall of Granada, which ended Muslim rule on the Iberian peninsula — an event for which he most certainly was not present.[22] His "heroism" is thus reinforced through violence against two racialized groups: an Italian "conquered" the indigenous people of the Americas and also fought against the "Moors" — and won.

The major epics of the period can provide a way to think through early modern Islamophobia at the height of Italian anxieties over the Ottoman Empire, as well as the intersection of early modern understandings of race vis-à-vis skin color. I think, for instance, of Bernardo Pulci's *Morgante* (1483), whose title character, a Muslim giant, is not allowed to become a Christian knight because of his "reo destino" (wretched destiny) and

21. As has been much discussed in the last few years, the myth of Columbus as the Italian "founding father" of America emerged in the late nineteenth century, and helped to recast Italian Americans, who faced discrimination and violence across the United States, into white Americans. Brent Staples and others have compellingly argued that the lionization of Columbus over the last century and a half has served not only to make Italian Americans white, but to reinforce antiblack racism. See especially Brent Staples, "How Italians Became 'White,' *The New York Times*, October 12, 2019.
22. Nathalie Hester, "Columbus Conquers the Moors" in *The New World in Early Modern Italy*, eds. Elizabeth Horodowich and Lia Markey (Cambridge, 2017), 270–87.

who does not survive his own poem.[23] Another example is Clorinda in Tasso's *Jerusalem Delivered* (1581), born, like her classical prototype Chariclea from Heliodorus' *Aethiopica*, white to Black parents. Italian texts that do not make their way into the college classroom as much as they might (including Cinthio's *Il capitano moro* and Basile's *Pentamerone*, which Suzanne Magnanini addresses in her insightful essay in this collection) can be centralized in new ways. In a unit on early modern women, the role that elite women played in racist practices in early modern Italy can be explored through the letters of Isabella d'Este, which detail her aforementioned purchase of Black African slaves.[24]

These possibilities work not only to center race in the Italian Renaissance classroom, but also to question and destabilize the primacy of the Italian canon, which still tends to sit, unquestioned, at the center of most Italian literature classes. Ayanna Thompson advocates for studying and teaching Shakespeare through authors who have engaged with his plays from across the world, through different perspectives, and in different historical moments; Noémie Ndiaye argues for understanding how race works in his plays by considering the broader context of capitalism-driven racial formation in the Global Renaissance.[25] How might our students' experiences be enriched by reading Dante, Petrarch, and Machiavelli — and our own understanding of the canon destabilized — by putting them into dialogue with other texts from other national traditions in the early modern world, but also with texts across time, by Salman Rushdie, by Toni Morrison, by Frantz Fanon? Our task should be to move toward teaching race in the Italian Renaissance in an intentional, antiracist way, one that allows students to think critically about the contemporary world as they learn about the past.

23. See Anna Wainwright, "Tied Up in Chains of Adamant": Recovering Race in Tasso's ArmidaBefore, and After, Acrasia," *Spenser Studies* 35, (2021): 181–211.
24. *Isabella d'Este: Selected Letters*, edited and translated by Deanna Shemek (ACMRS, 2017).
25. Ayanna Thompson, *Passing Strange: Shakespeare, Race, and Contemporary America* (Oxford University Press, 2011); Noémie Ndiaye, "Shakespeare, Race, and Globalization: Titus Andronicus," in *The Cambridge Companion to Shakespeare and Race* (Cambridge University Press, 2021), 158–174.

Suggestions for Further Reading

Britton, Dennis Austin. "*Contaminatio*, Race, and Pity in *Othello*." In *Rethinking Shakespeare Source Study*, edited by Dennis Austin Britton and Melissa Walter. New York: Routledge, 2018.

Elias, Karen, and Judith C. Jones. "Two Voices from the Front Lines: A Conversation about Race in the Classroom." In *Race in the College Classroom*, edited by Bonnie TuSmith and Maureen T. Reddy. New Brunswick, N.J.: Rutgers University Press, 2002.

Hester, Nathalie. "Columbus Conquers the Moors." In *The New World in Early Modern Italy*, 1492–1750, edited by Elizabeth Horodowich and Lia Markey, 270–87. Cambridge: Cambridge University Press, 2017.

Kaplan, Paul. "Isabella d'Este and black African Women." In *Black Africans in Renaissance Europe*, edited by T.F. Earle and K.J.P Lowe, 125–54. Cambridge: Cambridge University Press, 2005.

Ndiaye, Noémie. "Shakespeare, Race, and Globalization: Titus Andronicus." In *The Cambridge Companion to Shakespeare and Race*, 158–174. Cambridge: Cambridge University Press, 2021.

Staples, Brent. "How Italians Became 'White'." *The New York Times*, October 12, 2019.

Tylus, Jane. "Reasoning Away Colonialism: Tasso and the Production of the *Gerusalemme liberate*." *South Central Review* 10, no. 2 (1993): 100–114.

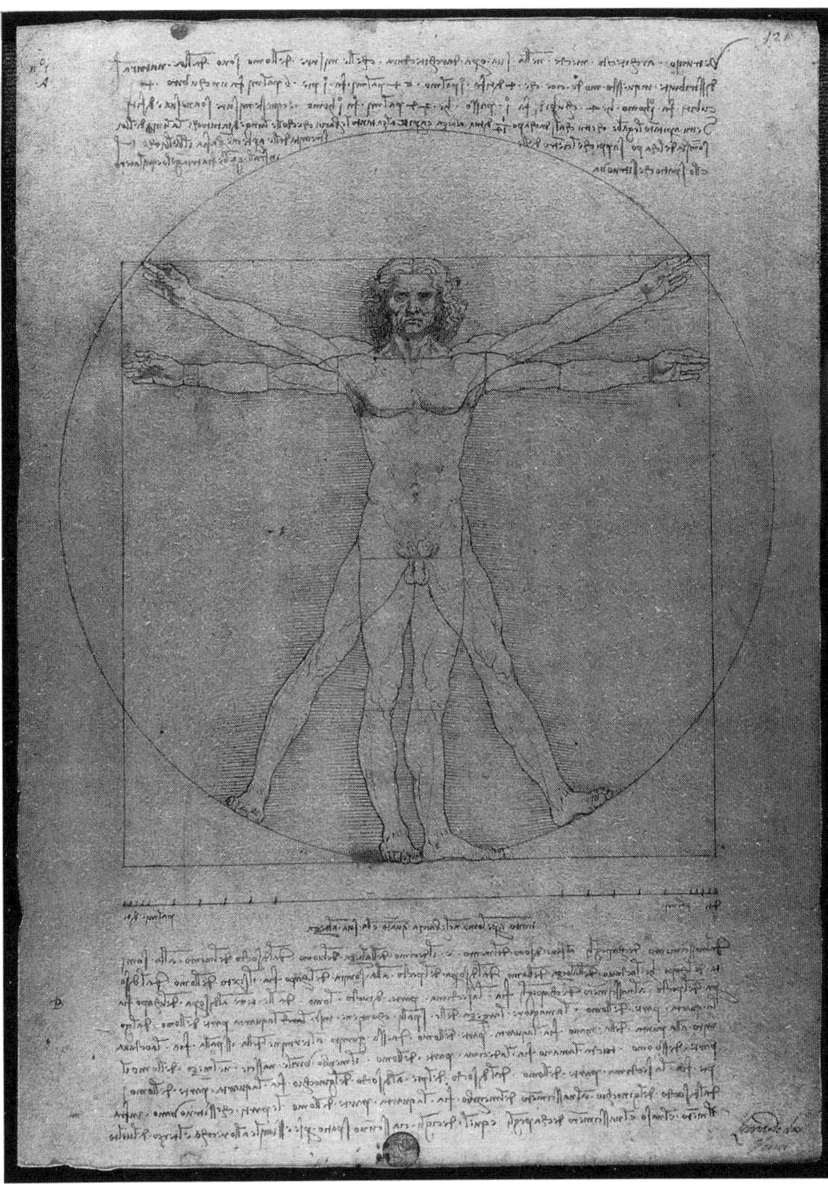

Figure 1. Leonardo Da Vinci, *L'uomo vitruviano* (*Vitruvian Man*), c. 1490. Photo by Luc Viatour, in public domain.

Figure 2. Sandro Botticelli — La nascita di Venere (The Birth of Venus) — c. 1485, Uffizi Galleries, Florence, Italy. Google Art Project

Ogres and Slaves: Representations of Race in Giambattista Basile's Fairy Tales

SUZANNE MAGNANINI

Written in Neapolitan dialect and titled *Lo cunto de li cunti overo lo trattenemiento de' peccerille* [*The Tale of Tales or Entertainment for Little Ones*] (1643–1636), Giambattista Basile's collection of fifty fairy tales opens with the extradiegetic narrator whose voice begins and concludes the overarching or frame tale by stating:

> A seasoned proverb of ancient coinage says that those who look for what they should not find what they would not, and it's clear that when the monkey tried putting on boots it got its foot stuck, just like what happened to a ragged slave girl who although she had never worn shoes on her feet wanted to wear a crown on her head. But since the millstone grinds out the chaff and sooner or later everything is paid for, she who deceitfully took from others what was theirs ended up caught in the circle of heels, and however steep her climb up was, her tumble down was even greater. It happened in the manner that follows.[1]

The overarching (frame) tale that follows this introductory paragraph does not, however, begin with a direct recounting of the enslaved Black woman's rise and fall. Instead, her storyline is subsumed by and subordinated to the adventures of the white princess for whom the slave functions as an antagonist, an obstacle to be overcome. Immediately after this

1. Giambattista Basile, *The Tale of Tales, or Entertainment for Little Ones*, ed. and trans. Nancy L. Canepa, foreword by Jack Zipes, illustrations by Carmelo Lettere (New York: Penguin Books, 2016), 3. For a Neapolitan-Italian bilingual version see Giambattista Basile, *Lo cunto de li cunti overo lo trattenemiento de' peccerille*, ed. and trans. Michele Rak (Milan, Garzanti, 1987).

introduction that momentarily foregrounds the slave, the narrator begins to tell the story of princess Zoza.

Once upon a time, in the kingdom of Valle Pelosa [Hairy Valley], there was a melancholy princess named Zoza. Despite her father's best efforts to cheer her with dancing dogs, jugglers, and singers, Zoza never cracks a smile. One day, an old woman and a court page fight viciously in front of an oil-spouting fountain that the king had constructed in the hope of amusing his sad daughter. After they both let loose an avalanche of curses, the frustrated hag flashes the lad by raising her skirts to reveal a "scena voscareccia" [woodsy scene].[2] Zoza's laughter at this ribald exchange provokes the old woman's wrath and she curses the princess to marry Prince Tadeo who lies as if dead in far off Campo Retunno [Round Field]. To wake him, Zoza must cry a pitcher full of tears. After a long journey during which each of three fairies gives Zoza a nut containing an enchanted automaton, she arrives in Round Field and begins to cry, but before her tears have reached the rim, she falls asleep exhausted. In that moment, a Black slave named Lucia seizes the pitcher, finishes the task, and marries the prince. Undaunted, Zoza will use the automatons to gain Tadeo's favor and enchant now pregnant Lucia with a craving to hear stories. Speaking in a patois, Lucia threatens to punch her belly and abort the child she is carrying if her desire for stories is not satisfied: "If people no come and with tales my ears fill, me punch belly and little Georgie kill."[3] Fearing for his heir, Prince Tadeo chooses ten old women from his kingdom and commands them to "content yourselves for these four or five days before she empties her belly to each tell one tale a day of the sort that old women usually entertain the little ones with."[4] Thus, the Black character's story serves as a negative exemplum, an example of pride punished. What will be her violent demise — still pregnant, she'll be buried alive — is necessary to facilitate the white princess's happy ending. Although many a fairy tale character has risen from an impoverished beginning to wear a crown on their head, Basile denies Lucia this sort of permanent transformation.

2. Basile, *The Tale of Tales*, 5.
3. Basile, *The Tale of Tales*, 10.
4. Basile, *The Tale of Tales*, 11.

The Tale of Tales is a seminal text of both the European fairy tale tradition and the Italian literary canon. Subtitled the *Pentamerone* for its structural resemblance to Boccaccio's *Decameron*, the collection includes some of the earliest printed versions of well-known tale types, including Cinderella, Puss in Boots, and Sleeping Beauty. The Italian philosopher, historian and literary critic Benedetto Croce (1866–1952) considered *The Tale of Tales* to be an essential text of the Italian literary canon and one of the most beautiful books of the Italian Baroque.[5] The Brothers Grimm considered Basile's collection to be a foundational text of European folklore and they created German adaptations of a number of his tales.[6] Today, Basile's fairy tales are positioned at the origins of the European literary fairy tale tradition in academic anthologies widely used in undergraduate classrooms.[7]

How might we use Basile's tales to teach literary representations of race in Renaissance Italy? How might a literary genre grounded in "long ago" and "far away" fantasies allow us to examine the complex social historical realities of race and slavery in the early modern Mediterranean? How do gender and genre shape representations of race? For students whose knowledge of the fairy tale is based primarily on the animated films of Walt Disney — *Cinderella*, *Sleeping Beauty*, *Snow White*, *Beauty and the Beast*, and so on — the fairy tale might seem an unlikely object of study to answer these questions. But Basile's tales will prove a fertile field of inquiry. In this essay, I will show how to use Basile's fairy tales to teach our students a number of lessons, including how dominant paradigms in our fields might discourage discussions of race; how identity was intersectional in the early modern period as it is today, with gender and race affecting whether a character achieves a happy ending; and how a pluri-

5. Benedetto Croce, ed. and trans., *Il Pentamerone* by Giambattista Basile, (Bari, Laterza, 1982), xl.
6. For an English translation of the Brothers Grimm's adaptations of Basile's tales see Armando Maggi, *Preserving the Spell: Basile's 'The Tale of Tales' and Its Afterlife in the Fairy Tale Tradition* (Chicago: University of Chicago Press, 2015), 287–346.
7. See for example, Jack Zipes, *The Great Fairy Tale Tradition: From Straparola and Basile to the Brothers Grimm* (New York: Norton, 2000).

vocal text with its many narrators and tales might simultaneously possess an openness to the imagined difference of fantastic characters (ogres) and a racist attitude toward characters whose identity is grounded in historical reality (slaves).

In her study "Visible Lives: Black Gondoliers and Other Black Africans in Renaissance Venice," the historian Kate Lowe concludes by making a "basic methodological point above all else: that views are formed on the basis of sources consulted, and in order to get a view in the round, it is necessary to work across a great many sources."[8] In illuminating the lives of Black freedmen in Venice, Lowe combines the analysis of historical documents (notarial and crime records, wills) with visual evidence (paintings by Carpaccio and Bellini, period prints). This same research methodology informs the design of a series of assignments and class discussions in which Basile's fairy tales provide a fuller view of the representation of race in early modern Italy, while the work of historians and art historians enrich our understanding of Basile's text. Employing an interdisciplinary approach to the text at hand has the added benefit for scholars of Italian literature to recognize and to question why our field lags behind others, such as history and other national literatures like English and Spanish, in exploring representations of race. Taking a cue from the Baroque penchant for multiple perspectives, I triangulate topics and tales as the class examines representations of Black female slaves, Black and/or Muslim male slaves,[9] and fantastic others such as ogres and ogresses.

8. Kate Lowe, "Visible Lives: Black Gondoliers and Other Black Africans in Renaissance Venice," *Renaissance Quarterly* 66, no. 2 (Summer 2013): 452.

9. All the female slaves in *The Tale of Tales* are described as either Black or dark-skinned, while there is more variety in the description of male slaves. In Basile's "The Golden Trunk," which I discuss later, a handsome man reveals to the heroine that he is actually a white prince cursed to live as a Black slave, albeit a handsome one, by day and becomes white at night. In "The Padlock," a handsome slave, whose skin color is not indicated, assists Luciella and her secretive white husband who visits her only at night. The name of a slave in "Penta with the Chopped-off Hands," Alì, seems to indicate he is a Muslim although he is not explicitly called a Muslim; his skin color is not mentioned in the tale. Two presumably white characters also lose their freedom, as captives or slaves. The prince of Clear Fountain in the tale "Rosella" is kidnapped while boating and

Putting multiple tales into play to explore each topic helps us to avoid falling into binary thinking while providing students a glimpse at the complexity that would arise from an analysis of all fifty tales. What follows is a series of lesson plans that may be employed in a course on early modern Italian literature, European fairy tales, or race in the Renaissance.

Lesson 1: Basile and *The Tale of Tales*: The "dream of an odd Mediterranean Shakespeare"[10]

Assigned Readings:

1. Nancy Canepa, "Introduction," *The Tale of Tales*, xxxiv–xl
2. Joaneath Spicer, "European Perceptions of Blackness as Reflected in the Visual Arts," 35–59
3. Kate Lowe, "The Lives of African Slaves and People of African Descent in Renaissance Europe," 13–33

Before diving into Basile's fairy tales, I think it is important to remind students that when a reader encounters a text, the text draws the reader into its orbit and exerts a gravitational force. In part, the reader's own identity and experiences determine the force of a text's pull, or the weight the reader feels in the presence of the text. I would then warn students of color and women that Basile's text might weigh heavily upon them; I would also ask those students who find the text "light" reading to reflect on why this is so for them.

We can begin our discussion of Basile and his tales by first noting that literary critics and folklorists to date have said precious little about the remarkable fact that at the center of one of the key texts of the European fairy tale tradition stands a Black woman. Using my own work as an exam-

taken to Constantinople where the ill-informed Grand Turk believes the prince's blood will cure his leprosy. In "The Little Slave Girl," Lisa, a sort of Snow White who lies in an enchanted death-like sleep, is revived by her uncle's wife who disguises her as a slave, dressing her in rags, cutting her hair, and beating her so that her face is black and blue.

10. Italo Calvino, *Italian Folktales*, trans. George Martin (New York: Harcourt Brace Jovanovich, 1980), 3.

ple, I suggest that both white privilege and our classification of Basile and his tales as "Italian" or "Neapolitan," categories scholars often constitute exclusively as white, cause us to ignore the presence of the Black character Lucia. In doing so, we commit a sort of violence to her, intellectually burying her, just as she will be buried alive and pregnant at the end of the text.

A first step, then, in re-evaluating this character and the representation of Blackness in the fairy tales, is to reconsider Basile's own identity. Using literary scholar Nancy Canepa's concise biography of Basile, we can remind our students of his identity as a Mediterranean author. As a young man, Basile was a soldier of fortune at the Venetian Republic's eastern outpost in Candia (Crete), facing the Ottoman Empire. For most of his adult life, he lived in Naples, a port city that had been under the rule of a Spanish viceroy since the beginning of the sixteenth century. We can thus take seriously Italo Calvino's description of Basile's tales as the "dreams of an odd Mediterranean Shakespeare" and think of him as Mediterranean *and* Italian *and* Neapolitan. Doing so positions him in a multicultural and multi-confessional context, where he was stationed in the Eastern Mediterranean to protect Venetian territories from possible invasions by the Ottoman Empire; he mingled with Italian and Spanish men of letters in Naples' Accademia degli Oziosi; he served at Neapolitan courts under the rule of Spanish viceroys, the counts of Lemos, who had former slaves who had converted to Christianity working for them;[11] and he lived in a city with a Muslim community and where up to 7% of the population was comprised of slaves coming from all around the Mediterranean including the Middle East, Eastern Europe, and North and sub-Saharan Africa.[12]

The readings by Spicer and Lowe are meant to foster a discussion of the configuration of race in Renaissance Europe; the unique features of the intersection of race, ethnicity, and slavery in the Mediterranean; and early modern stereotype of blackness, both positive and negative. After a mini-lecture on how race was theorized in the Renaissance based on Lowe's

11. Giuliana Boccadamo, *Napoli e l'Islam: Storie di musulmanni, schiavi, e rinnegati in età moderna* (Naples: M. Dauria Editore, 2010), 179.

12. Boccadamo, *Napoli e l'Islam*, 144–51.

observations, I put into play works of art and literature mentioned in sources which are contemporary to Basile's literary career: Pietro Tacca's bronze sculpture "Quattro mori incatenati" [Four Moors in Chains]; a statue of Saint Benedict of Palermo, sometimes called "the Moor," whose case for canonization was actively being compiled in 1625; and a sonnet, "Bella Schiava" (Beautiful Slave), by fellow Neapolitan poet Giambattista Marino (1569–1625). I focus on these three cultural artifacts in order to share the main concepts I want students to absorb from these readings. I show images of Tacca's sculpture, explaining that it was commissioned, executed, and erected in Livorno in the same years that Basile was likely writing his tales (1617–1626). Tacca's four enslaved figures are chained to the base of a statue of Ferdinando I de' Medici by sculptor Giovanni Bandini (1595), and were meant to celebrate the Medici Duke Cosimo I's victories over the Ottomans. Bandini's statue invites us to tell the story of Cosimo I's founding of the Knights of Saint Stephen, a military order charged with battling the Ottoman Empire on the Mediterranean and fighting piracy, but which also enslaved and sold or sent to the galleys people captured during these conquests, just as the Ottomans and North Africans captured and enslaved Christian Europeans and sub-Saharan Africans. Examining the four bronze figures created by Tacca based on wax casts taken from actual galley slaves allows us to underscore the diverse origins of enslaved individuals in the Mediterranean. The variation of the somatic features of Tacca's four "Moors" reminds us both of the array of skin colors and ethnic origins of slaves in Basile's day and of the imprecision of the language used to describe people of color. All four figures in Tacca's sculpture are referred to as "Moors," a word which could mean Muslim and/or Black, but only one figure possesses features that appear to be sub-Saharan African. As scholars have noted, terminology for skin color, ethnicity, and religion was not always precise; "Moor" and "Saracen" could describe North African or Middle Eastern Muslims, as well as Black Africans who might not be Muslim. As we will see, Basile refers to Lucia as both "black" and "Moorish," and uses "Saracen" to describe another enslaved Black woman.

As I guide this discussion, I introduce historian Giovanna Fiume's description of the unique aspects of slavery in the Mediterranean in order to help students to distinguish it from the Atlantic slave trade.[13] Mediterranean slavery was marked by *reciprocity*: Europeans, Ottomans, North Africans, and sub-Saharan Africans enslaved, traded, and ransomed or freed each other throughout the early modern period. Mediterranean slavery differed from Atlantic slavery in its *temporariness*: enslavement was often a period of one's life, not a permanent condition. Captured and enslaved individuals could be ransomed, and religious orders and legal procedures oversaw such transactions. Slaves were often manumitted upon the death of their owner and entered the local culture as freedmen and women. This meant that enslaved, freed, and free Black Africans could be found in Basile's Naples. In the Mediterranean, slavery could also be a *repetitive experience* with individuals captured, enslaved, and freed more than once.

Next, a statue of Saint Benedict the Moor (Attrib. José Montes de Oca, 1734) and the poem by Marino can be used to analyze the tropes employed in more positive representations of blackness, Black Africans, and slaves. The statue of Benedict provides a stark contrast to the enchained Black African sculpted by Tacca. Benedict (1526–1589) was the son of a couple from sub-Saharan Africa, Cristoforo Manasseri, enslaved, and his free wife Diana, who had converted to Christianity.[14] Born in San Fratello, near Messina, Benedict eventually moved to a monastery in Palermo. A Franciscan monk, he was revered for his charity and ability to heal the sick. He would find many devoted followers, first in his native Sicily and then in the New World, particularly among indigenous tribes and people of color (he is the patron saint of African Americans). Benedict can serve as an example of what Spicer calls "black and/but" beautiful.[15] Efforts to canonize Benedict were well underway in 1625 and Philip III of Spain, who ruled over both Sicily and Naples, ordered a silver casket to be built for

13. Giovanna Fiume, *Schiavitù mediterranee: Corsari, rinnegati e santi di età moderna* (Milan: Bruno Mondadori, 2009), x–xi.
14. Most of medieval and early modern Italy continued to follow the Roman law according to which the status the mother, enslaved or free, determined the status of the child. On this point see Stephen Epstein, *Speaking of Slavery: Color, Ethnicity, and Human Bondage in Italy* (Ithaca, NY: Cornell University Press, 2001), 84–85.
15. Spicer, "European Perceptions of Blackness," 37.

Benedict's bones. Praise for Benedict, however, sometimes celebrated him by erasing his Blackness. For example, a Spanish priest who wrote on the evangelization of people of color in the seventeenth century noted that "although black," Saint Benedict "was the whitest among all the spiritual men of the time."[16]

Marino's depiction of a beautiful Black slave in his sonnet "Bella Schiava" (Beautiful Slave), which begins "Black, yes, but you're beautiful," can be used in a similar fashion.[17] Here Marino plays on the Petrarchan tropes of female beauty that celebrated the white skin and golden hair of the poet's beloved lady, by praising the black skin of the slave.[18] In keeping with Marino's poetics of the marvelous through which he aims to amaze his reader, the slave's beauty is depicted as an exotic curiosity and she is described as a beautiful monster ("leggiadro mostro"). We can conclude by drawing attention to Spicer's observations that during the first decade of the seventeenth century, there appeared to be "a new level of acceptance for Africans in Europe," but, in hindsight, and from the vantage point of Basile's text, these events "look more like markers of the end of an era."[19]

16. These are the words of Father Alonso de Sandoval, author of *De instauranda Aethiopium salute* (Madrid, 1636) and cited in Fiume, *Schiavitù mediterranee*, 126.
17. For the poem see and a paraphrase in contemporary Italian see: http://www.treccani.it/magazine/strumenti/una_poesia_al_giorno/07_16_Marino_Giambattista.html.
18. For an English paraphrase of Marino's poem, see George R. Kay, ed. and trans., *Penguin Book of Italian Verse with Plain Prose Translations of Each Poem* (Hammondsworth, UK: Penguin, 1958).
19. These included: "the elaborate arrangements made by Pope Paul V to receive the Congolese ambassadors known in Europe as Antonio Manuel, Marquis of Na Vunda ... Morocco and the Dutch republic sign a landmark treaty establishing trade relations, the first between a European country and a non-Christian one; the Spanish playwright Enciso writes a play celebrating the life of the black humanist Juan Latino; Philip III of Spain orders a silver casket for the bones of Benedict the Moor (canonized in 1807)" (Spicer, 10).

Lesson 2: Zoza vs. Lucia: The Fairy Tale Frame Tale

Assigned Readings:

1. Basile, "Introduction to the *Tale of Tales* (Frame Tale)," 3–11; "The Cinderella Cat" (1.6), 56–62

For this lesson, students undertake a close reading of Basile's overarching tale, the story of Lucia and Zoza, that is informed by the background readings, and they analyze Basile's Baroque style through a reading of his version of Cinderella, a tale type most will know, in which the female protagonist, Zezolla, is also mockingly called "gatta Cennerentola" [Cinderella Cat]. I provide a series of questions and request that they cite the text in their answers. I begin with "The Cinderella Cat" because Basile's version of this classic tale challenges students' expectations. How does Basile's version differ from the one you know? How does his literary style differ from that of other tales you have read? Zezolla, or Cinderella Cat murders her first stepmother on the advice of the woman who will become her second abusive stepmother, manipulates and threatens her father in order to obtain the magic that will allow her to leave home, and in her finery is compared to a promenading prostitute. Basile employs a poetics of the marvelous, using surprisingly ingenious comparisons in long lists of metaphors, and making unexpected references to both learned and popular culture.

Turning to the frame tale, we can ask students to provide a description of Lucia based on textual citations: How is Lucia described physically? How does she speak and what does she say? What does she do? Which tropes of blackness is Basile employing in his descriptions of Lucia? In class, we can characterize Basile's representation of Lucia based on an analysis of the citations in student responses. Lucia's blackness is often negatively contrasted to whiteness ("the prince got out of his coffin of white stone as if he were awakening from a long sleep, took hold of that mass of black flesh, and carried her off to the palace").[20] Many comparisons liken her to animals in unflattering ways ("cricket-legged"; "monkey"). Blackness is set in antagonistic opposition to whiteness; it undoes or temporarily defeats Zoza ("two black things had brought her [Zoza's]

20. Basile, *The Tale of Tales*, 7.

downfall: sleep and a slave").[21] Comparing Basile's representation to the sonnet we studied in the previous lesson, they might note that while Marino calls the Black slave in his poem a "monster of beauty," Basile casts Zoza in this role, associating Lucia with the black night: "Tadeo, who like a bat was always flying round that black night of a slave but became an eagle when he fixed his eyes upon Zoza – that monster of nature's bounty, that 'I'm out' of the game of beauty."[22] They might also note that Lucia is described as a "Moorish slave" an "ugly slave.[23] Finally, Lucia's patois also marks her as linguistically different from both Princess Zoza and the lower-class narrators summoned to entertain her. When she speaks, she does so only to demand things and threatens, in a sing-song rhyme, to abort by beating her belly should her desires not be satisfied: "If people no come and with my tales ears fill, me punch belly and little Georgie kill."[24]

We can then contextualize these citations for students, beginning with Lucia's name and the many associations it would have evoked for early modern readers. Slaves were often renamed when they arrived in Italy, and Lucia was a particularly popular name for enslaved women.[25] Basile's Lucia speaks a patois that Michele Rak, who has edited the tales, calls Neapolitan-Moorish.[26] This was both a language spoken in the streets by foreign-born slaves and a literary language used by African characters in Neapolitan theater. A stock character named Lucia appeared in a micro-genre of street theater known as "Luciate," as well as in theatrical dances, such as the one listed as one of the entertainments Zoza's father hopes will cheer his melancholy daughter ("Lucia Cagnazza" or "Bitchy Lucia"). In this Moorish dance performed during Carnival, a man in blackface cross-dressed as a woman in Oriental garb mimed while a song referenced sexual acts, birth, and death and included a chorus calling Lucia a

21. Basile, *The Tale of Tales*, 8.
22. Basile, *The Tale of Tales*, 8.
23. Basile, *The Tale of Tales*, 9.
24. Basile, *The Tale of Tales*, 10.
25. Stephen Epstein, *Speaking of Slavery: Color, Ethnicity, and Human Bondage in Italy*, 25–28.
26. Michele Rak, ed. *Lo cunto de li cunti*, by Giambattista Basile (Milan: Garzanti, 1986), 29 n17.

bitch.[27] Although Basile doesn't particularly underscore Lucia's sexuality, her patois and name liken her to a highly sexualized character from Neapolitan street theater. Rak describes a published example of the micro-genre *La Luciata nuova. Posta in luce dal Rovinato Pover'Uomo, a compiacenza de' virtuosi* (The New 'Luciata,' Brought to light by a Ruined Poor Man, For the Satisfaction of the Virtuous, Napoli, 1628), with dramatis personae including Lucia, three male slaves, a master-slave, and a chorus.[28] Written in the theatrical language akin to the patois of Basile's Lucia, in this *luciata* Lucia is depicted as a flirt who dances uninhibitedly to the sound of percussion instruments with movements that mimic copulation and her infidelity produces a child at the end of the play.[29] We can ask students how knowing about this theatrical tradition, which Basile's first readers most certainly did, informs our perception of Lucia.

Students who are studying Basile as part of a course on fairy tales sometimes attribute Lucia's overwhelmingly negative portrayal as characteristic of the fairy tale genre. Fairy tales are often described as presenting characters and situations in stark terms and well-defined contrasts. For example, when writing about the style of oral fairy tales the Swiss folklorist and literary theorist Max Lüthi (1909–1991) observed, "The fairy tale is also fond of other extremes and contrasts: dreadful punishments and splendid rewards, giants and dwarfs, mangy skull and golden hair, good and evil, handsome and ugly, black and white. Thus, the fairy tale portrays a clearly and neatly fashioned world."[30] But it is important to remind stu-

27. Roberto De Simone, *Il Cunto de li Cunti di Giambattista Basile nella riscrittura di Roberto De Simone*, 2 vols. Piacenza: Einaudi, 2002. 1: 7 n4.
28. Michele Rak, *Napoli gentile: La letteratura in 'lingua napoetana' nella cultura barocca (1596–1632)* (Bologna: Il Mulino, 1994), 130.
29. Rak, *Napoli gentile*, 130–31.
30. Max Lüthi, *Once Upon a Time: On the Nature of Fairy Tales*, translated by Lee Chadeayne and Paul Gottwald, introduction by Francis Lee Utley (Bloomington: University of Indiana Press, 1970), 50–51. Similar observations have been made in general introductions to the fairy tale genre. For example, Marina Warner observes that the symbolism of fairy tales "comes alive through strong contrasts and sensations" (Warner xix) and, echoing the work of Lüthi, that "Fairy tales are one-dimensional, depthless,

dents that Basile does not always proceed according to this stricture of sharp contrasts and simplicity – one need only think of Zezolla, or Cinderella Cat, who is neither completely kind nor wholly evil. And, if we look at his depiction of a fantastic race, ogres and ogresses, we will see that Basile often introduces remarkable complexity into the fairy tale tradition that belies the sort of flat binaries attributed to the genre. We can use three tales depicting ogres told during the first day to make this point and to provide a richer context for Basile's representation of Lucia's difference.

Lesson 3: Ogres and Ogresses: A Spectrum of Difference

Assigned Readings:

1. Basile, "The Ogre" (1.1), 13–21; "The Flea" (1.5), 49–55; "The Enchanted Doe" (1.9), 83–90
2. Nancy Canepa, "Ogres and Fools: On the Cultural Margins of the Seicento," 222–46

For this lesson, I assign the three ogre tales recounted on the first day of storytelling, tales 1, 5, and 9, using three questions to guide students: What role does the ogre play in the tale? How is the ogre depicted? Does this representation challenge or conform to our assumptions about ogres and their roles in fairy tales?

In tale 1.1, the ogre adopts a foolish boy who has been chased from his mother's home and teaches the lad how to properly use three magic objects to provide for his family. The ogre is an adoptive father and effective teacher, whose guidance puts the boy on a path of self-sufficiency. When in tale 1.5 an ogre guesses that the hide which the King of Green Meadow has displayed is that of a monstrously large flea, he wins the hand of the princess in marriage. The ogre is terrifyingly ugly and lives in a house constructed from human bones. He is, however, also surpris-

abstract and sparse" (Warner xx). See Marina Warner, *Once Upon a Time: A Short History of Fairy Tale* (London: Oxford University Press, 2014).

ingly open to negotiating the preferences of his human wife, by accounting for her dietary practices. After seeing his wife Porziella repulsed by the human flesh he has brought home, he promises to hunt pigs the next day and then invite his family for a celebration of their matrimony. The ogre wants to integrate her into his cultural milieu without demanding that she assimilate completely. Though he seems far more accommodating to his wife's wishes than her father was, the ogre will be killed at the end of the tale. In tale 1.9, we find the traditional human flesh-eating ogre dwelling deep in the woods who must be killed in order for the hero's trajectory to a happy ending to continue. Thus, Basile's ogres perform different narrative functions in each tale and are not depicted solely as evil antagonists.

We can enrich the conversation by assigning literary scholar Nancy Canepa's insightful article "Ogres and Fools: On the Cultural Margins of the *Seicento*," in which she meticulously documents the multiple, nuanced depictions of ogres in Basile's tales. Particularly useful for our purposes is her observations that "Ogres' heads are repeatedly likened to food — ricotta, pears, — again hinting that the real cannibals are others. Basile has, of course, an illustrious precedent in contrasting 'innocent cannibalism' with the barbarity of civilization, where man, perhaps not as literally but much more cruelly, devours man, in [the sixteenth-century French intellectual Michel de] Montaigne's essay 'On Cannibals.'"[31] Basile himself will associate human flesh-eating ogres with New World people in tale 5.9, discussed below. In that tale, a human prince searches for a perfect wife by sailing to the New World and exploring various islands where he meets an ogress who will encourage him to leave quickly before her hungry son returns.

As Canepa shows, ogres function in Basile's text much like wild men did in early modern culture, as an imagined race used to critique the faults of civilized society. Though imagined others, Basile's ogres share many traits with actual minority groups living in Naples. They live on the geographical margins (deep in the woods, on mountain tops, on islands in the New

31. Nancy L. Canepa, "Ogres and Fools: On the Cultural Margins of the *Seicento*," *Monsters in the Italian Literary Imagination*, ed. Keala Jewell (Detroit: Wayne State University Press, 2001), 232.

World), but can also be found in small numbers amidst the dominant, civilized culture; they are marked by physical difference that is often deemed unseemly or ugly; they embrace different dietary practices; they are often victims to the unjust whims of the hegemonic powers; and while their children sometimes marry into the dominant culture, the price of assimilation can be high, demanding the death of a parent or guardian. When operating in a completely imaginary sphere, Basile musters sympathy for some members of this imagined race of ogres. He recognizes the systematic oppression they endure and provides readers with a wide variety of representations of individuals belonging to the race that are difficult to reduce to stereotypes.

Lesson 4: Fairy Tale Intersectionality: Tales of Male Slaves

Assigned Readings:

1. Basile, "The Padlock" (2.9), 185–88; "Penta with the Chopped-Off Hands" (3.2), 214–24; "The Golden Trunk" (5.4), 413–42

Having examined Basile's diverse depictions of ogres, we can examine three tales that depict male slaves to provide an intersectional view of the representation of race in *The Tale of Tales*. Here I am using Critical Race Studies scholar Kimberlé W. Crenshaw's concept of intersectionality. For Crenshaw, our understanding of an individual's difference and experience of that difference, if assessed solely along a single axis (e.g., race or gender), will necessarily be distorted and incomplete.[32] As with the previous lesson, questions regarding function and representation guide the reading: How are male slaves depicted? What are their functions in the tales? In two of the tales, male slaves play minor roles. In "The Padlock," a reworking of motifs from Apuleius's "Cupid and Psyche," the youngest of

32. Crenshaw first introduced this concept in the article "Demarginalizing the Intersection of Race and Sex: A Black Feminist Critique of Antidiscrimination Doctrine, Feminist Theory and Antiracist Politics," *University of Chicago Legal Forum*, Vol. 1989: 1.8 (http://chicagounbound.uchicago.edu/uclf/vol1989/iss1/8).

three sisters, a girl named Luciella, meets "a handsome slave" at the fountain who takes her to a "splendid underground palace."[33] He sees to her needs at the behest of the prince who will become her husband. When in "Penta with the Chopped off Hands," Penta's brother insists on marrying her because he, as if acting out a Petrarchan trope, is infatuated with her lovely white hands, she decides to extinguish his passion by persuading her slave Alì, "who didn't have much of a brain," to chop them off in exchange for a bag of gold coins. While his name marks him as Muslim, his skin color is not mentioned, although Penta's is. Perhaps referencing European books of secrets which contained all sorts of recipes for whitening skin, Penta speaks with words which recall Lucia's patois, "My dear Alì, you cut my hands, me want make nice formula and get more white," as if his stupidity would prevent him from understanding her unless she spoke this way.[34]

In another one of Basile's variations on "Cupid and Psyche" called "The Golden Trunk," Parmetella descends a porphyry staircase hidden under a golden tree trunk to find "a lovely plain on which stood a splendid palace."[35] Inside, among the lavish riches, she will meet a "handsome slave" who proposes marriage to her. This character provides Parmetella with a royal lifestyle and seems to have no master. He commands Parmetella to extinguish the candle when she goes to sleep, and after becoming "a beautiful young man" he crawls into bed with her after she has fallen asleep. Awoken in the night, she feels "her wool being carded without a

33. Basile, *The Tale of Tales*, 186. On Basile's use of Cupid and Psyche, see Armando Maggi's *Preserving the Spell*, 23–108.

34. Basile, *The Tale of Tales*, 216. This is the only moment in *The Tale of Tales* in which a free person uses this patois to address an enslaved person. On the use of "slave speech" in lyric poetry, see Mario Ferrara, "Linguaggio di schiave," *Studi di filologia italiana* 8 (1950), 320–28. While more recently Gianfranco Salvatore has described the language used in sixteenth-century *canzoni moresche* as a "*pidgin* afro-napoletano" that blends Neapolitan dialect and Kanuri words, I refer to the speech of Basile's tales as a patois because it uses non-inflected verbs without integrating words from Arabic or African languages. See Gianfranco Salvatore, "Parodie realistiche: Africanismi, fraternità e sentimenti identitari nelle canzoni moresche del Cinquecento," *Kronos* 14 (2011): 97–128.

35. Basile, *The Tale of Tales*, 414.

comb."[36] Like Psyche curious to see her nocturnal visitor, the next night the young woman lights the candle after her bedmate has fallen asleep. She lifts the covers and sees that "the ebony had turned to ivory, the caviar to the milkiest milk, and the coal to whitewash."[37] Unlike in the descriptions of Lucia, blackness here is associated positively with precious materials, "ebony" and "caviar," but we can note that these positive assessments appear in a phrase that serves to erase or undo the very blackness it describes. And despite his beauty, this character's blackness is literally a curse. We learn that the handsome slave is the son of an ogress who has been cursed to live for seven years as a Black man. After Parmetella has, like Psyche, endured many trials, he will eventually reclaim her as his wife, but their happy ending is founded on his return to whiteness and the death of his ogress mother, aunt, and newborn cousin. In sum, these three tales recall Tacca's statue which depicts diverse groups as enslaved.

Lesson 5: Lucia & Lucia: Doubling and Displacement

Assigned Readings:

1. Basile, "The Three Citrons" (5.9), 443–53; "End of the *Tale of Tales*," 454–55

In the fifth and final lesson, having examined the representation of ogres and male slaves, I circle back to the depiction of Lucia in the frame tale and her double, another enslaved Black woman named Lucia, who appears in the penultimate tale of the collection, "The Three Citrons" (5.9). As in previous lessons, I ask students to undertake a close reading that compares Lucia in the frame tale to Lucia in "The Three Citrons," during which they note similarities and differences. But I also now ask them to compare the representation of these Black enslaved women to those of male slaves and ogres.

36. Basile, *The Tale of Tales*, 415.
37. Basile, *The Tale of Tales*, 415.

I emphasize that the similarities between the two Lucias runs deeper than their shared name and status. In "The Three Citrons," Lucia's blackness is also described in negative terms and she, too, will supplant temporarily a white woman destined to marry a prince. Despite the resemblances, there are also key differences to note between the frame tale and "The Three Citrons." In the latter, the prince is fully alive and awake throughout the tale. Although initially reticent to marry, after cutting his finger and bleeding onto white ricotta cheese, the prince is determined to marry a woman of similar complexion (red and white) and "of his blood." He travels as far as the New World in search of his bride and returns home with a white fairy whom he has liberated from inside a citron. Wanting to provide his bride with a proper entrance, the prince leaves her in a tree outside the kingdom, stating he will return with fine clothes for her. As the fairy awaits his return, a Black slave named Lucia arrives at the fountain below the tree and, when she mistakes the fairy's reflection in the water for her own, she assumes she is now white, and rebels against her mistress by repeatedly refusing to fetch water. When the fairy spies Lucia inadvertently creating a comical fountain by piercing her mistress's goatskin filled with water, she laughs out loud and Lucia realizes her mistake. After offering to style the fairy's hair, Lucia attempts to murder the fairy who, to save herself, becomes a dove and flies away. When the prince returns, he is clearly upset to find the slave rather than the fairy in the tree, and his Baroque lament unfolds as a series of comparisons that celebrate whiteness and denigrate blackness: "Who put this ink blot on the royal paper where I planned to write my happier days? Who draped with black mourning the freshly whitewashed house where I thought I would take all my pleasures? Who would have me find this touchstone where I left a silver mine destined to make me rich and blissful?"[38] Lucia then lies, claiming to be under a curse, "Not to marvel my prince, for presto! Me be enchanted, one year white face, one year black ass!"[39] As in the frame tale, black skin is depicted negatively, equated here with a stain, mourning, and a less valuable dark stone (instead of a pre-

38. Basile, *The Tale of Tales*, 449–50.

39. Basile, *The Tale of Tales*, 450.

cious metal), the bottom of the body rather than the top. In the end the fairy-dove returns and reveals Lucia's deception, the slave is sentenced to death, and the fairy, once again in human form, will marry the prince.

"The Three Citrons" is followed by the conclusion of the frame tale, in which the prince's wife Lucia reacts to the tale of this other Lucia in a way that once again recalls the eponymous character from street theater: "And Lucia reacted like a Lucia, wiggling all over as the tale was told, and from the agitation of her body, could be understood the tempest in her heart, since she had seen in the tale of the other slave the spitting image of her own deceits."[40] But are the crimes of the two Lucias equal? Is "The Three Citrons" the "spitting image" of the frame tale? In the frame tale, Lucia murders no one, does not actively lie, but instead simply finishes off a task begun by another woman.

We can end this lesson by asking students to compare the representations of Black female slaves, male slaves, and ogres in *The Tale of Tales* and to draw some conclusions. Hopefully, they will be able to generate a series of ideas. For example, Basile's nuanced depictions of members of the imaginary race of ogres does not extend to human characters marked by difference (skin color, enslavement) or to characters with historical counterparts in early modern Naples. The depiction of race is intersectional in *The Tale of Tales*, with female slaves receiving worse outcomes than male slaves, and their skin color consistently denigrated. By reducing Lucia to a sort of *commedia dell'arte* mask, a stereotype that excludes individual variation, Lucia in the frame tale is conflated with other Lucias (in "The Three Citrons," in street theater) and burdened with their vices and sins (lust, murder, fraud), despite never having engaged in these acts. Through this association, her violent death, then, can be more easily justified. Also, a kind of white privilege exists in fairy land. Zezolla, the Cinderella Cat, murders and threatens, but still receives a happy ending. In the frame tale, Lucia, ignorant of Zoza's curse (and perhaps then innocent), merely completes a task begun by another. Rather than an outright lie, her victory involves a sin of omission, yet she suffers a torturous death as violent as the one meted out on the murderous Lucia in "The Three Cit-

40. Basile, *The Tale of Tales*, 454.

rons." And once the center of concern, the fate of the Giorgetiello, whom Lucia is carrying, is no longer mentioned. While Basile has been seen to use his tales to contest the institutions of power that oppressed courtiers like himself, ultimately his depiction of Lucia reifies the oppression of enslaved Black women by denying them representation as individuals, by reducing all Lucias to one negative stereotype.

Images:

For Pietro Tacca's statue see:
https://commons.wikimedia.org/wiki/Category:Monumento_dei_Quattro_Mori_(Livorno)

For the Statue of Saint Benedict the Moor see:
https://collections.artsmia.org/art/109582/saint-benedict-of-palermo-attributed-to-jose-montes-de-oca

Discussion Questions:

1. How might the literary fairy tale, a genre grounded in "long ago" and "far away" fantasies, help us to examine the complex social historical realities of race and slavery in the early modern Mediterranean? How do gender and genre shape representations of race?
2. How might redefining Basile's own identity as more complex than simply "Italian" help us understand his depictions of race in his fairy tales?
3. How does Basile's version of the Cinderella tale type differ from the one you know? How does the literary style of his tales differ from the style of other tales you have read?
4. How is Lucia described physically in the frame tale to *Lo cunto de li cunti*? How does she speak and what does she say? Which tropes of blackness is Basile employing in his descriptions of Lucia?
5. How does the street theater tradition/micro-genre of *Luciate* shape our understanding of Lucia and her actions in the frame tale?
6. Concerning Basile's ogre tales: What role does the ogre play in the tale? How is the ogre depicted? Does this representation challenge

or conform to our assumptions about ogres and their roles in fairy tales?

7. How are male slaves depicted in Basile's fairy tales? What are their functions in the plots of these tales? Does their role and description differ from those of female slaves?
8. Compare Lucia in the frame tale to Lucia in the tale "The Three Citrons." In what ways do they resemble each other? Are the "crimes" of the two Lucias comparable? Is story of "The Three Citrons" the "spitting image" of the frame tale?

Suggested Further Reading:

On slavery in the early modern Mediterranean:

Davis, Robert C. *Christian Slaves, Muslim Masters: White Slavery in the Mediterranean, the Barbary Coast, and Italy 1500–1800*. New York: Palgrave McMillan, 2003.

On the representation of Black Saints in early modern Europe:

Rowe, Erin Kathleen. *Black Saints in Early Modern Global Catholicism*. Cambridge: Cambridge University Press, 2019.

On the representation of power, race, and gender in early modern Italian fairy tales:

Maggi, Armando. "Abuse of Power, Gender, and Race in Tales by Straparola and Basile." In *A Cultural History of Fairy Tales in the Age of the Marvelous*, edited by Suzanne Magnanini, 191–212. Vol. 3 of *A Cultural History of Fairy Tales*, edited by Anne E. Duggan. London: Bloomsbury Academic, 2021.

On how lore and legends contribute to racecraft, or the construction of race:

Fields, Karen E., and Barbara J. Fields. *Racecraft: The Soul of Inequality in American Life*. New York: Verso Books, 2012.

The Black Female Attendant in Titian's *Diana and Actaeon* (c. 1559), and in Modern Oblivion

PATRICIA SIMONS

I begin with a confession. For many years, I found it difficult, even embarrassing, to teach about one aspect of Titian's *Diana and Actaeon* canvas produced in the 1550s (see figures 1 and 2). The Black figure in the retinue of the goddess Diana, on the right, was often passed over by scholars, or relegated to an allegorical function such as *Fortuna* or *Natura*, but that did not encompass its crucial effect, dramatic presence, or historical context. Whether there were Black students in the classroom or not, the figure needed to be seen and explained. This essay hopes to offer a way forward, trying to empower students, offering a degree of hope, and fitting them with tools of visual literacy as well as verbal skill. Racism is not timeless, and naming it can lessen its effectiveness. The history of power can reveal fissures in the edifices of control, and it is important to understand that ancestors from various minorities were sometimes victors in their quiet struggles.

The visual archive is not a collection of straightforward or transparent records about the existence of and attitudes toward a variety of ethnic and racial types in premodern Europe. Like texts, images must be situated in their time and place, and treated with nuance and respect as sophisticated, complex and sometimes contradictory materials. Artistic observation was always balanced with imagination, fascination co-existed with fear, and the production and reception of art was filtered through intellectual conventions and power differentials as well as aesthetic traditions, material practices, and cultural expectations. Similarly, today's modes of interpretation are multiple, overlapping, and changing. Art historians increasingly study the visual representation of Black figures "not only as

Figure 1. Titian. *Diana and Actaeon*. 1556–1559. Oil on canvas. 184.5 x 202.2 cm. National Gallery, London and Scottish National Gallery, Edinburgh.

an iconographic subfield or as an enterprise of recuperation, but rather as part of broader discursive constructions of race."[1]

In the Italian peninsula during the fifteenth and sixteenth centuries, such discourses were shaped by factors like increasing travel and pilgrimage, growing trade activity, contact and conflict with non-Christian peoples (including inhabitants of the Ottoman empire, primarily Turks and Egyptians), local labor conditions as well as the international slave trade, religious shifts and challenges both near and far, and the rise of imperialism, especially by the Hapsburgs. It was to a key member of that dynasty,

1. Angela Rosenthal and Agnes Lugo-Ortiz, "Envisioning Slave Portraiture," in *Slave Portraiture in the Atlantic World*, ed. Agnes Lugo-Ortiz and Angela Rosenthal (Cambridge: Cambridge University Press, 2013), 12.

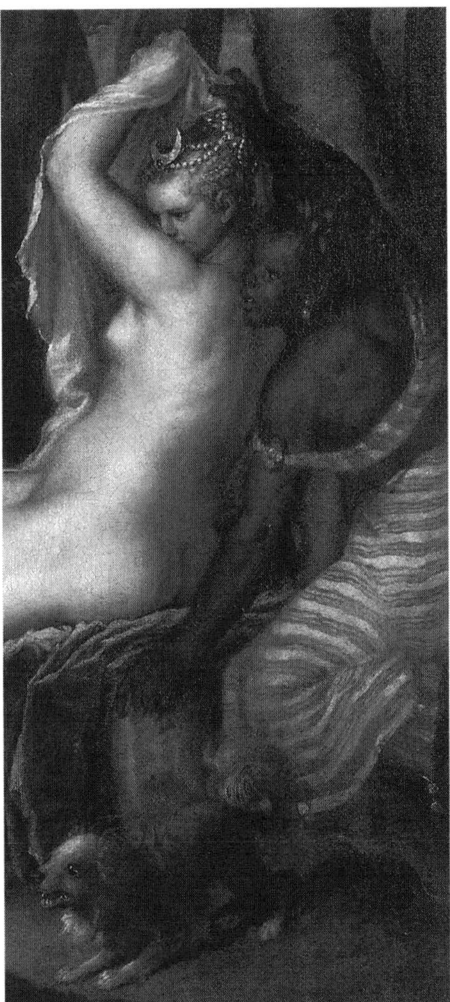

Figure 2. Detail of Figure 1.

King Philip II of Spain, that the Venetian painter Titian sent the canvas of *Diana and Actaeon* in 1559.[2] Moving beyond simply noticing this figure, this study treats not merely the matter of Black visibility, but of what kind, and in what context. The goal is to identify ways in which modern commentaries have marginalized or removed the figure, instead arguing for

2. Harold Wethey, *The Paintings of Titian*, vol. III (London: Phaidon, 1975), 73–74, 138–41.

its importance, and for the possibility that the character is endowed with a degree of agency.

Historical Context: Black Africans in the Mediterranean

In the sixteenth century, Black Africans were chiefly known in the Mediterranean area as slaves but they were not the major element of the slave trade until it waned in Europe and developed across the Atlantic. Meanwhile, European Christians purchased slaves from Central Asia, Eastern Europe, and Muslim lands; this ethnically diverse populace of slaves comprised Armenians, Mongols, Slavs, Tartars, Turks, Russians, and more. In 1483 the Swiss pilgrim Felix Fabri saw for sale at Cairo's slave market "many people, youths and children of both sexes, black and white (*nigri et albi*), female and male," though in another market with only blacks ("Ethiopians," then a standard term for Black Africans), Muslim slave traders would not sell to the Christians.[3] Slaves "did not form a clearly distinctive or definable group," and there were considerable differences not only in geographical origin and religious faith but also in practices, sources, types of trade, and legal regulations.[4]

Venice was one of the major cities involved in the slave trade, acting as a port of acquisition, transfer, and export. Around 1480, the visitor Fabri was struck by the abundance of non-European faces in the streets and canals of the metropolis, estimating that there were around 3,000 enslaved "Ethiopians and Tartars."[5] Black gondoliers and boatmen were common enough in the 1490s for Vittore Carpaccio to depict them in two of his paintings, cleverly constructing the appearance of realistic detail

3. Felicis Fabri, *Evagatorium*, edited by Konrad Dietrich Hassler (Stuttgart: Sumtibus Societatis Litterariae, 1849), vol. IV, 36–37.
4. Juliane Schiel and Stefan Hanß, "Semantics, Practices and Transcultural Perspectives on Mediterranean Slavery," in *Mediterranean Slavery Revisited* (500–1800), edited by Stefan Hanß and Juliane Schiel (Zurich: Chronos, 2014), 16.
5. Fabri, *Evagatorium*, 432. In 1509 the city's population was between 103,500 and 115,000: Kate Lowe, "Visible Lives: Black Gondoliers and Other Black Africans in Renaissance Venice," *Renaissance Quarterly* 66, (2013): 428. Assuming around 100,000 for the population nearly thirty years earlier, Fabri thus posits a slave population of around three percent, whereas scholars suggest a proportion closer to one or two percent.

Figure 3. Vittore Carpaccio. *Miracle of the True Cross at the Rialto Bridge*: detail. 1494–1501. Tempera on canvas. 365 x 389 cm. Galleria dell'Accademia, Venice.

(see figure 3).[6] It has been estimated that over four hundred Venetian images produced before 1800 show one or more African figures.[7]

On the other hand, Black Africans were a "very small minority" of slaves in any part of northern Italy, and they were less in demand than lighter-

6. Lowe, "Visible Lives," 412–52. The other example is *Hunting on the Lagoon* (c. 1490–1494, Getty Museum, Los Angeles).
7. Paul H. D. Kaplan, "Local Color: The Black African Presence in Venetian Art and History," in *Fred Wilson: Speak of Me as I Am* (Cambridge MA: List Visual Arts Center, Massachusetts Institute of Technology, 2003), 8.

skinned people.[8] There was also a noticeable decline in slavery by the late decades of the fifteenth century, in large part due to less access to Muslim lands, and slaves grew expensive. Of any origin, slaves became an "unusual extravagance," serving mostly in aristocratic circles as markers of European privilege.[9] Art skewed the representation of sub-Saharan Africans because most images present Black males, in outdoor settings, whereas the overwhelming majority of slaves were female, employed in household work (often entailing wet nursing, and sexual service to the master).[10]

Venice was also populated with freed former slaves, who, if they were Black men, usually worked in labor-intensive occupations like gondolier or marble-carver, whereas freedwoman tended to marry or continue as servants.[11] In 1386 the will of the Venetian painter Nicoletto Semitecolo stipulated that his Tartar slave would be freed after remaining with his widow for six years, during which time the slave was to continue to exercise the art of painting.[12] It is crucial not to mistake every picture of a non-European for a slave. There is no evidence that Titian's figure is meant to evoke slavery, though his actual model may have still been unfree.

In any case, the adorned woman who is the focus of this essay does not directly or simply record social reality. Like Carpaccio's gondolier clad in flamboyant dress, she is designed to catch the eye, add variety to the scene, draw cosmopolitan allusions, and demonstrate innovative, artistic skill. Yet, as with Carpaccio's figures, the female attendant is often men-

8. Sally McKee, "Domestic Slavery in Renaissance Italy," *Slavery & Abolition* 29 (2008): 311–12.
9. The quotation is from McKee, "Domestic Slavery," 321.
10. Steven Epstein, "Slaves in Italy, 1350–1550," in *At the Margins: Minority Groups in Premodern Italy*, edited by Stephen Milner (Minneapolis: University of Minnesota Press, 2005), 223, 224, 227; McKee, "Domestic Slavery," esp. 317–18, 320.
11. Lowe, "Visible Lives," 421–23, 446, and passim.
12. Vincenzo Lazari, "Del traffico e delle condizioni degli schiavi in Venezia nei tempi di mezzo," *Miscellanea di storia italiana* 1 (1862): 473. Two notarial documents in Genoa record slaves becoming pupils of artists, in February 1489 and January 1578: Luigi Tria, "La schiavitú in Liguria," *Atti della Societá Ligure di Storia Patria* 70 (1947): 108. For other examples see *Revealing the African Presence in Renaissance Europe*, edited by Joaneath Spicer (Baltimore: The Walters Art Museum, 2012), 83–84.

tioned simply as an example of the presence of Africans in Venice. Scholars might highlight her exoticism, along with the common description of the figure as an aesthetic "foil" to accentuate Diana's white purity. Or she is reduced to an allegorical symbol, with no social meaning. This essay tries to offer a more nuanced reading, between the polarities of reality and metaphor, document and allegory, naturalism and fantasy.

The Myth and Meaning of Ovid's Diana and Actaeon

The retelling of the myth of Diana and Actaeon by the first-century Roman poet Ovid was well known during the Renaissance: the young hunter unwittingly came upon Diana and her nymphs bathing in a secluded grotto.[13] Angry at the intrusion into her private sanctuary, the goddess punished Actaeon by turning him into a stag, so that his dogs set upon him, a brutal death that Titian showed on another canvas. Common allegorical readings of the tale regarded Actaeon as overly curious about mysteries beyond human ken, or as a man unable to control his passions. Being the goddess of chastity, Diana's vengeful punishment of him was interpreted as the right, if cruel, feminine response to improper, irrational, and passionate behavior.[14]

Titian focused on the first moments of the youth's interjection, when the women begin to react. The artist makes the issue of who sees what the crux of the painting, by taking on Diana's challenge to Actaeon, voiced as she begins the hunter's metamorphosis: "Now you are free to tell that you have seen me all unrobed – if you can tell".[15] Of course, the stag never can speak, and thus female chastity and divine secrecy remain sacrosanct. Depicting the initial stage rather than the event of bestial transformation, Titian adds suspense and not only sees the goddess naked, but lives to tell the tale. Thereby, he asserts his privileged access to visions of the divine as well as to knowledge of the naked female body, and he provides his

13. *Metamorphoses*, 3:138–193.
14. H. David Brumble, *Classical Myths and Legends in the Middle Ages and Renaissance. A Dictionary of Allegorical Meanings* (Westport, CT: Greenwood Press, 1998), 5–6, 98–100.
15. Ovid, *Metamorphoses*, 3:192–193.

audience with the same license. In normative terms, Actaeon's shock and Diana's anger remind viewers of the social values of masculine control and feminine chastity, core components of the honor of each gender. Simultaneously, Titian presents the enticing view of idealized female nakedness that is no longer held secret but seen by all.

Titian dramatizes the inter-related issues of sight and veiling. Between and beyond the narrative poles of Diana and Actaeon, six young women perform assorted actions and gazes. Closest to Actaeon, one nymph casts an anxious look toward her mistress while pulling at the red curtain for protection. Another looks down, concentrating on her task of drying her mistress's leg and thus missing the crisis entirely. In the central cluster, a blonde nymph lowers her eyes and starts to turn away. Behind her another woman has turned her back and is covering herself, while a third nymph hides behind a pillar yet peeks out, trying to understand what is happening. Playing the crucial role of closing the composition on the far right and returning the viewer's eyes to the action, a young Black woman opens her mouth in surprise and helps Diana cover herself.

Visibility/Invisibility: The Black Woman in Titian's Painting

The drama begins with Actaeon, and ends with the nameless Black figure who also raises her arm in alarm. Paid little or no attention by modern commentators, as we will see, the figure is exceptional yet essential. Ovid imagined that Diana's nymphs crowded around to shield her, but in the painting they have not had time to do so, thus enabling Titian to bare the bodies of all but one of the female characters. Diana has to fend for herself, except for the companion behind her, the clothed attendant who reinforces her gesture of lifting a veil. The goddess's rising anger (her face flushed with the blush of modesty that is blossoming into the heat of anger) and vehement defense of chastity is aided and accentuated only by the escort. They act in tandem.

The Black figure's features are individualized enough to suggest that Titian observed a particular model and he produced an attractive, animated face. Only beautiful, ever-youthful maidens could surround a goddess in her idyllic habitat. However, unlike the nymphs, who are semi-divine beauties populating remote locales, the Black woman is thinner, muscular, partly clothed and sumptuously adorned, thereby adding a unique note of contemporary relevance to the ancient yet supposedly timeless fable. Given the conventions of the day, carried over into modern assumptions about racial superiority, nymphs can only be pale-skinned and they are usually fair-haired or blonde.

This figure is more than an ordinary servant, and there are no indications that she was to be understood as a slave. Just the opposite. Venetian regulations that were expanded in 1541 forbade servants from wearing certain items of silk or velvet, and their common fabrics were white, black, or drab browns.[16] Nor were they allowed to wear anything regarded as inadequately respectable (*non honesto*), rules flaunted by Titian's arresting garb with multi-colored stripes, to say nothing of the bared shoulder.

Stripes at times connoted foreign, transgressive, or evil creatures.[17] But similarly striking attire was also depicted on servants and aristocrats. Young pages (one of whom is Black) and a woman in the elite entourage of the Pharaoh's daughter exhibit striped clothing in Bonifazio de Pitati's *Finding of Moses* (c. 1540–1545, Pinacoteca di Brera, Milan). A long shawl of white, pink, and gold stripes, akin to the cloth in Titian's painting, is worn by a brown-skinned female servant standing behind the princess in the fanciful Egyptian setting of Carpaccio's St *George Baptizing the Selenites* (c. 1505–1507, Scuola di San Giorgio degli Schiavoni, Venice).

Jewelry also distinguishes Titian's character: a sizeable pearl ornaments her armband, a large ruby hangs from her gold earring, and her hair is adorned with blue daubs (perhaps anemones or feathers, but probably ribbons). Aristocratic women wore earrings, though pierced ears supporting pendant earrings had something of the exotic and foreign about them. They were even disparaged by one Venetian gentleman in 1525 as "the Moorish mode."[18] At a lower level of society, Black women were renowned

16. Dennis Romano, *Housecraft and Statecraft. Domestic Service in Renaissance Venice, 1400–1600* (Baltimore: Johns Hopkins University Press, 1996), 28–32, 56, 247.
17. Michel Pastoureau, *The Devil's Cloth. A History of Stripes and Striped Fabric*, translated by Jody Gladding (New York: Columbia University Press, 2001).
18. Marino Sanuto, *I Diarii*, edited by Rinaldo Fulin et al., (Venice: Visentini, 1894), vol 40, col. 425 (6 December 1525, "costume di more").

for wearing many trinkets or charms.[19] Aspects of Titian's embellishments thus evoke and enhance her foreignness, but they are neither trashy baubles nor records of reality. They signify her eminence, bejeweled as she is almost as much as Diana. Her setting is not household, brothel, or plantation, but the fantastical world of courtly life and ancient legend. She exists in the close company of a goddess, and is one of the most honored members of the innermost circle. The figure is not present in the painting as a representative of all of exoticized Africa.

Nor is she a mere appendage to the goddess. Decades earlier, Titian devised the first portrait of a white woman accompanied by a Black servant, establishing a type that became popular during the seventeenth and eighteenth centuries when intercontinental imperialism and slavery flourished.[20] The pre-pubescent page in Titian's portrait of Laura Dianti (see figure 4) has been described as an objectified "luxury item," and a Black person working at any court was apparently only "a curious ornament or a diverting toy."[21] But just as not all Black people can be cast into a single mold, images of them cannot be left undifferentiated. Laura's servant is a child looking up to focus only on her, and the same gaze, along with the disparity in age, size, status and race, recurs in Titian's later portrait of Fabricius Salvaresius (1558, Kunsthistorisches Museum, Vienna).[22]

19. Francisco Delicado, *La Lozana Andaluza* (Madrid: Espasa Calpe, 1988), 83 (1.7): "lleva más dixes que una negra." The novel was written and published in Venice in 1528 but set in Rome.

20. Paul H. D. Kaplan, "Titian's 'Laura Dianti' and the origins of the motif of the black page in portraiture," *Antichità viva* 21 no 1 (1982): 11–18, and 21 no 4 (1982): 10–18; Jane Fair Bestor, "Titian's Portrait of Laura Eustochia: The Decorum of Female Beauty and the Motif of the Black Page," *Renaissance Studies* 17, (2003): 628–73; Joanna Woods-Marsden, "The Mistress as 'Virtuous': Titian's Portrait of Laura Dianti," in *Titian: Materiality, Likeness, Istoria*, edited by J. Woods-Marsden (Turnhout, 2007), 53–69.

21. Bestor, "Laura Eustochia," 633; Iris Origo, "The Domestic Enemy: The Eastern Slaves in Tuscany in the Fourteenth and Fifteenth Centuries," *Speculum* 30, (1955): 354.

22. Paul H. D. Kaplan, "Sicily, Venice, and the East: Titian's *Fabricius Salvaresius with a Black Page*," in *Europa und die Kunst des Islam, 15. bis 18 Jahrhundert* (Vienna: Bohlaus, 1985), 127–36.

Diana's aide is not infantilized or passive, and it is she who looks most directly at the intruder.

Figure 4. Titian. *Laura Dianti and a black page*. c. 1524–1529. Oil on canvas. H. Kisters Collection, Kreuzlingen.

Images of Black women, rather than men or children, were not common in Italian painting. Medieval images of the Queen of Sheba and her retinue occasionally showed them as Black, but that tradition did not continue in the Renaissance. African and dark-skinned women appear in a handful of Italian paintings and drawings from the fifteenth and early sixteenth centuries, as a turbaned figure among court ladies in the case of Mantegna's oculus in the Camera Picta of Mantua (c. 1465–1474), for instance, or aiding the Old Testament hero Judith, and caring for an infant in Lorenzo Lotto's *St Lucy altarpiece* (c. 1532).[23] The salacious stereotype of Black women informs Sodoma's *Marriage of Alexander and Roxana* (c. 1519, Villa Farnesina, Rome). The celebratory, sexual tone of epithalamia (nuptial poetry) is emphasized by a grinning Black woman who eagerly watches the groom approach the bridal chamber, her hands grasping the bed's red curtains so that the cloth between her hands forms the shape of a vulva.

Titian's figure in *Diana and Actaeon* fiercely aids in the defense of chastity, which meant consistent loyalty to the marital oath rather than virginity *per se*. She is situated in a visual context that does not pretend to be a vignette of everyday life. Rather, she appears in an *istoria*, a narrative considered especially noteworthy, and in a large canvas intended for a powerful king. Interpreting her as a mere appendage to Diana implies that she signifies no more than slavery and servitude. Attendant she may be, but she is bedecked, energetic, and engaged with the story and its central point about chastity.

While stereotypes were rampant, in practice Black women, like other servants and slaves, were expected to defend the honor of the household

23. The early case of Mantegna's fresco was discussed by Maria Maura in a paper delivered at the Feminist Art History Conference on 30 September 2018, "Beyond the Reality Effect: The African Woman in Mantegna's Oculus." For others see Paul H. D. Kaplan, "Isabella d'Este and Black African Women," in *Black Africans in Renaissance Europe*, edited by T. F. Earle and K. J. P. Lowe (Cambridge: Cambridge University Press, 2005), 125–54; Elizabeth McGrath, "Lotto's Lucy, her name and her black companion," in *Mantova e il Rinascimento italiano. Studi in onore di David S. Chambers*, edited by Philippa Jackson and Guido Rebecchini (Mantua: Editoriale Sometti, 2011), 191–11.

they served and to uphold its respectability.[24] However much they were or were not complicit with such patriarchal standards for others, most were certainly keen to guard their own honor, though despair, covert rebellion and personal assertion led to cases of drunkenness, illicit sexual activity, suicide, or murder. Records about the emotional lives of slaves and servants in premodern Europe are sporadic, mainly surviving in legal records, but in that restricted context there are glimpses of women who are proud to have been long-term concubines of their European master, or who use the word "companion" to describe their role. With pride and determination, some managed to mount court cases seeking freedom for themselves and their children or successfully accused masters of beating them. Under the prejudicial legal system and caught up in the stereotype that all Africans were lustful, there was little point trying to bring a charge of rape but some informally named the fathers of their offspring, implicating European owners and their friends. Complaints by masters about the disobedience, insolence, laziness, or pride of slaves point to a strong undercurrent of resistance and subversion. Titian's figure can be regarded as fighting for her own honor and reputation as well as for that of her goddess. Already clothed, she moves with alacrity to cover the personification of chastity.

The treatment of servants and slaves in Renaissance Italy varied widely, from beating and near-starvation to decent care and generous bequests. Not all bonds were antagonistic, despite the long-term influence of the phrase "domestic enemy" used in the ground-breaking article on Italian slavery published by historian Iris Origo in 1955.[25] She mentioned the fourteenth-century humanist Petrarch, whose statement — "we have as many enemies as we have slaves" — was actually about servants (he owned no slaves). Furthermore, he repeated an ancient saying from Seneca rather

24. The following is largely drawn from Romano, *Housecraft and Statecraft*, 52–53, 171, 193–222; Steven Epstein, *Speaking of Slavery. Color, Ethnicity, and Human Bondage in Italy* (Ithaca: Cornell University Press, 2001), 114–17, 124–32; Debra Blumenthal, *Enemies and Familiars: Slavery and Mastery in Fifteenth-Century Valencia* (Ithaca, NY: Cornell University Press, 2009), 46–47, 64–65, 68–76, 154–93.
25. Origo, "Domestic Enemy," 332 ("domestici hostes," mentioning Petrarch but with no endnote).

than inventing a new, emotional or personal one.[26] Sixteenth-century authors repeated the proverb "we have as many enemies in our house as we have slaves." Writing in Sicily – where the proportion of slaves was as high as four or five percent – Paolo Caggio, the author of *Iconomica* (1552), referred to it, but in the context of ruptures between levels of privilege and power, not slaves *per se*.[27] In 1575, Stefano Guazzo's conduct manual repeated it in his comments about servants, further echoing Seneca in saying that such enemies were made not born.[28] Historian Kate Lowe concludes that in Renaissance Italy, "slave status more often than skin color" was what mattered and "color was not considered a deep characteristic of a person."[29]

Working for rich patrons who were fellow European Christians, Titian was a man of his time who could not conceive of advocating for those of low status or different race. His painting assumes that chastity is a universal value, but it is not a conscious manifesto for the inclusion of all races under that banner. The superiority of himself, his viewers (primarily male and white), and the mythological divinity are assumed. The picture asserts patriarchal, hierarchical, and European values, but it is not without sympathy for the performers of the narrative.

26. Seneca, *Epistulae Morales*, 47.5 ("totidem hostes esse quot servos," "as many enemies as you have slaves"); Petrarch, *Familiarium rerum libri*, 4.14.1 ("familiarium hostium") and 10.3.31 (quoting Seneca); Conrad Rawski, *Petrarch's 'Remedies for Fortune Fair and Foul'* (Bloomington: Indiana University Press, 1991), vol. 3, 84–85 2.29, (citing Seneca); Rawski, *Petrarch's 'Remedies,'* vol. 4, 137–41 (including the Latin and an English translation of *Familiarium* 4.14); Epstein, *Speaking of Slavery*, 43–44. Perhaps Origo had in mind Cicero, *In Catilinam* 3.28 ("domestici hostes"), but the phrase referred to a political enemy in the Roman senate.
27. Paolo Caggio, *Iconomica* (Venice: al segno del Pozzo, 1552), 41r; Origo, "Domestic Enemy," 322.
28. Stefano Guazzo, *La civil conversatione* (Venice: appresso Bartolomeo Robino, 1575), 440, 454; Romano, *Housecraft and Statecraft*, 20.
29. Kate Lowe, "Isabella d'Este and the Acquisition of Black Africans at the Mantuan Court," in *Mantova e il Rinascimento italiano. Studi in onore di David S. Chambers*, edited by Philippa Jackson and Guido Rebecchini (Mantua: Editoriale Sometti, 2011), 71; Epstein, *Speaking of Slavery*, 108.

Goddess and assistant act in unison, bodies slightly overlapping and curving in similar arcs, arms raised to one purpose. Diana's eyes are lowered in modesty, but her companion looks across at Actaeon in disbelief and alarm. The represented alliance follows the social ideal. Slaves were to be treated with moderation according to the Bible, like a brother, and "as of thy own self," advice Guazzo reiterated.[30] Perfect, loyal servants were like a second self. That is not to say that servants were equals. There is a clear differential in Titian's pairing, for the goddess is obviously above everyone else in monumental size, status, fury, and pictorial focus. Yet the Black figure is a core player in the goddess's sanctuary, much more important than the white nymph obliviously attending to her mistress. Her purpose is not primarily as a subjugated attribute of Diana, however; rather, Titian places her there to accentuate certain visual and narrative distinctions.

Her significance is clear if we imagine the figure not there at all. In narrative terms, emphasis is added to the crucial act of noticing and the chaste act of covering, which thus also further underscore the expanse of alluring nakedness. Compositionally, she folds the action back into the dynamics of the picture; otherwise the edge is vacuous and Diana isolated, with literally no one having her back. These effects would, however, work almost as well with a pale figure in the same pose. Importantly, x-rays show that Titian did initially plan a white nymph in that position, though reaching her left arm around to cover Diana's genitals.[31] Some scholars believe the alteration was made so that Diana was not swamped by too high a tone in that area of the composition, and thus that the nymph was replaced by "the less conspicuous dark attendant."[32]

30. Ecclesiasticus 33:31 ("quasi anima tua"); Guazzo, *Civil conversatione*, 454–45, 461–62 ("quasi l'anima tua"); Romano, *Housecraft and Statecraft*, 20.
31. S. Kennedy North, "The Bridgewater Titians," *Burlington Magazine* 62 (1933): 15; Lars Skarsgård, *Research and Reasoning: A Case Study on an Historical Inquiry*: "*Titian's* Diana and Actaeon: A *Study in Artistic Innovation*" (Göteborg: Akademiförlaget, 1968), 55–59, 73–82; Jill Dunkerton et al., "Catalogue," *National Gallery Technical Bulletin* 36 (2016): 64–75, 129, esp 70, 72, and figs 123, 137.
32. Skarsgård, *Research and Reasoning*, 58.

While this may be somewhat true in terms of tone and light, the final effect hardly relies on an unobtrusive figure to close the composition. Titian took pains with the altered flesh, using layers of "lead white, yellow earth, black, umber, lead-tin yellow and even a little blue pigment" to build up "the sheen of black skin," whereas Laura's page was rendered in a less variegated brown and Salvaresius's page, close in date to the *Diana* canvas, also has less subtly executed, though darker, skin.[33] Moreover, the skillfully shaded flesh is supplemented by numerous exciting touches of color: sapphire daubs in the hair, ruby and gold at the ear, glistening pearl on the arm, and the eye-catching multi-colored fabric of stripes. I agree that the chief impetus for the alterations was likely to be Titian's unexpected access to an actual model.[34] Individualization of the face, as well as careful attention to capturing the nuances of dark skin suggest that the artist was inspired by the challenges of first-hand sight. The changes enhanced the narrative and compositional import of the figure, and the painting became more intriguing, emphatic, and varied after one bland, pale nymph was eradicated.

Modern Oblivion[35]

Yet the figure is "less conspicuous" in modern commentary, to the point of invisibility in some cases. Who sees what, and how, and when, remain important issues. Over the course of the sixteenth and seventeenth centuries, various copies and oil sketches of the canvas were produced, and the African woman always appeared.[36] Perhaps the rise in race theory dur-

33. The quotation is from Dunkerton et al., "Catalogue," 72.
34. Dunkerton et al., "Catalogue," 72.
35. The phrase is from Leo Steinberg, *The Sexuality of Christ in Renaissance Art and in Modern Oblivion*, 2nd ed. (Chicago: University of Chicago Press, 1986), a study of ways in which modern observers had denied any meaning to pictures that displayed Christ's genitals, some examples of which had also been overpainted.
36. The figure is severely cropped in Andrea Schiavone's c. 1559 version now in the Kunsthistorisches Museum, Vienna, which may be due to subsequent trimming on that edge. For details and reproductions, see Wethey, *Titian*, 140–141 (the painting there attributed to Teniers is now given to Frans Wouters and in the Scottish National

ing the eighteenth century fostered subsequent erasures, neglect, denigration, or dismissal of Titian's Black figure. Examining the language and tactics used by museums and scholars in the past helps us learn how to speak and see in more insightful ways.

In the worst cases, the figure is ignored entirely. A five-minute video about the painting produced by the National Gallery, London, in 2008 did not mention her, though it found time to refer to the fine glass that was shipped to Spain at the same time as the canvas.[37] At least she has not been painted out or had the pigment scraped off and re-painted, as has happened in the case of some portraits of sitters of mixed race.[38] But little attempt was made to remember her in the photographed tableaux-vivant staged in November 2008 by Tom Hunter as part of the campaign to raise money so that the painting could be purchased for a British public collection.[39]

Calvin Colvin's 1998 interpretation of the painting is more thoughtful (see figure 5), wryly updating the scenario by situating it in a living room crowded with such domestic objects as an ironing board and washing hanging on the line. Every figure is present, except for the Black woman, who is replaced by an upright vacuum cleaner displaying the brand name "Hot Point" on its lower, black section. Nearby, a large pair of black binoc-

Gallery, Edinburgh); Francis Richardson, *Andrea Schiavone* (Oxford: Clarendon, 1980), 54, 59–60, 163, 190–91, 194–95, nos 262, 327–28, 333; Terisio Pignatti, "*Abbozzi* and *Ricordi*: New Observations on Titian's Technique," in *Titian 500*, edited by Joseph Manca (Washington, DC: National Gallery of Art, 1993), 72–83.

37. https://www.youtube.com/watch?v=7Afr93w2WNE (published 25 November 2008; last accessed 17 November 2019). The figure is not mentioned in the excellent overview *Revealing the African Presence*.

38. In the twentieth century, the latter fate befell Louis Antoine Collas's *Portrait of a Free Women of Color Wearing a Tignon* (1829, New Orleans Museum of Art). Instances of figures painted out include Joaneath Spicer, "Pontormo's *Maria Salviati with Giulia de' Medici*," *The Walters Members Magazine* 54, no 3 (Summer 2001): 4–6; Rosenthal and Lugo-Ortiz, "Envisioning Slave Portraiture," 1, fig. I.1.

39. Arranged by *The Daily Mirror*, and published in the 25 November 2008 issue: https://www.mirror.co.uk/3am/celebrity-news/sex-and-the-citys-kim-cattrall-strips-361694. The ethnicity of the light-skinned woman on the far right is difficult to determine.

Figure 5. Calum Colvin. *Diana and Actaeon (after Titian)*. 1998. Collection: the artist.

ulars rests atop red fabric tossed on the floor, a reference to the story's themes of sight and voyeurism. Far removed from Renaissance investment in the authority of the classical world and its stories, Colvin presents a "Scottish 'working class domestic' version of the myth, where Diana is reduced herself to a kind of domestic servitude."[40] Regarded as a lowly servant, Titian's African figure is replaced by black objects that point ironically to sexual stereotypes about "hotness." On the one hand, the Black woman is expunged, but on the other hand thereby no Black person is objectified or pictured in a servile role.

Without any such sense of irony or critique, however, one art critic crassly suggested in 2008 that Titian's work is "in all likelihood a brothel scene cloaked in myth" and that the presence of the Black woman tends

40. Calum Colvin, email to the author, 14 October 2019. I am very grateful to Professor Colvin for his comments and his willingness to allow reproduction of the work.

to confirm that claim.[41] The derogatory proposition ignores differences between prostitutes and courtesans and between sensuality and pornography, flouts the story's import about chastity, and conflates models with narrative figures. Above all, it perpetuates the insulting, uninformed, and long-standing stereotype about Africans being sexually promiscuous, a stereotype already evident in the Renaissance.[42] While it is true that some slaves and former slaves, from any geographical region, were prostitutes or servants of sexual workers, it was not a predominant pattern.[43]

Most commonly, the Black woman is mentioned in passing, deemed inconsequential and no more than a "black maidservant." Thus the figure is usually identified as a possession or accoutrement of Diana, but nothing further is said, so she becomes invisible as a subject. Sometimes there is the hint of dismissal. In 1968, one author referred to Diana as a "woman" and all the nymphs as "girls," but noted "the little negro girl's face."[44] In 1985, she was consistently and only "the Negress," without an occupation.[45]

Rather, the latter author associated the figure with the allegorical aspect of Diana as *Natura*, thereby once more subsuming it under the role of secondary attribute. Allegorical readings of the figure cloak it in intellectual obscurity, evacuating from it any social, political, or artistic significance beyond symbolism. No attention is paid to features like costuming, pictorial handling, or facial expression, much less the context of chastity or the dynamics of sight. All that matters in such elaborate moves is the

41. Jonathan Jones, "The £ 50m brothel scene," *The Guardian* (17 December 2008) https://www.theguardian.com/artanddesign/2008/dec/18/titian-art-worth-jonathan-jones (accessed 17 October 2019). He concludes "Does Titian, too, include a black servant to show that he is actually portraying the courtesans of Venice? Is she the crucial clue that this is a brothel scene?"
42. Kate Lowe, "The stereotyping of black Africans in Renaissance Europe," in *Black Africans in Renaissance Europe*, edited by T. F. Earle and K. J. P. Lowe (Cambridge: Cambridge University Press, 2005), 29–30.
43. Certain places, such as Genoa and Sicily, explicitly outlawed the use of slaves as prostitutes: Epstein, *Speaking of Slavery*, 133–34.
44. Skarsgård, *Research and Reasoning*, 48.
45. Jane Nash, *Veiled Images. Titian's Mythological Paintings for Philip II* (Philadelphia: Art Alliance Press, 1985), 41, 42, 43, 46, 63, 64.

figure's blackness, which enables interpretations of the figure as Night or as an associate of *Natura* or *Fortuna*.[46]

Contrapposto and Complementarity

Another, subtle mode of marginalization has been the frequent observation that the Black woman is an aesthetic "foil" to the adjacent white figure. Thus, to cite just one example, "the dusky Negro girl ... provides a telling foil to the fair-skinned goddess."[47] The comment is considered a sufficient and sole explanation for her presence and visual effect. In a preliminary, cursory sense this is true enough, but it makes the Black figure dependent on and secondary to Diana, and leaves everything else about her insignificant. To be sure, the goddess is the leading character, but the Black attendant is more important than any of the pallid nymphs.

Certainly, ideal feminine beauty was described as white (akin to milk, snow, ivory, and alabaster) tinged with red (likened to blood and rose).[48] Yet treatises on the matter did not explicitly contrast this ideal with any other pigmentation, and the concept works equally well if the companion would be, say, olive-skinned, or distinctively different in any other way. Around 1590–1600, the minor French nobleman Pierre Brantôme remarked: "an excellent painter ... having executed the portrait of a very beautiful and pleasant-looking lady, places next to her an old hag, a Moor-

46. See Marie Tanner, "Chance and Coincidence in Titian's *Diana and Actaeon*," *Art Bulletin* 56, (1974): 535–50; Nash, *Veiled Images*, 64 and 82 n. 77; Marie Tanner, *Sublime Truth and the Senses. Titian's Poesie for King Philip II of Spain* (London: Harvey Miller, 2018), 101–15.
47. Wethey, *Titian*, 74.
48. Giangiorgio Trissino, *I Ritratti* (first published in 1524), in *Tutte le opera* (Verona: Jacopo Vallarsi,1729), vol. 2, 272–273; Agnolo Firenzuola, *On the Beauty of Women*, trans. Konrad Eisenbichler and Jacqueline Murray (Philadelphia: University of Pennsylvania Press, 1992), 15, 28, 31, 45–46, 49, 57, 60, 62, 63, 65, 67 (first published in 1548); Federigo Luigini, *Il libro della bella donna* (Venice: Plinio Pietrasanta, 1554), 35, 43–44, 47–48, 51, 54, 56, 72, and passim; Mary Rogers, "The decorum of women's beauty: Trissino, Firenzuola, Luigini and the representation of women in sixteenth-century painting," *Renaissance Studies* 2 (1988): 47–88.

ish slave or a hideous dwarf, so that their ugliness and blackness may give greater lustre and brilliance to her great beauty and fairness."[49]

However, the fundamental principle of *contrapposto* meant that a fair lady's beauty was enhanced when she wore a black dress, and not because the clothing was considered ugly.[50] Brantome simplified aesthetic theory, which ultimately deployed *contrapposto* as a mode, not of outright opposition, but of concord that arose from comparison and dialectical subtlety where each element enhances the other.[51] Harmony and diversity or *varietà* were the desired results, rather than binary contrast. In the 1430s, Leon Battista Alberti's treatise on painting picked up on ancient praise of the famous painter Apelles, recommending that the women in Diana's troop wear a range of colored garments, some light, some dark, leading to a pleasing, graceful whole.[52] Writing just a few years before the *Diana and Actaeon* was finished, Titian's friend Ludovico Dolce noted that painters had to find a mean between the extremes of light and dark, which "unites one contrary with the other."[53] Juxtapositions, of light and dark, young and old, near and far, and so on, were commonly applauded due to their mutual enhancement, and such charming variety extended beyond pairs alone, entailing also multiple types, postures, and colors.

Furthermore, many understood that perception and beauty were relative and that, in the words of the inscription on an Italian cameo made in the second half of the sixteenth century featuring the profile of an African

49. Lorne Campbell, *Renaissance Portraits* (New Haven: Yale University Press, 1990), 134; Woods-Marsden, "The Mistress as 'Virtuous,'" 61.
50. Trissino, *I Ritratti*, 273.
51. David Summers, "Contrapposto: Style and Meaning in Renaissance Art," *Art Bulletin* 59 (1977): 336–61. On comparison, see also Leon Battista Alberti, *On Painting and On Sculpture*, edited and translated by Cecil Grayson (London: Phaidon, 1972), 52–55 (1.18). I thank Mary Pardo for the latter reference.
52. Summers, "Contrapposto," 349.
53. Summers, "Contrapposto," 353.

man, "Varying like this, Nature is beautiful."[54] While the color black might have symbolized evil in some circumstances, in other contexts, including allegory and poetry, black was beautiful, a tradition going back to the Old Testament and Greek poetry.[55] Saying no more than that Titian presents a "foil" to Diana misses the subtlety of *contrapposto* and implies that the difference in skin color is the chief or only factor. It also infers that white beauty is always primary and that blackness is ugly, recessive, and dependent. But Titian offers many charming, concordant variations in the canvas, including fully naked, partly veiled, and partly clothed in the case of the Black attendant. As with Titian's representations of Black pages, there is a clear power differential in the *Diana and Actaeon* scene because the chief protagonist is an eternal goddess whereas the Black attendant, in clothing, ornamentation, and skin color is a person of the artist's time. But she is not infantilized, and her action and values are in concert with those of the deity.

Her proximity to Diana may indeed have symbolic meaning, though it is conveyed in more nuanced ways than solely by skin color. Diana is crowned with her sign of the crescent moon and allegorical interpretations of the painting claim that the Black attendant, because of her pigmentation, represents various aspects of the goddess in her dark and nighttime manifestations.[56] I would argue that we see co-ordination and affirmation in the pair. Slipping far off her shoulders, the attendant's upper dress forms a lunar arc, and the sweeping gesture of her two arms enfolds the goddess in a similar celestial curve. Her shimmering cloth with

54. Spicer, *Revealing the African Presence*, 46, fig. 22 (with a different translation). The line is from a poem by Serafino Aquilano (1466–1500): Serafino de' Ciminelli dall'Aquila, *Le Rime*, edited by Mario Menghini (Bologna: Romagnoli Dall'Acqua, 1894), 1:124, "e per tal variar natura è bella." See also, for example, Alberti, *On Painting*, 52–53; Summers, "Contrapposto," 359; Firenzuola, *Beauty of Women*, 10; *Complete Essays of Montaigne*, trans. Donald Frame (Stanford: Stanford University Press, 1958), 355–56 (mainly written in 1576); Tommaso Buoni, *I problemi della bellezza* (Venice: Ciotti, 1605), 24–25, 98.
55. See, for instance, *Song of Songs*, 1:4 ("Nigra sum, sed Formosa"); *Greek Anthology*, 5.210; Giambattista Marino, *La Lira*, Part 3 (Venice: Ciotti, 1614), 9 ("Bella Schiava").
56. See n. 44 above.

golden and white highlights is contrary to nighttime. In terms of *contrapposto*, her skin color adds variety and balance. Visible, colorful, active, and meaningful, the Black figure is a crucial player in Titian's drama.

Discussion Questions

1. How does the presence of the Black figure in Titian's painting change the narrative of the myth of Diana and Actaeon?
2. Can you think of some examples in contemporary popular culture in which secondary characters are racialized in ways that seem extraneous or unquestioned?
3. How does this reading change your idea of Renaissance Venice and Italy?

Suggestions for Further Reading

Epstein, Steven. "Slaves in Italy, 1350–1550." In *At the Margins: Minority Groups in Premodern Italy*, edited by Stephen Milner, 219–235. Minneapolis: University of Minnesota Press, 2005.

Kaplan, Paul H. D. "Local Color: The Black African Presence in Venetian Art and History." In *Fred Wilson: Speak of Me as I Am*, 8–19. Cambridge, MA: List Visual Arts Center, Massachusetts Institute of Technology, 2003.

Lowe, Kate. "Visible Lives: Black Gondoliers and Other Black Africans in Renaissance Venice." *Renaissance Quarterly* 66, (2013): 412–52.

McGrath, Elizabeth. "Lotto's Lucy, her name and her black companion." In *Mantova e il Rinascimento italiano. Studi in onore di David S. Chambers*, edited by Philippa Jackson and Guido Rebecchini, 191–211. Mantua: Editoriale Sometti, 2011.

Whitewashing the Whitewashed Renaissance: Italian Renaissance Art through a *Kapharian* Lens

REBECCA M. HOWARD

> *"You remember old-school cameras, where when you took a picture, you actually had to focus? Right? You'd put the camera up, and if I wanted you in focus, I would move the lens a little to the left and you would come forward. I could move the lens a little to the right, and you would go back and the folks in the background would come out. I'm just trying to do that here. I'm trying to give you that opportunity."* – Titus Kaphar[1]

This exercise asks students to refocus and amend long-held ways of viewing early modern Italian works of art that incorporate Black Africans alongside white Europeans. As its base and inspiration, the methodology utilizes the work of the contemporary African American artist Titus Kaphar. The following case study involves a detailing of background information that can be used for teaching existing scholarship on the images to be discussed, followed by pedagogical resources, detailed approaches, and discussion questions that instructors may use to engage with this material in the classroom. This methodology initiates a discussion of race in the Renaissance, specifically focusing on the Italian Renaissance, but applicable in a range of Western artworks from this period. First considering the aims of Titus Kaphar, who intends to *amend* history through his paintings and sculptures, this essay will then provide a brief study of blackness in early modernity, as well as information about certain early modern Italian works.

1. Titus Kaphar (August 2017), "Can art amend history?" TED talk (video file), retrieved from https://www.ted.com/talks/titus_kaphar_can_art_amend_history?language=en.

Born in 1976, Titus Kaphar is a contemporary African American artist, whose works act as physical deconstructions of a white-centered western past and as such, can be widely applied to a number of works from the Italian Renaissance and beyond. Kaphar received his MFA from Yale University and has seen a steady rise in fame and influence in recent decades. According to the artist's official website, his works "examine the history of representation by transforming its styles and mediums with formal innovations to emphasize the physicality and dimensionality of the canvas and materials themselves." In so doing, he aims to "dislodge history from its status as the 'past' in order to unearth its contemporary relevance," shining light on evident active absences or instances of marginalization found in certain works from the past.[2] In discussing race in the Italian Renaissance, the contemporary relevance of Kaphar's works can help us better understand and connect with the past, particularly by viewing certain works through what I call a *Kapharian lens*. Kaphar's choice of the word *unearth* in talking about his creative goals is of importance in what this essay aims to do – asking students to reconsider and amend the works that they are viewing in and out of the classroom. In Kaphar's artistic approach of exposing elements like structure, material, and compositional choices, he in fact unearths an entirely new way of viewing.

Many of Kaphar's works are quite clear, even straightforward, in what they intend to visually convey, thus providing a useful ignition for students to begin discussing and studying a difficult subject. As we will see, the artist frequently aims to provide a new lens – the *Kapharian lens* – for viewers to look through, inspiring new and careful ways of thinking about the works that they are seeing. Having learned about Kaphar's contemporary pieces and their intended impact, and then having considered specific early modern artworks with Kaphar's aims in mind, students will be able to apply this knowledge toward reconsidering said works, utilizing the *Kapharian lens* and thereby *re-focusing* their approach to both discussing and further researching many early modern pieces.

2. Titus Kaphar, official website, https://kapharstudio.com/, accessed March 4, 2019.

Titus Kaphar Reconsiders Frans Hals

Black characters appearing in Renaissance artworks are often marginalized, sidelined, and quite clearly not the intended primary focus of the majority of works in which they appear. As such, scholarship has continued for centuries to ignore or merely gloss over their presence. The careful composition of certain works of art is one of Kaphar's primary concerns. Any class activity or discussion inspired by this essay should begin with the artist's incredibly impactful TED talk of 2017, "Can Art Amend History?" In this talk, he explains that, having taken a number of art history courses in his past, he recognizes that "painting is a visual language where everything in the painting is meaningful, is important. It's coded." However, Kaphar notes that sometimes, "because of the compositional structure, because of compositional hierarchy, it's hard to see other things,"[3] meaning, our attention is not explicitly directed to them. He is largely referring to those people who have been pushed aside not only in the artworks themselves, but also, problematically, in the scholarship. Kaphar states that he wants his artworks to help people both think of history and *see* history in new ways. Noting that history – good or bad – is important, his intention is not to change or erase history, but instead to *amend* it, thereby *altering our focus*: "What I'm trying to show you is how to shift your gaze just slightly, just momentarily."[4] In his talk, Kaphar asks that we look at certain historical images as though we are looking through an "old-school camera." The artist wants viewers to shift the focus of one's looking in the way that we would shift the camera's focus.[5] When you move your lens, and instead use a *Kapharian lens*, different figures come in and out of focus, expanding and changing our understanding of race in the period.

3. Kaphar, "Can art amend history?" TED talk.
4. Kaphar, "Can art amend history?" TED talk.
5. Kaphar, "Can art amend history?" TED talk.

Figure 1. Titus Kaphar, *Shifting the Gaze*, 2017, 211 x 262 cm, oil on canvas, Brooklyn Museum, Courtesy of the artist and the artist's estate

Completed during his TED talk, which is an interesting and accessible addition to any classroom discussion on the topic of race in the Renaissance, Kaphar's 2017 work, *Shifting the Gaze*, now owned by the Brooklyn Museum, calls direct attention to these concerns about the way certain early modern works were composed, as well as the way we view them today (Figure 1). While *Shifting the Gaze* is not based on an Italian artwork, the original painting that Kaphar amends is from the early modern period and the refocused approach is entirely applicable to similar images. For the creation of this work, Kaphar first paints a group portrait largely inspired by (in fact, nearly a perfect copy of) the seventeenth-century Dutch artist Frans Hals' *Family Group in a Landscape* (c. 1645–1648), located in Madrid's Thyssen-Bornemisza Museo Nacional (Figure 2). Hals' piece depicts a group of four white individuals, presumably family members, accompanied by a Black figure. In Hals' painting, as well as in Kaphar's later version, this young Black man looks out directly into the viewer's space. Using this painting as a base, Kaphar alters the group portrait in front of a live audience, during his TED talk. While doing so, he states that he wants to know about the Black character, too. As he explains, "What I'm trying to do, what I'm trying to show you, is how to shift your gaze just slightly, just momentarily ... "[6] By looking through a *Kapharian lens*, we might now begin to consider what further research could bring to light.

Figure 2. Frans Hals, *Family Group in a Landscape*, c. 1645–1648), 202 x 285 cm, oil on canvas, Museo Nacional Thyssen-Bornemisza, Madrid, Courtesy of the Museo Nacional Thyssen-Bornemisza.

6. Kaphar, "Can art amend history?" TED talk.

As many scholars of early modernity have noted, when both white and Black figures are included in the same work, it is the Black characters that are typically placed in marginal positions – pushed to the background or sides.[7] And, as mentioned, this marginalization is apparent in most scholarship on Renaissance art historical topics, as well, especially scholarship that was conducted before the twenty-first century. "Historically speaking," Kaphar states, "in research on these kinds of paintings, I can find out more about the lace that the woman is wearing in this painting – the manufacturer of the lace – than I can about [the Black man's] character ... about his dreams, about his hopes, about what he wanted out of life."[8] This is exactly the long-established tendency with which Kaphar's works take issue. The hope behind his creation of pieces like *Shifting the Gaze* is that viewers will be inspired and reminded to look more closely at *any* image that includes both Black and white figures within the same piece. The artist is essentially asking us to always consider the lives of Black characters *beyond* only thinking of them in relation to an artwork's white characters.

A Shift in Our Gaze

This biased history does not need merely to be erased, then, but instead it is our gaze and our understanding that needs to be altered and shifted. When Kaphar paints over the members of the white European family in *Shifting the Gaze*, literally "whitewashing" the white figures, he makes sure that the audience is aware that this alteration is largely temporary. "I don't want you to think that this is about eradication. It's not," he says, explaining that the paint he uses is mixed with an oil that will cause it to fade overtime, thereby allowing the white characters to eventually reemerge, albeit partially.[9] Of course, this white paint will never fade

7. Kate Lowe, "The Lives of African Slaves and People of African Descent in Renaissance Europe," in *The Image of the Black in Western Art: From the "Age of Discovery" to the Age of Abolition, Artists of the Renaissance and Baroque*, Part III, edited by David Bindman and Henry Louis Gates, Jr. (Cambridge, MA: Harvard University Press, 2010), 19.
8. Kaphar, "Can art amend history?" TED talk.
9. Kaphar, "Can art amend history?" TED talk.

entirely, existing as a reminder of the necessity of *refocusing* our viewing of certain images. Kaphar is asking us to reset our lens, bringing others into focus and *amending* history, in order to better understand *all the characters of that history*. Just as other recent endeavors have attempted to do (such the 2013 exhibition, *Revealing the African Presence in Renaissance Europe*, at the Walters Art Museum in Baltimore, Maryland), Kaphar also aims to take prized pieces of art history, "polished to a glow by generations of attention," and turn each piece in an "unexpected direction, so it catches the searching, scouring rays of new investigative light."[10] As art historian Adrienne Childs notes, this kind of reclamation of humanity and assertion of the Black presence in history is popular within many artists' oeuvres in our contemporary moment.[11] While Kaphar's *Shifting the Gaze*, especially when paired with his TED talk during which he completes the work, is extremely powerful and quite straightforward in its intention (and thus useful in the context of teaching), the expectation is that, by discussing Kaphar's goal in *Shifting the Gaze*, students may develop an interest in various other contemporary artists who are working in a similar vein by connecting the lauded works of a dubious past to our own present.

Explaining his reasoning for works like *Shifting the Gaze*, Kaphar shares that his numerous art history classes led him to rethink certain artworks of the past, thus inspiring the creation of his exceptional works of today. In their deliberate connections to canonical moments in art history's past, this artist's creations are particularly well-suited for an exercise that is focused on the so-called *pinnacle* period of western art history — the Italian Renaissance. Kaphar speaks specifically about that moment that produced a certain cognitive spark and defined much of the course of his work. In an art history survey course in college, he noticed that only fourteen out of approximately four hundred pages in the course's required textbook were dedicated to Black people in painting. Despite issues with the section's organization and design, Kaphar exclaims that he was "really

10. Holland Cotter, "A Spectrum from Slaves to Saints," *The New York Times*, November 8, 2012.
11. Adrienne L. Childs, "Presence of Mind," *Transition*, no. 111, New Narratives of Haiti (2013): 159–65, at 164.

excited about it, because in all the other classes that I had, we didn't even have that conversation. We didn't talk about it at all."[12] Nevertheless, the section was skipped in his course. Despite being incorporated into the course's textbook, the professor chose not to discuss it with the class at all. This is what Kaphar's artworks aim to change by drawing attention to and refocusing our gaze toward works by Black artists, and Black individuals within white artists' works, that have been glossed over or even skipped entirely in the broad spectrum of the field of art history. And, when incorporated into the study of Italian Renaissance art, an exercise like the one I discuss in the following sections aims to do the same.

Blackness and Black Individuals in Renaissance Thought

Having introduced a classroom to the work of Titus Kaphar, I suggest that instructors now discuss some of the extensive scholarship that directly examines early modern artworks that include both white and Black individuals in the same space, a field of research that has been addressed on a larger scale only in recent decades. While considering various exemplary works, ask students to think about what new questions and concerns a *Kapharian lens* could help to unearth. What new ways of looking might finally be allowed if we "amend" certain early modern artworks? When white European characters are removed or whitewashed, even if temporarily, what is left and what should viewers make of it? What additional information can then be brought to light? Just as Kaphar's aim is to "reveal something of what has been lost and to investigate the power of a rewritten history," students should similarly be inspired to shift their looking, which can ultimately lead the field to new research and scholarship.[13]

Before discussing specific images, it is first important to understand and convey to students early modern views of blackness. In the catalogue accompanying the previously mentioned exhibition at the Walters Art Museum, *Revealing the African Presence in Renaissance Europe*, Joaneath

12. Kaphar, "Can art amend history?" TED talk.

13. Kaphar, official website.

Spicer, the museum's Curator of Renaissance and Baroque Art, explains how most Europeans perceived a polarity between blackness and whiteness, which was largely drawn from biblical sources. Long histories of understanding Heaven as a place of light and Hell as a place of darkness fostered attitudes toward black and white as reflecting certain opposing values. There was an overall negativity associated with darkness and blackness that stems from as far back as Old Testament sources. Spicer writes, for example, "that anything horrible might be described as 'black,' such as the deadly plague, which in the 1500s began to be called 'the black death,' not because of the color of victims but because of the horror it engendered."[14] Furthermore, biblical examples like Christ's declaration in the *Gospel of John* that, "I am the light of the world; he that followeth me shall not walk in darkness (8:12)," describe similar polarities between light and dark which seem to have been transferred to polarities between white and black.[15] Satan was also said to be black, as were his demons. And, according to other early modern figures such as the playwright Thomas Nashe, "As God is entitled the Father of Light, so is the devil surnamed the Prince of Darkness, which is the night."[16] Powerful metaphorical allusions like these, Spicer explains, placed black and white on a moral spectrum — blackness essentially reflecting evil and whiteness reflecting good, a concept that is explored further in Matthieu Chapman's essays in this collection, "Mapping Race in Early Modern Europe" and "Sight-Reading Race in Early Modern Drama: Dog Whistles, Signifiers, and the Grammars of Blackness," co-authored by Joshua Kelly. "Sin itself was black, blackening and corrupting the soul by soiling it with a rejection of God," Spicer

14. Joaneath Spicer, "European Perceptions of Blackness as Reflected in the Visual Arts," in *Revealing the African Presence in Renaissance Europe*, edited by Joaneath Spicer, The Walters Art Museum (Baltimore, MD: Trustees of the Walters Art Museum, 2012), 56, n16.
15. *Gospel of John*, 8:12; Spicer, "European Perceptions," 38; Craig Koslofsky, *Evening's Empire: A History of the Night in Early Modern Europe* (Cambridge: Cambridge University Press, 2011), 10.
16. *Works of Thomas Nashe, The Terrors of the Night, A Discourse of Apparitions* (London, 1594), edited by R.B. McKerrow (London: A. H. Bullen, 1904), 345–47.

writes.[17] Blackness was, thus, frequently seen as a sort of embodied, inherent vice.[18] Furthermore, for Europeans, "goodness" was also reflected in ideals of beauty. In Renaissance Italy, standards of beauty were held to ideals drawn from the poetic writings of Francesco Petrarca (or Petrarch), which included small features, long golden hair, and pale skin.[19] And in opposition, in the European Renaissance mind, the African continent was seen as "a place of freakish beasts and bestial, violence-prone, naturally subject peoples."[20]

At the same time, however, numerous court cities in Renaissance Italy treated Black individuals as *objects* to be collected and as symbols of prestige and wealth in their apparent exoticism. The mid- to late fifteenth century sees a slight increase in imagery and textual sources depicting Black Africans in Italy, and art historian Paul Kaplan explains that this is likely in part due to the rise of the West African slave trade.[21] One of the most intriguing cases of such collecting for the purposes of exotic display, however, is that of Isabella d'Este, Marchioness of Mantua, one of the Italian peninsula's northern court cities. It is well-recorded that Isabella was particularly invested in collecting objects of art and of rarity and interest, and Black servants were certainly considered as such. In 1491, Isabella d'Este instructed one of her agents in Venice to find her an African child, "as black as possible" and no older than four.[22] According to Kaplan, doc-

17. Spicer, "European Perceptions," 37–38.
18. Childs, "Presence of Mind," 161.
19. Spicer, "European Perceptions," 41.
20. Cotter, "A Spectrum from Slaves to Saints," *The New York Times*. For more on negative early modern views of darkness, and by extension, blackness, see, Spicer, "European Perceptions," in *Revealing the African Presence in Renaissance Europe*; Koslofsky, *Evening's Empire*; Michel Pastoureau, *Black: The History of a Color* (Princeton: Princeton University Press, 2009). See also, primary sources, including, St. Augustine, *Confessions*, book 13, chap. 14; St. Augustine, *Sermons on Selected Passages of the New Testament*, no. 75, section 5; and *Works of Thomas Nashe, The Terrors of the Night*.
21. Paul H.D. Kaplan, "Italy, 1490–1700," in *The Image of the Black in Western Art: From the "Age of Discovery" to the Age of Abolition, Artists of the Renaissance and Baroque*, Part III, ed. David Bindman and Henry Louis Gates, Jr. (Cambridge, MA: Harvard University Press, 2010), 93.
22. Kaplan, "Italy, 1490–1700," 102.

umentation shows that the marchioness already had at least one Black child; as Isabella wrote, "We couldn't be more pleased with our black girl [*moretta*] even if she were blacker, because from being at first a little disdainful she has now become pleasing in words and acts, and we think she'll make the best buffoon in the world."[23] Ultimately, Isabella also came to acquire another two-year-old Black girl from a Venetian orphanage, initiated negotiations for a Black boy enslaved in a Venetian household, and purchased a Black girl for her sister, along with additional Black servants for herself over the years.[24]

While it was not yet in vogue in the 1490s for portrait sitters to have themselves depicted with such prized exotic "possessions," there are later images that do exactly this. Despite the obsession that the Este family, among others, seemed to hold toward Black people, these figures remained relatively invisible in artworks until the 1520s, when the first known portrait of a sitter with their Black servant appears. Titian's *Portrait of Laura Dianti* (c. 1523), the official mistress of the Duke Alfonso d'Este, Isabella's brother, is the earliest known freestanding portrait that includes a Black African attendant.[25] Art historian Kate Lowe, who has contributed a wealth of scholarship to the subject of Black Africans in Renaissance artworks, explains that the very composition of this piece is particularly telling. "The position of the African in a scene vis-à-vis other humans can ... suggest inferiority, as in the case with the young Black children who were so prized at European courts, and who were sometimes painted alongside their owners or masters/mistresses ... "[26] The smaller stature of the child juxtaposed with Laura Dianti makes clear that he is meant to be seen as the less important of the two. And for Kaplan, the Black child is a clear marker of the sitter's aristocratic status and fashionable tastes. "The child's spectacular striped silk costume signifies the

23. Kaplan, "Italy, 1490–1700," 102.
24. Kaplan, "Italy, 1490–1700," 102.
25. This painting is currently housed in a private collection. However, it can be found through internet searches and is one of many of its type. There are also a number of copies based on the original.
26. Lowe, "The Lives of African Slaves," 17–19.

wealth at Laura's disposal," while also likely indicating one of the child's roles as an entertainer for the court.[27] Interestingly, though, some have seen the relationship between Laura and the child as somewhat affectionate, explaining that this may be attributed to Laura's own situation as a mistress from a lower-class family, which might, in some ways, be reflected in the situation of the child. As Kaplan concludes, Laura's "visual appeal had led to her acquisition by a member of the elite and to a privileged, if not very independent, life."[28]

Figure 3. Paris Bordone, *Portrait of a Man in Armor with Two Pages*, c. 1550, 117 x 157 cm, oil on canvas, Metropolitan Museum of Art, New York City, Courtesy of the Metropolitan Museum of Art.

27. Kaplan, "Italy, 1490–1700," 109.
28. Jane Fair Bestor, "Titian's portrait of Laura Eustochia: the decorum of female beauty and the motif of the black page," Renaissance Studies 17, no. 4 (2003): 628–73, at 636; and Kaplan, "Italy, 1490–1700," 109.

This particular portrait by Titian initiated a new fashion in the realm of portraiture, causing such compositions to appear with rapidly increasing frequency. The Venetian artist Paris Bordone's *Portrait of a Man in Armor with Two Pages* (c. 1550), for example, follows the same type (Figure 3). While the sitter is yet to be identified with certainty, the individuality with which his two young pages are depicted suggests that these figures may very well be portraits of specific boys working for the sitter, which in fact reflects a mid-sixteenth century fashion to have pairs of Black and white servant boys.[29] Unlike the awestruck gaze of the Black attendant in Laura's portrait, though, the unknown man here is doted on by his white servant, while the Black child works as the painting's interlocutory figure — looking out at and seemingly posing for the viewer in order to capture our attention. He functions as an interesting rarity, a way for the sitter to show his wealth, power, and connections, and making this message all the more overt by directly connecting with the viewer. This reading, while valid, can be strengthened by the use of a *Kapharian lens*. The Black child's value and interest has only been considered by way of his relationship with the white sitter, as well as in comparison with the white attendant. In applying a *Kapharian lens* and temporarily *amending* history, however, viewers should be inspired to question the boy's personal background, his family, and his future and dreams, as Kaphar recommends.

The Unique Case of Renaissance Venice

Considering that a majority of Italian Renaissance works that incorporate Black figures come from Venice and the Veneto (the mainland areas near the island city of Venice, once part of the Republic of Venice), we need to discuss in a bit more depth this cosmopolitan Republic in particular. In artworks from early modern Venice, one can find a variety of people from different races, which was clearly intended to reflect the diversity of this unique city. The so-called *eyewitness style* that experiences a vogue in late Quattrocento (1400s or fifteenth century) Venice is characterized by a journalistic approach, capturing every minute detail of the city when con-

29. Kaplan, "Italy, 1490–1700," 126.

veying a particular event, in order to make the reality of that event all the more believable. The eyewitness style is notably carried out in a number of works by late Quattrocento and early Cinquecento (1500s or sixteenth century) painters, Vittore Carpaccio and the Bellini brothers, Gentile and Giovanni.

Both Black servants and freed Black slaves were common in early modern Venetian society. While there is little known extant documentation regarding Black people in early modern Venice and the Veneto, paintings in the eyewitness style have afforded scholars a meticulous rendering of the Republic of Venice, and, "one of the salient features [that artists] made sure to include was the presence of black Africans," which was an often very social, visible presence.[30] Among the examples of such images are two particularly intriguing works by Vittore Carpaccio, his *Healing of the Madman* (c. 1496) (Figure 4) and his *Hunting on the Lagoon* (c. 1490–1495), both of which incorporate depictions of Black gondoliers.

The most comprehensive consideration of the role of Black gondoliers in Renaissance Venice, especially their appearance in works of art, has been carried out by Kate Lowe, whose work on the subject appears not only in the 2012 Walters Art Museum catalogue, but also in a fascinating study in a 2013 volume of *Renaissance Quarterly* entitled, "Visible Lives: Black Gondoliers and Other Black Africans in Renaissance Venice."[31] In fact, even though it is lengthy, this article is well-suited for discussing in greater detail the appearance of Black characters in early modern Italian paintings; I routinely assign it as a reading for students, especially those in upper-level courses. Lowe explains that, even though the assumption of modern western viewers is that Black figures in many Renaissance paintings are depictions of slaves, it is important to note that we cannot be certain about legal status. This is because, in Venice, "a niche occupation for freed black Africans existed, linked to their prior lives in West Africa: that of gondolier."[32] As such, it is not, in fact, unusual to find a Black gondolier

30. Kaplan, "Italy, 1490–1700," 95.

31. Kate Lowe, "Visible Lives: Black Gondoliers and Other Black Africans in Renaissance Venice," *Renaissance Quarterly* 66, no. 2 (2013): 412–52.

32. Lowe, "The Lives of African Slaves," 14.

Figure 4. Vittore Carpaccio, *Healing of the Madman (Miracle of the Relic of the True Cross at the Ponte di Rialto)*, c. 1496, 365 x 389 cm, tempera on canvas, Galleria dell' Accademia, Venice, photograph courtesy of Didier Descouens, Creative Commons, Public Domain.

in an eyewitness style work that is intended to capture the city in careful, journalistic detail.

As slavery in fifteenth- and sixteenth-century Europe was usually not for life, Black Africans were increasingly integrated into society.[33] Never-

33. Concerning early modern slavery in many European cities, Lowe writes that, "on the death of a master or mistress, either a slave was freed or a set period of further enslavement was fixed. In Europe, a future freed life for slaves was envisages, and consequently slaves always lived in hope that they would be freed from bondage." (Lowe, "The Lives of African Slaves," 13–14.)

theless, many scholars have continued to gloss over their presence and the variety of their experiences. Through a *Kapharian lens*, perhaps both current and future historians of visual culture can shift their viewing of a work like Carpaccio's *Healing of the Madman*, focusing their attention and study on that figure who was socially cast aside and who has long been academically cast aside — the Black gondolier in the foreground. Amending our viewing of such an image, and conducting important historical studies like Lowe's, helps to form new questions and to inspire new avenues of research and scholarship.

As noted above, even though images in fifteenth- and sixteenth-century Italy frequently incorporated Black characters, it has indeed not been until the last thirty years or so that scholarship has given much attention to these figures at all. The roles played by Africans were simply not factored into traditional histories of Renaissance Europe.[34] Yet, these figures were part of that history and exist within the oeuvre of Italian Renaissance art, necessitating much more study than they have been given. Representations of Black Africans in the European Renaissance are typically read very simply, as "servants to the elite, as markers of the ethnic diversity of the Islamic world, as components of the Magi story, and more broadly as emblems of Christian evangelical universalism," and it is assumed that the appearance of Black characters being incorporated in these ways began in the late Middle Ages.[35] In general, the names of these characters have been lost, but this does not negate the possibility that even generalized studies of their stories and their histories can still be conducted.[36]

33. Concerning early modern slavery in many European cities, Lowe writes that, "on the death of a master or mistress, either a slave was freed or a set period of further enslavement was fixed. In Europe, a future freed life for slaves was envisages, and consequently slaves always lived in hope that they would be freed from bondage." (Lowe, "The Lives of African Slaves," 13–14.)
34. Childs, "Presence of Mind," 159.
35. Kaplan, "Italy, 1490–1700," 93.
36. Cotter, "A Spectrum from Slaves to Saints," *The New York Times*.

Employing the *Kapharian Lens* in the Classroom

Having considered the history of blackness in the Renaissance and the goals of the contemporary American artist Titus Kaphar, I ultimately suggest that instructors ask their students to look at Renaissance images anew, through a *Kapharian lens*. What is left when we *whitewash* the whitewashed Renaissance? What *new* things become visible when we deliberately remove certain compositional features and focal points? Utilizing this approach in the classroom might involve asking students, either alone or in groups, to formulate discussion questions meant to focus the viewer's attention entirely on the Black figure(s) in an artwork, perhaps even utilizing a tool like Photoshop to temporarily paint over the white figures. Students should consider whether any given person is included for the sole purpose of displaying exoticism and/or cultural connectivity and hierarchy, as seen in works such as Titian's *Portrait of Laura Dianti*. Or might we be inspired to think more thoroughly and deeply about the roles of Black Africans in early modern Italian society? Who, specifically, is the young Black boy in Titian's painting? What might we be able to discover about his life and his social roles? These questions are particularly interesting in works like Carpaccio's *Healing of the Madman*, along with others in the eyewitness style, which were known to frequently be filled with identifiable portrait likenesses of real early modern people living in Venice. Might period viewers have been able to *recognize* Carpaccio's gondolier? Can we know if he was enslaved or freed? Can his attire, his boat, or even his patron tell us more about his social status? What was his life like? His future? What really happens if we, as viewers, amend this painting, removing everyone else and leaving only the Black gondolier? How could this shift in focus enhance our understanding of the figure's role, his status, his personality, even his life? Ultimately, this methodology intends to inspire students to approach and discuss canonical Renaissance images in an entirely new way, allowing for a better understanding of how history continues to resonate in our still-fractured modern world.

Possible Discussion Questions

1. For what purpose is any given marginalized/sidelined figure included in Renaissance art?
2. When our attention is refocused entirely to a single figure, what new questions arise?
3. Can research help us to identify who these figures are, or figures like them?
4. What can a figure's attire, actions, and surroundings tell us about their social role, personality, or life?
5. What new questions and concerns does a *Kapharian lens* enable us to unearth?
6. How does the *temporary* removal of other figures in an artwork help us to refocus our looking, and therefore, our understanding of a figure and an image as a whole?
7. When white European characters are — even temporarily — removed, what is left? What additional information is then allowed to be brought to light?
8. What new ways of looking finally come to the forefront when we *amend* early modern artworks?
9. How does a deliberate, yet temporary, change in an artwork's composition allow us to rethink its purpose and function?

Further Selected Images for Teaching and Research

Titian, *Portrait of Laura dei Dianti*, c. 1523
Vittore Carpaccio, *Hunting on the Lagoon*, c. 1490–1495
attributed to Annibale Carracci, *Portrait of an African Slave Woman*, c. 1580s
Mantegna, *Camera Picta / Camera degli Sposi* ceiling oculus, 1465–1474
Benozzo Gozzoli, *Journey of the Magi*, from the Palazzo Medici-Riccardi, c. 1459–1462
Follower of Leone Leoni, *Bust of Giacomo Maria Stampa*, 1553, marble
Titan, *Portrait of Fabrizio Salvaressa*, 1558
Titian, *Diana and Actaeon*, 1559
Paolo Veronese, *Marriage at Cana*, 1562–1563
Veronese, *Feast in the House of Levi*, 1573

Suggestions for Further Reading

Bestor, Jane Fair. "Titian's Portrait of Laura Eustochia: The Decorum of Female Beauty and the Motif of the Black Page." *Renaissance Studies* 17, no. 4 (2003): 628–73.

Bindman, David, ed. *The Image of the Black in Western Art: From the "Age of Discovery" to the Age of Abolition*. Vol. III, part I, *Artists of the Renaissance and Baroque*. Cambridge: Belknap Press at Harvard University Press, 2010.

Childs, Adrienne L. "Presence of Mind." *Transition*, no. 111, *New Narratives of Haiti* (2013): 159–65.

Debrunner, HansWerner. *Presence and Prestige: Africans in Europe*: A History *of Africans in Europe before* 1918. Basel: Basler Afrika Bibliographien, 1979.

Erickson, Peter. "Invisibility Speaks: Servants and Portraits in Early Modern Visual Culture." *Journal for Early Modern Cultural Studies* 9, no. 1 (2009): 23–61.

———. "Representations of Blacks and Blackness in the Renaissance." *Criticism* 35, no. 4 (1993): 499–527.

Fortini Brown, Patricia. *Venetian Narrative Painting in the Age of Carpaccio*. New Haven: Yale University Press, 1990.

Kaphar, Titus. official website: https://kapharstudio.com/

———. TED talk: https://www.ted.com/talks/titus_kaphar_can_art_amend_history?language=en

Kaplan, Paul. "Titian's *Laura Dianti* and the Origins of the Motif of the Black Page in Portraiture." *Antichità Viva* 21, (1982): 11–18.

Lowe, Kate. "Isabella d'Este and the Acquisition of Black Africans at the Mantuan Court." In *Mantova e il Rinascimento italiano: studi in onore di David S. Chambers* edited by Philippa Jackson and Guido Rebecchini, 65–76. Mantova, Semetti, 2011.

———. "Visible Lives: Black Gondoliers and Other Black Africans in Renaissance Venice." *Renaissance Quarterly* 66, no. 2 (2013): 412–52.

Mark, Peter. "Africans in European Eyes: The Portrayal of Black Africans in Fourteenth and Fifteenth Century Europe." MA thesis, Maxwell School of Citizenship and Public Affairs, Syracuse University, 1974.

———. “Africans in Venetian Renaissance Painting: The Social Status of Black Men in Late Fifteenth Century Venice.” *Renaissance 2, A Journal of Afro-American Studies* 4, (1975): 7–11.

McKee, Sally. “Domestic Slavery in Renaissance Italy.” *Slavery and Abolition* 29, no. 3 (2008): 305–26.

Spicer, Joaneath, ed. *Revealing the African Presence in Renaissance Europe.* Baltimore, MD: Trustees of the Walters Art Museum, 2012.

Giovanni Buonaccorsi (fl. 1651–1674): An Enslaved Black Singer at the Medici Court

EMILY WILBOURNE

Giovanni (or Giovannino) Buonaccorsi was an enslaved Black singer at the Medici court from at least 1651 until his death on August 15, 1674.[1] At the court in Florence, Buonaccorsi sang both chamber music and opera.[2] Buonaccorsi is unusual in that a substantial quantity of archival material allows scholars to trace his participation in elite musical genres; he is not unusual as an early modern Black European entertainer – of whom there were many. In this essay I will focus my discussion of Buonaccorsi on two main sources: first, a double portrait from c.1662 (shown as figure 1), painted by Baldassarre Franceschini (1611–1690), better known by his nickname *Volterrano* (meaning 'from Volterra'), and second, a scene from the opera *Ercole in Tebe* from 1661, with words (the *libretto* or lyrics) by Giovanni Andrea Moniglia (1625–1700) and music by Jacopo Melani (1623–1676).[3] Details of Buonaccorsi's life and performances can be gleaned from a number of account books, administrative documents, letters, costume designs, set drawings, libretti, scores, descriptions of performances and paintings, and in one remarkable instance, a poem that

1. "Gio: Buonaccorsi moro" is listed as a singer among the members of Prince Gio: Carlo Medici's household in ASF *Mediceo del Principato*, f.5358, c.657*v*. His death record, for "Gio: Buonaccorsi moro, turco battezzato" is located at ACAF S. *Felice in Piazza*, Morti dal 1627 al 1686, RPU 0025.13, c.236*v*.
2. Buonaccorsi also sang at least one season on the public operatic stage in Venice.
3. The libretto was published at the time, see Giovanni Andrea Moniglia, *Ercole in Tebe* (Florence: Stamperia all'Insegna della Stella, 1661); the score, which survives in manuscript, was published in a modern, facsimile edition, see Jacopo Melani, *Ercole in Tebe* (New York: Garland Publishing, 1978). On the Volterrano painting see Alessandro Grassi's catalogue entry in Maria Cecilia Fabbri, Alessandro Grassi, and Riccardo Spinelli, eds., *Volterrano: Baldassarre Franceschini* (1611-1690) (Florence: Ente Cassa di Risparmio di Firenze, 2013), 245.

Figure 1. Baldassarre Franceschini (1611-1690), detto il Volterrano. *Ritratto di suonatore di liuto con cantore moro* (Pier Gio: Albizzi, detto Panbollito, e Giovannino Buonaccorsi); c.1662. Oil on canvas: 95 x 144cm. Private collection.

he seems to have written.[4] Considering Buonaccorsi as a case study foregrounds the relevance of race to an analysis of European music history in three important ways. First, his very existence and his participation as a singer in the elite genre of opera makes it clear that race and racial difference were an important part of Florentine court life. Second, the operatic

4. My work on Buonaccorsi is central to a forthcoming book, *Voice, Slavery, and Race in Seventeenth-Century Florence* (Oxford, 2023). Some preliminary archival findings and the extant sources are discussed in "'... la curiosità del personaggio': *Il Moro* on the Mid-Century Operatic Stage," in *Seachanges: Music in the Mediterranean and Colonial Worlds, 1550–1850*, edited by Kate van Orden, I Tatti Research Series, 133–48 (Florence: I Tatti Studies, 2021); I discuss the poem at some length in the open access book chapter, "Little Black Giovanni's Dream: Black Authorship and the 'Turks, dwarves, and bad Christians' of the Medici Court," in *Acoustemologies in Contact: Sounding Subjects and Modes of Listening in Early Modernity*, edited by Emily Wilbourne and Suzanne G. Cusick, 135–65 (Cambridge: Open Book Publishers, 2021), https://www.openbookpublishers.com/product/1238. Paul Kaplan has presented several papers on Buonaccorsi, though to my knowledge none are in print.

roles Buonaccorsi played and the performance opportunities that were available to him demonstrate the structural importance of stereotypes to the development of musical and dramatic forms. Third, emergent expressive and metaphorical meanings of 'voice' — which coalesced in the new genre of opera — intersected with stereotyped characters (on stage and in real life) to distribute insidious stereotypes about the innate humanity of raced, classed, gendered, and differently abled bodies in formulations that are legible in Buonaccorsi's blackness and persist into the present moment.

"Portrait of a lute player with a black singer"

Volterrano's *Ritratto di suonatore di liuto con cantore moro* [Portrait of a lute player with a black singer] was commissioned by the Cardinal Prince Giovan Carlo de' Medici (1611–1663), a younger brother of the Medici Grand Duke Ferdinando II (1610–1670). Both of the sitters were members of the Cardinal's household: Buonaccorsi, on the right, and Pier Giovanni Albizzi (fl. 1651–1670), who was known in the court as *Pan Bollito*, on the left.[5] Albizzi's nickname refers to a cheap soup that was common in Tuscan peasant cuisine, translating quite literally as 'Boiled Bread.' Buonaccorsi, for his part, is frequently referred to in documents as *il Moro* (lit. 'the Moor' but in mid-seventeenth-century Florence more explicitly, 'the Black'), which at times makes him difficult to trace — particularly given the elevated number of enslaved Black Africans in the courtly environment, all

5. The lute player is identified in a 1663 inventory of paintings: "Un quadro in tela senza adornamento bislungo di braccia 2 1/2 largo, et alto braccia 1 3/4 entrovi il Ritratto di Pan Bollito che suona il Liuto, et il Moro con una Carta di musica in Mano, con il Violino et libri di mano di Baldassarre." ASF Miscellanea medicea, n.31, ins. 10, c.133*v*. Pier Gio: Albizzi is identified as "P. Bollito" in the "Ruolo dei Cortigiani del Ser.mo Car.le Gio: Carlo A' quali doppo la morte di S.A.Ill.mo doveva dargli impiego," ASF *Mediceo del Principato*, f.5358, cc.728–729.

of whom could be called by the same racially-marked epithet.[6] According to administrative documents, Buonaccorsi and Albizzi entered the Cardinal's service on the same day: September 14, 1651, Buonaccorsi as a chamber singer and Albizzi as a *staffiere* or 'footman.' Importantly, while Albizzi was paid a regular salary (and after the Cardinal's death, received a pension), Buonaccorsi was not.[7]

An inventory compiled shortly after Cardinal Giovan Carlo's death, in February 1663, describes the painting as unframed; it is thus assumed to be one of a recent delivery of new works by Volterrano to the Cardinal and tentatively dated to 1662.[8] We do not know how old Buonaccorsi was at that time, though the painting depicts him as a young man, possibly in his late teens or early twenties.

Importantly for our analysis, the work is a portrait, depicting recognizable individuals (Buonaccorsi and Albizzi) in a customary occupation (chamber music performance) in a recognizable location (Palazzo Pitti, with a section of the Boboli gardens and the famous artichoke fountain visible through the open window). Yet that does not mean that the scene is unmediated. Much like the curated photographs that characterize the modern social media stream, paintings such as this one make careful claims about the social status and public profiles of patrons and sitters through framing, costuming, and the inclusion (or exclusion) of specific items.

This image of Buonaccorsi and Albizzi has a studied casualness to the composition — as if Volterrano has captured a candid glimpse of an ordinary and intimate afternoon of musical performance. Formally, however,

6. The descriptor *moro* is notoriously difficult to translate as the meanings range from 'brunette,' to 'Muslim,' or 'Black African,' depending on the context or more precisely on the presumptions of a given author or scribe. In my research into Florentine sources, I have found the term used almost exclusively to describe Black Africans who predominantly entered Italy via the Middle East or the Ottoman empire, with the diminutives *morino* or *moretto* used to describe Black children. Muslims more generally were typically described instead with the term *turco*. I have chosen therefore to translate the term as 'Black' in recognition of the localized Florentine usage.
7. See ASF *Mediceo del Principato*, f.5358, c.657*v* and cc.728–729.
8. ASF Miscellanea medicea, n.31, ins. 10, c.133*v*.

the painter has constructed a striking contrast between the pale-skinned white lutenist, depicted in somber, dark clothing, and seated in shadow, and the Black-skinned singer who sits with the light behind him, wearing a brightly striped, non-Western tunic. This play of light and dark, outside and inside, exotic and European splits the painting right down the middle, belying the sense it exudes of a natural, frequent occurrence, happily captured by the painter-as-observer. Even as Buonaccorsi and Albizzi are markedly contrasted, their unity and coordination are emphasized by subtle visual cues — such as the parallel angle of Albizzi's left hand and the back of Buonaccorsi's right, and the similarly open collars of their two very different outfits. It is this deliberateness that allows us — as modern viewers — to read, and to read into the details of the image: nothing is included in Volterrano's frame by mistake or happenstance, not the music, not the outfits, and certainly not the enslaved Black singer.

In mid-seventeenth-century Italy, elite chamber music was largely written for the solo soprano voice and semi-improvised chordal accompaniment, whether at a keyboard or with a plucked string instrument such as the lute (shown in figure 1). I talk more about the specifics of this kind of music below, but for now we can note that both men direct their music making to a specific goal: both make eye contact with the viewer, initially identifiable as the Cardinal patron and/or his selected guests. Albizzi fingers a chord with his left hand, his right poised in anticipation; he seems to wait for a signal from the viewer. Buonaccorsi has his lips slightly parted. This is a common iconography of song or singing, though here it looks as if he is breathing in or holding a breath, poised like Albizzi and ready to begin. There are bound music books visible on the table, yet the performers are reading from loose sheets. The implication is that the listener is about to hear something fresh and new, likely something written expressly for the patron's enjoyment. Indeed, the literacy of the two musicians underscores their importance as playback devices (even as it testifies to their level of education): before recording technologies existed, only the wealthiest Europeans could listen to music on demand.

In this context of understated yet conspicuous consumption, the clothing of the two men calls attention to itself, with both depicted in costly, even luxurious outfits. Black fabric was particularly expensive, and the textured velvet and voluminous folds of Albizzi's jacket and undershirt make it clear that whoever paid for the outfit spared no expense. While the satiny fabric of Buonaccorsi's tunic also makes a claim to volume (and thus expense), the brightly striped pattern and the Middle Eastern style of dress have a dramatically different effect. Indeed, it is productive to consider Buonaccorsi's outfit as a costume, though he likely wore this outfit or something very similar as his everyday wear. In an age such as the Renaissance in which sumptuary legislation dictated what clothes could be worn by which types of people, "clothes maketh the man." Servants and retainers wore livery supplied by their employers, and enslaved foreigners typically wore clothing that marked them as such. Accounts from 1666, for example, document an outfit made for the *Morino* or 'black boy' belonging to Ferdinando II, presumably Ali Moro, who would have been about ten at the time.[9] He received an "outfit in the Moorish style (*alla morescha*) made of green cloth, full hose, and stockings made in one piece and a long cassock down to the knee, all decorated with green trim."[10] The (literal) costume that Buonaccorsi wore in *Ercole in Tebe* was described at some length:

> Iolao, the black servant of the Athenian monarch appeared on the shore. He wore a vest in the African style with satin sleeves, adorned with splendid embroidery; the dark color of his black legs was covered by soft stockings of pure silver, and the many jewels adorning him at every turn denoted the grandness of his master.[11]

This description makes apparent the clear link between the exoticized (African) style of a Black African servant's clothing and the glory thus reflected back onto the owner/patron through the manifestation of purchasing power.

9. For Ali's age see his baptismal details at I-Fd, reg. 58, fol. 22. Ali took the baptismal name Cosimo Maria Medici.
10. ASF Camera del Granduca f.35, 77r.
11. "Iolao moro servo del monarca Ateniese comparve sul lido. Egli vestia all'Affricana una giubba di raso manì, adornata con ricamo splendete; copriva l'oscuro colore della sua nera gamba gentile calzare di candido argento, e le molte gioie, che d'ogn'intorno il fregiavano, la grandezza dinotavano del suo Signore." Cited from the "Descrizione dell'Ercole in Tebe, feste teatrale," published as an appendix to the libretto, 134.

Everything about this painting portrays the fabulous wealth of the Medici court, including the decorative nature of the painting itself, the leisurely enjoyment of new music, the expensive clothing of the (relatively lowly) court functionaries, and the majestic architectural and botanical vistas glimpsed in the background. The pose of the waiting musicians flatters the patron directly, implicating him as the reason for and the controlling force over their imminent performance. This pose thus signals the patron's sovereignty over the bodies, products, and sounds depicted in the painting — this is true not only of the two visible musicians, but also the painter whose labor resulted in the image and the composer whose labor produced the newly composed song indicated by the loose sheets. Painting and musical performance were luxury goods.

So, too, were enslaved Black retainers. Indeed, within the visual economy of Volterrano's painting, Buonaccorsi's race is far from negligible. While the painter's artistry would seem to discount some of what we see as posed or constructed rather than a fully transparent documentation of court practice, we need to bear in mind that the court itself was a superficial and competitive environment in which courtiers and sovereigns staged their influence and power in order to claim influence and power. Thus the presence of this painting in Cardinal Giovan Carlo's collection suggests that the Cardinal would have enjoyed and staged similar performances in his everyday life: the artifice of this scene does not mean that it did not happen. (In a mundane and modern analogy, one might both enjoy a cup of coffee in a fashionable café and enjoy posting an artful snap on social media of the latte art.) Buonaccorsi was listed in Medici accounts as a chamber singer, thus we assume that he sung in intimate, chamber settings such as the one depicted here.

What Operatic Voice Conveys

In mid-seventeenth-century Italy, most notated vocal music was operatic in character. Indeed, opera as we know it was invented in Florence (where Buonaccorsi lived) around 1600, and thus was relatively new during his lifetime. Opera was incredibly successful, and the important vocal innovations associated with its invention spread rapidly through elite European networks, quickly becoming the dominant European musical language in chamber and theatrical contexts.

In the simplest possible terms, opera can be understood as a play set entirely to music and sung throughout. As in a play, actors and actresses impersonate characters and speak (or in opera, sing) their lines in the first person using "I" and "we." Costumes and sets substitute for the narration of an author, and the story unfolds through scenes and acts, monologues and dialogues. Unlike in a spoken play, however, in opera the music provides an integral element of the drama. Indeed, the success of opera and operatic music is predicated on the assumption that music does not merely accompany the words but that music can *narrate* the emotional life of a character more effectively than words alone.

Many theatrical performances prior to the invention of opera included music — sometimes lots of music — as songs, dances, or background sound, each a closed unit of musical performance embedded within a larger whole. What was fundamentally different about operatic music, however, was the constant first-person, present-tense demands of the theatrical form: this is the difference between a song about how the singer's heart was previously broken and a song sung as if the singer's heart were being broken at precisely that moment. To achieve this aim, opera composers turned away from repeating verse-chorus structures and invented a new kind of music — called *recitative* — that was understood to represent speech itself. Recitative eschews a constant pulse, predictable phrases, and memorable tunes, relying instead on a flexible musical texture than can set each word. It built upon a pre-existing form of poetry, the *versi sciolti* (freely mixed, blank verse in seven and eleven syllable lines) which itself was prized for an avoidance of repetitive rhythmic formulae and the singsong textures of patterned poetry.

While the earliest operas consisted almost entirely of recitative, by mid-century, a desire for aural and narrative variety had resulted in a sharp increase in the number of *arias* (songs) and *arioso* (song-like) passages. Crucially, given opera's fundamental premise that the sounds of the voice express the representational truth of the character, recitative and aria were distributed along a sounding axis of stereotyped associations, which mapped onto existing linguistic registers associated with various poetic and musical forms — from elite to popular. In this sense, opera was heavily reliant on the sonic profiles of various character types within the existing vernacular (spoken) theater, the *commedia dell'arte*.[12] Simpler, lower-class (comic) characters, such as servants, slaves, and soldiers, sung simple songs, with patterned, rhyming poetry, repetitive, singable melodies, and rhythmic, danceable accompaniments; these characters provided subplots and entertaining interludes. Educated, upper-class (serious) characters, such as princes, princesses, or priests, sung complex, emotional appeals to love or duty, written with elevated poetic vocabularies and complex, stirring, or beautiful music; these are the story's main characters and love interests. (Even today similar musical and characterological choices continue to structure contemporary music drama, as can be seen from a consideration of any given Disney musical.) There is thus a clear and highly stereotyped relationship between musical register and character type.

Black Voices and Stereotypes on the Stage

In Buonaccorsi's performances, musical identity coheres with vocal sound in powerful ways: all of the operatic roles that Buonaccorsi is known to have performed were Black slaves, Black servants, or Black gypsies. He is thus (visually) typecast and, by the logic of opera, musically typecast, too. The representational stereotype of Black characters in Italian drama centered on their speech as recent immigrants.[13] As Extract 1 (given below), I translate a scene from the anonymous libretto for *Scipione in Cartagine*, performed in Florence at the Cocomero theater in 1657.[14] This opera includes a Black galley slave character called Caralì, who sings a partic-

12. Emily Wilbourne, *Seventeenth-Century Opera and the Sound of the Commedia dell'arte* (Chicago: University of Chicago Press, 2016).
13. On theatrical representations of Africanized speech in early modern Spanish sources, see Nicholas Jones, *Staging Habla de Negros: Radical Performances of the African Diaspora in Early Modern Spain* (University Park, PA: Penn State University Press, 2019); on the relationship of Italian *moresche* to African (specifically Kanuri) words, see Gianfranco Salvatore, "Parodie realistiche: Africanismi, fraternità e sentimenti identitari nelle canzoni moresche del Cinquecento," *Kronos* 14 (2011): 97–130.
14. *Scipione in Cartagine, dramma musicale; Fatto rappresentare da gli Accademici Sorgenti, nel loro Teatro, sotto la protezzione* [sic.] *del Sereniss. e Reverendiss. Princ. Card. Gio: Carlo di Toscana* (Florence: Gio: Anton Bonardi, 1657).

Extract 1. Taken from Anon, *Scipione in Cartagine* (perf. 1657), I, xv.[15]

CARALÌ	O Quanto star contentu Baes miu andar, Marmorata trovar; Legressa grandu Diù, O fatma core miù.	Oh, how happy I am, To return to my country To find my beloved; How generous the great God, O, Fatima, my love.
1	Camarata nesciumù, Non biscottu mansgiar, Non corbasciù tuccar; Tenimu libertà; Scibiona gentilisco Fasito carità; *Salamalech Ikallà, Ikallà.*	Leave the cabin, We will not eat ships' biscuit, Nor be touched by the whip, We hold our liberty; Noble Scipione Has done us this good deed; *Peace be upon you, God willing!*
2	Ber chistu ligramente Frofalla, & Ebrahin, Corcùt, Dragùt, Selin, Soliman, Mustafà, Ballar, e ghimberì. Sonar, Alì, Cassa, *Salamalech Ikallà, Ikallà.*	For this happily, Frofalla, and Ebrahin, Corcùt, Dragùt, Selin, Soliman, Mustafà, Dance and [with] cymbals, Play, Alì, Cassa. *Peace be upon you, God willing!*

ularly dense example of stereotypical Black speech. This role was likely performed by the ex-galley slave Caralì who was owned by Prince Mattias de' Medici (brother to the Cardinal Giovan Carlo); Caralì was around sixteen at the time.[16] In this scene, the character Caralì has just learnt that Scipione has liberated all the slaves, and he sings in celebration. Given the heavily marked Italian, the deliberate grammatical errors, and the use of both foreign and dialect words, the translation offered here reproduces the meaning of the words with no attempt to reproduce the errors of the text.[17]

Though the score of this opera does not survive, the poetic meter of this scene indicates an introductory recitative followed by two verses of aria, both of which would have been sung to the same music. Direct refer-

15. *Scipione in Cartagine*, 34–35.

16. Previous scholarship has assumed that Buonaccorsi played all the Black roles on Florentine stages during this period, however I have argued otherwise, see my "... la curiosità." For details of Caralì's life and baptism see ACAF *Pia Casa dei Catecumini*, f.2, insert 18, cnn. [3] and I-Fd *Registri Battesimali*, Maschii, reg.51, fg. 236, 1 August 1657.

17. I would like to thank Riccardo Strobino and Giuliano Mori for their help with this translation.

ence is made to the life of the galley slave – No longer will they have to eat ship's biscuit! – while the names of Caralì's fellow slaves are recognizably ethnic, even Ottoman. The refrain cites the traditional Arabic greeting: "As-salāmu 'alaykum," or "Peace be upon you," possibly with the word "Allah" or "in sha Allah" ("God willing") tacked on the end. For readers who do not recognize Italian conventions, the distance of this text from correct linguistic formulations will be hard to judge. The first line of the last verse, for example, "Ber chistù ligramente," should read "Per questo allegramente." The *p* sound has been replaced with *b*; the opening *qu* of *questo* has been chewed into a sounding *ki* (*chi*), the final vowel replaced with an un-idiomatic *ù*; and syllables omitted from the last word. In other places verbs are left un-conjugated (*star* rather than *sto*, for example, in the opening line). Describing the speech of a Black character (also, for what it's worth, named Caralì) in a libretto by Giovanni Andrea Moniglia, the theater scholar Françoise Decroisette writes, "this figure of the *moro* is typical in the dramas of Moniglia, who gives him an exotic, macaronic language, dominated by a final *ù*, by the substitution of *b* for *p*, by the use of infinitive verbs, and by the omission of grammatical articles."[18]

Interestingly enough, however, in *Ercole in Tebe* (also by Moniglia) in which the role of Iolao was written specifically for Buonaccorsi, this "Black voice" is avoided. In this way, Buonaccorsi manages to sidestep one of the most insidious markers of Black foreignness, representing himself instead as fundamentally Italian. In other ways, however, his performance confirms and reiterates characteristics understood to be natural to a specific class or category of person. In *Ercole in Tebe*, act III, scenes v and vi, Buonaccorsi's character Iolao has his only solo and his longest section of dialogue. The action of these two scenes takes place on the banks of the river Styx – which, in Greek mythology, separates the land of the living from the land of the dead. Figure 2 shows the set design of scene vi, with Iolao and his interlocutor Sifone visible at the bottom right. Throughout

18. "[Q]uesta figura di moro è abituale nei drammi di Moniglia, che gli dà un linguaggio esotico maccaronico, dominato dalla ù finale, dalla sostituzione di -p- in -b-, dall'uso degli infinitivi verbali, e dalla soppressione degli articoli." See the editorial apparatus to Giovanni Andrea Moniglia, *Il vecchio balordo*, ed. Françoise Decroisette, Biblioteca Pregoldoniana (Venice: Lineadacqua, 2014), 149.

Figure 2. Unsigned etching, possibly by Valerio Spada, from Giovanni Andrea Moniglia's libretto for *Ercole in Tebe* (Florence: Stamperia all'Insegna della Stella, 1661), where it appears between pages 44 and 45.

both of these scenes Iolao is waiting for his master to return. He is understandably antsy, more than ready to leave the unsettling landscape and the land of death behind, and his opening aria is a series of complaints about the situation in which he finds himself. As his first solo scene, his immediate launch into song (into *aria* rather than *recitative*) marks him as a lower-status character; the rhythms and repeating melodic cells emphasize his expressive register. Interestingly, the poetic form is *versi sciolti*, so this could have been set as recitative, however the poet has repeated the last line, and then the composer has used more insistent repetitions — sometimes of whole lines, sometimes of single words — to break down the elevated poetic effect into something much simpler and more popular in style. When we look at the lyrics, the impression of simplicity and rustic naturalness are deepened: Iolao complains of bodily distress — terror and hunger — far removed from the political and romantic crises that trouble the serious characters. The punchline of the song confirms the character's low-brow essence: there is not even anything here worth stealing!

Figure 3a. "E a chi non scapperebbe la patienza?" Aria sung by Giovannino Buonaccorsi as Iolao Moro, Act III, scene v, *Ercole in Tebe* (1661). Text by Giovanni Andrea Moniglia, music by Jacopo Melani.

Figure 3b. "E a chi non scapperebbe la patienza?" Aria sung by Giovannino Buonaccorsi as Iolao Moro, Act III, scene v, *Ercole in Tebe* (1661). Text by Giovanni Andrea Moniglia, music by Jacopo Melani.

Figure 3.c "E a chi non scapperebbe la patienza?" Aria sung by Giovannino Buonaccorsi as Iolao Moro, Act III, scene v, *Ercole in Tebe* (1661). Text by Giovanni Andrea Moniglia, music by Jacopo Melani.

Extract 2. Taken from Gio: Andrea Moniglia, *Ercole in Tebe* (perf. 1661), III, v.[19]

IOLAO	E a chi non scapperebbe la pazienza?	And who wouldn't lose their patience?
	La paura mi tormenta	Fear torments me
	E la fame m'assassina;	And hunger assassinates me.
	La caritade in questi luoghi è spenta,	In such places, charity is exhausted
	E non c'è modo à viver di rapina.	And there is nothing to steal.
	Per qual grave peccato	For what grave sin
	Sono, ohime, condennato	Have I, alas, been condemned
	A tanta rigorosa penitenza?	To such a harsh punishment?
	E a chi non scapperebbe la pazienza?	And who wouldn't lose their patience?

The composer of this opera, Jacopo Melani, was on the payroll of Prince Mattias, and Melani served as singing teacher to at least one of Giovan Carlo's young musicians.[20] He can thus be assumed to have had a good grasp of Buonaccorsi's vocal and dramatic capacities. Notably, all of the surviving music written for Buonaccorsi is scored for the soprano voice, a high-pitched voice that in modern society is typically associated with female singers. Buonaccorsi may have sung *falsetto* (now often called "counter tenor"), but more likely was castrated before he reached puberty in order to preserve his youthful high voice into adulthood. The castrato voice was particularly favored in seventeenth-century Italian music, simultaneously celebrated for the ways in which breath control and melodic flexibility exceeded that of the unaltered male voice and viewed as explicitly "natural" — despite the surgical intervention required to produce the voice — as the singer retained his (natural) boyish voice into adulthood rather than artificially manufacturing a small, false voice (literally, 'falsetto') in the adult throat.

19. Moniglia, *Ercole in Tebe*, 54.
20. For Melani's presence on Mattias' rolls, see Sara Mamone, ed., *Mattias de' Medici serenissimo mecenate dei virtuosi. Notizie di spettacolo nei carteggi medicei. Carteggio di Mattias de' Medici (1629–1667)* (Florence: Le Lettere, 2013), lett. 1103-04. For the reference to Jacopo as a singing teacher, see Mamone, ed., *Serenissimi fratelli principi impresari: Notizie di spettacolo nei carteggi medicei. Carteggi di Giovan Carlo de' Medici e di Desiderio Montemagni suo segretario (1628–1664)* (Florence: Le Lettere, 2003), lett. 803.

Musically, the aria is structured into two halves, with the opening material (text and music) returning at the end as a form of refrain. The A section is in duple time, with the repeating pulse felt in groups of two. The bass line moves quickly and emphasizes the tonic and dominant chords of the d min key. This section is quite jaunty, giving a kind of rollicking, humorous energy to Iolao's energetic complaints. The musically literate will notice that the bass line cycles through a series of different stock formulae. From measure 9, for example, the bass moves up a step and down a third repeatedly until the end of the phrase; in the following phrase, from measure 14, the bass descends stepwise through an octave plus a fifth, and so on. Iolao reaches an energetic climax as he repeats the punchline ("E non c'è modo à viver di rapina") on an ascending sequence, which is followed by an orchestral ritornello. The contrasting B section is in triple time, with the pulse felt in groups of three. This would have been sung more slowly, allowing the singer to spoof the moment of introspection, before returning to the opening complaint, and repeating the first two lines of the A section to conclude the piece.

In the following scene, an old friend arrives: the (white) servant Sifone, a stuttering comic character played by the tenor singer Carlo Righenzi, also a member of Cardinal Giovan Carlo's household.[21] Sifone, too, is unsettled and looking to find his master. In the interaction between the two servants, Buonaccorsi's blackness takes on dramatic importance, as Sifone fails to recognize his friend, screaming instead that he is being accosted by an ugly demon (see Extract 3.)

21. ASF *Mediceo del Principato*, f.5358, c.657*v*. On Righenzi, see Sergio Monaldini, "Leandro: Carlo Righenzi musico e comico," Musicalia 8 (2011): 75–112.

Extract 3. Taken from Gio: Andrea Moniglia, *Ercole in Tebe* (perf. 1661), III, vi.[22]

SIFONE	Per tro-, trovare Alceste vò cercando per tutto oh, che paese bru-, bru-, bru-	To f-, find Alceste I am searching everywhere Oh, this place is ug-, ug-, ug-
IOLAO	In queste parti e come Per qual strana occasione …	In these parts, and how? For what strange reason …
SIFONE	bru-, bru-, bru-	ug-, ug-, ug-
IOLAO	… arrivasti Sifone?	… does Sifone arrive?
SIFONE	bru-, bru-, bru-	ug-, ug-, ug-
IOLAO	Che fai, non mi conosci?	What are you doing? Don't you recognize me?
SIFONE	bru-, bru-	ug-, ug-
IOLAO	Guardami, chi son io?	Look at me! Who am I?
SIFONE	bru-, bru-, brutto. Ohimè, un Demonio, ohimè	ug-, ug-, ugly. Oh no, a demon, oh no!
IOLAO	Di che paventi? Iolao son' io.	Why are you so scared? It is me, Iolao!
SIFONE	È quando sei venuto nella patria di Pluto?	And when did you arrive in the land of Pluto?

Importantly, since the role of Iolao was written specifically for Buonaccorsi, the lack of noticeable accent suggests that he spoke Italian well, as does his one surviving poem (which is written in excellent Italian). As evidenced by his literacy and his facility as a singer, Buonaccorsi presumably lived in Italy from a very young age (and may have been born there). The role of Iolao represents a blackness that was thoroughly Italianate, though importantly, the role of Caralì and of other Black characters and Black voices written in a similar vein also imply a Black Italian presence and the familiarity of white Italian authors and poets with Black individuals. The presence of Buonaccorsi, Caralì, and Ali Moro at the court makes it clear that the elite Italians of Medici Florence regularly interacted with enslaved Black retainers.

22. Moniglia, *Ercole in Tebe*, 54–55.

Modern Race and Early Modern *Razza*

Even as the characterological differences between Iolao (who is enslaved within the court) and Caralì (who is enslaved on the galleys) demonstrate a variety of Black experience in late Renaissance Italy, their shared categorization as entertaining, aria-singing servants emphasizes the limits of class or category mobility within the Italian imaginary. Understanding the circumscribed space accorded to Black voice here is crucial, for as the spread and wide popularity of opera disseminated the ideology of the expressive voice, it categorized a hierarchy of persons to whom such a voice was afforded.

Opera relies on the epistemological conceit that the voice (emerging from the hidden depths of the body) tells the truth — betraying the body and its history irrespective of the semantic content of any given act of speech (even as that natural, expressive voice is fabricated in the act of performance).[23] Such assumptions persist: we regularly deduce the health, happiness, age, gender, national origins, linguistic fluency, and sincerity of our interlocutors based on the sound of their voices.[24]

So what can we hear in Buonaccorsi's voice? What did contemporary audiences hear? Buonaccorsi is ascribed a strictly delimited emotional range. His music is "song like" — which by early modern European standards was securely located at the entertaining, popular, or "low brow" end of the spectrum. He never gets the flexible, emotional extremes of the princely hero. His character appears in (comic) episodes and never develops. In what the Black musician is permitted to sing we can hear the parceling out of full humanity only to certain characters and the association of a natural, musical predisposition with the marked bodies of enslaved Black individuals. Still today assumptions of natural musicality are mapped onto certain (racial) categories, imposing limits on the stories their bodies are permitted to live and assumed to tell.

23. See Emily Wilbourne, "Demo's Stutter, Subjectivity, and the Virtuosity of Vocal Failure," *Journal of the American Musicological Society* 68, no. 3 (2015): 659–63.
24. Amanda Weidman, "Anthropology and Voice," *Annual Review of Anthropology* 43 (2014): 37–51.

Scholars have emphasized that the early modern usage of the Italian term *razza* meant something closer to 'lineage' rather than 'race' as the term is currently understood.[25] Still, to come from a "race of kings" or a "long line of thieves" implies a passing down of inherited suitability, a categorization of potentiality that helps to explain the rigid stereotypes of the early modern theater. Buonaccorsi doesn't get to play the king, though neither does Righenzi (who played the stuttering, hunchback servant) – both men were visibly marked, though one we now call 'race' and the other 'disability.'[26] For elite, white, European audiences, the Black entertainers they watched on stages and in other public spaces were a category apart. Black voices, raised in song, were assumed to signal a contentment with and suitability for servitude that echoes – in disturbing ways – through modern assumptions about race, voice, and subjectivity.

Discussion Questions

1. In what ways are the stereotypical associations of Black performance that limited Giovannino Buonaccorsi still operating in contemporary society?
2. What information does the sound of your voice (including your accent, pitch, and linguistic habits) give to your auditors? In what ways might the sound of your voice prejudice others against you?
3. To what extent should we understand Buonaccorsi as African? To what extent should we understand him as Italian?

25. See Kate Lowe, "Isabella d'Este and the Acquisition of Black Africans at the Mantuan Court," in *Mantova e il Rinascimento italiano: Studi in onore di David S. Chambers*, edited by Philippa Jackson and Guido Rebecchini (Mantua: Editoriale Sometti, 2011), 65–76.
26. On early modern disability, see Amrita Dhar's essay elsewhere in the collection.

Suggestions for Further Reading

Bindman, David, and Henry Louis Gates, eds. *The Image of the Black in Western Art*. 10 vols. Cambridge, MA: Harvard University Press, 2010–2014, particularly vol. 3, which has a significant essay on Italy during the Renaissance and Baroque eras.

Jones, Nicholas. *Staging Habla de Negros: Radical Performances of the African Diaspora in Early Modern Spain*. University Park, PA: Penn State University Press, 2019.

Lowe, Kate. "Isabella d'Este and the Acquisition of Black Africans at the Mantuan Court." In *Mantova e il Rinascimento italiano: Studi in onore di David S. Chambers*, edited by Philippa Jackson and Guido Rebecchini, 65–76. Mantua: Editoriale Sometti, 2011.

Wilbourne, Emily. "'… la curiosità del personaggio': *Il Moro* on the Mid-Century Operatic Stage." In *Seachanges: Music in the Mediterranean and Colonial Worlds, 1550–1880*, edited by Kate van Orden. I Tatti Research Series, 133–148. Florence: I Tatti Studies, 2021.

Wilbourne, Emily. "Little Black Giovanni's Dream: Black Authorship and the 'Turks, Dwarves, and Bad Christians' of the Medici Court." In *Acoustemologies in Contact: Sounding Subjects and Modes of Listening in Early Modernity*, edited by Emily Wilbourne and Suzanne G. Cusick, 135–165. Cambridge: Open Book Publishers, 2021. https://www.openbookpublishers.com/product/1238

Barbouillage: Twenty Seventeenth-Century Poems on an Enslaved Black Woman

ANNA KŁOSOWSKA

As Noémie Ndiaye and Mame-Fatou Niang have long insisted, the French term *barbouillage* must be used in the French context instead of *blackface*, because using an English term may suggest it is a foreign phenomenon or de-emphasize the negative impact of blackface: a foreign borrowing functions as a euphemism.[1] To start a class discussion on this topic, we might begin with the current discussions of *barbouillage* in the mainstream Francophone and Anglophone media. We might open with the filmed panel on *barbouillage* with the participation of Niang and Norman Ajari that includes a handful of infamous examples — Justin Trudeau as Aladdin; the use of caricature in the painting by Hervé Di Rosa, *Abolition of Slavery*, in the French National Assembly; the *barbouillage* staging of the classical Greek tragedy *The Supplicants*; the often-defaced late 1800s advertisement in Paris, now at the Musée Carnavalet/Musée de l'histoire de Paris.[2] An introduction to the class might also include information about the French National Committee for the Memory and History of Slavery and recent publications by Niang and Maboula Soumahoro.[3]

Early modern examples in this chapter can help students articulate the connections between cultural phenomena that are often presented separately, which causes the throughline of racism to be buried: 1600s

1. Noémie Ndiaye, *Scripts of Blackness: Early Modern Performance Culture and the Making of Race* (Philadelphia: University of Pennsylvania Press, 2022). Mame-Fatou Niang, *Identités françaises: Banlieues, feminités et universalisme* (Leiden: Brill, 2020).
2. Michel Guerrin, "Barbouillage: appropriation culturelle, décolonialisme, liberté d'expression," with the participation of Niang, Ajari, Laurent Dubreuil and Isabelle Barbéris, 5 October 2019, https://www.dailymotion.com/video/x7md1lz.
3. See Maboula Soumahoro, *Black is the Journey, Africana the Name*, trans. Kayama L. Glover (New York: Critical South, 2021), translation of *Le Triangle et l'Hexagone: Réflexions sur une identité noire* (Paris: La Découverte, 2021).

barbouillage, formalist Baroque poetry, visual representations that incorporate hierarchies of power, and participation in slave trade – as well as the shockingly literal and direct reprisal of these traditions in the 1800s by Romantic authors such as Théophile Gautier and the Symbolists such as Charles Baudelaire.[4]

Thanks to that step back into the early modern period, the students are able to comprehend that contemporary *barbouillage* has a long history that has been occluded. A contributing factor is the periodization of the study of race and slavery, rooted in specific geographies, religions and chronologies. Scholars are often reluctant to counter the prevailing narrative that dates the emergence of modern racism linked to global slavery and colonization to the Enlightenment, but notable new studies mark the beginning of a new period of synthesis in the study of early modern race as well as slavery. Recently, Ndiaye and other scholars have shown that early modern culture is characterized by the rise of "skin color as a shorthand for racialized thinking."

By highlighting both the links and the differences between the 1600s, 1800s and the present, students are better able to understand and articulate the harmful effects of *barbouillage* in present-day France. The early modern culture classroom becomes a laboratory where students discuss representation and its opposite – cultural appropriation – and chart the path to mutual respect and full participation in cultural productions.

Two Types of *Barbouillage* — Mythologization and Blackface; Polysemy of *More* (Moor)

There are two related strands of *barbouillage* in the sense of fictional blackness written by white authors who represent and articulate the dominant racist culture in the 1600s in France. The first is *barbouillage* in court ballet, theater, and visual arts that consists of the representation of racialized people in supporting or comical roles. The second is the rep-

4. On Baudelaire, see Tracy Denean Sharpley-Whiting, *Black Venus: Sexualized Savages, Primal Fears, and Primitive Narratives in French* (Duke University Press, 1999). On Gautier, see later in this chapter.

resentation of enslaved and racialized people as leading, tragic or heroic fictional characters and allegorical or mythological figures. As I argue, both of these two very different modes of fictional representation are *barbouillage*, because they do the same cultural work: to intentionally delete on stage and in fiction the violence and horror of the French slave trade and plantation economy. Therefore, I will call both of them *barbouillage* throughout this essay.

First, I look to mythologization: in literature and the arts in Paris during the decades leading to the legalization of slavery by the French in the Antilles (1642), warfare, colonization, and slavery were staged in aestheticized, fantastical terms. Violence was presented as symbolic, not real; death as noble, not final; disappointed love as the worst thing that could happen, rather than captivity, torture, and genocide. Examples of that fantastical staging culminate in late 1600s palace décor that glorifies colonization, for example in Versailles from the 1670s to the 1680s: the *Allegory of Africa* in the *Salon d'Apollon* (c. 1675), *Different African Nations* in the *Escalier d'Ambassadeurs* (1674–1679).[5] The point of these allegorical visual representations was to imagine and project French and aristocratic superiority, often in terms of literal, positional superiority: the allegory of Africa as one of the four peripheral continents is subordinate to the central allegory of Europe in the *Salon d'Apollon*.

As for *barbouillage* in the sense of blackface as it is more traditionally understood, Parisian diarist and gossip Gédéon Tallemant de Réaux describes a portrait commissioned by his relation, Marie d'Harambure: "she was brown/a brunette, so she had the fantasy to have herself painted as an enslaved African woman [*esclave more*] with arms in chains." [6] (The

5. *The Allegory of Africa*, salle Apollon, Versailles, c. 1675, by Charles de la Fosse (1636–1716), INV 1850 2252 C; Charles Le Brun (1619–1690), *Different African Nations*, 1674–1679, study for *l'Escalier d'Ambassadeurs*, Versailles; *Cabinet du roi*, atelier Le Brun; Louvre, dépt. Arts graphiques INV 27706, recto, *Four parts of the world*.

6. "[P]ar vision, comme elle [Mme d'Harambure] estoit brune, elle [se] fit peindre en esclave more, qui avoit des fers aux mains," Tallemant des Réaux, *Historiettes*, ed. A. Adam (Paris: Gallimard, 1961), vol. 2, 552.Cited by Myriam Dufour-Maître, "De 'Précieuse, Egyptienne' à 'Mélisse, vieille Précieuse': naissance d'un personnage, applications mondaines et exténuation d'un type (1628–1724)," *Littératures classiques (issue: Le*

Tallemant were among the more prominent bankers in Bordeaux, having acquired in 1611 the office of the treasurer of the house of Navarre.) The French *More*, like the English "Moor" is a polysemous term used to denote categories distinct today: African, Muslim, Black, Jew, "Oriental," Turkish, racialized. For example, in political pamphlets against Philip II in the 1590s, he is described as "half-Moor, half-Jew, half-Saracen" who "treats the French as Tupinambas."[7] *Mores* and their multiple avatars — Jew, Muslim, Egyptian, Indian, Turk, African, Indian, Native American — were stereotypical characters performed in court ballet and masquerade, an integral part of visual culture in 1600s Paris staged by amateur and professional actors, whose performances often echoed concrete political events.[8] The figure of the *More* also functions as a thought experiment, a formalism or tropism in poetic contexts.

With this background, a class might then analyze a group of poems written in 1600s Paris, extant in manuscript or published in various print collections from c. 1640–1675. These poems, which as I argue must also be considered as a type of *barbouillage*, construct the fictional lyric portrait of a beautiful enslaved Black woman, *belle noire*. They are French adaptations of a group of "Dark Love" sonnets by Giambattista Marino including the notorious *Bella Schiava* (Beautiful Enslaved Woman). These 1600s French poems were first collected in an anthology under the title *L'Amour noir* (Dark/Black Love) by Albert-Marie Schmidt in 1959.[9] As most scholars of Marinist poetry, Schmidt was interested in Marino's formalism and his Baroque aesthetics of *amori notturni*, nocturnal landscapes in the

salon et la scène: comédie et mondanité au 17e siècle) 58:3 (2005), 115–30, at 117. All translations are mine unless otherwise indicated.

7. These pamphlets are cited in Marcel Paquot, "Les étrangers dans le ballet de cour au temps de Henri IV," *Revue du seizième siècle* 16 (1929), 21–39, 24 n1; see also Marcel Paquot, "Les étrangers dans le ballet de cour," *Revue du seizième siècle* 15 (1928), 43–55.
8. Marcel Paquot, *Les étrangers dans les divertissements de la cour, de Beaujoyeulx à Molière (1581–1673). Contribution à l'étude de l'opinion publique et du théâtre en France* (Bruxelles: Palais des Académies, Liège: H. Vaillant-Carmanne, n.d.). More recently, Daniel Heartz, "Un ballet turc à la cour d'Henri II: les branles de Malte," *Baroque* 5 (1972), n.p.
9. See prior.

love lyric tradition: "black Suns, merciful Night ... dark beauties, jade and ebony, the Bohemian, the African, androgyny, succubi."[10]

Belle noire poems use the recursive logic and paradoxical juxtapositions typical of Baroque and Mannerist poetry: the enslaved Black woman in turn enslaves her white male captor, the slave owner, who is now a slave to passion. The ivory-bright feminine beauty idealized in Petrarchism becomes subordinate to coal-black; coal-black shines brighter than the sun or gold. As mentioned above, these poems are adaptations of a cycle by Marino, including *Bella Schiava* and poems on the widow, the beggar, the Egyptian or the Romani fortune teller.

This group of poems, perhaps created as part of a *salon* challenge or *concorso*, as it often happened when we see a number of poems on one theme, consists of at least twenty poems by some fourteen men and women; the number is not precise because some poems are anonymous. The named authors include such leading figures as the playwright Paul Scarron; the poet, soldier, and courtier Marc-Antoine Girard de Saint-Amant and the brother of the celebrated novelist Madeleine de Scudéry, Georges.[11]

10. Paulette Choné, *L'Atelier des nuits: histoire et signification du nocturne dans l'art d'Occident* (Nancy: Presses Universitaires de Nancy, 1992), 133.

11. See Albert-Marie Schmidt, *L'Amour Noir: Poèmes baroques* (Monaco: Edition du Rocher, 1959). These Marinist poets are, in the approximate order of publication, François Tristan l'Hermite (1641); an anonymous poet, probably a woman, in a manuscript dated to before 1660; Georges de Scudéry (1649); Marc-Antoine Girard de Saint-Amant; Charles de Vion d'Alibray (1653); Hippolyte-Jules Pilet de La Mesnardière (1656); Jean Ogier de Gombauld (1657); Urbain Chevreau (1656); Claude de Malleville (1659); Jean de Boyssières, Jacques Carpentier de Marigny, and a few other anonymous authors. These Marinist poets are, in the approximate order of publication, François Tristan l'Hermite (1641); an anonymous poet, probably a woman, in a manuscript dated to before 1660; Georges de Scudéry (1649); Marc-Antoine Girard de Saint-Amant; Charles de Vion d'Alibray (1653); Hippolyte-Jules Pilet de La Mesnardière (1656); Jean Ogier de Gombauld (1657); Urbain Chevreau (1656); Claude de Malleville (1659); Jean de Boyssières, Jacques Carpentier de Marigny, and a few other anonymous authors.These Marinist poets are, in the approximate order of publication, François Tristan l'Hermite (1641); an anonymous poet, probably a woman, in a manuscript dated to before 1660; Georges de Scudéry (1649); Marc-Antoine Girard de Saint-Amant; Charles de Vion d'Alibray (1653);

Links to the Slave Trade

These poems serve as sociohistorical documents that help students understand the personal connections between literature and early modern racial exploitation. Some of these writers, visual artists, performers, and patrons were directly involved in the slave trade, including Scarron's wife, Françoise d'Aubigné, who later became Mme de Maintenon and wife to Louis XIV. Scarron sold his church *bénéfice* — as I understand, his marriage necessitated this, as it invalidated his minor orders, the rank in the Church ministry required to collect his income — and invested in the *Compagnie des Indes*. D'Aubigné married Scarron, three times her age (she was a teenager) because she was destitute. She nearly died crossing the Atlantic and lived briefly in the Antilles as a child, where her parents purchased enslaved people and made a failed attempt to make a fortune on a plantation. Her mother later sold these enslaved men and women to pay for her and her two children's return passage to France, following the father.

Saint-Amant also had a first-hand knowledge of slave trade and plantation economy. Under Richelieu, nobles did not compromise their title and its tax-exempt status by participating in trade if the trade was part of the colonial *compagnies*. Saint-Amant's brother was a sailor who died in the Red Sea, and Saint-Amant himself participated in more than one military colonial expedition. Financed by the *Compagnie du Sénégal*, he sailed from Lisbon in January 1626, via the Canary Islands along the coast

Hippolyte-Jules Pilet de La Mesnardière (1656); Jean Ogier de Gombauld (1657); Urbain Chevreau (1656); Claude de Malleville (1659); Jean de Boyssières, Jacques Carpentier de Marigny, and a few other anonymous authors. See Georges de Scudéry (1601–1667), *Poesies diverses* (Paris, 1649), 59. Charles de Vion d'Alibray (c. 1590–1654) *Les oeuvres poetiques* (Paris, 1653), 96, 111, 122. Hippolyte-Jules Pilet de La Mesnardière (1610–1663), *Les poésies* (Paris, 1656), 287. Jean Ogier de Gombauld (1576–1666), *Les épigrammes* (Paris, 1657), 132, Épigramme XVI. Urbain Chevreau (1613–1701) *Poésies* (Paris, 1656), *Ode Pour une belle Egyptienne.* Claude de Malleville (1597–1647) *Poésies* (Paris, 1659), 189. Schmidt, *L'Amour*, 92–93: an anonymous author, 1656 (Schmidt, *L'Amour*, 92); an anonymous author in the *Recueil de diverses poésies* (Paris, 1657), 29; an anonymous author in the collection *La muse coquette* (Paris: Loyson, 1665), vol. 2, 36 (Schmidt, *L'Amour*, 93).

of Africa, part of a military expedition that founded Saint-Louis in Senegal. Saint-Amant may have also participated in the expedition to the Antilles, to Saint-Christophe for eight months in 1629 with François de Rotondy, Sieur de Cahuzac/Cussac. He describes the Canary Islands in a handful of poems, and mentions his travels in Africa, the Canaries and America (Saint-Georges) in the preface to the collection of poems published in 1629. Some extant printings of this volume have a frontispiece framed by two palm trees, indicating that the Canaries theme was particularly worth foregrounding and resonated with the public.[12]

Race and Slavery in 1600s *Salons, Académie*, Court Ballet, and Theater

Barbouillage was not limited to these Marinist poems and authors in the 1600s — far from it. The legitimacy and function of slavery was discussed in salons: records show a debate on the topic in 1633 at the Académie Renaudot, soon to be institutionalized as the state-sponsored French Academy.[13] Plays and masquerades were performed at court and in the city, and the court and royal family regularly danced in *barbouillage*. Under Louis XIII, the ballet *La Douairière de Billebahaut* (The Dowager of Bilbao, 1626), including groups of dancers in costumes and *barbouillage* representing different sovereign nations paying homage to France, was performed at the Louvre and later for the Paris Parliament. Following the

12. Canaries are mentioned in Saint-Amand's "La métamorphose de Lyrian et de Sylvie," "La vigne." See Jean Lagny, *Le poète Saint-Amant*, 1594–1661 (Paris: Nizet, 1964), 49. "L'Automne dux Canaries," Saint-Amant, *Oeuvres*, *Troisième partie* (Paris: Toussainct Quinet, 1649 and 1669), part of the four-season cycle.
13. Yves Bénot, "Les Amis des Noirs et les 'déclamations' de Diderot," in *Esclavage et abolitions: Mémoires et systèmes de représentation* (Paris: Karthala, 2000), 221–32, at 221–22: "Seventh conference ... 1. On the Air 2. If it's better for a State to have Slaves" (*Première centurie des questions traitées ez conférences du bureau* d'adresse, depuis le 22 jour d'Aoust 1633 jusques au dernier Juillet 1634, Paris, Au bureau d'adresse, 1638, 41, 53–57).

hiatus of the Fronde, two ballets, *le Ballet de la Nuit* (1653) and *Noces de Pélée et Thétis* (1654) revived the *ballet des nations* tradition.[14]

In the *Douairière* (1626), Gaston d'Orléans, Louis XIII's brother, danced as an African. The libretto specifies: "Monsieur representant un Afriquain" ("The King's Brother, playing an African"), and his lines read: "do not disdain me because I am a Moor,/ Because like the son of Aurora,/ Although my complexion is black, I am from the Blood of Gods/ My race is adored at both ends of the Earth."[15] Among the best known *barbouillage* performances linked with the future Louis XIV is the Italian *La finta pazza* (The Fake Madwoman), which he watched as a six-year-old (December 14, 1645).[16] In his own first public performance as an adolescent, in *Noces de Thétis et Pélée* (1654) Louis danced in *barbouillage*, feathers, and a slave collar as the *Indien* or *académiste de Chiron* (a student of the centaur Chiron), one of six costume changes also including Apollo, a dryad, a courtier, and an allegory of War. *Noces* was so popular that it was performed three times a week for more than a month and the last two performances were open to a popular audience.[17] The stage designer of the *Noces* was Giacomo Torelli, famous for his machines, special effects, and dramatic scene changes; *La finta pazza* (1645) was his Paris début and a vast success, reprising his Venice designs. In turn, a generation after *Noces* (1654) when the ballet *Le triomphe de l'amour* (1681,1682) was performed to celebrate his eldest son's marriage, Louis was the spectator and the young aristocrats danced in *barbouillage*, including his eldest son in the traditional mythological costume of *Indien* following Bacchus. The classical mythol-

14. Marie-Françoise Christout, "Les Noces de Pélée et de Thétis, comédie italienne en musique entremelée d'un ballet dansé par le Roi (1654)," *Baroque* 5 (1972), n.p.
15. *Ne me desdaignez pas pource que je suis More,/ Car comme le fils de l'Aurore,/ Bien que mon teint soit noir, je suis du sang des Dieux/ Ma race est adorée aux deux bouts de la Terre*: René Bordier, Imbert and Charles Sorel, *Grand bal de la douairière de Billebahaut. Ballet dansé par Sa Majesté.* [n.p., n.p., n.d.], 45.
16. Drawings by Francesco Spada, see Philippe Beaussant, *Le ballet des singes et des autruches* (Paris: Gallimard, Le Promeneur, 2010). According to Philippe Beaussant, the future Sun King himself colored the album of engravings with scenes from the play, filling in with brown paint the images of men dancing in feather skirts.
17. April 14–May 20, Christout, "Les Noces," 12, 21.

ogy and iconography of Dionysus includes the conquest of India and the battle scenes with Indians as well as triumphal processions including Indians, lions, elephants and camels, which served in the 1600s as one of the prominent visual and literary sources of Baroque representations of colonization. The aristocrats danced alongside professional performers.[18]

Barbouillage and costumed representations of racialized stereotypes – so-called "ballets of the nations" – are a constant in 1500s–1600s triumphal entries and court ballets. Masquerades including *barbouillage* were usually danced every January at court and reprised after Easter in the city.[19] The titles speak for themselves. Even a few titles listed here in the body of the chapter will enable the students to appreciate the frequency and insistence with which *barbouillage* appears in the mainstream culture of the 1600s Paris. These titles include: 1600–1601, *Ballet*

18. However, it is also worth mentioning that the courtiers were not always able to participate in Louis XIV's entertainments: soon after the marriage ceremony the Dauphin fell ill, causing the performance to be postponed twice, and the various ladies of the court excused themselves due to a mourning in the family, also causing delays.
19. Paquot, "Les étrangers … Henri IV," 33–34. Full chronology of French court ballet: https://www.wikiwand.com/es/Anexo:Cronología_del_ballet_cortesano_francés_(1573–1671) is based in Margaret McGowan, *L'art du ballet de cour en France* (1581–1643) (Paris, CNRS, 1963), and Marie-Françoise Christout, *Le ballet de cour de Louis XIV* (1643–1672) (Paris, Picard, 1967); for earlier studies, see Pierre-François Godard de Beauchamps, *Recherches sur les Théâtres de France depuis l'année onze cents soixante et uns …* (3 vols, Paris: Prault, 1735); Pierre Lacroix, *Ballets et mascarades de cour sous Henri IV et Louis XIII* (6 vols, Geneva and Turin, Gay, 1686–1870); Henri Prunières, Le Ballet de Cour en France avant Benserade et Lully (Paris: H. Laurens, 1913), Paquot, "Les étrangers" and "Les étrangers … Henri IV," Olivia Bloechl, "Race, Empire and Early Music," in *Rethinking Difference in Musical Scholarship*, ed. Olivia Bloechl, Melanie Lowe and Jeffrey Kallberg (Cambridge: Cambridge University Press, 2015), 77–107; Katharine Baetjer, ed. *Watteau, Music, and Theater* (New Haven: Yale University Press and New York: Metropolitan Museum of Art, 2009), 90–91, describing and reproducing the illustration by Jean Dolivar after Jean I Berain, *Habit d'Indienne*, and citing Roger-Armand Weigert, *Jean I Berain: Dessinateur de la chambre et du cabinet du roi* (1640–1711) (Paris: Nogent-le-Rotrou, 1937), vol. 2, 112–13, no. 127, and Weigert, *Inventaire du fonds français: Graveurs du XVIIe siecle* (Paris: Bibliotheque nationale, departement des estampes, 1954), vol. 3, 469, no. 268.

des Turcs, *Ballet des Maures Nègres*, *Ballet des princes de la Chine*, *Ballet des princesses des îles*, 1604 *Ballet des Janissaires*, 1607 *Ballet des Maures adorant le Soleil*, *Ballet des blancs et des noirs*, *Le Maistre de l'academie d'Hyrlande* (Ireland), 1608 *Ballet de Maître Guillaume* including the figures of Moor, Tartar, Indian, Englishman, and Spaniard, 1609 *Ballet des Maures*, *Ballet des Juifs*, *Ballet des Sauvages*, *Ballet de la Reine* including Americans, 1610 *Ballet de Monseigneur le duc de Vendôme* including the description of the "black mask, silver eyebrows and moustache,"[20] c. 1620 Coffin's *Ballet des Indiens*, 1626 *Douairière de Billebahaut*, which left the record including Daniel Rebel's watercolor album of costume designs for *Ballet des nations*. 1645, *La finta pazza*, 1654 *Noces de Pelée et de Thétis*, 1658 *Ballet d'Alcidiane* with Louis in *barbouillage* as *Maure* in the final entry *chaconne des Maures*. The 1662 *Carousel* is well documented by Henri de Gissey's printed designs and Perrault's captions, including men in *barbouillage* ("Moors") and enslaved men.[21] We could multiply the examples.[22]

Not only court ballet but also theater, more accessible to the *bourgeois*, staged enslaved and racialized characters. *Comédiens italiens* — Francesco and Isabella Andreini, and then their son Giovanbattista and his wife, Virginia Ramponi, often performed in Paris, including in 1621–1623, and six of their plays were printed there. The theatrical and print success of Giovanbattista Andreini's *Lo schiavetto* (1612, 1620) whose Venetian 1620 frontispiece portrays the young enslaved Black boy — in reality, the noble

20. Paquot, "Les étrangers ... Henri IV," 36.

21. "Moors carrying monkeys, and leading bears;" Perrault's caption "suggests that the performers were royal domestics of unknown origin, some costumed as bears, others as enslaved men." Bloechl, "Race," 89.

22. In 1673 *Cadmus and Hermione*, an opera by Quinault and Lully, includes dancing "Africans" in Act I. In 1679 *Masquerade* in St. Germain-en-Laye features the duchess de Nemours dancing in *barbouillage* as *Mauresse*, documented by Jean Berrain's illustration. Berrain documents that African, Persian, and Moorish costumes of 1679 incorporate elements of costume design by Gissey from 1622. In 1681 *Ballet du Triomphe de l'amour* by Lully celebrates the marriage of the Dauphin who dances in *barbouillage* as *Indien*. In 1683 *Phaëton*, an opera by Quinault and Lully, with a printed *livret* (libretto) suggests a page in *barbouillage*. It was performed at Versailles (January) and in Paris at the Théâtre du Palais-Royal in 1683–1684, and revived six times before 1742.

heroine in *barbouillage* played by his wife Virginia Ramponi, who uses that disguise to follow her lover – undoubtedly also helped the popularity of different versions of Andromeda (on Andromeda, see below, figure 2) in the early decades of the 1600s.[23] Claude de l'Estoile (1597–1652), who collaborated on the libretto of the 1626 ballet *La Douairière de Billebahaut*, also wrote the tragicomedy *La belle esclave* (Beautiful Enslaved Woman). Printed in 1643, it was regularly performed from 1642 to 1669, testifying to its popularity. An *Andromède délivrée* dates to 1624.[24] A significant number of French plays performed in Paris in the 1600s have racially marked characters, including the most famous plays by Alexandre de Hardy (*Belle Egyptienne*, 1628), Pierre Corneille (*Medea* and *Cid*, 1635, 1637; *Andromeda* 1650–1660s and later; *Titus and Bérénice*, 1670), Molière (*Bourgeois gentilhomme*, 1670), and Jean Racine (*Bérénice*, *Bajazet* and *Mithridate*, 1670, 1672, 1673), to mention only the best known. Two of the poets we will mention below, Tristan l'Hermite and Georges de Scudéry, also authored plays and novels that foreground the themes of slavery and race.

Barbouillage in the Visual Arts: Sappho's Portrait in Ovid's *Heroides* and Representations of Andromeda

Because of limited space, I will not discuss here the frequent inclusion of the representations of Black men, women, and children in French portraits and art collections in the 1600s, especially by patrons and sitters with direct links to slave trade. Instead, I will limit myself to mythology. In visual arts, representations of Black men and women as allegorical or mythological figures existed and gained some prominence in public and private spaces in the 1600s. Raised on Ovid, French literary men and women would be automatically reminded of Black Sappho and Black Andromeda (see explanation below) by Marino's poem and its French

23. On *Lo schiavetto* and race see Emily Wilbourne, "*Lo Schiavetto* (1612): Travestied Sound, Ethnic Performance, and the Eloquence of the Body" in *Journal of the American Musicological Society* (2010) 63: 1–43.
24. *Andromède délivrée: intermède anonyme*, 1623. Ed. Benoît Bolduc, preface Françoise Signoret (Paris-Seattle-Tübingen: Supplément to *Papers on French Seventeenth Century Literature*/PFSCL 17 (70), 1992).

Figure 1. Black Sappho, a mainstream French print, c. 1620. Jean I Le Blond (1590/94–1680), part of a series of women's portraits based on drawings by Abraham Bosse.

adaptations. In parallel with the literary tradition, the visual representations — mythological and allegorical portraits of Black men and women, especially including Sappho, Andromeda, and Memnon — were circulated by popular engravings, printed in large quantities and cheaply bought to decorate the walls of shops and rooms.

For example, a portrait of Sappho printed in the 1620s, part of a series of "worthy women" portraits, uses as her identification not only her name written on the lute, the instrument that she is traditionally credited with having perfected, but also, as I argue, visual and especially textual clues to her appearance, which traditionally includes a reference to her dark beauty. In Ovid, the wording of the Sappho epistle presupposes a hierarchy of female beauty where the appeal of dark beauty is not self-evident, it has to be argued and proven by a reference to a famous precedent: Perseus's love-at-first-sight for Andromeda. That is the section of Ovid's poem cited on the print, where Sappho compares herself to an irresistibly attractive Black figure, Andromeda. The figure in the print has the fashionable, tightly curled, almost spherical, voluminous hairstyle, suggesting that the image may date to the 1620s. I thank Suzanne Karr Schmidt for brilliantly pointing out a near-contemporary print in which, in a *mise en abyme*, a print from the Sappho series is represented hanging on the wall of a Paris shoe shop, giving us both the *terminus ante quem* and an idea of the popular distribution of the series. Although I am not an expert, I think that two elements of Sappho's clothing might be a shorthand for "Turkish" style: first, the deeply cut lambrequins of the patterned overgarment, edged in gumball-sized pearls. Second, the long, fringed shawls used as a scarf and a belt, which appear to float around Sappho's upper and lower body. Another shawl is woven into her coiffure, its two-fringed, patterned ends resting on her shoulders and upper torso in a liquid drape. These two elements, lambrequins and decorative scarves, appear repeatedly throughout the 1600s in prints that portray women dancers in *barbouillage* as allegories for India, America, Africa, and the Ottoman Empire.

Sappho is looking directly into our eyes, with a tiny smile: she seems amused with us. A delicate twist to her head and torso creates an illusion of life. With one arm she cradles her lyre, her hand framing her name. Her other arm points down. Her elegantly bent wrist and languid port-de-bras look ballet-like. She holds up her scarf, with her index finger pointing to the well-known lines of Ovid's *Heroides* 15 where Sappho describes herself as brown — brown like Black Andromeda. The French text reads:

> My brown skin color displeases you — a pathetic excuse:
> Andromeda was black, and Perseus loved her.

Alas, to see a volcano, no need to go to Sicily:
Come, see it in my heart, where your eyes set it ablaze.

Created about the same time as the Sappho print, an iconic image of Black Memnon and Black Andromeda, part of a series of mythological scenes no longer extant, decorated the *cabinet* of Jacques Favereau, one of Paris's elite literary figures.[25]

Figure 2. Black Andromeda, from Marolles's *Temple des Muses*, fifteen printings from 1655 to the 1720s.

25. Michel de Marolles, *Tableaux du Temple des Muses tirez du cabinet de feu Mr. Favreau* (Paris: Antoine de Sommaville, 1655), Memnon at p. 131, Andromeda at p. 315. The drawings for the *Temple* were completed c. 1635–1638 by a disciple of Rubens, Abraham van Diepenbeeck (1596–1675). The prints are by Cornelis Bloemaert (1603–1692) and Pierre Brebiette (1598–1642).

While the oil-on-canvas originals were only known to those admitted to Favereau's *salon*, a series of engravings based on them was widely published as a small album, *Temple des Muses*. Facing each *tableau* was a page of French commentary by Michel de Marolles, the well-known author who prolifically published both pious texts and translations of canonical school texts from Latin, and a notable print collector. Marolles's collection was later purchased by Colbert and formed one of the core collections of the royal *Cabinet*. Marolles's title, *Temple des Muses*, echoes another famous *Musaeum*–that is, a temple of the Muses–which gave its name to our ubiquitous public institutions: Paolo Giovio's portraits gallery in his villa on the lake Como begun in 1512 and finished in 1540s, copied by the duke Cosimo I de' Medici for his Uffizi Gallery, with Giovio's descriptions, known as *Elogia*, widely circulating in print since 1546–1551. Portrait galleries in aristocratic houses throughout Europe were conceived on the scheme of Giovio's museum, creating patterns of portraiture for famous historical and contemporary figures as well as including family portraits. A hundred years after Giovio, published in Paris in 1655, Marolles's *Temple*, like Giovio's portraits, circulated in print for a century, and scholars often assume that both his print collection and his *Temple* served as a visual reference for decorators and artists. It was reprinted in French a dozen of times, and published in English in Antwerp at least three times, as late as the end of the 1740s.[26]

The portrayal of Black Andromeda preoccupied Parisians in the 1600s. Corneille includes it in the "Argument" of *Andromeda*, where he justifies his departures from Ovid. He writes about the play's location:

> [Ovid] only says that Cepheus [the father of Andromeda] reigned in Ethiopia, and he does not indicate in what climate. The modern topography of these parts is not very well known, and even less in Cepheus's time. Suffice it to say that Cepheus had to be a ruler of some coastal land, that the capital was on the coast, and that his people were white, although Ethiopian. It's not that the blackest

26. Three times from 1655–1733, nine times from 1733–1749, three times in English in 1733, in a folio format, including by the printer-librarian Abraham Wolfgang (1634–1694).

> Moors [*Mores*] don't have beauties, after their fashion, but it's not likely that Perseus — a Greek born in Argos — would fall in love with Andromeda if she were of their color [*si elle eust esté de leur teint*]. I have the opinion of all the painters on my side, and above all — the authority of the great Heliodorus [author of *Aethiopica*] who specifically links the whiteness of the divine Chariclea to a representation of Andromeda.[27]

In other words, there were two traditions for the representation of Andromeda. Sappho of our print justifies her loveliness by comparing herself to Black Andromeda, but the character of Chariclea in the widely read and admired *Aethiopica* "proves" that Andromeda was white. To understand Corneille here it is necessary to mention that skin color is the pretext to the abandonment-and-recognition plot of *Aethiopica*: Chariclea's pregant mother supposedly looked at a print of Andromeda, so that Chariclea was born white, instead of Black like her father; of his coloring, only a spot remained, sufficient to effect a recognition and reunite them in the end.

The topic of Andromeda's appearance is discussed by the prolific Marolles in print at least twice, in 1655 and 1661. In the 1655 edition of the *Temple des Muses*, Marolles's commentary is explicit: he is against representing Andromeda as Black, a direct critique of the image of Black

27. "Il dit pour toute chose the Cephée regnoit en Ethiopie, sans designer sous quel climat. La Topographie moderne de ces contrées-là n'est pas fort connuë, et celle du temps de Cephée encor moins. Je me contenteray donc de vous dire qu'il falloit que Cephée regnast en quelque pays maritime, que sa ville capitale fust sur le bord de la mer, et que ses peuples fussent blancs quoy qu'Ethiopiens. Ce n'est pas que les Mores les plus noirs n'ayent leurs beautez à leur mode, mais il n'est pas vray-semblable que Persée qui estoit Grec et né dans Argos, fust devenu amoureux d'Andromede, si elle eust esté de leur teint. J'ay pour moy le consentement de tous les Peintres, et sur tout l'authorité du grand Heliodore qui qui ne fonde la blancheur de sa divine Chariclée que sur un tableau d'Andromède." Pierre Corneille, *Andromède* (Paris: C. de Sercy, Rouen: Laurens Maurry, 1651), "Argument," n.p. The text is the same in the first and second editions of 1651, by the same printer (Maurry) but in different typeface and the second, accompanied by engravings.

Andromeda on the facing page of the book, our Figure 2. But six years later (1661), in the notes to his translation of Ovid's *Heroides* 15, "Sappho to Phaon," Marolles takes the opportunity to say in print that his opinion has evolved: "*Andromeda daughter of Cepheus for being brown*: Given she was Ethiopian ... What I wrote about Andromeda regarding the color of her skin [*la couleur de son teint*], in my *Livre des Tableaux des Muses*, needs some correction."[28]

Barbouillage in Marino and his Parisian Epigones: A Closer Look

With this context in mind, a class might now turn to the close reading of Marino's sonnet *Bella schiava* and its French adaptations. The *belle noire* tradition predates Marino, but the French 1600s versions are undoubtedly linked to his Paris sojourn.[29] Marino was considered as Italy's most important poet at the time. Exiled at the end of a tumultuous career marked by three incarcerations for sex with men and manslaughter, he lived in Paris from 1615 to 1623 on a royal French pension. It was in Paris that he published and dedicated to Louis XIII his masterpiece, *L'Adone*, the final version of a much-revised narrative poem on the loves and feats of Venus and Adonis. *L'Adone*'s success enabled him to return to Italy, where he died in 1625. His first claim to fame was the collection of poems known as *La lira* – two volumes of *Le Rime* published in 1602, becoming *La lira* in 1608, expanded in 1614. Our text, *Bella schiava* figures in the section "Love Sonnets."

Bella schiava was so common that, in another of Marino's pastorals, *La bruna pastorella*, Marino's own fictional Alpine shepherds adapt it. Adjacent to but different from the debasing, comic portrayals of racially marked characters, or the baroque tradition of the poem of praise of an

28. "Ce que j'ay écrit d'Andromede pour la couleur de son teint, dans mon Livre des Tabelaux des Muses, a besoin de quelque correction": Ovid, *Les Epistres Heroides d'Ovide*, trans. Michel de Marolles, Abbé de Villeloin (Paris: Pierre Lamy, 1661), 338 n35.
29. On the *belle noire* tradition before Marino in Italian poetry, see Patrizia Bettella, *The Ugly Woman: Transgressive Aesthetic Models in Italian Poetry from the Middle Ages to the Baroque* (Toronto: University of Toronto Press, 2005), 135–52.

ugly woman, *stanze in lode della donna brutta*, where "ugly" often means old, racialized, disabled, or poor, *belle noire* texts provide another version of fictional exploitation of racialized, enslaved women protagonists, one written in the noble, lyric love poetry register:

> You are black but beautiful, o pretty marvel of nature
> among the beauties of love;
> the dawn next to you is dusky, ivory is lost and shadowed
> next to your ebony
> When or where, in our world or among the ancients,
> was ever seen such a brilliant — or felt such a pure —
> light come from the dark ink
> or such a glow emerge from cinders?
> I am the slave of her who is my slave
> Brown locks are a lock around my heart,
> which can never be untied by a white hand.
> Even if you burn your hardest, o Sun,
> You will only come short, because a Sun is born
> a Sun that, in her beautiful face
> holds the Night; the Day shines in her eyes.[30]

A related group of Parisian poems on the "dark lady" — a beggar, a widow, or a "Beautiful Egyptian" — is similarly fictionalized. As noted by Myriam Dufour-Maître, the "dark lady" sells fortunes, but she is more properly on sale herself, as in the remarkable poem by Georges de Scudéry, "Beautiful Egyptian" (1649):

30. Giovanbattista Marino, *La lira*, 3rd part, 1614, *La Bella Schiava*: Nera si, ma se'bella, o di natura/ fra le belle d'amor leggiardo mostro;/ fosca è l'alba appo te, perde e s'oscura/ presso l'ebeno tuo l'avorio e l'ostro.// Or quando, or dove il mondo antico o il nostro./ vide si viva mai, senti si pura/ o luce uscir di tenebroso inchiostro,/ o di spento carbon nascere arsura?// Serva di chi m'è serva, ecco ch'avolto/ porto di bruno lacio il core intorno,/ che per candida man non fia mai sciolto.// La've più ardi, o Sol, sol per tuo scorno/ un Sole e nato; un Sol, che nel bel volto/ porta la Notte, ed ha negli occhi il Giorno.

Somber Divinity, whose black splendor
Shines with obscure fires which can burn everything down,
Snow has nothing equal to you,
And today, Ebony wins over Ivory.

From your obscurity comes the splendor of your glory;
And I see in your eyes of which I dare not speak;
An African Cupid who is about to fly,
And hopes to win with an Ebony Bow.

Sorceress without Demons, who predicts the future:
Who entertains us looking at our hands,
And who charms our senses with an amiable imposture:

You don't seem very practiced in the art of guessing the future,
But without further delay, happily,
Somber Divinity, you can give it to us.[31]

The poem by Scudéry exemplifies two main tendencies of Marinist poetry: its Petrarchism and *concettismo* — the intention to astonish, expressed in Marino's *devise*: E *del poeta il fin la meraviglia*, the poet's aim is the marvelous. The enslaved woman "enslaves" the master; the Black beauty is so luminous that she shames the sun.

As Dufour-Maître shows, Cervantes's 1613 novella *Preciosa* is the avatar of this figure as well as of the French *préciosité* tradition. This connection

31. La belle Egiptienne: Sombre Divinité, de qui la splendeur noire,/ Brille de feux obscurs, qui peuvent tout brusler,/ La Neige n'a plus rien, qui te puisse égaller,/ Et l'Ebene auiourd'huy, l'emporte sur l'Ivoire.// De ton obscurité, vient l'esclat de ta gloire;/ Et ie voy dans tes yeux, dont ie n'ose parler;/ Un Amour Affriquain, qui s'apreste à voller,/ Et qui d'un Arc d'Ebene, aspire à la victoire.// Sorciere sans Demons, qui predis l'advenir;/ Qui regardant la main, nous viens entretenir;/ Et qui charmes nos sens, d'une aimable imposture:// Tu parois peu sçavante, en l'art de deviner;/ Mais sans t'amuser plus, à la bonne avanture;/ Sombre Divinité, tu nous la peux donner." Georges de Scudéry, *Poésies diverses dediées à Monseigneur le Duc de Richelieu* (Paris, Augustin Courbe, 1649), 59.

to *barbouillage* is important, because *préciosité* and the women *salonières* — the *Précieuses* — are a significant part of the canonical narrative of the 1600s, especially of proto-feminism. The *Précieuses* are such an important cultural commonplace that they are proverbial at the time, caricatured by Molière in *Précieuses ridicules* and *Femmes savantes*. Dufour-Maître's contribution highlights the racialization at the very heart of the canon — a racialization that is an integral part and the origin of a mainstream cultural reference, but that was completely elided before her important work brought it to the light once again.

The theme of *Précieuse* in this racialized *barbouillage* context was adapted in lyric poetic tradition by Tristan l'Hermite (*Belle gueuse*, 1648), Urbain Chevreau (*Belle gueuse*, 1648), Claude de Malleville (*Belle Gueuse* and an additional two sonnets and madrigal, 1649). It, too, was infamously reprised by the Romantics and, later, Baudelaire (*A une mendiante rousse*).

The earliest published (1641) of the numerous French adaptations of Marino's *Bella schiava* is a close translation by Tristan l'Hermite:

> The Beautiful Enslaved Moor Woman: A Sonnet
> Beautiful Marvel of Nature, it is true that your face
> Is black to the last degree, but perfectly beautiful;
> And the polished Ebony that serves as your ornament
> Wins over the whitest ivory.
>
> O divine marvel, unknown in our age!
> That a shadowed object may shine so brightly,
> And that an extinguished coal is burning more lively
> Than the ones that keep producing flames!
>
> Between these black hands I put my freedom;
> I, who was invincible to every other Beauty,
> A Moor sets me aflame, a Slave subdues me.
>
> But, o Sun, hide, you who come from these parts [i.e., the Orient]
> From which this Star has come, who wears — shame on you, [i.e.,

she shines brighter]
Night on her face, and daylight in her eyes.[32]

Tristan l'Hermite paraphrases Marino ("I put my freedom in her black hands"), where Marino speaks of "brown fetters around the heart, that will never be untied by a white hand" (*porto di bruno lacio il core intorno,/ che per candida man non fia mai sciolto*). This play on fetters, locks, and heart is older than Marino: a Petrarchan reference that, in English, is a pun on *locks* of hair that become *locks* or chains that bind the lover.[33]

An anonymous translation in a manuscript in the BnF (ms fr 20605) is even closer to Marino's original than Tristan l'Hermite. The manuscript contains a note that this version was by a woman (*une dame*) and that it was corrected (*réformé*) by no less than Paul Scarron — one is tempted to imagine that the *dame* might have been Françoise d'Aubigné, the future Madame de Maintenon:

I am the captive of my captive, following her, fettered
With black gold, which will never be unfettered
By a white hand, so strong is her spirit.[34]

32. Tristan l'Hermite, *La Lyre du sieur Tristan: suivi de l'Orphée, mélanges* (Paris: Augustin Courbe, 1641), 165: La Belle Esclave More, Sonnet: Beau Monstre de Nature, il est vray, ton visage/ Est noir au dernier point, mais beau parfaitement:/ Et l'Ebene poly qui te sert d'ornement/ Sur le plus blanc yvoire emporte l'avantage.// O merveille divine incognuë à nostre âge !/ Qu'un objet tenebreux luise si clairement;/ Et qu'un charbon esteint, brusle plus vivement/ Que ceux qui de la flâme entretiennent l'usage!// Entre ces noires mains ie mets ma liberté ;/ Moy qui fut invincible à toute autre Beauté,/ Une More m'embrase, une Esclave me domte.// Mais cache toy Soleil, toy qui viens de ces lieux/ D'où cèt Astre est venu, qui porte pour ta honte/ La nuict sur son visage et le iour dans ses yeux."

33. I thank Anna Wainwright for that reference.

34. *Captif de ma captive ainsy suivre enlacé/ De l'or noir qui jamais ne sera deslacé/ D'aucune blanche main, tant son esprit est forz*: BnF ms fr 20605, *Recueil de pièces historiques, originaux et copies.* (13e–18e siècle). Vol. 3, *Pièces de vers latins, français, etc. la plupart anonymes, des XVIe et XVIIe siècles*, Fo 396: "Sonnet reformé par Mr. Scarron"; the annotation in the margin reads "d'une dame."

The Petrarchism of this *concetto* is inescapable: already in Petrarch, the locks (hair)/locks (fetters) are connected to slavery, Africa, and racialization, via Petrarch's source in Ovid's version of the myth of Andromeda. In the *Triumph of Love*, Petrarch mentions the Ovidian Black Sappho and Andromeda:

> Perseus was one; and I want to know how
> Andromeda was pleasing to him in Ethiopia,
> The brown maiden, with the beautiful eyes and hair. (Petrarch, *Triumph of Love*).

As we discussed above (figure 1), Ovid's Sappho (*Heroides*, Epist. 15 "Sappho to Phaon") compares herself to the dark (*fusca*) Andromeda:

> If I am not fair, what of it? Perseus loved the Cepheian
> Dark Andromeda, who was the color of her country.[35]

As we already mentioned, the Parisian authors discussed in this chapter knew each other. For example, as the former preceptor to Louise-Marie de Gonzague-Nevers (1611–1667), twice the queen of Poland, Marolles secured from her a pension for Saint-Amant (1645–1659), one of the Parisian translators of Marino's *Bella schiava*. As does Marolles in the *Temple* and his translation of the *Heroides*, Saint-Amant also discusses the color of Andromeda's skin in his poem *Andromeda*, dedicated to the same Gaston d'Orléans who danced in *barbouillage* to portray an African prince in the *Douairière* — performed in 1626, the year when Saint-Amant sailed for Senegal in an armed expedition financed by the *Compagnie du Sénégal*. Saint-Amant cites the climate theory of race only to say how spectacularly

35. Candida si non sum; placuit Cepheia Perseo/ Andromede, patriae fusca colore suae" (Ovid, *Heroides*, Epist. 15 "Sappho Phaoni"). Andromeda is the daughter of Cepheus, the king of Ethiopia. See Elizabeth McGrath, "Ludovico il Moro and His Moors," *Journal of the Warburg and Courtlaud Institutes* 65 (2002), 67–94; McGrath, "Veronese, Callet and the Black Boy at the Feast," *Journal of the Warburg and Courtlaud Institutes* 61 (1999): 272–76; McGrath, "The Black Andromeda," *Journal of the Warburg and Courtlaud Institutes* 55 (1992), 1–18.

Andromeda contradicts it. Perseus almost falls off his flying mount upon first seeing her:

> Besides, was it believable
> And could one conceive
> That in such a frightening climate
> Anything pleasant can be seen?
> Or that, in the middle of Africa,
> Where the heat that prickles it
> Blackens even the blood,
> Among the dark visages
> Where bodies resemble shadows
> Can be found one so white?[36]

It is unbelievable that:

> one whose extreme beauties
> would captivate Gods themselves
> Should now be in chains.[37]

In this view of the world, blackness, like being enslaved, is unbelievable in one so white, and both blackness and slavery are characteristic of the climate of Africa. Or, in other words, if you are in Africa and white, you are not enslaved, but if you are Black and out of Africa, you can be. There is a conceptual slippage here characteristic of the racialization and hierarchy

36. "D'ailleurs estoit-il croyable/ Et pouvoit on concevoir,/ Qu'en un climat effroyable/ Rien de si doux se peust voir?/ Ny qu'au milieu de l'Afrique/ A qui le chaut qui la pique/ Noircit mesme jusqu'au sang,/ Parmy des visages sombres/ Où les corps passent pour ombres/ Il s'en trouvast un si blanc?" "L'Andromède, à Monsieur frère unique du Roy," Marc Antoine Girard de Saint-Amant, *Les Oeuvres du sieur de Saint-Amant, reveuës, corrigées, et de beaucoup augmentées dans cette derniere Edition* (Paris: Guillaume de Luyne, 1661), 33.
37. "Et dont les beautez extremes/ Captiveroient les Dieux mesmes,/ Fust maintenant dans les fers?" Marc Antoine Girard de Saint-Amant, *Les Oeuvres du sieur de Saint-Amant, reveuës, corrigées, et de beaucoup augmentées dans cette derniere Edition* (Paris: Guillaume de Luyne, 1661), 34.

that we may recognize as Enlightenment or modern, at work in the premodern period: from the hot climate of Africa to being Black and enslaved, and from whiteness, to beauty, to the impossibility of being enslaved.

Saint-Amant's poem, published posthumously in 1661, was undoubtedly inspired by the long-lasting success of Pierre Corneille's *Andromède*, staged from 1650–1660, with music by d'Assouci and set design by Torelli, some recycled from the opera *Orfeo* by Luigi Rossi (1647). Scheduled for 1648, Corneille's *Andromeda* was delayed by the Fronde. Performed in 1650, with Madeleine Béjart as Andromeda and young Molière as Perseus, the play travelled from Paris to Brussels and Metz, and again to Paris in 1655 (with sets by Buffequin). It was adapted a generation later, in 1682, by Quinault with Lully's music. Their *Perseus* was a lasting success: thirty-three consecutive performances, forty-five *in toto*. The parallel Comédie-Française's 1682 revival of Corneille's *Andromeda* with music by Marc-Antoine Charpentier included a real-life horse as Pegasus. The play was performed again in 1693. In Corneille, Andromeda is also white, a tradition inherited — as Corneille explicitly says, see citation above — from Heliodorus's *Aethiopica or Love adventures of Theagenes and Chariclea*. As we mentioned, the novel was favored by seventeenth-century readers, famously including Jean Racine who (in his son's recollection) memorized it as a schoolboy after repeated confiscation by his disapproving Jansenist pedagogues.[38] As we noted, Heliodorus's character, Chariclea is born white to her Black parents, because her mother looked at a representation of a white Andromeda. Abandoned at birth, after countless adventures, Chariclea is recognized by her father thanks to the black mark on her skin.[39] Translated numerous times, including into French by Amyot

38. Printed in Basel in 1526, translated into French by Jacques Amyot in 1547 and into English by Thomas Underwood in 1569. Jacques Amyot, *L'histoire aethiopique*, ed. Laurence Plazenet (Paris: Champion, 1928). The first book of *Aethiopica* was also translated by Lancelot de Carle, BnF ms français 2143, around the same time as Amyot's. For 1600s novels and plays inspired by *Aethiopica* and recent scholarship, see the bibliography of Hardy's play (2015), below.

39. Heliodorus of Emesa, *Les adventures amoureuses de Theagenes et Cariclée* (Paris: Pierre Valet, 1613) and trans. Montlyard, *Les amours de Théagène et Chariclée, histoire æthiopique. Traduction nouvelle* (Paris: S. Thiboust, 1623). The 1613 edition was one of

(1548) and Montlyard (1623), Chariclea inspired numerous Parisian playwrights, including Alexandre Hardy, whose play appeared in print in 1623 and 1628: a lasting success. [40]

As Kim F. Hall, Dennis Britton, Kimberly Coles, and Anna Wainwright have shown, the references to hair as links, nets, chains or ties that capture the lover — depending on the color of the hair, brown or gold links — are frequent in Petrarchist poetry.[41] Suffice it to mention Pierre de Ronsard's golden nets, *retz d'or* that seamlessly evoke the three meanings, the net cast by the god of Love that captures and binds his prey, the locks of the beloved's hair, and precious metal, as well as the patronage of the maréchal de Retz and his wife's, Catherine de Clermont's *salon*:

From here to there, under my lady's eyes
A golden net dropped from a hundred blooms.
Love cast the blond descent that fell, thoroughly curled,
In undulating waves to bind my soul. [...]
What could I do? the archer went so slow,
His fire so soft, his golden knots so mild,

the first French books with etchings, while the new 1623 translation by Monlyard had a new set of copper plate illustrations. Chariclea also inspired Torquato Tasso's warrior woman Clorinda, born white to Black Ethiopian parents, in *Gerusalemme liberata* (1581).

40. Octave-César Genetay, *L'étiopique, tragédie des chastes amours de Théagène et Chariclée* (Rouen: T. Reinsart, 1609; Alexandre Hardy, *Les chastes et loyales amours de Théagène et Cariclée* (Paris: Quesnel, 1623; second corrected edition 1628; ed. Antonella Amatuzzi, Paola Cifarelli, Michele Mastroianni, Monica Pavesio and Laura Rescia, general editor Daniela Dalla Valle, Paris: Garnier, 2015).

41. Kim Hall, "'A New Scholarly Song': Rereading Early Modern Race," Shakespeare Quarterly 67, no. 1 (2016): 1–13 and Hall, *Things of Darkness: Economies of Race and Gender in Early Modern England* (Ithaca, NY: Cornell University Press, 1995); Dennis A. Britton and Kimberly A. Coles, "Spenser and Race: An Introduction," *Spenser Studies* 35 (2021). On the sixteenth-century Italian context, see Anna Wainwright, "'Tied Up in Chains of Adamant': Recovering Race in Tasso's Armida Before, and After, Acrasia' *Spenser Studies* 35 (2021).

That in his nets I am forever lost. [...]
The fire burns, and the curly gold binds me.[42]

The transposition of the chains of slavery into chains of gold is an invention of the anonymous French poet-translator of Marino's *Bella schiava.* Here, the bondage of the lyric subject is a sublimated slave chain, made of an exotic precious metal, "black gold" that mirrors the condition of the fictional Black beloved. The incongruously gold, fictional slave chains echo the fictional chains and slave collars in contemporary Parisian novels, *barbouillage* ballet performances, and aristocratic portraits of noblemen accompanied by children wearing silver and gold slave collars, frequent in the period 1670–1710, especially in the atelier of the major court portraitist Hyacinthe Rigaud and his disciples, but also at court and in Paris print shops. Gold slave chains and collars appear in Mme de Scudéry's novel *Almahide, or Slave Queen* (in three parts and eight volumes, 1661–1663). The lover, Morayzel, enters sumptuously attired and "surrounded by twelve Slaves in long Pants of silver cloth, whose Cassocks and Hats were of cloth of gold, and Collars and Chains of massive gold."[43] In the third part of the novel, the splendid funerary procession of Lucane includes twenty-four "Slaves in Mourning, with silver Collars and silver Chains on arms and legs."[44]

Five of the dozen or so Parisian poets imitating Marino's *Bella schiava* foreground the theme of captive captor: the enslaved woman is the master. These five are, in tentative chronologial order: Tristan L'Hermite (1641), the anonymous woman poet of BnF ms fr 20605, Claude de Malleville (before 1647, printed in 1649), Charles de Vion d'Alibray (1654), and the anonymous author of the poem printed *La muse coquette* (1665). In

42. Puis çà puis là pres les yeulx de ma dame/ Entre cent fleurs un retz d'or me tendoit,/ Qui tout crespu blondement descendoit/ A flotz ondez pour enlasser mon âme./ Qu'eussay-je faict? L'archer estoit si doulx/ Si doulx son feu, si doulx l'or de ses noeudz,/ Qu'en leurs filetz encore je m'oublie.

43. Marie-Françoise and Georges de Scudéry, *Almahide*, parts 1–3 (Paris: Louis Billaine, 1660–1663), part 1, 133.

44. Marie-Françoise and Georges de Scudéry, *Almahide*, parts 1–3 (Paris: Louis Billaine, 1660–1663), part 3, 549.

this group, in all but d'Alibray, her black hair becomes fetters, sometimes brown, sometimes "black gold," of which are fashioned the bonds that enslave her lover. As in the theatrical plots frequently used in the same period, where the enslaved Black adolescent is in fact a noblewoman in disguise searching for her lover, lyric poetry produces a fiction of slavery that erases the violence inflicted upon the enslaved. Similar to the *barbouillage* ballets danced by Louis XIII and Louis XIV, or the *Masque of Blackness* danced by the English queen, blackness and slavery are a costume: a wealthy aristocrat hides underneath, as in Marie de Harambure's portrait "as an enslaved Moor woman, in chains"; Haramboure was exceptionally wealthy and the target of fortune hunters. The fictional female object of admiration in these poems and staged portraits is a simulacrum: in Paris, she performs the fictional version of the labor that violently enslaved women actually performed in the colonies.[45]

1800s Poets Borrowing 1600s *Barbouillage*

These poems can offer students — as well as scholars — an important connection between early modern French understandings of skin color as race and the more familiar racialized representations of later centuries.[46] 1600s *barbouillage* was often cited and adapted by the Romantics and Symbolists, imbued with the new racism of the 1800s. To understand the survival and continuity, as well as specificity and differences between 1600s *barbouillage* and the texts and images of 1800s Paris, students can examine, for instance, the literary portrait of the performer Jenny Colon (1837) by Gautier, part of his nauseatingly misogynist series of narrative portraits of contemporary women. Gautier reimagines Colon as a seventeenth-century print of a white noblewoman accompanied by a Black page by Abraham Bosse, the prolific 1600s draftsman. In other narra-

45. I thank Masnoon Majeed for this comment.

46. See Tracy Denean Sharpley-Whiting, *Black Venus: Sexualized Savages, Primal Fears, and Primitive Narratives in French* (Durham, N.C: Duke University Press, 1999) on racism and misogyny in nineteenth-century French tradition including Baudelaire, theater, poetry, Orientalist and Troubadour painting, and popular culture.

tive portraits from this series, Gautier constructs physical characteristics of race as a sign of gender and sexual difference. Gautier's portrait of brown women as men or intersex people, as opposed to the "completely feminine" (his phrase) white blond women, envisions two parallel gender systems for brown versus white women: brown women and men are nonbinary, they "present much fewer differences" and can "easily pass" for male or female, while white women are part of a normalized binary and are "woman in every sense of the word," "biblical Eve" (his words).[47] A generation later, Baudelaire infamously borrows from 1600s Marinist *barbouillage* in his erotic poems on the racialized (*Chevelure*), widowed (A *une passante*) and poor (A *une mendiante rousse*) female object of male gaze.

• • •

If Pierre Nora says that some places, texts and objects become the ground collective remembering and imagining, *lieux de mémoire*, we have shown in this chapter that national literary traditions also have ways to erase collective memory. After centuries of smoothing over the inconvenient and shameful truths, today Francophone cultures are reckoning with the past in the hope of building a more equal future. After a class or unit on these poems, students of the French Grand Siècle should be able to point to concrete examples of the links between premodern France's cultural icons and slave trade. The Enlightenment, abolition of slavery, and modernity relegated these links to inaccessible recesses where the shameful and inconvenient cultural memories dwell. The Symbolists and twentieth-century formalists, and later their twentieth-century commentators, critics, high school and college manuals of French literature evacuated the political and historical content of Baroque and 1800s *barbouillage*, focusing instead on the formal aspects of the poetic tradition. Today, we excavate and foreground the history of racism, especially in the classroom. The French people I encountered uniformly believe that to acknowledge France's part in the genocide of slave trade and colonization will prevent injustices and help heal in the present the wounds that begun in the past: that, as the historian Marc Ferro said, is the essential role of

47. Théophile Gautier, *Portraits contemporains: littérateurs, peintres, sculpteurs, artistes dramatiques* (Paris: Bibliothèque Charpentier, 1898), 383.

history and pedagogy. It seems to me that the context presented here, of the racialized fictions in mainstream cultural productions of the 1600s and their reverberations in the 1800s, helps to more fully understand the racist gestures in the present and build a better future through education. The debates in French press of the previous years that, in a way that clearly appeared racist to American commentators, framed *barbouillage* in the arts as a question–"Freedom of expression or racism?"–seem to finally have found a firm answer, thanks to the repeated interventions of Black intellectuals and activists. After having studied how the racist *barbouillage* of the 1600s is reprised in the 1800s by formative French canonical authors including Baudelaire, it is my hope that the students will have no trouble deciding on their own.

Suggestions for Further Reading

Bettella, Patrizia. *The Ugly Woman: Transgressive Aesthetic Models in Italian Poetry from the Middle Ages to the Baroque*. Toronto: University of Toronto Press, 2005.

Ndiaye, Noémie. *Scripts of Blackness: Early Modern Performance Culture and the Making of Race*. Philadelphia: University of Pennsylvania Press, 2022.

Niang, Mame-Fatou. *Identités françaises: Banlieues, feminités et universalisme*. Leiden: Brill, 2020.

Niang, Mame-Fatou and Julien Suaudeau, *Universalisme*. Paris: Anamosa, 2022.

Learning to Listen: A New Approach to Teaching Early Modern Encounters in the Americas

CHARLOTTE DANIELS AND KATHERINE DAUGE-ROTH

In 2016, at Bowdoin College, the "French" program became "Francophone Studies," reflecting a collective desire to work toward transcending within our curriculum persistent and problematic disciplinary boundaries between the study of continental France and of other French-speaking regions of the world. Following the lead of our colleagues whose research and teaching focus most directly on postcolonial issues, we made this shift from our elementary language courses forward so that our students at every level of the curriculum would experience more fully and in a more integrated way the issues, histories, traditions, and questions raised in different parts of the broad French-speaking world. Our new introductory survey course, "Spoken Word and Written Text," reflects a more global understanding not only of literature, that is the written tradition, but of the oral tradition as well. Spanning the period from the Middle Ages through the 1848 abolition of slavery in the French Antilles, the course is one of two chronologically organized "Introduction to Francophone Studies" surveys required to complete the major. Taught in French, it is designed for students who have had five semesters of college-level language or the equivalent, mostly first-years and sophomores. In this course, we have put into practice for earlier periods what our colleagues in postcolonial studies have long understood: that French-speaking regions and people across the globe are not independent but rather exist, and have existed for centuries, in dynamic relationship to each other.[1] In the following pages, we share one unit of the course, "Indigenous Peo-

1. Please see our "Globalizing the Early Literature Survey: Challenges and Rewards," *French Review* 93.1 (2019): 92–107 and its accompanying *dossier pédagogique* at frenchreview.frenchteachers.org/Dossiers.html.

ple and French Colonizers in North America," to present a new approach to teaching the (long) Renaissance period that considers perspectives and traditions excluded from more Eurocentric narratives of the period. We show how by widening our corpus to include texts not typically assigned in a literature survey as well as oral sources where Native American voices both past and present come to the fore, we and our students have learned to listen and subsequently to tell a more complete story of the Renaissance that has poignant resonances today.[2] From the outset, the authors would like to emphasize that the course and the unit we present here would not have been possible without our colleague Hanétha Vété-Congolo's tireless visible and invisible work over the course of many years to bring about an epistemic shift in our department's curriculum. We are deeply grateful to both her and to our colleague Meryem Belkaïd for their leadership and crucial contributions to enriching and complicating ours and our students' understanding of the French-speaking world, without which this article and the perspective it promotes would not exist.

Until quite recently, the Renaissance, both in France and in Europe at large, has been presented as a period of scientific innovation and artistic genius, a very European and very white affair. France's Renaissance has been most celebrated for innovations in the realm of literature, especially poetry. The French poets of the Pléiade, whose principal members were Pierre de Ronsard (1524–1585), Joachim Du Bellay (c. 1522–1560), and Antoine de Baïf (1532–1589), made of the sonnet and other poetic forms such as the ode, a literary expression of French style and beauty. The poems of La Pléiade are taught in almost every survey class, usually alongside Du Bellay's *Defense and Illustration of the French Language* (1549). This classic work explicitly links poetic innovation to political power and the

2. Henceforth, we use the terms "Native American" and "First Nations," as well as the adjectives "Indigenous" and "Native" to describe, in what are today the United States and Canada, those whose ancestors first inhabited these territories. See more detailed discussion of these terms and others in Olive Patricia Dickason with David T. McNab, "Introduction," *Canada's First Nations: A History of Founding Peoples from Earliest Times*, 4th ed. (Oxford, England: Oxford University Press, 2009), xii–xiii.

formation of a proud national identity, indeed, of Frenchness itself.[3] The French language, Du Bellay argued, if properly tended and nurtured by its poet-stewards, would become as magnificent as had been ancient Greek and Latin. Typically, beyond a short paragraph entitled something like "The Great Discoveries," students learn little about how this new notion of Frenchness tied in with social and political changes across the globe. After all, like the Ancients whom they claimed as their illustrious ancestors, the French were ambitious colonizers. In the sixteenth century, at the same time as King François I cultivated the arts at home and promoted French as the kingdom's official language, he sent forth multiple transatlantic expeditions as part of a colonial enterprise that would expand significantly in the seventeenth century with the establishment of French settlements in what would become known as North America. As Sara Melzer reminds us in *Colonizer or Colonized*, the inclusion of this "second France" deserves attention, pushing us to interrogate established narratives.[4] The unit we created to introduce students to this period follows Melzer's lead, drawing on several non-canonical sources, both written and oral, to tell a more interconnected and more accurate story. Students still read the familiar *carpe diem* sonnets of Ronsard and Du Bellay's *Defense*, but they make connections between the cultural renewal taking place on French soil and what was happening simultaneously in the territories inhabited by the Wabanaki, Algonquin, Huron, Iroquois, and Innu.[5]

After reading poems and excerpts from Du Bellay's *Defense*, students consider images and texts created by Frenchmen in Native American territories that have not usually figured in literature surveys. They thus gain access to on-the-ground interactions between First Nations people and

3. Joachim Du Bellay, *Deffence et illustration de la langue françoise*, in *Œuvres choisies*, ed. Adrien Cart and M.-Th. Beyret (Paris: Larousse, 1934).
4. Sara Melzer, *Colonizer or Colonized: The Hidden Stories of Early Modern French Culture* (Philadelphia, PA: University of Pennsylvania Press, 2012) and "Une 'Seconde France'? Re-penser le paradigme 'classique' à partir de l'histoire oubliée de la colonisation française," in *La littérature, le XVIIe siècle et nous: dialogue transatlantique*, ed. Hélène Merlin-Kajman (Paris: Presse Sorbonne Nouvelle, 2008), 75–85.
5. For a consideration of the difficulties around accurate naming of North American tribes, see Dickason with McNab, *Canada's First Nations*, xii.

new European arrivals, first from a European perspective. Even if French readers of the period never set foot on land in the Americas, their voracious consumption of narratives and images created by travelers and missionaries provided a sense of being there, of becoming part of the action among a community of "savages" who were a source of both fascination and fear. Safe in France, armchair travelers internalized ideas about faraway cultures that bolstered their own sense of belonging to a "civilized" world that existed in relation to this newly discovered "uncivilized" one. Students see the development of racist tropes just as they are emerging in the French imaginary. Then, in a rather dramatic shift, they engage with Native American legends and oral histories already in existence for millennia by the time European colonization began. This venerable oral archive, transmitted from generation to generation across time, continues to play an essential and vibrant role in tribal life today.[6] At Bowdoin, a small liberal arts college in Maine, we are fortunate to have as a frequent guest Maria Girouard, a member of the Penobscot nation, former tribal leader, Penobscot historian, author, educator, and environmental activist, who is an expert on the oral tradition. Through their interactions with Girouard, students see the oral tradition as something vibrant, an essential part of who the Penobscot are today in deep relation to who they were in the past. While students are at first surprised to find in "a French class" the inclusion of Native American tales and oral histories, they quickly see the intersections between the European texts discussed and this other part of the story, so close to home. Through their readings and discussions of both the written and the oral tradition, students come to think in exciting new ways about the early modern period.

Beyond the Literary Canon: The Written Archive

The first half of this unit invites students to experience the vision of the "New World" provided by print culture of the sixteenth and seventeenth

6. We are particularly lucky to have access to sources written and spoken in French in Maine and nearby Québec. However, we do not limit ourselves to French in our interactions with members of the Native American community.

centuries. Students are introduced to European perceptions of the Americas and its Native people through a series of engravings by the Fleming Theodor de Bry (1528–1598) depicting Native life, published and widely circulated in 1590 and 1591 in two volumes known as *America*, parts I and II.[7] The engravings are based on the work of the Frenchman Jacques Le Moyne de Morgues (1533–1588) and the Englishman John White (c. 1540–c. 1593) who, as artists, accompanied the first European travelers to North America and inaugurated a European iconography of the "New World." Students study these images to make initial observations about how Europeans perceive themselves and how they perceive the Indigenous people they encounter.[8] They note the interest in daily activities and rituals, the use of Christian symbols, and the obsessive attention paid by Europeans to Native Americans' bodies. Their preliminary analyses set up a series of themes and questions that they explore further in their readings of short passages from the three French voyages sent forth by King François I: Giovanni da Verrazzano's 1524 coastal expedition from Florida to the mouth of the Saint Lawrence River; Jacques Cartier's three expeditions (1534, 1535–1536, 1541–1542) to the areas that are today Montreal and Quebec; and Jean Ribault and René de Goulaine de Laudonnière's 1562 attempt to establish a Huguenot colony in today's Florida.[9] Our students, already

7. De Bry's first volume reproduced Thomas Harriot's narrative, *A Briefe and True Report of the New Found Land of Virginia*, adding engravings made from the drawings by the expedition's artist John White, *Admiranda narratio, fida tamen, de commodis et incolorum ritibus Virginiae* (Frankfurt: Johann Wechel, 1590). The second contained *relations* by René de Laudonnière and his artist, Jacques Le Moyne de Morgues, of their expedition in Florida, featuring engravings of the Timucua made from Le Moyne's watercolors, *Brevis narratio eorum quae in Florida Americae provicia Gallis acciderunt* (Frankfurt: Johann Wechel, 1591).
8. Travel narratives of the sixteenth and seventeenth centuries read and quote each other frequently, perpetuating stereotypes that influence their perceptions of those they encounter and become part of the permanent record. Moreover, printed versions often differ from their manuscript originals, thanks to publishers' modifications intended to make them better correspond to readers' expectations.
9. Ribault's voyages were documented in drawings by artist Le Moyne de Morgues, the engravings of which students have already considered. We thank Nicolas Hebbinckuys for having generously shared with us selections from these texts.

savvy readers of race and gender, find much to discuss. In Verrazzano's remarkable descriptions of the Native Americans' and European travelers' mutual fascination, students immediately note the central role that bodily ornamentation and skin color play in the establishment of difference. The Native Americans "walk around completely naked, except for covering their shameful parts with the skins of small animals like weasels or mink, and a narrow belt made of reeds, to which are knotted the tails of animals that hang from their bodies, all the way to their knees; ... they are black, not unlike Ethiopians."[10] According to Verrazzano, the Native Americans, for their part, are welcoming and curious about the European strangers in their midst. He reports that they first ran away but "reassured by our gestures, some of them approached us, showing great joy upon seeing us, amazed by our clothing, our appearance and our whiteness, indicating by gestures where the boat could land most easily and offering us some of their food."[11] Students see here, as they have in visual form through their analysis of the De Bry images, descriptions that highlight racial difference, while also suggesting a gendered and sexualized relationship between the cultures, this encounter representing a seduction scene in which the Native Americans must be coaxed but are ultimately willing. This tendency is even more marked in Jean Ribault's text, written forty years later. He describes the coastal lands of Florida in manifestly feminized terms, the sailors "enjoying [*jouissant*] with an unspeakable pleasure the suave perfumes she breathed and her beauties."[12] Ribault's word choice, suggesting sexual climax, underscores conquest as ravish-

10. Giovanni da Verrazano, *Relation* [1524] in Jacques Habert and Michel Mollat du Jourdin, *Giovanni et Girolamo Verrazano Navigateurs de François Ier. Dossiers de voyages* (Paris: Imprimerie Nationale, 1982), 15–16. All translations are our own.
11. Habert and Mollat du Jourdin, *Giovanni et Girolamo*. Elsewhere Verrazzano uses the word race in referring to a tribe and their skin tones: "This race is the most beautiful and the most civilized of those that we have met during this campaign. They are taller than we are; they have a bronze complexion, some of them are lighter colored, others more so;" Habert and Mollat du Jourdin, *Giovanni et Girolamo*, 27–28.
12. Ribault, Jean. *La Complète et Véridique Découverte de la Terra Florida* ... in *Les Français en Amérique pendant la deuxième moitié du xvie siècle*, ed. Charles-André Julien (Paris: PUF, 1958), 1–26, at 7.

ment, an apt metaphor, as we will see, for the uniquely French colonial enterprise more broadly. As nineteenth-century historian Francis Parkman wrote, "Spanish civilization crushed the Indian. English civilization scorned and neglected him. French civilization embraced and cherished him."[13]

Our students next move on to consider the French assimilationist project in Jesuit travel narratives known as *relations*, focusing on excerpts of the most famous of these, missionary Paul Le Jeune's (1591–1664) *Relation of* 1634.[14] By the seventeenth century, *relations* had become a well-known and widely read genre, surpassing even novels in their popularity. The Jesuits, who led the monarch's "civilizing mission" in "New France," converting Native Americans to the Catholic fold, were key players in the development of this new literary form, sending lengthy narratives of their experiences among "the savages" back to France for publication and distribution. These eagerly anticipated volumes appeared every year from 1632 to 1673.[15] Unlike the sixteenth-century explorers whose observations were based on limited contact with the Indigenous people of the Americas, Jesuits became part of local communities and remained with them for extended periods of time, learning their customs and languages. As such, they exemplify the distinctly French approach to colonization that sought to dominate the Native people and lands of the Americas not by extermination but by assimilation into the French state — conquest by a gentler name.[16]

13. Francis Parkman, *France and England in North America*, vol. 2, *The Jesuits in North America in the Seventeenth Century*, 3rd ed. (Boston: Little, Brown and Company, 1868), 44.
14. Paul Le Jeune, *Relation de ce qui s'est passé en la Nouvelle-France en l'année* 1634 [Sébastien Cramoisy, 1635], in *Monumenta Novae Franciæ*, vol. 2, *Établissement à Québec*, 1616–1634, ed. Lucien Campeau (Rome and Québec: Monumenta Hist. Soc. Jesus, 1979), 531–740. We are grateful to Sara Melzer, Micah True, and Ellen Welch for having shared sources and provided helpful recommendations regarding teaching the *Relation*.
15. Melzer, "Une 'Seconde France,'" 79.
16. On the French assimilationist model, see Melzer, *Colonizer or Colonized* and "Une 'Seconde France,'" and Gorden M. Sayre, *Les Sauvages Américains: Representations of Native*

Paul Le Jeune spent seventeen years living among First Nations people, arriving in Tadoussac in 1632 as a forty-two-year-old man and returning to France in 1649. His *Relation of* 1634 recounts his first winter among people whom he refers to as "the Montagnais" in what would become the French-speaking province of Quebec. As part of his project "for the conversion of these savages," he studies their belief system and cultural practices in depth, bringing alive and preserving in the written archive the cultural practices, beliefs, and day-to-day realities of a whole world that had existed long before contact with the French, when what was not yet known as the Americas belonged to Indigenous people.[17]

Even faced with the challenges of Le Jeune's seventeenth-century French prose, our students, like the French three hundred years earlier, find it a fascinating read. However, they are also quick to see in his work an extension of the troubling treatment of Native Americans already glimpsed in the artistic and written representations of sixteenth-century French travelers. At first, they are puzzled by Le Jeune's hyper-valorization of Native Americans combined with a systematic denigration of their behaviors and their culture more broadly. Le Jeune's chapters 5 and 6, for example, juxtapose what he sees as the "good" and then the "bad" traits of the Montagnais. During class discussions, students begin to see that this is part of a strategy. In Chapter 5, "Of the Good Things One Finds in the Savages," Le Jeune extolls their numerous qualities that show they are, so to speak, conversion-ready. The men are "tall, with good posture, strong, well-proportioned, agile," the reincarnation of the greats of the Roman Empire, so admired by the French of the period: "I see on the shoulders of this people, the heads of Julius Caesar, Pompey, Augustus."[18] "They are like us and we share a common ancestry," Le Jeune seems to be telling the French. Or, as King Louis XIV's Minister of Finance, Jean-Baptiste Colbert, would affirm some thirty years later, we are "one people

Americans in French and English Colonial Literature (Chapel Hill, NC, and London: The University of North Carolina Press, 1997), 3 and 7.

17. Le Jeune, Letter to his superior, Berthélémy Jacquinot, in *Relation de* 1634, 538.

18. Le Jeune, *Relation de* 1634, 595 and 597.

and one blood."[19] Le Jeune connects the Montagnais's well-formed bodies with bright souls and minds, no different from those of the French: "Having a well-formed body and well-arranged organs, their minds must operate with ease. The only things missing are education and instruction."[20] Le Jeune's positive assessment of the Montagnais's intellectual abilities reassures the French public that the people they are reading about have the potential to become French Catholics. Le Jeune goes on to share a list of the Montagnais's other positive traits: they do not anger easily, they are not stingy but instead generous and mutually supportive, forgiving, and patient, a long list of Christian virtues. Indeed, Native Americans often surpass Christians in these attributes: "The savages exceed us so much in this regard that we should feel ashamed."[21] These passages serve as a humoristic scolding of the readers themselves, who would do well to use these "savages" as models.[22]

Our students often wonder: if the Montagnais are so heroic, so virtuous, and indeed, in certain domains, worthy of emulation, what then justifies "Frenchifying" them? In keeping with the doctrine of Catholic universalism, Le Jeune has shown they have what it takes to see the light (i.e., be converted to the French religion and culture).[23] This is where the negative spin comes into play. Throughout his *Relation*, Le Jeune underlines the need for conversion by devaluing and denigrating Montagnais practices. He does so with a jocular tone that invites his readers to share in a humor-

19. Letter from Colbert to Talon, April 5, 1667, in *Rapport de l'Archiviste de la Province de Québec*, Redempti Paradis Imprimeur de Sa Majesté le Roi, 1930, 58, original cited in Melzer, "Une 'Seconde France,'" 77.
20. Le Jeune, *Relation de* 1634, 596.
21. Le Jeune, *Relation de* 1634, 597.
22. They foreshadow the genre of spy tales from abroad that the French will devour during the eighteenth century, most notably with Montesquieu's *Lettres Persanes*, Voltaire's *Ingénue*, Graffigny's *Lettres d'une Péruvienne*, in which the foreigners have a thing or two to teach the French about themselves.
23. The Greek roots of the word "Catholic" combine *κατά* (kata) meaning "concerning," with *ὅλος* (holos), "the whole"; "Catholic, adj. and n.," OED *Online*, June 2019 (Oxford: Oxford University Press), https://www-oed-com.ezproxy.bowdoin.edu/view/Entry/28967?redirectedFrom=Catholic (accessed June 29, 2019).

ous camaraderie that views the Native Americans as distinctly other. As in Du Bellay's call in his *Defense* for poets to cultivate the French language, which has been neglected for too long, so that it might "flower" and "bear fruit," Le Jeune, too, uses an agricultural metaphor to incite French support of the Jesuit project: "Their soul is fertile soil, but full of all the evils that a land abandoned since the beginning of time may bear."[24] In his chapter devoted to "their vices and imperfections," Le Jeune underlines what he sees as the numerous faults of the "savages" who, despite their good qualities, are "ignorant," and "barbaric," rationalizing the need for the French to come to their rescue. He invites his readers to share his disgust at their laziness, their gluttony, and especially their lust, exclaiming, "My God, what blindness!"[25] Le Jeune infantilizes the Montagnais as "real jokesters, real children who wish only to laugh."[26] As "children," who live only for the present, without the missionaries' help they are not yet capable of participating in the "civilized" French culture of which Le Jeune is so proud.[27]

In his chapter on the Montagnais religion, Le Jeune again invites his readers to laugh at and thereby dismiss the validity of "their religion or, more appropriately, their superstition."[28] He mocks the Montagnais's animism — the belief that all parts of the interconnected natural world have souls — ridiculing their prayers to porcupines, beavers, and moose. He invites his readers to be both mystified and astonished by their seemingly endless hours of repetitive "massive, ... somber and unpleasant" chanting.[29] He takes literally and then attempts to disprove the Montagnais belief that souls migrate across the waters in the afterlife to a "country where the sun sets" by invoking the European cartographic mastery of the globe.[30] Through their reading and discussion, Le Jeune's strategy becomes clearer to students: he at once reinforces the idea that this is

24. Du Bellay, *Deffence et illustration*, 18. Le Jeune, *Relation de* 1634, 596.
25. Le Jeune, *Relation de* 1634, 606; see also 604–7.
26. Le Jeune, *Relation de* 1634, 602.
27. Le Jeune, *Relation de* 1634, 585.
28. Le Jeune, *Relation de* 1634, 585 and 595.
29. Le Jeune, *Relation de* 1634, 576; see also 576–77.
30. Le Jeune, *Relation de* 1634, 572–75.

a gifted people with whom the French share traits and ancestry – and is therefore susceptible to successful assimilation – and degrades their beliefs and practices to affirm their need of the French to become truly civilized, arguments that together function once again as a seductive justification for the French colonial enterprise.

For Lejeune, bringing "the beautiful light of truth" to the Montagnais links with a series of concrete actions. His *Relation* lays out three proposals intended to disrupt the Montagnais way of life: 1. suppressing the Iroquois, whose warring ways are interfering with the conversion enterprise; 2. persuading the Montagnais to leave their itinerant life and settle down to an agrarian lifestyle; and 3. establishing seminary schools for Indigenous children. The second and third of these evoke a great deal of discussion among our students. According to Le Jeune, the Montagnais are "so busy scrambling for sustenance in the woods, they do not have time to save themselves."[31] The challenge for the French missionaries lies in inciting the Montagnais to give up their migrant hunting habits and to adopt instead a French agrarian model that would tie them to the land and facilitate sustained contact with French priests who could complete their catechism.[32] Seminary schools have a similar mission through a focus on young people. Le Jeune explains that seminaries will keep children away from their parents, a distance necessary because of what in Le Jeune's view is an unreasonable protectiveness: "These barbarians cannot abide by our punishing their children, not even with words, being completely unable to refuse anything to a crying child."[33] His words belie the brutal treatment that Native children will experience at the hands of priests in residential schools for centuries thereafter. As an added "benefit" of this project, Le Jeune believes that by effectively holding children hostage, their parents will treat the French with more respect and not resist their colonial efforts. By stealing children and placing them in schools free from parental interference, the Jesuits imagine the creation of a future generation of Christians, a vision that comes at a frightening cost. While Le

31. Le Jeune, *Relation de* 1634, 560.
32. Le Jeune, *Relation de* 1634, 559–62.
33. Le Jeune, *Relation de* 1634, 563.

Jeune's vision of residential boarding schools did not see the light of day in his lifetime, his model led to the later creation of Canadian schools that exploded into the news early in the summer of 2021 with the discovery of the remains of hundreds of First Nations children near what had been residential boarding schools in British Columbia, as we examine further in depth later in the unit.[34]

Though Le Jeune's first-person text asks readers to identify with the author's perspective, our students rebel against his invitation. They become what Judith Fetterly calls "resisting readers" who, as the term suggests, refuse the generic call of the text by a kind of "reading against the grain."[35] Many students, especially those who have experienced being "othered" themselves, are quick to imagine perspectives that radically challenge the authority of Le Jeune's text. More broadly, students are deeply uncomfortable with Le Jeune's efforts to force assimilation on a people at the cost of their centuries-old way of life. Thinking about why these texts exist and whose interests they serve gives students the language to pursue these questions in increasingly sophisticated ways, especially as we turn towards oral versions of the story.

Beyond the Literary Canon: The Oral Archive

In May 2001, Christiane Taubira, while deputy of French Guyana in the National Assembly, successfully introduced legislation calling for official French-government recognition of the slave trade as a crime against humanity. Among other measures, the proposal, passed into law unanimously, funded the development of new school curricula, scholarly research, and the establishment of a national day of remembrance. It underlined the importance of a new kind of history that included the per-

34. Ian Austin, "With Discovery of Unmarked Graves, Canada's Indigenous Seek Reckoning," *New York Times*, June 26, 2021, https://www.nytimes.com/2021/06/26/world/canada/indigenous-residential-schools-grave.html.
35. Judith Fetterly, *The Resisting Reader: A Feminist Approach to American Literature* (Bloomington: Indiana University Press, 1978). The phrase "reading against the grain," is taken from *Ways of Reading*, 3rd. ed., edited by David Bartholomae and Anthony Petrosky (Boston, MA: St. Martins Press, 2003).

spectives of those whose voices had not been heard in the history taught in schools. This involves reading written texts in new ways, from the position of those whose histories cross with European history, but who have very different stakes in that history. The Taubira law proposed a formal recognition of sources beyond the scope of the written archive. In particular, Article 2 emphasizes the value of "coordination to allow dialogue between the written archives available in Europe and oral sources and archeological knowledge gathered in Africa, the Americas, the Caribbean, and all the other territories where slavery had taken place."[36] Since the law's passage in 2001, more visibility has been given to what a broad variety of African and Caribbean sources — many of them oral — contribute to a more global history and to the dynamic potential that emerges when written and oral archives are placed into dialogue, each both questioning and serving as a source of knowledge for the other. The resulting scholarship, much of it carried out by scholars whose ancestors personally bore the brunt of enslavement and colonial violence during the early modern period, is changing the way we tell the story of both France and the broader world. What Taubira encouraged for rethinking the role of enslavement and the slave trade in this history is just as apt as we think about the role of the contemporaneous conquest of land inhabited by Indigenous people of the Americas.[37] Given the oral nature of their collective heritage, the only way that the voices of Native Americans have found a place in the historical archive has been through the highly subjective eyes and pens of writers like Le Jeune. Historian Olive Patricia Dickason underlines the limitations of a notion of history in which only documents "count" as history, one that excludes anything that has not been inscribed as letters on paper:

> [H]istory has been described as a document-bound discipline. If something was not written, preferably in an official document, it

36. "La loi Taubira du 21 mai 2001" in *Les routes de l'esclavage: histoire d'un très grand "dérangement,"* eds. Claude Fauque and Marie-Josée Thiel (Paris: Hermé, 2004), 186.
37. Article 1 of the Taubira law includes Indigenous people in the law without accounting for the specifics of their situation.

> was not historical. Thus were pre-literate societies excluded from history and labeled pre-historic, or perhaps proto-historic. The best [founding nations] could hope for was to become historic by extension, when they came into contact with literate societies.[38]

Despite their racist lens of European superiority, written sources such as Le Jeune's *Relation* allow important glimpses into Native American culture and society of the period, including their oral tradition. Le Jeune recounts and glosses numerous stories told by the Montagnais and provides a wealth of ethnographic detail used by First Nations historians today. Yet, as Dickason points out, becoming historic through texts like Le Jeune's is problematic, to say the least. First, suggesting that the written archive be the unique authoritative source for Native American actions, beliefs, and practices of earlier periods perpetuates a Eurocentric idea of history that refuses to acknowledge that Native Americans did not come into existence when Europeans encountered them, but had a thriving culture for millennia before the arrival of white seamen in search of a new route to India.[39] Second, as we have seen, Le Jeune's text and other contemporary written narratives are riddled with biases central to France's colonial efforts, which leave them sorely lacking in their ability to represent with accuracy and cultural sensitivity the views and values of the ancestors of today's First Nations communities. However closely Le Jeune observed Montagnais practices and beliefs during his time living among them, reporting everything he "saw with [his] own eyes ... while following them through the woods to learn their language," his ultimate goal in seeking to understand their culture was to eradicate it through replacement with French social and religious customs.[40] The systematic exclusion of the oral tradition — the only kind of "archive" created from the First People's point of view for their sixteenth- and seventeenth-cen-

38. Dickason with McNab, *Canada's First Nations*, viii.

39. Dickason notes that, rather than face this fact, Canadian historians have "found it much easier to ignore the earlier period; hence the blinkered view of Canada as a 'young' country;" *Canada's First Nations*, ix.

40. Le Jeune, Letter, in *Relation de* 1634, 539.

tury encounters with the French — is, then, indefensible. Taubira's call to incorporate the oral archive when telling the story of the Atlantic world challenges us as early modernists to rethink how we construct our syllabi.

Given the concerns about reliability and anachronism that have been ingrained in us by our academic training, the incorporation of oral sources poses challenges. For those of us steeped in the written tradition, accepting the validity of oral sources, to which we gain access through persons, recordings, and transcriptions rather than through period documents, sometimes inspires skepticism. Colleagues may question whether the tales and oral histories shared by First Nations people today are reliable sources for earlier periods: "Why do you use modern Native American sources to tell a seventeenth-century story?" These concerns reveal how conditioned we early modernists are to think with what Walter Ong calls "a literate mind," a mindset that privileges the written and makes certain assumptions about its superiority over the oral. As Ong highlights, it is symptomatic that we still often talk about oral sources as "oral literature": "This strictly preposterous term remains in circulation today even among scholars now more and more acutely aware how embarrassingly it reveals our inability to represent to our own minds a heritage of verbally organized materials except as some variant of writing, even when they have nothing to do with writing at all."[41] Inclusion of oral sources demands a kind of listening to what many of us have not been trained to hear. In our course, the quest for this kind of listening starts close to home when our course shifts to the point of view of Indigenous people, heard through the words of living Native Americans and Indigenous Canadians, carriers of the stories and histories of past generations. While the descendants of

41. Walter Ong, *Orality and Literacy: The Technologizing of the Word* ([Methuen, 1982] London: Routledge, 2002), 11. Indeed, seventeenth- and eighteenth-century missionaries were keen to find written traditions among Native Americans because they saw these as a sign of civilization. For example, Jesuit Joseph-François Lafitau (1681–1746) saw tattoos and carvings on trees as participating in a signifying system that uses symbols "that serve them as Hieroglyphics, writings, and memoirs," a substitute for "the missing Alphabet;" Joseph-François Lafitau, *Mœurs des sauvages amériquains comparées aux mœurs des premiers temps*, 2 vols. (Paris: Saugrain l'ainé and Charles Estienne Hochereau, 1724), 2:43–44.

the Montagnais studied by Le Jeune live in the nearby Quebec region, we begin even more locally, in the state of Maine where we teach.

It is at this point in the semester that students meet author, educator, and environmentalist Maria Girouard whose contribution to our course cannot be overstated. Executive Director of Maine-Wabanaki REACH, she is a member of the Penobscot nation, one of five tribes in Maine – the Mi'kmaq, Maliseet, Passamaquoddy, Abenaki, and Penobscot – who together make up the Wabanaki people from "the land first touched by the light of dawn." By the time Girouard visits our class, students have read her article, "Penobscots and the Sacred Mountain," in which she shares the story of the origin and sacred significance of Maine's tallest mountain, K'taadn, that rises up in the heart of the Wabanaki homeland, the source of the Penobscot River.[42] In addition, they have watched the lecture "Genocide and Maine: Shining the Light of Truth" that she delivered at the University of Southern Maine Portland Campus on November 20, 2014, available on YouTube.[43] They also have viewed a series of recorded testimonials from Indigenous Canadians living in Quebec, to which we will return after considering Girouard's contributions. In her article on K'taadn, Girouard discusses and describes a series of legends, beliefs and practices associated with the mountain – including an annual pilgrimage to its base participated in by hundreds of Wabanaki men, women, and children. Our students, many of whom have climbed K'taadn during pre-orientation or outing club trips, are amazed to learn of a vast and living Wabanaki tradition surrounding a mountain that they have until now seen simply as a beautiful landmark, the endpoint of the Appalachian Trail.[44] But it is Girouard's presence with them that brings the stories to life. When she enters the classroom her first words are "Kwai kwai," "hello" in her ancestral Penobscot language. Students have read transcriptions

42. Maria Girouard, "Penobscots et la montagne sacrée: K'taadn," *De L'Ossau à Katahdin, La revue de l'Association de L'Ossau à Katahdin* 7 (décembre-janvier 2017), 3–11, at 4–5. Girouard published the article discussed below in French as part of a transatlantic scholarly project.

43. Maria Girouard, "Genocide and Maine: Shining the Light of Truth," Maine-Wabanaki REACH, posted February 16, 2015, https://www.youtube.com/watch?v=G1DRIzt0Zgc.

44. Girouard's spelling; also transliterated as "Katahdin."

of the Montagnais language in Le Jeune, and Girouard's greeting connects the languages spoken by First Nations people long ago with the here and now. From the beginning, Girouard listens carefully to the students and wants to hear about their readings. She emphasizes that they are with her in this project of learning and sharing, that what they are learning from Le Jeune and what she brings to them are the means to arrive together at a broader base of knowledge. Throughout her conversation she shares bits of tales that she adopted after hearing them told in her youth by elders in the home and at tribal gatherings. Girouard, a passionate advocate for environmental protection, uses legends to tell us about her work to protect the Penobscot, a waterway that has been inseparable for centuries from Wabanaki livelihood and identity. She cites Wabanaki hero Gluskape's victory over the giant water monster Aglebemu, who had dammed up the great river and let it go dry.[45] She shows rather than explains how the spoken word functions, the historical and the present blending in a kind of sharing with its own rules. Students see the powerful role of storytelling in supporting a collective knowledge and protecting a way of life under grave threat. Through their experience with Girouard, our students, many of whom are active in the fight for sound environmental policy, feel grateful for the contributions of Native Americans, environmentalists long before others took up the cause. The inclusion of this material immediately links their awareness of the continued fight for the rights and recognition of First Nations people today to their study of francophone literatures and cultures. They are moved by the experience of Native Americans here in Maine and note how important having a broad sense of history is to understanding the problems around race and exclusion that live on in both American and French culture today.

The consideration of sources drawn from Native American oral tradition brings students face to face with a lot of pain. Girouard's lecture on "Genocide and Maine" graphically depicts the horrific violence and racism of the English and French colonization of Wabanaki lands, where ninety-

45. For more on the Penobscot River Restoration Project, see the website created by the National Resources Council of Maine in collaboration with the Penobscot Nation: https://www.nrcm.org/projects/waters/penobscot-river-restoration-project/.

five percent of the Native population was decimated, twenty tribes were reduced to five, and voting and religious rights were severely restricted until late in the twentieth century. As they listen to Penobscot versions of events that took place in Maine and recognize the names of nearby towns and regions, the violent history of colonial conquest becomes all the more real. Girouard shares with students Governor Phipp's 1755 proclamation that encouraged scalping Native Americans and her knowledge that inhabitants in nearby Woolwich, Maine, took up the offer of a bounty for this chilling practice, each scalp serving as proof of the capture and murder of a local tribe member.[46] The combination of Girouard's orally transmitted knowledge of tribal history and this document from the written archive is powerful. What students learn from Girouard deepens and challenges their understanding and their own relationship to the land and to the people that make up their adopted state. Indeed, Girouard's public lecture at Bowdoin in October 2018, "Our Story: Traversing the Homelands," explicitly called on her largely non-Native American audience to make Wabanaki history part of their own history by acknowledging the role each of us plays in what is a complexly interconnected story.[47]

Learning *with* a member of the local Native American community heightens the stakes of the encounters between First Nations people and Europeans in ways that written texts alone cannot.[48] Students connect with Girouard, and through her, with a larger group of descendants of the very area in which they are living. When the signs go up on campus

46. In 2009, the offer for sale on the internet of Native American scalps and bones was investigated by the FBI. Patricia Erikson, "Bones and Scalps coming out of the Closet," September 3, 2009, Heritage in Maine blog: https://heritageinmaine.blogspot.com/2009/09/bones-and-scalps-coming-out-of-closet.html.
47. Maria Girouard, "Our Story: Traversing the Homelands," October 25, 2018, Bowdoin College.
48. In some ways, we are catching up at the university level with what is happening at the elementary and secondary levels. Since 2001, a Wabanaki Studies curriculum has been mandated in all Maine schools, though not all have put it into practice: Robbie Feinberg, "A 2001 Law Says Maine Schools Must Teach Native American History, But Many Still Don't," February 7, 2019, npr.org, https://www.mainepublic.org/post/2001-law-says-maine-schools-must-teach-native-american-history-many-still-don-t.

each fall, their white letters on a green background declaring "You are on Indigenous land," it reverberates more for them. Girouard's testimony also brings alive a vision that goes far beyond the Penobscot. The values she shares traverse First Nations cultures, countering a European mindset that since the sixteenth century has placed "man" at the center. As Dickason underlines,

> [The] dazzling variety of cultural particularities [of different tribes] has tended to obscure the underlying unity of the Amerindian world view, which saw humans as part of a cosmological order depending on a balance of reciprocating forces to keep the universe functioning in harmony. This contrasts with the Judeo-Christian view of a cosmos dominated by a God in the image of man. In this perspective man is in the privileged position, as up to a certain point he can control nature for his own benefit.[49]

Her words remind us that the kinds of partnership we have forged here in Maine can be forged anywhere across the United States. American universities are *all* built on Indigenous land. We encourage our colleagues to reach out to members of local tribal communities to share in the telling of a more complete and more vibrant story of the early modern period.

Videos of testimonials from First Nations people living in the province of Quebec, who are closer descendants of those Le Jeune refers to as "les Montagnais," have been a useful complement to our partnership with Girouard. Students are moved by the horrific history of so-called "Indian Schools." Le Jeune's seminary schools, though initially unsuccessful, were brought to fruition with the advent of greater state control — still hand in hand with the church — in the nineteenth and twentieth centuries.[50]

49. Dickason with McNab, *Canada's First Nations*, ix–x.

50. For a detailed account of the history of "Indian Schools" in Canada, see The Truth and Reconciliation Commission of Canada, *Canada's Residential Schools: The History, Part 1: Origins to 1939*, vol. 1 of *The Final Report of the Truth and Reconciliation Commission of Canada* (Montreal: McGill-Queen's University Press, 2015).

These schools, established to "kill the Indian, and save the man" vividly show the costs of the assimilationist project as it unfolds over time.[51]

Our students listen to oral histories told in French by older Canadians who as children were forced to enroll in schools far from their families and tribes, where traditional braids were sliced away and tribal languages banished. They watch a short Radio-Canada news report produced in 2013, just as the Canadian Commission on Truth and Reconciliation was preparing to hold public meetings in Québec, part of a six-year series of events in cities across the country to reeducate citizens through finally hearing and honoring the testimonies of survivors.[52] Our students listen to the testimony of Marcel Petiquay, first sent at the age of six to a boarding school for Indigenous Canadian children. He describes his rape by a priest at the age of seven, the beginning of a long series of sexual aggressions that would be the source of enduring self-hatred, abuse of alcohol and drugs, and recurrent suicidal thoughts. He makes plain the heartbreaking cycle of violence that sweeps up the next generation, and his concerns for his children. Students recognize in Petiquay's lived experience of state-sanctioned cultural denial and violence the modern-day persistence of the very schooling project advanced by Le Jeune in the seventeenth century. As through conversations with Girouard, who recounts her memories of Penobscot mothers' terror at the approach of an unknown car, hiding their children from social workers for fear they would be taken away to boarding schools, students see in these testimonies the long-term costs of European-style progress. At the same time, students observe the remarkable resilience of tribal heritage and rituals that, in Petiquay's words, "a century of internment did not succeed in destroying."

As noted by *Washington Post* journalist Brenda J. Child, herself a grandchild of Native American grandparents, "for many in the United States,

51. Richard H. Pratt's 1892 speech, quoted by Maria Girouard, in-class discussion at Bowdoin College, April 2, 2019. One hundred and thirty such residential schools existed across Canada during the nineteenth and twentieth centuries; "Les pensionnats de la honte," *YouTube*, Radio-Canada, January 21, 2013. "Indian Schools" in the United States, were even more numerous, with a few off-reservation schools still operating today.
52. "Les pensionnats de la honte."

the conversation is, perhaps, just beginning."[53] She reminds us that the question of Indigenous schools is an American tragedy as much as it is a Canadian one, calling attention to the mass deaths of children in similar boarding schools right here in the United States, "beginning with Carlisle in Pennsylvania in 1879 and ending with the Sherman Institute in California in 1903." These stories go a long way toward connecting Le Jeune's colonial ambitions in the "time of encounters" to the here and now, a time when many non-Native students have had little to no contact with Native Americans. First Nations youth attend college at rates much lower than the average for Americans overall and they often face enormous obstacles to attending prestigious schools like Bowdoin.[54] This unit is a reminder of the importance of learning to listen for Native American history in the past but also in the present.

When considered together, oral and written sources enrich and complicate each other. Students see how the textual accounts they have read have provided them a context that helps them better understand the stakes of First Nations stories and testimonials. At the same time, reading, listening to, and interacting with Girouard in person and with the oral testimonials of Indigenous Canadians indirectly changes and enriches their understanding of the texts they have studied, making for some insightful essays. Students note the remarkable consistency between the themes and characterizations of First Nations people that fill Le Jeune's seventeenth-century written account and those of Penobscot oral tradition as shared by Girouard. Yet despite similarities, Girouard's Penobscot account has a very different tone from Le Jeune's. What was scorned in Le Jeune's *Relation*, is treated with respect and veneration. While Le Jeune denigrates the Montagnais's intimate relationship with the earth, Girouard deeply values the Wabanaki's sacred connection with the land. While Le Jeune mocks Montagnais belief in the presence of a spirit in all

53. Brenda J. Child, "U.S. Boarding Schools for Indians Had a Hidden Agenda: Stealing Land," *Washington Post*, August 27, 2021, https://www.washingtonpost.com/outlook/2021/08/27/indian-boarding-schools-united-states/.
54. Postsecondary National Policy Institute (PNPI), "Factsheets: Native American Students," last modified November 20, 2020, https://pnpi.org/native-american-students/#.

elements of the natural world, the Penobscot assert the intrinsic value and sacredness of all creation. They see the earth as an interconnected web of which human beings are just a part and affirm their role as its sacred stewards.[55] The two taken together go a long way towards fulfilling Christiane Taubira's wish (and ours) to arrive at a truer and richer story through collaboration.

Following their work with oral tales and testimonials, students return to Le Jeune with new eyes, reading between the lines and against the grain with greater sophistication. Having read and heard the story of Gluskape, who, "furious at the betrayal by those newly arrived in Wabanaki lands," spends his time making arrowheads "in anticipation of the future when the Indians will need him once again," they are even more aware than they had been of perspective and genre.[56] They highlight how Le Jeune's inclusion of quotations of the Montagnais's negative reactions to him destabilize his narrative. When his hosts respond with irony or with statements such as "[y]ou are ignorant," "you are stupid," students see that whatever Le Jeune wishes to communicate, his hosts do not seem to be buying it.[57] Some note that Le Jeune's juxtaposition of what he casts as the First Nations people's fantastical beliefs with equally incredible beliefs espoused within Catholicism undermines the authority of his critique. Others find evidence of resistance to the French project that differs markedly from the joy portrayed in the De Bry engravings or Verrazzano narrative that students first considered. What they have learned in this unit deeply informs their approach to sources considered later in the semester, in particular those regarding the French participation in enslavement and the experience of African captives in the Atlantic colonies.[58]

55. Girouard, "Penobscots et la montagne sacrée," 5.

56. Girouard, "Penobscots et la montagne sacrée," 6.

57. Le Jeune, *Relation de* 1634, 573 and 589.

58. For further details, see our "Globalizing the Early Literature Survey." Ashley Williard provides a helpful model for this approach to reading missionary texts in the context of the French Caribbean, "Ventriloquizing Blackness: Citing Enslaved Africans in the French Caribbean, c.1650 to 1685," in *Early Modern Black Diaspora Studies: A Critical*

Conclusion

We began our unit, and this piece, with a consideration of the Renaissance through the poetics of La Pléiade. In his *Defense and Illustration of the French Language*, with chapter titles like "That the French language must not be called barbarous" and "Call to the French to write in their own language, including praise for France," Du Bellay defends the value of French. He champions the dignity and potential of a language that had long been considered "savage," an oral and unworthy bastardization of Latin. Two generations later, with French well established as the language of the kingdom, Le Jeune, in the name of God and country, associates Montagnais oral tradition with barbarity. The French language, writing, and print become signs of civilization, while the oral languages of the Indigenous people of New France mark them as *un*civilized. Drawing a direct parallel between writing and cultural superiority, Le Jeune reports that the Native people he frequents "think only of living" and do not recognize the value of the text. They should therefore be considered inferior beings, stuck in a more primitive world of base concerns: "This people does not believe that there is any science in the world other than living and eating. This is their whole philosophy. They are astonished at the importance we give our books, because the knowledge they contain does nothing at all to lessen their hunger."[59] For Le Jeune, Montagnais language itself betrays a lack of civilization, devoid of all the terms that make Europe Europe. It is missing "the language of theologians, of philosophers, mathematicians, doctors, in short, of all educated men, all the words that concern the administration and governance of a town, a province, an empire, everything having to do with justice, reward and punishment, the names of an infinity of arts that we have in our Europe … of thousands upon thousands of inventions, of a thousand beauties and a thousand riches."[60] Le Jeune's effusive celebration of the glories of "our Europe" are linked by way of

Anthology, ed. Cassander L. Smith, Nicholas Jones, and Miles P. Grier (London: Palgrave Macmillan, 2018), 83–105.

59. Le Jeune, *Relation de* 1634, 637.
60. Le Jeune, *Relation de* 1634, 645.

contrast to all that is missing among the supposedly less advanced people of what he calls New France: "None of these things is found in the thought or the words of the savages who have neither true religion nor knowledge of virtues, nor order, nor governance, nor kingdom, nor republic, nor sciences, or anything else mentioned previously .... What an enormous deficiency." Le Jeune suggests that the French are thus doing the Native Americans a great service, helping them move out of an eternal childhood characterized exclusively by "primitive" preoccupations so that they can enter (French) history and, with it, civilization and progress.[61]

This clash of world views is not something we left behind as we moved into more modern times. Our university system, like Le Jeune some four hundred years ago, privileges a kind of knowledge associated almost exclusively with the written tradition. Earlier we considered Dickason's distinction between, on the one hand, the Judeo-Christian view "of a cosmos dominated by a God in the image of man" with "man ... in the privileged position ... controll[ing] nature for his own benefit" and, on the other hand, a Native American world view that "saw humans as part of a cosmological order depending on a balance of reciprocating forces to keep the universe functioning in harmony."[62] In *Teaching Cultural Strengths*, Alicia Fedelina Chávez and Susan D. Longerbeam similarly distinguish two broad cultural epistemologies in today's classrooms. On the one hand is a "culturally individuated worldview" that values privacy, compartmentalization and abstraction, and, on the other, a "culturally integrated worldview" in which interconnectedness and mutual dependence

61. This vision of the non-French other lives on today, as was made clear by Nicolas Sarkozy's infamous "Discours de Dakar," delivered on July 26, 2007, at the Cheikh-Anta-Diop University in Dakar, Sénégal, where the then French president declared that "Africans have not sufficiently come into History .... The problem with Africa is that she lives the present through a nostalgia for the lost paradise of childhood .... Within this imaginary where everything is always rebeginning, there is room for neither the human adventure nor the idea of progress;" https://www.youtube.com/watch?v=6k9tgDABYvw.

62. Dickason with McNab, *Canada's First Nations*, ix–x.

matter.[63] Western institutions, including American and European universities, have traditionally given overwhelming preference to the "individuated" model, often leading students from "integrated" cultures to feel self-doubt and a sense of not belonging. Our focus on the value of Native American "integrated" cultures in this unit offers a helpful counterpoint. As Chávez and Longerbeam have shown, greater emphasis on the "integrated worldview" in the classroom encourages students from more "integrated" cultures to feel more included and to find their perspectives legitimized. For many of these students, the oral tradition has played an important role in their own cultures and upbringing. Witnessing the spoken word valued in an academic setting transforms the playing field and invites different kinds of knowledge to take center stage for all students, even in a course like ours that introduces the early modern period. Including the oral thus not only helps us tell a more complete story of the period we are studying but also makes our classroom more inclusive.

Discussion Questions

1. How does the adoption of more "global" perspectives and the consideration of a wider range of sources change the way we read and think about European texts and, in particular, how we tell the story of the Renaissance?
2. What concrete steps can we take to include a more diverse set of voices in telling the tale of the long Renaissance period?
3. In what ways can the approach taken in the unit presented here be applied to other early modern sources and contexts?
4. What shifts in our thinking and our course structures are required to include the study of oral sources as well as written ones?
5. How do our academic institutions participate in the exclusion of certain voices, values, and approaches to learning and sharing knowledge?

63. Alicia Fedelina Chávez and Susan D. Longerbeam, *Teaching Across Cultural Strengths: A Guide to Balancing Integrated and Individuated Culture Frameworks in College Teaching* (Sterling, VA: Stylus Publishing, 2016).

6. What changes must we consider in our curricular structures, course materials, and assignments to create more inclusive courses that welcome and engage a more diverse student population?
7. Studying the colonial context necessarily means witnessing other people's trauma. How do we prepare students to create a community that honors the subjectivity and truth shared by the speaker and allows us to welcome their testimony without judgement or voyeurism?[64] How do we increase solidarity through bearing witness to another's pain rather than reinforce the speaker's otherness?
8. What can the field of early modern studies learn from the fields of postcolonial studies and what has been called "Francophone" studies?
9. Who has the right to tell these stories? For those of us trained in earlier periods, engaging with this work means reaching outside our specialty, and therefore entering the specialty of other scholars. How do we do this and at the same time avoid a sort of academic neo-colonialism?

Suggestions for Further Reading

Chávez, Alicia Fedelina and Susan D. Longerbeam. *Teaching Across Cultural Strengths: A Guide to Balancing Integrated and Individuated Culture Frameworks in College Teaching.* Sterling, VA: Stylus Publishing, 2016.

Chun, Wendy Hui Kyong. "Unbearable Witness: Toward a Politics of Listening." In *Extremities: Trauma Testimony and Community*, edited by Nancy K. Miller and Jason Tougaw, 143–165. Urbana, IL: University of Illinois Press, 2002.

Daniels, Charlotte and Katherine Dauge-Roth. "Globalizing the Early Literature Survey: Challenges and Rewards." *French Review* 93, no. 1 (2019):

64. On creating an effective and respectful "listening community," see Wendy Hui Kyong Chun, "Unbearable Witness: Toward a Politics of Listening," in *Extremities: Trauma Testimony and Community*, edited by Nancy K. Miller and Jason Tougaw (Urbana, IL: University of Illinois Press, 2002), 143–65.

92–107, and accompanying pedagogical dossier: frenchreview.frenchteachers.org/Dossiers.html

Dickason, Olive Patricia with David T. McNab. *Canada's First Nations: A History of Founding Peoples from Earliest Times*. 4th ed. Oxford, England: Oxford University Press, 2009.

Girouard, Maria. "Penobscots et la montagne sacrée: K'taadn." *De L'Ossau à Katahdin, La revue de l'Association de L'Ossau à Katahdin* 7 (décembre-janvier, 2017): 3–11.

Melzer, Sara. "Une 'Seconde France'? Re-penser le paradigme 'classique' à partir de l'histoire oubliée de la colonisation française." In *La littérature, le XVIIe siècle et nous: dialogue transatlantique*, edited by Hélène Merlin-Kajman, 75–85. Paris: Presse Sorbonne Nouvelle, 2008.

———. *Colonizer or Colonized: The Hidden Stories of Early Modern French Culture*. Philadelphia, PA: University of Pennsylvania Press, 2012.

Sayre, Gorden M. *Les Sauvages Américains: Representations of Native Americans in French and English Colonial Literature*. Chapel Hill, NC, and London: The University of North Carolina Press, 1997.

Taiaiakie, Alfred. *Peace, Power, Righteousness: An Indigenous Manifesto*. Oxford: Oxford University Press, 2009.

True, Micah. *Masters and Students: Jesuit Mission Ethnography in Seventeenth-Century New France*. Montreal: McGill-Queen's University Press, 2015.

The Truth and Reconciliation Commission of Canada. *Canada's Residential Schools: The History. Part 1: Origins to 1939*, vol. 1 of *The Final Report of the Truth and Reconciliation Commission of Canada*. Montreal: McGill-Queen's University Press, 2015.

Williard, Ashley. "Ventriloquizing Blackness: Citing Enslaved Africans in the French Caribbean, c.1650 to 1685." In *Early Modern Black Diaspora Studies: A Critical Anthology*, edited by Cassander L. Smith, Nicholas Jones, and Miles P. Grier, 83–105. London: Palgrave Macmillan, 2018.

Yaeger, Patricia. "Consuming Trauma: or, The Pleasures of Merely Circulating." In *Extremities: Trauma Testimony and Community*, edited by Nancy K. Miller and Jason Tougaw, 25–51. Urbana, IL: University of Illinois Press, 2002.

Wiseman, Frederick Matthew. *The Voice of the Dawn: An Autohistory of the Abenaki Nation*. Lebanon, NH: University Press of New England, 2001.

Racial Profiling: Delineating the Renaissance Face

NOAM ANDREWS

What does the face of another tell us? What inferences can be made about character, emotional state, intelligence, morality, and social status? And by what means may the individual be aggregated into similar types and prepared for visual reproduction and analysis, in turn used to make broader assumptions about the behavior of similar looking people? At the digital dawn of facial tuning and face recognition software, and in policing practices spanning airport security to the dangers of "driving while black" (and other everyday activities), questions such as these have penetrated the cultural consciousness as never before, drawing attention to the insidious effects of racial profiling as well as the collusion of societal structures in perpetuating bias. But the operative use of external human features to determine inner character or qualities has a deep history stretching back through the Enlightenment and post-Enlightenment sciences to pseudo-Aristotle, Theophrastus, and beyond, from philosophy and anatomical study to parody and propaganda.[1] Termed "physiognomy" and expanded into anthropometry, craniometry, and phrenology (the measurement of the shape of the skull to establish mental traits) in the

1. For further reading on classical physiognomy, see Benjamin Isaac, *The Invention of Racism in Classical Antiquity* (Princeton: Princeton University Press, 2004); Tamsyn Barton, *Power and Knowledge: Astrology, Physiognomics, and Medicine under the Roman Empire* (Ann Arbor: University of Michigan Press, 2002); Elizabeth C. Evans, "Physiognomics in the Ancient World," *Transactions of the American Philosophical Society* 59.5 (1969): 1–101. For a cross-cultural analysis of classical physiognomy, see Su Fang Ng, *Alexander the Great from Britain to Southeast Asia: Peripheral Empires in the Global Renaissance* (Oxford: Oxford University Press, 2019).

nineteenth century, these clusters of practices were responsible for generating an untold number of treatises and tractates.[2]

Though his scientific work has not often been analyzed within this framework, Albrecht Dürer (1471–1528), Germany's most famous artist, published just before he died a highly influential if eccentric treatise called *Vier Bücher von menschlicher Proportion* [Four Books on Human Proportion] (1528) (hereafter *menschlicher Proportion*) which contributed to developing and reinforcing these practices. While it refrained, importantly, from designating or labeling what we would describe today as nationality or ethnicity, or any descriptive aspects of character, it nevertheless proved important to the establishment of what would later become the prevailing parameters for a self-consciously "objective" representation of the human face in profile (figure 1). Much like other contemporary Renaissance treatises that sought to analyze and categorize the human body, Dürer stressed that geometry was fundamental to defining well-ordered and proportional rules of appearance.[3] But in moving beyond the pursuit and visualization of a singular and stable ideal proportion (for "no single man can be taken as a model for a perfect figure") or moralistic critiques of "licentious" proportions, *menschlicher Proportion* was unique in its evocative framework for mapping transformational relationships between body types and faces, and thus gave credence to the idea that mathematics could reveal the hidden rules underlying all bodies.[4]

2. See the classical *Physiognomica*, a peripatetic text dating from the third century B.C. that maintained its popularity through the Middle Ages and into the early modern period; *Essays on Physiognomy* [1777] by Johann Kaspar Lavater; Petrus Camper's *Dissertation physique* (1791); and *Rassenkunde des deutschen Volkes* [Racial Ethnology of the German People] (1922) by Hans F. K. Günther (1891–1968), an academic whose physiognomic writings was celebrated during the Nazi regime, among many other examples.
3. See *Body and Building: Essays on the Changing Relation of Body and Architecture*, edited by George Dodds and Robert Tavernor (Cambridge: MIT Press, 2002).
4. Albrecht Dürer, "Drafts for the Introduction to the Book of Human Proportions," *A Documentary History of Art*, edited by Elizabeth G. Holt, translated by William Martin Conway (Garden City, NY: Doubleday Anchor, 1957), 311–318, here 316. On "licentious" form

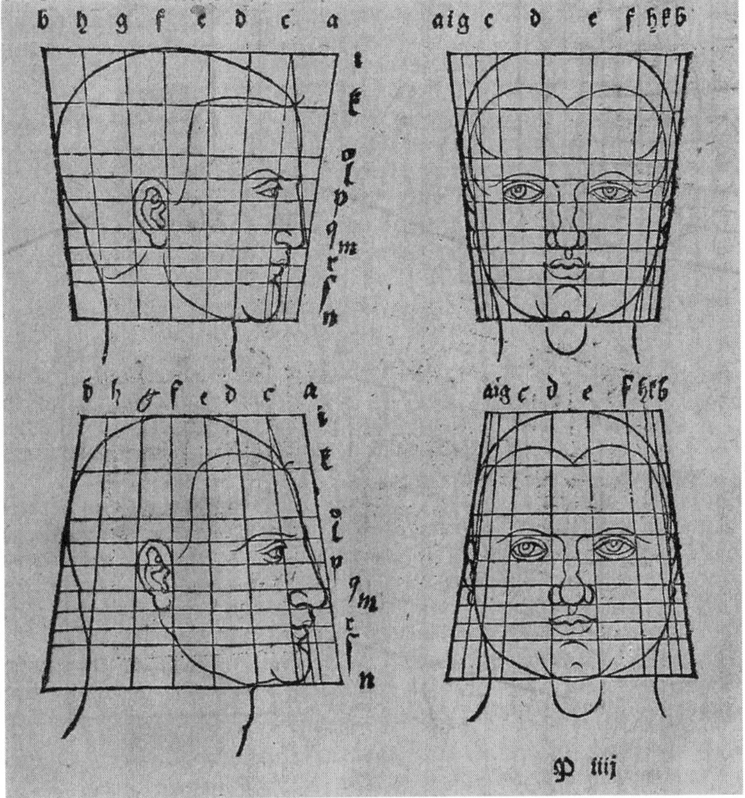

Figure 1. The construction of a narrow and broad head, *Vier Bücher von menschlicher Proportion* (Nuremberg: Hieronymous Andreae, 1528), Albrecht Dürer. Fol. P4r. Glasgow School of Art Library.

Dürer's incursion into the physiognomy of the human profile was anything but unprecedented. Amongst topical forays into the mathematics of ideal proportion and animal physiognomy, the Renaissance face was theorized through a disparate array of diagnostic graphemes whose primary and overlapping purpose was to discern the most profound nature of self (figure 2 and figure 3).[5] The journals and private papers of the Renaissance

and proportion, see *Sebastiano Serlio on Architecture*, edited by Vaughan Hart and Peter Hicks (New Haven: Yale University Press, 2001), 99v.

5. Martin Kemp, *Visualizations: The Nature Book of Art and Science* (Berkeley: University of California Press, 2000), 15.

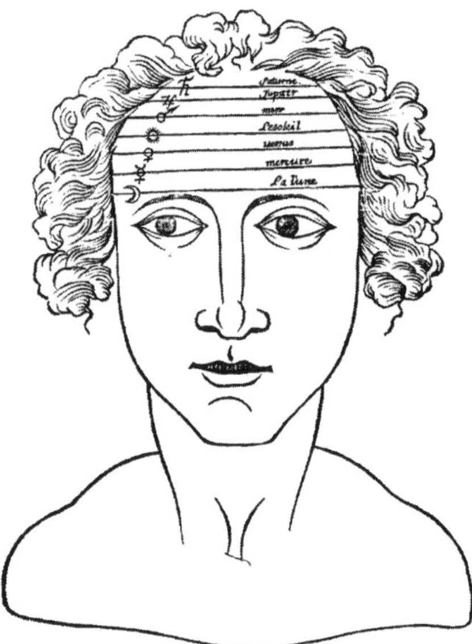

Figure 2. The construction of a narrow and broad head, *Vier Bücher von menschlicher Proportion* (Nuremberg: Hieronymous Andreae, 1528), Albrecht Dürer. Fol. P4r. Glasgow School of Art Library.

Figure 3. *Tranquilla frons* [The tranquil brow], Giambattista della Porta (1535–1615), *De humana physiognomia, libri ii*, p. 59 (Vico Equense: Giuseppe Cacchi, 1586), National Library of Medicine, Bethesda, Maryland.

artists Leonardo da Vinci and Peter Paul Rubens, among many Old Masters, reveal myriad experimental and evolving approaches to the theorization and construction of the face, traversing the Vitruvian man to the grotesque — the opposing and equally idealized poles of human perfection and deformity.[6]

In this context, it is important to include Dürer when we teach history of the concept of race in Europe, because of the direction history would go, particularly in Germany with the rise of fascism, and moreover Dürer's enduring symbolism, embraced from Vasari to Hitler, as *the* German artist *par excellence*. Dürer's contribution to physiognomy is acutely significant, even though *menschlicher Proportion* would only become reinterpreted in racial terms long after his death (figure 4).[7] Though Dürer could not have known the ways in which his work would be used, a pertinent question remains to be debated. Were his theoretical diagrams on the proportions and transformation of the human body already seeded from their inception with bias? And if so, does this not mean that his treatises on measurement should be studied in relation to the long and violent history of race in Europe and beyond.

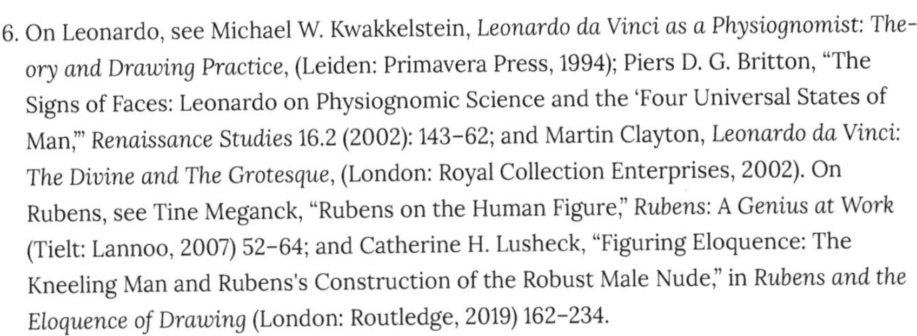

6. On Leonardo, see Michael W. Kwakkelstein, *Leonardo da Vinci as a Physiognomist: Theory and Drawing Practice*, (Leiden: Primavera Press, 1994); Piers D. G. Britton, "The Signs of Faces: Leonardo on Physiognomic Science and the 'Four Universal States of Man,'" *Renaissance Studies* 16.2 (2002): 143–62; and Martin Clayton, *Leonardo da Vinci: The Divine and The Grotesque*, (London: Royal Collection Enterprises, 2002). On Rubens, see Tine Meganck, "Rubens on the Human Figure," *Rubens: A Genius at Work* (Tielt: Lannoo, 2007) 52–64; and Catherine H. Lusheck, "Figuring Eloquence: The Kneeling Man and Rubens's Construction of the Robust Male Nude," in *Rubens and the Eloquence of Drawing* (London: Routledge, 2019) 162–234.
7. David B. Dennis, *Inhumanities: Nazi Interpretations of Western Culture*, (Cambridge: Cambridge University Press, 2012), 404. See also Thomas Schauerte, "Hitler's Dürer? The Nuremberg Painter between Self-Portrayal and National Appropriation," *The Primacy of the Image in Northern European Art, 1400–1700*. (Leiden; Boston: Brill, 2017), 315–28.

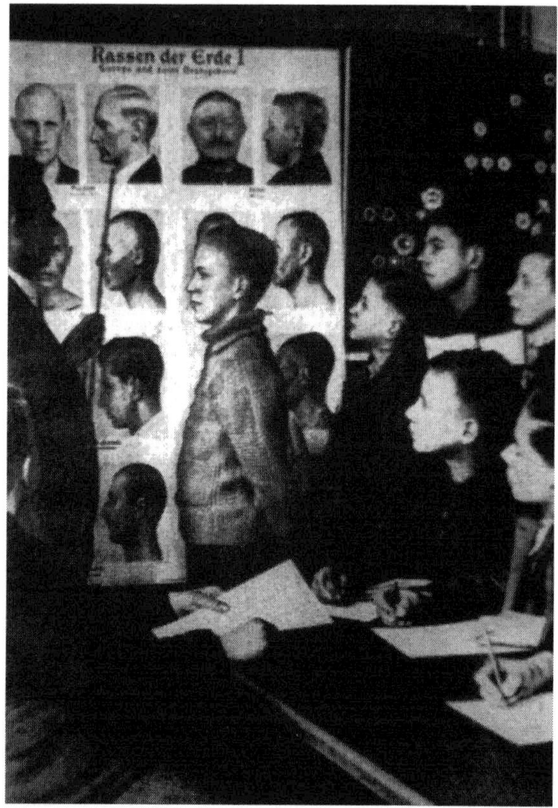

Figure 4. Photograph documenting instruction on the world races (*Rassen der Erde*), organized by profile, in a German elementary school during the Third Reich. *Neues Volk* (1934), Bundesarchiv Koblenz. Reproduced from Richard T. Gray, *About Face* (2004), 258.

In teaching race in the Renaissance, then, it is crucial to study the way visual strategies were used to parcel up humanity into distinct groups of operationally interchangeable individuals. Dürer is due the unwelcome credit of having proffered decisive steps toward the establishment of the human profile as both site and tool for the fixing of identity, thus instantiating a visual language that would become increasingly central to what would ultimately devolve into modern racist typologies based upon physical appearance. Among the most celebrated of the initial forays into the development of systems to classify human variety based upon experimentation, testing, and the scientific method, Enlightenment physiognomy would prove to be widely read and disseminated, influencing the science of Johann Wolfgng von Goethe and the evolutionary theories of Charles Darwin, and in the process directly contributing to a fraught if modern concept of race as well as its fascistoid manifestations.[8] Dürer and his Enlightenment afterlife deserve reassessment though we must balance our expectations of these historical actors' motivations with our knowledge of the entrenched systems of exploitation that their work may have inadvertently, or calculatedly, tapped into, triggered, or offered itself up to. Querying what we see when we see, and, moreover, who the *we* is that sees (or is being seen), is a perceptual terrain neither originating nor terminating with Dürer, though Dürer's measured approaches to the representation of the face would have a profound impact upon the visualization of racial difference in the centuries to come.

• • •

Media imbedded with "techno-racism" is an old problem whose institutional roots in the western world far predate the contemporary realization that modern technology, no matter how allegedly objective or utopian in aim, is no better than its programmers, and thus inexorably performs the uninterrogated biases of its creators or majority users.[9] Classical physiognomy and its visual elaborations are no exception. Both extensively plotted the overall contours of a value system celebrating ethnic stereotypes on the basis of skin color, gender, corporeal attributes, and the effects of the environment. Although the determinative judge-

8. David Bindman, *Ape to Apollo: Aesthetics and the Idea of Race in the 18th Century*, (Ithaca: Cornell University Press, 2002), 12–13. See also Robert Bernasconi, "Who Invented the Concept of Race?," *Theories of Race and Racism: A Reader*, edited by Les Back and John Solomos, 2nd ed. (London; New York: Routledge, 2009), 83–103; and Miriam Eliav-Feldon, Benjamin H. Isaac, and Joseph Ziegler, *The Origins of Racism in the West*, (Cambridge: Cambridge University Press, 2009). On Goethe and physiognomics, see Richard T. Gray, *About Face: German Physiognomic Thought from Lavater to Auschwitz*, (Detroit: Wayne State University Press, 2004), 137–76.
9. See the work of Joy Buolamwini (1989–) and the *Algorithmic Justice League*, https://www.ajlunited.org/ (accessed December 11, 2019).

ments made varied between texts and could substantially contradict each other, the fundamental anthropological battle lines of modernity presented itself in full visibility: light vs. dark, north vs. south, and here vs. there (the *there* standing in for any number of distant locales).[10] Further shaping the discourse on physiognomy through the dominant Christian paradigm, medieval scholars expanded upon the Bible, splicing humanity into tribes or races descended from the three sons of Noah — Shem, Ham, and Japheth — each of whom were responsible for populating Asia, Africa, and Europe, respectively.[11] Evocatively illustrated in books of wonders or breathlessly regaled in popular travel literature such as *The Travels of John Mandeville* (mid/late fourteenth century), medieval authors sutured together relative geographic distance from Europe with a moral turpitude reflected in the appearances, behaviors, and customs populating the margins of the European imagination. In this context, non-Western catchall quasi-ethnicities such as "Ethiopians" were designated "the remotest and foulest of mankind" as per Augustine of Hippo, at once human and humanoid, their blackness incorporated into a fertile slew of monstrous attributes.[12]

Against this backdrop, *menschlicher Proportion*, which was published in the same year as Dürer's death in 1528 and forms the intellectual pinnacle of his numerous contributions to the theorizing of the human body, appears incongruous — which to a large extent it is.[13] Conceptualized as a more advanced text on applied mathematics to be studied after his treatise on Euclidean geometry, *Underweysung der Messung* [Treatise

10. Isaac, *Invention of Racism*, 151.
11. Debra Higgs Strickland, "Monstrosity and Race in the late Middle Ages," *The Ashgate Research Companion to Monsters and the Monstrous*, (Farnham, UK: Routledge, 2017), 405–26.
12. Psalm 72/71:0. Quoted from Strickland, "Monstrosity," 382.
13. The full title reads *Hierin sind begriffen vier bûcher von menschlicher Proportion durch Albrechten Dürer von Nürnberg erfunden und beschriben/zu nutz allen denen so zu diser kunst lieb tragen.* (Nuremberg: Hieronymus Andreae, 1528). See Peter Parshall, "Graphic Knowledge: Albrecht Dürer and the Imagination," *The Art Bulletin* 95.3 (2013): 393–410; and Rainer Schoch, Matthias Mende, and Anna Scherbaum, *Albrecht Dürer: Das Druckgraphische Werk*, 3 vols. (Munich: Prestel Verlag, 2001–2004), 3:319–29.

on Measurement] (1525), *menschlicher Proportion* is devoted primarily to exploring the corporeal ratios and measurements of different bodies and is wholly bereft of the lurid exposition later characteristic of physiognomy and its offshoots. By contrast, contemporary notes by Dürer contained at the British Museum acknowledge what he felt to be the book's greatest challenge: namely, not the circumscribing of human difference through narrative illustration, but the representation of the many irregularities of the body and the structured dimensions of component body parts. As he observes, "The 'measure' of a human figure is especially hard to comprehend, amongst other reasons because the human figure is composed neither by rule nor compass but is contained within irregular curved outlines, it is specially hard to write and treat of it."[14]

Dürer's sketches evidence many attempts at working through competing graphical techniques, though he would eventually move toward effecting systems of mathematical proportions that more closely reflected those contained within the printed edition of *menschlicher Proportion*. Like Leon Battista Alberti and Leonardo da Vinci before him, both of whom surveyed classical statues, living models, and even architecture to compile statistical data on the well-proportioned body, Dürer accumulated his own measured surveys of bodies, though at a much larger and more comprehensive scale than the Italians.[15] In pursuit of a balance between ideal proportionality and the mean values he had determined through direct measurement of human subjects, *menschlicher Proportion* elides a penultimate proportional ratio. The treatise accordingly contains a spectrum of adult physiques, as well as measurements of toddlers, and defines a range of idealized human specimens divided into several types

14. Albrecht Dürer, translated in William Martin Conway, *Literary Remains of Albrecht Dürer*, (Cambridge: Cambridge University Press, 1889), 175. With reference to the Dürer manuscripts at the British Museum, Vol. 4, 132a and b.
15. Erwin Panofsky, *The Life and Art of Albrecht Dürer*, (Princeton: Princeton University Press, 2005), 264; and Robert Tavernor, *On Alberti and the Art of Building* (New Haven: Yale University Press, 1998), 40–41. For Dürer's reference to the measurement of human models, see *menschlicher Proportion*, fol. T3r.

(thinner, stouter, shorter, taller, more or less muscular) reflective of the physical variation of humanity.[16]

The inclusion of multiple competing proportional systems and physiques lends *menschlicher Proportion* an uncanny fluidity, since Dürer was as expressly interested in how bodies might be transformed into one other as he was in fixing the measurement of specific bodies in stasis. In particular, his striking demonstrations in Book III (fol. P3v – fol. Q6r) of the geometrical rules underlying the metamorphosis of the human face, the diagrams which would so capture the imagination of the Swiss physiognomist Johann Kaspar Lavater (1741–1801), the Dutch physician Petrus Camper (1722–1789), and later the Scottish biologist D'Arcy Wentworth Thompson (1860–1948), represents one of, if not the first, sustained, geometrical dissections of the (male) profile in Western art and science. As we saw in Figure 1, Dürer maps an ideal human head upon a three-dimensional grid (*cubus*) in order to explain how varying this grid will result in reciprocal changes to the form of the head, "and how thus various forms of the face can be made."[17] He begins by compressing the x- and y-axes, which in turn generates thinner or squatter heads, and then moves to skewing the outer edges of the grid at an angle so that "the first head has a tapered forehead, but the other has a flared head" and inflating or deflating the head to fit within convex (*aufßgebogen*) or concave (*eyngebogen*) curves (figure 5).[18] These archetypal changes to the structure of the human head, for Dürer, gesture toward the infinite variations of nature.[19] Accordingly, to learn his graphical techniques and furthermore to combine them, was to attain the ability to reproduce nature's ever-shifting

16. For exposition on the evolution of Dürer's proportional theories, see Berthold Hinz, "'Von menschlicher Proportion': Ablauf und Gliederung" and "Die 'Messung': Fragen und Antworten," in *Albrecht Dürer: Vier Bücher von menschlicher Proportion* (1528), edited by Berthold Hinz (Berlin: Akademie Verlag, 2011) 331–37 and 339–53.
17. "vnnd wie so manicherley gestalt der angesicht zu machen seyen." Dürer, *menschlicher Proportion*, 1528, fol. P5r.
18. "Das erst haubt gewindt ein spizige stirn/ aber das ander hinden ein hoch haubt," Dürer, *menschlicher Proportion*, fol. P4r and fol. Q2r.
19. "Wie dann des die natur villerleu gibt." Dürer, *menschlicher Proportion*, fol. Q3r.

essence, of more use "to describe difference than the shape of beauty."[20] In this one short passage, Dürer had hinted at a new avenue of exploration for the studying of types of faces that were not generally exposed to mathematical scrutiny.

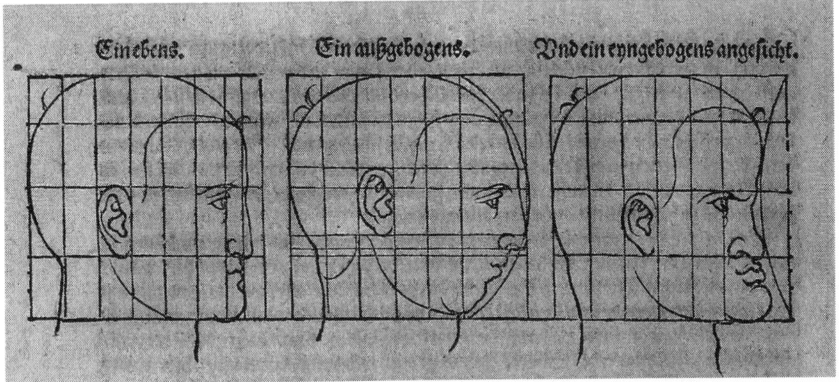

Figure 5. The construction of heads according to convex and concave curvature, *Vier Bücher von menschlicher Proportion* (Nuremberg: Hieronymous Andreae, 1528), Albrecht Dürer. Fol. Q2v. Glasgow School of Art Library.

Dürer admits that a convincing restructuring of the human head on paper requires a significant amount of essential detail to be filled in by the artist. It was not enough solely to translate or alter the head according to locating lines (*ort lini*), prefigurings of what Camper would designate as the *linea facialis* [facial line]. The morphology of facial features could be further mapped by framing the face within control points (figure 6), denoted here with the letters to the right of each profile and which stretched and condensed the nose, chin, eyes, and mouth when slid up and down, though he does not go into the specifics of how to render this detail. The framing text simply enumerates the shifting of the determining construction lines, leaving any impression one might have about the nature of

20. "aber solche ob beschrybne meynung diendt als mer zu vnderchyd dann zu gestalt der hübsche." Dürer, *menschlicher Proportion*, fol. Q3v.

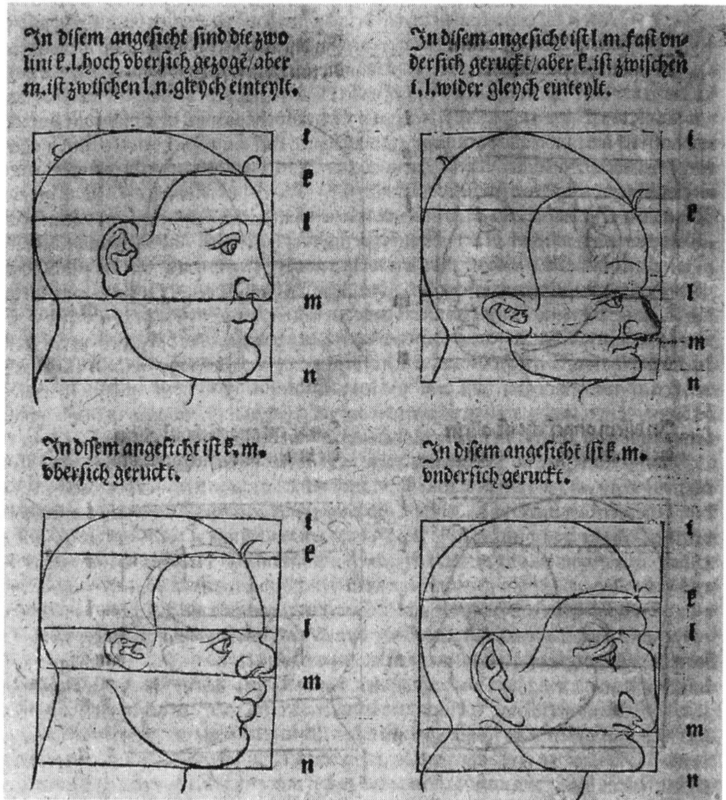

Figure 6. Four profiles [Detail], *Vier Bücher von menschlicher Proportion* (Nuremberg: Hieronymous Andreae, 1528), Albrecht Dürer. Fol. Q1v. Glasgow School of Art Library.

these subjects unsaid. By not being proscriptive, *menschlicher Proportion* goads the viewer into making further assumptions — about beauty, but also intelligence, social standing, age, and emotional state. These faces, simply through having been positioned in comparative profile, seem to divulge their unique interiorities, interiorities predicated upon the deformation of proportional relationships and the capacity of the artist to convincingly render their exteriority in shorthand.

Dürer's broader oeuvre testifies to an ambivalent relationship to the representation of racial difference. Physiognomy lingers at the conceptual edges of his profile studies, most of which, in their exaggeratedness, verge

Figure 7. Coat of Arms (1523), Albrecht Dürer. Accession Nr. 52.581.1. The Elisa Whittelsey Collection, The Elisha Whittelsey Fund, 1952. Metropolitan Museum of Art, New York.

into the realm of caricature and test a viewer's desire *not* to read character traits into them. On the other hand, *menschlicher Proportion*, which otherwise eschews stereotypical, ethnic indicators in favor of constructing general, vaguely Eurocentric facial features, does include one singular head that presents as an African stereotype. The last profile in the treatise's sequence of profiles, the figure's exaggerated nose, lips, and chin echo the family crest Dürer composed for himself in 1523, which contains a bust in profile of a winged Black man distinguished by an earring in his right ear (figure 7). But whereas the figure in the crest is singled out for special attention by virtue of its centrality in the image, the head from *menschlicher Proportion* is not highlighted in any way nor referenced in language different from that of the other drily geometric-based descriptions typifying the section. On the contrary, the head asks to be judged as just one more manifestation of the infinite possibilities of human variation.

The inclusion of such heads did not necessarily indicate derogatory assumptions. In the case of the Dürer crest, the head may well have been added to signify Dürer's worldliness and cosmopolitan outlook, though the recasting of an African head as a covetable exotic inevitably springs from an established system of signifiers of European imperialism. Dürer's earlier charcoal *Portrait of an African* (1508) and silverpoint drawing, *Portrait of Katharina* (1521) remain amongst the most touching and humane European depictions of peoples of non-Western origins from the period, owning nothing to visual stereotyping and enlivened by Dürer's sensitive penmanship. Little is known of the first subject, but Katharina is believed to have been a twenty-year-old servant of João Brandão, the representative of the King of Portugal in Antwerp and Dürer's host when he visited the city during his trip to the Netherlands in 1520–1521.[21] Dürer's diaries recount that he "portrayed with metalpoint his [Brandão's] negress."[22] It is notable that he composed his own family crest after these earlier artistic endeavors.

Though two hundred plus years would elapse, encompassing myriad advances in the science of human and animal biology, Renaissance treatises such as *menschlicher Proportion* continued to serve as references in the eighteenth century and beyond.[23] The evocative woodcut images of

21. "Albrecht Dürer's Sketches," *Black Central Europe*. https://blackcentraleurope.com/sources/1500-1750/albrecht-durers-sketches-1508-1521/ (Accessed January 2, 2020). On Katharina, see Diane Wolfthal, "Household Help: Early Modern Portraits of Female Servants," *Early Modern Women* (2013), 5–52, at 14–22.
22. Quoted from Joseph Leo Koerner, "The Epiphany of the Black Magus circa 1500," *The Image of the Black in Western Art: Volume III: Part 1. "From the Age of Discovery" to the Age of Abolition: Artists of the Renaissance and Baroque*, edited by David Bindman and Henry Louis Gates Jr., (Cambridge: Harvard University Press, 2010), 7–92, at 56.
23. For a list of the editions of *Vier Bücher von menschlicher Proportion*, see Berthold Hinz, ed., *Albrecht Dürer: Vier Bücher von menschlicher Proportion* (1528), 1–4.

human-animal affinities from Giambattista della Porta's *De humana physiognomia* (1586) hover spectrally above the proto-evolutionary sequences from later physiognomic treatises such as Camper's *Dissertation physique* (1791), and were surely known to the court painter Charles Le Brun (1619–1690), whose physiognomic drawings of animal and human heads were posthumously published in 1806.[24] Dürer, for his part, explicitly served as both foil and counterpoint for eighteenth-century theorists of race and biological morphology. Lavater, the author of *Essays on Physiognomy* (1777), directly refers to Dürer multiple times, while Camper positions himself in dialogue with Dürer, claiming in one instance that Dürer's heads were generally "too broad," a determinant Camper had made through "modelling in clay, after the finest heads of antiquity."[25] Dürer was still in use as a reference in the early twentieth century, for instance in Thompson's *On Growth and Form* (1917), a weighty text on the morphogenesis of animals and plants illustrating how diverse species might be deformed into each other by varying their coordinates upon a grid (figure 8).[26] *On Growth and Form* owed the privileged position of its descriptive diagrams to *menschlicher Proportion* and its landmark contributions to the geometrical foundation of difference and similarity.

• • •

The overriding perception of *menschlicher Proportion* is as a set of investigations on human proportion tied together by Dürer's interpretive *Meynung* [opinion]. Still, Dürer was not immune to what the philosophers Theodor W. Adorno and Max Horkheimer would later identify as the "dialectic of Enlightenment," where even a catalogue of difference is prone

24. On Le Brun, see Jennifer Montagu, *The Expression of the Passions: The Origin and Influence of Charles Le Brun's "Conference Sur L'expression Générale Et Particuliere,"* (New Haven: Yale University Press, 1994); Sarah R. Cohen, "Searching the animal psyche with Charles Le Brun," *Annals of Science* 67.3 (2010): 353–82.
25. Petrus Camper, *The Works of the Late Professor Camper*, translatd by T. Cogan, (London: Printed for C. Dilly, in the Poultry, 1794), 6, 38–39.
26. D'Arcy Wentworth Thompson, *On Growth and Form*, edited by John Tyler Bonner, (Cambridge: Cambridge University Press, 2000 [1917]), 290–91.

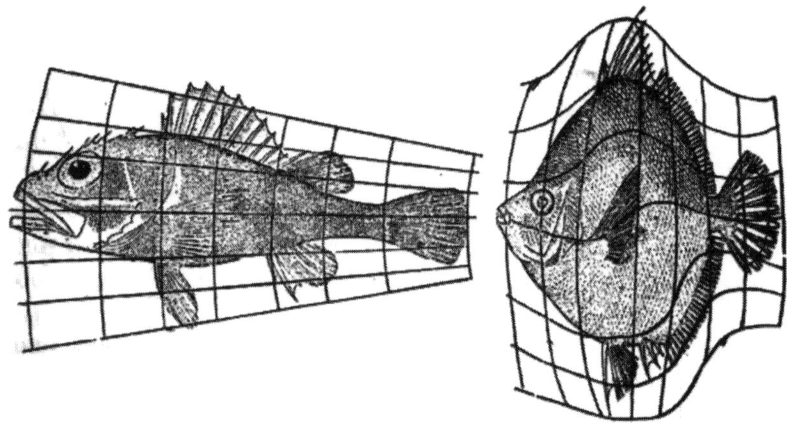

Figure 8. Deriving the *Antigonia capros from the Scorpaena*. Reproduced from D'Arcy Wentworth Thompson, On Growth and Form (Cambridge: Cambridge University Press, 1942 [1917]), 1063.

to collapse and to the defeat of its intrinsic logic.[27] Dürer's methodological wavering, his calculated indecision and representation of multiple systems of measurement, may have tacitly accommodated for a cascade of misappropriating and racialized views and opinions. Despite his attempt to create a graphic apparatus to account for the natural diversity of the human figure, one of the most significant outcomes of *menschlicher Proportion* was its rampant use by others to exclude the same variation it had sought to describe.

That the following centuries weaponized these visual strategies to great and devastating effect is already history, albeit a still-present history continuously unveiling itself. From catalogues echoing Lavater's and Camper's physiognomic stereotypes in the outlining of the silhouettes of African slaves in the Americas to the pervasive, anti-Semitic propaganda of the Third Reich, the ensuing cultural history of the profile became a media shorthand for unbridgeable difference and the indisputable aesthetic

27. See "The Concept of Enlightenment," Theodor W. Adorno and Max Horkheimer, *Dialectic of Enlightenment*, translated by E. Jephcott (Stanford, Stanford University Press, 2002 [1947]), 1–34.

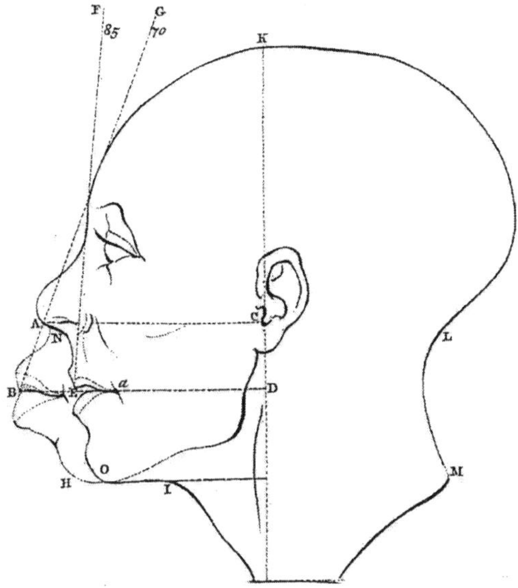

Figure 9. Superimposition of two heads, one African and one Caucasian, illustrating the 15 degree difference in facial angles, Petrus Camper (1722–1789), *Dissertation Physique, sur les différences réelles que présentent les traits du visage chez les hommes de différents pays et de differénts ages ...* (Utrecht: B. Wild & J. Altheer, 1791), Tab. VI. University of Michigan.

superiority of white Christians.[28] Unlike the many medieval depictions of non-Europeans, which appeared as ornamental embellishments or as manuscript images seeking to encapsulate the subject in his most representative behavior, the Enlightenment-era treatises made use of the potent, de-contextualized visual language so effectively innovated by Dürer. By way of example, the shocking and inexcusable images in *Dissertation physique* dramatize the development of the skull in profile, mapping its evolution from ape to that of a person of color and unto a spectrum of white Europeans. Superimposed one on top of the other (figure 9) or encapsulated in a series of profiles whose angular facial lines (running

28. On the visual history of the silhouette and its intersection with the racial politics of American culture, see Asma Naeem, *Black Out: Silhouettes Then and Now*, (Princeton: Princeton University Press, 2018).

from forehead to lip) progress closer to a desired value approximating ninety degrees, Camper strove to define the facial line as the most appropriate method for analyzing anthropological variety, defending his studies on the basis of direct examination of human and animal skulls.[29]

According to Camper, graphically tweaking the facial line to different degrees generated the entire spectrum of human and animal cranial anatomy, with the proportions of classical antiquity constructing a skull defined closer to an imaginary vertical at one end and the far more oblique angle of the ape at the other.[30] Recalling his study of his collection of human skin specimens, Camper concluded that pregnancy has the capacity to cause shifts in the skin's hue so that the "membrane becomes as black in our fairest women, during their pregnancy, as that of the blackest negro or Angolese." By his reasoning, the "fairest skin may become black, and the darkest become fair" as a result of natural biological processes, environmental influence, or without discernable cause, and furthermore as perception of color itself depends upon how "rays of light are refracted" upon the surface of the eye. Düreresque diagrams such as his that isolated and revealed the essential mathematics of the facial

29. "When in addition to the skull of a negro, I had procured one of a Calmuck [a branch of the Mongolian race], and had placed that of an ape contiguous to them both, I observed that a line, drawn along the forehead and the upper lip, indicated this difference in national physiognomy; and also pointed out the degree of similarity between a negroe and the ape. By sketching some of these features upon a horizontal plane, I obtained the lines which mark the countenance, with their different angles. When I made these lines to incline forwards, I obtained the antique head; backwards, the head of the negroe; still more backwards, the lines which mark an ape, a dog, a snipe [a wading bird species], &c." Camper, *Works*, 9. With slight modifications to the translation by author.

30. Notwithstanding the dated problematics of the enterprise, Camper elsewhere stressed the overall unicity of the human race, claiming that the zoological comparison was morphological only and not indicative of any *a priori* affinities between any one human group and animal species. Moreover, he remained categorically opposed to using skin color, that which is commonly used today as the prevailing visual marker dividing majority from minority, as indicative of human difference. His position against discrimination on the basis of skin color is most fully articulated in *Redevoering over den oorsprung en de kleur der zwarten* (Oration on the origin and color of the blacks), 1795.

line provided the most objective approach to a comparative study of the human head.[31]

The import projected upon the human profile reached the apex of its legitimacy in late eighteenth-century science.[32] Prevailing opinion held, per Lavater, that the many and variegated attempts of man "to appear wiser, better, and honester than, in reality" were bound to flounder upon the unforgiving shores of physiognomy. As he asserts, "There are many features, or parts of the body, which are not susceptible to dissimulation ... and, indeed, such features are indubitable marks of internal character."[33] To dispassionately study the face was to turn man inside out and to reduce him to his indelible physiological traces, those hard or firm parts of the body that eluded the power of his will to mold. As he concludes, "What man ... would be able to alter the confirmation of his bones ... Can any fashion the flat and short into the well-proportioned nose? Who can make his thick lips thin, or his thin lips thick?"[34]

Critically, that which needed to be cast aside and held in furthest opposition to a Western European ideal varied wildly. Camper's ape, so to speak, has at different moments in time stood in for the Black, but also the woman, the criminal, and the Jew among other oppressed or marginalized groups. This innate flexibility of the profile construct only reinforced the operational impact of the visual strategy and the ease with which diverse, if innately prejudicial, value systems could be effectively superimposed upon the human outline. Reducing man or woman to a two-dimensional reproduction of his or her profile and subjecting this image to measurement, or measuring subjects against this image, proved to be a perniciously successful visual argument. This evaded the potential for sympathy and identification spurred by looking directly into the eyes of the other, much as the mugshot or the lineup continue to harness and

31. Camper, *Works*, 16–17.
32. There were, however, dissenting views that stressed the schema's over-reductiveness. See for example *The Anthropological Treatises of Johann Friedrich Blumenbach*, edited by Thomas Bendyshe (London, 1865); and Bindman, *Ape to Apollo*, 209.
33. Johann Caspar Lavater, *Essays on Physiognomy* [1777], translated by Thomas Holcroft, (London: W. Tegg, 1878), 83–84.
34. Johann Caspar Lavater, *Essays on Physiognomy*, 84. See also Gray, *About Face*, 340.

exploit the malleable otherness required by the institutional gaze. From counter-terrorism to modern policing, the split-second judgements that enact the power of the law owe their existence to robustly constructed corridors of premodern thought that far predate any modern form of governmentality — and to the Renaissance history of a companion visual culture of diagrams flexible enough to accommodate for potential shifts in interpretive reading, namely, in the priorities and targets of power. Thus, as with *menschlicher Proportion*, even if the links between the profiles and their original meanings remain up for interpretation now, obscured as they may be behind five hundred years and the "period eye," the diagrams themselves, supported by the discourse on physiognomy, bolstered with learned knowledge of classical texts, and framed by informational graphics and explanatory markings, strip the primary field of expressive action from the face of the other and transplant it onto the page. Positioned at a perpendicular to the dispassionate gaze of the trained observer and denied its capacity for dissimulation, the face is delegated an ethical position in absentia, a profile without profile, not a double but a terrible sameness leaving no room for alterity.

Curiously, there are instances of Dürer's private explorations breaking with the graphic convention of the printed human profile (figure 10). Hidden in a sheet of drawn studies from 1513, Dürer arrays a compressed sequence of ten faces bookended by two classic stereotypes that he would describe in his "Aesthetic Excursus," appended to Book III of *menschlicher Proportion*, as "two species of mankind, whites and negroes; in these a difference in kind can be observed as between us and them."[35] It has been noted that it is only the last, Africanized profile who is "rendered conscious of the series to which it belongs."[36] As variable as the adjacent folds of drapery, there are, for Dürer, "many varieties and causes of beauty ... " as well as "a great harmony in diversity."[37] And yet it is only the last man, the only man, his one eye swiveling in its socket towards us in this final image, who by virtue of his difference is able to pierce the veil of representation and in so doing become privy, in horror, to what is to come.

35. Albrecht Dürer, "Aesthetic Excursus," *A Documentary History of Art*, 318–29, at 324–25.
36. Koerner, "Black Magus," 84.
37. Dürer, "Aesthetic Excursus," 317.

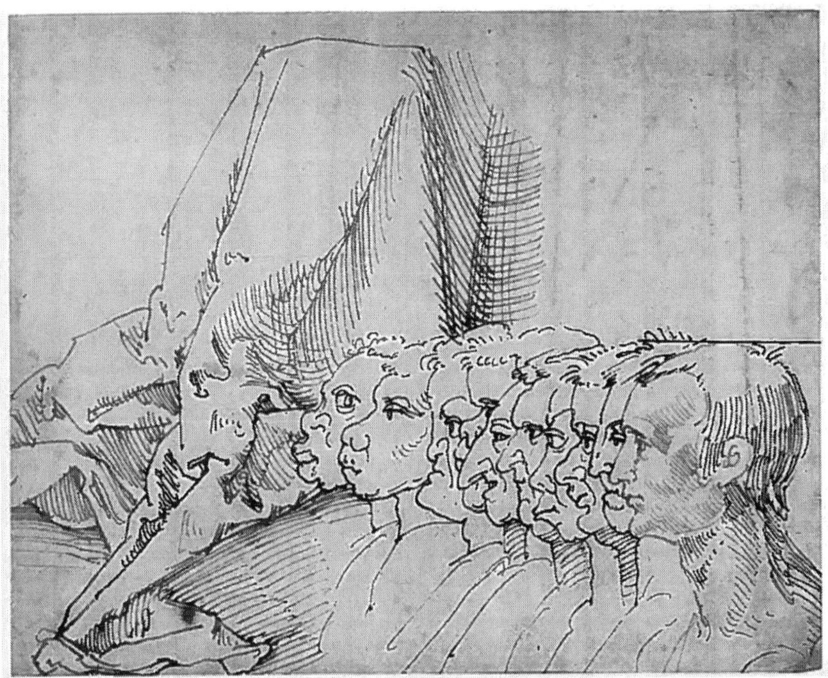

Figure 10. Sheet of Studies with physiognomic heads and drapery (1513), Albrecht Dürer. Staatliche Museen zu Berlin.

Suggestions for Further Readings

Bindman, David, *Ape to Apollo: Aesthetics and the Idea of Race in the 18th Century*. Ithaca: Cornell University Press, 2002.

Dennis, David B. *Inhumanities: Nazi Interpretations of Western Culture*. Cambridge: Cambridge University Press, 2012.

Panofsky, Erwin. *The Life and Art of Albrecht Dürer*. Princeton: Princeton University Press, 2005 [1943].

Strickland, Debra Higgs. "Monstrosity and Race in the late Middle Ages." In *The Ashgate Research Companion to Monsters and the Monstrous*, 405–426. Farnham, UK: Routledge (2017).

Contextualizing Race in Leonhard Thurneysser's Account of Portugal

CAROLIN ALFF

"They have mostly a broad face and all of them pitch-dark or coal-black curly hair [...]"[1] or so the Swiss traveller Leonhard Thurneysser zum Thurn (1531–1596) begins his eighteen-page long observation on the African diaspora in sixteenth-century Lisbon. In this passage he addresses three features that have marked the stereotypical appearance of people of color in European discourses: black skin, a broad face, and curly hair. Many further examples in Thurneysser's text will seem outright racist to today's readers, since a number of his descriptions became degrading tropes for people of color in later centuries and therefore resemble aspects of modern racism. Studying this text with students today requires a strong discussion of context, for reading it will challenge students especially when they have experienced racism themselves. This paper aims to provide tools and examples for teachers to deconstruct the text and tropes of this historic source so that a discussion of race can be integrated into the study of early modern European culture. The underlining question of this essay is: Does Thurneysser's description of the African diaspora in Lisbon offer us insights into constructions of race in the sixteenth century?

Scientific racism — the belief that a person's origin and physical attributes determined their unchangeable social and natural position in this

1. "Sie habenn gemeiniglich ein breit Angesicht, vnnd alle samblich ein gar pech oder kohlschwartzes krauses Haar[...]." Berlin, Staatsbibliothek zu Berlin – Preußischer Kulturbesitz, Germ. Fol. 97, (hierafter, Germ. Fol. 97), fol. 133v; Unless otherwise specified all transcriptions and translations were taken from Bernardo J. Herold, "The Diary of the Swiss Leonhard Thurneysser and Black Africans in Renaissance Lisbon," *Renaissance Studies* 32.3 (2017): 463–88. The manuscript should soon become available in the digital collection of the Staatsbibliothek in Berlin.

world — was not fully formulated until the nineteenth century.[2] According to Ivan Hannaford, the general use of the term "race" in European languages commenced in the sixteenth century, precisely when Thurneysser wrote his description.[3] Thurneysser's account, however, does not use the term. As such, many disciplines view discussing race in this period as an anachronistic and problematic approach to historical sources, although most agree that historic sources frequently include prejudice and discriminate against people based on skin color and place of origin.[4] Instead, these disciplines focused on the process of othering, outlining how sixteenth-century texts describing people of color establish tropes through the process of fusing observed information gleaned from travels with philosophical, scientific, and theological ideas of otherness at the time.[5] According to these authors, the sixteenth-century accounts seem to fall

2. For a general definition of racism see Ian Law, *Racism and Ethnicity: Global Debates, Dilemmas, Directions* (London: Pearson Longman Publishers, 2010), 3–11; George M. Fredrickson, *Racism: A Short History* (Princeton, NJ: Princeton University Press, 2002), 5–6. For an overview of the discussion of this anachronistic approach see David Davis, "Constructing Race: A Reflection," *The William and Mary Quarterly* 54: 1 (1997): 7–18. For a critical discussion of the literature on race see Wulf D. Hund, "Vor, mit, nach und ohne 'Rassen': Reichweiten der Rassismusforschung," in *Wandel des Politischen: Die Bundesrepublik Deutschland während der 1980er-Jahre*, eds. Beatrix Bouvier et al., Archiv für Sozialgeschichte 52 (Bonn: J.H.W. Dietz. Nachf., 2012), 723–61.
3. Ivan Hannaford, *Race: The History of an Idea in the West* (Baltimore: Woodrow Wilson Center Press and John Hopkins University Press, 1996).
4. Among others see the contributions in Thomas F. Earle and Katherine Lowe, eds., *Black Africans in Renaissance Europe* (Cambridge: Cambridge University Press, 2005).
5. For a discussion of otherness in context of sixteenth-century encounters between Europeans and people of color see Anthony Pagden, *The Fall of Natural Man: The American Indian and the Origins of Comparative Ethnology* (Cambridge: Cambridge University Press, 1982). For a discussion of the monstrous races see Lorraine Daston and Katherine Park, *Wonders and the Order of Nature, 1150–1750* (New York, NY: Zone Books, 1998); John B. Friedman, *The Monstrous Races in Medieval Art and Thought* (Cambridge, MA: Harvard University Press, 1981).

short of describing race as it is understood today because a person's hierarchical position could change based on religion and wealth.[6]

What did and did not constitute race in the early modern period is worthy of reassessing and discussing with students today. Thurneysser's text is an apt case study because of the detail in which he describes the people of color he encountered living in sixteenth-century Lisbon. His profession as a physician provides a context within the medical and natural sciences. Thurneysser's text offers teachers and students a clear way to study race formation in the early modern world, revealing that the pseudoscience of skin color and its racist meanings were happening before the Enlightenment. Using an early modern text, students and teachers can interrogate the formation of racist stereotypes and the way they were given legitimacy.

The text about Thurneysser's travels through Portugal is bound in a manuscript alongside other texts and kept in the State Library in Berlin (henceforth referred to as *Berlin Manuscript*).[7] A practical benefit of using Thurneysser's account as teaching material is the availability and the amount of material still existing to this day. A digital copy and a transcription of the text are available online.[8] They provide access to primary source material for teachers and students. The vast number of letters and publications left by Thurneysser offers valuable additional context for

6. Among others see Surekha Davies, *Renaissance Ethnography and the Invention of the Human: New Worlds, Maps and Monsters* (Cambridge: Cambridge University Press, 2016), 39, 223; The contributions in T.F. Earle and K.J.P Lowe, eds., *Black Africans in Renaissance Europe*; Jean Massing, *The Image of the Black in Western Art: From the "Age of Discovery" to the Age of Abolition: Europe and the World Beyond*. Vol. III.2 of *The Image of the Black in Western Art*. Ed. David Bindman and Henry Gates, Jr. (Cambridge: The Belknap Press of Harvard University Press, 2011), xviii, 2, 397, 398, 399; Fredrickson, *Racism*, 24.
7. Germ. Fol. 97.
8. Bernardo Herold, Thomas Horst and Henrique Leitão, A *História Natural de Portugal de Leonhard Thurneysser zum Thurn, ca.* 1555–1556 (Lisbon: Academia das Ciências de Lisboa, 2019) [http://www.acad-ciencias.pt/document-uploads/2695205_herold,-b,-horst,-t,-leitao,-h---historia-natural-portugal-transcricao-final2019.pdf].

understanding his pseudoscientific motives in collecting and processing information gained in his travels.

This essay covers a selection of material to use when studying Thurneysser's account of Portugal. In studying historic travel accounts it is paramount to bear in mind and remind students that the historic accounts are subjective narratives. Therefore, it is important to convey the methodological challenges that arise when studying such a source. A close reading of Thurneysser's text, for instance, requires comparisons with other relevant travel accounts containing descriptions of the body of a person of color to determine the general significance of the text.[9] Furthermore, as it is not possible to discuss the meaning of his words with the author, an interpretation depends on understanding the text in context of the author's life and other work. Lastly and more generally, racist tropes can be triggering to students and therefore it is important to produce an environment that protects students and teachers from being personally subjected to racism while also aiming to discuss and deconstruct racist tropes. To create this environment, teachers may choose to look into general approaches to discussing racism with students before using this material in a classroom.[10]

The analysis of sixteenth-century travel accounts frequently argues that they either contain ethnographic information or deploy unscientific tropes. I will present a multilayered approach to Thurneysser's description to show that, contrary to such a binary analysis, a travel account such as Thurneysser's can present a range of historic evidence. Although often claiming scientific objectivity, many sixteenth-century travel accounts contain discrimination, stereotypes, and othering of people of color that arise from outside direct physical observation.[11] At the same time, these

9. For an introduction and discussion of micro-history see István Szijártó and Sigurður Magnússon, *What Is Microhistory? Theory and Practice* (London: Routledge, 2013).
10. There are many general resources to consult when preparing for discussing racism in a classroom. One example that provides free information is the ADL: https://www.adl.org/education/resources/tools-and-strategies/race-talk-engaging-young-people-in-conversations-about. Accessed March 6, 2020.
11. See among others Fracanzano da Montalboddo, *Newe unbekanthe landte Und ein newe weldt in kurtz verganger zeythe erfunden* (Nuremberg: Georg Stuchs, 1508); Balthasar

texts may also represent an interest in the cultures of people from other continents and a desire to understand cultural and physical differences, paving the way to a form of early ethnography.[12] Studying such historic descriptions, like Thurneysser's account of the African diaspora in Lisbon, also allow students to discuss relations of race formation and ethnography in the sixteenth century and the value of such sources as historic evidence.

To discuss the range of this evidence, I suggest teachers look at the text from three perspectives. The first perspective analyzes how Thurneysser's text contained firsthand information and tropes to exhibit ethnographic and historical information. This section forms the basis for how Thurneysser described the appearance and habits of the African diaspora in sixteenth-century Lisbon. The second perspective qualifies this information by concentrating on the specific context in which his work was produced. The third perspective will explore the bias of such reports and the tropes resulting from such information introduced in the first section more fully.

I will first set the scene by briefly describing the historic details of the African diaspora in Lisbon and Thurneysser's manuscript. Sixteenth-century Lisbon was a "global city," housing and hosting inhabitants from many

Springer, *Die Merfart vn(d) erfarung nüwer Schiffung vnd Wege zu viln onerkanten Inseln und Künigreichen, von dem groſsmechtigen Portugalischen Kunig Emanuel Erforscht. . . . wie ich, Balthasar Spre(n) ger sollichs selbs [. . .]gesehen vn(d) erfaren habe* (etc.) (Oppenheim, 1509); Walther Raleigh, *Kurtze Wunderbare Beschreibung: Deß Goldreichen König=reichs Guianae in America* (Nuremberg: Lievin Hulsius, 1599).

12. For an example of a discussion of the meaning of ethnology in the sixteenth century see Anthony Pagden, *The Fall of Natural Man*. For a visual record of such cultural encounters as a form of early ethnography see Stephanie Leitch, *Mapping Ethnography in Early Modern Germany: New Worlds in Print Culture* (Basingstoke: Palgrave Macmillan, 2010); Surekha Davies, *Renaissance Ethnography and the Invention of the Human: New Worlds, Maps and Monsters* (Cambridge: Cambridge University Press, 2016); Mary B. Campbell, *The Witness and the Other World: Exotic European Travel Writing, 400–1600* (Ithaca, NY: Cornell University Press, 1988).

parts of the world.[13] Trade fueled the existence of this multiethnic community. The city was visually described as "games of chess, with as many blacks and whites" living in Lisbon at the time, although the majority of people making up the African diaspora came to the city as slaves.[14] Thurneysser's observations from Portugal were recorded in four parts (plants, small animals, miscellaneous, and larger animals). His description of the African diaspora is part of the miscellaneous section, where he recorded information that was obviously important to him but that did not fall into the other categories. This section included a description of Lichens, the hazing practiced by Norwegian tradesmen and his observations of sea tides. The four parts of his observations in Portugal were written consecutively in the same handwriting on paper that possesses the same watermark. Each section however is meant to stand on its own, as all but one (missing) possess a title page (Figure 1) and begin with a new page count.[15] The *Berlin Manuscript* is a compendium, which is a collection of many texts, that contains eleven sections in total. Except for the four components regarding Portugal, all other parts are independent of each other and penned by several different scribes with varying topics and many incomplete.[16] In the *Berlin Manuscript*, Thurneysser's workshop recorded and bound together the information about the African diaspora with pharmaceutical and botanical explorations from other sources.

13. The description of "global city" was used in the following publication: Annemarie Geschwend and Katherine Lowe, eds., *The Global City: On the Streets of Renaissance Lisbon* (London: Paul Holberton, 2015).
14. This description and many more were published in Katherine Lowe, "The Global Population of Renaissance Lisbon: Diversity and its Entanglements," in *The Global City: On the Streets of Renaissance Lisbon*, edited by Annemarie Jordan Geschwend and K.J.P. Lowe (London: Paul Holberton, 2015), 61.
15. The title page of the fourth section is missing.
16. For a detailed analysis and description of the entire manuscript see Thomas Horst, "A Rediscovered Manuscript about Portuguese Plants and Animals: Preliminary Observations," in *Renaissance Craftsmen and Humanistic Scholars: Circulation of Knowledge between Portugal and Germany*, edited by Thomas Horst, Marília dos Santos Lopes, and Henrique Leitão (Frankfurt: Peter Lang, 2017), 133–74.

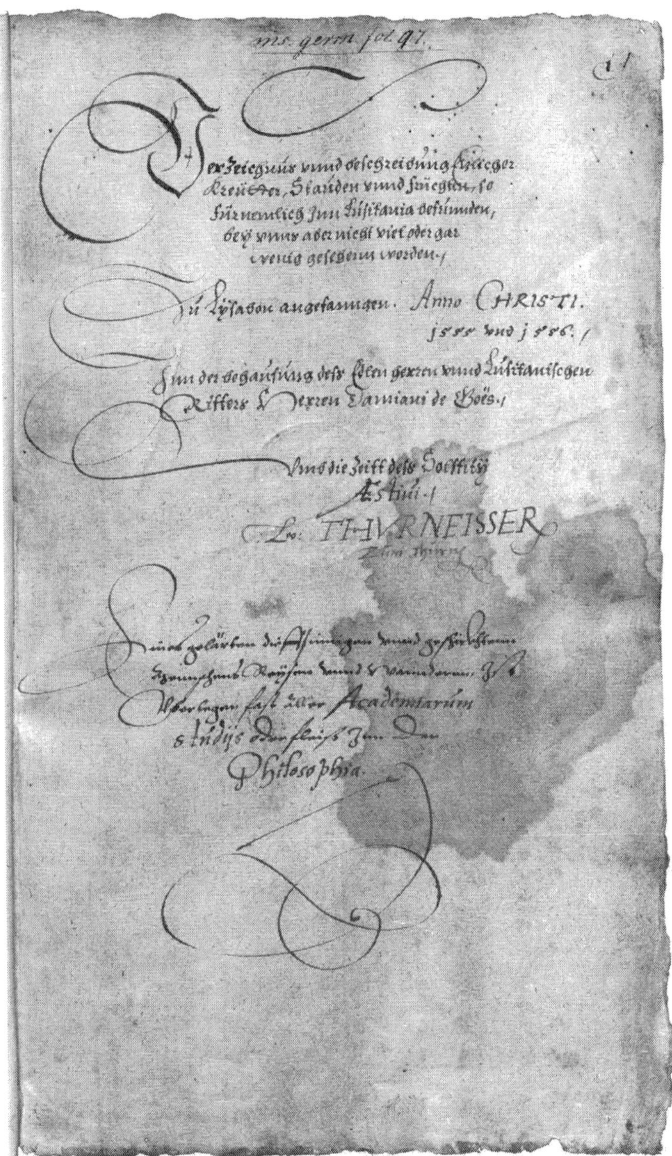

ms. germ. fol. 97.

Anno CHRISTI.

THURNEISSER

Academiarum

Philosophia

Figure 1. Leonhard Thurneysser, *Nutural History of Portugal*, Berlin, 1570–1579, Staatsbibliothek zu Berlin – Preußischer Kulturbesitz; Handschriftenabteilung; Signatur: Ms Germ. Fol. 97, fol. 1r.

Ethnographic and Historic Information

The first perspective to Thurneysser's text requires students to closely read and characterize the information in the account as well as the way Thurneysser obtained it. By analyzing the text from this angle, students are led to identify the uniqueness of the detail of Thurneysser's text and what value it has as a historic source for the lives of the African diaspora in Lisbon. They are equally meant to learn how to distinguish between information gathered directly and information conveying preconceived tropes. A close reading of the text should additionally introduce students to the type of information on physical appearance and habits of the African diaspora circulating in the sixteenth century.

Thurneysser's observations of the African diaspora suggest that he was in close proximity to his subjects when he described them. Thurneysser reconstructs in writing the face of a person of color by specifying the texture, which suggests he himself had touched the person he was describing.[17] Continuing from the quote beginning this paper, he writes that "[...] both the men, as well as the women" possess black curly hair, "which they shear away or raze down to the skin, and which, as soon as it grows again a little, becomes strangely curly."[18] The text carries on by describing the feel of the hair: "the same feels also very hard to the touch."[19] His language uses tactility and personal observation as the method for perceiving and understanding the faces of a Black man and woman. It suggests that he collected his information from firsthand experience.

It should be conveyed to students that the amount of detail with which Thurneysser describes the body of a person of color has no parallel in other accounts of the sixteenth century. His intricate information reaches an invasive depth, as he goes as far as to describe the genitals of the man

17. Herold, "Thurneysser and Black Africans," 471.
18. "[...]die Menner eben so wol alls die Weiber [...] wellches sie gar biß auf die Haut weckscheren vnnd schneidenn, und wellches, so baldt es inen nur gar ein klein wenig widerumb wechst, gar wunderlichen krauß wirrdt." Germ. Fol. 97, fols. 134r. More and similar examples can be found on fol. 135r and 136r.
19. "desselb ist auch am Angriff sehr hart." Germ. Fol. 97, fol. 134r.

he was observing and touching.[20] He adds to his account instances of body mutilations as beautifications: "Several among them had been strangely adorned as youths by cutting them on both sides of their mouth, […] which they consider to be a great adornment."[21] In almost equal detail as his portrayal of the faces, he concludes his description of the body of a man of color with descriptions of the appearance and feel of the legs, hands, and feet, the last of which follows: "Thus they have also very small and cracked heels, which look more whitish, but otherwise are, together with the foot soles very hard, […]."[22] Students may be able to understand the uniqueness of Thurneysser's text when contextualized through the information that was available in popular sixteenth-century publications. His text, for instance, refrains from referring back to medieval representations of the monstrous races to communicate a different appearance.[23] For a clear contrast between Thurneysser's description and the monstrous races, students can study creatures with traits of animals and excess or missing body parts (Figure 2) that were still depicted as populating the African continent in contemporary cosmographies and accompanying maps, such as in Sebastian Münster's *Cosmographiae universalis*, published in Basel in several editions from 1544 onwards.[24] Comparing Thurneysser's account to other literature circulating at the time allows students to debate in what ways Thurneysser's detailed description of the African body exhibits an interest in understanding the appearance of a foreign culture and people from Africa. This type of information is termed ethnographic by studies of early modern culture. The label should be

20. Germ. Fol. 97, fol.136r
21. "Etzliche vnnder denselbigen warden zu einer sunderlich[en] Zier inn der Jugenndt an allen beyden Seitten deß Munndes, vonn dem Haupt oder Stirnn an, biß zu dem Munndt durchschnitten, […] wellches sie vermainen ein groß Zier zu sein." Germ. Fol. 97, fol. 135v.
22. " Sie haben sie auch gar kleine vnnd verkerbte Hackhen, wellche etwas weißlechtiger anzusehenn, sonnst aber, samt der Füessolen gar hart seindt, […]." Germ. Fol. 97, fols. 136r–136v.
23. For context on monsters and the monstrous see Asa S. Mittman with Peter J. Dendle, *The Ashgate Research Companion to Monsters and the Monstrous* (London: Routledge, 2013).
24. Sebastian Münster, *Cosmographiae universalis* (Basel: Heinrich Petri, 1550).

Liber VI. 1151

stes, sæpeꝗ; illos lædit. Quando occiditur & mactatur, dicuntur inueniri in stomacho eius lapides & interdū ferrum, quæ & per digestionē longam absumit. Parat nidum suum in fouea arenę, atque circumædificat propugnaculū in modum muri, quo aquas pluuiales abarceat ne ingrediantur nidum & lædant pullos. Sunt qui scribunt illum aut fœmellam oua sua non excludere, sed committunt ea calidæ arenæ, quousque pulli egrediuntur, tunc parentes nutriunt pullos suos. Dicitur esse simplex & obliuiosum animal: nam quàmprimū oua edit, obliuiscitur eorum quousꝗ; pulli prodeunt.

De mirabilibus & monstrosis creaturis quæ in interioribus Africæ inueniuntur.

REcensent ueteres, præsertim Pomponius Mela, Plinius & Solinus, multa mirabilia quæ in interiori Africa siue in Aethiopia inueniunt, ex quibus aliqua hic breuiter cōmemorabo. Iuxta insulam Meroe est lacus quidam, cuius aquæ sunt instar olei lubricę & subtiles, & quicquid in ipsum cadit, quantumlibet leue sit, cadit ad fundum. Nullum lignum sed nec arboris folium enatat. Apud Sambales populos, quadrupedia carent auribus. Monstrosorum multa hominum genera post linguarū uarietatem à Deo factam uarijs in locis producta fuisse, etiam diuus Augustinus 16. de ciuitate Dei cap. 8. commemorat dicens. Deus ipse cum sciret, quarum partium similitudine uel diuersitate cōtexeret pulchritudinem uniuersi, etiam monstrosos homines in mundum producere uoluit. Dicuntur reperiri Cynomolgi siue cynocephali, quorum canina sunt capita, caninaꝗ; ora, qui ipso latratu magis bestias quam homines se esse profitentur. *Cynocephali.* Alij deinde esse dicunt, Artapathitæ dicti, qui instar qadrupedum incedunt per manus & pedes, nec habent propriam mansionem. Et alij qui in media fronte unum tantum habent oculum, monoculi appellati. *Monoculi.* Alijs aiunt ora non esse, sed per nares solo halitu uiuere. Alios statura esse cubitales, quos Pygmęos Græci uocant, qui annum octauum uiuendo nō excedunt. *Pygmæi.* Pugnare dicuntur cum gruibus sed uincunt. Horum mulieres quinto anno pariunt & senescunt octauo, reponitꝗ; eos Plinius in Indiæ mōtibus. At Strabo reponit eos in extremitate Africæ, si modo Pygmęi sunt in rerū natura. Nam nemo fide dignus, inquit Strabo, id ex uisu narrat. Item aliæ cōmemorantur gentes, in quibus singuli singula crura in pedibus maximis habent, non flectentes poplitem & tamen mirabilis sunt celeritatis, quos Sciopodas uocant. Hi Plinio teste per æstiuū tempus in terra supini iacentes, pedum se umbra protegunt. *Sciopodæ.* Quosdam alios sine ceruice esse aiunt, habentes oculos in humeris. Item Plinius scribit in Arabia nasci Camelopardalim, collo similem equo, pedibus & cruribus boui, camelo capite, albis maculis rutilum colorem distinguentibus. Inueniri aiunt & parandrum animal, magnitudine bouis, habens caput ceruinum cum ramosis cornibus. Nascitur quoꝗ; in Africa Hystrix, animal ex herinaceorum genere fœtidum, paulo minus lupo. Longi aculei dorsum & latera eius exasperant. Vulgo uocant ipsum porcum spinosum & marinum, quum tamen animal sit terrestre. Quum irritatur intendit cutem & missiles aculeos iaculatur in canes sequentes, lęditꝗ; eos in facie. Nugantur quoꝗ; aliqui in Africa esse Pegasum auem, quæ dicitur habere corpus equinum atque aures equi & alas uolucris: & Trogopam aliam auem, in capite instar arietis cornutam. Horum tam mirabilium animalium causam, signat Plinius aquæ penuriam. Nam quum tot diuersæ animalium species iuxta aquam cōueniunt, quædam ex aliorum pruritu & salacitate: quæ non sunt ex sua specie, compręssa, concipiunt & generant monstrum, prolem ex diuersa natura constitutam. *Quare in Africa tot portentosa animalia.*

Hhh 2

Figure 2. Sebastian Münster, *Cosmographiae universalis*, Basel, Heinrich Petri, 1550, Bayerische Staatsbibliothek, Signatur: Hbks/E 4, p. 1151.

treated critically, as it does not automatically question the invasive nature of such a description. Calling a text ethnographic also neglects to fully contextualize the implicit biases that exist between the author, a Swiss doctor, and the subject, the African Diaspora, based on social positions and culture.

Following a very comprehensive description of the faces, students should be encouraged to analyze his portrayal of the body, which focuses on skin color. He writes: "They are also very coal-black or pitch-black on the whole body."[25] When studying the skin, he does differentiate certain physical traits, such as skin texture and skin color, that are softer or lighter between people from different African countries: "they (Ethiopians and Arabs) are the mightiest and most beautiful ones. They also have a most smooth, glossy and even skin, and also their bodies are the most perfect and strong, as compared to other moors […]."[26] Thurneysser associates a positive judgment with the lighter-skinned inhabitants of North Africa as opposed to people from sub-Saharan Africa. Thurneysser also describes his perceptions of difference in skin tone and the country of origin. He writes: "the moors […] who came from the islands of *D. Thomae* or the *Capotos Viridis* or the green head or from *Malagetta* or have been brought, are not that black, but rather of a dark-brown color and mainly in their faces, but they have mostly the same shape, kind and appearance of their hair, noses, lips, skin, pudenda, and their feet."[27] He even takes note of irregular appearances to the norm such as the existence of people that were born "from two coal-black parents, which nevertheless was com-

25. "Sie seindt auch sunst am ganntzen Leib gar kol und pichschwartz." Germ. Fol. 97, fol. 134r.
26. "seindt sie (Æthijopice and Arabiæ) zum aller schwerist[en] vnnd schonnsten, habent auch gar ein glatte, ja glanntzenndt vnnd ebene Hautt, so seindt sie auch am Leib folkhumlichen vnnd sterckher dann die anndere Mohren, […]." Germ. Fol. 97, fol.135r.
27. "Die Mohren […] auß den Innsulis D. Thomae, oder deß Capitis Viridis oder des grünen Haupts, vnnd auß Malagetta khumen vnd gebracht werdenn, seindt nicht so gar sehr schwartz, sunderen seindt einer dunckhelbraunen Farb vnnd sunderlich im Angesicht, aber sie haben doch gemeiniglichen alle einerley Form, Artt vnd Gestallt, der Haaren, Nasen, Lippen, Hautt, Schams, vnnd der Füeß." Germ. Fol. 97, fol. 135v.

pletely white, yes, even whiter than a German can be [...]."[28] For Thurneysser, skin color becomes the main differentiating attribute between people of color from the African continent and their varying places of origin.

After describing their appearance, Thurneysser writes about the behaviors found among the African diaspora. He describes women and men of African descent as especially violent, ambivalent to pain, and revengeful.[29] Their sexuality is painted as unchaste and hypersexual.[30] He explicitly compares white women and women of color to stress the sexual nature of the latter by stating, "that the women are quite merry, adroit and delightful in love-making, yes much sweeter, passionate and lustful than ours."[31] Thurneysser does not specify how he gathered this information and whether it was firsthand. Students can compare the detailed description of the body with his general descriptions of habits and behavior — the differences in the amount of detail suggests that Thurneysser recorded some information from first-hand experience and some from common stereotypes circulating in Lisbon at the time.[32]

28. "von zwey gar kolschwarzen Elterenn, darr doch gar weiß, ja, viel weisser dann die Teütschen, [...]." Germ Fol. 97, fol 142r,
29. Germ. Fol. 97, fol. 137r.
30. Germ. Fol. 97, fol. 138r.
31. "seindt die Weiber fein lustig, behanndt vnd lieblich in opera Venereo, ja viel lustiger, wercklicher, vnd begiriger dann die vnnseren." Germ. Fol. 97, fol. 138r.
32. When putting this analysis of Thurneysser's text into context, students may discover that many sixteenth-century travel descriptions, especially published accounts, mixed original information with bits from other travel narratives to a much greater extent than Thurneysser. These descriptions also drew on cosmographies, texts that explained the earth's consistency, climate and appearance, including descriptions of people, animals, plants and geographic features.(For a discussion of authenticity of travel accounts see Mary B. Campbell, *The Witness and the Other World: Exotic European Travel Writing*, 400–1600 (Ithaca, NY: Cornell University Press, 1988). An example with which teachers can demonstrate this contrast is the travel account of Walter Raleigh (1552/1554–1618), whose description of his stay on the American continent stated that there "are divers nations of *Canibals*, and of those *Ewaipanoma* without heads." (Walther Raleigh, *The Discovery of the Beautiful Empire of Guiana*, ed. by Sir Robert H. Schomburck [London: Hakluyt Society, 1848], 108.) These texts also contain statements specifying that their information had been verified by hearsay or observa-

Thurneysser's description of the slave market in Lisbon is one of the most detailed to exist today. Earlier texts, such as Nuremberg physician Hieronymus Münzer's (1437/47–1508) account, for example, only casually mentioned the existence of slaves in Lisbon.[33] In contrast, Thurneysser's account paints an image of the gruesome sale of people on the shores of Portugal in the sixteenth century. Thurneysser describes the sale of enslaved people that he calls "Nigriten" (Blacks) as follows:

> Among the same, however, who are being walked about and offered for sale, there are plenty of men, women, youths and maids stark naked or nude, some of them, however, have their private parts covered, but are otherwise naked. The merchants feel or touch them everywhere, specially around the navel, which when sticking out of the belly, and if the belly is swollen or inflated, they do not buy them, because they believe that it is the symptom of a dangerous malady. Thus they also have to show their private parts or genitals and open them, stretch their feet, as well as raise and lower their arms repeatedly, allowing them [the merchants] to evaluate and recognize their strength by lifting and lowering something [...].[34]

tion. The German publication of Raleigh's travel refers to "Mr. Raleigh witnessed" to lend additional authority to the information presented in the translation.

33. Munich, Bayerische Staatsbibliothek, Clm 431, 122v. For a translation of this sections see Jeremy Lawrence, "Black Africans in Renaissance Spanish literature," in *Black Africans in Renaissance Europe*, edited by Thomas F. Earle and Katherine Lowe (Cambridge: Cambridge University Press, 2005), 71.
34. "Vnnder denselbigen aber, weil sie also herumb gefürrt und zum Kauf gestellt warden, seindt etzliche Menner vnnd Weiber, Jüngling und Jungfrawen gar mueter nackhet, oder blos, etzlich aber habendt die Scham bedeckht, vnnd seindt sunnst auch ganntz mueter nackhendt. Die Kaufleüt befühlen oder tasten sie allenhalben, vnnd sunderlich vmb den Nabel, wellcher, wann er inen ausserhalb dem Bauch heraussen steht, vnnd der Leib aufgedehnet oder aufgeblasen ist, so kauffen sie sie nicht, dann sie dasselbige für ein Anzeizeigung einer geferlichen Kranckheit an inen hallten. So müssen sie inen auch die Scham oder Geburtsglider zeigen vnd öffnen, ire Füesse außstreckhen wie den auch die Arm auf vnnd nider vnnd hin vnd wider heben, darauß sie dann ire Sterckhe abnehmen vnd erkhennen lassen sie etwas auf und niedergehen [...], begreiffen ire Duttennn vnd Brüste, [...]." Germ. Fol. 97, fols. 138v–139r.

As a useful resource to prepare for a discussion of this description, teachers and students can refer to the analysis of the historian Bernardo Herold, who published a transcription and English translation of Thurneysser's text in 2017.[35] Without Thurneysser's travel account and a small amount of other texts, we would not have a literary record of such an event and how it took place, and no firsthand account penned by an enslaved person of color from the sixteenth century has so far come to light.[36] However, despite their relevance as contemporaneous sources and as testimonials of an African history otherwise lost, their value does not exclude them from containing stereotypes and degrading tropes. The particular context of Thurneysser's account, which I will describe in the next section, qualifies the historic and ethnographic information contained within it and establishes the ground on which Thurneysser investigated and formulated terms of race.

The Body as Research

This section provides details of Thurneysser's life and professional practice so that students can discuss his motivation for recording both firsthand observations and cultural tropes in his work. Bernardo Herold argues that, as "a naturalist," Thurneysser described the bodies of women and men of color "as if they were mere botanical and zoological species," but Herold neglects to explore this further.[37] My analysis aims to provide students with the knowledge to discuss whether Thureysser's text, from a contemporaneous perspective, acts as a scientific exploration of the black body.

Although the text about his voyage to Portugal carries the dates 1555–1556, it was during his years in Berlin that one of his scribes, presumably Adam Seidel (dates unknown), penned the text of Thurneysser's

35. Herold, "Thurneysser and Black Africans."

36. Next to travel accounts, other archival documents can show a less subjective view of the life of the African diaspora in Portugal as investigated in Thomas F. Earle and Katherine Lowe, eds., *Black Africans in Renaissance Europe* (Cambridge: Cambridge University Press, 2005); Katherine Lowe, "Visible Lives: Black Gondoliers and Other Black Africans in Renaissance Venice," *Renaissance Quarterly* 66, no. 2 (2013): 412–52.

37. Herold, "Thurneysser and Black Africans," 463.

journey to Lisbon.[38] From 1570–1579 Thurneysser was the personal doctor to the Elector of Brandenburg, Johann Georg (1571–1598).[39] The steady income and social recognition that he received from this position enabled Thurneysser's intellectual life to flourish.[40] He maintained a vivid correspondence with many humanists, alchemists, doctors, printers, and members of the European nobility.[41] Thurneysser ventured into many fields, including printing, alchemy, botany (he set up a botanical garden and a small zoo), pharmacy, metallurgy, and astronomy.[42]

Thurneysser's workshop in Berlin processed empirical information to determine the natural properties of living beings. The four parts of the *Berlin Manuscript* contain enquiries into the properties of the natural world in the form of botanical lists and descriptions as well as notes on materials and cures for diseases. Overall, the manuscript highlights gathering empirical knowledge about plants and animals to comprehend the

38. Based on the opinion of Gabriele Kaiser who has studied the penmanship of both Thurneysser and Seidel. Mentioned in a conversation on August 18, 2019.
39. For Thurneysser's first biography see Johann K. W. Moehsen, *Beiträge zur Geschichte der Wissenschaften in der Mark Brandenburg: von den ältesten Zeiten an bis zu Ende des sechszehnten Jahrhunderts* (Berlin: George Jakob Decker, 1783). Gabriele Kaiser (formerly Gabriele Spitzer) published extensively on Thurneysser's life and work, see Gabriele Spitzer, *… und die Spree führt Gold: Leonard Thurneysser zum Thurn, Astrologe – Alchimist – Arzt und Drucker in Berlin des 16. Jahrhunderts* (Berlin: Staatsbibliothek zu Berlin, Beiträge aus der Staatsbibliothek zu Berlin – Preußischer Kulturbesitz 3, 1996); Gabriele Kaiser, "Leonhard Thurneysser zum Thurn (1531–1596) und sein Nachlass in der Staatsbibliothek zu Berlin," in *Renaissance Craftsmen and Humanistic Scholars: Circulation of Knowledge between Portugal and Germany*, edited by Thomas Horst, Marília dos Santos Lopes, and Henrique Leitão (Frankfurt: Peter Lang, 2017), 121–31.
40. He received as steady income (1352 Taler) from his position at the Brandenburg court and from his expertise in analyzing urine samples for the European aristocracy. For further information see Spitzer, *… und die Spree führt Gold*, 23.
41. His estate in Berlin includes the letters he received from 1564–1583 in Berlin, Staatsbibliothek zu Berlin – Preußischer Kulturbesitz, Germ. Fol. 420–426 (provenance: in the Prussian royal library since its foundation in 1661); Berlin, Staatsbibliothek zu Berlin – Preußischer Kulturbesitz, Bor. Fol. 680–687 and 691 (provenance: in the Prussian royal library since its foundation in 1661).
42. Printing, setter, and form cutter. See Spitzer, *… und die Spree führt Gold*, 37–55.

world, as well as healing methods and the human body.[43] On the title page of every section, Thurneysser puts this approach of gathering empirical information into his own words by stressing that the experiences of a traveler will "surpass almost all / studies in academies / and diligence in philosophy."[44] Another docphysician, Nicolaus Müller (dates unkown), with whom Thurneysser corresponded in 1577, mirrored this way of gathering information for practicing medicine by writing that he was a "student in nature."[45] Observing and collecting information becomes Thurneysser's scientific approach. As such, the description of people of color in Lisbon thus takes on the impression of a scientific survey to identify their attributes.

Thurneysser's approach differed from those of other authors of European travel accounts.[46] Contemporary texts of this kind focused on African countries and their inhabitants as commodities that could be exploited economically for European advantage.[47] For example, *Newe unbekanthe landte* from 1508 provides an example for the stark contrast of customary travel accounts in German and Thurneysser's approach.[48] In the preamble to the text, Jobst Ruchamer (1486–1515), the translator of the text from Italian to German, promises "strange wonderful animals,

43. Thurneysser's approach to learning is also discussed in Tobias Bulang, "Die Welterfahrung des Autodidakten: Fremde Länder und Sprachen in den Büchern Leonhard Thurneyssers zum Thurn," *Daphnis* 47 (2017): 510–37
44. "vberlegen fast aller Academiar[um] studijs vnnd fleiß in Philosophia." Germ. Fol. 97, fols. 1r, 111r, 129r.
45. "Schühler in der Natur." Germ. Fol. 421b, fols. 358r–359r.
46. For a suitable comparison see Richard Hakluyt, *The Principal Navigations, Voyages, Traffiques and Discoveries of the English Nation*, Vol. VI (London: James MacLehose and Sons, 1906) [https://www.biodiversitylibrary.org/item/30430#page/11/mode/1up].
47. See for example: Balthasar Springer, *Die Merfart vn(d) erfarung nüwer Schiffung vnd Wege zu viln onerkanten Inseln und Künigreichen, von dem großmechtigen Portugalischen Kunig Emanuel Erforscht ... wie ich, Balthasar Spre(n) ger sollichs selbs [. . .]gesehen vn(d) erfaren habe (etc.)* (Oppenheim, 1509). For the economic impetus for the German journeys to other countries see Christine R. Johnson, *The German Discovery of the World: Renaissance Encounters with the Strange and Marvelous* (Carlottesville, Va: University of Virginia Press, 2009).
48. Montalboddo, *Newe unbekanthe landte.*

birds, delicious trees, spices, several precious stones, pearls, and gold."[49] The text focuses primarily on the economic potential of such a journey, including the possibility of purchasing enslaved people by recounting Alvise Ca'da Mostos's (1432–1483) journey around the African coast in which Ca'da Mosto was given the opportunity to purchase one hundred enslaved people from a king on the West African coast.[50]

Thurneysser's detailed description, in contrast, is primarily concerned with the body. He details the appearance of Africans from head to foot as outlined in section one. He also makes note of signs for possible illnesses when describing the sale of enslaved people.[51] His text is only occasionally interspersed with entries about bartering practices, religion, fertility of the land, and payment methods.[52] The descriptions of habits and behavior primarily aim to characterize the people and not the commodities for trade.

Students may now discuss what focusing on the people means for Thurneysser's understanding of the African diaspora. For Thurneysser, the physical determinates, such as facial features and skin color, characterized people he termed *Mohren* (Moors), *Nigiten* (Blacks), and *Aethiopier* (Ethiopians or Africans).[53] By doing so he presents the appearance, especially skin color, of the African diaspora as unchangeable characteristics through which he defines them. Thurneysser thereby determines racial markers without using the term explicitly.

To convey whether Thurneysser used racial markers for people other than the African diaspora, it is necessary to discuss whether he used the same approach for people from other countries. Unfortunately, in Thurneysser's account of his voyage to Portugal, there is no description of the bodies of people from other nations that students could compare to the detailed analysis with which Thurneysser describes the bodies

49. "seltzame(n) wunderlichen thyren/ geflügeln, köstlichen bawmen/spetzereyen/ mancherley edeln gestayne/ perlen und golde." Germ. Fol. 97, fol. 1v.
50. Germ. Fol. 97, fol. 9v.
51. as quoted in the section above.
52. Germ. Fol. 97, fols. 137r, 137v, 141v, 142r,
53. Germ. Fol. 97, fol. 133v,

of the African diaspora. The miscellaneous section also describes Thurneysser's encounter with Norwegian tradesmen and their unusual rituals, but the tone of this description is entirely different. It describes the hard life of merchants from "Lappia und Pilappia," countries where "nothing grows from the ground."[54] His main concern is to describe the brutal hazing procedures with which every new member of this trade group was confronted with: "many who did not have a very strong nature or physical condition died in the act and were murdered by them."[55] Thurneysser recorded this description of Norwegian tradesmen because they are gruesome and exceptional. This account next to the description of the African diaspora alone highlights that he aimed to address what was to him the unusual nature of the African diaspora, which included people from North Africa and sub-Saharan Africa in Portugal. The motivation of describing unusual characteristics presupposes difference, and therefore produces an underlying implicit bias toward the subject throughout the text.

Students may contextualize Thurneysser's description of the African body further by comparing it to his medical practice in Berlin. As a physician, Thurneysser customarily described female and male bodies intimately. His publications, such as an anatomical study he published in Berlin in 1576, demonstrate that he treated the body in general as a source for empirical information.[56] The bust and stomach of the represented human body (Figure 3) in this publication could be opened and anatomical features removed.[57] Thurneysser's correspondence also reflects his medical approach of providing treatments through an analysis of a patient's body. Frequently, the patients would describe their ailments, and on this basis, Thurneysser would provide an ointment or recommendation. In many

54. "ganndz vnnd gar nichts auß der Erdenn wechst." Germ. Fol. 97, fol. 130v (author's translation).
55. "gar viel, so nicht ser starckher Natur od[er] complexion gewesen, inn dem actu gestorben, vnnd vonn inen vmb das Leben gebracht worden sein." Germ. Fol. 97, fol. 131r.
56. Spitzer, *... und die Spree führt Gold*, 84.
57. Leonhard Thurneysser, *Confirmatio Concertationis* (Berlin, 1576).

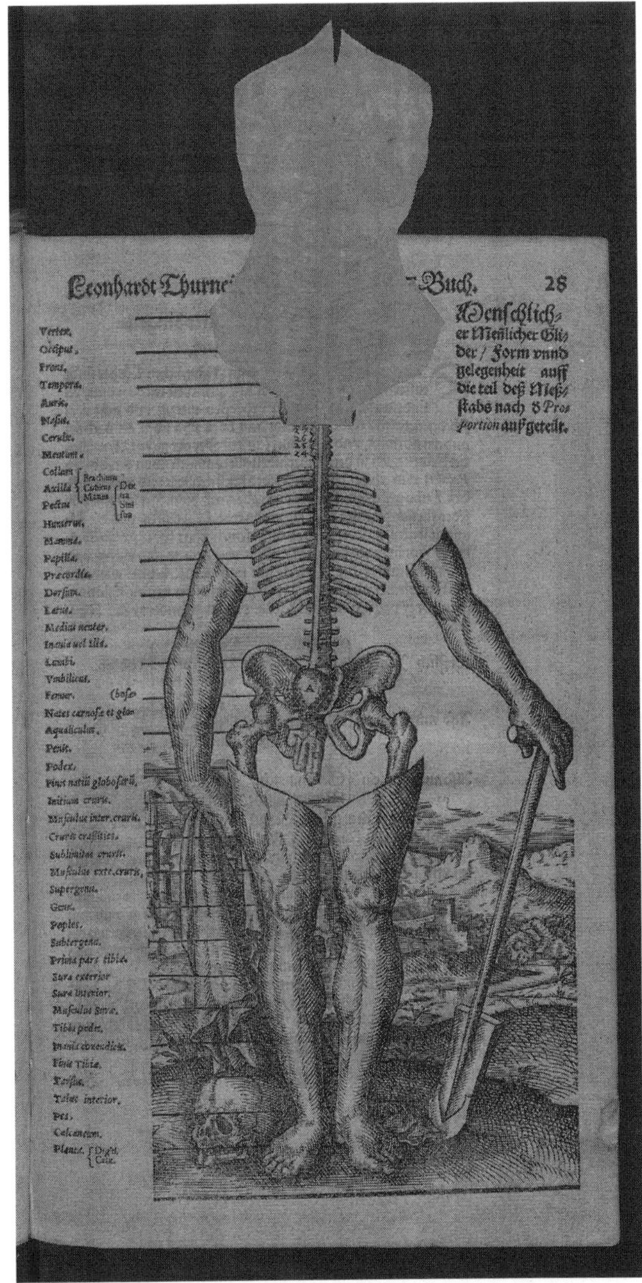

Figure 3. Leonhard Thurneysser, *Confirmatio Concertationis*, 1576, Staatsbibliothek zu Berlin – Preußischer Kulturbesitz; Abteilung Historische Drucke; Signatur: 4" Kc 920 : R, fol. 28r.

instances, they would also send him urine samples,[58] which Thurneysser would analyze. The descriptions included detailed and very private information about the body. One example is a note by an unknown author, found alongside a letter sent in 1577 by a book merchant named Samuel Selfiste (dates unknown). The note details that the writer's wife's "body from below appears firm together with the genitals as well as from the back up to the naval is very swollen and hurts very much."[59] In another, Jacob Maijer (dates unknown), a painter from Austria, describes himself as suffering from the following: "several years after another with sickness and severe stomach pain, weighed down with fever and crying, and when I am rid of the fever and crying, I still always have the mentioned stomach sickness […] and open blisters on me […]."[60] The correspondents also did not hesitate to analyze the sexual lives of others. Such as Anna Bürgermeister (dates unknown), who wrote to Thurneysser explaining that her daughter's husband "could not consummate their marriage" and asked Thurneysser to prescribe a remedy.[61] These insights into his medical practice can show students that Thurneysser's invasive approach to the body of the Africa diaspora matched his general approach to the human body as a physician. It included the analysis of physical details that encroached on an individual's privacy, regardless of race. Thurneysser applied his medical practice to his observation of the Africa diaspora with an implicit bias and one important exception: nowhere else in his medical profession does he analyze skin color as the defining trait for the origin of a person. This indicates an inherent racial bias toward the African diaspora centered on the discussion of skin color that will be explored fully in the next section.

58. For example of a sample sent by Fugginer Ritter, see Germ. Fol. 426, 42.

59. "leibe von undem auff sei hart samptt dem gemecht mit zudem der hintern bis ain der nabell gahr sehrr geschwollen ist und thutt ihr so wehe[…]." Germ. Fol. 421b, 66b.

60. "etliche Jar nach ainander mit krankhait und sond=erlich magen weh fiebern und geweinen bela=den, und so ich gleich vo[n] gemelte[n] fieberein und gewein ledig so hab ich doch stetts gemelte magen krankhaitt […] und auff platzung an mir, […]." Germ. Fol. 426, fols. 119r–119v.

61. "die eheliche pflicht nicht pflegen kan." Germ. Fol. 425, fol. 246r.

Degrading Tropes and Stereotypes

As students may already have found when discussing the content and context of Thurneysser's text in sections one and two, his description of the body of a person of color in the African diaspora in Lisbon goes beyond the mere sensory observation and forms explicit judgments.[62] Students may observe that parallels exist between Thurneysser's description of the body of a person of color and his description of the assessment slave purchasers made of the bodies of enslaved people being sold at the slave market. He articulates his descriptions of people of color as things he had seen and touched. His senses reveal the nature of their bodies, habits, and feelings. Thurneysser progresses from head to feet. He also describes touch and sight as the instruments used at the slave market to assess the price of a person. As quoted in the first section, he details the brutal treatment of enslaved people and writes of the examinations of male and female reproductive organs by the slave masters which he had detailed and assessed in his preceding description. The process of observation taken by Thurneysser mirrors the objectifying and dehumanizing approach of people in Lisbon purchasing enslaved men and women of color.

Students may discover that Thurneysser's account lists exaggerated bodily features as generalizations to describe the physical appearance of a person of color. Black people are described as possessing "strangely curly" hair,[63] "flat and depressed noses,"[64] "an uncommonly large and ugly gap or mouth hole,"[65] and "very white teeth."[66] Students can compare this description with the image and text in *Four Books on Human Proportion* and an appended essay on aesthetics by famous artist Albrecht Dürer (1471–1528), which was published in 1528 about thirty years prior to the

62. For an overview of the Black presence in renaissance Germany see contributions in Mischa Honeck, Martin Klimke and Anne Kuhlmann, eds., *Germany and the Black Diaspora: Points of Contact 1250–1914* (Oxford and New York: Berghahn, 2013).
63. "wunderlichen krauß." Germ. Fol. 97, fol. 134r.
64. "nidere oder eingetruckhte Nasenn." Germ. Fol. 97, fol. 134v.
65. "ein gros vnnd scheützlich orificium das ist Munndtloch." Germ. Fol. 97.
66. "gar weisse Zeene." Germ. Fol. 97, fol. 135r.

genesis of Thurneysser's text.[67] In this treatise, the artist outlines faces in profile of different proportions. One such face (Figure 4) displays similar characteristics with exaggerated bodily features to those described in Thurneysser's text. Students may observe that Thurneysser explicitly formulates an aesthetic judgment when describing facial physiognomies. He writes about the eyes that "they open them horribly wide and slowly […] when they are alone" and "the noses being built at their tips with a repugnant or ugly wideness."[68] His description of the body uses more neutral terms and even some positively inclined adjectives such as "strong" and "solid."[69] The dichotomy between the face and the body of a person of color also appears in Dürer's *Essay on Aesthetics*.[70] Dürer draws a line between the face of a person of color as ugly and the body as beautiful.[71] Thurneysser's aesthetic judgment of these goes beyond his own medical approach and reveals his biased judgment that was not free from general stereotypes. Dürer's publication and Thurneysser's account both present stereotypical facial features associated with the appearance of a person of color in the German-speaking regions of sixteenth-century Europe. Although the term race is not explicitly used by either of these authors, it is present in their general stereotypes associated with the face and body of a person of African descent.

67. Written by Albrecht Dürer 1518–1520 and published in 1528. Albrecht Dürer, *HJeriñ sind begriffen vier biicher von menschlicher Proportion/ durch Albrechten D[ue]rer von Nurenberg erfunden vnd be/schriben/ z[uo] nutz allen denen/ so z[uo] diser kunst lieb tragen* (Nuremberg: Hieronymus Andreae, 1528).
68. "so sperren sie sich gar grewlich weitt vnd langsam vonneinannder […] wann sie aber allain sein" and "die Naasen an irer Spitzen inn einer scheützlichenn oder heßlichen Breitte gestaltet ist." Germ. Fol. 97, fols. 134r–134v.
69. "starckh" and "fast." Germ. Fol. 97, fol. 136v.
70. Written by Albrecht Dürer 1518–1520 and published in 1528. Transcribed and brought into modern German, see Berthold Hinz, *Albrecht Dürer: Vier Bücher von menschliche Proportionen* (1528): *mit einem Katalog der Holzschnitte* (Berlin: Akademie Verlag, 2011), 229.
71. Hinz, *Albrecht Dürer*.

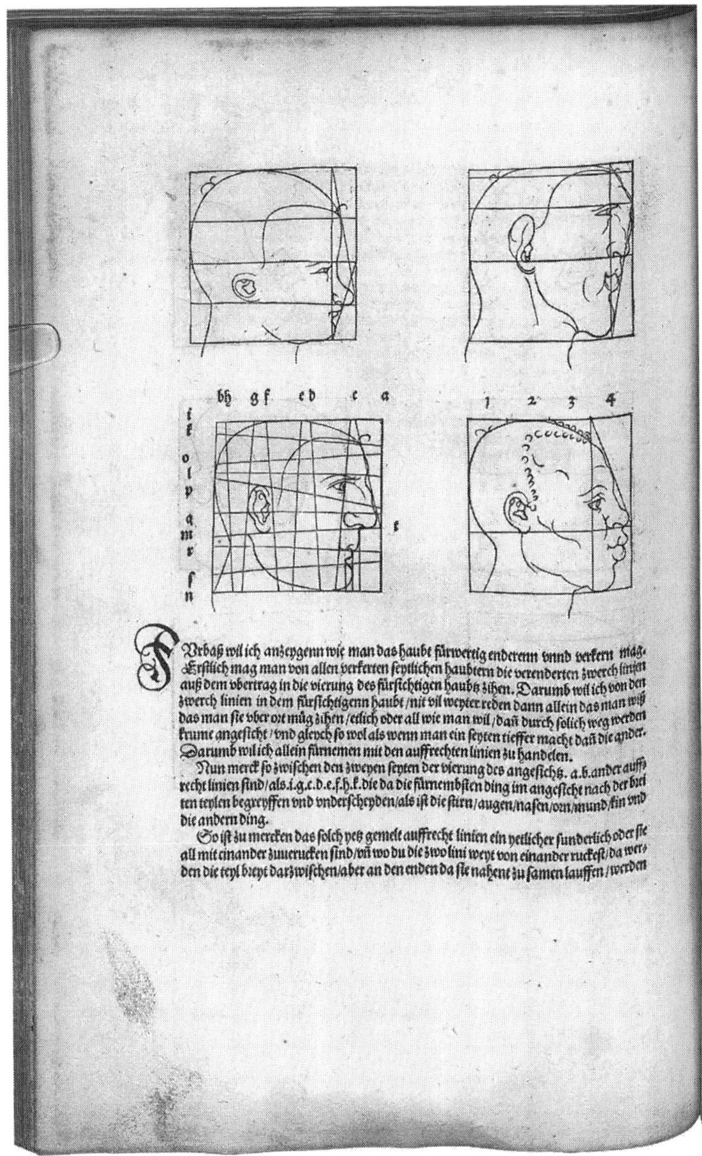

FVrbaß wil ich anzeygenn wie man das haubt fürwertig enderenn vnnd verkern mag.
Erstlich mag man von allen verkerten seytlichen haubtern die verenderten zwerch linien
auß dem vbertrag in die vierung des fürsichtigen haubts zihen. Darumb wil ich von den
zwerch linien in dem fürsichtigenn haubt / nit vil weyter reden dann allein das man wiß
das man sie vber ort müg zihen / etlich oder all wie man wil / dañ durch solich weg werden
krume angesicht / vnd gleych so wol als wenn man ein seyten tieffer macht dañ die ander.
Darumb wil ich allein furnemen mit den auffrechten linien zu handelen.
Nun merck so zwischen den zweyen seyten der vierung des angesichts. a.b. ander auffrecht linien sind / als. i.g.c.d.e.f.h.k. die da die fürnembsten ding im angesicht nach der dri-
ten teylen begreyffen vnd vnderscheyden / als ist die stirn / augen / nasen / orn / mund / kin vnd
die andern ding.
So ist zu mercken das solch yetz gemelt auffrecht linien ein yetlicher sunderlich oder sie
all mit einander zuuerucken sind / vñ wo du die zwo lini weyt von einander ruckest / da werden die teyl breyt darzwischen / aber an den enden da sie nahent zu samen lauffen / werden

Figure 4. Albrecht Dürer, *Four Books on Human Proportion*, 1528, Nuremberg, Hieronymus Andreae, Bayerische Staatsbibliothek, Signatur: Rar. 612, fol. 90v.

Students may identify strong emotions and a lascivious nature as further tropes for habits that characterize people of color in such accounts.[72] The earlier-mentioned account of Alvise Ca'da Mosto describes polygamy on several occasions.[73] The count of Budomel whom he meets and befriends likes to "sleep with the maidens, as well as with his wives. And his wives do not regard such [behavior] as wrong/ as it is often the tradition/ This is why the count often changes accommodation."[74] He goes on to describe the men and women as "very unchaste."[75] The account of Jan Huygen van Linschoten (1563–1611) published in 1597 utilizes a similar description as *Newe unbekanthe landte*: "Their wives are very unchaste, especially with [men from] foreign nations and they do not think of it as a disgrace."[76] None of these authors specifies whether their descriptions arise from firsthand knowledge or observation. They thus reproduce the trope of a hypersexual and polygamous society inhabiting the African continent throughout the sixteenth century. These tropes are present in Thurneysser's description of the hypersexual nature of women of color living in Lisbon. Although this type of comment may still fall within his medical domain, as evidenced by the example of his letters mentioned above, his judgment of their presumed social practices as a hypersexual society, which he describes as "unchaste" and "impertinent," falls outside of his professional opinion. It depends on Thurneysser's moral framework (and the general moral framework in Christian Europe), and shows that racial thought connecting physical characteristics with judgments of their habits already existed in the early modern world.

72. For an analysis of how sixteenth-century travel accounts highlighted the sexual nature of people encountered in South America see Peter Mason, *Deconstructing America: Representations of the Other* (London: Routledge, 1990).

73. Montalboddo, *Newe unbekanthe landte*, fols. 8r, 10r.

74. "schlaffen bey den mayden/ als bey seinen weybern. Und achten solches seyne weyber nicht fur unrecht/ so es der massen der gebrauche ist/ Und deswegen verwandelt der fürst offt die herberge." Montalboddo, *Newe unbekanthe landte*, fol.10r

75. "vest unkewsch." Montalboddo, *Newe unbekanthe landte*.

76. "Ihre Weiber sind sehr unkeusch und insonderheit mit frembter Nation/ und man helt es da im Land fur keine schande." Jan Huygen van Linschoten, *Ander Theil der Orientalischen || Jndien* (Frankfurt: Johan Saur, 1597), 10.

Thurneysser brackets these unscientific descriptions with a broad display of contemporary scientific arguments regarding the origin of black skin, thus giving an air of legitimacy to the entirety of his observations. He shows a desire to understand the mystery of black skin, which "is almost hidden to human reason."[77] This desire becomes a central point toward the end of his account. Framed as a scientific challenge, Thurneysser elaborately formulates the "cause of the swarthiness or blackness." [78] Thurneysser debunks a widespread assumption that black skin is caused by the sun by pointing out that this cannot be so because "they are born from their mother's womb as black, and that not only in their countries, but also in *Lusitania Hispania*, and all other places where they have been led."[79] Instead, he concludes that next to the sun blackening the skin and altering the "semen" of the parents, the color came from the "property of the same soil," and "the principal reason for their blackness sprouts or flows from a certain [combination of] position[s] of a number of stars, which have a special relationship with said countries."[80] Thurneysser thus lists astrology as a reason for black skin, which inevitably categorizes a geographic area by divine creation. Furthermore, students may consider that the theoretical basis for Thurneysser's practice in medicine was also based in

77. "ist mennschlicher Vernuunft fast verborgenn." Germ. Fol. 97, fol. 139v.
78. "Vrsach der Nigredinis oder Schwertze." Germ. Fol. 97, fol. 140r
79. "sie werden also schwartz vom Muter Leib gebohrenn, vnd zwar nicht allein inn iren Lanndtschafften, sunderen auch in *Lusitania Hispania*, vnnd allen annderen dahir sie gefürret warden." Germ. Fol. 97, fol. 139v. Ancient sources including Ptolemey's *Geography* and Ovid's *Metamorphoses* associate the heat of the sun with skin color. The Flemish cartographer Abraham Ortelius disputed this in his atlas *Theatrum Orbis Terrarum* (Antwerp: Aegidius Coppens, 1570). See Jean Michel Massing, *The Image of the Black in Western Art: From the "Age of Discovery" to the Age of Abolition: Europe and the World Beyond*, vol. III.2 of The Image of the Black in Western Art, edited David Bindman and Henry Louis Gates, Jr. (Cambridge, MA: The Belknap Press of Harvard University Press, 2011), 65, 79; Davies, *Renaissance Ethnography and the Invention of the Human*, 170–71.
80. "Sperma," "Proprietet desselbigen Erdreichs," and "daß sollcher irer nigredinis fürnehmer Vrsach, auß einem gewiss[en] potitu etzlicher stellarum, so mit denselbigenn Lennderen, auch ein besunder Familiaritet habenn, entrpriesse oder herfliesse." Germ. Fol. 97, fols. 140r–141r.

Christian theology, as Peter Morys has argued.[81] His reasons for black skin take it to be an unchangeable characteristic based on the properties of the respective countries of origin. In this it still remains different from today's definition of black skin as a hereditary characteristic. Although Thurneysser does not note explicit moral or theological judgments for his observations of black skin,[82] he presents his arguments within a scientific context indebted to contemporary theological principals, and which lent the work particular legitimacy.

Lastly, anecdotal evidence as part of his description of a Norwegian who's skin is covered in soot brings to light and can show students the bias Thurneysser possessed in regards to black skin. The first challenge for northern tradesmen as part of the hazing rituals, which Thurneysser describes in the same section as his description of the African diaspora, commences in such a fashion where "they first hang him into a dirty chimney or wall with his feet into the air they let him hang there for several hours."[83] Underneath him, they burn dead animals until he "totally stinks of carcass, yes, that he resembles more a black moor than a white Norwegian."[84] This comparison to a person of color does not only pertain to the skin color, but, in connection with his comment of smelling like rotting carcasses, reveals Thurneysser's general negative use of the reference to a person of color in this context.

81. Peter Morys, *Medizin und Pharmazie in der Kosmologie Leonhard Thurneissers zum Thurn* (1531–1596) (Husum: Matthiesen Verlag, Abhandlungen zu Geschichte der Medizin und der Naturwissenschaften 43, 1982), 25.

82. Thurneysser's faith was driven more by circumstance rather than a fierce belief. He was a Lutheran but later converted to Catholicism to integrate into the society in Rome, where he resided from 1584 to 1590. See Spitzer, *... und die Spree führt Gold*, 13–14; Paul H. Boerlin, *Leonhard Thurneysser als Auftraggeber: Kunst im Dienst der Selbsdarstellung zwischen Humanismus und Barock* (Basel: Birkhäuser Verlag, 1976), 27.

83. "hang[en] sie denselbigenn erstlich inn einen vnsauberenn Scharstein oder Feürmaur, bey den Füsse inn die Höche, vnnd lassen in allda etzliche Stund[en] henngen, [...]." Germ. Fol. 97, fols. 132r.

84. "gantz vnd gar wie das Aas stinnckhe, ja, daß er vielmer einem schwartzenn Mohren, dann weissen Norttweger enlich sey." Ibid.

Pseudoscientific Racism and Historical Record

Stereotypical facial features, an excessive amount of strength, ambivalence to pain, a hypersexual nature, and other tropes expressed by Thurneysser in his descriptions of Africans exist to this day. Studying sixteenth-century sources such as Thurneysser's text shows that twentieth-century racism does not exist in a vacuum, but that it is based on a long tradition of bias and tropes that predate the Enlightenment. Only by reconstructing the history of racial thought may one come to understand the processes that produced implicit racism and racist tropes. This paper offers an important contribution to researching Thurneysser and the formation of race in the early modern period. Deconstructing his text allows students to study race in the early modern world.

Thurneysser's unique description shows that he used a pseudoscientific approach based on the collection of empirical information to cultivate definitions and characteristics for people of African descent in Lisbon with an underlying implicit bias. He associates these characteristics with tropes and judgments of their habits and behavior, thereby formulating racist categories that connect these behavioral markers with physical markers. A concept of race, although Thurneysser does not use the term explicitly, where physical attributes define the social character of a person of color, underlies his observations. The uniqueness of Thurneysser's text may call into question whether his description formulated a widely disseminated view of the African diaspora in Lisbon. The lack of comparable descriptions also means that it is not possible to answer this question. I can conclude that while his pseudoscientific approach to such a description may be unique, the tropes are common in comparable contemporary accounts of the sixteenth century. Connecting scientific theory and common tropes was an important step in the formation of race. Thurneysser's text can offer a first insight into this process.

This paper also frames the study of race formation and tropes in early modern sources in their particular historic context. It looks at a range of evidence gained from them. A sixteenth-century travel account never has just one perspective. Thurneysser's text is a rare historical record of the life of the African diaspora and the slave trade in Lisbon, it is the most extensive example of a pseudoscientific exploration of the body of a person of color by a sixteenth-century physician known today, and it contains implicit and explicit biases and tropes in its description of people of African descent in sixteenth-century Lisbon. Studying his text allows students to discuss the value of such historical records in light of the bias they also contain.

Discussion Questions

1. What kind of definitions of race exist? How can we think of race historically? (See further reading.)
2. What is the difference between the pseudoscientific racism discussed in this chapter, and what we call scientific racism?
3. To what extent does Leonard Thurneysser's text reflect the opinions of his contemporaries?

Suggestions for Further Reading

Davis, David. "Constructing Race. A reflection." *The William and Mary Quarterly* 54 no. 1 (1997): 7–18.

Goldenberg, David M. *The Curse of Ham: Race and Slavery in Early Judaism, Christianity, and Islam*. Princeton: Princeton University Press, 2005.

Heng, Geraldine. *The Invention of Race in the European Middle Ages*. Cambridge: Cambridge University Press, 2018.

Murphy, Hannah. "Re-writing race in early modern European medicine." *History Compass* 19 no. 11 (2021): e12692.

Strickland, Debra Higgs. "Monstrosity and Race in the Late Middle Ages." In *The Ashgate Research Companion to Monsters and the Monstrous*, edited by Asa Simon Mittman with Peter J. Dendle, 365–386. 2nd Edition. New York: Routledge, 2016.

Settler Colonialism, Families, and Racialized Thinking: Casta Painting in Latin America

DANA LEIBSOHN AND BARBARA E. MUNDY

The history of race and of racialized thinking took a distinctive turn when Europeans became settler colonists in the Americas after 1492. So decisive were these changes that they still inflect thinking about identity, image-making, and family histories today. Consider the digital print created in 1998 by the artist Iñigo Manglano-Ovalle. Part of a series, collectively named *The Garden of Delights*, the panels of the triptych each show an enlarged scan of a DNA sample (figure 1).[1] These samples came from individuals named in the image's title: *Glenn, Dario and Tyrone*, all of whom made willing donations of their biomatter for Manglano-Ovalle's project. For the purposes of this artwork, the trio chose to be grouped as a "family." The triptych thereby riffs on the traditional idea of a family portrait: each individual appears not as they look but as "they really are" — at least in contemporary genetic terms.

1. The series, of forty-eight individual prints arranged into sixteen triptychs, is named after Hieronoymous Bosch's sixteenth-century triptych, *The Garden of Earthly Delights*. For his project, Manglano-Ovalle not only enlarged the DNA scans, he accentuated their color patterns and mounted the prints on acrylic panels approximately five feet in height (not quite life size). See Ron Platt, ed., *Iñigo Manglano-Ovalle: The Garden of Delights* (Winston-Salem, NC: Southeastern Center for Contemporary Art, 1998). For a description of this triptych: https://www.guggenheim.org/artwork/10464.

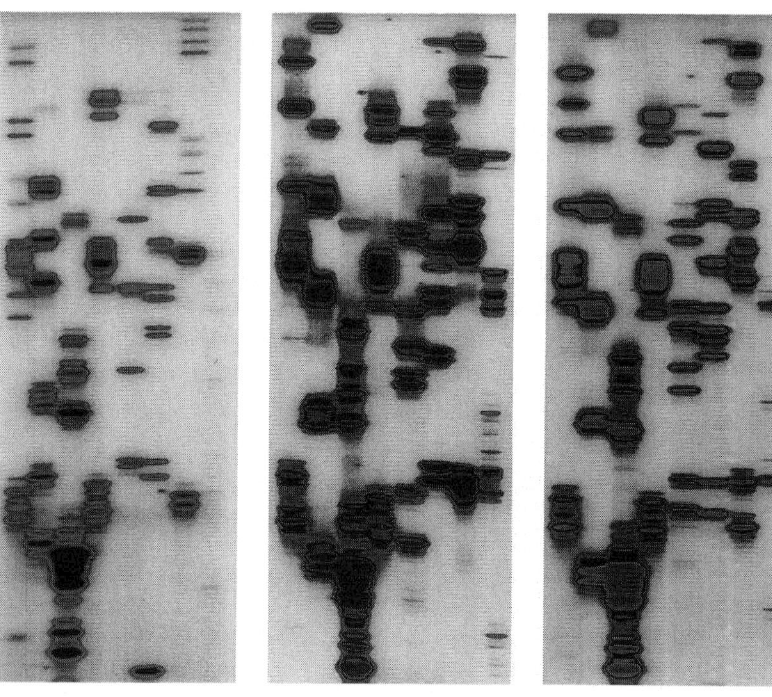

Figure 1. Iñigo Manglano-Ovalle, *Glenn, Dario and Tyrone*, 1998, three chromogenic prints face-mounted to acrylic, 152.4 x 58.4 x 3.2 cm, Guggenheim Museum of Art, New York City, Copyright Iñigo Manglano-Ovalle. Photograph: The Solomon R. Guggenheim Foundation / Art Resource, NY, ART457106. Reproduced by permission.

As a family portrait, *Glenn, Dario and Tyrone* invites deeper thinking about the persistent ideas produced by Euro-American histories of race, using some of the tools that art history offers to interpret visual works of the past and the present. On one register, the digital print references social identities and forms of belonging that individuals can choose to enact and embody. That is, they are largely performative: the title gives personal names, and the composition sets Glenn, Dario, and Tyrone alongside the others they chose as family, people whose genes they do not necessarily share. On another register, this artwork taps into conventional ideas about genetics. The use of DNA to represent Glenn, Dario, and

Tyrone tethers the group portrait to the hard "facts" of biology, and in this, the artwork asks its viewers to question whether aspects of identity are immutable. Since the artwork offers no mimetic imagery (that is, no images of faces or bodies), it is impossible to know how Glenn, Dario, and Tyrone look. Nothing is shown of their complexion or height, hair color, or musculature; nothing reveals how these three people dress as they move through the world. Instead, in viewing their DNA scans, cues to their uniqueness in the world, we glimpse something more private and personal. Read in this way, the work of art seems to reinforce a well-known racialized logic: chosen social identities do not erase the biological histories encoded in one's chromosomes.

This is not, however, the only interpretation this work of art allows. All of the identities that its subjects, the Glenn, Dario, and Tyrone of the title, could claim, be they biological, ethical, or performative, derive from histories of racialized thinking. Manglano-Ovalle was also thinking of the visible forms of that history, in that he took inspiration from eighteenth-century *casta* paintings (*cuadros de casta*, in Spanish) made in New Spain, the part of the Spanish Americas roughly coterminous with Mexico and Central America today.[2] These paintings, usually fashioned of oil paint on stretched canvas, depict family groupings of father, mother and child.[3] In this, the painting *Español y Mestiza, producen Castiza* [Spaniard and Mestiza produce *Castiza*], by José Joaquín Magón, c. 1770, is typical (figure 2).

2. In this essay, the "Spanish Americas" refers to those parts of North and South America and the Philippines under Habsburg and Bourbon control, from roughly 1520 to 1820.
3. The scholarship on *casta* painting is extensive, and growing. For a range of perspectives and a selection of foundational works, see bibliography.

Figure 2. José Joaquín Magón, #2. *Español y Mestiza, producen Castiza* [Spaniard and Mestiza produce Castiza], c. 1770, oil on canvas, 115 x 141 cm, Museo Nacional de Antropología, Madrid, Spain. Photograph: José Pérez Pérez. Reproduced by permission.

Here the painter depicts and names each figure as "types" rather than individuals. The label designating their social caste (thus the name *casta* in Spanish) appears in a cartouche at the upper edge of the scene: 2, *Español y Mestiza, producen Castiza.* This painting, like the Manglano-Ovalle DNA prints, would have been one of a set, often a set of sixteen. To show the full extent of the *casta* "types," figure 3 offers a rare surviving example of a *casta* painting that includes all sixteen within the space of single canvas.[4] It was created by Ignacio María Barreda in 1777 (figure 3).

4. While some *casta* series are still intact, most museum collections have partial sets or individual paintings.

Figure 3. Ignacio María Barreda, *Casta Painting*, 1777, oil on canvas, 77 x 49 cm, Real Academia Española de la Lengua, Madrid, Spain. Image: Wikimedia Commons, Public Domain.

As viewers moved from the first painting in a *casta* series to the last, the imagery would show the permutations that could occur when members of the three primary social "castes" of the period – labeled *español* [Spaniard], *indio* [Indian], and *negro* [Black] – produced children.[5] Typically, series of *castas* show those labeled as *español* or *española* as being better dressed, and enjoying leisure activies rather than working. In figure 3, for instance, the leisure of the four families at the top of the canvas, each of which includes a person labeled as *español* or *española*, contrasts markedly with the laboring members of other castes in the rows below. In the bottom row of the left column, a family fight erupts. Figure 2 is the second panel of a different *casta* series, and in it, a male of Iberian origins (labeled as *español*) and a woman of Indigenous and Iberian parentage (labeled as *mestiza*) have produced a child labeled as *castiza*. As Magón renders it, the daughter's skin color appears slightly darker than that of her father but lighter than that of her mother. This was not the painter's invention, rather, he depended upon a representational system and racialized thinking that was common in *casta* paintings: since the child's combined ancestry would have been calculated at one-quarter Indigenous and three-quarters Spanish, she has been depicted as lighter than her mother but darker than her father. Whether fashioned by painters of local renown or those of mediocre skill, *casta* paintings suggested to their viewers that ethnic designations in New Spain could be distinguished by skin color. These artworks also tied wealth and social standing to biological ancestry. And because of this, *casta* images fueled a version of the racialized imaginaries of their era.

In referencing *casta* paintings, the contemporary artist Manglano-Ovalle envisioned a genealogy of artworks, that is, he was thinking about how his own work descended from, and was indebted to, earlier portraits

5. *Casta* was not the sole category used to distinguish among different social groups. *Calidad* (quality) was another dominant term, which "transcended phenotype by revolving around questions of individual status and the behaviors appropriate to different social ranks," Joanne Rappaport, *The Disappearing Mestizo, Configuring Difference in the Colonial New Kingdom of Granada* (Durham and London: Duke University Press, 2014), 7.

of families. In this essay, we follow his lead, exploring genealogies of racialized thinking as they were expressed in the Spanish Americas in images. Central to our claims about the history of race is that visual imagery, especially imagery focused on family lines, played a crucial role (and indeed, still does) in both articulating and obscuring the instabilities that come into play as human bodies are racialized. The term "race" may have developed in the early modern period, but it was not generally used in the Spanish Americas. Yet, some of the themes that figure most prominently in constructions of race, at least as now recognized, found expression in this visual culture. In what follows, we enlist the term "racialized" to underscore how varied are the historical processes that people, today, associate with the concept of race. We do not believe that the *casta* system of the Spanish Americas was the only precursor to today's constructions of race.[6] Rather, as Manglano-Ovalle's print suggests, elements of the past filter into the present, but they never come unchanged (a DNA scan is not a *casta* painting, after all). Central to this essay, then, are the ways in which family portraits and *casta* paintings sustain — but also challenge — ideas of difference and belonging, sociality and biology. Using genealogy as a lens, along with the interpretive tools of art history, we seek to better understand how habits of racialized thinking and practices of visual evocation supported each other over time in colonial Latin America, a place that was a crucible of ethnic mixing.

Colonialism and the Renaissance World

The Americas, we must emphasize, are crucial for any consideration of "race in the Renaissance" because the colonial experiences that unfolded there transformed the early modern world. Western European decisions to cross the Atlantic in the fifteenth century and, upon arrival, to extract wealth (silver, gold, dyestuffs) via human labor led to dramatic relocations that remodeled the globe. Some travel, largely from the Iberian peninsula

6. For the legacy of castes in modern Latin America from the point view of sociology, see Mara Loveman, *National Colors: Racial Classification and the State in Latin America* (New York: Oxford University Press, 2014).

and other parts of Europe, was voluntary. By the mid-sixteenth century, however, many who came to the Spanish Americas were brought by force from Africa, especially west and central Africa via the massive expansion of the slave trade, and from Asia, via the Philippines. This global movement of human bodies fueled the development of colonial societies, particularly urban societies, and contributed to unprecedented linguistic and cultural diversity. Well before the sixteenth century drew to a close, cities in the Spanish Americas — Lima, Mexico City, Santo Domingo, and Potosí — could be counted among the most cosmopolitan and ethnically complex settings of early modernity.

Urban experiences would not have been unfamiliar as urbanism had long been important in the Americas. Under both Inka rulers (c. 1438–1534) and their Mexica counterparts (who are often better known today as the Aztecs, c. 1345–1521), bustling, multi-ethnic cities functioned as economic engines, driving sophisticated imperial ambitions. These cities were contemporaneous with Florence, led by Medici scions, Istanbul, ruled by Ottoman sultans after 1453, and Beijing, steered into prosperity by Ming emperors. And while America's cosmopolitan history does not usually come first to mind when one thinks of the Renaissance, it probably should. When Hernando Cortés (1485–1547) and his troops and allies wrested the Mexica capital of Tenochtitlan from Motecuhzoma (c. 1466–1520) and Francisco Pizarro (1478–1541) and his soldiers took the Inka capital of Cuzco from Atawalpa (c. 1502–1533), their regicides and brutal tactics established patterns of violence that spread rapidly across the Americas. This is one implication of Walter Mignolo's now familiar phrase, "the darker side of the Renaissance."[7] Of course, military campaigns were not the only force in the transformation from Abya Yala, Tawantinsuyu, and Aztlán into "the Americas," and Indigenous histories should not — in fact, cannot — be written only in relation to Europe. Yet the unchecked practices of enslavement, the violent overthrow of Indigenous empires, the imposition of religious beliefs by the Catholic church and the economic cravings of the Habsburg rulers that drove them to occupy foreign lands,

7. Walter Mignolo, *The Darker Side of the Renaissance: Literacy, Territoriality, and Colonization* (Ann Arbor: Michigan University Press, 1995).

gave rise to patterns of oppression and social reordering whose effects persist. Eventually, settler colonialism fostered new patterns of belonging and exclusion that, often, were most keenly felt in cities of the Spanish Americas. This essay presumes that neither settler colonialism in the Americas nor the racialization that it fostered were ever just American stories, nor are they strictly early modern histories: the "Americanization" of the "Renaissance world" forced understandings of the globe to shift fundamentally.

The projects of settler colonialism radically altered the daily life of millions of people, from the island of Cuba to the highlands of Bolivia, as disease, enslavement, famine and war took the lives of thousands upon thousands of Indigenous people in the first decades after Habsburg emperors laid claim to the Americas. However, it was in the cities that foreign ambitions made some of their strongest visible marks. This can be seen in architecture and urban planning. Even more profound were new forms of sociability. Under the imperial rule of Charles V (1516–1556) and his son Phillip II (1556–1598), enslaved people — from Africa and India, Southeast Asia, and the Philippines — and their descendants labored in and learned to share urban spaces, with each other and with those who claimed Indigenous or Iberian ancestry. Urban residents met face to face in colonial courts, watched each other dress in finery for Catholic festival processions, and bargained for goods in markets. By 1600, people with complex ancestral ties regularly courted and married; they also had extramarital relationships (whether coercive or not) and, along the way, bore and raised children. While many early modern cities drew people from around the world, creating cosmopolitan communities, it is our contention that the complexity and extent of ethnic mixing in what is today Latin America, both physically and conceptually, set this region's history apart. Within the Habsburg American empire, settler colonialism demanded many levels of social control to build extractive economies. Central to this colonial project was the social recognition of ethnic difference, and the concomitant creation of new hierarchies based on ethnicity. One ideal enlisted consistently in the project of settler colonialism was the monogamous family, and with it, representations of genealogical connections that bolstered ideological positions that it was "natural" for some people to belong together, but not others. As we understand early modern history, embedded in the naturalized monogamous family is a dominant thread of racialized thinking that later gets twisted into concepts of race. These ideas were made present via the visual culture of the period.

Family Ties: Painting Genealogies in the Sixteenth Century

Indigenous people living in central Mexico in the 1540s and 1550s, along with enslaved people transported forcibly from Africa and Asia, remembered and commemorated their forebears and lineage through acts and images that built upon centuries of oral tradition and ritual practice. Painted imagery created by Africans and Afro-descendant communities does not survive in great quantities from the early colonial period. Surviving Indigenous manuscript scenes of rulers, their children, and their ancestors, however, represent an important form of memory-keeping. Because political and territorial rights were shifting dramatically in the mid- to late-sixteenth century, such paintings might be kept locally; others were presented in legal contexts, some being made expressly for that purpose. Nearly all of the works known today rely upon modes of image-making with diverse origins. This is the case with the ink-on-paper painting that presents the family tree of Gaspar Antonio Chi (c. 1532–1575), a well-educated Maya man and member of a powerful family in the Yucatán (figure 4).

Having been taught Catholic doctrine and practice by friars in the town of Maní, and having worked with Spanish officials as an interpreter, Chi knew more than a little about Christian forms of painting and European writing. A man of noble descent who would later become the *bacab* [leader] of Maní, Chi created many images in the sixteenth century that charted his family's claims to status and territory.[8] The image shown here depicts his family tree by reworking the Biblical theme of the Tree of Jesse. Typically, Trees of Jesse show this Old Testament prophet reclining at the bottom of the image. A great tree grows from his crotch and his descendants

8. On Gapar Antonio Chi's social and political roles, see C. Cody Barteet, "Maya Heraldic Arms: the Merging of Spanish and Maya Visual Cultures in the Memorial Shield to the Massacre at Otzmal," *Konsthistorisk tidskrift/Journal of Art History* (2017): 1–22.

Figure 4. Gaspar Antonio Chi, *Genealogical Tree of the Xiu Family*, c. 1550–1560, ink on European paper, 41 x 31 cm, Tozzer Library Special Collections, Harvard University, Cambridge. Reproduced by permission.

are pictured on its branches. At the top of this genealogical tree is Jesus. Here, instead of representing Jesse as the progenitor, Chi paints his Maya ancestor, Tutul Xiu. As the progenitor, he rests upon one elbow and holds an Indigenous-style fan in the other hand. The leg tattoos are familiar from Maya tradition, although upon Tutul Xiu's head perches a crown that resembles those worn in central Mexico by Mexica (but not Maya) royalty. Since the image has deteriorated over time, the name of the woman dressed in an Indigenous-style garment who kneels beside Tutul Xiu is no longer known, although she may well have been his wife. Along with its direct biblical reference, this painting enlists metaphors drawn from the plant world: a tree grows from the male ancestral body; its branches bear dozens of blossoms, each with the name of Tutul Xiu's lineal descendants. One of them is Ix Kukil, the mother of the painter, Gaspar Antonio Chi. This painted work, kept by Chi and later generations in Maní, makes it clear that knowing one's blood relations was an important part of colonial thinking in the Spanish Americas — and not only among settlers from Europe. As if to reaffirm the point, in the foreground of the scene two crossed deer legs, set aflame, smolder in front of a cave, a likely reference to ancient Maya rites for commemorating ancestors.[9]

Chi's image makes the connections among family members seem to be naturally occuring processes, like the growth of a plant, so that all who belong to his family are rooted in the body of a single, primordial ancestor. The biological metaphor fuses with one that is Christological, since, in Christian belief, the Tree of Jesse gives rise to the Christian savior, connecting Chi's family line to the right and natural order of things. Not all sixteenth-century family portraits, however, invested so heavily in natural and religious metaphors. Not even in Europe. A painting from the mid-sixteenth century of King Henry VIII of England (1491–1547) and his relatives, offers a case in point (figure 5).

9. Connie Cortez, "New Dance, Old Xius: The 'Xiu Family Tree' and Maya Cultural Continuities after European Contact," in *Heart of Creation: The Mesoamerican World and the Legacy of Linda Schele*, ed. Andrea Stone (Tuscaloosa and London: University of Alabama Press, 2002), 201–15; Dana Leibsohn and Barbara E. Mundy, "Genealogical Tree of the Xiu Family, in *Vistas: Visual Culture in Spanish America, 1520–1820*. http://www.fordham.edu/vistas, 2015.

Figure 5. Painter whose name is currently unknown, *The Family of Henry* VIII, c. 1545, oil on canvas, 144.5 x 355.9 cm, Hampton Court Palace, RCIN 405796, Royal Collection Trust / Copyright Her Majesty Queen Elizabeth II 2021. Reproduced by permission.

The monarch, seated on his throne with his stockinged legs splayed, anchors the scene. His body aligns with the central axis and serves as pivot for the painting, as other figures have been positioned like parentheses to frame him. Closest to Henry is his third wife, Jane Seymour (1508–1537), and their son, Edward (1537–1553), Henry's first and only surviving legitimate male child. Farther from the king and his heir and mother, stand two of Henry's daughters. Neither of these women is the child of Jane Seymour; rather, one is Mary (1516–1558), daughter of Catherine of Aragon (1485–1536), Henry's first wife; the other is Elizabeth (1533–1603), daughter of Anne Boleyn (c. 1501–1536), his second wife. Toward the edges of the painting, in the outdoor scenes, are members of the court, not relatives. Along with proximity to the monarch, the contrast between interior and exterior space offers a visual cue as to who "belongs" to Henry's family line. While the meaning of some of the painted imagery in this scene is still debated by scholars, the central theme of the painting is crystal clear: this is the family of the king, potential heirs to his throne.[10]

10. On debates about the painting's iconography, see Christopher Lloyd and Simon Thurley. *Henry* VIII: *Images of a Tudor King*. London: Phaidon Press Limited, 1990; Kent Rawlinson, "Architectural Culture and Royal Image at the Henrician Court," in *Henry* VIII *and the Court: Art, Politics and Performance*, edited by Thomas Betteridge and Suzannah Lipscomb (Burlington, VT: Ashgate Publishing Company, 2013); Hampton

At first glance, both Chi's family tree and the portrait of Henry VIII and his family stake claims about the politics of lineage that seem to shed little light on questions of race. This is because the paintings draw upon and reaffirm normative habits of thinking and practice. The "whiteness" of the figures in the English royal portrait might strike modern eyes as inevitable, but it actually describes a long history of exclusionary customs. Although Afro-Europeans were among the members of the English court, they are not pictured here.[11] Furthermore, this image negotiates lineage in relation to (if not also through) Henry's body: Mary, Elizabeth, Edward, and the king all share some genes. Yet the scene is a fiction, and not only because Jane Seymour had been dead for years when the painting was created. While the painting situates Edward closer to his father than his sisters, this was a legal rather than genetic "truth." Following English law of the time, the male prince would inherit Henry's throne first. This portrait, then, projects a hope: that the male line matters more than other blood relations. In the case of Chi's family tree, the question is certainly not one of whiteness, nor is it one of Indigeneity, at least not in any straightforward way. By the time that scene was painted, the political prerogatives of elites in the Yucatán depended upon possession of verifiable Maya — not simply Indigenous — identity and heritage. It is the claim to this possession that Chi's painting makes visible.

Setting Chi's painting of Tutul Xiu and his descendants alongside that of Henry VIII and his kin, pairs two Renaissance-era paintings that together highlight the distinct ways that imagery could be enlisted in the mid-sixteenth century to visualize elite commitments to a male progenitor and to describe one's family ties to others. Both paintings trade in cultural certainties about ancestry and genealogy that were widely shared in the Christian worlds of their day, be they English Christian or Maya Christian. Indeed, these images show how lineage could be tracked and traced, not only remembered. Both paintings also minimize aberrations and breaks,

Court Palace, "Henry VIII: Renaissance Prince or Terrible Tudor?" Website accessed at https://www.hrp.org.uk/hampton-court-palace/history-and-stories/henry-viii/#gs.813urj.

11. See Onyeka Nubia, *Blackamoores. Africans in Tudor England, Their Presence, Status and Origins* (London: Narrative Eye, 2013).

if not also the shifting fortunes among family members. In so doing, these works stress how "natural" it is to organize human connections through biological metaphors and genealogical premises. Viewed today, when contemporary ideas of belonging and exclusion, and of family, are quite different than in the sixteeenth century, these two paintings offer insight into how people in the past used images to make sense of family relations and lineage. Later *casta* paintings offer somewhat different possibilities, because they were created in settings where the urban environment, immigration, and slavery produced far more complex ethnic and social differences than those of the sixteenth century. Because of the colonial economies and habits of negotiating inclusion and exclusion in the late seventeenth and early eighteenth centuries in the cities of the Spanish Americas, *casta* paintings evoke very particular kinds of daily work and creative labor.

Painting *Castas* in the Eighteenth Century

Since the violent imposition of settler colonialism in the Spanish Americas depended upon social hierarchies that privileged people of European (and especially Spanish) descent and their heirs over others, it is hardly suprising that concerns with the naturalization of social difference take new and more potent forms over time. Hence, an increasingly explicit articulation of a hierarchical system of *castas* surfaces in paintings of the eighteenth century, and this differs from the kinds of hierarchies depicted in the paintings of Henry VIII and by Gaspar Antonio Chi that we have been considering. At their core, *casta* paintings, similar to the sixteenth-century examples, are founded on the forced union of social identities with genealogy. They also implicitly reject the idea that social identities were or could be fluid and performative. But, in distinction to what came before them, *casta* paintings never portray a phonetypically homogeneous or "pure" *casta* family. There are, for instance, no known examples of a mestizo child with mestizo parents. Instead — and this is fundamental — these images are interested strictly in categories that arose when different *castas* produced children. *Casta* paintings therefore address a driving concern with cultural mixing and its manifestation in phenotypes, or visible features, like skin color. No less significantly, these paintings seem to offer irrefutable documentation of what was, in reality, an unstable system, given that the categories that the *casta* paintings promoted were not necessarily the ones people used to classify themselves. Indeed, in their neat assignment of every person pictured into one of sixteen available categories, *casta* paintings imply certainties rather than instability.

In the Spanish Americas, as noted above, the terms and concepts of "*casta*" and "*castas*" represented but one way to think about ethnic difference. Most days one's *casta* designation would not have been voiced aloud, although the concept of *castas* formed a distinctive way of categorizing and thinking about people. Just who belonged to what caste was a source of anxiety, particularly among the elites of Spanish America who considered themselves one of the pure *español* [Spanish] castes. It is not surprising, then, that *castas* were surveilled and commented upon in censuses, legal documents and personal letters. Across the early eighteenth century, long after *castas* had become a familiar part of colonial society, they also became the focus of a unique form of visual representation: *casta* painting. Today, these paintings are recognized as some of the most explicitly racialized images created in the early modern period. As paintings that depict histories of miscegenation in seemingly benign terms, these works are both confounding and unsettling. Rarely are the social and economic permissions and exclusions of a society so frankly expressed in painting.

As with the paintings by Magón and Barreda (see figures 2 and 3) or the example discussed below by a painter whose name is no longer known (figure 6), all works in this genre rely upon mimesis, depicting domestic scenes and other aspects of daily life as if the painters witnessed what they painted. This taken-from-life quality adds to the illusion that these paintings document lived experience. In the Magón painting, for instance, the man has been working at his desk. The feathered pen resting in an inkwell and the brightly colored parrot perched upon his finger imply he has just taken a break from his correspondence, perhaps having been interrupted by the woman cradling the well-fed, well-dressed child. A small bouquet of flowers and two avocados, a fruit with origins in the Americas, sit at the table's edge. The stack of papers confirms the father is an educated man; he is also a person who can afford luxuries. Although artfully composed, the scene does not over-stretch one's imagination: this all could have existed.

Despite their mimetic claims, their true-to-life quality, all scenes in *casta* paintings are conjured and imagined. As part of this constructed urban world, people in *casta* paintings appear primarily as examples of genetic mixing. Moreover, in these scenes, people of presumed "purer origins," be they "purely" Spanish, Indigenous, or Black, and lighter skin are shown occupying the highest rungs in colonial social and economic hierarchies. Along with their emphasis on the nuclear family, which forms one consistent feature of *casta* painting, these artworks feature descriptive ethnonyms, each of which carried distinctive connotations. For instance, the term *español* did not necessarily root identity in one's place of birth as *España* [Spain]. An *español* might be born in New Spain or Iberia, but the label signaled those with ancestors who were both Spanish-born and Christian (Catholic). The term *indio* had stronger geographic connotations, referencing people who came from the Indies (as Spain's overseas possessions were called). And according to the *casta* painting labeling scheme, *negros* [Blacks], were largely untethered from geographic origins, defined instead by skin color. Taken together, these labels make clear that a significant part of the work of settler colonialism lies in racializing people and geographies, inventing and using logics that this form of colonialism authorizes.

There is still much unknown about the *casta* genre, including how people of the past read such images or why, precisely, one might purchase such a painting or send it across the Atlantic Ocean to Spain, where many, including Magón's and Barreda's paintings, are found today. *Casta* paintings nonetheless invite thinking about what constitutes a normative family and an acceptable human body in colonial contexts. For instance, *casta* paintings, featuring family portraits, rule out procreation via extramarital relationships or rapes. They also exclude elders and extended groups of relatives from the family group. Instead, these paintings suggest that in the Spanish Americas all families were composed of heterosexual pairs who give birth to one or two children (at most). In this painted world, both poverty and wealth are bound to one's genetic code and any hope of changing *castas* — of racial passing — is foreclosed.

In lived reality, as revealed by historical documents, *castas* were never so neatly or definitively fixed, nor were families and households so narrowly circumscribed. For although the *casta* paintings imply that naming ethnic types was of paramount importance, people in the Spanish Americas also recognized that aspects of one's identity could be chosen and enacted: they were performative. In Mexico City, for instance, different facets of social identities came into play, day by day and year by year. In the marketplace, one's economic standing was preeminent; whereas in the viceregal courts, rank and genealogy mattered most. When the census taker came knocking on the door, he might well want to know how many males resided in a particular house, and also whether they were *españoles* or *mestizos*. Yet census counts reveal that while some categories, like *español* and *mestizo* and *mulatto* were legally recognized in the eighteenth century, other terms that surface in *casta* paintings were not, such as *albino* (technically, a person with a congenital absence of pigment, but used in *casta* paintings for a person with one Black great-great-grandparent among otherwise *español* forebears) and *negro torna atrás* [Black throwback]. Moreover, even recognized *casta* terms were not securely affixed to individuals — in lived experience (although not painting) people could slip into more desirable *castas* should circumstances permit.[12]

By stating *casta* categories so concretely, and by supplying images that attest to their veracity, *casta* paintings seem to crowd out other means of social divisions used in their day. However, *casta* paintings are contradictory in that they also offer visual evidence of one of the most important means of enacting social fluidity: clothing. In the painting titled *De Albina y Español produce Negro torna atrás* [Albina and Spaniard Produce a Black Throwback], c. 1770–1780 (see figure 6), each family member depicted in the foreground of the scene belongs to a different *casta*, yet all are dressed in luxury fabrics, carefully tailored. This implies the trio shared the same economic status: nice clothes were expensive, and poor people had access only to simple fabrics, often undyed. But in Mexico City and other urban settings, costly fabrics were an unstable marker of economic status, in part because in wealthy households, servants sometimes had access to cast-off clothes, and open markets meant that luxury

12. See Rappaport, *The Disappearing Mestizo* for a sophisticated discussion of the slippages in identity categories. Nancy van Deusen, *Global Indios: The Indigenous Struggle for Justice in Sixteenth-Century Spain* (Durham and London: Duke University Press, 2015) focuses on the sixteenth century.

Figure 6. Painter whose name is currently unknown, *De Albina y Español produce Negro torna atrás* [Albina and Spaniard Produce a Black Throwback], c. 1770–1780, oil on copper, 46 x 55 cm, Banco Nacional de México, Mexico City. Reproduced by permission.

cloth was available to everyone who could afford it. The unreliability of clothing-as-status-marker was an irritant to the Spanish crown government, who frequently issued edicts meant to rein in the wearing of luxury clothes by non-elites. Nevertheless, clothes continued to circulate in spite of sumptuary laws. In *casta* paintings, then, what people wore is a catalogue of possibility, not necessarily tied inextricably to one's ethnicity. Even so, *casta* painters sought to convince their viewers that the genetic codes of people of the Spanish Americas were predictable and largely immutable, and that these, rather than individual choice or performances, determined social order. Painters therefore lavished more care on the clothes of elite *castas* than they did of those who were impoverished. This is part of their commentary on social and ethnic norms, implying that clothing the wealthy, who were also the least "mixed" *castas*, required both others' labor and an eye for aesthetics, not merely money.

The scene in figure 6 also seems to contradict the idea that social personhood could transcend biological or genetic "destiny." At first glance, this *casta* painting presents an idyllic scene. The Alameda, a public park at the edge of Mexico City, fills much of the image. The painter has tilted the picture plane so that viewers can appreciate the strict geometry of park paths, their crossings marked by fountains. If we compare this scene to the *casta* painting by Magón (see figure 2), we sense how painters shaped the genre to fit different visual tastes. Here, in contrast to Magón's intimate interior, we see a busy setting. Small figures, mostly in pairs or groups of three, stroll through the park. In an ambiguous space in the left foreground, perhaps a rooftop with a view onto the park beyond, appear three figures: a white-skinned man and woman and a Black child, all dressed in elegant and fashionable clothing. The woman and child both turn to look at the man, who raises a telescope to survey the park. The painted caption at the lower center edge of the painting – *De Albina y Español produce Negro torna atrás* – tells viewers that the three people are, indeed, biologically related. The terms, "albino/a," "Spaniard," "Black throwback," are all well-known descriptors in *casta* paintings. According to the logic of such paintings, *español* or *española* was one of the three original, unmixed castes, along with Indian and Black. In contrast, an albino/a (according to the same typological logic), was not purely white. Although the text doesn't specify who is who in the scene, it is not hard to parse the image. Since it takes two sexually mature people to produce a child, the albina and *español* are the adults in the picture – the gender specificity of Spanish (*albina* is feminine, *español*, masculine) distinguishes them even further. The Black child is their issue, but he is not just any child. The descriptor "*torna atrás*" is meant to explain how light-skinned parents could produce a child of very dark skin. In using this phrase, the painting offers visual testimony on genetic destiny: that children with one Black great-great-grandparent could "*torna atrás*" (literally, turn around) and manifest the skin color of this one ancestor. In *casta* paintings, there was no escaping one's family genetics, no amount of inter-marrying that could "whiten" a Black ancestral line. Yet this kind of indelible marker of ethnicity did not exist, the sets of *casta* paintings suggest, for those with

Indigenous ancestors, where, after four generations of marriage of one member of the *indio casta* with the *español casta*, the resulting child was unreservedly *español*. This contrast makes clear that the *torna atrás* is premised on anti-Blackness, which was hardly a fantasy of *casta* paintings. It was, and remains a social reality in the Americas. Both in settler colonial societies and today anti-Blackness persists, and who can lay claim to a particular ethnicity remains crucially important.

Casta Complications and Bodily Limits

No viewer in the past looked at a *casta* scene in isolation. Rather, these paintings formed part of a rich visual culture in urban environments, themselves awash in imagery. In urban painters' studios where *casta* paintings were created, other images were being produced as well. On the easels of a painter's workshop, one might find a *casta* painting, as well as a painting of a miraculous intervention of a religious statue that had cured a sick person. Outside the studio, being hawked on the streets were printed images, some documenting religious miracles, others showing marvelous and monstrous events, like the birth of a baby with a pig's head or conjoined twins.[13] Setting the *casta* painting of the *español*, *albina*, and *torna atrás* against these kinds of images, reveals that visual imagery in this period was often about the *outer limits* of the possible, not strictly (or even largely) meant to document the normative. Most people did not fear that their children would emerge with different phenotypes than their parents, and most did not really worry that their children would be born with pig's features. But people did look to images to ruffle up staid traditions, to be sensational, to show the unexpected. Given this, we might well read figures like the *torna atrás* not only as a cautionary tale about the longevity (if invisibility) of African-derived bloodlines but also as a figure, like the miraculous, that exists at the boundaries of known realities.

13. For Lima in the colonial period, see Emily Floyd, "Privileging the Local: Prints and the New World in Early Modern Lima," in *A Companion to Early Modern Lima*, edited by Emily Engel (Leiden and Boston: Brill, 2019): 360–84.

Figure 7. Detail of *De Albina y Español produce Negro torna atrás* [Albina and Spaniard Produce a Black Throwback], c. 1770–1780, oil on copper, Banco Nacional de México, Mexico City. Reproduced by permission.

In addition, some *casta* paintings seem to reveal an awareness of the limits of their own racialized propositions. If we return to Alameda in Figure 6 and look beyond the *casta* family, we see a small boy chasing after a heavily veiled woman and her attendant (figure 7). He is delivering a cup — almost certainly chocolate, a beverage enjoyed by elite women in Mexico City; he is running, we suspect, so that the chocolate would reach the women while still frothy. Nothing pictorial marks his *casta*, but his activity makes it clear he is a servant. And the veiled woman, as the recipient of the chocolate, is certainly elite, her status emphasized by the quantity of fabrics she wears. In another part of the park, a male figure holds a wide basket on his head, and carries a narrow-necked vessel, implying he is a street vendor (figure 8). In showing a world divided between the servants and the served, the background of this painting suggests that people knew full well that social distinctions other than caste were at play in their daily lives. This may not have been the primary tale that *casta* painters wished to tell or the patrons of their paintings wished to see. As with much racialized imagery from early modernity, however, cracks and

Figure 8. Detail of *De Albina y Español produce Negro torna atrás* [Albina and Spaniard Produce a Black Throwback], c. 1770–1780, oil on copper, Banco Nacional de México, Mexico City. Reproduced by permission.

seams are inevitable. They, too, are part of the system and logic of racialized thinking.

If one looks at *casta* paintings through a historical-materialist lens, wherein images are superficial justifications for an underlying social order determined by even deeper economic forces and relationships, it is possible to argue that their painted surfaces offer little more than falsified justification for social hierarchies, many of which are rooted in economic exploitation, including enslavement. And in fact, paintings do describe one general economic truth: the families they depict that are headed by men identified as *español* are commonly shown as more prosperous, and more likely to engage in leisure activities than families headed by other *castas*. The basis for such claims about Spanish economic power had its roots in Iberian conquests of the Americas in the sixteenth century and the particularities of settler colonialism. To many viewers of the day, the rejection of hierarchies would have been unthinkable: to them, societies were properly hierarchical, and a naturally-based hierarchy, beginning with human dominion over animals, men's dominion over women, and adults' dominion over children, offered the best blueprint for a successful, functioning society.

Many modern eyes tend to see *casta* paintings as misguided representations, evidence of errant ideologies. Not only were their patriarchal and racialized hierarchies inextricably intertwined with practices of colonial oppression, they also express a deep anti-Blackness. For some viewers today, who see themselves as having overcome absurd and suspect notions such as resurgence of a Black phenotype, *casta* paintings produce not a little *schadenfreude*. Indeed, it would not be wrong to take these images to task. In very fundamental ways, they describe ways of thinking and understanding human biology and lineage that misalign with twenty-first-century understandings of lived experience. While *casta* paintings were popular for only a few decades, they were commissioned by art collectors, colonial officials, foreign diplomats and local residents. They have since become canonical in Latin American art. So, what were *casta* paintings good for in the past? Why might people have wanted one?[14]

In Mexico City, as in other cities of the early modern world, the visual expression of identities was rarely happenstance. One's clothing and habits of speech, the ways one moved through parks and plazas — with servants, in coaches, or on foot with children in tow — offered cues to one's social and economic status and, by extension, one's family history. *Casta* paintings told their viewers that choices were few if one wanted to shift one's place in society: biology was destiny. This was neither wholly accurate, nor completely wrong. Shifts could be made, but ambition was never enough to climb out of poverty or take a leadership role in metropolitan government. In the Spanish Americas — as in many places of the world today — mobility was also tied to phenotype. In colonial society, the lighter one's skin, the more opportunities one might have. Such privilege could of course be squandered, but if the *torna atrás* shown in Figure 6 came to life, he would have a tougher path to tread than would his mother and father, no matter their wealth, no matter that their lineage was primarily *español*. What people could see about a person, especially in the public realm, set the parameters and permissions of daily life.

14. While not the most expensive purchase one might make in the Spanish Americas, such paintings could be pricy.

It is hard not to say the same of the present. Yet in closing, we wish to forestall any over-quick elisions. As the digital prints of Manglano-Ovalle with which this essay opened suggest, the kinds of racialized thinking and pressure put upon visibility and phenotype in eighteenth-century Mexico City is not quite the same as in the twenty-first century. *Casta* paintings invite us to ask: Is who we are and who we wish to become more negotiable today than it was in the past? Are some identities easier to perform than others? As Patrick Wolfe has argued, settler colonialism is a structure, and so, the social, economic, and racializing relationships it constructed across Europe, Africa, the Americas, and Asia will forever be difficult to dismantle.[15] What happened in the fifteenth and sixteenth centuries — events and practices that invented the Americas, turned them into a "New World," and then through violent dislocations of Brown and Black bodies, brought them into closer contact with other parts of the world — still shapes the world today. Among other things, this form of settler colonialism bound genealogy and genetics to skin color and identity. Given modern desires to see, and thus to know who someone "really is," is it possible to trace a legacy of *casta* paintings that endures today?

Discussion Questions

1. The chapter posits that many parts of identity are performative. Are some identities easier to perform than others?
2. The chapter uses the methods of art history to ask, and answer, questions raised by paintings. In what significant ways does this approach differ from chapters in this volume that focus upon historical documents or literary texts?
3. The rigid "caste" structure that *casta* paintings present was never reflected in lived experience. In the contemporary world, can you identify instances of similar fictionalized representations of the social order? How would you analyze their relationship to lived experience?

15. Patrick Wolfe, "Settler Colonialism and the Elimination of the Native," *Journal of Genocide Research* 8, no. 4 (Dec. 2006): 387–409.

Suggestions for Further Reading

Bryant, Sherwin, Rachel O'Toole, and Ben Vinson III., eds. *Africans to Spanish America: Expanding the Diaspora.* Urbana: University of Illinois Press, 2012.

Carrera, Magali. *Imagining Identity in New Spain: Race, Lineage and the Colonial Body in Portraiture and Casta Paintings.* Austin: University of Texas Press, 2003.

Deans-Smith, Susan, and Ilona Katzew, eds. *Race and Classification: The Case of Mexican America.* Stanford: Stanford University Press, 2009.

Lugo-Ortiz, Agnes, and Angela Rosenthal, eds. *Slave Portraiture in the Atlantic World.* Cambridge and New York: Cambridge University Press, 2013.

Memories of Underdevelopment: Art and the Decolonial Turn in Latin America, 1960–1985 // Memorias del subdesarrollo : arte y el giro descolonial en América Latina, 1960–1985. San Diego: Museum of Contemporary Art, 2018.

Seijas, Tatiana. *Asian Slaves in Colonial Mexico: From Chinos to Indians.* New York: Cambridge University Press, 2014.

Bibliography

Barteet, Cody C. "Maya Heraldic Arms: the Merging of Spanish and Maya Visual Cultures in the Memorial Shield to the Massacre at Otzmal." *Konsthistorisk tidskrift/Journal of Art History* (2017): 1–22.

Cortez, Connie. "New Dance, Old Xius: The 'Xiu Family Tree' and Maya Cultural Continuities after European Contact." In *Heart of Creation: The Mesoamerican World and the Legacy of Linda Schele,* edited by Andrea Stone, 201–215. Tuscaloosa and London: University of Alabama Press, 2002.

Deans-Smith, Susan. "Creating the Colonial Subject: *Casta* Paintings, Collectors, and Critics in Eighteenth-Century Mexico." *Colonial Latin American Review* 14, no. 2 (December 2005): 169–204.

Earle, Rebecca. "The Pleasures of Taxonomy: *Casta* Paintings, Classification, and Colonialism." *William and Mary Quarterly* 73, no. 3 (July 2016): 427–66.

Floyd, Emily. "Privileging the Local: Prints and the New World in Early Modern Lima." In *A Companion to Early Modern Lima*, edited by Emily Engel, 360–384. Leiden and Boston: Brill, 2019.

García Saíz, María Concepción. *Las castas mexicanas: Un género pictórico Americano*. Milan: Olivetti, 1989.

"Glenn, Dario and Tyrone," Guggenheim Online Resources. Accessed at: https://www.guggenheim.org/artwork/10464.

Hampton Court Palace. "Henry VIII: Renaissance Prince or Terrible Tudor?" Website accessed at: https://www.hrp.org.uk/hampton-court-palace/history-and-stories/henry-viii/#gs.813urj

Katzew, Ilona. *Casta Painting: Images of Race in Eighteenth-Century Mexico*. New Haven: Yale University Press, 2004.

Leibsohn, Dana, and Barbara E. Mundy. "Genealogical Tree of the Xiu Family." In *Vistas: Visual Culture in Spanish America, 1520–1820*. http://www.fordham.edu/vistas, 2015.

Lloyd, Christopher, and Simon Thurley. *Henry VIII: Images of a Tudor King*. London: Phaidon Press Limited, 1990.

Loveman, Mara. *National Colors: Racial Classification and the State in Latin America*. New York: Oxford University Press, 2014.

Mignolo, Walter. *Darker Side of the Renaissance: Literacy, Territoriality, and Colonization*. Ann Arbor: Michigan University Press, 1995.

Platt, Ron, ed. *Iñigo Mangalo-Ovalle: The Garden of Delights*. Winston-Salem: Southeastern Center for Contemporary Art, 1998.

Rappaport, Joanne. *The Disappearing Mestizo: Configuring Difference in the Colonial Kingdom of New Granada*. Durham: Duke University Press, 2014.

Rawlinson, Kent. "Architectural Culture and Royal Image at the Henrician Court." In *Henry VIII and the Court: Art, Politics and Performance*, edited by Thomas Betteridge and Suzannah Lipscomb. Burlington, Vermont: Ashgate Publishing Company, 2013.

Van Deusen, Nancy. *Global Indios: The Indigenous Struggle for Justice in Sixteenth-Century Spain*. Durham and London: Duke University Press, 2015.

Wolfe, Patrick. "Settler Colonialism and the Elimination of the Native." *Journal of Genocide Research* 8, no. 4 (Dec. 2006): 387–409.

Teaching Race in the Global Renaissance Using Local Art Collections

LISANDRA ESTEVEZ

This case study[1] focuses on three paintings currently on view in North Carolina museum collections that I integrate into teaching one of my art history surveys, Art 2302 (Art History II), which encompasses Renaissance to contemporary art.[2] They include *A Man Scraping Chocolate* (c. 1680–1780, oil on canvas, Raleigh, North Carolina Museum of Art, figure 1), *Saint Martín de Porres* (c. 1750–1775, oil on cloth, The Mint Museum, Charlotte, North Carolina, figure 2), and *The Defense of the Sacrament (or Defense of the Eucharist)* (c. 1750–1775, oil on cloth, The Mint Museum, Charlotte, North Carolina, figure 3). These images significantly enrich my teaching of Iberian and Latin American art to students at Winston-Salem State University (WSSU), an HBCU (or historically Black college or university) within the University of North Carolina system.[3] Discussions of race and periodization become especially relevant when teaching undergraduates at WSSU about the Renaissance and Baroque eras (1400–1800) in art history.[4] In addition, active and engaged discussions about diversity

1. Special thanks go to Dr. Matthieu Chapman and Dr. Anna Wainwright for including my work in this volume and for their support. I am also grateful to Dr. Cecile Yancu and the anonymous reviewer whose thoughtful comments and feedback greatly improved this text.
2. Art 2302 (Art History II) is designed as a class that serves diverse student populations. It is offered to non-art majors as a general education course with fine arts as the area of knowledge and critical thinking as a student learning outcome. Art majors take this course as one of the foundation requirements in the degree.
3. For a history of Winston-Salem State University, see E. Louise Murphy, rev. and ed., Frances Ross Coble, Simona Atkins, and Wilma Levister Lassiter, *The History of Winston-Salem State University, 1892–1995* (Virginia Beach, VA: The Donning Company/ Publishers, 1999).
4. Race and periodization were the focus of a ground-breaking conference on medieval and early modern history: "Race and Periodization: a #RaceB4Race Symposium," September 5–7, 2019, Washington, D.C.: https://acmrs.asu.edu/public-events/symposia/race-and-periodization (Accessed November 19, 2019).

Figure 1. A *Man Scraping Chocolate* (c. 1680–1780, oil on canvas, Raleigh, North Carolina Museum of Art

Figure 2. *Saint Martín de Porres* (c. 1750–1775, oil on cloth, The Mint Museum, Charlotte, North Carolina.

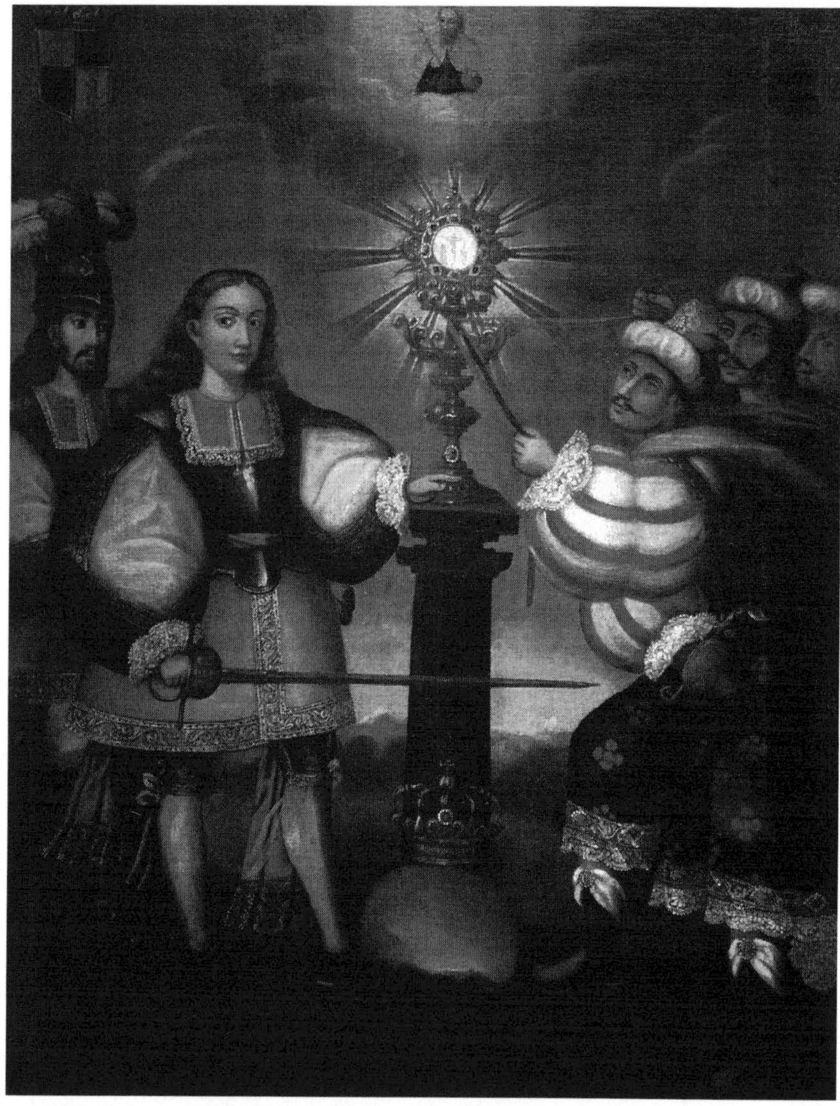

Figure 3. *The Defense of the Sacrament (or Defense of the Eucharist)* (c. 1750–1775, oil on cloth, The Mint Museum, Charlotte, North Carolina.

in the visual arts constitute a high-impact practice in the classroom that becomes especially meaningful in thinking about histories that, until recently, have not been widely represented in Renaissance and Baroque art history and visual culture.[5]

As an instructor, one often asks: what does the inclusion of this material in visual studies courses tangibly *mean* in pedagogical practices and curricular cohesion? Instilling these works of art into an art history survey expands the globalized aspects of its content and responds to my university's curriculum that centers on overarching equity and social justice issues. In studying racial or racialized imagery, students can visualize "difficult differences" that originate in the pre-modern world, especially regarding the construct of the "other" in Renaissance and Baroque art history.[6] These case studies thus address questions of identity and race and how they relate to other paradigms such as class, nation, and faith in the visual arts of Spain and Latin America during the sixteenth to eighteenth centuries.

Closely reading these three works of art elicits questions that allow students to weigh the value of regional collections in broader, global presentations of race and identity in Renaissance and Baroque Iberian and Latin American art. Part of analyzing these pictures involves "slow looking": taking the time in class to parse these paintings carefully for their content, representation, and context. Engaging students in this process helps

5. High-impact practices are educational approaches that have demonstrated a significant impact on student success. They consist of learning communities, writing-intensive courses, undergraduate research, and diversity/global learning, among other methods that promote increased student engagement and participation. These methods are especially impactful when they engage traditionally underserved student populations. While there is an extensive body of education literature that underscores the benefits of these practices, an essential reference for their impact on underserved student populations is George D. Kuh, *High-Impact Educational Practices: What Are They, Who Has Access to Them, and Why They Matter* (Washington, DC: Leap, 2008), eBook.

6. The following exhibition catalogue is an excellent introduction: Joaneath Spicer, ed., *Revealing the African Presence in Renaissance Europe* (Baltimore: The Walters Art Museum, 2012). See also Carmen Fracchia, *"Black but Human" Slavery and the Visual Arts in Hapsburg Spain, 1480–1700* (New York: Oxford University Press, 2019).

them to look closely at these artworks (albeit in projection using powerpoint presentations) and ask specific questions about them.[7] Moreover, these three paintings (figures 1–3) help students 1) to interrogate notions of otherness that informed early modern constructs of African diasporic identity and 2) to provide points of historical reference for how modern and contemporary African American artists such as John Biggers, Kehinde Wiley, Amy Sherald, and others will confront and challenge notions of culture, identity, and race.

This case study provides close readings of the paintings and includes instructive comparisons to guide students in thinking about how these global objects from North Carolina collections relate to others in national and international art collections. Class discussions address how the *A Man Scraping Chocolate*, *Saint Martín de Porres*, and the *Defense of the Eucharist* (figures 1–3) ended up in these regional collections and what it means for these works to be in these specific museums in the U.S. South.[8]

We begin with a thought-provoking work, which is the North Carolina Museum of Art's *A Man Scraping Chocolate* (figure 1). This painting represents an African laborer grinding chocolate on a *metate*, a Mesoamerican grinding stone traditionally used for processing maize. This distinct canvas introduces students to a complex transcultural nexus that joins the cultures of Africa, Europe, and the Americas vis-à-vis the globalized culture of chocolate and the African labor that sustained it.[9]

In a distinct turn, the Mint Museum's *Saint Martín de Porres* (figure 2) offers a different perspective on representations of Africans in colonial Latin America. Martín, who was of biracial ancestry, both African and Spanish, became Peru's patron saint associated with social justice and

7. For the concept of "slow looking," or the cultivation of observation skills that foster critical reasoning, namely in the visual arts, see Shari Tishman, *Slow Looking: The Art and Practice of Learning through Observation* (London: Routledge, 2017).
8. For the provenance of *A Man Scraping Chocolate*, see Lisandra Estevez, "(Re)-presenting Africans in Early Modern Spain and Latin America." *Notes on Early Modern Art*, vol. 4, no. 1 (2017): 14–16. The Mint Museum's *Defense of the Eucharist* and *Saint Martín de Porres* were acquired from the Paul and Virginia Clifford Collection. The Cliffords were known for their extensive collection of South American art.
9. Estevez, "(Re)-presenting Africans in Early Modern Spain and Latin America," 11–22.

racial harmony.[10] This image allows students to see how Andean painters depicted the sanctity and spirituality of Afro-descended saints.

In considering cross-cultural connections among these artworks, the dynamics of politics, power, and exclusion often come into play. For example, the Mint Museum's Peruvian *Defense of the Eucharist* (figure 3) depicts a Spanish king protecting a radiant monstrance while, stereotypically, exoticized Turks try to topple it. A close reading of this painting helps students comprehend the exertion of European social control over other non-European peoples as part of a mentality of conquest carried over from medieval Spain into colonial Latin America. Furthermore, this idiosyncratic iconography creates correspondences between the Muslims in Spain and indigenous peoples in the Americas that demonstrate the transfer of racialized concepts such as anti-Muslim animus, or Islamophobia, from Europe to the New World. The comparisons between these different examples can help students to comprehend the implications of the racial "othering" of individuals and communities of other faiths and nations in the early modern period and the persistence of this othering today.[11]

When taken together, these paintings generate class discussions that challenge and complicate the students' perspectives on race and culture in the global Renaissance using works of art found in local art collections. Class discussions allow students to compare these paintings to other examples in the respective histories of early modern Iberian and Latin American art with specific reference to sixteenth- and seventeenth-century artists such as Luis de Vargas, Andrés Sánchez Gallque, and Diego Velázquez.

From a pedagogical standpoint, discussing these pictures also develops in-depth critical thinking skills that help students to move beyond a comparative model of art history that consists of "compare and contrast."

10. For a comprehensive study of Saint Martín de Porres's hagiography, see Celia Cussen, *Black Saint of the Americas: The Life and Afterlife of Martín de Porres* (New York: Cambridge University Press, 2014).
11. Lisandra Estevez, "Imagining the Other in a Cuzco Defense of the Eucharist," *Renaissance Papers* 2018 (2019): 67–92.

Instead, looking at the paintings from different cultural, political, and socio-economic contexts helps students understand a more expansive paradigm. In analyzing these images critically, students learn to challenge, complicate, or even contradict their views of racial otherness and ask relevant questions: Who is an "other"? By whose biases, judgments, or standards? How? Why?

Useful Resources for Course Readings

Before I turn to the individual case studies I mentioned, a brief overview of the study of the African presence and contribution to Renaissance and Baroque art history is necessary. Groundbreaking publications authored by American and European art historians Carmen Fracchia, Joaneath Spicer, Victor Stoichita, and Tanya Tiffany have profoundly reshaped this field within Renaissance studies.[12] Both Grace Harpster and Erin Kathleen Rowe have also compellingly written how colorism affected perceptions of sanctity and spirituality in early modern Spanish visual culture.[13] On a broader scale, the landmark *The Image of the Black in the Western Art* series has specific volumes dedicated to representing Africans in early

12. Carmen Fracchia has extensively published on this topic. See the following link for her publications: https://www.worldcat.org/search?qt=worldcat_org_all&q=Fracchia, Carmen. (Accessed November 19, 2019). Among Victor Stoichita's many publications, see *Darker Shades: The Racial Other in Early Modern Art* (London: Reaktion Books, 2019); Tanya Tiffany, "Light, Darkness, and African Salvation: Velázquez's Supper at Emmaus." *Art History*, vol. 31, no. 1 (2008): 33–56; and also Spicer, ed., *Revealing the African Presence in Renaissance Europe*.
13. Grace Harpster, "The Color of Salvation: The Materiality of Blackness in Alonso de Sandoval's *De instaurando Aethiopium salute*." In *Envisioning Others: Race, Color, and the Visual Arts in Iberia and Latin America*, ed. Pamela A. Patton (Leiden: Brill, 2016), 83–110; Erin Kathleen Rowe. "After Death, Her Face Turned White: Blackness, Whiteness, and Sanctity in the Early Modern Hispanic World" *American Historical Review* (2016): 727–54; idem, "Visualizing Black Sanctity in Early Modern Spanish Polychrome Sculpture." In *Envisioning Others: Race, Color, and the Visual Arts in Iberia and Latin America*, ed. Pamela A. Patton (Leiden: Brill, 2016), 51–82; and idem, *Black Saints in Early Modern Global Catholicism* (New York: Cambridge University Press, 2019).

modern European art.[14] These particular publications are highlighted because they are written in English and accessible to students. Students who are Spanish speaking should seek out publications by Aurelia Martín Casares and Luis Méndez Rodríguez.[15]

Case Studies of Paintings in North Carolina Collections

A Man Scraping Chocolate

Painted by an anonymous artist sometime between the late-seventeenth and eighteenth centuries, *A Man Scraping Chocolate* (figure 1) represents a young man of African ancestry who kneels on the ground as he processes a large block of chocolate. His eyes engage directly with the viewer, and his lips parted to suggest a smile as he rolls the chocolate on a *metate*, a Mesoamerican stone tool used in Mexico and Central America for milling corn. A small brazier underneath the *metate* softens the chocolate so it can be processed more quickly. Grinding cacao into chocolate in this traditional fashion required much physical exertion. Nevertheless, this process had an alluring quality for the viewer, as extolled in verses by the Spanish writer Marcos Antonio Orellana (1731–1813): "Oh, divine chocolate!

14. See *The Image of the Black in Western Art: From the Early Christian Era to the "Age of Discovery." From Demonic Threat of the Incarnation of Sainthood*, eds. David Bindman and Henry Louis Gates, Jr., vol. 2, part I (Cambridge, MA: The Belknap Press, 2010) and *The Image of the Black in Western Art, From the "Age of Discovery" to the Age of Abolition, Part 1: Artists of the Renaissance and Baroque*, edited by David Bindman and Henry Louis Gates, Jr., vol. 3, part I (Cambridge, MA: The Belknap Press, 2010).
15. See the essays by both scholars in Aurelia Martín Casares and Margarita García Barranco, eds., *La esclavitud negroafricana en la historia de España. Siglos XVI y XVI* (Granada: Editorial Comares, S.L., 2010) and Luis Méndez Rodríguez, *Esclavos en la pintura sevillana de los siglos de Oro* (Seville: University of Seville, 2011).

/They grind thee kneeling, /Beat thee with hands praying. And drink thee with eyes to heaven."[16]

Part of my instructive style encourages students to note descriptive details that support a focused visual analysis of a work of art. For example, despite his hard labor, the man is neatly dressed. He wears brown breeches and a white shirt with a broad collar that extends down his back. The shirt is buttoned on the front and tied with a red ribbon at the waist and chest. He also sports brown boots. Although kneeling, the man occupies the center of the composition at eye-level. The man's prominent placement at the center of the composition emphasizes the dignity of this labor, even though grinding chocolate was exhausting work. A bowl to his left contains the chocolate shavings pushed off the stone as he processes the chocolate. A letter supports five large chocolate disks. A partially covered box containing chocolate disks and three smaller disks are seen on the right, while another is partially visible on the left. The man's position in the lower half of the composition thus raises attendant questions about the viewer's gaze in objectifying the Black male subject. How are we, as viewers, meant to engage with him? Do we look at, above, down at, or with him? How do we dismantle the racial biases imposed by the sense of sight?

Furthermore, chocolate grinding as a profession attached to African labor merits further explanation. For Spaniards, chocolate was an important American product that bridged conquest with commerce and bound economic interests with human capital.[17] Cacao production in the Americas was interconnected with enslaved African labor. South American plantations cultivated this crop for export to Europe well into the nineteenth century. Thus, it is known that chocolate grinding in North America was an occupation held by Black men, whether freed or enslaved. This fact is especially relevant for WSSU students in making visual connections

16. "¡O, divino chocolate! Que arrodillado tu muelan, Manos plegadas te baten Y ojos al cielo te beban." Cited from Sophie D. Coe and Michael D. Coe, *The True History of Chocolate* (London: Thames and Hudson, 1996), 210. See also Estevez, "(Re)presenting Africans," 12, no. 8.

17. For a recent study on this topic through the lens of literary production, see Erin Alice Cowling, *Chocolate: How a New World Commodity Conquered Spanish Literature* (Toronto: University of Toronto Press, 2021).

among art, labor, and economic production in the early modern Iberian and Atlantic worlds.[18]

However, certain ambiguities complicate the task of evaluating this painting. The nature of the letter on which the five disks in the foreground rest is hard to ascertain as the handwriting is nearly illegible. Edward Sullivan has reasonably suggested that it is a legal document, based on his identification of some words, such as "casa" or "house" in Spanish.[19] In my examination of the letter, I have discerned the name "Luis" and the letters "Rs," which can stand for "reales," or Spanish currency. This letter, then, perhaps records the man's name or that of the individual for whom he grinds the chocolate. The documents on the ground can be interpreted in different ways. They might indicate the wage he was paid for grinding it or the fee for his release from bondage, whether indentured servitude or slavery. Given its conspicuous location in the foreground, the letter could be a statement of manumission proclaiming the man's freedom, but this remains highly speculative as the script is difficult to decipher.[20]

Saint Martín de Porres

The Mint Museum's *Saint Martín de Porres* (figure 2) complements the North Carolina Museum of Art's A *Man Scraping Chocolate* (figure 1) in its illustration of African labor. Born the illegitimate son of a Spanish nobleman and freed African mother, Saint Martín de Porres (Martín de Porres Velázquez, O.P. December 9, 1579 – November 3, 1639) was a Peruvian lay brother of the Dominican order. He was nicknamed the "fray escoba" ("friar of the broom") as he was the patron saint of custodians and service workers. He is often shown sweeping to demonstrate the worthiness of that labor, often perceived as menial. He was eventually beatified in 1837 by Pope Gregory XVI and canonized by Pope John XXIII in 1962.[21]

18. Estevez, "(Re)-presenting Africans," 21.
19. Cited in Estevez, "(Re)-presenting Africans," 14.
20. Estevez, "(Re)-presenting Africans," 12, 14.
21. See Cussen, *Black Saint of the Americas*, 19–102.

The Mint Museum's painting represents both the saint's humility and sanctity. He wears the habit of the Dominican order with a rosary around his neck. The saint sweeps a small spare space that is warmed by a lit brazier. Animals often accompany Saint Martín de Porres. In this painting, a dog, cat, and mouse harmoniously share food from the same bowl while another mouse nibbles on a food scrap.[22] While he appears in the mundane task of sweeping the floor with a broom, his saintly or holy nature also reveals itself. The saint's gaze turns to the heavens, with his head framed by a radiant halo; the golden clouds reiterate that effect in the background.

In the classroom, we further navigate the juxtapositions between *A Man Scraping Chocolate* (figure 1) and *Saint Martín de Porres* (figure 2). There is ample evidence that Saint Martín de Porres had to negotiate racial and racist attitudes toward him as a Black friar. In considering the complexities of racialization posed by the latter image of Saint Martín, one can deliberate the question: how does this image express racial anxieties toward Black sanctity?[23]

The Defense of the Eucharist

Even though the paintings discussed above present us with plural representations of Black labor and varying perceptions of blackness, the Spanish transferred exclusionary concepts of personhood from Europe to America, whereby both African and Ingenious communities were subjected to similar racialized agendas and policies of disenfranchisement

22. Chris Garces, "The Interspecies Logic of Race in Colonial Peru: Saint Martín de Porres's Animal Brotherhood," in *Sainthood and Race: Marked Flesh, Holy Flesh*, edited by Molly H. Bassett and Vincent W. Lloyd (New York and London: Routledge, 2015), 82–101.
23. See Cussen, *Black Saint of the Americas*, 119 and Geraldine Heng, "An African Saint in Medieval Europe: The Black Saint Maurice and the Enigma of Racial Sanctity," in *Sainthood and Race: Marked Flesh, Holy Flesh*, eds. Molly H. Bassett and Vincent W. Lloyd (New York and London: Routledge, 2015), 18–43.

and exclusion.[24] For example, Europeans transferred the Islamophobic stereotype of the "Turk" and the "Moor" as an arch-enemy of Christianity to Andean communities in South America. Likewise, Spaniards often conflated distinct groups, such as Turks, Muslims, and indigenous peoples, as apostates and threats to the sanctity of the Eucharist. The Mint Museum's *The Defense of the Eucharist* (figure 3) represents the king of Spain, possibly Charles II (r. 1665–1700), and plausibly Muslim bystanders beholding the Eucharist to promote the Spanish monarch as a defender of the Catholic faith. A soldier sporting a feathered helmet protects the king. A lion and orb appear underfoot as symbols of the monarch's power. This imagery capitalizes on negative depictions of the Turks using racial stereotypes signified by elements of dress and costume such as turbans and scimitars. The king brandishes his sword to guard the Eucharist, the consecrated bread wafer (ensconced in a jeweled, gold monstrance), from three Turks who are portrayed as the king's enemies as they unsuccessfully try to topple the Eucharist by pulling on a thin ribbon. Two coats-of-arms, presumably the king's, flank an icon of Christ as *Pantocrator* (or ruler of the universe) at the composition's top and center, who miraculously protects the king against the Turks.[25]

This imagery also draws poignant parallels between Iberian Morisco communities and South American indigenous populations that complicate the racialization of the other in early modern South America. Complex layerings need to be dismantled in making these connections among the Turks, Moriscos, and indigenous Andean populations. While significant cultural and religious distinctions exist between the Moriscos and Turks, the Spanish perceived both groups as a monolithic threat to Christianity.[26] Thus, in portraying the Turks as the purported enemies of the Christian faith, the image transfers the visual rhetoric of othering the Moriscos

24. Sylvia Wynter writes about this exclusionary constitution of the human: idem, "Unsettling the Coloniality of Being/Power/Truth/Freedom: Towards the Human, After Man, Its Overrepresentation — An Argument." CR: *The New Centennial Review* 3 (2003): 257–337.
25. Estevez, "Imagining the Other in a Cuzco Defense of the Eucharist, 67.
26. Andrew C. Hess, "The Moriscos: An Ottoman Fifth Column in Sixteenth-Century Spain," *The American Historical Review* 74 (1) (1968): 1–25.

(Spanish Muslims who converted to Christianity) to indigenous populations who were similarly perceived by the Spanish as "heathen" and were consequently (and forcibly) converted to Christianity. The painting's mimetic representation of the figures is troubling because it imposes the medieval mentality of conquest onto indigenous communities using the pictorial language of realism.[27]

Developing Connections in Classroom Comparisons

Building on the analysis above, the following comparisons aid in thinking deeply about how African men were represented in early modern Iberian and Latin American art, and offer additional opportunities for analytic comparisons.

Comparison 1: *A Man Scraping Chocolate* and Diego Velázquez's *Juan de Pareja*

In visualizing how Afro-Hispanic men were represented, the painting of *A Man Scraping Chocolate* (c. 1680–1780, oil on canvas, Raleigh, North Carolina Museum of Art, figure 1) is an instructive example that lends itself to comparison with Diego Velázquez's portrait of *Juan de Pareja* (1650, oil on canvas, New York, The Metropolitan Museum of Art, figure 4).

The portrait of Juan de Pareja is a singular image because it is the only known portrait of an enslaved African man in seventeenth-century Spain. Velázquez painted Pareja's likeness during his Roman sojourn from 1649 to 1651 while the latter was still indentured to the former. A notarial act freed Pareja on November 23, 1650, eight months after the painting's completion. Pareja is set against a dark background in this portrait and posed in three-quarters view. Dressed in a courtier's suit, though with worn elbows, Juan de Pareja appears poised and confident with an intense gaze framed by the soft mass of his black hair. As Carmen Fracchia rightly notes, "Velázquez's choice of a non-European subject at the papal court would have signified the visualization of not only the imperial power of

27. Estevez, "Imagining the Other in a Cuzco Defense of the Eucharist," 68–69.

Figure 4. Diego Velázquez, *Juan de Pareja* (1650, oil on canvas, New York, The Metropolitan Museum of Art.

Spain but also his challenge to his virtuosity. The function of *Juan de Pareja* was to heighten Velázquez's social status and self-promotion."[28]

28. Carmen Fracchia, "Metamorphoses of the Self in Early-Modern Spain: Slave Portraiture and the Case of Juan de Pareja," In *Slave Portraiture in the Atlantic World*, edited by Agnes Lugo-Ortiz and Angela Rosenthal (New York: Cambridge University Press, 2013), 153.

This comparison allows students to raise questions regarding the agency and representation of enslaved and freed African men in early modern Spanish society. Juan de Pareja's portrait was publicly exhibited in Rome on March 19, 1650; at the time, Velázquez was in residence at the court of Pope Innocent X. When the canvas was displayed in the Pantheon, critics proclaimed that it represented "the truth in painting."[29] Nevertheless, Velázquez's portrait of Pareja presents certain paradoxes or exceptions; painted while Pareja was still enslaved, Velázquez strikingly represents him in a courtier portrait, an art genre that was restricted to Spain's elite.[30] After his emancipation, Juan de Pareja became an artist in his own right and included a self-portrait in his *The Calling of Saint Matthew* (1661, oil on canvas, Madrid, Museo Nacional del Prado).[31]

Comparison 2: Saint Martín de Porres and Luis de Vargas, *Preparations for the Crucifixion*

In considering Saint Martín's sanctity in colonial-era Peru, one can also draw comparisons to earlier Spanish paintings to make deeper historical connections between Spain and Latin America. For students, Spanish sixteenth-century images not only provide an instructive context for envisioning African Christianity but also support thinking critically about the relevance of art in framing transatlantic diasporic experiences. Sixteenth-century European altarpieces representing African men in donor portraits are rare in early modern art history. Luis de Vargas's *Preparations for the Crucifixion* (figure 5) illustrates a donor portrait of an African man who solemnly kneels in perpetual prayer before the scene of the Crucifixion. Early modern Spanish art rarely depicts this narrative from Christ's Passion. In this panel, Christ appears in repose on the Cross itself as he

29. For an extensive bibliography on Velázquez's *Juan de Pareja*, see the Metropolitan Museum of Art's online entry: https://www.metmuseum.org/art/collection/search/437869 (Accessed November 19, 2019).

30. Artist Julie Mehretu presents a compelling interpretation of this painting in *The Artist Project*, a video series supported by the Metropolitan Museum of Art: http://artistproject.metmuseum.org/5/julie-mehretu/. (Accessed November 19, 2019).

31. Carmen Fracchia and Hilary Macartney, "The Fall into Oblivion of the Works of the Slave Painter Juan de Pareja," *Art in Translation* 4 (2) (2012): 163–83.

Figure 5. Luis de Vargas, *Preparations for the Crucifixion.*

despondently awaits his Crucifixion. Aside from the donor, Roman soldiers surround Christ amid preparations for the Crucifixion.

While the African donor was most likely the individual who commissioned this work, his identity precludes a definitive identification. He wears a black suit with a white ruffled collar. Courtiers, nobility, and clergypersons wore this type of austere clothing that followed the fashions set out by the Hapsburgs who ruled Spain then. Thereby, the Black donor's clothing signifies his elevated social rank; for example, the elegant collar in Velázquez's portrait of *Juan de Pareja* (figure 4) is meant to illustrate an elevation in social status. Likewise, Vargas's portrait of the Black donor provides a counterpoint to the humble representation of Saint Martín de Porres (figure 2).

Comparison 3: *The Defense of the Eucharist* and Andrés Sánchez Gallque, *Don Francisco de Arobe and His Sons Pedro and Domingo*

This comparison focuses on the projection of identity conditioned by race, nation, and faith. In contrast to the grouping of figures in the *Defense of the Eucharist* (figure 3), Andrés Sánchez Gallque's group portrait (figure 6) allows for multiple comparisons regarding race, religion, and national allegiances. In contrast to how the Spanish demonized the Turks as apostates or non-believers who attempted to desecrate the Eucharist in the *Defense of the Eucharist* and required the Spanish king's intervention to control them (figure 3), Gallque's group portrait focuses on the allegiance and obedience of his subjects to the Spanish monarchy. The portrait was commissioned in 1599 by Juan Barrio y Sepúlveda, a judge in the *audiencia* (regional court) of the Viceroyalty of Peru, who sent it to King Philip III; a lengthy inscription and signature confirm the date of the painting as 1599 as well as Gallque's authorship of it. This painting was exported to Madrid as a gift to King Philip III and remained in the Spanish royal collection until it was transferred to the Prado Museum in the nineteenth century.

More importantly, Gallque's remarkable group portrait is the first significant representation of multiracial individuals of African and Indigenous ancestry and the "oldest surviving signed portrait" from South America.[32] Francisco de Arobe is shown with his two sons, Pedro and Domingo, during an official visit to Quito, Ecuador, in 1598; inscriptions above their

32. Tom Cummins, "Three Gentlemen from Esmeraldas: A Portrait fit for a King," in *Slave Portraiture in the Atlantic World*, edited by Agnes Lugo-Ortiz and Angela Rosenthal (New York: Cambridge University Press, 2013), 129.

Figure 6. Andrés Sánchez Gallque's group portrait.

heads identify their names. The elder de Arobe was the son of an indigenous Nicaraguan woman and an escaped enslaved African. He brokered an agreement with the Spanish Crown and pledged his loyalty to the king. In return, he was granted a governorship that gave him control over the Esmeraldas, an expansive region in Ecuador populated chiefly by African and Indigenous peoples and rich in natural resources. Portrayed in three-quarters length against a pale background, the men sport elaborate attire that incorporates Spanish-style collars and suits, Andean textiles, shell necklaces, and gold nose and ear ornaments. They all hold steel-tip spears that illustrate their defense of Ecuadorian territories against English and Dutch piracy.[33]

33. Thomas B.F. Cummins, "Don Francisco de Arobe and His Sons Pedro and Domingo," in *The Arts in Latin America* 1492–1820, edited by Joseph J. Rischel and Suzanne Stratton-Pruitt (New York and London: Yale University Press, 2006), VI-40, 418; Susan Verdi Webster, "Of Signatures and Status: Andrés Sánchez Gallque and Contemporary Painters in Early Colonial Quito," *The Americas*, Vol. 70, No. 4 (April 2014): 603–44; Tom Cummins, "Three Gentlemen from Esmeraldas: A Portrait Fit for a King," in *Slave Portraiture in the Atlantic World*, edited by Agnes Lugo-Ortiz and Angela Rosenthal (New York: Cambridge University Press, 2013), 119–145; and Baltasar Fra Molinero, "Los mulatos de Esmeraldas (1599): afrofuturismo en el museo," In *La negritud y su poética.*

Moreover, this approach to the three paintings from North Carolina collections prompts students to consider the implications of race in the Atlantic world to assess early modern artists' cultural identities. While the artists who painted these works remain anonymous, one can plausibly speculate that Afro-descended or Indigenous indigenous artists could have made them.

While the case studies focus on late-seventeenth- and eighteenth-century paintings by anonymous Spanish and South American artists, named artists of African origins such as Juan de Pareja in Madrid (figure 4),[34] Juan Correa in Mexico,[35] Andrés de Liébana in Lima, and the Indigenous Ecuadorian painter Andrés Sánchez Gallque[36] achieved recognition and success despite the barriers imposed by racial discrimination and social restrictions.[37]

The Visual Complexity of the African Diasporic Experience

In sum, these three paintings in North Carolina collections allow students to visualize the complexity of the African diaspora both in Spain and Latin America.[38]

Prácticas artísticas y miradas críticas contemporáneas en Latinoamérica y España, ed, Andrea Díaz Mattei (Montevideo: BMR-Cultural Sevilla Publicaciones Enredars, 2019), 51–67.

34. See Fracchia and Macartney, "The Fall into Oblivion of the Works of the Slave Painter Juan de Pareja," and also Fracchia, "Metamorphoses of the Self in Early-Modern Spain: Slave Portraiture and the Case of Juan de Pareja."
35. Aaron M. Hyman, "Inventing Painting: Cristóbal de Villalpando, Juan Correa, and New Spain's Transatlantic Canon," *The Art Bulletin*, Vol. 99, No. 2 (2017): 102–35.
36. See note 33 for references.
37. Joaneath Spicer, "Free Men and Women of African Ancestry in Renaissance Europe," In *Revealing the African Presence in Renaissance Europe*, edited by Joaneath Spicer (Baltimore: The Walters Art Museum, 2012), 81–99.
38. The following articles allow students to reflect further on the implications of early modern history and different aspects of the African diaspora: Tiffany Ruby Patterson and Robin D.G. Kelley, "Unfinished Migrations: Reflections on the African Diaspora and the Making of the Modern World," *African Studies Review* 43, no. 1 (2000): 11–45, and

Students cultivate a more nuanced perspective on Renaissance and Baroque art once they see representations of African and Indigenous peoples as individuals with agency and who were endowed with spirituality and sanctity, despite the obstacles they encountered in both European countries and Latin American societies. Evaluating these images helps them to visualize the extent to which Europeans exercised cultural control over colonized populations in the early modern era and how African diasporic communities endured and defied these challenges and were indeed visible in early modern Spanish and Latin American societies. These topics are incredibly complex to extricate as they are also entangled with the traumatic history of transatlantic slavery.

To contextualize the African contribution to global histories better, historians Kennetta Hammond Perry and Kira Thurman have re-circulated the term "Black Europe" to understand the ties between African diasporic and European communities, especially during the Renaissance. As both authors rightly note, this critical model of analysis "provides a framework for us to ask questions, rethink relationships, and reimagine linkages, and boundaries ... Thus, by examining Black lives and experiences in Europe's past, historians unsettle what it means to be European, and they unsettle what it means to be Black."[39] In the specific context of this essay, this framework underscores the contributions of Afro-descended peoples as imperative to the formation of artistic, cultural, intellectual, and social milieus in the early modern Atlantic world; in doing so, it decenters and resists racialized, hegemonic narratives of Renaissance art history and addresses the complexity of African diasporic identity in early modern Europe and Latin America.[40]

Nadi Edwards, "Diaspora, Difference, and Black Internationalisms," *Small Axe* 9, no. 17 (2005): 120–28.

39. Kennetta Hammond Perry and Kira Thurman, "Black Europe: A Useful Category of Analysis," http://www.aaihs.org/black-europe-a-useful-category-of-historical-analysis/ (Accessed November 19, 2019).

40. See T.F. Earle and K.J.P Lowe, eds., *Black Africans in Renaissance Europe* (New York: Cambridge University Press, 2005) and Paul Gilroy, *The Black Atlantic: Modernity and Double-Consciousness* (Cambridge, MA: Harvard University Press, 1995).

This category of historic analysis is valuable in understanding the implications of race in images of Black Africans in Spain and the Americas, such as *A Man Scraping Chocolate* (figure 1), *Saint Martín de Porres* (figure 2), and *The Defense of the Eucharist* (figure 3). *A Man Scraping Chocolate* (figure 1) shows how Black labor, particularly chocolate grinding, was perceived in early modern Spanish society. In comparison, *Saint Martín de Porres* (figure 2) illustrates how artists portrayed the sanctity and spiritual lives of Black saints in early modern Latin American visual culture. Finally, in a distinct and different visual turn, *The Defense of the Eucharist*'s (figure 3) transfer and imposition of negative racial and religious stereotypes on American communities allows for an extended analysis of racialized imagery in seventeenth- and eighteenth-century South American art.

Additionally, this approach to analyzing early modern Iberian and Latin American imagery has profoundly impacted students; many undergraduates are surprised by these images. Most students associate pre-modern European art and history with the physical horrors and psychological trauma of slavery and racial violence, and not necessarily with the representation of non-European subjects. Studying these images, particularly in the context of an HBCU, allows more in-depth discussions about social justice and injustices concerning the representation of Africans in early modern visual culture. For example, are the men in these paintings objectified following European definitions of blackness, or do their likenesses convey their agency as individuals?[41] Moreover, in viewing these specific images of Afro-Hispanic and Afro-Latin American men, students are prompted to think more deeply about African Europeans and African Latin Americans to sort out the challenging global implications of colonialism, race, and nation.

41. For an excellent discussion of these issues in early modern European art, see Kim F. Hall, "Object into Object?: Some Thoughts on the Presence of Black Women in Early Modern Culture," in *Early Modern Visual Culture: Representation, Race, and Empire in Renaissance England*, ed. Peter Erickson and Clark Hulse (Philadelphia: University of Pennsylvania Press, 2000), 346–79.

Suggestions For Application: Discussion Questions

These five, multi-part questions are intended to engage students in art historical analysis and interpretation that encompasses both breadth and depth of critical thinking. In particular, the first question helps students understand the relevance of Renaissance imagery to contemporary art practices. The fifth question allows students to make connections throughout the extended timeline of the course that encompasses the Renaissance to contemporary art. In-class writing exercises could be guided by prompts such as:

1. How do artworks in local or regional (North Carolina, in this case study) collections connect to ones in other national and international collections? How can we find globality in local contexts?
2. How was African labor envisioned in early modern Iberian or Latin American art?
3. How was African spirituality presented in Latin American and Spanish art and visual culture?
4. How do these paintings challenge your point (or points of view) on identity and nation? Race? Otherness? Selfhood?
5. How do modern and contemporary African American artists such as John Biggers, Kehinde Wiley, Julie Mehrutu, and Amy Sherald engage or confront these European visual traditions in their artistic praxes?

Suggested Course Assignments

Different options for research-based course assignments on the topic of the African presence in European and Latin American early modern art history include an analytic comparison of two works of art supported by research; a Tiki-Toki timeline that covers a variety of objects from different cultures and periods within 1400–1800; a zine that, similarly to the timeline, is expansive in chronology and scope; or an exhibition proposal plan that contains an introduction, a checklist of twenty images, and an annotated bibliography, which can be formatted as an Adobe Spark presentation or archived in an online platform such as Omeka. These projects are scaffolded, meaning specific benchmarks such as the preparation of a proposal, the compilation of an annotated bibliography, and the write-up of drafts shape the undergraduate research process. These steps are constructive for students who need research experience in the arts and humanities disciplines.[42]

Suggested Further Readings

Fracchia, Carmen. "(Lack of) Visual Representation of Black Slaves in Spanish Golden Age Painting." *Journal of Iberian and Latin American Studies* 10, no. 1 (June 2004): 23–34.

———. "The Place of Slaves in Early Modern Spain." In *The Place of the Social Margins, 1350–1750*, edited by Andrew Spicer and Jane L. Stevens Crenshaw, 117–134. U.K.: Routledge, 2017.

———. "Constructing the Black Slave in Early Modern Spanish Painting." In *Others and Outcasts in Early Modern Europe*, edited by Tom Nichols, 179–195. Aldershot, U.K., and Burlington, VT: Ashgate, 2007.

Kaplan, Paul H.D. "Introduction." In *The Image of the Black in Western Art: From the Early Christian Era to the "Age of Discovery." From Demonic*

42. For the integration of in-person and virtual exhibitions as part of the undergraduate research experience, see Ian F. MacInnes, Alexa Sand, and Lisandra Estevez, "Using Exhibitions for Undergraduate Scholarship," CURAH: *The Arts and Humanities Division of the Council on Undergraduate Research*, http://curartsandhumanities.org/2019/11/18/undergraduate-exhibitions/ (Accessed November 21, 2019).

Threat of the Incarnation of Sainthood, edited by David Bindman and Henry Louis Gates, Jr., vol. 2, part I, 1–30. Cambridge, MA: The Belknap Press, 2010.

Lowe, Kate. "The Lives of African Slaves and People of African Descent in Renaissance Europe." In *Revealing the African Presence in Renaissance Europe*, edited by Joaneath Spicer, 13–34. Baltimore: The Walters Art Museum, 2012.

———. "Black Africans' Religious and Cultural Assimilation to, or, Appropriation of, Catholicism, 1470–1520." *Renaissance and Reformation* 31, no. 2 (Spring 2008): 67–86.

———. "The Stereotyping of Black Africans in Renaissance Europe." In *Black Africans in Renaissance Europe*, edited by T.F. Earle and K.J.P. Lowe, 17–47. Cambridge: Cambridge University Press, 2005.

Spicer, Joaneath. "European Perceptions of Blackness as Reflected in the Visual Arts." In *Revealing the African Presence in Renaissance Europe*, edited by Joaneath Spicer, 35–59. Baltimore: The Walters Art Museum, 2012.

———. "Free Men and Women of African Ancestry in Renaissance Europe." In *Revealing the African Presence in Renaissance Europe*, edited by Joaneath Spicer, 81–99. Baltimore: The Walters Art Museum, 2012.

Stoichita, Victor I. "The Image of the Black in Spanish Art: Sixteenth and Seventeenth Centuries." In *The Image of the Black in Western Art, From the "Age of Discovery" to the Age of Abolition, Part 1: Artists of the Renaissance and Baroque*, edited by David Bindman and Henry Louis Gates, Jr., vol. 3, part I, 191–234. Cambridge, MA: The Belknap Press, 2010.

Podcasting Las Casas and Robert E. Lee: A Case Study in Historicizing Race

ELIZABETH SPRAGINS

Classes that focus on early modern history, literature, and thought have lost much cachet amid today's academic interest in "marketable skills" and a fast-moving news cycle.[1] This may be due to our society's commitment to what some early modernists decry as a prevailing "ideology of presentism," the challenges of making pre-modern culture relevant to students trying to make the most out of an expensive education, or part of a broader crisis in the humanities.[2] In the face of waning humanities graduate programs and job markets, why should undergraduates read sixteenth- and seventeenth-century literature? What does Bartolomé de las Casas, sixteenth-century Spanish friar and social reformer, have to do with twenty-first century political or social activism? How can a Portuguese chronicle from the fifteenth century possibly help us to better understand the United States or, even more microscopically, a small college in rural Virginia, such as the one where I taught this course?[3] These questions and so many others about the Renaissance and early colonial American history may be difficult for undergraduates to answer because of the devaluation of historical awareness in American secondary education and the myth that a degree in the humanities leads to poor employment prospects.

1. Benjamin Schmidt, "The Humanities Are in Crisis. Students are abandoning humanities majors, turning to degrees they think yield far better job prospects. But they're wrong." *The Atlantic*, August 23, 2018, https://www.theatlantic.com/ideas/archive/2018/08/the-humanities-face-a-crisisof-confidence/567565/.
2. Sidney Donnell, "*Don Quixote* in the Balance: Early Modern Studies and the Undergraduate Curriculum," in *Approaches to Teaching Cervantes*'s Don Quixote, 2nd ed., edited by James A. Parr and Lisa Vollendorf (New York: MLA, 2015), 200.
3. As I discuss in greater detail later, this institution was a small liberal arts college with an enrollment of approximately 1,800 undergraduates and 400 graduate students.

The danger of "presentism" becomes even more urgent when we focus on the history of racist ideology and systems. A key feature of these systems of oppression is the insidiously widespread common-sense understanding of race as a timeless, biological category that divides humans into inevitable and natural categories.[4] If we accept that the notion of preordained racial categories remains a major factor in the perpetuation of systematic racism throughout the world and particularly in the United States, it is historically and ethically incumbent upon university instructors to debunk these preconceptions. In my experience teaching "Comparative Critical Race Theory and the Early Modern Creation of Race," in this iteration, an intensive, four-week, bridge course aimed at second- and third-year Spanish majors, asking students to historicize race by listening to and creating podcasts engages them through a medium that is innovative and approachable. It also encourages them to develop empathetic and careful listening skills, and it provides a model for composing their own ideas into written and spoken form. Put in other terms, podcasting as a method for historicizing race asks students to think carefully about whose voices they are listening to, both literally and metaphorically; what voices should be amplified; and how to add their own voices to this important conversation. This essay presents the contours of one course that used podcasting to address the conundrum of how to historicize racial and racist ideology for students living in the United States after 2016, when Donald Trump was elected President.

4. This misconception is common, despite ample scholarship and mainstream media that attests to the contrary. Disseminating information about the history of race as a constructed category also pushes back against white-washed images of pre-modern Europe, a live issue among pre-modern scholars in light of recent controversies about white supremacist appropriation of medieval studies. See, for example, Jennifer Schuessler, "Medieval Scholars Joust with White Nationalists. And One Another," *The New York Times*, May 5, 2019, https://www.nytimes.com/2019/05/05/arts/the-battle-for-medieval-studies-white-supremacy.html.

Questioning Audible Voices in the Classroom

As a teacher trained and experienced in teaching Spanish as a second language and tasked with teaching a bridge (200-level/intermediate) course for undergraduate Spanish majors, I approached the ethical and historical problem of how to teach early modern race in part as a question of language pedagogy. In part thanks to Elizabeth Bernhardt-Kamil's more expansive understanding of second language pedagogy and learning, proficiency and literacy, I regard upper-level classes in Spanish as continuations of the language sequence and as opportunities to expand my students' language proficiency as well as cultural, historical, and social literacy.[5] How could undergraduate students gain second-language proficiency by reading, writing, listening, and speaking about the history of race in the Western Hemisphere? How does developing their proficiency in those linguistic domains also enable them to think critically about their position within systems and ideologies of race and racism in the twenty-first century? In this course, analyzing and discussing emotionally charged issues like race in a second language allowed second-language learners to gain critical distance from ideas which, in their first language, they might take for granted along with their first-language fluency. Similarly, the course demonstrated that a greater depth of knowledge of systems of human classification in other languages, societies, and time periods allowed students to gain perspective on their own language, society, and time.

Since the election of Donald Trump as President of the United States in 2016, the audibility and visibility of white supremacy in the nation has skyrocketed. Widely covered events like the white-supremacist dominated Unite the Right rally in Charlottesville (August 11–12, 2017); the Tree of Life shooting in Pittsburgh, PA, targeting Jewish people (October 27, 2017); and the El Paso shooting targeting Latinx people (August 3, 2019) have drawn media attention to what many critical race theorists and social justice activists have been arguing for decades: racism is alive and well in

5. I am indebted to Bernhardt for this training. See her *Understanding Advanced Second-Language Reading* (London: Routledge, 2010).

the United States, and many of the country's most respected institutions are not just steeped *in* but built *on* white supremacy. It has become clear that how academia deals with racism both inside and outside the classroom must extend far beyond calls for diversity, equity, and inclusion, and embark instead on the more challenging work of grappling with academia's own complicity as historical beneficiary of literal and ideological violence directed at racialized minorities.

At the small college in rural Virginia where I taught my course on "Comparative Critical Race Theory and the Early Modern Creation of Race," local concerns about race and racism were highly charged and urgent. Students and faculty alike were dissatisfied with the college administration's tepid response to the Charlottesville rally and a KKK leafleting campaign on campus.[6] These troubling events were exacerbated by the college's long-term commitment to the Confederate General Robert E. Lee, its historical aversion to and ongoing difficulties with admitting a diverse student body and hiring and retaining diverse faculty, and the conservative leanings of some alumni.[7] Finally, some members of the com-

6. Will Dudley, "KKK Leafleting," *W&L Messages to the Community*, October 26, 2018, https://www.wlu.edu/the-w-l-story/leadership/office-of-the-president/messages-to-the-community/2018-19/kkk-leafleting/. Alison Graham, "W&L condemns hate group's flyers found on campus," *Roanoke Times*, October 29, 2018, https://roanoke.com/news/education/w-l-condemns-hate-groups-flyers-found-on-campus/article_aa16a3ef-6e97-501d-a2d5-fd118a37008c.html.
7. I taught this course in a previous appointment in the Romance Languages Department at Washington and Lee University. US News & World Reports currently ranks WLU's "campus ethnic diversity" in the bottom third of their list of national liberal arts colleges. "Campus Ethnic Diversity: National Liberal Arts Colleges," *US News & World Reports*, accessed August 5, 2019, https://www.usnews.com/best-colleges/rankings/national-liberal-arts-colleges/campus-ethnic-diversity. Certainly, such statistics are not the only way of thinking about race or diversity in academia, but I use this here as a metric of the extent of the institution's particular limitations on this point, both historically and at present. I am not the first to draw attention to WLU's struggles with race, diversity, and its history of white supremacy. See, for example, Taylor Dolven, "Faculty consider leaving college named for Robert E. Lee after president rejects recommended changes to campus," *Vice News*, September 9, 2018, https://news.vice.com/

munity immediately surrounding the college engaged in a number of troubling practices, including holding annual parades of people dressed as Confederate soldiers on Martin Luther King Jr. weekend and openly displaying Confederate flags in the downtown area. The few Latinx students I taught in this context frequently expressed frustration at the institutional expectation that they would stand as representatives for their ethnic and cultural groups when these issues were addressed. These concerns were pressing for all the students entering my classroom, and they regularly entered our discussions from their various ethnic and cultural positions.

I realized that I could not solve any of these problems as an individual. During an intensive four-week term, however, I sought to make my classroom a community that opened a conversation about the history of race and racism as a Transatlantic phenomenon shaped by the influence of power and economic interests. At an institution where student and alumni voices can motivate change in the administration, it was my hope that the students I reached would go on to push for broader institutional changes both while they were students and after graduation. Even if the institution does not satisfactorily resolve these issues, I wanted my students to leave our class with a better understanding of what created our modern understanding of race, as well as a greater ability to engage in educated and civil conversations about the impact of race and racism on the world.

Amplifying Underrepresented Voices to Link Past and Present

In designing my syllabus, I sought a balance among podcasts, secondary sources that surveyed the major tenets and concerns of critical race theory, primary sources that situated the histories we were covering, and other materials that addressed contemporary issues in which the students were emotionally invested. The auditory component of the class emerged from one of its organizing principles: to disrupt institutional

en_us/article/kz5eye/faculty-consider-leaving-college-named-for-robert-e-lee-after-president-rejects-recommended-changes-to-campus.

silence on these points through conversation. In choosing a guide for the theoretical underpinnings of critical race theory, a movement originally based in law schools, I prioritized selections that were accessible and engaging but that challenged students to think critically about the role of race not just in a legal setting but more broadly in society.[8] Ultimately, I saw the early modern texts playing multiple and important roles in raising my students' awareness about the historicity of race and the prevalence of racism in the present day. These texts were intended to be relatively safe sites in which to practice evaluating strategies of racism. Here, too, was evidence of the artificiality of racialized systems: the economic, political, and cultural underpinnings of fifteenth-century racism are all abundantly clear. By learning to question these texts, students began to practice habits of antiracist thought.[9] While in other academic settings, I might have more heavily weighted the syllabus with primary texts from Transatlantic, Iberian, and Latin American literature, for this place and this time, I chose to teach the class as a primer for my predominantly white, American-born students.

The backbone of the syllabus was a collection of podcasts that deal with race from diverse perspectives and across a number of time periods, including *Seeing White*, *Code Switch*, and *Uncivil*.[10] Some of these pod-

8. For graduate students already familiar with some of the basic concepts of critical race theory, for example, the comprehensive edited volume *Critical Race Theory: The Key Writings That Formed the Movement*, eds. Kimberlé Crenshaw, Neil Gotanda, Gary Peller, and Kendall Thomas (New York: The New Press, 1996), would directly expose students to foundational articles that shaped this school of thought. Given my undergraduate students' lack of familiarity with these ideas, I instead adopted the more accessible summary given by Richard Delgado and Jean Stefancic in their volume *Critical Race Theory: An Introduction*, with a foreword by Angela Harris (New York: New York University Press, 2001).
9. On such habits, see Ibram X. Kendi, *How to Be an Antiracist* (New York: One World, 2019).
10. *Scene on Radio: Seeing White*, season 2, February–August 2017, produced by John Biewen, podcast, MP3 audio, https://www.sceneonradio.org/seeing-white/. Shereen Marisol Meraji and Gene Demby, *Code Switch*, produced by Shereen Marisol Meraji and others, podcast, MP3 audio, https://www.npr.org/sections/codeswitch/. *Uncivil*,

casts spoke to the early modern origins of race; some addressed particular contours of American racism in the nineteenth, twentieth, and twenty-first centuries; still others highlighted the negative health effects of racism on particular human bodies through telomere shortening and other results of chronic stress. These podcasts accordingly gave students a sense of ongoing contemporary conversations (emotional, factual, and historical) about the devastating history and effects of race and racism on lives in this country. At an institution with a disproportionately high white population, the question of voice was a live and constantly present issue in my classroom.[11] Throughout her work on education as a practice of freedom, Black feminist bell hooks emphasizes the importance of "voice" in engaged classrooms. She asks: "Who speaks? Who listens? And why?"[12] Similarly, Delgado and Stefancic, in *Critical Race Theory: An Introduction*, discuss the centrality of the "voice of color thesis" to justice for some critical race theorists: namely, the contention that "minority status [...] brings with it a presumed competence to speak about race and racism."[13] On the one hand, it was important for students to hear voices of color speak to their experiences of race and racism, but on the other, it was an unfair burden to impose on the few students of color in my classroom that they be solely responsible for making voices of color heard.

The medium of podcasts was an obvious resource that introduced and amplified voices of color both in and out of the classroom and expanded the viewpoints to which students had access. It also redirected my students' attention away from my own voice toward the voices on podcasts and toward one another's voices. The visceral emotional impact of these podcasts on my students is best expressed in their own words. One course evaluation remarked: "There was never a time that I read something for class or listened to a podcast and didn't have some sort of deep

produced by Kimmie Reglar and others, podcast, MP3 audio, https://gimletmedia.com/shows/uncivil.

11. bell hooks, *Teaching to Transgress: Education as the Practice of Freedom* (New York: Routledge, 1994), 40–41; 148–51.
12. hooks, *Teaching to Transgress*, 40.
13. Delgado and Jean, *Critical Race Theory*, 9.

thoughts about it. In fact, there were several times when I gasped aloud or audibly said, 'Wow,' because a shocking fact or story had been presented." While, of course, many podcasts are just as edited and produced as written sources are, audible media can convey a personal and affective impact in ways difficult to achieve in writing, often because of the ineffable emotional effect of the human voice on its listener or the apparent spontaneity of the spoken word. On a more mundane level, presenting my students with a broad range of podcasts gave them an archive of models to imitate and adapt when they were asked to create their own podcasts for the final project, which I will discuss in greater detail below.

In addition to the assigned podcasts, students read Delgado and Stefancic's *Critical Race Theory: An Introduction* to gain familiarity with the basic tenets and major contours of critical race theory, as well as to learn key terminology that scholars use to discuss race and racism.[14] This text proved useful for a number of reasons, many of which were due to its design as a text to be used in a classroom: the accessibility of its language, the clarity with which it defined and used terms, the thought-provoking questions found at the end of each section, and the extensive bibliography which directed students to more specialized resources depending on particular areas of interest. In blog entries for each class meeting, students often shared that they found what they had read in this text eye-opening, while in their final projects they incorporated frameworks and key terms that they had learned in this primer. While a wider selection of critical material about theories of race and ethnicity is available, Delgado and Stefancic is pitched at a level that is accessible to undergraduates while surveying the landscape of this sophisticated field.[15]

14. Delgado and Stefancic, *Critical Race Theory*.
15. The bibliography is now extensive. Some more sophisticated options addressing race past and present might include: Crenshaw, Gotanda, Peller, and Thomas, eds., *Critical Race Theory*; Thomas Foster Earle and K. J. P. Lowe, eds., *Black Africans in Renaissance Europe* (Cambridge: Cambridge University Press, 2010); Geraldine Heng, *The Invention of Race in the European Middle Ages* (Cambridge: Cambridge University Press, 2018); Hazel Rose Markus and Paula M. L. Moya, eds., *Doing Race: 21 Essays for the 21st Century* (New York: Norton, 2010); Michael Omi and Howard Winant, *Racial Formation in the United States*, 3rd ed. (London: Routledge, 2015).

Correspondingly, students learned about the historical and legal origins of twenty-first-century American racist ideologies by reading some of the early modern texts that scholars of race identify as the origins of white supremacist thought in the Western Hemisphere.[16] We start with the court historian Gomes Eanes de Zurara (c. 1410–c. 1474), who chronicled Portuguese conquests along the African littoral during the middle of the fifteenth century. Students read the first chapter of an English translation of his *Chronicle of the Discovery and Conquest of Guinea* (1453), which establishes Prince Henry the Navigator as Zurara's patron and thus delineates clear economic, political, and social motivations for portraying in a positive light the beginnings of what would become the Transatlantic slave trade.[17] They later read chapters twenty-five and thirty-six of the same chronicle, which depict the first slave markets in Lagos and Lisbon (Portugal) in the 1440s. Providing more context for Zurara's text were excerpts from critical race scholar Ibram X. Kendi's *Stamped from the Beginning*, as well as an interview Kendi recorded with John Biewen in Part Two of *Seeing White*. Students remarked on the dramatic cognitive dissonance at work in these scenes, in which Zurara simultaneously describes in detailed terms the suffering inflicted on these first victims of the global slave trade while also seeking to dehumanize them or justify that suffering in religious terms. The clear influence of the royal family's economic interests in exploiting these human beings as assets became a touchstone for the remainder of the term. Referring back to Zurara as a tainted and unreliable source, students readily identified or questioned the economic interests underlying racial language in later works, while also doubting the credibility of certain faith-based pretexts for exploitative behavior and practices.

Students went on to read excerpts from the first voyage from Christopher Columbus's *Diary*, in which they encountered depictions of Euro-

16. Kendi, *Stamped from the Beginning: The Definitive History of Racist Ideas in America* (New York: Nation Books, 2016), 15–30. James H. Sweet, "The Iberian Roots of American Racist Thought," *The William and Mary Quarterly* 54, no. 1 (1997): 143–66.
17. Gomes Eanes de Zurara, *The Chronicle of the Discovery and Conquest of Guinea*, trans. Charles Raymond Beazley, vol. 1 (Cambridge: Cambridge University Press, 2010).

peans' first encounters with the indigenous populations of the Caribbean basin.[18] In preparing students to read these sections, it was particularly useful to contextualize the intellectual underpinnings of the voyage as a continuation of "Reconquest" ideology, which pitted Christians against Muslims in stark religious, linguistic, territorial, and racial terms.[19] Constructive for unpacking these medieval precursors to Columbus's worldview was historian David Nirenberg's article on "Race and the Middle Ages," which cogently summarizes concerns in the scholarly community as to whether "race" is anachronistic to the medieval period, while also acknowledging the productivity of drawing comparisons between medieval and modern understandings of human difference.[20] Key to their discussion of Reconquest discourse throughout the *Diario* was recognizing the extent to which prescribed language, actions, and concepts dictated what Columbus attempts to present as an unscripted encounter. A crucial point in our discussion of both Zurara's and Columbus's representations of European imperialism was unpacking the language of environmental determinism, the belief that race and its traits commonly associated with it (appearance, intellectual abilities, work ethic, etc.) are the result of environmental factors. Our discussion of this theory of race, and the closely related Curse of Ham, which exegetically assigns certain regions of the known world to sons of Noah and their descendants,

18. Christopher Columbus *The Four Voyages of Christopher Columbus*, ed. and trans. J. M. Cohen, (New York: Penguin Books, 1969).
19. The ideologically loaded, nineteenth-century historiographical term "Reconquest" or "*Reconquista*" broadly refers to the period of conflict between 711 and 1492 in which Christian forces "re"-conquered tracts of territory throughout the Iberian Peninsula under Muslim control following the Umayyad conquest of the region during the first half of the eighth century. For a survey of the idea of reconquest in medieval Iberia, see Luis García-Guijarro Ramos, "*Reconquista* and Crusade in the Central Middle Ages. A Conceptual and Historiographical Survey," in *Crusading on the Edge: Ideas and Practice of Crusading in Iberia and the Baltic Region, 1100–1500*, eds. Torben Kjersgaard Nielsen and Iben Fonnesberg-Schmidt, 55–88 (Turnhout: Brepols Publishers, 2016).
20. David Nirenberg, "Race and the Middle Ages: The Case of Spain and Its Jews," in *Rereading the Black Legend: The Discourses of Religious and Racial Difference in the Renaissance Empires*, edited by Margaret R. Greer, Walter D. Mignolo, and Maureen Quilligan (Chicago: University of Chicago Press, 2007), 71–87.

opened a conversation about the suspect role of science and scientific discourse in perpetuating systematic racism.[21]

The third major primary text that anchored the course was Bartolomé de las Casas's *Brevísima relación de la destrucción de las Indias* [A Short Account of the Destruction of the Indies] (1543), a critique of atrocities committed by Spaniards against the indigenous inhabitants of the Americas in the first decades of Spain's colonial project.[22] In many ways, this was the text with which students most identified ideologically — Las Casas does not sugarcoat his descriptions of the abuses perpetrated in a wide range of contexts, and the grotesque behavior of the Spaniards makes it easy for readers to choose sides — but had the most difficulty getting through emotionally. While earlier in the class, students were eager to point out logical fallacies or contradictions committed by Zurara and Columbus, the graphic depictions of rape, murder, and torture in the *Brevísima relación* often left them at a loss for words. Despite their discomfort with these passages, they also recognized the discursive and moral force these sections marshalled to galvanize the reader to act against injustice.

This wide-ranging syllabus sought to make early modern texts accessible to students working in their second language by relating them to issues of immediate and urgent concern, as well as by assigning secondary materials, both written and aural, that provided historical and cultural context for what they were reading. The accessibility of the early modern materials, in turn, gave students a more comfortable arena to practice evaluating and criticizing racist behaviors and strategies of early modern people before being asked to turn the same lens on their own communities. The rich class discussions that emerged from the students' deep engagement with these materials and the fluency with which they moved

21. See Benjamin Braude's excellent survey of the relationship of the Curse of Ham to medieval and early modern discourses of race in "The Sons of Noah and the Construction of Ethnic and Geographical Identities in the Medieval and Early Modern Periods," *The William and Mary Quarterly* 54, no. 1 (1997): 103–42.

22. Bartolomé de las Casas, *Brevísima relación de la destrucción de las Indias*, ed. André Saint-Lu (Madrid: Cátedra, 2003); Las Casas, *A Short Account of the Destruction of the Indies*, ed. and trans. Nigel Griffin, with an introduction by Anthony Pagden (New York: Penguin Books, 2004).

between the pre-modern and contemporary issues speaks to the productivity of putting these materials in conversation with each other.

Students' Voices in the Classroom

The central purpose of the course was to encourage students to develop the tools, linguistic and otherwise, to examine their beliefs and attitudes surrounding race and those expressed by others. Second-language literacy scholar Alan Hirvela insightfully identifies reading as a process and skill that is inextricable from writing; students who wish to become effective writers must first learn what it means to be a good reader.[23] It follows that students who wish to become proficient speakers must also learn to be good listeners. The assignments for which they were responsible asked them to use all modalities of language — reading, writing, listening, speaking — in different ways and contexts to enhance their proficiency in engaging with and discussing these issues. Assignments were designed to encourage them to rehearse language and ideas in lower-stakes environments so as to increase their confidence and willingness to participate in such conversations outside of the classroom. By engaging in formal and informal writing and speaking assignments both individually and collaboratively, students practiced using a broad range of registers and language to examine a wide range of issues.

In the first class, we agreed to create a community of mutual respect and understanding and to hold one another accountable for our shortcomings. We established a regular practice of reading, listening, and writing on low-stakes assignments, like blog entries and written responses to podcasts, to develop a common language for analyzing and examining racism at the level of individuals and systems.[24] Given the added compli-

23. Alan Hirvela, *Connecting Reading and Writing in Second Language Writing Instruction* (Ann Arbor, MI: The University of Michigan Press, 2004), 1–8.

24. Chenjerai Kumunyika speaks eloquently to the importance of focusing on the systematic rather than the individual. "Part 1: Turning the Lens," February 15, 2017, in *Scene on Radio: Seeing White*, produced by John Biewen, podcast, MP3 audio, 10:15–12:50, http://www.sceneonradio.org/episode-31-turning-the-lens-seeing-white-part-1/.

cation that the majority of my students were speaking and writing in a second language – Spanish – the question of appropriate vocabulary was a particularly present one for the class. One important activity from the first week of instruction came on the first day of class: students spent an hour before the next class looking for resources in Spanish for how to discuss race conscientiously. The next day, students worked in small groups to create an initial glossary of terminology that we as a community were comfortable using. Some of this vocabulary was, by necessity, literally translated from an American context into Spanish, since it reflected the particular needs and preferences of individuals in our classroom in the rural American South. As our discussions evolved over the course of the term, new vocabulary continued to flesh out this shared lexicon. The collaborative nature of this assignment was meant to get them thinking about community and the inescapable fact that racism can only be combated when groups of people mobilize to change systems.

Despite the lexical challenges presented by discussing issues of race in a second language, these proficiency limitations actually lowered affective barriers for the challenging conversations we were trying to have. During breaks, I would occasionally solicit informal feedback from students about how they felt discussions were going, and if they would prefer to continue a particular conversation in English rather than Spanish. While I knew these students were invested in maintaining a Spanish-speaking space for their pursuit of linguistic proficiency, almost without exception they explained that their linguistic preferences were dictated by a greater sense of safety in that second-language learning space. This sort of learning environment implied a greater degree of cooperative communication among language learners and generosity in listeners. On my students' account, listeners in this setting would be more likely to assume that errors in communication or slips of the tongue were an inevitable result of the language-learning process, rather than of underlying ill intent on the part of the speaker. In other words, discussing race in a second language

See also The People's Institute for Survival and Beyond, "Our Principles," Undoing Racism®, accessed July 23, 2019, https://www.pisab.org/our-principles/.

meant that everyone assumed that everyone else would make mistakes, and those mistakes were just part of the process.

Discussions of both primary and secondary sources were initiated alternately through direct contributions to the class blog or comments on classmates' entries, due by midnight the night before class. Each class meeting began with discussions of the most recent blog contributions in pairs or small groups. A fixture in second language classrooms, discussions in pairs and small groups are widely recognized to do critical work for student learning: it gives students more opportunities to practice and produce language; it gives less-vocal students the chance to rehearse language in lower-stakes situations; it can serve as motivation if students compete with one another, and so on. In this class on critical race theory, the small group or pair was critical for allowing students to rehearse ideas in a more private setting. Many students expressed considerable anxiety about saying the wrong thing and inadvertently offending their classmates. By giving them the chance to first articulate ideas in writing on the blog, and then to discuss their ideas with a few classmates they trusted, students had several chances to settle on language they were comfortable with as well as question and refine underlying assumptions before having to speak their ideas in front of the entire classroom.

On days for which students had listened to a podcast, class began with time for individual, written reflections in Spanish on the podcast that had been assigned for the day. Students produced concise summaries, identified surprising or compelling facts or perspectives they had learned from listening, and related them to critical race theory concepts we had discussed thus far. Subsequent small-group discussions of these reactions meant that students uncomfortable speaking in front of the entire class could begin to explore these challenging and complex ideas with just a few peers before having to articulate their reactions more publicly. These initial conversations were opportunities for self-reflection and for beginning to build toolkits of antiracist habits of thought. The discussions acted as the backbone of the class as students got more comfortable with each other and with seeing, voicing, and starting to unravel their own internalized biases. Over the course of the four weeks, the conversations students had about "the problem of race" more frequently began to include recognitions of the ways in which they themselves participated in perpetuating it, as well as race and racism as an abstract issue.

As they witnessed this conversation, students learned vocabulary and terminology to structure and monitor their own language, and looked for spaces to make their own, local contributions. Their final project was to deploy the critical framework we had begun to develop over the course of the term to produce a podcast that engaged in a meaningful way with an issue concerning race or racism. Students worked in pairs to create a podcast in which they used an element of critical race theory to frame an issue, text, or event of particular interest to the students. The assignment encouraged students to go out into the university community and engage classmates and mentors in conversation about some of the issues we were discussing in the classroom — thus expanding the range of contexts in which students felt competent to participate in and initiate conversations about race in their broader community. Using the free audio-editing software *Audacity*, groups edited and mixed ten-to-fifteen-minute episodes with music, sound effects, interviews, and recorded commentary in which they examined their topic. Along with their final edited podcasts, they created "show-notes" to accompany the sound file that provided background and context for the podcast. In these show-notes, students gave brief summaries of their theoretical framework, links to related articles, and research that allowed listeners to more fully appreciate their podcasts. The resulting podcasts discussed a range of local topics and concerns, including intersectionality and the margins of identity, the experience of students of color in the university's system of fraternities and sororities, and the differences in racial discourse between Panama and the US, this final topic informed by a student's bicultural background. The students presented their projects to the rest of the class during the final week of the course, with time for questions from classmates. This question-and-answer period productively pushed students to engage in spontaneous conversation about topics to which they had devoted considerable thought.

Conclusions and Suggestions for Podcasts for Teaching Race in the Renaissance

One of the single greatest challenges of discussing race and racism for students in a predominantly white classroom, or in more general forums, is the fear of getting it wrong. What if I open my mouth and say the wrong thing, and, all of a sudden, everyone in the room sees me for what I am: a racist? Or, what if I'm asked to speak as the representative, token person of color in a predominantly white space? What if I'm made the object of racist microaggressions? Writing about race and racism is, if possible, even scarier. In the classroom scenario, there is at least the possibility that the faux pas one just committed will have been missed by other inattentive students, too busy scanning Twitter on open laptop screens to pay attention to a companion's stuttering slip-up. Writing, on the other hand, leaves a record, a time-stamped mark on the page that indelibly records the time that you got it wrong. Such high stakes mean that conversations about race in the US are often superficial, "designed to protect our fortresses of identity and to spare us from excavating those places where guilt and hurt, bitterness and anger, lie not at all deeply buried."[25]

As a new and diverse medium, podcasts exist in a liminal place between these two extremes. In generic terms, podcasts may provide one model for how civil conversations about race can take place going forward: on the one hand, citizens engaging in careful consideration and research in controlled environments, but on the other hand, those same citizens participating actively and spontaneously in interactions with other members of society. Wanting that conversation, believing that it is acutely important, and knowing how to engage in it are entirely different things. Approaching this problem through the frame of language proficiency gives the students concrete tools for thinking deliberately about what they do with their voice, while also giving them the space in which to use it. Producing a podcast requires extensive preparation and planning but can also emerge as the result of spontaneous conversations between

25. Leonard Pitts, Jr., "The Challenges of Writing for White People," *Literary Hub*, February 12, 2019, https://lithub.com/the-challenges-of-writing-for-white-people/.

two or more people that happened to be captured digitally. A return to the Renaissance roots of modern-day racism through podcasts encourages students to develop their own voices and engage with others as they examine the ways power and economic interests shaped the earliest versions of present-day ideology.

Discussion Questions

1. How should we adapt our pedagogical approaches to the racial and ethnic, composition of the class? Especially in predominantly white classrooms, how can we make space for voices of color without tokenizing them or making students of color into native informants?
2. How do we create a classroom environment that fosters multi-racial dialogue and combats microaggressions and other forms of aggressive comments and behavior? In other words, how do we minimize harm to all students while still fostering dialogue and reflexivity in the classroom?
3. How might engaging with contemporary issues of race from an early modern perspective open space for discussing race as a historical, social ideology not a biological inevitability, and, perhaps, provide a more affective distance for us to observe, reflect upon, and critique racist and racializing ideologies?
4. How can podcasting and other forms of new media provide unique strategies for historicizing race? In what way do these media prompt us as a learning community to think carefully about voice: voices we are listening to, both literally and metaphorically; what voices should be amplified; and how to add our own voices to this important conversation?
5. How might second language pedagogy give us new tools and approaches for teaching race in the Renaissance? Using these strategies, how might we constitute classrooms that lower affective filters (emotional variables associated with success and failure); empower learners to become socially aware risk-takers while learning; create safe environments for learners to share their thinking, make mistakes, and assimilate corrections?

Suggestions for Further Reading

Bernhardt-Kamil, Elizabeth. *Understanding Advanced Second-Language Reading*. London: Routledge, 2010.

Branche, Jerome. *Racism and Colonialism in Luso-Hispanic Literature*. Columbia, MO: University of Missouri Press, 2006.

Crenshaw, Kimberlé, Neil Gotanda, Gary Peller, and Kendall Thomas, eds. *Critical Race Theory; The Key Writings That Formed the Movement*. New York: The New Press, 1995.

Delgado, Richard, and Jean Stefancic. *Critical Race Theory: An Introduction*. With a foreword by Angela Harris. New York: New York University Press, 2001.

Earle, Thomas Foster, and K. J. P. Lowe, eds. *Black Africans in Renaissance Europe*. Cambridge: Cambridge University Press, 2010.

Heng, Geraldine. *The Invention of Race in the European Middle Ages*. Cambridge: Cambridge University Press, 2018.

Hirvela, Alan. *Connecting Reading and Writing in Second Language Writing Instruction*. Ann Arbor, MI: The University of Michigan Press, 2004.

Jones, Nicholas R., Cassander Smith, and Miles P. Greer, eds. *Early Modern Black Diaspora Studies*. New York: Palgrave MacMillan, 2018.

Omi, Michael, and Howard Winant. *Racial Formation in the United States*. 3rd ed. London: Routledge, 2015.

American Moor: Othello, Race, and the Conversations Here and Now

MARJORIE RUBRIGHT AND AMY RODGERS

In their 2019 MLA essay in *Profession*, "BlacKKKShakespearean: A Call to Action for Medieval and Early Modern Studies," Kimberly Anne Coles, Kim F. Hall, and Ayanna Thompson provide five axioms for expanding our reach in what we teach and why, to whom we teach, and how we diversify the pipeline of students entering early modern studies.[1] Starting with the acknowledgement that "our fields of study are not politically neutral," Coles, Hall, and Thompson propose that the work of attracting a multiplicity of students to pre- and early modern fields will require that we: Start Early; Provide Mentors; Create Inclusive Events; Support Professional Training Across Institutions; and Cite Scholars of Color. While this crystalizing call to action was published after the *American Moor* Five College residency that we discuss in this chapter, this artistic and scholarly project pursued similar goals, and, we hope, offers an interdisciplinary, performance-forward model for meeting them.

The brainchild of stage and television actor Keith Hamilton Cobb, *American Moor* explores the legacy of William Shakespeare's *Othello* via the perspective of a Black American actor auditioning for the eponymous lead role.[2] At the request of the "director" character (typed as a young, white man fresh out of an MFA program), Cobb performs only one monologue from the play – Othello's Act I address to the Venetian senate, the governing body of white, European aristocrats who call Othello to appear before them to answer, simultaneously, their call to lead the Venetian fleet against the advancing Ottoman force and the charge that he has

1. Kimberly Anne Coles, Kim F. Hall, and Ayanna Thompson, "BlacKKKShakespearean: A Call to Action for Medieval and Early Modern Studies." *Profession* (MLA: 2019) https://profession.mla.org/blackkkshakespearean-a-call-to-action-for-medieval-and-early-modern-studies/
2. On *American Moor*, visit http://keithhamiltoncobb.com/site/american-moor/

"abducted," and married, one of their most prominent citizen's only daughter. From here, *American Moor* diverges sharply from *Othello* in content while following some similar, and transhistorically relevant, thematic avenues. If Cobb's narrative takes us on journey of the African American actor's relationship to one of the two Shakespeare roles that he is "destined" to play (the other being Aaron the Moor from *Titus Andronicus*), both plays explore the profound consequences of what W.E.B. Du Bois called double-consciousness: the reality of living as a Black subject in a hegemonically white world. As Du Bois claims, "After the Egyptian and Indian, the Greek and Roman, the Teuton and Mongolian, the Negro is a sort of seventh son, born with a veil, and gifted with second sight in this American world – a world which yields him no true self-consciousness, but only lets him see himself through the revelation of the other world. It is a peculiar sensation, this double-consciousness, this sense of always looking at one's self through the eyes of others, of measuring one's soul by the tape of a world that looks on in amused contempt and pity."[3] That the twenty-first century African American actor's journey should intersect with a fictional seventeenth-century Black, Venetian general's seemed sufficiently extraordinary (and yet painfully unsurprising) to create an interdisciplinary, multi-campus event dedicated to exploring the histories of (and cross-currents between) these two stories separated by more than three centuries and yet still traveling hand-in-hand through our own contemporary racial moment.

Playwright Keith Hamilton Cobb is probably most well-known for his extensive television work on ABC's daytime drama *All My Children* and the Syfy original series *Andromeda*; however, he is also a classically trained actor with an extensive theater resume.[4] According to Cobb, *American Moor* "was born out of a perpetual state of disquiet with the experience of African American manhood. *Othello*, the role, and the play, and the real

3. W.E.B Du Bois, *The Souls of Black Folks*. Edited by David W. Blight and Robert Gooding-Williams (Boston: Bedford Books, 1997), 38.
4. See, http://www.keithhamiltoncobb.com

estate that both have occupied in my life are intrinsic to that experience."[5] In her introduction to the 2020 publication of *American Moor*, Kim F. Hall, one of the leading figures in premodern critical race studies, describes the play as following: "a veteran Black actor auditioning to play Shakespeare's Othello for an unseasoned, white director. It is the story of how his blackness and his love of Shakespeare collide with the largely white Shakespeare industry — the teachers, acting coaches, agents, directors (and scholars?) — who subtly maintain ownership over Shakespeare while at the same time insisting that Shakespeare is a universal public good."[6]

The *American Moor* residency began on Friday, November 2, 2018, and ran for just under three weeks with events transpiring across three campuses. Western Massachusetts is home to the Five College Consortium, consisting of four liberal arts colleges (Amherst, Hampshire, Mount Holyoke, and Smith) and the flagship state university of Massachusetts (University of Massachusetts - Amherst).[7] Once the four-show, sold-out run ended at Mount Holyoke, Cobb spent a further week at the University of Massachusetts - Amherst, and a day at Amherst College. Structurally, the residency was organized so that most of the Mount Holyoke events took place prior to the performances and the University of Massachusetts - Amherst and Amherst College events took place in the days immediately

5. Ferri, Josh. Interview with Keith Hamilton Cobb. *Five Burning Questions with American Moor Playwright and Star Keith Hamilton Cobb*. Broadway Box, August 21, 2019. https://www.broadwaybox.com/daily-scoop/five-burning-questions-with-american-moors-keith-hamilton-cobb/.
6. Hall, Kim F., "Introduction," *American Moor: A Play by Keith Hamilton Cobb* (New York: Methuen Drama, Bloomsbury Publishing, 2020), ix.
7. Among the consortium's many advantages are a shared library system, a Five College course exchange, and a rich intellectual and pedagogical matrix. There are a number of Five College interdisciplinary organizations and seminars, as well as the Kinney Center for Interdisciplinary Renaissance Studies, which fosters and supports programming with faculty and students across the consortium (https:// http://www.umass.edu/renaissance). While collaboration across the institutional entities is widely encouraged, it often proves difficult, as each institution simultaneously exists (and indeed must exist) as a distinct, even unique, higher educational entity. As such, each institution conceptualizes (and to some extent enrolls) a discrete student body, with differing needs, interests, concerns, and hence administrative apparatuses.

following the run. The arc of events followed a sine curve, in which the performances and conference (discussed below) formed the peak activity, and the individual campus events formed the slopes.

The *American Moor* residency endeavored to create an affective and intellectual network — a community — that came together around a series of events dedicated to the topic of Shakespeare, race, and America. Of equal significance were the key questions that this community raised and returned to over the residency's sixteen-day span, and that the conversations inspired by these questions diversified not only who was included but who shaped them. It invested students as creators and leaders of the conversation from the start, empowering them to become advocates, teachers, and community ambassadors. At this essay's conclusion, we return to the call to action with which the chapter opens to propose a sixth axiom that proved crucial to our collaborative pursuits in 2018: foster local community that extends beyond the university.

The residency began with a simple impulse: Amy Rodgers, a faculty member at Mount Holyoke College, saw the show at Boston's O.W.I theater, found it deeply moving, and wanted her students to see it as well.[8] In particular, she felt that the play contained a unique ability to vocalize the affective, intellectual, and discursive aphasia around American race relations. Like many college campuses, Mount Holyoke consistently seeks new methods for engaging community discourse around diversity, equity, and inclusion; however, the performing arts had been surprisingly absent from these college-wide conversations.

Initially, Rodgers aimed to bring *American Moor* to the Mount Holyoke campus as a contribution to the institution's evolving diversity, equity, and inclusion (DEI) initiatives; in conversing with Marjorie Rubright, a professor of English at the University of Massachusetts - Amherst, about bringing the play to the Connecticut River Valley area, a more ambitious

8. O.W.I (Bureau of Theatre) was part of the Boston Center for the Arts. Named after the Office of War Information, the small, black-box organization programs theater that explicitly engages with issues of racial identity. The company no longer appears among BCA's theatrical affiliations, and, as O.W.I does not maintain a website; it is difficult to tell whether it still exists in any capacity.

and wide-ranging set of programming and conversational opportunities emerged. Our shared goal was to generate a robust series of integrated, creative, public-facing, and scholarly programming across multiple campuses that put race squarely at the discussion's center. We oriented our energies around two open questions: how do *Othello*'s legacies speak to urgent questions about race in America today; and how might the performing arts serve as a centerpiece for both pedagogical innovation and enriched scholarly and creative cross-pollination between our campus communities, particularly around matters of race and racism?

After ten months of planning, programming, and significant fundraising efforts at both Mount Holyoke and the University of Massachusetts – Amherst (UMass), the *American Moor* residency came to fruition. Our aim here in chronicling and reflecting on this endeavor is to articulate how it succeeded in meeting a number of college, university, consortium, and community goals, as well as the ways in which we gained greater insight into how to engage diverse students, faculty, and the larger community in wide-ranging, multi-campus, events-based residencies, particularly those that feature a performance event as the centerpiece. The 2018 *American Moor* residency was a robust — and scalable — residency. In outlining its contours, we offer one model from which readers might pluck selectively or build upon in an effort to design future cross-institutional collaborations that center conversations about race.

The Embodied Residency: Voices, Questions, and Conversations

"What do we do when they laugh, but I want to cry?" With a voice tremulous with both courage and apprehension, an African American English major ventured his question from the back of the theater, breaking the silence that hung among us following Keith Hamilton Cobb's performance of *American Moor*. In the still-darkened Mount Holyoke College Rooke theater, filled with undergraduate students from various humanities departments across multiple campuses, this was but the first of many powerful questions that arose in the weeks of the Five College residency. Responding intuitively, intellectually, and emotionally, Cobb extended both his gaze and arms out into the audience in response, as if drawing this student into the orbit of his confidence: "I hear the silences, too, you know?" Elaborating, he explained that sadness, pain, and rage registers in an audience's silence – inside that particular student's feeling of wanting to cry when others laugh – and that this makes its way to the actor's ears, too. "Not everyone is laughing, and I hear that." The larger question – "What do *we* do"? – was met with Cobb's explicit, intimate, and immediate answer, "we cry – you and I cry – we *should!*" and with a more implicit answer that forecasted conversations to come in the days ahead: "we must listen to one another – and we're not *really* doing that yet, are we?" Cobb thus began a conversation that did more than transform how students in one corner of New England think about race in America today. Through his performances and conversations with students across multiple campuses, Cobb transformed the nature of the questions that students feel they can ask, and who feels welcome to ask them.

The audience on that particular afternoon had spent the weeks running up to the performance studying the racial and racist logics circulating in Shakespeare's *Othello* with Amy Rodgers (a white, cisgendered woman) and Marjorie Rubright (a white, queer, feminist and director of the Kinney Center for Interdisciplinary Renaissance Studies at UMass Amherst). Together, we asked our students to embark on various ventures in understanding early modern systems of power and epistemologies of race and to consider their on-going legacies today: they'd written analyses of singular words from Shakespeare's play (Barbary, Moor, tupping, etc.) for how language gestates and produces race-thinking in the period; they explored the interconnections between ethnic and racial representations of human kinds on the stage and representations of human difference on the pages of early modern world maps;[9] they anatomized entire speeches for how Othello seems to master the threatening discourses of Othering in the play; they wrote reviews of various film adaptations of *Othello* with

9. For a discussion of this assignment, see Rubright, Marjorie, "Charting New Worlds: The Early Modern World Atlas and Electronic Archives." *Teaching Early Modern English Literature from the Archives*, edited by Heidi Brayman Hackel and Ian Frederick Moulton (The Modern Language Association of America, 2015), 201–11.

an eye toward the implicit biases of casting, cutting, and the direction of mise-en-scene; they wrote their own twenty-first-century versions of a single scene of *Othello*, illuminating or deliberately rejecting the legacies of early modern race-thinking alive in Shakespeare's play; they read and discussed Kim F. Hall's introductory chapters on race and cultural geography in her Bedford *Othello* in preparation for discussions they would have with her upon her visit to campus.[10] Students also wrote labels for a Mount Holyoke Art Museum exhibit featuring Curlee Raven Holton's etchings of *Othello* completed during a Venice residency in 2012. They crafted teaching plans for the play and visited various first-year seminars that were working with Shakespeare's *Othello*. Students also met regularly at the Kinney Center for Interdisciplinary Renaissance Studies, where, using the rare book collection on site, they helped to curate an exhibit of books: "*Othello* in Context, Then and Now." Finally, mentored work-study and internships offered Mount Holyoke and UMass Amherst students opportunities to work together over the course of the residency as "*American Moor* Ambassadors." Designing outreach across the campuses, developing pop-up events, and organizing with other student groups on our campuses, the Ambassadors put students' investments and questions at the forefront of the residency. Simply put, our students were thick into *Othello* before *American Moor* came to town.

Chronicling the Residency

The residency opened with a gallery exhibition entitled "Othello Reimagined in Sepia," displayed in the Anne Greer and Frederic B. Garonzik Family Gallery, Mount Holyoke College. The brainchild of Rodgers and Ellen Alvord, Associate Director of Education and Weatherbie Curator of Academic Programs at Mount Holyoke, the Museum event brought together Cobb's performance with an exhibit featuring the founding director of Lafayette College's Experimental Printmaking Institute, Curlee Raven Holton's series of prints entitled "Othello Reimagined in Sepia".

10. Shakespeare, William, *Othello, The Moor of Venice: Texts and Contexts*, edited by Kim F. Hall (Boston: Bedford/St. Martin's, 2007).

Figure 1. Curlee Raven Holton, *Othello's Reflections before Venice; The trauma of death, memories of birth and renewal-the cycle of life.* Mount Holyoke College Art Museum, South Hadley, Massachusetts (MH 2016.2.13.10a-b).

Created during a 2012 residency at the Venice Printmaking Studio, Holton's images chart new terrain into Othello's inner life – his affective past and psychic present – as a means of offering an alternative (or perhaps supplemental) narrative to Shakespeare's play. Professor, painter, and master print maker Curlee Raven Holton engaged in public conversation with Cobb on "African American Perspectives on Othello," with Rodgers as facilitator.

During their time at Mount Holyoke, the *American Moor* team (Cobb, director Kim Weild, actor Josh Tyson, and stage manager Caleb Spivey) were in tech for six days preceding the play's four-day public run; Cobb and Weild also visited twelve Mount Holyoke classes and attended two community events (the Holton event at the art museum and another for the Students of Color Committee on the topic of "Engaging Race through the Arts"). In addition, Caleb Spivey, *American Moor*'s stage manager, ran a workshop for theater students interested in stage management, and Cobb, Weild, and Spivey were available for less-formal student meetings and conversations.

The scholarly programming was inaugurated earlier in the fall with the Normand Berlin Lecture, delivered by Professor Mazen Naous (Dept. of English, UMass Amherst) who spoke on Diana Abu-Jaber's Arab-American novel *Crescent*, thereby launching a Five College-wide discussion of *Othello*'s global afterlives.[11] These conversations flowed into the curriculum across the campuses where Shakespeare's *Othello* was a shared text. During the *American Moor* residency, Kim F. Hall (Lucyle Hook Professor of English and Professor of Africana Studies, Barnard College, Columbia University) delivered a historically wide-ranging keynote at the UMass Amherst Fine Arts Center, "'Othello Was My Grandfather': Shakespeare and Race in the African Diaspora." A preeminent scholar of Black feminist studies, critical race theory, slavery studies, and early modern literature and culture, Hall is also the editor of the influential Bedford edition of *Othello*, which Keith Hamilton Cobb holds in his hands throughout *American Moor* and our students studied from throughout the semester. Her

11. A fuller version of this talk is published in Naous, Mazen, *Poetics of Visibility in the Contemporary Arab American Novel* (Columbus: Ohio State University Press, 2020)

talk explored connections between Shakespeare and freedom dreams in the African Diaspora, outlining a tension between the ways that Shakespeare and blackness have been valued in the 400 years since Shakespeare's birth. It opened onto the ways that Black writers and actors in the early twentieth century used Shakespeare when grappling with constructions of blackness and race in the United States.

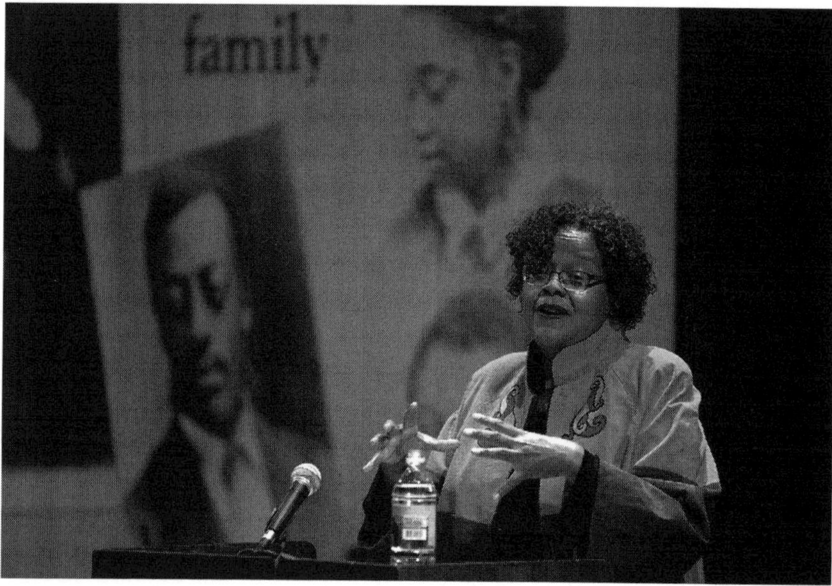

Figure 2. Professor Kim F. Hall

Our conversations bridged research and the creative arts by way of an afternoon conference, loosely based on the concept of the Ovation Network's series "Inside the Actors Studio," facilitated by the Trinidad and Tobago-born actor, movement artist, teacher, and director, Jude Sandy. Currently a Resident Artist at the Trinity Repertory Company, Sandy has performed numerous roles on, off-, and off-off-Broadway, including two years in the Tony Award-winning *War Horse* at Lincoln Center Theater. Together, Weild, Cobb, Hall, and Sandy engaged our academic and public communities in urgent conversations about Shakespeare, race, and America today, conversations in which the humanities' role in excavating new avenues of discourse and forms of political action featured prominently, particularly around the potency of narrative and performance to communicate across difference.

Following this event, UMass Amherst students returned to the classroom with tremendous enthusiasm for the kinds of questions these artists and academics were asking. In her recent essay, "Why Black Lives Matter in the Humanities," Felice Blake, a professor of English at the University of Santa Barbara, admonishes: "It isn't enough to include texts by historically aggrieved populations in the curriculum and classroom without producing new approaches to reading" (309).[12] On its face, Cobb's dramatized audition for the role of Othello is just that: a heart-wrenching appeal for new approaches to reading which can only be activated by deepened capacities for listening to the presence of the past in our present moment. Hall's talk engendered significant interest from students of color for how, throughout, she claimed not only to relate to stories of the African Diaspora but be related to that history. She offered our students a new approach to reading. "It was personal while also being scholarly," one student remarked. "I think more often we're taught that we're supposed to stand outside history, looking back at it like an object in a museum, untouchable" another offered. When asked if they felt there were similarities between Hall's scholarly keynote and the conversation that followed between Hall and the actors and director, a white theater-studies student remarked that "history felt present." Her Black friend nodded, then reshaped the formulation: "I felt present in that history of black oppression and resistance. I mean, I could *feel* it . . . in me and in the room." "I think that's what *American Moor* does in a different way," another student added. "Isn't Keith's audition all about who does and doesn't feel history as present 'in the room'?"

12. Blake, Felice, "Why Black Lives Matter in the Humanities." *Seeing Race Again: Countering Colorblindness across the Disciplines*, edited by Kimberlé Williams Crenshaw, Luke Charles Harris, Daniel Martinez HoSang, and George Lipsitz (Oakland: University of California Press 2019), 307–26.

Following his residency at Mount Holyoke, Cobb spent a week in residence at the Kinney Center for Interdisciplinary Renaissance Studies at the University of Massachusetts – Amherst, holding workshops and roundtables with students from the departments of English, history, theater, Afro-American studies, and women, gender, and sexuality studies. He also participated in classroom conversations with students. During Cobb's visit to Rubright's introductory Shakespeare course (a large lecture course of sixty students), as well as to a more intimate masters-level theater seminar, students asked the author/actor questions ranging from his "decision to use the N-word in the play and how we should think about that," to whether "it's different to say that word aloud to a NYC audience than in Western Mass," which is predominately white. They also ventured questions more personal and biographical: "when did you know you were a writer and an actor and did your family support those choices?" At the conclusion of Cobb's week-long residency, the Shakespeare students were invited to write a private letter to Cobb reflecting on their experience of *American Moor*, their conversations with him over his week in residence, and/or on the feelings his residency sparked in them. This epistolary extension of the conversation was private, not to be shared with Rubright or other students. In this way, students continued the conversation off stage, and many reported that writing their letter was "harder than anything" they'd written before. As one student elaborated in a class review, "Cobb was so honest and open with us, I felt I needed to find the words to be as honest" in return.

At Mount Holyoke, Cobb visited Rodgers' "Activist Shakespeare" class the Monday following the conclusion of *American Moor*'s run. Students and Cobb together debriefed on the experience of being in the audience (students) and performing the play (Cobb) in Western Massachusetts (and in front of what was a predominantly white audience). As one student of color said to Cobb, "So often I feel like no one sees me here. How do you deal with that, especially since you are putting yourself and your story out there for everyone to see?" Cobb responded with understanding and empathy: "Even if people don't see exactly what I want them to see, they *are* seeing me and listening to what I have to say. And they see you. I see you!" This moment of genuine vulnerability was deeply felt by the class community as a whole (many were in tears), and marks precisely the coordinates that demarcate a place where actual change, at the level of heart and head, can occur.[13]

Reflections on the Residency

Despite the consortium structure of the Five Colleges, engaging community across different campuses presents numerous challenges even when institutions co-sponsor high-profile speakers and artists.[14] Event saturation permeates individual campuses, a fact that compounds across the consortium. The *American Moor* residency occurred in the final third of the semester, when demands on students and faculty are at their height. Even so, the residency managed to gain considerable interest and momentum, evinced by the four sold-out shows, the packed house at UMass's *American Moor* Actors Studio and Keynote events, and the fact that Mount Holyoke's president, dean of faculty (provost), vice-president of diversity, equity, and inclusion, and vice-president of student life all attended the performances – an unprecedented turnout for Mount Holyoke's officers at a performance-based event, even one at their own campus.

13. This Five College residency drew audiences from all Five Colleges and the broader New England community and gained local and national media attention. Amy Rodgers' interview with Mount Holyoke College, "Race, Shakespeare and America" is available online (https://www.mtholyoke.edu/media/race-shakespeare-and-america). An interview with Cobb and Rubright appeared in *The Daily Hampshire Gazette* (https://www.gazettenet.com/American-Moor-21221674) and another was printed in *The Los Angeles Review of Books* (https://lareviewofbooks.org/article/all-this-life-made-this-play-an-interview-with-keith-hamilton-cobb/). In her op-ed piece, Morgan Reppert, Op-A Ed Editor for *The Massachusetts Daily Collegian*, lauded the immersive and hands-on learning experiences that *American Moor* offered to undergraduate students (https://dailycollegian.com/2018/11/umass-students-should-learn-by-doing/).
14. Mount Holyoke College and the Office of the Provost at the University of Massachusetts – Amherst generously partnered to provide full financial support for this programming, whose costs otherwise exceeded the discretionary budgets of single departments, humanities units, and colleges.

Student response to the residency was highly positive. During their exit interviews, a number of theater majors stated that *American Moor* provided an experiential zenith in their college experience. One student, from Rodgers' Activist Shakespeare course, stated "Getting to work with Keith Hamilton Cobb on his *Othello* adaptation was one of the highlights of my time at Mount Holyoke. During the class he visited, students laughed, cried, and had the most open conversation about race that I've had during my three and a half years here." Elizabeth Young, Carl and Elsie A. Small Professor of English at Mount Holyoke, shared that "[t]he visit by Keith Hamilton Cobb was an excellent experience for students in my course English 199, Introduction to the Study of Literature. It was one of several extraordinary activities for these students related to Shakespeare's *Othello*, which also included attending Mr. Cobb's play *American Moor*; visiting the exhibition at the Mount Holyoke College Art Museum of 'Othello Reimaged in Sepia,' by artist Curlee Raven Holton; and attending the conversation between Mr. Holton and Mr. Cobb at the Museum. Discussions about race in the play, and about Black responses to it, that might otherwise have been abstract or speculative were concrete, vivid, and dynamic, ranging across two media (theater and visual art) and emerging from in-person conversation with an actor/playwright." Indeed, one of the residency's more successful tactics was its consistent and multidisciplinary imbrication of different artistic and scholarly approaches to *Othello* and its many artistic and cultural legacies. So too, involving students from the start in the planning and organization of the residency — and doing so with a group of cross-campus Ambassadors who had time to work together, face-to-face, and develop trust with one another — was essential to the groundwork upon which the residency was built.

Students took increasing risks in raising questions — of each other and of *American Moor* — over the course of the residency. The multi-week timescale of the residency, as well as its traffic through different campus cultures, allowed students time to digest the thoughts of others. Faculty across the disciplines integrated Cobb into their courses: faculty from English, history, Latinx studies, theater, and Africana studies invited Cobb to speak with their students on race, identity, performance, masculinity, and Shakespeare. Students at UMass reported appreciating face-to-face engagements with the performance artist, whom they had opportunities to interview in classroom visits and roundtable events over the course of the week of residency. In particular, students found the combination of interacting with the author/actor both at the intimate level of small class discussion and the public level of the show's performance and post-show discussions particularly fruitful. Students who initially reported being concerned about "call out culture" – about whether they might ask questions about race in the past and present "without offending" or seeming "not woke," and others who doubted whether they could tell their own stories about encounters with white supremacy "without getting too emotional" – began to practice, in the more intimate contexts, genuinely searching lines of inquiry that were not stifled by what Black feminist Loretta Ross characterizes as "cancel culture, where people attempt to expunge anyone with whom they do not perfectly agree, rather than remain focused on those who profit from discrimination and injustice."[15] Cobb's own style of Q&A in the after show talk backs helped to model the kind of listening these conversations require. Cobb's interlocutory style encouraged students to raise challenging questions about *American Moor* itself, which gender-studies students indeed did especially in inquiring about the portrait of Desdemona's agency in the production: "I wanted more of her voice, her perspective – less her father's and Othello's," one student appealed. Moving from the local (their individual experience of and with race on their campuses) to the national (a performance piece that adapts a canonical Western text to speak to the contemporary experience of a Black American actor seeking validation and expressive agency through the Shakespearean canon within American theater) was an essential part of the exercise and reward of these conversations. Ultimately, it was the saturation of a variety of engagements over the course of the residency that fostered the trust necessary for the challenge of the conversations sparked by *American Moor*.

15. On the toxicity of call-out culture in Western Massachusetts, see Ross, Loretta, "I'm a Black Feminist. I think Call-Out Culture is Toxic." *The New York Times* online (August 17, 2019). https://www.nytimes.com/2019/08/17/opinion/sunday/cancel-culture-call-out.html

In terms of the larger Western Massachusetts community (particularly that outside of the elite Five College milieu), we found that three events drew the most interest: foremost, the performances themselves and the Q&As that followed; secondly, the Mount Holyoke College Art Museum event and related pedagogical opportunities; and third, the Actors Studio at the UMass Fine Arts Center and conversations that it ignited. In addition to the performances, which themselves sparked powerful conversations each evening, these two distinct events share in their endeavor to join public-facing artistic production or public-facing artistic conversations with pedagogical and research investments. Crucially, we discovered that when no one in the room was cast as the 'expert' on the topic or the 'master' of a craft, everyone joined creatively and more openly in conversation.

The Actors Studio was an occasion to set Keith Hamilton Cobb, Kim Weild, and Professor Kim F. Hall into conversation with one another, thus further dissolving divisions between performance, scholarly research, and the real-world questions about systemic racism at the center of our discussions. What worked especially well was the introduction of a talented intermediary who brought questions to the stage that animated actor, director, and scholar alike. Jude Sandy, an award-winning actor and celebrated teacher, is not part of the *American Moor* team, though he was familiar with the show. His questions emerged from the position of an informed 'outsider,' someone who stood just on the edges of the *American Moor* project. This bifocal perspective – one foot in the acting world, one foot in the teaching world – made a successful formula for conversation. Students jumped into the Q&A period, as did the community, in large part because Sandy positioned himself – as well as the audience – as possessed of many questions, and few certain answers. What began as a conversation between Cobb, Weild, and Hall soon spilled into a Q&A with an entire auditorium.

'What's Past Need Not Be Prologue'

> *American Moor* is as exuberantly hopeful as it is deeply critical. It is a play with uncommon faith in us. As the audience, we are simultaneously the Director, the Venetian Senate, and ourselves: we can stop the racism in the theater and in our lives, if we can make space and time for learning and listening. We don't have to passively play the roles as others imagine them. What's past need not be prologue. — Kim F. Hall[16]

Where to go from here? Starting with his generous and generative practice of holding a Q&A following every performance of *American Moor*, Keith Hamilton Cobb offers one proposal for where to go from here: continue the conversation. The challenge of this straightforward proposal is significant in that it presses those of us teaching race in early modern literature, contemporary theater, and performance studies to ask how we generate these conversations and work to expand the community of interlocutors who shape it. This leads us to suggest a possible sixth axiom in support of Coles, Hall, and Thompson's call to action: foster local community that extends beyond the university. While Coles, Hall, and Thompson's five axioms suggest this endeavor tacitly, we believe that making it explicit is imperative, particularly for those who might wish to mount such an initiative at their own institution. As a corollary, colleges and universities must do more to encourage, support, and recognize endeavors like the *American Moor* residency that arise from the social-justice commitments of faculty, particularly pre-tenure and adjunct faculty. As two mid-career tenured faculty, we encountered skepticism from some professional peers about whether the significant time and work entailed in organizing this residency was "at our own professional peril." Cues like this can have chilling effects, particularly on early career scholars and faculty in temporary appointments. If we are to continue the conversation, it must not exclude the creative energies of already over-burdened junior faculty of color who may be best suited to continue these conversations

16. Kim F. Hall, "Introduction" to *American Moor: A Play by Keith Hamilton Cobb* (Methuen Drama 2020), xii.

around racial injustice but may, nonetheless, feel restricted by the narrowly proscriptive path of publication-toward-tenure. Departments, colleges, and universities must rethink and redesign the evaluative systems of promotion review in an effort to convey the value of this kind of work to adjunct and pre-tenure faculty, and thereby endorse and support it.

Among the residency's successes was its ability to bring students and faculty from the Five Colleges together to act and imagine themselves as a larger, more wide-ranging force for discussion and (ex)change. Intermingled with those students, staff, and faculty were community members – people who live in the three towns that house the Five Colleges (Amherst, Northampton, and South Hadley). South Hadley (the most working-class of the three) also hosted *American Moor*'s performances, and Rodgers, with the help of several Mount Holyoke students, publicized it widely to the town, in particular, to the middle and high school. And yet, more could have been done in this area. Holyoke, the city that lies directly south of South Hadley, has a predominantly Latino population (52% according to the United States 2019 Census).[17] Springfield, the third-largest city in Massachusetts, is part of the Connecticut River Valley, and has the largest Black population in the area and the second-largest Latino population.[18] By contrast, Hampshire county where the Five College Consortium is situated is 88% White, 4.3% Black or African American, 5.9% Hispanic or Latino, and 5.7% Asian.[19] Admittedly, little outreach was done in these areas, outside of advertising to postsecondary institutions in the two cities and encouraging UMass students who commute from these communities to bring family and friends. Ideally (and, should such a large-scale performance event occur in the future), we would spend more time

17. US Census Bureau. QuickFacts, Holyoke city, Massachusetts, 2019. https://www.census.gov/quickfacts/holyokecitymassachusetts.
18. US Census Bureau. QuickFacts, The Census Bureau's 2019 report cites Springfield's Black population as 20.9% and its Latino population as 44.7%.
19. US Census Bureau. QuickFacts, Hampshire county, Massachusetts, 2019 https://www.census.gov/quickfacts/fact/table/hampshirecountymassachusetts/PST045219.

and resources toward tracing a larger geographical circumference in terms of outreach and thinking through how such outreach and (hopefully) engagement, might help us begin to break down the silos that separate our communities into taxonomies of race, affluence, and ideology. Perhaps, then, the optimism of *American Moor* would manifest more fully: "what's past need not be prologue."

Mapping Race Digitally in the Classroom

ROYA BIGGIE

In the last two decades, the availability of GIS (geographical information technologies) has provided scholars across disciplines with new tools to pursue cultural geographical research. For literary scholars, particularly those interested in the relationship between literary texts and the material worlds they represent, mapping tools, such as Google maps, offer interactive interfaces that visualize "spatial patterns that remain hidden in texts and tables."[1] Recent work includes the Stanford Literary Lab's "The Emotions of London." Led by Ryan Heuser, researchers at the lab have mapped eighteenth- and nineteenth-century novels' affective representations of London, demonstrating in part how fictionalized and sociological accounts of the city diverge.[2] At Lancaster University, Ian Gregory and Christopher Donaldson have mapped a corpus of eighty texts (spanning from 1622 to 1900) on England's Lake District. Their maps provide starting points for comparative analyses that attend to both representations of the region and the Lake District's material terrain.[3] While scholars acknowledge the limitations of geospatial tools, noting that they are more equipped to convey precise data than ambiguity, such technologies provide new "ways of [generating] questions" rather than "binding interpre-

1. David J. Bodenhamer, John Corrigan, and Trevor M. Harris, "Introduction," in *The Spatial Humanities: GIS and the Future of Humanities Scholarship*, ed. David J. Bodenhamer, John Corrigan, and Trevor M. Harris (Bloomington, IN: Indiana University Press, 2010), vii.
2. Ryan Heuser, Mark Algee-Hewitt, Annalise Lockhart, Erik Steiner, and Van Tran, "Mapping the Emotions of London in Fiction, 1700–1900: A Crowdsourcing Experiment," in *Literary Mapping in the Digital Age*, ed. David Cooper, Christopher Donaldson, and Patricia Murrieta-Flores (London, UK: Routledge, 2016); See also, Ryan Heuser, Franco Moretti, and Erik Steiner, "The Emotions of London," Pamphlets, Stanford Literary Lab, accessed January 18, 2020, https://litlab.stanford.edu/LiteraryLabPamphlet13.pdf.
3. Ian Gregory and Christopher Donaldson, "Geographical Text Analysis: Digital Cartographies of Lake District Literature," in *Literary Mapping*.

tations."[4] As Barbara Piatta explains, "the best literary maps ... [return] the reader to the text with new questions and ideas."[5] Likewise, in the classroom, digital mapping projects grant students the opportunity to form innovative questions about literary and historical texts while developing visual interpretation and digital literacy skills.[6] Moreover, such projects also offer students an alternate medium through which to examine and represent histories of migration, exploration, and conquest.[7] In this chapter, I discuss a digital mapping project I assigned while teaching a course on race and cross-cultural exchanges in early modern English literature. Though I had no prior experience with digital mapping tools, I was interested in exploring how mapping technologies might yield new insights about the impact of European colonization and the exploitation of non-European land and people. In explaining the scaffolding of the assignment and reflecting on its challenges and pitfalls, my aim is to provide a project blueprint to other instructors of early modern literature, especially in courses devoted to the study of race in the European Renaissance.

Digital Mapping in the Humanities

The digital mapping assignments I have encountered demonstrate a common investment in students as researchers who can evaluate and manipulate technology and who can create and circulate new knowledge. In her recent book, *New Digital Worlds: Postcolonial Digital Humanities in Theory*, postcolonial and digital humanities scholar Roopika Risam argues that mapping projects, particularly in the postcolonial studies classroom,

4. Barbara Piatti, "Mapping Fiction: The Theories, Tools and Potentials of Literary Cartography," in *Literary Mapping*, 91. See also, Bodenhamer, "The Potential of the Geospatial Humanities," in *The Spatial Humanities*, 23.
5. Piatti, "Mapping Fiction," 100.
6. See Chris Johanson and Elaine Sullivan, "Teaching Digital Humanities through Digital Cultural Mapping," in *Digital Humanities Pedagogy: Practices, Principles and Politics*, ed. Brett D. Hirsch (Cambridge, UK: Open Book Publishers, 2012), 123.
7. "Mapping," Digital Pedagogy in the Humanities: Concepts, Models, and Experiments, MLA Commons, accessed October 1, 2019, https://digitalpedagogy.mla.hcommons.org/keywords/mapping/.

help students to "see a new dimension of texts that span multiple locations, while increasing their understanding of the world, allowing them to learn not only how to use but also how to critique geospatial technologies and develop their critical thinking skills about geospatial data."[8] In an effort to help students think about "the complexity of how race is negotiated in postcolonial texts ... [and] the cultural contexts that shape blackness," Risam has co-created the interactive database and digital map, *A Cultural Atlas of Global Blackness*, with her students. By clicking on the map's various pins, viewers can read annotations on "postcolonial cultural texts ... that engage with race."[9] As Risam explains, students not only developed digital literary skills by assessing various GIS platforms, but also deepened their readings of postcolonial texts by gaining familiarity with their cultural and geographic contexts.[10] At the University of North Dakota, literary and digital humanities scholar David Haeselin has had students in his "American Migrations" course create a collaborative map of geographic locations in Junot Diaz's *The Brief Wondrous Life of Oscar Wao*.[11] Some of these locations are central to the novel's plot while others are passing references only mentioned once in the text. Using ZeeMaps, students annotated each location, discussing the location's relevance to both specific characters and the novel's overall plot. Haeselin aimed to show students how even brief details influence our reading of a

8. Roopika Risam, "Postcolonial Digital Pedagogy," *New Digital Worlds: Postcolonial Digital Humanities in Theory, Praxis, and Pedagogy* (Evanston, IL: Northwestern University Press, 2018), 106.
9. Risam, "Postcolonial Digital Pedagogy," 110.
10. More broadly speaking, Risam argues that digital projects are particularly useful in the postcolonial studies classroom because they help students understand the "omissions and inequalities" of the digital cultural record as directly tied to the "ongoing influences of colonial power" (90). Projects that trouble canonical formations or recover historically silenced voices help students "see themselves not simply as consumers of knowledge but as creators" (93).
11. David Haeselin, "Beyond the Borders of the Page: Mapping *The Brief and Wondrous Life of Oscar Wao*," *The Journal of Interactive Technology and Pedagogy* 13 (June 2018): https://jitp.commons.gc.cuny.edu/beyond-the-borders-of-the-page-mapping-the-brief-wondrous-life-of-oscar-wao/.

text, oftentimes even more so than those that are repeated. Haeselin was also interested in how "an interface that most of [his] students use regularly" could help students "more easily identify with [Diaz's] characters, and perhaps, start to see them as peers."[12]

Prior to teaching "Early Modern Transnational Encounters," I was only vaguely familiar with the digital mapping work of other scholars and educators. My aim in this course was for students to analyze what Renaissance and postcolonial studies scholar Ania Loomba terms early modern "vocabularies of race," language used to construct whiteness, emphasize ontological, religious, and cultural difference, and strengthen socio-economic systems that disproportionately granted power and influence to white Europeans.[13] As a class, we read early modern literary texts, including William Shakespeare's *Othello* and *The Tempest*, John Fletcher's *The Island Princess*, Edward Lord Herbert's poetry, as well as contemporaneous travelogues, royal proclamations, and scientific treatises. We contextualized these literary and archival sources by turning to foundational scholarship on early modern race and colonization by critics such as Loomba, Kim F. Hall, Ian Smith, Bernadette Andrea, Ayanna Thompson, Jane Degenhardt, and Daniel Vitkus.[14] Because these literary, archival, and critical texts concerned cross-cultural exchanges, I was interested to see how the visual potential of a map might convey the consequences of racist, Eurocentric ideologies. Yet, I assigned the project without a clear

12. Haeselin, "Beyond the Borders of the Page."
13. Ania Loomba, *Shakespeare, Race, and Colonialism* (Oxford, UK: Oxford University Press, 2002).
14. Bernadette Andrea, "Black Skin, The Queen's Masques: Africanist Ambivalence and Feminine Author(ity) in the Masques of *Blackness* and *Beauty*," *English Literary Renaissance* 29, no. 2 (1999): 246–281; Jane Hwang Degenhardt, *Islamic Conversion and Christian Resistance on the Early Modern Stage* (Edinburgh, UK: Edinburgh University Press, 2010); Kim F. Hall, *Things of Darkness: Economies of Race and Gender in Early Modern England* (Ithaca, NY: Cornell University Press, 1995); Ian Smith, *Race and Rhetoric in the Renaissance: Barbarian Errors* (New York, NY: Palgrave, 2009); Ayanna Thompson, *Performing Race and Torture on the Early Modern Stage* (London, UK: Routledge, 2008); Daniel Vitkus, *Turning Turk: English Theater and the Multicultural Mediterranean, 1570–1630* (New York, NY: Palgrave Macmillan, 2003).

picture of a final product in mind. As a result, my instructions were at once vague and straightforward: Tell the story of your research to someone beyond our classroom through the medium of a digital map.

In designing the project, I was also eager to create more opportunities for collaboration and for students to think about publics beyond our classroom. As a teacher and scholar, I recognize the value of sharing research and written work; my own work is made better by the feedback I receive from generous colleagues, and my excitement for that work increases when I have the opportunity to talk through ideas and questions with willing listeners. I have noticed similar responses from my students. They are more enthusiastic about continuing their writing and research after discussing their thoughts in class and after a one-on-one or group conference, often refreshed by new questions, ideas, and lines of inquiry. I however felt that these opportunities to share their work and writing were not enough. They did not fully levy my students' skillsets, and they did not help students develop or practice skills that they would likely need post-graduation. Put differently, in writing a traditional research paper, my students were writing and speaking to members of the class or those familiar and interested in a particular academic field. Though I was hesitant to forgo the more traditional elements of the research project, including a fifteen-page final essay, I believed that the addition of a public-facing digital project would help students develop writing and digital literacy skills that they could draw on later in their academic, personal, and professional lives.

About three quarters of the way through the semester, students began working on their research proposals, and as a class, we considered what it means to read, use, and create a map. Students read the introduction to Mark Monmonier's seminal *How to Lie with Maps*, which conceptualizes maps as highly intentional cartographic representations that thus influence a viewer's interpretation of data.[15] As Monmonier, a scholar of geography and cartography, reminds readers and as we all readily admitted, it is remarkably easy to forget — particularly with the advent of digital maps

15. Mark Monmonier, "Introduction" in *How to Lie with Maps, 3rd ed.* (Chicago, IL: University of Chicago Press, 2018).

and features like Google Street View — that "a single map is but one of an indefinitely large number of maps that might be produced for the same situation or from the same data."[16] Seeking to cultivate "a healthy skepticism about maps," Monmonier urges his audience to approach maps as they would any other authored, interpretive work.[17] Rather than turning to the contemporary maps and charts Monmonier cites, we analyzed sixteenth- and seventeenth-century regional and world maps, many of which depict human figures from Europe, Asia, Africa, and the Americas alongside the maps' borders.[18] Drawing on recent work on cartography and embodiment by Renaissance studies scholar Valerie Traub, we discussed how the spatial medium of the map "inaugurated new ways to 'know' gendered, ethnic, racial religious, tribal, and national groups."[19] In scrutinizing how spatial techniques contributed to conceptions of the foreign and familiar, students began to view maps as tools that — beyond assisting us to move through space — can produce and shape ethnographic and racialized knowledge.

To further expand my students' thinking about what maps can do, I introduced the class to cartographic representations that most would not readily identify as maps. We examined, for example, Sensory Maps created by the artist Kate McLean.[20] McLean's "New York's Smelliest Blocks" represents the city's gridded streets and provides viewers with a color-coded key of smells, olive green indicating "stagnant water," pink "cheap

16. Monmonier, "Introduction," 2.
17. Monmonier, "Introduction," 2.
18. We discussed, for example, Willem Janszoon Blaeu's *Nova Universi Terrarum Orbis Mappa* (1605/24) and *Asia* (1617); John Speed's "The Kingdom of Ireland" (1611/13); and Joannes Jansonnius's *Gallia Nova Galliae* (1632).
19. Valerie Traub, "History in the Present Tense: Feminist Theories, Spatialized Epistemologies, and Early Modern Embodiment," in *Mapping Gendered Routes and Spaces in the Early Modern World*, ed. Merry E. Wiesner-Hanks (Farmham, UK: Ashgate, 2015), 36. See also, Traub, "Mapping the Global Body," *Early Modern Visual Culture: Representation, Race, and Empire in Renaissance England*, ed. Peter Erickson and Clark Hulse (Philadelphia, PA: University of Pennsylvania Press, 2000).
20. Kate McLean, "Sensory Maps," accessed October 1, 2019, https://sensorymaps.com.

perfume."[21] Multicolored brushstrokes of varying size adorn the map, conveying the intensity of the odor on a particular corner or street. In her tactile map of Edinburgh, Scotland, McLean uses collagraphy, a printmaking technique, to create different textures on paper that capture the affective and physical "feel" of the city's various neighborhoods.[22] As students observed, McLean's aesthetically seductive portfolio of smell, tactile, and taste maps — which orbit around questions of place, memory, and emotion — demonstrate the deeply subjective and visually experimental possibilities of cartography.

Students and I also examined maps that attempt to raise public consciousness by offering a visual form of political intervention. We discussed, for example, mortality maps of migrant deaths in the Sonoran Desert created by Humane Borders, a non-profit corporation in Tucson, Arizona, working in partnership with the Pima County Office of the Medical Examiner (OME). On their website, Humane Borders issues the following warning: "The information presented is stark and perhaps unsettling. However, both Humane Borders and the Pima County OME believe that the availability of this information will contribute to fulfilling our common vision."[23] While they acknowledge that each organization has a unique mission, they explain that they are "committed to ... raising awareness about migrant deaths and lessening the suffering of families by helping to provide closure through the identification of the deceased and the return of remains."[24] The map is powered by Google GIS and looks initially familiar; however, viewers are confronted with densely dispersed and overlapping red pins; in fact, one must zoom in a few times to see

21. McLean, "New York's Smelliest Blocks," Sensory Maps, accessed October 1, 2019, https://sensorymaps.com/portfolio/nyc-thresholds-of-smell-greenwich-village/.
22. McLean, "Tactile Map: Edinburgh," Sensory Maps, accessed October 1, 2019, https://sensorymaps.com/portfolio/tactile-map-edinburgh/.
23. "Arizona OpenGIS Initiative for Deceased Migrants," Humane Borders, accessed October 1, 2019, http://humaneborders.info.
24. "Arizona OpenGIS Initiative for Deceased Migrants."

individual points.[25] Each pin contains a case report that includes, if known, the identity and age of the person, the date of the report, the exact location, the cause of death, and the county in which the body was found. In studying this map, students discussed how a familiar platform can represent data that is at once highly specific and visually impactful. As they observed, the barely distinguishable pinpoints underscore the severity of the crisis while each annotation reminds viewers of the individuality of the deceased. Through such conversations, students began to consider maps as more than navigational tools.

Before students began working on their maps, Grinnell's Humanities and Digital Scholarship Librarian, Elizabeth Rodrigues, introduced students to two digital platforms: Omeka and Neatline.[26] Omeka is an open-source content management system that uses the Dublin Core Schema to include metadata for digital resources. Omeka's plug-ins allow users to import resources from their collections onto other platforms, such as Neatline, a geotemporal exhibit builder. As the Omeka site explains, "Neatline adds a digital map-making environment that makes it easy to represent geospatial information as a collection of 'records' plotted on a map, which can be bound together into interactive exhibits that tell stories and make arguments."[27] During a series of hands-on workshops, Dr. Rodrigues walked students through these platforms, showing students aspects of the site, including Neatline's vector drawing tools. Once students had written their research papers, they used Omeka to curate

25. "Custom Map of Migrant Mortality," Arizona OpenGIS Initiative for Deceased Migrants, Humane Borders, accessed September 30, 2019, http://www.humaneborders.info/app/map.asp.

26. Dr. Rodrigues led two tutorials and held office hours during different phases of the project, providing students individual, personalized support. Had it not been for Dr. Rodrigues's generosity of time and spirit, I would not have been able to teach a content heavy course and assign a digital project. I would also like to acknowledge that the project was enabled by the immense privilege of an institution with the resources to run a class of only five students.

27. Scholars' Lab, "Neatline," Omeka Classic, accessed October 1, 2019, https://omeka.org/classic/plugins/Neatline.

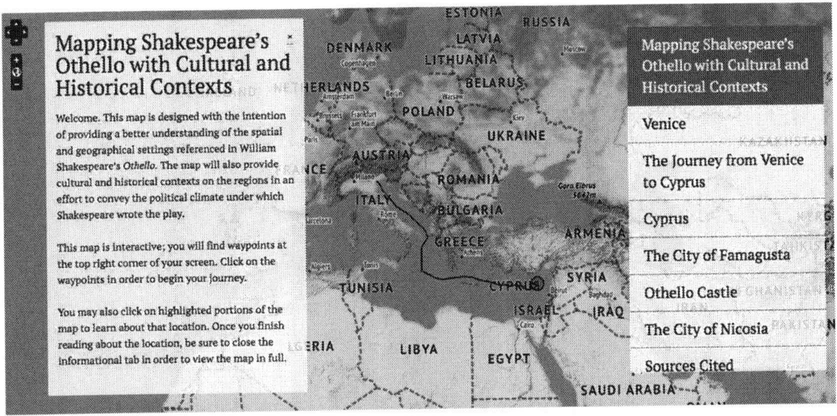

Figure 1. Mapping Shakespeare's *Othello* with Cultural and Historical Contexts.

collections, incorporating critical and archival sources relevant to their research.

As students started to think about how they could visualize their analyses, we began, as a class, to revise the project's initial prompt. Taking into account both time constraints and the limitations of the platforms, we decided that rather than attempt to represent the entirety of their claims, they would instead visualize a crucial aspect of their work that would benefit from the inclusion of a digital map. Thus, the maps, rather than offering another iteration of their research, served to supplement their essays, acting almost as visual guides to their papers. While I initially envisioned a project that could "stand alone," thinking, with my students, about what they could feasibly do during the last few weeks of the semester led to a valuable discussion of the platforms as well as how the genre of a geotemporal map differs from that of a research paper.

One student chose to represent the martial and political contestation over the island of Cyprus, mentioned though not staged in *Othello* (figure 1). Her map guide includes several waypoints that correspond with moments in the plot and various locations, some of which, though not referenced in the play, reflect her research on sixteenth- and seventeenth-century Cyprus. As she explains, she added these waypoints in an effort "to convey the political climate under which Shakespeare wrote the play." By clicking on the map's locations, located on the left, the map offers a

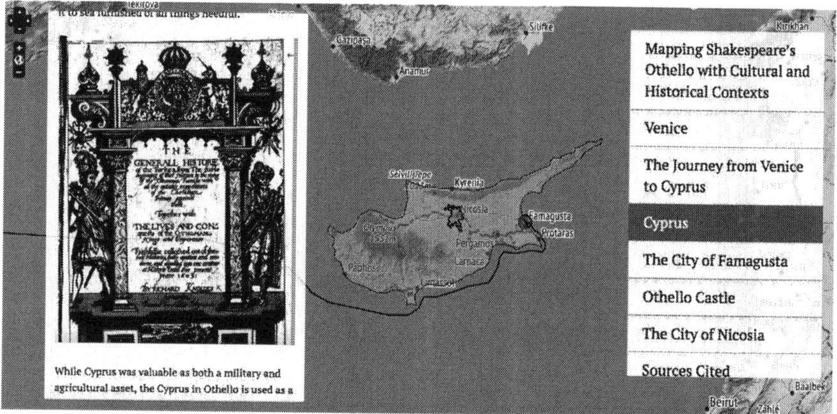

Figure 2. Cyprus.

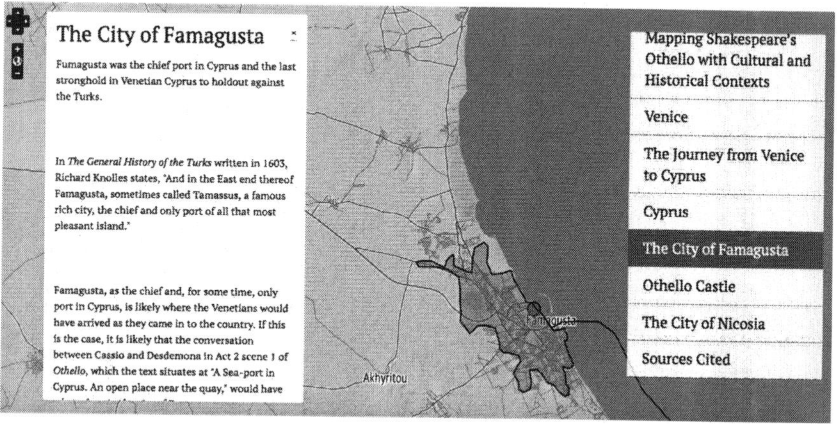

Figure 3. The City of Famagusta.

closer look at, for example, the city of Famagusta and the city of Nicosia. The student couples information about these various locations with readings of the play and non-literary sources, such as Richard Knolles's *The Generall History of the Turkes*.

Another student chose to use the map to underscore the emphasis on physical and cultural distance in *The Tempest*. As she writes in her map guide, "The visual aspect of the map allows one to consider how the geographic interaction of the different spaces are either reflected in the rhetoric of historical documents, or, as I will discuss, substituted for a rhetoric that connotes an entirely different (false) physical geography"

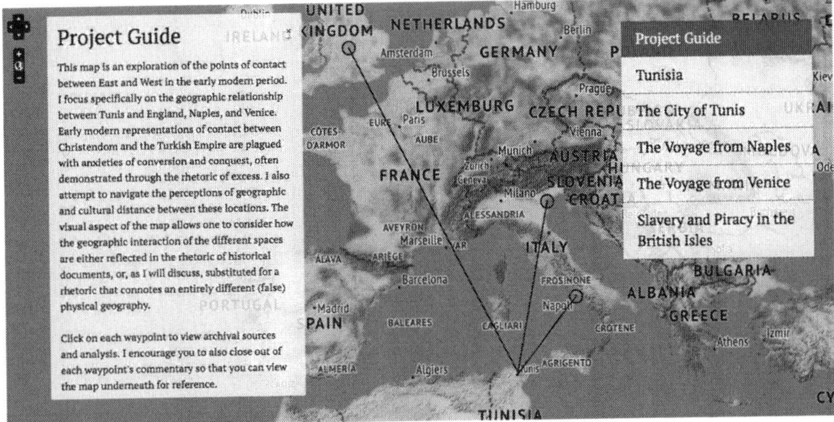

Figure 4. Project Guide.

(figure 4). The student used Neatline's geometric tools to draw viewers' attention to this thread of her argument.

As is evident from these maps, students interested in demonstrating how a more precise understanding of the plays' geographical contexts shape our interpretations and understanding of cross-cultural conflict, moments of tension, both alluded to and dramatized, between Venetians and Turks in *Othello* and between Neapolitans and Tunisians in *The Tempest*. The students include more nuanced analyses of these locales and characters' journeys from one port city to another in their annotations of various waypoints. Although Europe and North Africa's geography influenced students' analyses — which was, in part, conveyed through the use of Neatline's geometrical vector tools — they still relied heavily on text to communicate their claims.

During finals week, students presented their research papers and maps, explaining what they decided to represent and why they felt it necessary to visualize some but not other parts of their research. Although our audience was limited to the class itself, two students and I applied to and presented at the HASTAC (Humanities, Arts, Science, and Technology Alliance and Collaboratory) meeting, a professional, interdisciplinary conference. The conference offered these students another opportunity to think about the ways we communicate our research, both textually and visually, to audiences beyond the early modern literature — and even humanities — classroom.

Overall, the project allowed students to develop an understanding of maps as mediums through which scholars can represent an argument and offer a particular perspective. Given students' research topics and class discussions on early modern cross-cultural contact, students thought carefully about how spatial visualizations can foreground patterns and stories regarding colonization and human migration. They also began to consider how such visualizations can offer historical and literary analyses in a way not fully possible through writing alone. Though initially apprehensive about learning a new platform, students became more confident with these technologies as the semester progressed; I often reminded them that because they can now navigate Omeka and Neatline, they will find other new platforms less daunting. I also encouraged them to describe their work with Omeka and Neatline to potential employers. Although these specific platforms are not used in most industries, they demonstrate students' digital literacy skills (i.e., if a student can master these platforms, they can presumably master others) as well as their capacity for self-directed learning.

Challenges and Recommendations

As is the case with most new assignments (digital or otherwise), ours faced several challenges. Due largely to time constraints, which included in-class workshops on Omeka and Neatline, peer-workshopping sessions, as well as additional course content, students struggled to familiarize themselves with the platforms while creating a digital map for the first time. Although conversations on maps such as those created by McLean and Humane Borders expanded students' thinking about what a map can do and look like, fuller discussions on digital humanities maps (specifically, those built on Neatline) could have aided students early on in the process as they explored different ways of visualizing their research.[28]

28. Although students created waypoints to illuminate their research on specific locations and used Neatline's vector tools to signify various voyages, they relied heavily on text, demonstrating I think their hesitancy to allow their maps to represent visually their questions and analyses.

Moreover, more explicit instructions and more transparent evaluative criteria could have helped students feel more at ease while both designing their maps and navigating unfamiliar digital platforms.

I conclude by offering several suggestions for instructors based on my initial piloting of this assignment:

1. Involve students in the design of the project. As a class, discuss the advantages of illustrative maps versus those that draw the viewer back to the text and, as Franco Moretti puts it, "[bring] to light relations that would otherwise remain hidden."[29] Such conversations may help students think through the advantages and limitations of the medium as they consider which research questions may benefit from spatial visualizations more so than others. Instructors might also lead students in developing a shared class "symbology."[30] This common cartographic language will likely encourage students to experiment with and take advantage of the platform's vector tools.
2. Begin the project during the first few weeks of the semester. As I note above, having students discuss cartography, pursue research, and learn new digital platforms all while writing a research paper and creating a digital map is too much for the last several weeks of the term. Also consider cutting the research paper altogether and having students focus instead on their digital maps. While I believe the research proposal and annotated bibliography are still necessary components of the overall project, I am inclined to forgo the essay, in part because of time constraints, but also because assigning both a mapping project and a research paper risks positioning the map as secondary to what students may perceive as the traditional and therefore more important assignment. Moreover, having students

29. Franco Moretti, *Atlas of the European Novel 1800–1900* (London, UK: Verso, 1997), 3. See also, Sally Bushell, "The Slipperiness of Literary Maps: Critical Cartography," *Cartographica* 47, no. 3 (2012): 149–60.
30. See Piatti, "Mapping Fiction," 93. Piatti describes creating a subject-specific symbology while working on A *Literary Atlas of Europe* with colleagues at ETH Zurich. Her team, for example, used different color scales "to distinguish between settings and projected spaces/places" (93).

visualize their research after having written the research paper potentially forecloses some of the experimental possibilities of the digital map. While I was interested in seeing how my students' research questions and textual analyses changed as they worked on their maps, I wonder if they were perhaps too committed to their initial work to entertain fully other interpretive possibilities.

3. Introduce students to mapping projects and scholarship by those who work at the intersection of the humanities and digital cartography. As I have mentioned, familiarizing students with a range of mapping projects will help students conceptualize their own work and understand that they are contributing to a still emerging field. Texts I recommend include David J. Bodenhamer "The Potential of Spatial Humanities," Roopika Risam's "Postcolonial Digital Pedagogy," and the collection, *Literary Mapping in the Digital Age*, edited by David Cooper, Christopher Donaldson, and Patricia Murrieta-Flores.[31] Instructors may also want to have students locate a digital map (created ideally by a literary scholar) and present that map to the class. In doing so, students will become acquainted with recent and foundational work in the field and can practice evaluating the successes and drawbacks of these projects.

Ultimately, I encourage instructors to view mapping assignments as works-in-progress, particularly given time constraints and the complexity of balancing course content and introducing students to new technologies. In part, it is because of these challenges that the project lends itself to student collaboration. I recall, still fondly and with excitement, some of our most enthralling class sessions in which students workshopped their visualizations. Students drew inspiration from one another's maps and were quick to point out to their peers what exactly in their maps worked — what seemed both innovative and informative — as they reconsidered and reconceptualized their own work. They were excited to share not just their research, but their increasing knowledge of

31. Bodenhamer, "The Potential of the Geospatial Humanities"; Cooper, Donaldson, and Murrieta-Flores, *Literary Mapping*; Risam, "Postcolonial Digital Pedagogy."

the platforms, offering their classmates advice and specific "tricks," different ways of utilizing the platforms' features. Their collaborative generosity during these workshops — their willingness to work collectively through a specific issue even when that issue was particular to a single student — is ultimately one of the many things that made this project a success.

Discussion Questions

1. How might digital mapping tools offer new possibilities for tracing the performance histories and literary legacies of sixteenth- and seventeenth-century drama? Why might a scholar, for example, utilize a geotemporal exhibit builder, such as Neatline, to record the proliferation of Shakespearean appropriations or "revisions"?[32] What patterns, questions, or new lines of inquiry might such maps yield?
2. Most GIS technologies were not designed to represent textual analysis. What other tools, symbols, legends, and borders do humanities scholars and students need to convey the nuances of a text and complex, misrepresented, or undocumented histories? What might a new, more ideal map look like, and what might it be able to do?
3. The development of cartography is inextricably linked to colonialism and the exploitation of indigenous populations, lands, and resources. In what ways can digital maps in the humanities classroom address and account for such legacies? How can these maps resist replicating imperialist codification and taxonomic impulses?

Suggestions for Further Reading

Aydelotte, Laura. "Mapping Women: Place Names and a Woman's Place." In *Travel and Travail: Early Modern Women, English Drama, and the Wider World*, edited by Patricia Akhimie and Bernadette Andrea. Lincoln, NE: University of Nebraska Press, 2019.

32. Peter Erickson, *Citing Shakespeare: The Reinterpretation of Race in Contemporary Literature and Art* (New York, NY: Palgrave MacMillan, 2007).

Benjamin, Ruha. *Race After Technology: Abolitionist Tools for the New Jim Crow*. Cambridge, UK: Polity Press, 2019.

Bodenhamer, David J., John Corrigan, and Trevor M. Harris, eds. *Deep Maps and Spatial Narratives*. Bloomington, IN: Indiana University Press, 2015.

Davies, Surekha. *Renaissance Ethnography and the Invention of the Human: New Worlds, Maps and Monsters*. Cambridge, UK: Cambridge University Press, 2016.

Hess, Janet Berry, ed. *Digital Mapping and Indigenous America*. New York, NY: Routledge, 2021.

McKittrick, Katherine. *Dear Science and Other Stories*. Durham, NC: Duke University Press, 2021.

Pewu, Jamila Moore. "Digital Reconaissance: Re(Locating) Dark Spots on a Map." In *The Digital Black Atlantic*, edited by Roopika Risam and Kelly Baker Josephs. Minneapolis, MN: University of Minnesota Press, 2021.

Ridge, Mia, Don Lafreniere, and Scott Nesbit. "Creating Deep Maps and Spatial Narratives Through Design." *International Journal of Humanities and Arts Computing: A Journal of Digital Humanities* 7, no. 1/2 (2013): 176–89.

(Re-)Editing the Renaissance for an Antiracist Classroom

ANN C. CHRISTENSEN AND LAURA B. TURCHI

[1]In the spirit of John Lewis and making good trouble, our collaboration has supported and gently provoked our students and English-teaching friends with what we call the "sticking places" of Shakespeare plays: that is – to embrace the intellectual and emotional work of grappling with textual snarls and disturbing meanings.[2] Rooted in the social-justice engagement demanded by the material, this embrace necessarily troubled our students and the teachers whom we prepared and engaged. For two years, we co-edited the column, "Teaching Shakespeare," for the NCTE's (National Council of Teachers of English) flagship publication for secondary school teachers, *English Journal.*[3] Before that, we co-founded Teaching Shakespeare in Houston, a teacher network intended to spread news about local productions and connect teachers to visiting scholars, workshops, and other professional development opportunities. Our Shakespeare column advanced teacher voices, writing with them on casting, #MeToo, on teaching to counteract educational inequities, and more. For local teachers and others, we sponsored a viewing and talk-back on a powerful documentary about young people in Richmond, CA, who recast the story of *Romeo and Juliet* as a protest against gun violence *Romeo is Bleeding.*[4] We organized mini-conferences, such as *Strangers and Exiles* at The University of Houston in 2018 with funding from a faculty research grant, which offered English teachers alternative approaches to plays

1. Ann presented a version of this paper, titled "The Loss of Gloss: Re-editing the Renaissance" at the MLA meeting in Seattle, 2020.
2. For a discussion of John Lewis and his achievements, see Wilburn's essay in this volume.
3. "Teaching Shakespeare" appears in volumes 108 and 109.
4. Russell Simms (Executive Producer) and Jason Zeldes (Director), *Romeo is Bleeding.* (Leo Persham Pictures 2017).

in the curriculum, highlighting compelling scholarship on early modern globalism and constructions of race as replacements to textbook-centric whitewashed histories. And we co-led a seminar for the Shakespeare Association of America (SAA 2018 Los Angeles) on projects where scholars use Shakespeare in community organizing. All this work foregrounded both the complexity of Shakespeare and our confidence that teachers and their students can engage and appreciate, if not totally resolve, textual and other kinds of problems.

Given our ongoing commitment to exploring these sticking places, this essay is part reflection on our sense that while much *scholarship* denies the "absolute historical boundaries between early modern and contemporary constructions [of race]," as the contributions to the 2016 *Shakespeare Quarterly* special issue on "Shakespeare and Race" attest, and though scholars invoke the impact on classroom practice, that *practice* often lags behind.[5] We as a profession still too often leave historical background on race at the threshold of today's racism rather than inside the secondary school and college curricula. To paraphrase Kim F. Hall, one of the co-editors of that ground-breaking special issue, Renaissance texts have race in them, as do our classrooms; denying this "serves to maintain white privilege" in our field.[6] As much as our own scholarship and activism commit to antiracism, we know, too, as white teachers we have challenging work to do in our respective classroom spaces. As we recognize sticking places in the texts we teach, we are developing approaches for making difficult conversations fruitful, turning challenges into opportunities for important individual and communal learning.

Last year Ann piloted her edition of the anonymous domestic tragedy, *A Warning for Fair Women*, with her Shakespeare class (the 1599 play

5. See Peter Erickson and Kim F. Hall, eds., "[Special Issue on Race]." *Shakespeare Quarterly* 67, no. 1 (2016): 1–135.
6. Kim F. Hall, *Things of Darkness: Economies of Race and Gender in Early Modern England*. (Ithaca, NY: Cornell UP, 1995), 255; see also Kimberly Anne Coles, Kim F. Hall, and Ayanna Thompson, "BlacKKKShakespearean: A Call to Action for Medieval and Early Modern Studies," MLA: The Profession. Modern Languages Association, November 25, 2019. https://profession.mla.org/blackkkshakespearean-a-call-to-action-for-medieval-and-early-modern-studies/.

is in the Lord Chamberlain's repertory, which was the theatre company for which Shakespeare wrote and performed) and her students did a full read-through of the play aloud. When the only Black student in the class happened to enter late during the reading, Ann watched him settle into the vast circle of readers and find his place in the text at the precise moment when his peer, playing the lover/murderer, Browne, delivered a random line about a "foul Negro." With the eyes of everyone else cast downward on the page, that student looked up just then; he and Ann locked eyes, and she found herself mouthing pathetically, "I'm sorry." She was instantly filled with shame, for though her edition did gloss the phrase in some detail and with attention to the racial slur (to be discussed below), she knew she missed the chance to connect more meaningfully with the class as a whole at that moment. How could she have interrupted the flow of words just then to question the way that such an insult imbedded itself in this text?

This essay proposes the idea of "re-editing the Renaissance" (following the spirit of literary scholar and editor Leah Marcus's germinal work, "Unediting the Renaissance") with our Shakespeare students and future teachers as a better framework than best intentions and with better results than painful failures.[7] By building research, discussion, and writing assignments that take on references to race, we model ways for students to enter the work of editing for current times. We can proactively locate the places in the text that seem racist, as Ann did, and yet not be quite prepared to address what we might otherwise want to apologize for or avoid. Good teaching connects the hard work of textual analysis (sticking places) with the equally hard work of cultural responsiveness. More than responding with apologies, we seek to be proactive. Shakespeare instructors at the university level should consider themselves not only early modernists, but also teacher educators, modeling the intellectual and cultural engagement required in their own classrooms and for the

7. See Leah Marcus, *Unediting the Renaissance: Shakespeare, Marlowe and Milton*. Routledge, 1996. *ProQuest Ebook Central*, www.ebookcentral.proquest.com/lib/uh/detail.action?docID=168237 and "Shakespearean Editing and Why It Matters." *Literature Compass* 2, no. 1 (2005): 1–5.

diverse classrooms where their students may one day teach. This sometimes gets personal, like making eye contact at a painful moment, but we have to go public too and lead the class to new and relevant Shakespeares. We are energized by the recent "Call to Action" for early modernists to recruit and mentor students of color, engage in race studies, and create a field that is antiracist, and by the BLM activism in and out of the academy.[8] In order to make our field relevant, critical, and thriving (not only enduring), we need to face race, own it, and get students involved in it. In this way, our textbooks and classrooms teach and learn about the past, grapple with the present, and act for a future that is different from both.

• • •

To illustrate what we mean by re-editing, we take a play that hangs upon the high-school curriculum like drips of Elmer's school glue. We consulted popular classroom editions and online study guides for their treatment of racialized language in *Romeo and Juliet*, in particular, Romeo's metaphor that Juliet "hangs upon the cheek of night / Like a rich jewel in an Ethiope's ear" (1.5.42–43). This line may alert students of color (and international students) to early racial constructions while white students, teachers (and perhaps the editors of the texts we teach) are oblivious. As a way to include questions and comments about such phrases, we propose a series of small assignments that introduce students to textual analysis as antiracist intellectual work. These can be done in class, in small groups or independently, and over the course of a unit.

---

a. **Research** various versions of the play for interpretations/glosses that may be more and less aware of race.

b. **Un-edit** to unpack the historical and contemporary biases and power structures that may have informed this textual history.

c. **Re-edit** to address how this play functions in modernity and engages the zeitgeist.

---

8. Coles, Hall, and Thompson, "BlacKKKShakespearean." This was a public forum piece printed in a publication of the Modern Language Association (MLA): *Profession*.

Research. Most texts that we consulted offered no gloss at all.[9] Some doled out a neutral-sounding claim: "In Romeo's metaphor, a jewel shines brighter against an Ethiopian's proverbial dark skin."[10] *No Fear Shakespeare* translates the line to "she stands out against the darkness like a jeweled earring hanging against the cheek of an African."[11] Some student editions and "guides" engage and dismiss racism in one fell swoop. *Cliff's* Notes, published by the textbook company Harcourt Brace, engages with the racist import of the phrase by asking and instantly answering: "Is this phrase racist? Most likely, by today's standards." But the authors hastily reassure, "Shakespeare's audiences, though, would not have given the underlying ethics of the phrase a second thought."[12] Setting to one side the problematic assumption about what Shakespeare's audiences might think, *we* do give thought to this, as do our students. We want them to recognize pre-modern constructions of race and pay attention to these as a legacy of canonical texts.

Un-edit. The *Cliff's* Notes version, to cite only the most obvious example, giveth and taketh away the chance to talk about racism and the no-gloss texts seem to assume the line is merely an aesthetic claim that speaks for itself. Shakespeare's imagery does present light and black as aesthetic foils, but No *Fear*'s "African" narrows the lobe onto a Black person from a particular continent in a way that "Ethiope's" etymology leaves it open, as we shall explore below.[13] So, although "African" might work

9. Dympna Callaghan, ed., *Bedford Texts and Contexts* (1.5.43); Lena Cowen Orlin and Russ McDonald, eds., *Bedford* (p. 288, 1.5.45); and David Bevington, *Norton Complete* (p. 886, 1.5.43).
10. Gordon McMullan, *Norton Critical edition*, 1.4.161, 24n2.
11. "No Fear Shakespeare: Romeo and Juliet: Act 1 Scene 5 Page 2." *Sparknotes*, sparknotes.com/nofear/shakespeare/romeojuliet/page_60/. On the debate about the validity of "modernizing" Shakespeare's language, see Mike LoMonico. "Shakespeare … in other words," esp. Julia Perlowski comment. January 6, 2012, at 5:40 pm.
12. Annaliese F. Connolly, *CliffsNotes on Romeo and Juliet*. Accessed 15 July 2021. /literature/r/romeo-and-juliet/romeo-and-juliet-at-a-glance.
13. Teachers could show students the following illustrative citations from the OED, and discuss the centrality of Shakespeare and the negative cast to the examples: 1. Of or relating to Ethiopia; Ethiopian 1600 Shakespeare *Much Ado about Nothing* V. iv. 38 "Ile

as a synonym, that replacement silences the noise of an echo we hear in another familiar early modern phrase: "to wash the Ethiope white," which the OED (the Oxford English Dictionary) quietly cross-references (you can click on "wash" in the online version and get to centuries of antiblack statements).[14] Editors can quash the cultural inheritance that labels black skin as inferior just as *Cliff's Notes* quashes curiosity about audiences' responses to racism, but students can un-edit and respond as twenty-first-century readers and viewers. Imagine students from their various positions, being called (or allowed) to undo assumptions that go into glossing such terms and phrases as they locate texts in their own time.

For example, per the OED, "Ethiop" bears a surprisingly jumbled etymology with Greek roots meaning 'kindle,' 'burnt-face,' and 'fiery looking' (thus independent of the association with the African continent), though Italians and other Europeans traded in North Africa. The word implies phenotype information (many Ethiopians are dark skinned, though so are some Italians) and bears some implication of racial inferiority (the jewel is 'better'/prettier in contrast to the 'backdrop'/foil). Romeo's line posits a comparison that we could syllogize as earring/Juliet/white/light/valuable(rich)/beautiful::cheek/Ethiope/black/dark(less valuable)/ugly.

Re-edit. While many of us ask students to use the OED for such multivalent terms as "black" and "fair" or uncommon terms like "blackamoor," in order to nuance them historically, we are often less successful in bridging racism back then and racism now. This is why we need the perspectives of

hold my mind were she an Ethiope" 2. Black or dark (literally or figuratively) a1616 SHAKESPEARE As *You Like It* (1623) iv. iii. 36 "Ethiop words, blacker in their effect /Then in their countenance." The coloring of Juliet/earring underscores a related pedagogical matter — the "West-Side-Storification" of the play that renders the "two households both alike in dignity" instead two races irreconcilably different. See Carla Della Gatta. "From West Side Story to Hamlet, Prince of Cuba: Shakespeare and Latinidad in the United States." *Shakespeare Studies* 44, (2016): 151–56; and Laura B. Turchi and Ann C. Christensen. "When the 'House' (of Montague) Is a Color, Not a Clan." *English Journal* 108, no. 1 (November 1, 2018): 111–14.

14. "Ethiop, n. and adj." *OED Online*, Oxford University Press, September 2021, www.oed.com/view/Entry/64772. Accessed 19 October 2021.

Black, Indigenous, and People of Color (BIPOC) in class and in footnotes. Inviting students to take on editorial decisions like this shows that multiple perspectives are valued. We recommend prompts like the following to spur such interventions, followed by an assignment on "do it yourself" footnotes:

- Ask why an English playwright like Shakespeare or an Italian youth like Romeo might have such an image at the ready.
- Search *Opensource Shakespeare* for other racially marked terms in plays from the same period such as *Love's Labour's Lost* and *The Merchant of Venice*.[15]
- Imagine audiences of students worldwide chancing upon phrases about "foul negroes" and "old black rams" and try to account for these imagined students.
- Ask students to explain where in current pop culture (or high culture) are comparisons like this still entrenched; how are they being (re)written?

Student activity — DIY footnotes

Gloss Romeo's line with race in mind by locating and summarizing information about early modern Anglo-African relations. Add a map to your note.

Review footnotes and 'translations' in other editions and ask your readers to consider what is gained or lost when such a phrase goes unremarked or treated as if race did not matter.

Use Source Shakespeare to scour the play for references to "black." What is significant about the fact that in *Romeo and Juliet* it modifies melancholy "humor," "fate," "strife," and funeral cloths, while "fair" mostly concerns beauty?

Explain how these color conceptions impact or contextualize the earring image. How do they make you feel?

• • •

While scholars now attend to the range of possibilities within and between textual variants to correct for sexist and racist interpolations that have constrained period texts for centuries, teaching editions of the

15. https://www.opensourceshakespeare.org/concordance/

plays rarely reflect this work (as seen with *No Fear*). Leah Marcus argued that centuries' old editorial suppositions shape our reception of Shakespeare — from listing all the male character names before the female characters, regardless of relative importance, to "downplay[ing] possible instances of female authority," and ignoring colonialist editorial legacies that whitened or blackened or othered the language of the plays ("Shakespearean," 2–3). Whereas Marcus and others' editorial remediation "unedits" the renaissance, stripping away ahistorical — or worse — editorial baggage, the kind of *re*-editing that we are calling for prioritizes frank talk about race that is student directed.[16] We must respond with more than apologies to students who happen to "look up" from the book; we must perform the requisite preparation and accept our obligation of instructors to bring all students into dialogues about race, not only BIPOC students. Thus, we design our assignments to build from un-editing projects to move outward, claiming editor's prerogatives to pointedly invite students to connect their observations and experiences with race and racism in their own and the world of Shakespeare. We offer ways to present (or "package," if you will) classroom editions of early modern texts and to create classroom activities that recognize and acknowledge racism. Our purpose is to encourage Shakespeare instructors to model responsive and responsible teaching, present our field as one that is relevant, and invite students to investigate problems of racism today though historical material. All of these are possible through the practice of re-editing with our students.

Re-editing Shakespeare requires the instructor to teach explicitly the very deep and long history of the association between whiteness and purity on the one hand, and blackness and sin, on the other — and the fact that variations on these associations persist today, implicating early modern studies in ways that we do well to confront. We note that this editing approach is equally appropriate whatever play one is teaching; "race" need not be a central theme, as David Sterling Brown has demonstrated

16. Marcus. *Unediting*, esp. Introduction "The blue-eyed hag," 1–37.

with his category of "the other race plays."[17] One of the editors of this volume, Matt Chapman, along with other scholars, shows that these ideological oppositions informed the color concepts as racialized categories. For Chapman, these racialized meanings that emerged in early modernity on various fronts, including stage blackface, helped "create the world … and … notions of humanity."[18] As Shakespeare scholars Peter Erickson and Kim Hall show, "our own historical moment shapes our questions" about race, the significance of which changes over time. They urge scholars to think "'cross-historical[ly]'" not as a "conflation of past and present," but as coordination of "two historical moments with distinct ideas of race … in interpretive relation to produce a comparative perspective."[19]

Given the heft of these premises that race has shaped the very idea of the human and that a comparative historical perspective is vitally important for understanding the "intractability" of current racial problems, students today can learn to reject neutral, etymological footnotes and blasé historical mini-lectures, and seize the chance to confront racism with us. This new kind of editorial work, especially when done *with* students, better accounts for/responds to twenty-first-century students' needs, granting their curiosity about and responses to phrases such as *tawny Tartars*, *old black rams*, and *white ewes*, to name a few (from *Midsummer Night's Dream* and *Othello*, respectively). Such practices underscore both the need for and the limits of history (and the scholarly tools, including the OED, that mediate that history), as well as the validity of engaging with

17. David Sterling Brown, "White Hands: Gesturing Toward Shakespeare's Other 'Race Plays,'" Shakespeare Association of America Conference, Washington, D.C., April 2019. The excellent critical work on race in the early modern period that we consulted for this essay includes Loomba and Burton, Charry, Hall, Little, Erickson and Hall, Newman, and Thompson.
18. Chapman, Matthieu. *Anti-Black Racism in Early Modern English Drama: The Other "Other."* (Routledge, 2017), 10. Chapman discusses the generalized history of black/white opposition to concur with Loomba and others in that "notions of whiteness as pure and blackness as sin in religious doctrine predate discourse on whiteness as racialized categories" (7, 29n20, 21).
19. Peter Erickson and Kim F. Hall, ed., "[Special Issue on Race]." *Shakespeare Quarterly* 67, no. 1 (2016): 7.

the present in order to promote an antiracist pedagogy. As literary critic Barbara Sebek explains, "keeping a critically inflected Shakespeare in the curriculum performs important work, given the historical uses to which 'Shakespeare' has been put" as *the* quintessential sign of Englishness, or as a container of 'timeless' human values."[20]

•••

High school students often resort to, and many entire school districts adopt, *No Fear Shakespeare*-type materials for classroom use. These and popular college editions, including the Folger and Bedford, as we showed, minimize, neutralize, ignore, or explain away racist phrases. Thus, they miss opportunities to teach history and Shakespeare, and to create an antiracist pedagogy.[21] When race-based slurs, insults, and epithets pop up, students notice and want to know, "Is this racist?" When those sometimes-bizarre instances are simply rewritten or unnoted, so goes the inevitable discomfort and horror that students and teachers feel and ought to confront. Critical introductions, editorial glosses, and in-class editing activities that prioritize race present a Renaissance that is both "the facts" and inevitably more interesting. These practices address Ayanna Thompson's detection of "a certain anxiety about ... the critics' own identity politics through the employment of prologues, forewords, afterwords, afterthoughts, and epilogues."[22]

For the instructor, teaching a critically inflected Shakespeare means preparing for sticking places, the textual and performance problems that we are often tempted to ignore. We see two equally important strategies to avoid leaving intellectual exercises about race at the threshold of today's racism: 1) proactively engage students to react to these words and phrases (rather than waiting to see if race 'comes up'), and 2) purposefully

20. Barbara Sebek, "Different Shakespeares: Thinking Globally in an Early Modern Literature Course." *Teaching Medieval and Early Modern Cross-Cultural Encounters*, edited by Karina F. Attar and Lynn Shutters. (Palgrave Macmillan, 2014), 115.
21. The Folger Education Blog has an official stand on the kind of paraphrase found in Spark Notes products; see Caitlin Griffin, "More to Fear from 'No Fear,'" February 23, 2012.
22. Ayanna Thompson, "The Future of Early Modern Race Studies: On Three Ambitious (Enough?) Books." *The Eighteenth Century* 49, no. 3 (2008): 259.

direct their reactions in and out of the text (highlighting and annotating while also inquiring and expressing). We find the footnote and other textual apparatus are productive and inclusive spaces where antiracist work can happen. Explanatory and discursive notes, introductions, and sidebars are freer spaces than formal essays, where these editorial and pedagogical commitments can flourish. This is not to suggest that glossing race is marginalizing it; rather this practice uses the local or concrete as an entrée into the abstract and general.

Below we will illustrate this practice by considering editing choices for some of the seemingly "throw-away" racist lines from early modern plays. A look at questions posed on the internet and engaged in discussion forums like Reddit about the color of Shakespearean characters shows that teachers and students are hungry for the chance to name the problem, find definitions for the offensive references, and unpack the implications for then and now.[23] These are important conversations, and if we don't welcome them in class, students will pick up information on the street, as it were, from the information superhighway where certainty and anger often trump ambiguity and social justice. The practice we advocate also helps our students to see their own interpretive labor as contributive. We chose these local expressions rather than, say, *Othello*, that centrally thematizes racial difference with a major Black character, or the sonnets' "fair friend" and "dark lady," because the suddenly appearing "Ethiope" or "foul Negro" strikes like a micro-aggression that can stun, shock, and stump some readers, while also potentially being overlooked by others, including, as we have shown, editors and instructors. Antiblack racism that is literally marginal (as in not obviously central to a given play) but culturally central for us need not be marginal*ized* in texts and classrooms.

In our teaching, we begin with modeling our own editing. In Ann's edition of *A Warning for Fair Women*, she created an extensive footnote

23. Reddit is a popular social news website and forum for questions, comments, and advice. Users, called redditors, curate and promote material by voting. According to a 2016 study by the Pew Research Center, 71% of Reddit's audience is composed of men. See Christian Stafford, "Reddit Definition" Search CIO, December 2016 https://searchcio.techtarget.com/definition/Reddit.

attendant on one of those seeming gratuitous lines. The lover-figure Captain Browne weighs the pros and cons of murdering his rival by proclaiming:

> And if I do [fail], let me be held a coward,
> And no more worthy to obtain her bed
> Than a foul Negro to embrace a Queene.[24]

Proverbial sounding, this was the phrase that caused Ann's one Black student to look up and Ann to issue an awkward apology. Although the footnote in her edition had re-edited the line to address the racist content, students in the moment were fixed on the text and anxious about their pronunciation of words. Here is what they would have seen at the bottom of the page in a more in-depth reading:

> Clearly racist, the comparison is meant to express the insurmountable disparity between Browne, afraid to commit murder, and his beloved, in the same way that a Black man (of any rank) has no right to 'embrace' (touch, have a relationship with) a (presumably white) queen. Embedded in such language is a fear of miscegenation and a sense of white/English superiority, though it is also true that Englishmen travelled to, were taken captive, or voluntarily resettled in areas throughout the Mediterranean, where they might turn "renegade" (abandon Christianity) and marry local non-white, non-Christian women. Another phrase for "that will never happen" was anti-Semitic, illustrated in Andrew Marvell's poem "To His Coy Mistress," where the male lover jokes that a woman might refuse to comply with his desires indefinitely, or "until the conversion of the Jews" (line 10). Theatre historian Andrew Gurr suggests that the negro/queen saying in *A Warning* may be an allusion to Aaron, the black Moor and his lover, Tamara, the Queen of Goths, both taken captive to Rome in Shakespeare's

24. Ann Christensen, ed., *A Warning for Fair Women.* (Lincoln: University of Nebraska Press, 2021), 7.1–12.

> first tragedy, *Titus Andronicus* performed by the same theatre company as *A Warning* (*The Shakespeare Company* 134). Also notable is that Aaron appropriates anti-black racism to claim his own racial pride:
>
> > Coal-black is better than another hue,
> > In that it scorns to bear another hue;
> > For all the water in the ocean
> > Can never turn the swan's black legs to white,
> > Although she lave them hourly in the flood. (4.2.103–107).
>
> Finally, consider the fact that in the play Browne is Irish, another kind of "other" in the sixteenth century, when English people occupied and ruled colonies (or "plantations") in Munster, the southwest part of Ireland, which was also called "the Pale." English texts and maps frequently represented Ireland, Scotland, and Wales, not unlike Africa and the Atlantic world, as the uncivilized, "dark corners" of the land, often brutally treating native inhabitants. The play is not specific about what Captain Browne's Irish parentage, but he elsewhere defends Ireland as civil, orderly, and law-abiding. See Ohlmeyer, Jane. 2002. "Literature and the New British and Irish Histories." Edited by David J. Baker and Willy Maley, 245–55. http://search.ebscohost.com.ezproxy.lib.uh.edu/login.aspx?direct=true&db=mlf&AN=2002581478&site=ehost-live.

This extensive footnote is explicitly written to acknowledge that the phrase is disturbing, imagine students' questions, furnish examples from contemporary texts both of antiblack racism and resistance, and lead back to the text and to the related "Irish problem." In fact it was this other racist, colonialist issue that led to a productive class discussion later about "colorblind" casting. Ann assigned a video recording of the world revival of *A Warning for Fair Women* performed by the Resurgens Theatre Company in Atlanta, Georgia, in November 2018 and using her draft edition; the cast members for this show were white with the exception of South Asian Tamil Periasamy, who played Browne and spoke the line about the "foul negro." In their initial reviews of the show, some students criticized it as racially biased (or insensitive) casting of "the black man" as the villain, though, as we processed the casting choices together, we also considered that his height (tall) and fit physique suited his role as the romantic rival, noting too that his excellent performance as the male lead "stole the show." This was a nuanced analysis in which skin color was one of other markers. Looking further at details from the play about character's Irish origins and using information about the Munster plantation, the class concluded that Periasamy's dark skin in a cast of otherwise white actors emphasized his outsider status as an Irishman in London. Following the in-class reading with this investigation of sticking places and fruitful complexity also took the pressure off the one Black student in the class (a common occurrence in predominantly white institutions) and widened the topic to casting and color in film and television.

The task is for Shakespeare instructors to proactively plan to highlight, probe, and question, and to give space and time for students to have a guided part in this same work. By lecture, discussion notes, or hand-outs, the planning creates a sort of "teacher's edition" to have at the ready the kinds of textual information and additional resources necessary to point to and then translate and contextualize potentially racial or racist implications but not explain that material away. Of course, time and intention are required to demonstrate to students that they should not be expecting an easy acquisition of answers.

• • •

Shakespeare instructors must do the kind of preparation/proactivity that makes for what social science describes as culturally responsive pedagogy. According to social scientist Carol Lee,

> ... robust learning environments must address goals beyond cognitive skills alone ... [must] draw from extant research on how people learn: the importance of drawing on relevant prior knowledge, of making problem solving public and explicit; the need to address generative concepts and to socialize epistemologies, to

> facilitate dialogue and metacognition; and opportunities to interrogate multiple points of view and misconceptions.[25]

In the last thirty years, teachers and teacher educators have worked to develop viable antiracist strategies for classrooms, using the perspectives of critical race theory. Some preparation programs provide courses or seminars that use social justice frameworks, asking teacher candidates to become conscious of the institutional structures that systematize racial thinking and unacknowledged discriminations.[26] Surely Shakespeare studies can be allied with this effort. Our notions of re-editing are in line with Carlin Borsheim-Black and Sophia Tatiana Sarigianide's proposal that teacher education needs a conception of "racial literacy," so that future teachers recognize expressions and expectations of race, language, literacy, and power.[27] Because future-teacher knowledge is essential but not sufficient, *culturally responsive pedagogy* (CRP) as both a theoretical basis and strategic method addresses and meets the needs of marginalized youth in schools.[28] Such pedagogy for Shakespeare means pointing out the language that is part of the foundation of what has previously excluded certain students.

Just as the "BlacKKKShakespeareans" call for dramatic change for the good of the early modern scholarship and the professoriate, teacher educators and social science researchers are similarly eager to support significant pedagogical change. Julia Schleck's essay on the antiracist classroom

25. Carol Lee, "An Ecological Framework for Enacting Culturally Sustaining Pedagogy," in Django Paris and H. Samy Alim, *Culturally Sustaining Pedagogies: Teaching and Learning for Justice in a Changing World*. (New York: Teachers College Press, 2017), 269–70.
26. Conra D. Gist, *Preparing Teachers of Color to Teach: Culturally Responsive Teacher Education in Theory and Practice*. (New York: Palgrave Macmillan, 2014), 291.
27. Carlin Borsheim-Black and Sophia Tatiana Sarigianides, *Letting Go of Literary Whiteness: Antiracist Literature Instruction for White Students*. (New York: Teachers College Press, 2019), 24.
28. See Geneva Gay, *Culturally Responsive Teaching: Theory, Research, and Practice*. Third edition. (New York, NY: Teachers College Press, 2018); and Gloria J. Ladson-Billings, "Preparing Teachers for Diverse Student Populations: A Critical Race Theory Perspective." *Review of Research in Education* 24, (1999): 211–47.

acknowledges that "we need to change this impression" that an early modern curricula covers a period remote from our own when race wasn't yet invented, taught by white instructors with texts "explicitly and exclusively" by white authors, if we hope to have a more inclusive profession and more inclusive classrooms.[29] Shakespeare instructors can do better than endorsing "resources" that merely shake up or shut down race talk. In *So you want to talk about race*, educator Ijeoma Oluo warns that talking is necessary but insufficient without action to counteract racism.[30] For editors and instructors, tackling words such as *Ethiope* is action.

• • •

Proactivity, or preparation, for such teaching is important, because of the promise and peril of "teachable moments." Drawing on influential psychologist Carl Jung's theory of synchronicity, Stephen R. White and George Maycock find "intense, insightful, and meaningful learning" that occurs when teachers are ready and able to respond to the unexpected in their instruction.[31] Educators who take advantage of teachable moments have developed their professional identities in ways that are flexible, focusing less on command and control and allowing for change and improvisation within their orchestration of a classroom discussion.[32] White and Maycock focus on college teaching and the instructors who "empathetically put themselves in the place of the learners."[33] However, there is a danger in assuming that troublesome or even distressing textual

29. Julia Schelck, "Stranger than Fiction: Early Modern Travel Narratives and the Anti-Racist Classroom." *Teaching Medieval and Early Modern Cross-Cultural Encounters*, edited by Karina F. Attar and Lynn Shutters. (New York: Palgrave Macmillan, 2014), 98.
30. Ijeoma Oluo, *So You Want to Talk About Race*. First edition. (New York, NY: Seal Press, 2018).
31. Stephen R. White and George A. Maycock, "College Teaching and Synchronicity: Exploring the Other Side of Teachable Moments." *Community College Journal of Research and Practice* 36, no. 5 (2012): 321–29. https://doi.org/10.1080/03601277.2010.500595. 324.
32. See, for instance, Hristina Keranova, "Grab Those Teachable Moments! (On Teacher Identities and Student Learning)," *English Teaching: Practice & Critique* 15, no. 2 (2016): 276–84.
33. White and Maycock, 322.

moments will be equally obvious to all, will organically "come up" in class, and that the wise instructor will be able to respond in the flow of the discussion. In reality, as educators Mary Mueller and Dina Yankelewitz write, taking advantage of perfectly timed opportunities to intervene, seizing on just that moment when a learner appears ready to engage in an important topic — leaves too much to chance.[34] Instead, Shakespeare instructors can and should predict what words in their text selections can and should expect a response. English language arts specialist Valerie Kinloch describes how this preparation takes the pressure off the diverse students who *might* voice a question, making central their "language, literacies, and cultural practices," that dominant practices might relegate to the margins.[35]

The glosses we imagine and create with our students need not *resolve* textual or racial problems, but they can at least identify them, furnish some information, and invite students to engage. We know these conversations happen outside of classrooms, and we need to make it clear they belong inside. For instance, we found a brisk debate on Reddit, the popular online forum, from 2017 spawned from one original poster's (OP's) question, "Is Midsummer's Hermia black?" The discussion included voices of the kind of curiosity and open-mindedness we want to foster in our classrooms as well as the certainty more typical of *Cliff's Notes* and footnotes, such as claims about "Shakespeare's intent" and unambiguous definitions of what was considered beautiful (whiteness) and ugly (blackness) in the period. The OP was the user u/MsNyleve:

> My colleague and I are teaching Midsummer to high school freshmen right now, and today we read the cat fight between Helena and Hermia. At one point, Lysander (under the influence of the flower juice) tells Hermia "Away, you Ethiope!" My colleague thinks

34. Mary Mueller and Dina Yankelewitz, "Teaching Mistakes or Teachable Moments?" *Kappa Delta Pi Record* 50, (2014): 124–29.
35. Valerie Kinloch, "'You Ain't Making Me Write': Culturally Sustaining Pedagogies and Black Youths' Performances of Resistance," in Paris and Alim, *Culturally Sustaining Pedagogies*, 38.

> Hermia's black. I assume not, since she's nobility and black nobility would be preposterous at the time. What say you, is Lysander just insulting her, or is she really black? For what it's worth, she's also described as tawny elsewhere.

The ensuing Reddit comments called up external "evidence," such as the notion that white skin stands for elite status (proof that a person does not labor outdoors and is hence "attractive"), and internal, textual "clues" about Hermia's appearance. For our purposes, we appreciated how those who identify as teachers initiated and pursued the conversation about a character's skin color, noting their professional and personal commitments to the topic of race prompted by the play. We suspect that the question arose in the forum because textbooks were silent on the matter. If teachers seek a community to debate a problem staring them in the face in class, and if students look up from reading for answers about an insulting word choice, why not acknowledge these needs in our editions? Editors and instructors can mentor students using these apparent one-off insults, such as "Ethiope," where currently, they find either a one-word "clarification" as when *The Bedford Shakespeare* supplies "Blackamoor," or through the spurious logic illustrated in the *Norton Shakespeare*'s explanation that "dark hair and complexion" = "Ethiopians or Tartars" = "ugly."[36] Since unguided readers consult the Ouija Board of the Internet with questions like "What color is Cleopatra?" and "Is Othello black?," the text books that we create could stimulate and guide, if not "control," the way students encounter race in Shakespeare.

There was a heated exchange in that Reddit thread about Hermia's potential blackness that illustrates some posters' seeming ease with open-endedness and updating and others' desire to close down possibility. The user called sprigglespraggle attests that "it is clear that Shakespeare's

36. See *Bedford*, 376n357 and *Norton*, 362n7. Since many editions now provide introductory and historical discussions of race, when a racially inflected term comes up in a given play, a footnote could direct readers to those sections and also provoke connections to modern lived experience closer to the reference itself. For example, the Bedford features discursive, historical "Context" chapters on topics such as "Race," "Religion," and "Empire."

intent with this line was hyperbole" and Jacksaintmonica erases race in this way: "I think that since white as a color was considered more virtuous and truthful, being called an Ethiope was more of a reflection on Hermia's character than her skin color." Another member, the-roaring-girl, returns to the original post, "I like your colleague's line of thinking! It's 2017; Shakespeare is dead, so we can't ask him what he thinks. If your colleague thinks Hermia may be POC, then let's cast a POC actress in the role!" Rcrow2009 pushes against the other posters' certain claims about Hermia's whiteness and the standards of beauty: "Again, I just don't see why people are so opposed to the notion that characters in this play could be non-white. Given the setting and textual clues especially .... But the play isnt set in britian. Its set in ancient greece and features hippolyta, an Amazon, and the fairies (who are mentioned being from india) ... .She's definately black. Not only is she called ethiope, but also a "nut" and a "raven". Given that the play is set in greece, her being black and nobility truly usnt that unusual." [37] Next, Iwillfuckingbiteyou asks for "a source" to support Rcrow's observation that Greeks were not white; BeeDice closes down the thread with two words and signs for a frustrated face: "'cat fight'? :/," by which that they might mean to refer to the scene in *Midsummer* when Helena and Hermia skirmish or to the very discussion on Reddit.

You go, Rcrow![38] Unfortunately, teachers and students reaching for online aids and even mainstream textbooks for racial questions rarely find

37. Rcrow2009 brings up other "textual clues" re: the character: "I think she was depicted as short, definitely shorter than Helena. I just don't see why we are discounting the reading of her being black despite several textual clues she was, when the only reason seems to be 'Maybe it was hyperbole.'" iwillfuckingbiteyou objects: "But she's referred to as a dwarf. She calls herself "dwarfish." That's pretty unambiguous, right? Those are definite textual clues." Rcrow2009 counters with the idea that "Dwarfish has a much more metaphorical meaning within colloquial contexts than Ethiope."
38. Many scholars agree with Rcrow2009. See Armelle Sabatier "Eulogizing Black in Love's Labour's Lost." *Actes des congrès de la Société française Shakespeare* [En ligne], 32 | 2015, 10 March 2015. *OpenEdition*, 10.4000/shakespeare.2925. Sabatier looks at the pattern of "unconventional discourses on female beauty" that include blackness in *The Two Gentlemen of Verona*, *A Midsummer Night's Dream*, and *Love's Labour's Lost*, noting the contexts of male rivalry and friendship.

debate. Much more common is the pattern illustrated in the *York Study Notes and Revision Guide* for A-Level students, for example, which uses the subject heading, "HERMIA'S APPEARANCE" to close down discussion:

> Hermia is the darker and shorter of the two young women. 'Who will not change a raven for a dove?' asks Lysander (II.2.120), contrasting her complexion and hair colour with Helena's. Later he calls Hermia an 'Ethiope' and a 'tawny Tartar' (III.2.257 and 263).

The Guide clinches the case thus without providing evidence: "Dark hair and skin were considered unfashionable in this period." This explanation fails to account for Hermia as an exception to this rule; the *York Study* allows, "but before the magic juice distorts their reactions, both men still perceive Hermia as highly attractive."

Is Black so base a hue? Is Hermia Black? These questions trouble us as scholars, high-school teachers, Shakespeare fan forum users, and students. The re-editing that we advocate is a hands-on way to question and refute assertions endlessly repeated that non-whiteness was unfashionable and unattractive and to counter bullying silence and pallid apologies with text and intellect. With this kind of work, future students might indeed look up and find connection to peers and teachers and look down to textual notes and see their questions valued.

Discussion Questions for Instructors

1. Reflect on a time that you seized a "teachable moment" on a difficult topic in class. How might you ensure the treatment of this topic in future classes? Alternatively, recall a time that you missed such an opportunity. What do you see as the "promise and peril" of these classroom moments?
2. Discuss some ways to adapt your current writing and in-class activities to focus on race. How can you keep students' attention on both what they sometimes imagine as a very different "back then" and now?
3. Create a "side-bar" assignment for your class using "race words." Include a model to illustrate the kind of apparatus you hope your students will create.